OPERATIONAL AMPLIFIER CIRCUITS

Preface

The objective of this book is to present a logical approach to analyzing practical circuits that use operational amplifiers, thereby enabling the reader to develop a familiarity with some fundamental application circuits widely utilized in electronics today. A secondary objective is to enable one to determine the performance limitations of an op amp circuit due to amplifier imperfections. Finally, it is intended that this book serve the engineer as a valuable reference source of application ideas.

It is also important to stress from the outset that this text is not concerned with the design details of internal circuitry of op amps; many books and articles contain such information. This text concerns itself mainly with op amps already available from manufacturers, and using available data sheets to design operational circuits to meet an overall design objective.

OUTLINE

Chapter 1, an introductory chapter, begins with the simplest possible concept, the ideal operational amplifier. This material expands in Chapter 2 to cover the basic building block of linear active circuits, the single-pole op amp used in fundamental inverting and noninverting configurations.

Chapter 2 is also concerned with amplifier performance limitations due to dc signals imposed on an op amp due to bias constraints. Here, the input voltage and current errors in practical devices, and their effect on the output dc voltage and current is considered. The error budget analysis concept, not usually covered in texts though quite important, is treated here. Effects of common-mode signals, power supply changes, and temperature are considered.

Chapter 3 is devoted to real-world performance limitations due to multiple poles in signal-loop transmission. Several frequency-compensation circuits and techniques that have proven universally useful are covered, as well as slew-rate limitations.

Chapter 4 presents a detailed analysis, with some simplifying circuit techniques, of the limitations of signal amplification due to electronic noise. This subject, though increasingly important in modern-day systems, has generally been ignored in most texts. The reader should find the material presented here easier to comprehend than many of the more fundamentally mathematical concepts available in open literature.

Chapters 5 and 6 concentrate on many of the widely used linear application circuits employed with op amps. Such examples as instrumentation amplifiers, linear regulators, and chopper-stabilized circuits are covered in Chapter 5, and the subject of RC active filters is exclusively treated in Chapter 6. A rather complete coverage of lowpass, highpass, bandpass (as well as band-reject) application circuits are covered in detail as are the recent switched-capacitor filters.

Chapter 7 concentrates on the increasingly important topic of nonlinear and other functional op amp circuits, presenting concepts and applications for various comparators, function generators, rectification circuits, sample-and-hold, logarithmic vs. antilogarithmic, V/F and F/V converters, as well as a brief discussion of several analog-to-digital converter examples. Finally, various multivibrator and oscillator circuits are presented.

Chapter 8 concludes, covering several important systems applications that involve op amps, such as temperature measurement, pressure indication, strain-gage circuits, and other signal-conditioning examples.

Several important appendices are included in the book. The practicing engineer should find the op amp data sheets useful, and the techniques for modeling op amps for computer circuit analysis programs such as SPICE should be most helpful.

The text can be used in either a one semester (45 meetings) or one-quarter (30 meetings) course taught at the senior level. Prerequisites are an understanding of s-domain analysis as well as awareness of frequency-response techniques, plus a basic sequence in electronic circuits. For either semester or quarter course a suggested sequence might be:

Chapter 1—Review material depending on student background. 1–3 meetings.
Chapter 2—Some review. Important material otherwise. 2–5 meetings.
Chapter 3—Complete coverage recommended for a Senior or Advanced Level course. 2–5 class meetings.

Chapter 4—Depends on the particular emphasis of the course. Cover in entirety for semester courses or choose parts for a course with primarily applications emphasis. 3–6 meetings.

Chapter 5—Cover by topics of interest. 4–6 meetings.

Chapter 6—If active filters are covered elsewhere in the curriculum, such as in an analysis and synthesis networks course, this could be left out. Otherwise, it could be covered by particular topics. 3–7 meetings.

Chapter 7—Much of this material is probably not available in other undergraduate courses. Various topics can be covered as time permits. 3–7 meetings.

Chapter 8—Use to end the semester (or quarter) with these and other assigned topics. 2–4 meetings.

Appendix—Topics here could be omitted or covered as time permits. Some topics may be of more interest to the practicing engineer, whereas op amp computer modeling is of significance to both the student and practitioner. The author has found it particularly enlightening to require students to model an existing commercial op amp, using the techniques of Appendix D, and correlate the SPICE analysis with laboratory results.

ACKNOWLEDGEMENTS

Considerable thanks are expressed to the many students who raised helpful criticism of the class notes that provided the incentive for this text. My appreciation is expressed also to my fellow faculty members at the University of Tennessee, Knoxville, notably Drs. T. V. Blalock, R. E. Bodenheimer, and J. M. Rochelle who offered suggestions for much of the manuscript. Certainly, the excellent typing by Ms. Denise Smiddy is gratefully acknowledged. The encouragement of many, most importantly Dr. Walter Green, Department Chairman, was essential to the success of the book.

The encouragement and motivational help of the Editor, Ms Deborah L. Moore, was outstanding and is gratefully acknowledged as is the effort of Chuck Wahrhaftig, Senior Project Manager, in producing this book. The suggestions of reviewers Eugene Chenette, University of Florida; J. Alvin Connelly, Georgia Institute of Technology; Doug Hamilton, University of Arizona; Paul Lewis, Michigan Technological University; Robert Samuels, Catawba Valley Technological College; Edgar Sanchez-Sinencio, Texas A & M University; David Shattuck, University of Houston; Dan Thomas, University of Texas-Austin; M. E. Van Valkenburg, University of Illinois-Urbana; and Henry Winton, Rose Hulman Institute of Technology are certainly appreciated.

E. J. Kennedy

OPERATIONAL AMPLIFIER CIRCUITS

Theory and Applications

E. J. Kennedy

UNIVERSITY OF TENNESSEE

HOLT, RINEHART AND WINSTON, INC.

New York   Chicago   San Francisco   Philadelphia
Montreal   Toronto   London   Sydney   Tokyo

To my wife, Lynda, and our daughters,
Marilyn, Ruth, and Rachel

Publisher	Ted Buchholz
Acquisitions Editor	Deborah Moore
Senior Project Manager	Chuck Wahrhaftig
Production Manager	Paul Nardi
Design Supervisor	Bob Kopelman

Library of Congress Cataloging-in-Publication Data

Kennedy, E. J. (Eldredge Johnson), 1935–
  Operational amplifier circuits.

  Includes index.
  1. Operational amplifiers. I. Title.
TK7871.58.06K46 1987   621.381'735   87-1483

ISBN 0-03-001948-6

8 9 0 1 039 9 8 7 6 5 4 3 2 1

Holt, Rinehart and Winston, Inc.
The Dryden Press
Saunders College Publishing

Contents

Chapter 6   ACTIVE RC FILTERS   **232**

APPENDIXES 533

INDEX 621

Chapter 1

The Ideal Operational Amplifier

The concept of the **operational amplifier** (usually referred to as an **op amp**) originated in the late 1940s with vacuum-tube dc amplifier designs developed by the George A. Philbrick Co. Later transistor designs by Philbrick, Burr-Brown, and others preceded the introduction of the first monolithic integrated-circuit (IC) op amp in 1965, the μA709 (designed by Bob Widlar, then with Fairchild Semiconductor). The 709 op amp was widely used by engineers throughout the world for several years, uses that led to numerous applications-oriented circuits and systems. While premium op amps in the late 1950s and early 1960s cost over $100 each, good monolithic IC op amps are available today at prices close to those of discrete transistors. Indeed a modern circuit designer should consider the use of an op amp in the same category as the use of another discrete transistor, since both are now similarly priced and offer equal reliability.

The term *operational* in the op amp designation probably applied more to its use in early analog computer circuits, since various *operations* such as addition, integration, and differentiation could be carried out easily with those dc-coupled amplifiers. For example, the solution of the differential equation

$$\frac{d^2y}{dt^2} + k\,\frac{dy}{dt} + my = f(t)$$

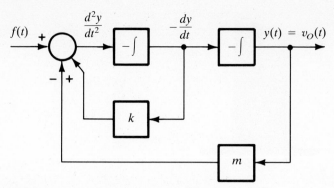

Figure 1.1 A differential equation solution.

is illustrated by the analog computer circuit of Fig. 1.1, where each block may contain an op amp (see Prob. 1.7).

In this first chapter the simplest possible circuit—the ideal op amp—is introduced. After the basic equations are developed, we gradually move in Chapter 2 to the more standard circuit, the op amp with one dominant open-loop pole and finite input and output impedance. In Chapter 3 techniques are presented for analyzing even more complex circuits that have multiple poles and zeroes.

1.1 THE IDEAL OP AMP

An ideal op amp* is a dc-coupled amplifier (illustrated in Fig. 1.2) with the following characteristics:

1. The gain A_O from input to output (usually referred to as the **open-loop gain**) is infinite. Stated another way, since the output signal is finite the input signal to the op amp (v_ε) must approach zero.
2. The input resistance R_{IN} of the amplifier is infinitely large, while the output resistance R_O is zero.
3. The gain is not a function of frequency; i.e., there are no poles or zeroes in the input-to-output gain expression. The bandwidth is infinitely large.
4. The amplifier draws no current at the input. Conversely, the output of the amplifier can either sink or source an infinitely large current to the load.
5. The common-mode rejection and the power-supply rejection are infinitely large. This statement implies that the amplifier has no output change due to changes in the dc power supplies and that the op amp only amplifies the *differential* signal appearing between the two inputs, and has no gain to a signal that is *common* to the two inputs. More practical definitions of common-mode and power-suply rejection for real op amps are given later (in Section 2.3).

---

* Much of the analysis on ideal op amps may have been covered by the student in earlier Sophomore or Junior courses. In that case the material in Sections 1.1–1.3 can be used merely for review purposes, and more careful study spent beginning with Section 1.4.

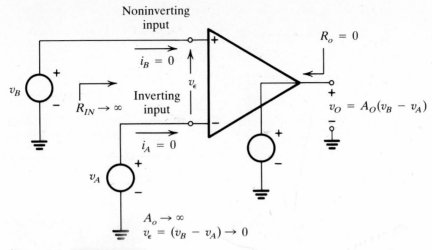

Figure 1.2 Ideal op amp.

Although the above requirements for an ideal op amp appear impossible to achieve, we will find that many present-day devices actually come very close to many of the specifications.

The symbol for the ideal op amp is shown in Fig. 1.2, where the input signals are applied as v_A and v_B, and the output signal is the voltage

$$v_O = A_O(v_B - v_A)*$$ (1.1)

Since A_O is infinite, the above equation would seem to state that the output voltage also is infinite. However, two important fundamentals limit the output signal: (a) a linear op amp circuit must *always* be used with negative feedback, and (b) since the gain A_O is so large, then the input error signal $v_\epsilon (= v_B - v_A)$ *must approach zero.*

This last statement could be expressed another way: The signal at the noninverting input *always* attempts (due to feedback) to achieve the same value as the signal at the inverting input. Thus, if the v_A signal of Fig. 1.2 is at ground (0 volts) v_B will try to reach ground potential; if v_A is at $+5$ V then v_B will be essentially at $+5$ V, etc.

1.2 THE INVERTING-AMPLIFIER CIRCUIT

The standard inverting-amplifier connection is shown in Fig. 1.3. The input signal v_I is applied to R_1 and negative feedback is furnished by resistor R_F. If we assume

---

* At the very first it is useful to define the general notation to be utilized in this text:

1. Uppercase letters are used for dc (or average), peak, and rms values (V for voltage, I for current, etc.), while lowercase letters (v, i, p) indicate instantaneous time-varying values.

2. The total value of a signal comprising both a dc (or average) value plus the time-varying value is indicated by an uppercase subscript, such as $v_A = v_a + V_A$.

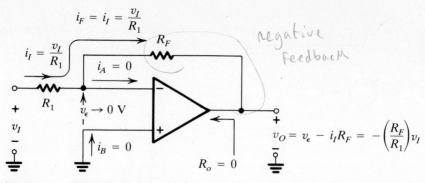

Figure 1.3 Ideal inverting amplifier.

an ideal op amp, the error signal v_ε must be zero. Also, since the input current drawn by the op amp is zero ($i_A = 0$), the input current i_1 must all flow through the feedback resistor R_F into the output of the amplifier. Since the noninverting input terminal is at *ground*, the inverting input terminal v_A is also at ground, so

$$i_1 = \frac{v_I - v_\varepsilon}{R_1} = \frac{v_I - 0}{R_1} = \frac{v_I}{R_1}$$

and since $i_I = i_F$, we have (writing the voltage equation around the loop from the output through R_F to the input to ground)

$$v_O = -i_1 R_F + v_\varepsilon = -i_1 R_F$$

or

$$v_O = -\left[\frac{R_F}{R_1}\right] v_I$$

Thus, the **closed-loop gain** is

$$\left(\frac{v_O}{v_I}\right) = -\left(\frac{R_F}{R_1}\right)$$

For the circuit of Fig. 1.3 the closed-loop output resistance can be obtained by grounding the input resistor R_1 (shorting v_I to ground), applying a voltage source to the output, and calculating the current furnished by the voltage source. Since the open-loop output resistance R_o is zero the closed-loop output resistance must obviously be zero. The only exception would be if the feedback were such as to force an opposing current back into the output-voltage source; however, this is not possible for the linear negative-feedback circuit of Fig. 1.3.

EXAMPLE 1.1

For the circuit diagram of Fig. 1.3 find the closed-loop input impedance defined by $r_{\text{in}} = v_I/i_I$.

Solution

Since there is a virtual short (virtual ground) at the input, the input resistance r_{in} seen by the signal source v_I is

$$r_{in} \equiv \frac{v_I}{i_I} = \frac{v_I}{\left(\dfrac{v_I - v_\varepsilon}{R_1}\right)}$$

or

$$r_{in} = \frac{R_1}{1 - 0} = R_1$$

In summary, the characteristics of the inverting amplifier (assuming the op amp is ideal) are

$$\mathbf{Gain} = \frac{v_O}{v_I} = -\left(\frac{R_F}{R_1}\right)$$

$$\textbf{Input Resistance} = R_1 \tag{1.2}$$

$$\textbf{Output Resistance} = 0$$

1.3 THE NONINVERTING-AMPLIFIER CIRCUIT

The basic noninverting-amplifier circuit is shown in Fig. 1.4(a). Here the input signal is applied to the non-inverting input and the feedback signal is connected via R_F and R_1 back to the inverting input.

Since the ideal op amp has zero input current and infinite input resistance R_{IN}, we find immediately that

$$r_{in} = \frac{v_I}{i_I} = \frac{v_I}{0} = \infty$$

Since the error signal must approach zero

$$v_I = v_\varepsilon + v_F = 0 + v_F = v_F$$

Since no current flows into the inverting input either, then

$$i_1 = i_F = \frac{v_F}{R_1}$$

and therefore the output voltage v_O is

$$v_O = i_F(R_F + R_1) = \left(\frac{R_F + R_1}{R_1}\right)v_F$$

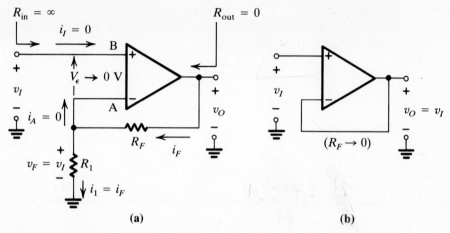

Figure 1.4 Ideal noninverting amplifier: (a) basic circuit, (b) unity-gain version.

Hence the gain is

$$\frac{v_O}{v_F} = \frac{R_F + R_1}{R_1} = 1 + \frac{R_F}{R_1}$$

Just as for the inverting amplifiier, the output resistance must be zero. Thus, the ideal noninverting amplifier is characterized by the following equation

$$\begin{aligned}
\textbf{Gain} &= \frac{v_O}{v_I} = 1 + \frac{R_F}{R_1} \\[6pt]
\textbf{Input Resistance} &= \infty \\[6pt]
\textbf{Output Resistance} &= 0
\end{aligned}$$

(1.3)

EXAMPLE 1.2

Show that the noninverting amplifier becomes a unity-gain buffer amplifier if $R_F = 0$. Such a circuit is indicated in Fig. 1.4(b).

Solution
From Eq. (1.3), if $R_F \to 0$ the gain becomes

$$\frac{v_O}{v_I} = 1 + \frac{0}{R_1} = 1$$

The concept of a buffer amplifier is indeed appropriate since the signal v_I is loaded by the infinitely large input impedance of the op amp and is then transferred to a zero-output impedance by $v_O = v_I$. Unity-gain noninverting circuits have many applications, as we shall see later.

1.4 OTHER CIRCUIT EXAMPLES

Before we proceed with more detailed analysis involving nonideal operational amplifiers, it is useful to look at some basic circuits that are widely used to see how simple the analysis can be, using an ideal op amp concept.

Figure 1.5 shows an **inverting-integrator circuit** (this circuit is used, for example, in the "integrator" box of the analog-computer circuit of Fig. 1.1). Since the error signal approaches 0 V the inverting input of the op amp is at ground potential, so

$$i_I(t) = \frac{v_I(t)}{R_1}$$

and the output signal is, summing the voltage across C and $v_\varepsilon(t)$,

$$v_O(t) = -V(0) - \frac{1}{C}\int_0^t i_I(t)dt$$

where $V(0)$ is the voltage existing on the capacitor at time $t = 0$. Substituting the equation for $i_I(t)$ gives

$$v_O(t) = -V(0) - \frac{1}{R_1 C}\int_0^t v_I(t)dt \qquad (1.4)$$

From Eq. (1.4) the output voltage is equal to the negative integral of the input voltage, divided by a gain constant $(R_1 C)$, minus any initial voltage on the capacitor at time $t = 0$. In the s-domain the equation for the transfer function V_O/V_i becomes [for $V(t = 0) = 0$ V]

$$\frac{V_O(s)}{V_I(s)} = -\frac{1}{R_1 Cs} \qquad (1.5)$$

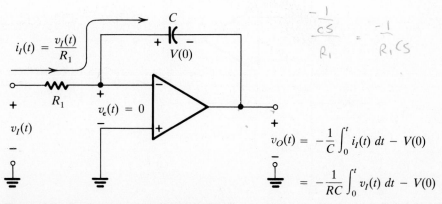

Figure 1.5 Basic inverting integrator circuit.

and correspondingly in the frequency domain

$$\frac{V_O(j\omega)}{V_I(j\omega)} = -\frac{1}{j\omega R_1 C}$$

(1.6)

EXAMPLE 1.3

Using the circuit of Fig. 1.5, design an inverting integrator satisfying the relation

$$\frac{V_O}{V_I} = -\frac{100}{s}$$

The input signal v_I is to see an input resistance of 100 kΩ.

Solution
The gain constant $1/R_1 C$ must be 100. Since the input resistance is to be 100 kΩ, then C must be 0.1 μF.

A noninverting integration is shown in Fig. 1.6. For the present, assume the initial voltage on C is zero [$V(t = 0) = 0$ V]. Since the signal $v_\varepsilon(t)$ is zero $v_A = v_B$ so

$$v_B = v_A = \left(\frac{R_2}{R_2 + R_2}\right)v_O = \frac{v_O}{2}$$

Hence, summing currents at the v_B node

$$i_I + i_1 - i_C = 0$$

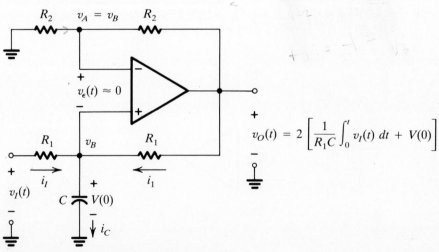

$$v_O(t) = 2\left[\frac{1}{R_1 C}\int_0^t v_I(t)\ dt + V(0)\right]$$

Figure 1.6 Noninverting integrator circuit.

or, in the s-domain

$$\frac{V_I - V_B}{R_1} + \frac{V_O - V_B}{R_1} - V_B(sC) = 0 \tag{1.7}$$

After substituting the expression for v_B above, we obtain the transfer function

$$\frac{V_O}{V_I} = \frac{2}{sR_1C} \tag{1.8}$$

■ **Exercise 1.1**

Obtain Equation (1.8) from (1.7) by appropriate substitutions. Also, include the effect of an initial voltage $V(0)$ on the capacitor (Hint: use superposition) and show that in the time domain

$$v_O(t) = 2\left[V(0) + \frac{1}{R_1C} \int_0^t v_I(t)dt \right] \tag{1.9}$$

■ **Exercise 1.2**

In the circuit of Fig. 1.6 show that the current i_C through the capacitor is given by

$$i_C = \frac{v_I}{R_1}$$

and is therefore *not* a function of the capacitor's value. Can you think of a possible application for this circuit, where C could be any impedance? Are there any practical disadvantages to using this circuit?

If we swap the location of the resistor and capacitor in Fig. 1.5 a differentiator circuit is obtained, as shown in Fig. 1.7(a). Since the error signal $v_\varepsilon(t) \to 0$ the input current is

$$i_I(t) = C\frac{d}{dt}\left[v_I(t) - v_\varepsilon(t) \right]$$

or

$$i_I(t) = C\frac{dv_I(t)}{dt} \tag{1.10}$$

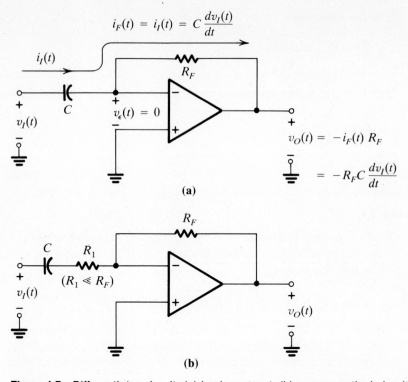

Figure 1.7 Differentiator circuit: (a) basic concept, (b) more practical circuit.

Thus, the output voltage is the product of the feedback current, which is equal to $i_I(t)$, and the feedback resistor, or

$$v_O(t) = -i_F(t)R_F$$

which is

$$v_O(t) = -R_F C \frac{dv_I(t)}{dt}$$

or in the s-domain

$$\frac{v_O}{v_I} = -R_F Cs \qquad \qquad \text{(1.11)}$$

and in the frequency domain

$$\frac{v_O}{v_I} = -j\omega R_F C \qquad \qquad \text{(1.12)}$$

The term $R_F C$ in Eqs. (1.11) and (1.12) is often called the **differentiator gain constant**.

The circuit of Fig. 1.7(b) is more often utilized as a differentiator, where a small resistor is placed in series with C to limit the gain at high frequencies.

However, this does restrict the range of frequencies useful for operating as a differentiation circuit. It can be shown (see Prob. 1.2) that the gain function for Fig. 1.7(b) in the s-domain is

$$\frac{v_O}{v_I} = \frac{-R_F C s}{1 + R_1 C s} \tag{1.13}$$

An inverting summing circuit is illustrated in Fig. 1.8(a), and a more general inverting and noninverting connection in Fig. 1.8(b). Since v_ε is zero and no input

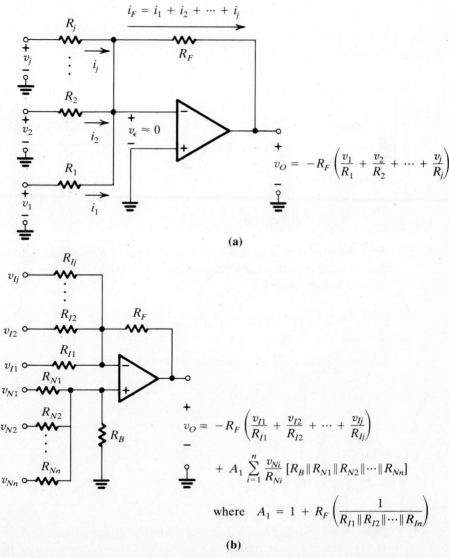

(a)

(b)

Figure 1.8 Summing circuits: (a) basic inverting circuit, (b) general circuit.

current flows into the op amp, then in Fig. 1.8(a)

$$i_F = i_1 + i_2 + \cdots + i_j$$

or

$$i_F = \frac{v_1}{R_1} + \frac{v_2}{R_2} + \cdots + \frac{v_j}{R_j}$$

Hence,

$$v_O = -R_F\left(\frac{v_1}{R_1} + \frac{v_2}{R_2} + \cdots + \frac{v_j}{R_j}\right) \tag{1.14}$$

The inverting summing amplifier circuit can be combined with signals summed at the noninverting input to produce a more general summing circuit, as shown in Fig. 1.8(b). Here, it can be shown (see Problem 1.4) that the equation for v_O is, in general,

$$v_O = -R_F\left(\frac{v_{I1}}{R_{I1}} + \frac{v_{I2}}{R_{I2}} + \cdots + \frac{v_{Ij}}{R_{Ij}}\right) + A_1 \sum_{i=1}^{n} \frac{v_{Ni}}{R_{Ni}} (R_B \| R_{N1} \| R_{N2} \| \cdots \| R_{Nn}) \tag{1.15}$$

where

$$A_1 \equiv 1 + R_F\left(\frac{1}{R_{I1} \| R_{I2} \| \cdots \| R_{In}}\right) \tag{1.16}$$

An inverting amplifier does not have to be formed using strictly one-port (two-terminal) networks. For example, the circuit shown in Fig. 1.9(a) has a general gain relationship

$$\frac{V_O}{V_I} = -\frac{Z_{FSC}}{Z_{1SC}} \tag{1.17}$$

where in this case the impedances are the short-circuit transfer impedances defined by

$$Z_{1SC} \equiv \left. \frac{V_I}{-I_1} \right|_{v_\varepsilon = 0} \tag{1.18}$$

and

$$Z_{FSC} \equiv \left. \frac{V_O}{-I_F} \right|_{v_\varepsilon = 0} \tag{1.19}$$

Thus, from the definitions of Eqs. (1.18) and (1.19), it is obvious that the ratio of Eq. (1.17) holds, since in Fig. 1.9(a) we have $I_1 = -I_F$, due to our ideal op amp conditions.

$\dfrac{V_I - 20I_1}{=10} \le I_1$

$I_1 = \dfrac{V_1}{30}$

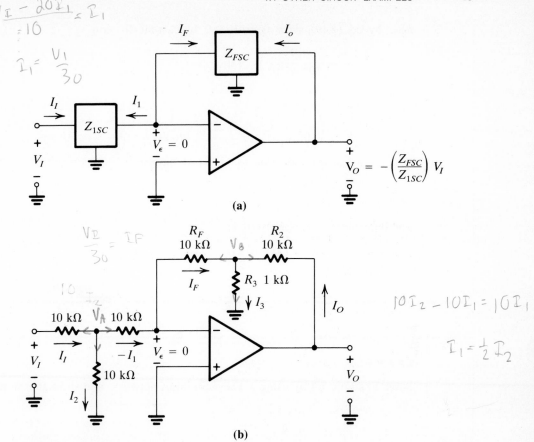

$\dfrac{V_I}{30} = I_F$

$10 \dfrac{}{+2}$

$10I_2 - 10I_1 = 10I_1$

$I_1 = \dfrac{1}{2} I_2$

Figure 1.9 Inverting amplifier using two-port networks: (a) general configuration, (b) circuit for Example 1.4.

EXAMPLE 1.4

Using the definitions of Eqs. (1.17)–(1.19) find the gain and input resistance seen by V_I in the circuit of Fig. 1.9(b).

Solution

Using the circuit values shown in Fig. 1.9(b), and using Eq. (1.18), since V_ε is zero then $I_I = V_I/15 \text{ k}\Omega$. Therefore

$$-I_1 = \frac{1}{2}\left(\frac{V_I}{15 \text{ k}\Omega}\right) = \frac{V_I}{30 \text{ k}\Omega}$$

so

$$Z_{1SC} = \left.\frac{V_I}{-I_1}\right|_{v_\varepsilon = 0} = 30 \text{ k}\Omega$$

Also, by Eq. (1.19), since again $V_\varepsilon = 0$, by current division

$$-I_F = I_O\left(\frac{10^3}{10^3 + 10^4}\right) = I_O\left(\frac{1}{11}\right)$$

or

$$-I_F = \frac{1}{11}\left(\frac{V_O}{10^4 + 10^3 \| 10^4}\right) = V_O\left(\frac{1}{120 \text{ k}\Omega}\right)$$

So $Z_{FSC} = 120$ kΩ and from Eq. (1.17) we have

$$\frac{V_O}{V_I} = -\frac{120 \text{ k}\Omega}{30 \text{ k}\Omega} = -4$$

The input resistance seen by V_I is

$$r_{\text{in}} = 10 \text{ K}\Omega + 10 \text{ k}\Omega \| 10 \text{ k}\Omega$$
$$= 15 \text{ k}\Omega$$

EXAMPLE 1.5

Solve Example 1.4 by using a Thevénin input network, and show that in general

$$\frac{V_O}{V_T} = -\left[\left(1 + \frac{R_2}{R_3}\right)\left(\frac{R_F}{R_T}\right) + \frac{R_2}{R_T}\right] \tag{1.20}$$

where R_T is the Thevénin impedance of Z_{1SC} as seen from the input of the op amp, and V_T is the Thevénin (open-circuit) input voltage.

Solution

We can convert the input circuit to a Thevénin equivalent network, with the result that the circuit now appears as in Fig. 1.10, where R_T is the Thevénin equivalent resistance and V_T is the Thevénin equivalent voltage. From the figure we have

$$I_T = \frac{V_T}{R_T} = V_I\left(\frac{1}{30 \text{ k}\Omega}\right)$$

and

$$V_f = -I_T R_F = -V_T\left(\frac{R_F}{R_T}\right) = -\frac{V_I}{3}$$

so

$$I_3 = \frac{V_f}{R_3} = -\frac{V_I}{3 \text{ k}\Omega}$$

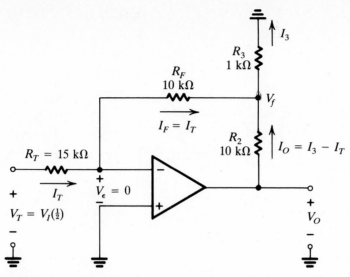

Figure 1.10 Equivalent circuit for Example 1.5.

and therefore

$$V_O = I_O R_2 + V_f = (I_3 - I_T)R_2 + V_f$$

or

$$\frac{V_O}{V_T} = -\left[\left(1 + \frac{R_2}{R_3}\right)\left(\frac{R_F}{R_T}\right) + \frac{R_2}{R_T}\right]$$

Substituting values we get (as previously)

$$\frac{V_O}{V_I} = -4$$

To limit noise from the input, it is often desirable to reduce the gain at higher frequencies. A simple first-order lowpass network can be implemented with the inverting amplifier, as shown in Fig. 1.11(a), or a noninverting connection as in Fig. 1.11(b).

For the inverting circuit the gain is

$$A(s) = \frac{v_O}{v_I} = -\frac{Z_F(s)}{R_1} = -\frac{R_F \| \dfrac{1}{sC_F}}{R_1}$$

or

$$\frac{v_O}{v_I} = -\left(\frac{R_F}{R_1}\right)\left(\frac{1}{1 + sR_F C_F}\right) \tag{1.21}$$

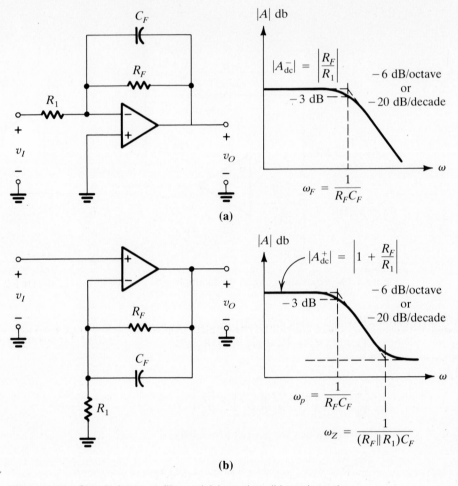

Figure 1.11 Simple lowpass filters: (a) inverting, (b) noninverting.

In the frequency domain we thus have a single pole

$$\frac{V_O}{V_I} = A_{dc}^- \left(\frac{1}{1 + j\dfrac{\omega}{\omega_F}} \right) \tag{1.22}$$

where $\omega_F = 1/R_F C_F$ and $A_{dc}^- = -(R_F/R_1)$.

Correspondingly, for the noninverting circuit

$$\frac{v_O}{v_I} = 1 + \frac{Z_F(s)}{R_1}$$

or

$$\frac{v_O}{v_I} = 1 + \left(\frac{R_F}{R_1} \right) \left(\frac{1}{1 + sR_F C_F} \right)$$

Reducing to a common denominator gives

$$\frac{v_O}{v_I} = (A_{dc}^+)\left[\frac{1 + s(R_F \| R_1)C_F}{1 + sR_F C_F}\right] \tag{1.23}$$

or, in terms of frequency

$$\frac{V_O}{V_I} = A_{dc}^+ \left[\frac{1 + j\left(\dfrac{\omega}{\omega_Z}\right)}{1 + j\left(\dfrac{\omega}{\omega_p}\right)}\right] \tag{1.24}$$

where $A_{dc}^+ = 1 + R_F/R_1$, $\omega_p(=\omega_F$ for the inverting circuit$) = 1/R_F C_F$, and ω_Z (which is $> \omega_p) = 1/(R_F \| R_1)C_F$.

Not so apparent from Eqs. (1.23) or (1.24) is that as frequency increases, the gain v_O/v_I becomes unity; i.e., the reactance of C_F approaches zero as $\omega \to \infty$, so the noninverting circuit of Fig. 1.11(b) becomes the unity-gain circuit of Fig. 1.5(b).

A frequency-response sketch of the two circuits is also illustrated in Fig. 1.11.

EXAMPLE 1.6

For the inverting circuit of Fig. 1.11(a), specify component values for a corner frequency (-3 dB frequency) of 1 kHz, a low-frequency gain (A_{dc}^-) of -10, and an input resistance seen by the source of 10 kΩ.

Solution
Since r_{in} is to be 10 kΩ, $R_1 = 10$ kΩ. Then, since the low-frequency gain is equal to -10, R_F must be equal to 10×10 kΩ, or 100 kΩ. The -3 dB frequency determines C_F, which now must be

$$C_F = \frac{1}{2\pi(10^3 \text{ Hz})(100 \text{ k}\Omega)} = 1600 \text{ pF}$$

■ **Exercise 1.3**

Using the noninverting circuit of Fig. 1.11(b), specify circuit-component values for a pole frequency $f_p = 1$ kHz and a dc gain of $+100$. Sketch the frequency-response plot (Bode plot) for the circuit, using asymptotes.

Many other circuits will furnish the desired pole and zero combinations with only one capacitor. For example, the circuit of Fig. 1.12(a) has a dc (low-frequency) gain less than the high-frequency gain, hence a zero occurs first and the pole second in the frequency response, or the transfer function should be

$$\frac{V_O}{V_I} = \frac{K_0(1 + s\tau_1)}{(1 + s\tau_2)} \tag{1.25}$$

with $\tau_1 > \tau_2$. The term K_0 is the gain at dc, and therefore is

$$K_0 = -\left(\frac{R_F}{R_1 + R_2}\right)$$

Conversely, the circuit of Fig. 1.12(b) has a dc gain greater than its high-frequency gain. The pole should therefore occur first in the frequency response, and

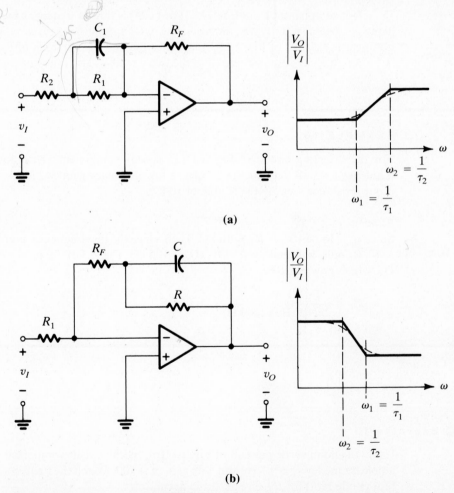

(a)

(b)

Figure 1.12 Other single-capacitor networks: (a) zero occurs first, (b) pole occurs first.

then the zero. In this circuit the same basic transfer function as Eq. (1.25) holds, however now $\tau_1 < \tau_2$ and the gain at dc is

$$K_0 = -\left(\frac{R + R_F}{R_1}\right)$$

■ Exercise 1.4

Assume an ideal op amp and derive the relation of Eq. (1.25) for both circuits of Fig. 1.12. Find the equation for τ_1 and τ_2 in both cases. Sketch the frequency response, indicating both limiting values of gain for each circuit.

One of the most widely used circuits is the differential amplifier. The basic circuit diagram is shown in Fig. 1.13(a). For the present, assume $R_2 = R_1$, $R_3 = R_F$ and the input signal is a truly **differential** signal v_{diff} applied between points 1 and 2. Then $i_1 = i_2 = i_F$ or, since v_ε is zero

$$i_1 = \frac{v_{\text{diff}}}{2R_1}$$

Further, writing the Kirchhoff's-voltage-law equation from the output

$$v_O = -R_F i_F + v_\varepsilon(=0) - i_2 R_3$$

Since the currents are equal and $R_3 = R_F$

$$v_O = -2R_F i_1$$

Substituting

$$\boxed{\frac{v_O}{v_{\text{diff}}} = -\frac{R_F}{R_1}} \tag{1.26}$$

Note also from the above equations that the **differential-input resistance**, R_{diff} is

$$R_{\text{diff}} = \frac{v_{\text{diff}}}{i_1} = R_1 + R_2 = 2R_1$$

Now, let us assume that the differential input v_{diff} is removed, and replaced by a signal v_{CM} that is *common* to the input, as shown in Fig. 1.13(b). Then the voltage at the input of the op amp is

$$v_A = v_B = v_{CM}\left(\frac{R_3}{R_3 + R_2}\right) = v_{CM}\left(\frac{R_F}{R_F + R_1}\right)$$

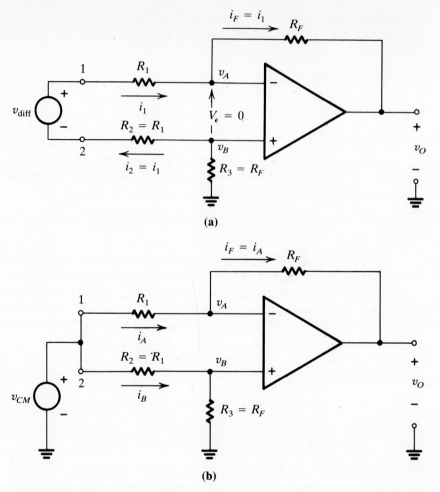

Figure 1.13 Differential amplifier: (a) basic circuit with signal v_{diff}, (b) circuit with a common-mode signal v_{CM} applied.

since $R_3 = R_F$ and $R_2 = R_1$. The current i_B is

$$i_B = \frac{v_{CM}}{R_2 + R_3}$$

and since $v_B = v_A$ and $R_1 = R_2$ the current i_A must be equal to i_B. Further, since the current into the inverting or noninverting input of the op amp is zero, then $i_A = i_F$. Thus, we can write the equation for v_O as

$$v_O = -i_F R_F + v_\varepsilon + i_B R_3$$

or substituting equalities, with $v_\varepsilon = 0$,

$$v_O = -v_{CM}\left(\frac{R_F}{R_2 + R_3}\right) + 0 + v_{CM}\left(\frac{R_F}{R_2 + R_3}\right)$$

or the gain for a signal v_{CM} *common* to the inputs is

$$\frac{v_{OCM}}{v_{CM}} = 0 \qquad (1.27)$$

So we see that an ideal differential amplifier will amplify a *differential-input signal*, but will have zero gain for a signal that is *common* to the two inputs.

EXAMPLE 1.7

The differential amplifier of Fig. 1.14 has a signal applied that consists of a differential input v_{diff} as well as a dc signal common to the inputs, $v_{CM} = +10$ V. To include both signals adequately the representation of the total signal input of Fig. 1.14 is often used. Find the differential gain, differential-input resistance (seen by v_{diff}), common-mode* gain, dc potentials at v_A and v_B, and the resistance seen by the v_{CM} signal.

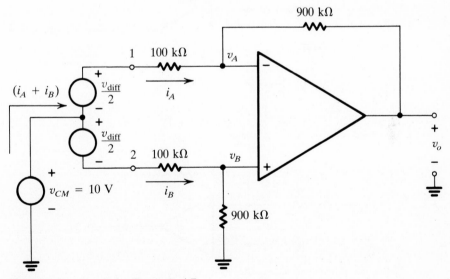

Figure 1.14 Circuit for Example 1.7.

---

* Common-mode gain is here defined as in Eq. (1.27); i.e., the gain to a signal *common* to the inputs at terminals 1 and 2.

Solution

The differential gain by Eq. (1.26) is -9, while the common-mode gain (since $R_3 = R_F$ and $R_2 = R_1$) is zero, as given by Eq. (1.27). The differential-input resistance is

$$R_{\text{diff}} = R_1 + R_2 = 2R_1 = 200 \text{ k}\Omega$$

while, due to the $+10$ V common-mode signal

$$i_B = i_A = \frac{10 \text{ V}}{1 \text{ M}\Omega} = 10 \text{ } \mu\text{A}$$

since $v_A = v_B$. Therefore the input resistance seen by v_{CM} is

$$R_{\text{INPUT}\,CM} = \frac{10 \text{ V}}{i_A + i_B} = 500 \text{ k}\Omega$$

The signals common to the inputs are

$$v_A = v_B = +10 \text{ V}\left(\frac{900 \text{ k}\Omega}{1 \text{ M}\Omega}\right) = +9 \text{ V}$$

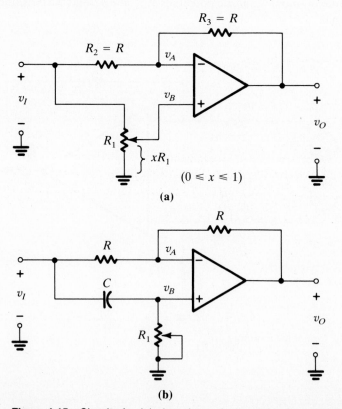

Figure 1.15 Circuits for (a) changing polarity and gain, and (b) shifting phase.

The circuit of Fig. 1.15(a) offers a simple way of adjusting the output voltage over a range from $v_0 = +v_I$, through zero, to $v_0 = -v_I$. This circuit is thus a convenient way to change both polarity and gain in a system. When the potentiometer R_1 is at its minimum position $(x = 0)$, then $v_B = 0$, so $v_0 = -v_I$. However, when the resistance value is maximum $(x = 1)$ the input signal is equal to v_B. But v_A must also be equal to v_B, so no current can flow through R_2 and likewise no current will flow through R_3. Thus, v_O must be equal to $+v_I$. The output is zero when x is equal to $\frac{1}{2}$, since we then have a true differential-amplifier connection with v_I a common-input signal, so v_O must be zero.

■ **Exercise 1.5**

Find the output voltage v_O in Fig. 1.15(b) as a function of R_1 and show that an adjustable phase shift is produced by varying R_1.

SUMMARY

We hope this first chapter has been mostly review material. If not, then careful attention should be paid to the problems that follow. Solutions to several problems are given in Appendix B. Our discussion so far has assumed an ideal op amp, and generally this has led to simple equations for gain, input impedance, output impedance, etc. Although the equations will become more complex in the next chapter (Chapter 2), and for the remainder of the text, we still will find that an awareness of the ideal-op-amp solution will usually lead to considerable simplification of the results. Indeed, even without an awareness of the nonideal nature of the op amp we will find that the basic gain relationships developed in this chapter are usually sufficient for a first-order approximation for circuit analysis.

PROBLEMS

1.1 Show that the output resistance of Fig. 1.4(b) is zero and the input resistance is infinite, assuming an ideal op amp.

1.2 Assuming an ideal op amp, derive the relation of Eq. (1.13).

1.3 In the circuit of Fig. 1.7(a) if the maximum value of C is 1 μF, what should R_F be for a gain constant of unity? What is the magnitude of gain v_o/v_I at a frequency of 1 MHz for this circuit? If we desire to lower the gain at 1 MHz to

1000, what should R_1 be in Fig. 1.7(b)? For this latter case sketch a frequency-response plot (magnitude only) for the transfer function, using asymptotes.

1.4 For the circuit of Fig. 1.8(b) derive the general result of Eqs. (1.15) and (1.16).

1.5 In the circuit of Fig. 1.8(a) if $j = 2$, with $R_1 = 10 \, k\Omega$, $R_2 = 20 \, k\Omega$ and $R_F = 100 \, k\Omega$, find the expression for v_O.

1.6 In the circuit of Fig. 1.8(b) let all resistors be equal to $10 \, k\Omega$. There are two inputs at each terminal (i.e., v_{N1}, v_{N2} and v_{I1} and v_{I2}). Find the equation for v_O, and the input resistance seen by each signal generator.

1.7 Using the basic building blocks of an integrator and summer (Figs. 1.5 and 1.8), show a complete circuit using ideal op amps that would implement the solution of the differential equation as shown in Fig. 1.1. Assume the coefficients are $k = 5$ and $m = 6$. The largest capacitor that can be used is $1 \, \mu F$.

1.8 One wishes to build an inverting amplifier with a gain of -100 and an input resistance of $1 \, M\Omega$. First, using the basic inverting circuit of Fig. 1.3 specify the required resistor values R_1 and R_F. Then, using the circuit of Fig. 1.10 specify the values of R_T and R_3 required if R_F is $1 \, M\Omega$. Which circuit would be less expensive to build?

1.9 Use the summing amplifier circuit and specify all resistor values for a single op amp circuit to produce
(a) $v_O = -3v_1 - 4v_2$
(b) $v_O = -3v_1 - 4v_2 + 6v_3$
Use resistors of $100 \, k\Omega$ or smaller.

1.10 Combine the summing amplifier and integrator to produce a single-op-amp circuit giving $[V_O(t = 0) = 0]$

$$v_O = -10 \int_0^t v_1(t)dt - 50 \int_0^t v_2(t)dt$$

1.11 If a square wave of amplitude 10 volts (20 V p-p) and frequency 1 kHz is applied to an integrator having $C = 1 \, \mu F$ and $R_1 = 100 \, k\Omega$, sketch the output signal of the integrator under steady-state conditions.

1.12 The concept for a simple digital-to-analog converter (DAC or D/A) is illustrated in Fig. P1.12. Show that the output can be written as

$$V_O = -V_{REF}\left(\frac{1}{2}a_1 + \frac{1}{4}a_2 + \frac{1}{8}a_3 + \cdots + \frac{1}{2^n}a_n\right)$$

where the a_n terms are either 0 or 1.

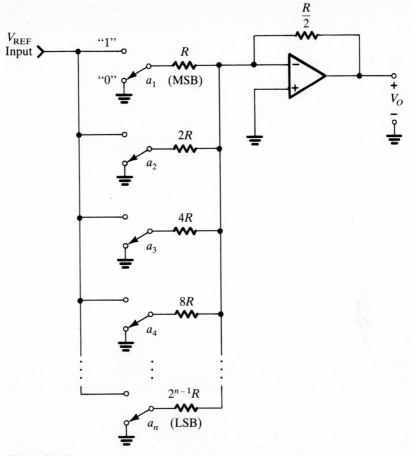

Figure P1.12

1.13 Specify circuit values for a single-op-amp circuit that would produce the function

$$\frac{v_O}{v_I} = \frac{-100}{1 + j\dfrac{f}{10^4}}$$

1.14 Show for the noninverting lowpass circuit of Fig. 1.11(b) that one cannot independently specify ω_p, ω_z and A_{dc}^+.

1.15 Design a noninverting single-op-amp circuit that will produce the transfer function

$$\frac{V_O}{V_I} = 50 \left[\frac{1 + j\dfrac{f}{10^3}}{1 + j\dfrac{f}{10^2}} \right]$$

1.16 For values $R_1 = 9\,\text{k}\Omega$, $R_2 = 1\,\text{k}\Omega$, $R_F = 100\,\text{k}\Omega$ and $C_1 = 1\,\mu\text{F}$, sketch the frequency-response plot (magnitude and phase) for the circuit of Fig. 1.12(a).

1.17 For the circuit of Fig. 1.12(b), we desire to have a low-frequency gain of -50 and a pole frequency of 100 rad/sec, with a zero location of 10^4 rad/sec. If the maximum value of C that can be used is $1\,\mu\text{F}$, specify all values for the required circuit.

1.18 It is desired that a differential signal v_{diff} from a sensor of value 10 mV be amplified to give an output signal of 100 mV. The internal impedance of the signal is a balanced 10 kΩ resistance in series with each input (20 kΩ total), while the sensor has, due to pickup, a 5 V rms, 60 Hz signal common to its terminals. Specify all values for resistors, using the basic circuit of Fig. 1.13(a).

1.19 A lowpass filter can be implemented in the form of a differential amplifier, as indicated in Fig. P1.19. Show, for zero common-mode gain at higher frequencies, that $C_3 = C_F$. For $R_1 = R_2 = 100\,\text{k}\Omega$, $R_F = R_3 = 500\,\text{k}\Omega$ and $C_3 = C_F = 1000\,\text{pF}$, find the differential gain and the -3dB corner frequency.

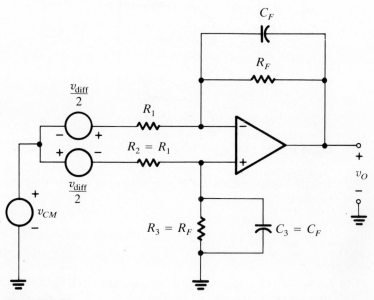

Figure P1.19

1.20 Show that the two-op-amp circuit of Fig. P1.20 will also function as a differential amplifier, producing a gain

$$\frac{v_O}{v_{\text{diff}}} = \frac{R_F}{R}$$

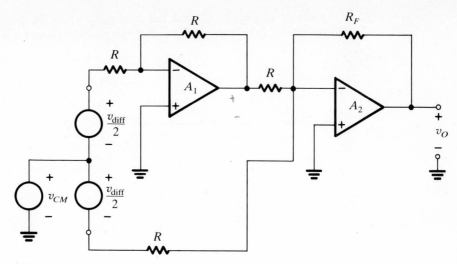

Figure P1.20

and

$$\frac{v_O}{v_{CM}} = 0.$$

1.21 Show that the circuit of Fig. P1.21 produces an output

$$\frac{v_O}{v_{\text{diff}}} = \frac{v_O}{v_{I1} - v_{I2}} = -\left(1 + \frac{R_F}{R}\right)$$

and a common-mode gain $v_O/v_{CM} = 0$, provided that $R_2 = R$ and $R_1 = R_F$. Does this circuit have any advantage over those of Fig. P1.20 or Fig. 1.13(a)?

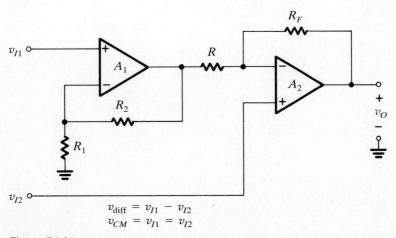

$$v_{\text{diff}} = v_{I1} - v_{I2}$$
$$v_{CM} = v_{I1} = v_{I2}$$

Figure P1.21

1.22 In the circuit of Fig. P1.22 find the gain v_O/v_I when the potentiometer is adjusted so that (a) x is zero, (b) x is 1. What position should x be for $v_O = 0$?

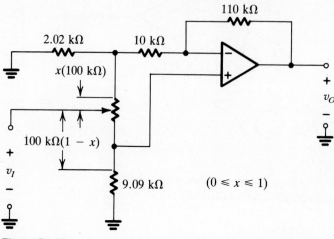

Figure P1.22

Chapter 2

The Nonideal Operational Amplifier

Today, operational amplifiers are available that come quite close to many of the ideal conditions described in Chapter 1. For example, although the dc open-loop gain A_O is not infinite, it is easily greater than 10^5, and often 10^7. The input resistance R_{IN}, although not infinite, may be greater than 10^{12} ohms if an op amp having an FET-input circuit is used. Further, although input currents i_A and i_B are not zero, in actuality they can easily be less than 10^{-8} amp, and in some circuits even less than 1 picoamp (10^{-12} A).

The most significant deviation from ideal conditions occurs in the frequency characteristics. The ideal device assumed that gain was not a function of frequency. Unfortunately, it is presently impossible* to obtain an op amp that comes close to fulfilling this assumption. All commercial devices have at least one pole in their open-loop response, as indicated by Fig. 2.1. Note that we are now defining our

---

* One should be cautioned against the use of words such as *impossible* in scientific texts. However, the author suspects in this case that an op amp having an infinitely large gain-bandwidth product is probably impossible, due to entropy considerations and the second law of thermodynamics.

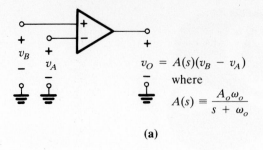

$$v_O = A(s)(v_B - v_A)$$

where

$$A(s) \equiv \frac{A_o \omega_o}{s + \omega_o}$$

(a)

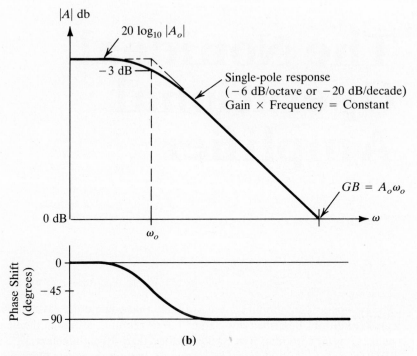

(b)

Figure 2.1 Characteristics of a single-pole op amp.

open-loop gain A_O to be the **dc open-loop gain**. Thus, the output voltage is now a function of frequency

$$v_O(s) = A(s)(v_B - v_A)$$

where, for a single pole in the gain equation

$$A(s) = \frac{A_0 \omega_0}{s + \omega_0} \qquad \qquad (2.1)$$

where ω_0 is the frequency (rad/sec) at which the gain is -3 dB below the dc value. Shown in Fig. 2.1(b) is the phase response, which obviously must change from $0°$ to $-90°$, with a value of $-45°$ at $\omega = \omega_0$.

Manufacturers of operational amplifiers go to great lengths to achieve a dominant-pole (single-pole) open-loop response. As one might expect, however, the greater the **gain-bandwidth product** (*GB*)* of the amplifier the more difficult this task becomes, and a second, or even third, significant pole can exist, thereby influencing the frequency response and ultimately limiting the useful frequency range of the op amp. We will first concentrate on the single-pole circuit, leaving the more detailed analysis of multiple poles for Chapter 3.

2.1 ANALYSIS OF THE SINGLE-POLE INVERTING OP AMP

2.1.1 Gain Relationships

A model for the standard inverting amplifier of Fig. 1.3 is redrawn in Fig. 2.2(a), with finite input and output resistance indicated. The open-loop gain $A(s)$ is assumed to be given by Eq. (2.1). The circuit can be reduced to that of Fig. 2.2(b) by the use of a Norton equivalent circuit.

The two nodal equations for Fig. 2.2(b) can be written in matrix form as

$$\begin{bmatrix} I_I \\ 0 \end{bmatrix} = \left\{ \begin{matrix} \left[\dfrac{1}{R} + \dfrac{1}{R_F} \right] & \left[-\dfrac{1}{R_F} \right] \\ \left[-\dfrac{1}{R_F} + \dfrac{A(s)}{R_O} \right]\left[\dfrac{1}{R_L} + \dfrac{1}{R_F} \right] \end{matrix} \right\} \begin{bmatrix} v_\varepsilon \\ v_O \end{bmatrix} \tag{2.2}$$

Solving for v_O from Eq. (2.2) gives

$$\frac{v_O}{I_I} = \frac{\dfrac{1}{R_F} - \dfrac{A(s)}{R_O}}{\left[\dfrac{1}{R}\left(\dfrac{1}{R'_L} + \dfrac{1}{R_F} \right) + \dfrac{1}{R_F R'_L} + \dfrac{A(s)}{R_F R_O} \right]}$$

Substituting the relationship for the single-pole open-loop gain of Eq. (2.1) and rearranging gives the expression for the **closed-loop gain** of the inverting amplifier $A^-_{CL}(s)$

$$A^-_{CL}(s) = \frac{\left(-\dfrac{R_F}{R_1} \right)\left(1 - \dfrac{R_O}{A_O R_F} \right)\left[1 - \dfrac{sR_O}{A_O \omega_0 R_F \left(1 - \dfrac{R_O}{A_O R_F} \right)} \right]}{1 + \left[\left(\dfrac{R + R_F}{A_O R} \right)\left(1 + \dfrac{R_O}{R_L} + \dfrac{R_O}{R + R_F} \right) \right] + \left(\dfrac{s}{\omega_0} \right)\left[\left(\dfrac{R + R_F}{A_O R} \right)\left(1 + \dfrac{R_O}{R_L} + \dfrac{R_O}{R + R_F} \right) \right]} \tag{2.3}$$

---

* The gain-bandwidth product (usually abbreviated *GB*) is the frequency at which the gain magnitude $|A(j\omega)|$ is unity. For a single-pole system, it must also be equal to the product $A_O \omega_0$ (rad/sec), or $A_O f_0$ (Hertz).

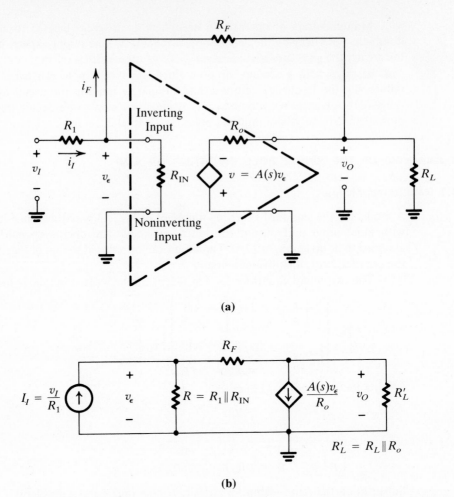

(a)

(b)

Figure 2.2 Models for the (a) nonideal inverting circuit, and (b) Norton equivalent circuit.

Several important observations from the results of this rather complicated equation can be made:

1. The first term in the numerator of Eq. (2.3) is identical to that of the ideal circuit, Eq. (1.2), namely

$$A_{CL}^{-}(\text{ideal}) = -\left(\frac{R_F}{R_1}\right) \tag{2.4}$$

2. The term within each bracket in the denominator of Eq. (2.3) is the reciprocal of the gain from a signal that would be returned to the output if a signal v_T were applied as indicated in Fig. 2.3; i.e. this is representative of

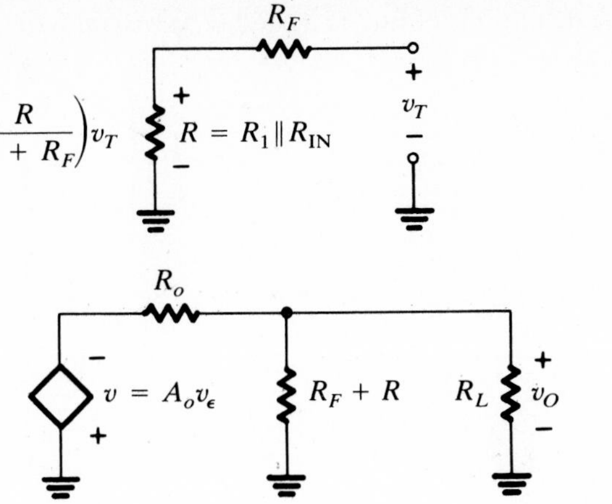

$$v_\epsilon = \left(\frac{R}{R + R_F}\right)v_T \qquad R = R_1 \| R_{\mathrm{IN}}$$

$$T_0 \equiv \frac{v_O}{v_T} = -\left(\frac{R}{R + R_F}\right)(A_o)\left[\frac{(R_F + R)\|R_L}{(R_F + R)\|R_L + R_o}\right]$$

Figure 2.3 Concept of dc loop transmission T_0 for the circuit of Fig. 2.2.

Bode's return difference*, or in modern signal analysis, the **dc loop transmission** T_0, where we can define

$$T_0 \equiv \frac{v_O}{v_T}$$

or for the circuit of Fig. 2.2 and 2.3,

$$T_0 = -A_O\left(\frac{R}{R + R_F}\right)\left(\frac{1}{1 + \dfrac{R_O}{R_L} + \dfrac{R_O}{R + R_F}}\right) \qquad R = R_1 \| R_{IN} \tag{2.5}$$

3. Since the open-loop output resistance R_O of the op amp is small (ideally, zero), and the open-loop dc gain A_O is very large (ideally approaching infinity), all terms in Eq. (2.3) multiplied by the ratio R_O/A_O are negligible. In fact, these terms involving $-R_O/A_OR_F$ in the numerator of Eq. (2.3) are a result of the **feedforward** of the signal from the input directly to the output by the feedback resistor R_F. Since these terms are negligible, we will generally ignore them in future analysis.

---

* Bode, H. W., *Network Analysis and Feedback Amplifier Design*, (Princeton: Van Nostrand, 1945). Also, much of the original analysis in feedback amplifiers was described by H. S. Black, Bell Telephone Laboratories, in his patent (No. 2,102,671) of December 21, 1937. Further early work is by R. B. Blackman, *Bell System Tech. J.*, Vol. 22, pp. 269–77, (Oct., 1943).

Thus, using the definitions of Eqs. (2.4) and (2.5) we can write the equation for the inverting gain as

$$A_{CL}^-(s) \approx A_{CL}^-(\text{ideal}) \left[\frac{1}{\left(1 - \frac{1}{T_0}\right) + \frac{s}{\omega_0}\left(-\frac{1}{T_0}\right)} \right]$$

or simplifying

$$A_{CL}^-(s) \approx \frac{A_{CL}^-(\text{ideal})\left(\dfrac{-T_0}{1 - T_0}\right)}{1 + \dfrac{s}{\omega_0(1 - T_0)}} \tag{2.6}$$

or since T_0 is negative*

$$A_{CL}^-(s) \approx \frac{A_{CL}^-(\text{ideal})\left(\dfrac{|T_0|}{1 + |T_0|}\right)}{1 + \dfrac{s}{\omega_0(1 + |T_0|)}} \tag{2.7}$$

Thus, we see that the nonideal op amp having a single pole in the open-loop gain also has a single pole in the closed-loop gain, but at a frequency increased by the loop transmission

$$\omega_{CL} = \omega_0(1 + |T_0|) \tag{2.8}$$

Since $|T_0|$ is typically much greater than unity

$$\omega_{CL} \approx \omega_0 |T_0|$$

We can also relate the closed-loop frequency to the gain-bandwidth product *GB*. For a single pole in the open-loop response $GB = \omega_0 A_0$. Hence, from Eqs. (2.5) and (2.8) the value of ω_{CL} is

$$\omega_{CL} \approx GB\left(\frac{R}{R + R_F}\right)\left(\frac{1}{1 + \dfrac{R_o}{R_L} + \dfrac{R_o}{R + R_F}}\right) \quad \approx \omega_0 |T_0| . \tag{2.9}$$

$$GB = \omega_0 A_0$$

2.1.2 Input and Output Impedance

The input impedance of the inverting nonideal circuit can be obtained from Fig. 2.2 by solving for the impedance looking into the inverting terminal, or from Fig. 2.2(a)

$$Z_{\text{in}} = R_{\text{IN}} \| \left(\frac{v_\varepsilon}{i_F}\right)$$

---

*Equation (2.7) can also be written more generally as

$$A_{CL}^- = A_{CL}^-(\text{ideal})\left[\frac{-T(s)}{1 - T(s)}\right]$$

Summing the currents flowing into the output node we obtain

$$\frac{v_\varepsilon}{i_F} = \frac{R_F}{1 + \dfrac{A(s)[1 - R_O/R_F A(s)]}{(1 + R_O/R_F + R_O/R_L)}}$$

Substituting the relation of Eq. (2.1) and simplifying, two distinct relationships arise (assuming $R_O \ll R_L, R_F$); for $\omega < \omega_0$

$$Z_{\text{in}} \approx R_{\text{IN}}\|\left(\frac{R_F}{1 + A_O}\right) \qquad\qquad (2.10)$$

and for $\omega > \omega_0$

$$Z_{\text{in}} \approx R_{\text{IN}}\|R_F\| \frac{R_F}{A_O}\left(1 + \frac{s}{\omega_0}\right) \qquad\qquad (2.11)$$

Thus, an equivalent-circuit representation of the input impedance of an inverting amplifier is as indicated in Fig. 2.4, for $R_O \ll R_L, R_F$.

The output impedance can be obtained from the circuit model of Fig. 2.2 by shorting the input signal v_I to ground, applying a signal v_t to the output, and finding the current I_t. From Fig. 2.2(a) we would have (since resistor R_L is present in parallel with the output, it is removed for simplicity)

$$v_\varepsilon = \frac{(R_1\|R_{\text{IN}})v_t}{(R_1\|R_{\text{IN}}) + R_F}$$

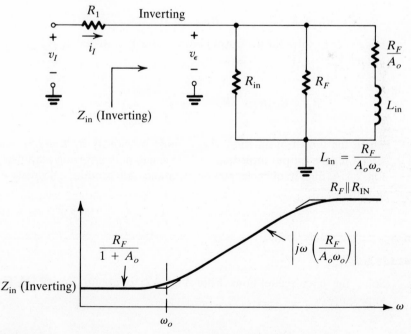

Figure 2.4 Input impedance of the single-pole inverting amplifier.

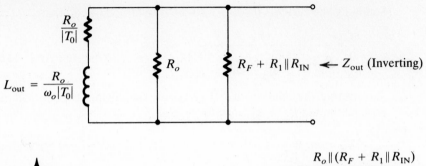

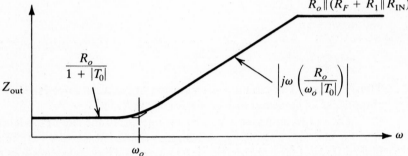

Figure 2.5 Output impedance of the single-pole inverting (or noninverting) amplifier.

This gives an output current

$$I_t = \frac{v_t}{R_F + R_1 \| R_{IN}} + \frac{v_t + v_\varepsilon A(s)}{R_O}$$

It is easier to solve for the output admittance Y_{out}. Reducing the previous equation to find $Y_{out} = I_t/V_t$

$$Y_{out} \approx \frac{1}{R_F + R_1 \| R_{IN}} + \frac{1}{R_O} + \frac{1}{\dfrac{R_O}{|T_0|}\left(1 + \dfrac{s}{\omega_0}\right)} \qquad (2.12)$$

where the loop transmission was defined previously by Eq.(2.5). An equivalent circuit for the output impedance of the single-pole inverting amplifier is shown in Fig. 2.5. At high frequencies stray capacitance will produce a decrease in the output impedance.

■ **Exercise 2.1**

Solve the circuit equations from Fig. 2.2 to obtain Eq. (2.11) for the input impedance.

■ **Exercise 2.2**

Similarly, solve the circuit equations of Fig. 2.2 that result from shorting v_I and applying a voltage v_t to the output, and find the output admittance

$$Y_{\text{out}} = \frac{I_t}{v_t}$$

EXAMPLE 2.1

A basic inverting amplifier circuit as in Fig. 2.2(a) has $R_1 = 1 \text{ k}\Omega$, $R_F = 100 \text{ k}\Omega$ and $R_L = 10 \text{ k}\Omega$. The op amp has a single pole at $\omega_0 = 2\pi \times 100$ rad/sec. The op amp also has an open-loop gain $A_O = 10^5$, with input and output resistance of 1 MΩ and 100 Ω, respectively. Find the closed-loop gain at dc $[A_{CL}^-(\text{dc})]$, the bandwidth, and the input and output resistance seen by the signal and the load, respectively. Also, find at dc the **fractional error** (defined as the difference between the ideal gain and the actual gain).

Solution
For this circuit the loop transmission as defined by Eq. (2.5) is

$$T_0 = -(10^5)\left(\frac{1 \text{ k}\Omega}{1 \text{ k}\Omega + 100 \text{ k}\Omega}\right)\left(\frac{1}{1 + \dfrac{10^2}{10^4} + \dfrac{10^2}{10^6}}\right) \quad = -A_0\left(\frac{R}{R+R_F}\right)\left(\frac{1}{1 + \frac{R_F}{\cdots} + \frac{R_4}{\cdots}}\right)$$

or

$$T_0 \approx -A_0\left(\frac{1}{102}\right) = -980.3$$

where $R = R_1 \| R_I = 1 \text{ k}\Omega \| 1 \text{ M}\Omega \approx 1 \text{ k}\Omega$. At dc the closed-loop gain is thus

$$A_{CL}^-(\text{dc}) = A_{CL}^-(\text{ideal})\left[\frac{-T_0}{1 - T_0}\right]$$

We could also write

$$A_{CL}^-(\text{dc}) = A_{CL}^-(\text{ideal})\left[1 - \frac{1}{1 + |T_0|}\right]$$

so that the difference between actual and ideal gain is

$$\text{fractional error} \equiv \frac{1}{1 + |T_0|} \tag{2.13}$$

With these values

$$A_{CL}^-(\text{dc}) = -\left(\frac{10^5}{10^3}\right)\left(1 - \frac{1}{981.3}\right)$$

or $A_{CL}^-(\text{dc})$ is equal to -100, the ideal gain, to within 0.1%. The bandwidth is, by Eqs. (2.8) or (2.9),

$$\omega_{CL} = 2\pi(100)(1 + 980.3) = 6.2 \times 10^5 \text{ rad/sec}$$

or

$$f_{CL} = 98.2 \text{ kHz}$$

Note that since the gain-bandwidth product for the op amp is

$$GB = 100 \times 10^5 = 10 \text{ MHz}$$

we would also have obtained the closed-loop bandwidth by

$$f_{CL} \approx GB\left(\frac{R}{R + R_F}\right) = 10 \text{ MHz}\left(\frac{10^3}{1.01 \times 10^5}\right) = 99 \text{ kHz}$$

The input resistance seen by the signal is, from Fig. 2.4, or Eqs. (2.10) and (2.11)

$$\frac{v_I}{i_I} = R_1 + Z_{\text{in}}(\text{inverting})$$

which at frequencies less than ω_0 is

$$r_{\text{in}} = 1 \text{ k}\Omega + \frac{10^5}{10^5} \approx 1 \text{ k}\Omega$$

Above ω_0 the input impedance increases as

$$Z_i \approx 1 \text{ k}\Omega + j\left(\frac{f}{100}\right)\left(\frac{10^5}{10^5}\right)$$

until a constant value (ignoring stray capacitance) is reached of $Z_i = 1 \text{ k}\Omega + 100 \text{ k}\Omega \| 1 \text{ M}\Omega = 91.9 \text{ k}\Omega$, which occurs at a frequency of approximately 9.1 MHz. The output resistance at dc from Fig. 2.5 or Eq. (2.12) is

$$r_O = \frac{R_O}{1 + |T_0|} = \frac{10^2}{981.3} = 0.11 \ \Omega$$

Likewise, the output impedance increases for frequencies beyond ω_0 until the limiting value of the open-loop resistance R_O is obtained at a frequency of approximately $f_0|T_0|$, or 98 kHz.

2.2 ANALYSIS OF THE SINGLE-POLE NONINVERTING OP AMP

We considered the ideal noninverting case previously in Fig. 1.4. Our circuit model remains the same, except we include finite input and output resistance, with a single-pole response

$$A(s) = \frac{A_O \omega_0}{s + \omega_0}$$

just as was defined earlier for the inverting amplifier.

2.2.1 Gain Relationships

The circuit diagram for the noninverting single-pole op amp is shown in Fig. 2.6. The equations are

$$v_I = v_\varepsilon + v_F$$

or

$$v_I = i_I(R_{\text{IN}}) + (i_I + i_F)R_1$$

and

$$A(s)v_\varepsilon = R_O(i_O + i_F) + i_F R_F + v_F$$

$$A(s)v_\varepsilon = R_O(i_O + i_F) + i_O R_L \tag{2.14}$$

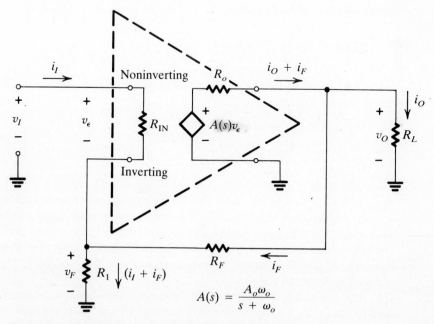

Figure 2.6   Model for the nonideal noninverting circuit.

Solving for the gain v_O/v_I gives the same basic form as the inverting Eq. (2.6)

$$A_{CL}^+(s) = A_{CL}^+(\text{ideal})\left[\frac{-T(s)}{1 - T(s)}\right] \approx \frac{A_{CL}^+(\text{ideal})\left(\frac{|T_0|}{1 + |T_0|}\right)}{1 + \frac{s}{\omega_0(1 + |T_0|)}} \qquad (2.15)$$

where

$$A_{CL}^+(\text{ideal}) = \frac{R_F + R_1}{R_1}$$

and the loop transmission is identical to that of Eq. (2.5) for the inverting amplifier

$$T_0 = -A_O\left(\frac{R}{R + R_F}\right)\left(\frac{1}{1 + \frac{R_O}{R_L} + \frac{R_O}{R_F + R}}\right) \qquad R = R_1 \| R_{IN} \qquad (2.5)$$

with $R = R_{IN} \| R_1$. So we see the same form of the gain equation as we obtained for the inverting case.

2.2.2 Input and Output Impedance

The input impedance can be obtained from the circuit of Fig. 2.6 and Eq. (2.14) by solving for the ratio of v_I to i_I

$$Z_{in}(s) = \frac{v_I}{i_I}$$

and if the output resistance R_O is small (i.e. $R_O \ll R_F$) the relation becomes

$$Z_{in}(s) \approx R_{IN}\left(1 + \frac{|T_0|}{1 + \frac{s}{\omega_0}}\right) + \frac{R_1 R_F}{R_1 + R_F} \qquad (2.16)$$

where the loop transmission T_0 was stated previously. In actuality, the value of $Z_{in}(s)$ of Eq. (2.16) is in parallel with a limiting resistance between each input of the op amp and ground, which is defined as the **common-mode input resistance**, R_{CM}. This resistance is the maximum value Z_{in} could ever achieve, and is obtained by applying a signal *common* to the two inputs of the op amp (See Problem 2.5). Normally $R_{CM} \gg R_{IN}$. An equivalent-circuit representation of Eq. (2.16) with R_{CM} included is shown in Fig. 2.7.

The equivalent circuit to obtain the output impedance is the same as the one used to obtain $Z_{out}(s)$ for the inverting amplifier. Thus, the circuit results shown in Fig. 2.5 and Eq. (2.12) also apply.

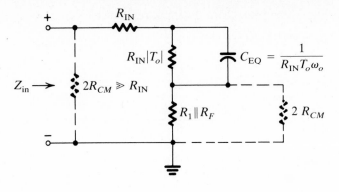

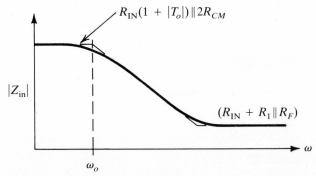

Figure 2.7 Input equivalent circuit for a noninverting amplifier.

EXAMPLE 2.2

Use the same parameter values for an op amp as in Example 2.1 with $R_1 = 1\ k\Omega$, $R_F = 100\ k\Omega$ and $R_L = 10\ k\Omega$. Assume the op amp also has $R_{CM} = 250\ M\Omega$. Find the dc voltage gain, bandwidth, and input and output resistance for the noninverting op amp. By what percentage would the signals v_I and v_F (see Fig. 2.6) differ if $\omega < \omega_0$ and $v_O = 10$ V.

Solution
The loop transmission is the same as for Example 2.1. Thus, from Eq. (2.15)

$$A_{CL}^+(\text{dc}) = A_{CL}^+(\text{ideal})\left[1 - \frac{1}{1 + |T_0|}\right]$$

or

$$A_{CL}^+(\text{dc}) = 101$$

and the fractional error is 0.1 %.

From Fig. 2.7 and Eq. (2.16) the input resistance is

$$r_{in} = 500 \text{ M}\Omega \| 1 \text{ M}\Omega (1 + 980.3)$$

or

$$r_{in} = 331 \text{ M}\Omega$$

The output resistance is the same as for Example 2.1

$$r_O = 0.11 \ \Omega$$

The closed-loop bandwidth is also the same as Example 2.1, or 98 kHz. For $\omega < \omega_0$ the input signal and the signal v_F differ only by the error signal v_ε which is

$$v_\varepsilon = \frac{v_O}{A_O} = \frac{10 \text{ V}}{10^5} = 0.1 \text{ mV}$$

But

$$v_I = \frac{v_O}{101} = 99 \text{ mV}$$

so

$$v_F = v_I - v_\varepsilon = 98.9 \text{ mV}$$

and the two signals differ by only 0.1 % or *by the fractional error.*

E X A M P L E 2.3

Find the characteristics for the unity-gain noninverting amplifier of Fig. 1.4(b) as was done in Example 2.2.

Solution
For the unity-gain noninverting circuit the feedback resistor R_F is zero, and resistor R_1 can be combined with the load resistor. Thus the feedback signal v_F is equal to v_O. Using the op amp parameters of Examples 2.1 and 2.2

$$|T_0| = A_O \left(\frac{1}{1 + \dfrac{R_O}{R_L} + \dfrac{R_O}{R_{IN}}} \right) \tag{2.17}$$

or

$$|T_0| = 10^5 \left(\frac{1}{1.01} \right) \approx 10^5 = A_O$$

Hence, at dc

$$r_{in} = 500 \text{ M}\Omega \| 10^{11} \ \Omega \approx 500 \text{ M}\Omega (= 2R_{CM})$$

and

$$r_O = \frac{R_O}{1 + |T_0|} = \frac{R_O}{1 + A_O} = 0.01\ \Omega$$

The closed-loop bandwidth is now the same as the gain-bandwidth product, or

$$f_{CL} = GB = 10\ \text{MHz}$$

2.3 DEFINITION OF OP AMP PARAMETERS

We have already described several of the nonideal characteristics of op amps, such as input and output resistance, open-loop gain A_O and open-loop bandwidth ω_0. Before we proceed further it is probably useful to define various other parameters we will use to characterize the performance of op amps in various circuits. In the following list the circuit symbols are also included.

Input Offset Voltage (V_{OS}). This is the dc voltage that must be applied between the input terminals of an op amp to reduce the dc output voltage to zero. Its value is usually stated as $\pm V_{OS}$, since it may be either polarity. The V_{OS} value is usually due to an imbalance in input-stage currents for a bipolar-transistor circuit, and to mismatches between pinchoff or threshold voltages for JFET or MOS designs. The offset voltage will drift with temperature as $\Delta V_{OS}/\Delta T$ (usually expressed in $\mu V/^\circ C$), and may also drift over long periods of time. For bipolar-transistor op amps V_{OS} is typically in the range of $\pm 10\ \mu V$ to 10 mV, while for some FET designs it can be greater than ± 50 mV (indeed, a recent gallium-arsenide op amp has $V_{OS} = \pm 500$ mV!).

Input Bias Current (I_B). This is the average of the dc currents flowing into (or out of) the inputs, expressed as

$$I_B \equiv \frac{I_B^+ + I_B^-}{2} \tag{2.18}$$

where I_B^+ is the input current of the noninverting terminal and I_B^- is the input current of the inverting terminal. For bipolar-transistor inputs I_B is in the range of 10 nA to 1 μA, while FETs have I_B values less than 100 pA and in some cases less than 10^{-14} A. The value of I_B will decrease with increasing temperature for bipolars, while for JFETs the input current (this is a reverse-bias pn-junction current) will double for every 8–12 $^\circ$C increase of temperature.

Input Offset Current (I_{OS}). The offset current is the difference of the two input bias currents, or

$$I_{OS} \equiv \pm |I_B^+ - I_B^-| \tag{2.19}$$

and for a well-matched differential-input stage should have a value easily one-fifth that of I_B (an exception occurs for the case of input circuits using current cancellation of I_B). The value of this parameter is also temperature dependent with $\Delta I_{OS}/\Delta T$ expressed in pA/°C.

Input Common-Mode Linear Range (V_{ICMR}). This is the maximum positive and negative voltage that we can apply to the op amp inputs and still have linear circuit operation. For power-supply voltages of ± 15 V, the common-mode range typically extends from $+13.5$ V to -13.5 V, although some op amps are designed for use with one power supply, so that the negative range can extend slightly beyond the negative power-supply value. For some P-channel JFET input designs the common-mode positive input voltage can equal the positive power-supply voltage.

Input Differential Range (V_{IDIFF}). This is defined as the maximum differential signal that can be applied between the two inputs without degrading the op amp characteristics.

Input Impedance (R_{IN}, C_{IN}, R_{CM}). This input impedance can generally be modeled by a resistance R_{IN} in parallel with a small capacitor C_{IN}. Typical values of R_{IN} range from 10 kΩ to 100 MΩ for bipolar designs, and up to 10^{14} Ω for some FET designs. C_{IN} is nominally 1–10 pF. As stated earlier, the common-mode input resistance R_{CM} is also in parallel with R_{IN}, but normally $R_{CM} \gg R_{\text{IN}}$.

Input Noise [e_n, i_n, e_n(p-p)]. This is the inherent noise of the op amp due to resistor noise and active-device noise. The input-noise voltage e_n is generally noise in some frequency bandwidth, specified in rms volts or as the square root of the short-circuit input-power spectral density, usually stated in nV/$\sqrt{\text{Hz}}$. Conversely, low-frequency noise is usually specified as an observed-input-equivalent, peak-to-peak noise (probably determined by a total peak-to-peak amplitude observation on an oscilloscope), with typical units of μV(p-p). The low-frequency bandwidth used most often is 0.1 Hz to 10 Hz. The input noise current i_n is an rms value of current specified as the square root of the open-circuit input-noise power density, usually specified as pA/$\sqrt{\text{Hz}}$. We will develop equations for calculating noise effects in Chapter 4.

Common-Mode Rejection Ratio (CMRR). This term is defined as the absolute value of the ratio of the differential open-loop gain to the common-mode open-loop gain, expressed as

$$\text{CMRR} \equiv \left| \frac{A_{\text{diff}}}{A_{CM}} \right| \tag{2.20}$$

or in decibels as

$$\text{CMRR(dB)} \equiv 20 \log_{10} \left| \frac{A_{\text{diff}}}{A_{CM}} \right| \tag{2.21}$$

Most inexpensive general-purpose op amps have values of CMRR in the range from 60–90 dB, while more expensive precision op-amps can achieve values of

120 dB. Another way of specifying CMRR is that it is the ratio of the change in the common-mode voltage to an equivalent change in the input voltage. Thus, an op amp having a CMRR of 80 dB would produce a ± 1 mV change in the input voltage for a 10 V change in common-mode input voltage. One further comment is necessary; values of CMRR (and PSRR defined below) stated by the manufacturer are low-frequency values (less than ω_0) and are not indicative of the degradation that occurs at higher frequencies. Generally the CMRR (and PSRR) values decrease like the gain function past ω_0. For example, a typical 741 op amp has a CMRR of 90 dB from dc to 100 Hz, but then decreases to a value of 20 dB at 1 MHz.

Power-Supply Rejection Ratio (PSRR). PSRR is the change in an op amp's input voltage per unit change in power-supply voltage. This term is expressed either in dB as

$$\text{PSRR(dB)} \equiv 20 \log_{10} \left| \frac{\Delta V_{\text{supply}}}{\Delta V_{\text{in}}} \right| \tag{2.22}$$

or, more typically on op amp data sheets, as the power-supply-voltage sensitivity S in units of μV/V. Values of S (and therefore PSRR) for the positive and negative power supplies are usually different. Typically, PSRR values for an op amp are in the same range as CMRR values.

Maximum Output-Voltage Swing (V_O). This is the maximum linear positive and negative output voltage allowed in an op amp before nonlinear effects due to transistor saturation or cutoff occur. For general purpose designs biased with ± 15 V power supplies, the output can usually swing a maximum of ± 13.5 V (about 2 V_{BE} voltages from the power supplies). For some op amps having MOS transistors in the output, it is possible to drive nearly to the "rail" (close to $\pm V_{\text{supply}}$).

Slew Rate (SR). This is the maximum rate (volts/time) at which the output voltage can change. It is normally expressed in units of volts/μsec with values of 0.1–1 V/μsec for general purpose op amps, but can exceed 1000 V/μsec for special high-frequency units. It has become standard practice for manufacturers to specify SR in a unity-gain noninverting configuration. Values of SR usually differ depending on whether the output signal is driving positive or negative.

Gain-Bandwidth Product (GB). This term was described earlier as the product of the open-loop gain A_O times the frequency of the dominant open-loop pole: $GB = A_O \omega_0$ (rad/sec) or $A_O f_0$ (Hertz). Alternatively, for an op amp having two or more open-loop poles the gain-bandwidth product is stated by the manufacturer to be measured for a given value of closed-loop gain (usually a gain of 10 or 100), for which the response is still dominated by a single-pole.

Full-Power Bandwidth (BW_p). This term is directly proportional to the slew rate of an amplifier. However, the value of BW_p is involved with the output response to a sinusoidal signal; it is defined as the maximum frequency of a sinusoidal input signal for which we can obtain a given peak-to-peak, large-signal output voltage without significant distortion. The full-power bandwidth can be much less than the small-signal bandwidth for an output-voltage swing approaching the maximum value $\pm V_O$.

Settling Time (t_s). This is the time required for the output signal of an op amp to settle to within some defined error band of the steady-state value. Typically, this band is $\pm 0.1\%$; for a 10 V steady-state output, this would be the time required for the output to be within ± 0.01 V of 10 V. This specification is very important for application circuits such as Analog-to-Digital and Digital-to-Analog converters.

Short-Circuit Output Current (I_{SC}). This is the maximum value of the current furnished by the op amp under shorted output conditions. Generally, the value is different for sourcing conditions as opposed to sinking conditions. Most inexpensive circuits have I_{SC} values of 20–40 mA, but special high-current output op amps may have I_{SC} greater than 1 A.

Phase Margin (PM or ϕ_m) and Gain Margin (GM or A_m). These terms are carryovers from Bode plots, and feedback-system analysis. The **phase margin** is defined as $180°$ plus the phase angle of $T(j\omega)$ where the magnitude of $T(j\omega)$ is unity. The **gain margin** is defined as the magnitude of $1/T(j\omega)$, in decibels, at the frequency for which the phase angle of $T(j\omega)$ is $180°$. Thus, for a stable system it is necessary that both GM and ϕ_m be greater than zero. A typical rule of thumb for good design is to have $\phi_m \geq 45°$ and $GM \geq 10$ dB. Of course, if we have only a single pole for the closed-loop response, then $\phi_m = 90°$.

2.4 EFFECTS OF DC OFFSETS

The dc parameters that will directly influence the output voltage are the input offset voltage V_{OS}, the input bias and offset currents I_B and I_{OS} and the common-mode and power-supply rejection ratios, CMRR and PSRR. We will examine each of these terms and their output effects separately and later combine them through an error budget analysis.

2.4.1 Input Offset Voltage, Bias, and Offset Currents

Practically all op amps have a differential-input bias network, either bipolar or FET, as shown in Fig. 2.8. The offset voltage at the input for a bipolar circuit is therefore

$$V_{OS(\text{Bipolar})} \equiv \pm |V_{BE1} - V_{BE2}|$$

and for a FET input circuit

$$V_{OS(\text{FET})} \equiv \pm |V_{GS1} - V_{GS2}|$$

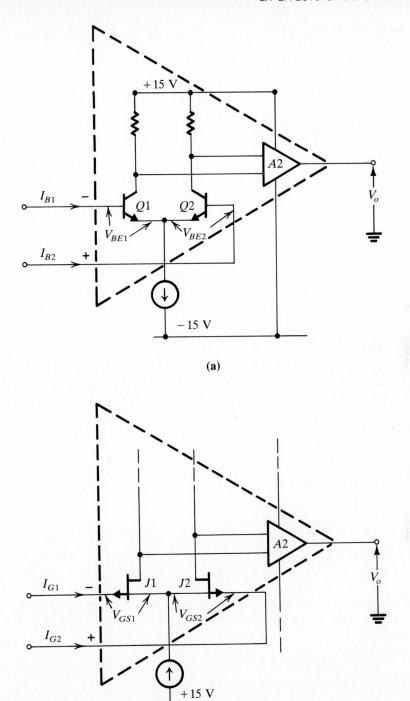

(a)

(b)

Figure 2.8 Circuits illustrating the input networks for typical op amps.

Similarly, the input bias and offset currents for the bipolar circuit would be

$$I_{B(\text{Bipolar})} \equiv +\left(\frac{I_{B1} + I_{B2}}{2}\right)^*$$

and

$$I_{OS(\text{Bipolar})} \equiv \pm|I_{B1} - I_{B2}|$$

while for the FET circuit

$$I_{B(\text{FET})} \equiv +\left(\frac{I_{G1} + I_{G2}}{2}\right)^*$$

and

$$I_{OS(\text{FET})} \equiv \pm|I_{G1} - I_{G2}|$$

To analyze effects due to V_{OS} we can insert a voltage generator in series with either input terminal of the op amp and calculate the gain to the output, as shown in Fig. 2.9. For the standard inverting circuit of Fig. 2.9(a), it is apparent that

$$V_{\text{out}}(\text{due to } V_{OS}) = \left(1 + \frac{R_F}{R_1}\right)V_{OS} \tag{2.23}$$

If there is no external resistance in series with the noninverting input, then I_{B2} has no effect. However, I_{B1} must flow through R_1 and R_F, giving an apparent input voltage

$$V_I = \left(\frac{R_1 R_F}{R_1 + R_F}\right)I_{B1}$$

At the output

$$V_{\text{out}} = I_{B1}\left(\frac{R_1 R_F}{R_1 + R_F}\right)\left(1 + \frac{R_F}{R_1}\right)$$

or since $I_{B1} \approx I_{B2} = I_B$

$$V_{\text{out}}(\text{due to } I_B) = I_{B1}R_F = I_B R_F \tag{2.24}$$

If a resistor is added in series with the noninverting input, the equation for the output voltage using superposition in Fig. 2.9(c) and the results of Eq. (2.24), becomes

$$V_{\text{out}} = I_{B1}R_F - \left(\frac{R_1 + R_F}{R_1}\right)(I_{B2}R)$$

---

* By convention I_B is positive if the current flows *into* the input and negative if current flows *out* of the input.

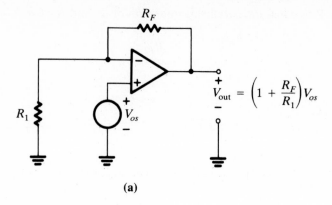

(a)

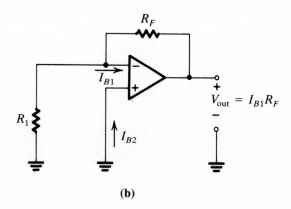

(b)

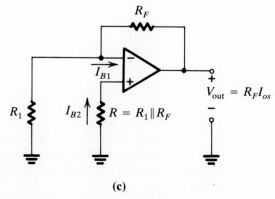

(c)

Figure 2.9 Calculation of effects due to (a) V_{OS}, (b) I_B, and (c) I_{OS}.

If we choose R to equal the parallel combination of R_1 and R_F then

$$V_{\text{out}} = I_{B1}R_F - \left(\frac{R_1 + R_F}{R_1}\right)\left(\frac{R_1 R_F}{R_1 + R_F}\right)I_{B2}$$

or

$$V_{\text{out}} = R_F(I_{B1} - I_{B2})$$

Using the definition of the offset current

$$V_{\text{out}} = R_F I_{OS} \tag{2.25}$$

Thus, the output voltage due to the combined effects of V_{OS}, I_B and I_{OS} is, for the circuit of Fig. 2.9(c)

$$V_{\text{out}} = \left(\frac{R_F + R_1}{R_1}\right)V_{OS} + R_F I_{OS} \tag{2.26}$$

One could estimate the change of V_{out} due to changes in operating temperature from Eq. (2.26) by taking appropriate derivatives, or

$$\frac{\Delta V_{\text{out}}}{\Delta T} \approx \left(\frac{R_F + R_1}{R_1}\right)\frac{\Delta V_{OS}}{\Delta T} + R_F \frac{\Delta I_{OS}}{\Delta T}$$

$$+ R_F\left(I_{OS} + \frac{V_{OS}}{R_1}\right)\left(\frac{\Delta R_F}{R_F \Delta T}\right) - \left(\frac{R_F V_{OS}}{R_1}\right)\left(\frac{\Delta R_1}{R_1 \Delta T}\right) \tag{2.27}$$

where the temperature coefficient of the resistors is included as a $\Delta R/R$ term.

EXAMPLE 2.4

Using the specifications for a 741C op amp (see Appendix C), with $R_F = 100 \text{ k}\Omega$ and $R_1 = 5 \text{ k}\Omega$, estimate the worst-case limits for the output offset voltage ($V_{\text{out(wc)}}$) at 25 °C, using the circuits of Fig. 2.9.

Solution

From the data sheet for the 741C in Appendix C, at 25 °C, $V_{OS}(\text{max}) = \pm 6 \text{ mV}$, $I_B = 0.5 \ \mu\text{A}$ and $I_{OS} = \pm 0.2 \ \mu\text{A}$ (the $\pm$ signs are required for V_{OS} and I_{OS} since we do not know which of the inputs has the larger V_{BE} voltage or I_B current).

Thus, for the circuit of Fig. 2.9(a) or (b)

$$V_{\text{out(wc)}} = \left(\frac{105 \text{ k}\Omega}{5 \text{ k}\Omega}\right)(\pm 6 \text{ mV}) + 0.5 \ \mu\text{A}(100 \text{ k}\Omega)$$

$$= \pm 126 \text{ mV} + 50 \text{ mV}$$

or the output voltage is constrained to be within a zone

$$-76 \text{ mV} \leq V_{\text{out(wc)}} \leq 176 \text{ mV}$$

Actually, for typical values of $V_{OS} = \pm 2$ mV, $I_B = 80$ nA and $I_{OS} = \pm 20$ nA, we have

$$-34 \text{ mV} \le V_{\text{out}}(\text{typ}) \le 50 \text{ mV}$$

However, for the circuit of Fig. 2.9(c) we have

$$V_{\text{out(wc)}} = \left(\frac{105 \text{ k}\Omega}{5 \text{ k}\Omega}\right)(\pm 6 \text{ mV}) + 100 \text{ k}\Omega(\pm 0.2 \text{ }\mu\text{A})$$

or

$$-146 \text{ mV} \le V_{\text{out(wc)}} \le 146 \text{ mV}$$

and the typical results are

$$-44 \text{ mV} \le V_{\text{out}}(\text{typ}) \le 44 \text{ mV}$$

Note the interesting phenomenon that the V_{out} negative limit is greater for the case of Fig. 2.9(c) where the compensating resistor R is used.

The above results are illustrated by the graphs of Fig. 2.10(a) and (b).

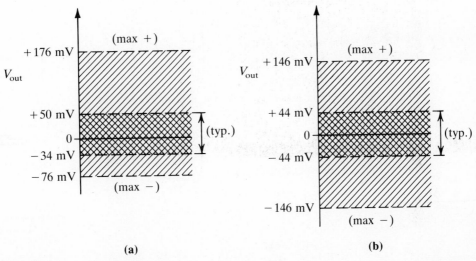

(a)   **(b)**

Figure 2.10 Output offset limits for a 741C op amp: (a) basic circuit; (b) compensated circuit.

■ **Exercise 2.3**

Repeat Example 2.4 for the case of an OP-27E op amp. From your results, which device would be better for a precision application, a 741C or an OP-27E?

EXAMPLE 2.5

For an inverting integrator circuit, find the effects of V_{OS}, I_B and I_{OS} on the circuit's performance.

Solution

The model for the integrator, with the offset voltage and bias current included, is shown in Fig. 2.11. The total current through the capacitor must be

$$I_F = I_B^- + \frac{V_{OS}}{R_1}$$

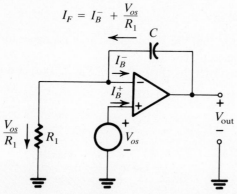

Where I_B^- is the input bias current for the inverting input, and I_B^+ is the input bias current for the noninverting input.

Figure 2.11 Integrator circuit for Example 2.5.

Hence, the output voltage must be

$$V_{\text{out}} = V_{OS} + \frac{1}{C} \int I_F \, dt$$

or

$$V_{\text{out}} = V_{OS} + \frac{I_B^- t}{C} + \frac{V_{OS} t}{R_1 C} \tag{2.28}$$

2.4.2 CMRR and PSRR Offsets

The dc offset effects of common-mode rejection and power-supply rejection of the op amp can also be modelled by circuit analysis. Since the common-mode rejection of a signal was defined earlier by the amplifier's CMRR where

$$\text{CMRR} \equiv \frac{A_{\text{diff}}}{A_{CM}} = \frac{A_O}{A_{CM}}$$

then the output signal due to both a differential-input signal and the common-mode signal is

$$V_{out} = A_O v_{diff} + A_{CM} v_{cm}$$

or

$$V_{out} = A_O \left(v_{diff} + \frac{v_{cm}}{CMRR} \right)$$

(2.29)

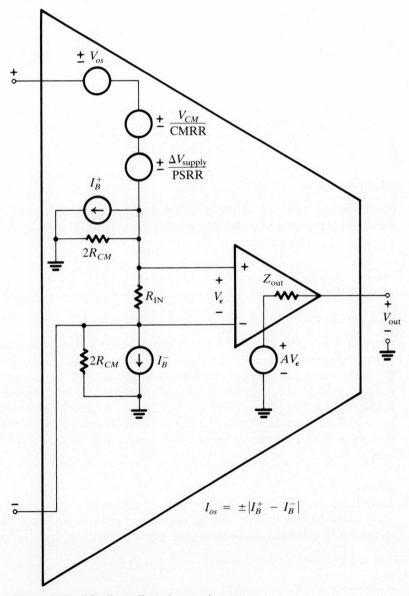

Figure 2.12 DC offset effects in a real op amp.

Similarly since the power-supply rejection was defined in terms of the PSRR by

$$PSRR = \frac{1}{S}$$

where the power-supply-voltage sensitivity term S was defined as the change in input voltage per volt change in power-supply voltage, then the output due to both a differential-input signal and power-supply changes would be

$$V_{out} = A_O v_{diff} + S\Delta V_{supply} A_O$$

or

$$V_{out} = A_O \left(v_{diff} + \frac{\Delta V_{supply}}{PSRR} \right) \tag{2.30}$$

The effects of dc offsets can be summarized as shown in Fig. 2.12 for a practical op amp, where each effect is referred to the input as an equivalent-signal generator.

2.4.3 Error Budget Analysis

The combined effect of all the dc offset conditions can be summarized for a particular application in a logical fashion by performing an error budget analysis for the circuit. This technique probably can best be illustrated by an example.

EXAMPLE 2.6

Consider the circuit of Fig. 2.13, which approximates a signal transducer whose internal resistance, nominally 10 kΩ at room temperature, may vary (due perhaps to temperature, nonlinearities, etc.) by as much as ±20%. Assume all other resistors used in the op amp circuit are metal-film*, ±0.5% tolerance (type RN55C) whose temperature coefficient is ±50 ppm/°C (max). The power supplies are ±15 V, but can vary by ±5%. The circuit is to operate over a temperature range of 0–70 °C. Evaluate the use of a 741C op amp versus a precision OP-27E op amp.

Solution
There is an error due to the finite open-loop gain, which was defined from Eq. (2.13) as the fractional error. The maximum gain error occurs when we have an op amp with minimum open-loop gain. For the 741C, A_O(min) is 15,000 (for

---

* Available resistor values for various tolerances are listed in Appendix E.

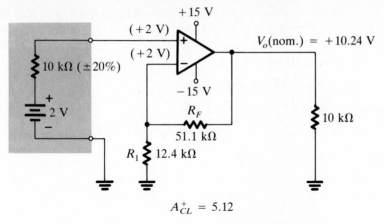

$$A_{CL}^{+} = 5.12$$

Figure 2.13 Circuit for error budget analysis of Example 2.6.

$0\,°C \leq T \leq 70\,°C$) while for the OP-27E, $A_O(\text{min})$ is 750,000. From Eq. (2.15), the gain at dc(A_{CL}^{+}) for a noninverting amplifier can be written as

$$A_{CL}^{+}(\text{dc}) = \left(1 + \frac{R_F}{R_1}\right)\left(1 - \frac{1}{1 + |T_0|}\right)$$

Therefore, the maximum output-voltage error due to finite gain for the 741C is

$$\Delta V_{\text{out}}(\text{max}) = V_{\text{out}}(\text{ideal}) - V_{\text{out}}(\text{actual})$$

or

$$\Delta V_{\text{out}}(\text{max}) = \frac{2\,\text{V}\,(5.12)}{1 + 1.5 \times 10^4 (0.188)} = -3.63\,\text{mV}$$

and for the OP-27E is

$$\Delta V_{\text{out}}(\text{max}) = \frac{10.24\,\text{V}}{1 + 7.5 \times 10^5 (0.193)} = -70.84\,\mu\text{V}$$

The output error due to the input offset voltage, using worst-case offset values of 50 μV for the OP-27E and 7.5 mV for the 741C, is

$$\Delta V_{\text{out}(741C)} = (5.12)(7.5\,\text{mV}) = \pm 38.41\,\text{mV}$$

and

$$\Delta V_{\text{out}(OP-27E)} = \pm 0.256\,\text{mV}$$

The offset-voltage change due to temperature is worst for a 25–70 °C change ($\Delta T = 45\,°C$). However, the maximum values of V_{OS} used in the above analysis included temperature-drift effects.

In the circuit of Fig. 2.13 the parallel combination of R_1 and R_F is equal to the nominal source resistance of 10 kΩ, thus input I_B currents are first-order compensated. However, in this example the source resistance can change by $\pm 20\%$, so the output-voltage error introduced due to I_B is

$$\Delta V_{out} = I_B \times \Delta R \times \text{Gain}$$

or for a 741C op amp

$$\Delta V_{out(741C)} = 0.8 \ \mu\text{A} \times 2 \ \text{k}\Omega \times 5.12 = \pm 8.19 \ \text{mV}$$

while for the OP-27E

$$\Delta V_{out(OP-27E)} = \pm 0.615 \ \text{mV}$$

The output voltage error due to I_{OS} is, for the 741C

$$\Delta V_{out(741C)} = 300 \times 10^{-9} \times 10 \ \text{k}\Omega \times 5.12 = \pm 15.4 \ \text{mV}$$

and for the OP-27E

$$\Delta V_{out(OP-27E)} = 50 \times 10^{-9} \times 10 \ \text{k}\Omega \times 5.12 = \pm 2.56 \ \text{mV}$$

The values of I_B and I_{OS} also change with temperature. However, since worst-case values over the range from 0 °C to 70 °C were used in the previous calculations, we do not have to add temperature effects.

The effect of CMRR is to add an equivalent-input dc offset of value V_{CM}/CMRR, as shown earlier. Using worst-case values for CMRR—here, we only have the data given at 25 °C, CMRR(min) = 70 dB, or 3162—we obtain for the 741C

$$\Delta V_{out(741C)} \approx 2 \ \text{V}\left(\frac{1}{\text{CMRR}}\right) \times 5.12 = \pm 3.24 \ \text{mV}$$

and for the OP-27E [CMRR(min) = 110 dB, or 3.16×10^5],

$$\Delta V_{out(OP-27E)} \approx 2 \ \text{V}\left(\frac{5.12}{3.16 \times 10^5}\right) = \pm 32.4 \ \mu\text{V}$$

The effects of power supply voltage changes of $\pm 5\%$ will be a ΔV_{supply} worst-case change of $2 \times 15 \ \text{V} \times 10\% = 3\text{V}$. Hence the output effect is a voltage change (we are using 150 μV/V as a worst-case estimate of S) of

$$\Delta V_{out(741C)} = 3 \ \text{V} \times 150 \ \mu\text{V/V} \times 5.12 = \pm 2.3 \ \text{mV}$$

and for the OP-27E

$$\Delta V_{out(OP-27E)} = 3 \ \text{V} \times 15 \ \mu\text{V/V} \times 5.12 = \pm 0.23 \ \text{mV}$$

The change in the output voltage due to the temperature coefficient (TC) of the resistors was discussed earlier, with the result stated in Eq. (2.27). Using these results we obtain for the circuit of Fig. 2.13 an output-voltage change of

$$\Delta V_O \approx 2 \ \text{V}\left(\frac{R_F}{R_1}\right)\left(\frac{\Delta R_F}{R_F} - \frac{\Delta R_1}{R_1}\right) \tag{2.31}$$

If resistor changes are equal there is no effect on the output voltage. However, the worst case would occur when one resistor has the maximum positive TC change of $+50$ ppm/°C and the other resistor has the maximum negative TC of -50 ppm/°C. For this case Eq. (2.31) obtains, for $\Delta T = 25\text{--}70$ °C,

$$\Delta V_{O(\text{wc})} = \pm 2 \text{ V}\left(\frac{51.1 \text{ k}\Omega}{12.4 \text{ k}\Omega}\right)(100 \times 10^{-6}/°\text{C})(45°\text{C})$$

or $\Delta V_{O(\text{wc})} = \pm 37.1$ mV.

The effects described in Example 2.6 are summarized for the two op amps in Table 2.1. Also included in Table 2.1 is a low-frequency noise specification in the 0.1–10 Hz region. Since this frequency range is so low, it is difficult to determine whether an output change is due to noise or drift. In either case, the inclusion of low-frequency noise is negligible as compared to the rest of the output errors.

The result of the analysis is that, for the most probable case, the errors add as the square root of the sum of the squares, or

$$\text{rms Error} \approx [V_{O1}^2 + V_{O2}^2 + \cdots + V_{ON}^2]^{1/2} \tag{2.32}$$

Table 2.1 SUMMARY OF DC ERROR BUDGET, EXAMPLE 2.6

Parameter	741C Output Error	OP-27E Output Error
Gain	-3.63 mV	-0.07 mV
V_{OS}	± 38.41 mV	± 0.26 mV
I_B	± 8.19 mV	± 0.62 mV
I_{OS}	± 15.4 mV	± 2.56 mV
CMRR	± 3.24 mV	± 0.032 mV
PSRR	± 2.3 mV	± 0.23 mV
Resistor TC	0 (typ) ± 37.1 mV (wc)	0 (typ) ± 37.1mV (wc)
Low-Frequency Noise (0.1 Hz to 10 Hz)	—	0.18 μV $\times A = 0.009$ mV (p-p)
Total Algebraic Worst-Case Error	71.17 mV* or 108.27 mV†	3.77 mV* or 40.9 mV†
Percentage Worst-Case Error	$\dfrac{71.17 \text{ mV}}{10.24 \text{ V}} = 0.70\%$* or 1.06%†	0.037%* or 0.4%†
Probable RMS Error	42.5 mV (0.41%)*	2.66 mV (0.026%)*

* Assumes TCs of R_1 and R_F are equal.
† Assumes TCs of R_1 and R_F are opposite.

For this example, the rms output-voltage error using a 741C could be as high as 42 mV, or 0.41% of the output voltage (42 mV/10.24 V × 100%), but for the OP-27E op amp the result is only 2.7 mV, or 0.026% of 10.24 V. These values are important, since if the output voltage were directly digitized by an Analog-to-Digital (A/D) converter, then a ±42 mV error is equivalent to ± one bit in an 8-bit A/D conversion (10.24 V/2^8 = 40 mV). However, a ±2.7 mV error is nearly equivalent to ± one bit in a 12-bit A/D conversion (10.24 V/2^{12} = 2.5 mV).

It is important to note how dominant would be the effect of a mismatch in the temperature coefficients of resistors R_1 and R_F; in either circuit the contribution could be a worst-case output of ±37 mV, a factor of 10 higher than all the rest of the errors combined for the OP-27E circuit. For precision applications it is therefore essential that metal-film or wirewound types of resistors be used, and that temperature coefficients track as closely as possible.

2.5 LARGE-SIGNAL CONDITIONS

We have already seen how the gain, loop transmission, and open-loop bandwidth ω_0 determine the gain-bandwidth product GB, and therefore the bandwidth for either inverting or noninverting designs. The high-frequency −3 dB value (f_{high} or f_{-3dB}) is, however, strictly a *small-signal* value. The logical question that arises is when does a signal output satisfy small-signal conditions and when does it not (and therefore require some type of large-signal calculation)? The answer lies in a parameter specified for op amps as the **slew-rate limit** SR, or the **full-power bandwidth**, BW_p (sometimes also called **maximum-power bandwidth**).

The slew-rate limit for an op amp is the maximum rate of change of the amplifier's output voltage, and in a typical integrated circuit design is due to the fact that the compensation capacitor has only a finite current available for charging or discharging. This is illustrated in Fig. 2.14, a circuit diagram characteristic of most inexpensive single-pole op amps. Here the current source I provides equal currents to the differential-input transistors Q_1 and Q_2. If a large differential signal is applied, say for example Q_2 is turned off, then Q_1 must be driven more into conduction, so that the collector current of Q_1 becomes equal to I while the collector current of Q_2 goes to zero. Because of the current-mirror action of Q_3, $I_{C3} = I_{C4} = I$. So the current flowing through the compensation capacitor C_c is limited to I, and since the rate of change of voltage across the capacitor is

$$\frac{dv_c}{dt} = \frac{I}{C_c}$$

the output voltage of A_2 is the same value. Since it is also the same as V_{out} we have for the positive output limit

$$SR^+ = \frac{dv_O}{dt} = \frac{I}{C_c} \tag{2.33}$$

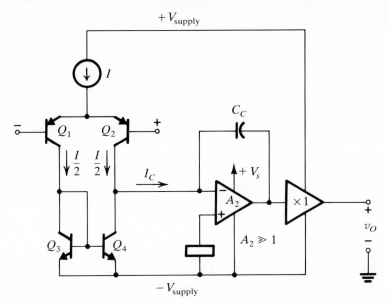

Figure 2.14 Simplified schematic diagram of a standard IC op amp.

The same scenario could be stated for the opposite condition, when the input signal forces the collector current of Q_1 to zero, thereby forcing the collector current of Q_2 to increase from $I/2$ to I, with the result that now, for the negative output limit

$$SR^- = \frac{dv_O}{dt} = -\frac{I}{C_c} \tag{2.34}$$

For example, in a 741 op amp the value of I is typically 20 μA, while the compensation capacitor C_c is 30 pF. Thus, the slew-rate limit should theoretically be

$$SR(741) = \frac{20 \ \mu\text{A}}{30 \ \text{pF}} = 0.67 \ \text{V}/\mu\text{sec}$$

The published data sheet value is typically 0.5 V/μsec for a 741.

The slew-rate limit is most appropriate when a circuit has a step function applied at the input, resulting in a linear rise or fall of the output signal, according to Eqs. (2.33) or (2.34). For a sinusoidal input signal, the output will also be limited when its maximum rate of change equals the slew-rate limit SR of the amplifier. Consider a sinusoidal output signal of peak value V_p

$$v_O(t) = V_p \sin \omega t$$

The derivative of the output is

$$\frac{dv_O(t)}{dt} = \omega V_p \cos \omega t$$

The maximum rate of change occurs at $t = 0$, or

$$\frac{dv_O(t)}{dt}(\text{max}) = \omega_{\text{max}}V_p \equiv 2\pi(BW_p)V_p$$

But this must equal the slew rate. We therefore have a relation between the slew rate and the full-power bandwidth, or

$$BW_p(\text{Hz}) = \frac{SR}{2\pi V_p} \tag{2.35}$$

Equation (2.35) shows that the borderline between small-signal and large-signal (slew-rate–limited) response is not just an amplifier effect; by trading off either frequency or peak amplitude (V_p), one can continue to have a low-distortion output.

As an example, the curve of peak-to-peak (p-p) output-voltage swing as a function of frequency for a 741 op amp is shown in Fig. 2.15. The full-power bandwidth for a 28 V (± 14 V) p-p output is approximately 10 kHz (this would correspond to a value for SR of $2\pi \times 14$ V $\times 10$ kHz $= 0.88$ V/μsec). However, if we lower the output voltage to 2 V p-p ($V_p = 1$ V), then the undistorted bandwidth reaches about 100 kHz.

The relationship between small-signal and large-signal response is illustrated by Example 2.7.

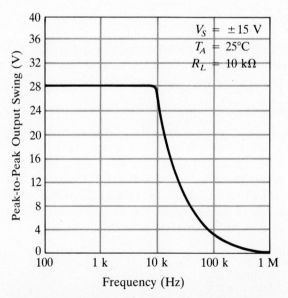

Figure 2.15 Peak-to-peak output voltage for a 741 op amp vs frequency. Source: Fairchild Camera and Instrument Corp.

EXAMPLE 2.7

The inverting circuit of Figure 2.16 is utilized to provide a gain of -5 for a square-wave input signal V_i. If a 741 is employed for the op amp, estimate the small-signal rise time (10–90%) of the output signal, and find the amplitude of V_i at which the small-signal rise time becomes equal to the large-signal slew-rate limit.

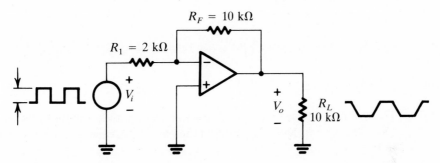

Figure 2.16   Circuit for Example 2.7.

Solution

If we use a typical value for *GB* of 1 MHz for the 741, the small-signal $-3\,\text{dB}$ bandwidth (f_{high}) for the circuit is

$$f_{\text{high}} \approx 1\,\text{MHz}\left(\frac{R_1}{R_1 + R_F}\right) = 167\,\text{kHz}$$

Since we have approximately a single-pole reponse for the amplifier, as

$$V_O(\text{s}) \approx V_i(\text{s})\left(\frac{-5}{1 + \dfrac{s}{\omega_{\text{high}}}}\right)$$

then, considering an initial step input of value

$$V_i(\text{s}) = \frac{V_i}{s}$$

the output signal is

$$V_O(\text{s}) = \frac{-5V_i\omega_{\text{high}}}{s(s + \omega_{\text{high}})}$$

In the time domain the solution is

$$v_O(t) = +5V_i[1 - \exp(-\omega_{\text{high}}t)]$$

Now, the small-signal output rise time τ_r between 10% and 90% of the output signal, is found by solving for the time required for the output to reach 90% of its final value (-4.5 volt) and 10% of its final value (-0.5 volt)

$$\tau_r = (t_{90} - t_{10}) \approx \frac{1}{\omega_{high}} (2.3 - 0.1)$$

or

$$\tau_r \approx \frac{2.2}{\omega_{high}} = \frac{0.35}{f_{high}} \qquad (2.36)$$

Hence, the small-signal 10–90% rise time for the circuit of Fig. 2.16 should be

$$\tau_r \approx \frac{0.35}{167 \text{ kHz}} = 2.1 \ \mu\text{sec}$$

The small-signal rise time is not a function of amplitude, but the output slew rate is.

The output slew-rate limit and the rise time τ_r become equal* when, from Eq. (2.36)

$$\frac{0.35}{f_{high}} \approx \frac{V_{out}(\text{p-p})}{SR}$$

or when the output p-p amplitude reaches

$$V_{out}(\text{p-p}) \approx \frac{0.35 \ SR}{f_{high}} \qquad (2.37)$$

or when the input p-p amplitude is

$$V_{in}(\text{p-p}) \approx \frac{1}{A_{CL}} \left(\frac{0.35 \ SR}{f_{high}} \right) \qquad (2.38)$$

For this example, using a 741 op amp

$$V_{out}(\text{p-p}) \approx -\frac{0.35 \times 0.5 \text{ V}/\mu\text{sec}}{167 \text{ kHz}} = -1.05 \text{ V}$$

or the input signal is

$$V_{in}(\text{p-p}) \approx \left(\frac{-1.05 \text{ V}}{-5 \text{ V}} \right) = 0.21 \text{ V}$$

Thus, in this example any output step signal of value greater than 1 V will be dominated by large-signal effects, while outputs below this value are controlled by

---

* This statement is not precisely correct, since the ratio $V_{out}(\text{p-p})/SR$ is 100% of the output, while τ_r relates to 10–90% of the output.

the small-signal rise time. It is possible to estimate the output rise time due to both effects by a method similar to Eq. (2.32), as*

$$\tau_{\text{out}} \approx [\tau_r(\text{small signal})^2 + \tau_r(\text{large signal})^2]^{1/2} \tag{2.39}$$

For this example, if the V_{out} value were indeed 1.05 V p-p, then approximately

$$\tau_{\text{out}} \approx \sqrt{2}(2.1 \ \mu\text{sec}) = 3 \ \mu\text{sec}$$

If the output amplitude were 10 V p-p, large-signal slew-rate limiting would occur and

$$\tau_{\text{out}} \approx \left[\left(\frac{10 \ \text{V}}{0.5 \ \text{V}/\mu\text{sec}} \right)^2 + (2.1 \ \mu\text{sec})^2 \right]^{1/2}$$

or

$$\tau_{\text{out}} \approx 20 \ \mu\text{sec}$$

---

* The fact that overall system rise time is approximately equal to the square root of the sum of the squares of individual rise times was first observed empirically by Valley and Wallman [Ref. 2.1], and stated mathematically by Elmore [Ref. 2.2]. For Eq. (2.39) to hold, overshoot should be small.

■ **Exercise 2.4**

If the input in Example 2.7 were a sinusoidal signal, for what value of output peak amplitude would the small-signal -3 dB bandwidth f_{high} equal the full-power bandwidth BW_p for the 741? For the LF351?

■ **Exercise 2.5**

From the specifications for typical slew rate for the LF351, what is the expected value of drain current for each input JFET?

2.6 OTHER USEFUL CIRCUITS

We could analyze many other very useful circuits for the effects of nonideal operation. For the present, however, we will look at only three important categories to illustrate some additional practical limitations.

Table 2.2 COMMERCIAL UNITY-GAIN DRIVERS

Device	Construction	f_{high} (MHz)	SR (V/μsec)	R_{in} (Ω)	R_{out} (Ω)	ΔV_{out} (or I_o) into R_L
3329	Hybrid	5	60	10 k	10	± 10 V (100 Ω)
3553	Hybrid	300	2000	10^{11}	1	± 10 V (50 Ω)
BUF-03	Mono.	63	250	10^{11}	2	70 mA (peak)
EL 2004	Hybrid	350	2500	10^{11}	4	± 9 V (100 Ω)
HA 2635	Mono.	8	500	2 M	2	± 12.5 V (50 Ω)
HA 5002	Mono.	110	1300	3 M	3	± 10 V (50 Ω)
HA 5033	Mono.	250	1300	1.5 M	5	± 10 V (100 Ω)
HOS 100	Hybrid	125	1400	200 k	8	± 10 V (100 Ω)
LH 0002	Hybrid	30	200	400 k	6	± 10 V (100 Ω)
LH 0033	Hybrid	100	1400	10^{11}	6	± 9 V (100 Ω)
LH 0063	Hybrid	200	6000	10^{11}	1	± 13 V (50 Ω)
MC 1438	Mono.	8	94	400 k	10	I_O adj. to 300 mA

2.6.1 Output Driver Circuits (Buffers)

Most commercially available, present-day monolithic op amps are capable of furnishing up to ± 20 mA into a load. Varieties such as the 741, 351, OP-27, and others also have output short-circuit protection to limit the output current to a safe value, typically less than 30 mA.

If we want to drive a low-value load resistance, or when output currents greater than 30 mA are required, we must either add a high-current driver stage* to the op amp, or buy a much more expensive op amp that has an internal driver. To avoid degrading the op amp characteristics, we must keep the driver inside the feedback loop. This latter requirement necessitates a unity-gain type of driver stage, or additional constraints on the loop transmission $T(j\omega)$ if additional gain is used.

Some representative commercial high-current unity-gain drivers useful for adding to op amps are shown in Table 2.2.

Since the commercial drivers indicated in Table 2.2 are fairly expensive, it is usually more advantageous to add a simple emitter follower, or other equivalent circuit, to the output of the op amp. Figure 2.17(a) shows probably the simplest possible driver circuit one could use. However, this circuit has two distinct disadvantages: (1) no short-circuit protection; and (2) considerable crossover distortion, since only one of the output transistors can be conducting at any particular time. Both disadvantages are removed in the accompanying circuit of Fig. 2.17(b).

The circuit of Fig. 2.17(b) allows both Q_1 and Q_2 to be biased in a linear mode. Furthermore, short-circuit protection is provided by D_3 and D_4. The resistors R_5 and R_6 are chosen so that the maximum current required from Q_1 or

---

* High-current drivers are often referred to as **buffers**.

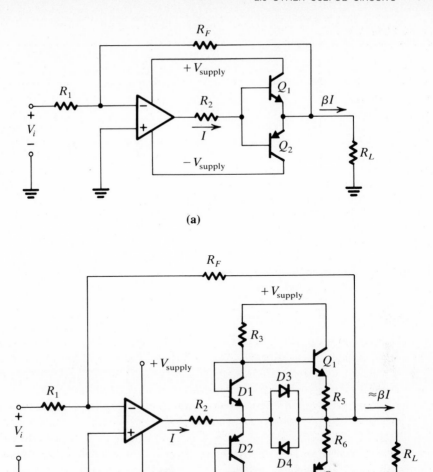

(a)

(b)

Figure 2.17 (a) A very simple driver circuit. (b) A way to include short-circuit protection and reduce cross-over distortion.

Q_2 is equal to the short-circuit limit required; thus, the product of $I_{sc}(Q_1) \times R_5$ is set equal to the forward-conduction voltage of D_3 (typically 0.7 V). Hence, when the maximum positive short-circuit-current limit is reached, D_3 conducts, thereby limiting the base current to Q_1. Similarly, $R_6 \times I_{sc}(Q_2)$ causes forward conduction of D_4. The actual output short-circuit current will include the current available from the op amp, which will also flow as well through D_3 or D_4. Although the circuits shown in Fig. 2.17 are for an inverting amplifier connection, the same driver circuits can also be used in noninverting applications.

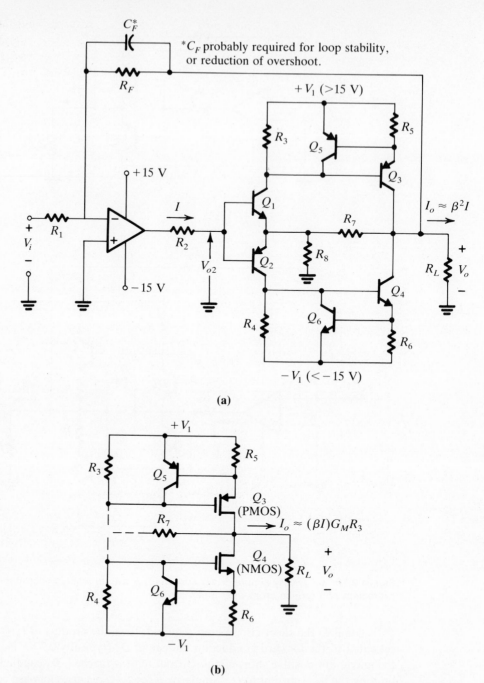

Figure 2.18 Output buffer circuits with higher output voltage: (a) bipolar output; (b) power MOS output.

For applications that require higher output voltages as well as high power, the circuits of Figs. 2.18(a) and (b) can be used. The circuit of Fig. 2.18(a) can theoretically furnish $\beta^2 \times I$ current to the load. Transistors Q_5 and Q_6 provide short-circuit protection for Q_3 and Q_4, respectively. R_5 and R_6 would be chosen such that

$$R_5 = \frac{V_{BE5}}{I_{sc}(Q_3)}$$

while correspondingly

$$R_6 = \frac{V_{BE6}}{I_{sc}(Q_4)}$$

If resistor R_7 is zero, the voltage gain from the output of the op amp to the load is unity. However, with R_7 present, the gain from the op amp output to the load is multiplied by the booster gain

$$A_{\text{booster}} \approx \left(\frac{R_7 + R_8}{R_8} \right)$$

For example, if the normal linear output of the op amp is ± 10 V (V_{O2}), and we wish to drive the load to ± 45 V, we would probably choose $\pm V_1$ to be ± 50 V, and let the booster gain be 4.5; so we would choose $R_7 = 3.5 R_8$, or we might let $R_8 = 110 \ \Omega$, so $R_7 \approx 390 \ \Omega$.

■ **Exercise 2.6**

We wish to use a 741C op amp, in a gain of $+10$ (V/V) circuit, and to drive a 100-ohm load resistor to ± 5 volts peak. Using the circuit of Fig. 2.17(b) specify all component values to meet the requirements, and provide an SC current limit at ± 75 mA. Specify transistors to use for Q_1 and Q_2, and specify whether a heat sink is required, if operation to an ambient of 50 °C is required.

Some additional power-output circuits are shown in Problems 2.32, 2.35 and 2.36 at the end of the chapter.

2.6.2 Single-Power-Supply Biasing

Often, an application will require that op amp circuits be designed into systems having only one power supply (automotive systems, for example). This creates some special, although not insurmountable, problems. In general, bias connections using one power supply are considerably simplified if one remembers that the error signal v_ε between the inputs of an op amp must approach zero, or as stated in Section 1.2, the signal at the noninverting input always attempts to achieve the same value as that on the inverting input. If we raise the noninverting input to a given potential [usually a value such that $V_{out}(dc) = V_{supply}/2$], we also force the inverting input to the same potential. As an example, consider the circuit in Fig. 2.19. Here, raising the noninverting input potential to $+7.5$ V causes an equal voltage to appear at the inverting input, and essentially also at the output, since

$$V_{out} = V_{inv.} + I_B^-(20 \text{ k}\Omega) \approx V_{inv.} = +7.5 \text{ V}$$

In the circuit of Fig. 2.19 the linear output of the op amp will swing from approximately $+13.5$ V to $+1.5$ V, or V_O (across the load) goes from $+6$ V to -6 V.

A basic limitation to the use of one power supply occurs because of the input common-mode range V_{ICMR} of the op amp. For the basic 741-type op amp the input signal to either input for linear circuit operation must typically be between $+V_{supply} - 1$ V and $-V_{supply} + 1.5$ volts, or for operation with one supply voltage of $+15$ volts, between $+14$ volts and $+1.5$ volts. Thus, signals which cause either input to go below $+1.5$ volts would produce distorted outputs. Fortunately, several of the more recent dual and quad op amps, such as the LM124-324, LM158-358, LM2900, MC3401-3403, MC34074, OP421, HA5144, and others provide a pnp common-collector input stage that allows the input voltage to go to the $-V_{supply}$ value, and still have linear operation.

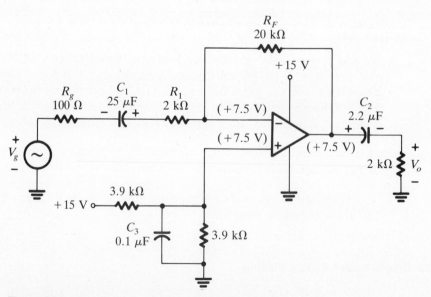

Figure 2.19 Op amp circuit using one power supply.

For circuits using P-channel JFETs in the input stage, such as the LF351 op amp, the input common-mode linear range will include the positive power-supply voltage.

EXAMPLE 2.8

For the circuit of Fig. 2.19 estimate values of $f_{low}(-3 \text{ dB})$, $f_{high}(-3 \text{ dB})$, and A_{mid}, if a 741 op amp is utilized in the circuit.

Solution
Regardless of the type of op amp used, if the low-frequency open-loop gain is large, then the inverting input appears as an ac virtual ground. Thus, the low-frequency input RC time-constant is

$$\tau_{in} = C_1(R_g + R_1) = 52.5 \text{ msec}$$

or the low-frequency -3 dB value due to C_1 is

$$f_1 = \frac{1}{2\pi\tau_{in}} = 3 \text{ Hz}$$

Similarly, since T_0 is large, the output impedance seen by C_2 is small; hence,

$$\tau_2 \approx C_2 R_L = 4.4 \text{ msec}$$

or

$$f_2 = \frac{1}{2\pi\tau_2} = 36.1 \text{ Hz}$$

The effect of C_3 is negligible, since it does not directly affect the gain. Hence the approximate f_{low} for the circuit is

$$f_{low}(-3 \text{ dB}) \approx 36.1 + 3 = 39 \text{ Hz}$$

The midband gain occurs when the reactance of C_1 and C_2 is small (effectively C_1 and C_2 appear shorted), so since $T_0 \gg 1$,

$$A_{mid} \approx -\left(\frac{20 \text{ k}\Omega}{2.1 \text{ k}\Omega}\right) = -9.52$$

The f_{high} is given by

$$f_{high}(-3 \text{ dB}) = GB\left(\frac{R_1 + R_g}{R_1 + R_g + R_F}\right)$$

or for the inverting amplifier

$$f_{high} \approx 1 \text{ MHz}\left(\frac{1}{1 + |A_{mid}|}\right) = 95 \text{ kHz}$$

■ **Exercise 2.7**

Suppose one desires to eliminate the capacitor C_1 (short out C_1) in Fig. 2.19, but still have $V_O(dc) = +V_{supply}/2 = +7.5$ V. What should be the dc voltage value at the noninverting input to accomplish this? What restriction would this place on the type of op amp that could be used?

2.6.3 Nonideal Differential-Amplifier Problems

The basic differential-amplifier circuit was shown in Fig. 1.13, and a two-op-amp version in Problem P1.20. In both circuits it was assumed that resistors were perfectly matched (in Fig. 1.13, for example, that $R_2 = R_1$ and $R_3 = R_F$). However, resistors always have a tolerance factor, with values guaranteed to be $\pm 5\%$, $\pm 2\%$, $\pm 1\%$, etc. The matching can create real problems when one must have a large value of CMRR for a particular application.

To illustrate this problem, the differential amplifier is redrawn in Fig. 2.20, for a nominal gain of -10 for the differential signal. We assume that the resistors are metal-film type, with a $\pm 1\%$ tolerance (for example, type RN55C), and that a common-mode signal of $+10$ V is present. We will use an OP-27 precision op amp, which has a guaranteed CMRR ≥ 110 dB.

In Fig. 2.20, since $T_0 \gg 1$, the gain for the differential signal is

$$A_{diff} = \frac{v_O}{v_{diff}} = -\left(\frac{R_F}{R_1}\right) = -10$$

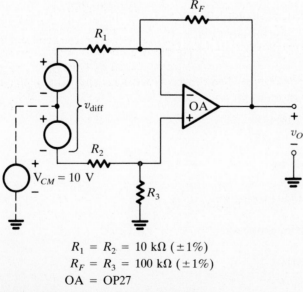

$$R_1 = R_2 = 10 \text{ k}\Omega \ (\pm 1\%)$$
$$R_F = R_3 = 100 \text{ k}\Omega \ (\pm 1\%)$$
$$OA = OP27$$

Figure 2.20 Basic differential amplifier.

Using superposition, and with R_{IN} very large for the op amp*, the gain for the common-mode signal is

$$A_{CM} = \frac{V_O}{V_{CM}} = -\left(\frac{R_F}{R_1}\right) + \left(\frac{R_3}{R_2 + R_3}\right)\left(\frac{R_F + R_1}{R_1}\right) \tag{2.40}$$

Now assume a worst-case situation, that R_F and R_2 will be $+1\%$ *above* the stated value, while R_3 and R_1 will be 1% *below* the stated value. Thus, Eq. (2.40) becomes

$$\left(\frac{V_O}{V_{CM}}\right)_{\text{worst case}} = -\left(\frac{R_F + 1\%}{R_1 - 1\%}\right)$$
$$+ \left[\frac{R_3 - 1\%}{(R_2 + 1\%) + (R_3 - 1\%)}\right]\left[1 + \frac{(R_F + 1\%)}{(R_1 - 1\%)}\right] \tag{2.41}$$

Substituting values we have

$$\left(\frac{V_O}{V_{CM}}\right)_{\text{worst case}} = -10.20202 + 10.16498 = -0.037034 \tag{2.42}$$

or for a $+10$ V common-mode input signal

$$(V_{OCM})_{\text{worst case}} = -0.37 \text{ V}$$

Thus, the actual common-mode rejection ratio for the circuit is

$$\text{CMRR}_{\text{worst case}} = 20 \log_{10}\left|\frac{A_{\text{diff}}}{A_{CM}}\right| = 20 \log_{10}\left|\frac{10}{0.037}\right| = 48.6 \text{ dB} \tag{2.43}$$

Hence, the limiting factor is not the CMRR of ≥ 110 dB for the OP-27, but rather the *precision of the resistors*.

It is possible to increase the CMRR to a value approaching that of the op amp itself by making one of the resistors in Fig. 2.20 variable. For example, resistor R_3 could be replaced by a 9.09 kΩ resistor in series with a 2 kΩ potentiometer. With the circuit operating and the $+10$ V common-mode voltage present, the potentiometer would be adjusted for minimum common-mode output signal.

Later we will examine other circuits that improve upon the characteristics of the basic differential amplifier. These circuits come under the general category of **instrumentation amplifiers** and will be treated in detail.

SUMMARY

This chapter has gone beyond the "ideal" op amp concept of Chapter 1 to the practical nonideal device approximated by one dominant open-loop pole, a finite open-loop gain (A_{OL}), as well as a large (but not infinite) input resistance, and finite output resistance. We have also found how the dc errors at the input of the op amp

---

* The input resistance R_{IN} is not effective in this case because it is driven by the same V_{CM} on both ends of R_{IN} (this is often referred to as "bootstrapping"). Here, R_{IN} reduces to R_{CM}, which for an OP-27 is typically 2000 MΩ.

(due to V_{OS}, I_B, CMRR, and PSRR) can be analyzed, and how these dc offsets affect the performance of the op amp circuit.

The concept of loop transmission was introduced, and techniques presented for analyzing some of the practical circuits most often used. The most significant deviation from the ideal op amp, the frequency response, often proved to be the most challenging limitation to the actual use of op amp circuits, particularly when output-signal amplitudes are limited by the slew-rate response of the device. For this reason, the frequency (and transient) response of actual commercial op amps is explored more fully in the next chapter.

It is hoped that the student has now begun to develop a reasonable familiarity for standard inverting and noninverting circuits, and their general analysis.

PROBLEMS

2.1 Starting with the basic Eq. (2.2) derive the relationships of Eqs. (2.3) and (2.7).

2.2 Using the same op amp parameters as Example 2.1, find the closed-loop bandwidth, input and output resistance, and fractional error for $R_1 = 10$ kΩ and $R_F = 1$ MΩ for the inverting circuit.

2.3 Rework Problem 2.2, but use a 741C op amp. The parameters for a 741 op amp are shown in Appendix C.

2.4 Rework Problem 2.2, but use an LF351 op amp. The parameters are in Appendix C.

2.5 Using Eqs. (2.14), obtain the relation of Eq. (2.15). You may ignore the zero term in the numerator of v_O/v_I.

2.6 For a 741 op amp estimate the common-mode input resistance, R_{CM}. Use the circuit indicated on the data sheet, and assume the same signal v_{CM} is applied to the inputs of Q_1 and Q_2. The collector current of Q_8 is 20 μA, and npn transistors have

$$\beta_N = 200, \qquad r_{CE(N)} = \frac{100}{I_C}$$

while pnp transistors have $\beta_P = 50$, and $r_{CE(P)} = 60/I_C$.

2.7 Using the typical parameters for a 741C op amp, find the dc gain, input resistance and output resistance for a noninverting circuit having $R_F = 200$ kΩ, $R_1 = 10$ kΩ, and $R_L = 10$ kΩ. Find also the -3 dB bandwidth for the circuit. To what frequency is the approximation $Z_{in} = R_{IN}(1 + |T_0|)\|2R_{CM}$ good, for 10% accuracy? Assume $R_{CM} = 250$ MΩ.

2.8 If the signal source in Problem 2.7 has an internal resistance of 100 kΩ, discuss how this would affect the results of Problem 2.7.

2.9 A 741C op amp is used in a unity-gain noninverting circuit. Using typical parameters find r_{in}, r_{out}, the -3 dB bandwidth and $|T_0|$. Assume $R_L = 10$ kΩ.

2.10 A 741C op amp is used in a unity-gain inverting circuit, with $R_F = R_1 = R_L = 10$ kΩ. Find r_{in}, r_{out}, the -3 dB bandwidth and $|T_0|$. Compare with the results of Problem 2.9.

2.11 Use an LF351 op amp in the basic integrator circuit of Fig. 1.5, with $R_1 = 100$ kΩ and $C = 1$ μF. Plot the loop transmission $T(j\omega)$ versus frequency (i.e., a Bode plot) using typical parameter values of the LF351. Over what frequency range would this circuit be useful as an integrator?

2.12 A summing circuit is formed, as in Fig. 1.8(a), with three inputs v_1, v_2 and v_3. The resistors are $R_1 = 20$ kΩ, $R_2 = R_3 = R_L = 10$ kΩ and $R_F = 100$ kΩ. If a 741C op amp is utilized, find the values of input resistance seen by v_1, v_2, and v_3, the output resistance seen by the load, and the -3 dB bandwidth for the circuit.

2.13 The integrator and differentiator circuit can be combined as shown in Fig. P2.13. Assuming an ideal op amp, show that the transfer function is

$$\frac{V_O}{V_{in}}(j\omega) = \frac{-K_O j\left(\dfrac{\omega}{\omega_3}\right)}{\left(1 + j\dfrac{\omega}{\omega_1}\right)\left(1 + j\dfrac{\omega}{\omega_2}\right)}$$

(a) For values $R_1 = 1$ kΩ, $R_F = 100$ kΩ, $C_1 = 8.2$ μF, and $C_F = 82$ pF, and assuming an ideal op amp, sketch the Bode plot (dB vs frequency).

(b) If the op amp is not perfect, but has a single pole in the open-loop response, what is the minimum value of GB necessary for $T \geq 100\,(40$ dB$)$ for all frequencies of interest?

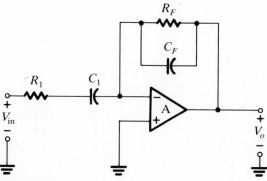

Figure P2.13

2.14 Make a table comparing the 741C, LF351, and OP-27E op amps in terms of the parameters V_{OS}, I_B, I_{OS}, V_{ICMR}, V_{IDIFF}, R_{IN}, C_{IN}, R_{CM}, CMRR, PSRR, V_O, SR, BW_p, t_s (for unity gain), and I_{SC}. Assume an output of ± 10 V. Some values may not be indicated for all op amps.

2.15 Using circuit analysis, show that for $T_0 \gg 1$, Eq. (2.24) is true.

2.16 For a noninverting amplifier such as the basic circuit of Fig. 1.4(a) with $R_1 = 1\ \text{k}\Omega$ and $R_F = 1\ \text{M}\Omega$, find the worst-case output offset limits due to V_{OS}, I_B, and I_{OS}, both positive and negative, using (a) a 741C and (b) an LF351 op amp. Compare your results. What do the results suggest as to the type of op amp required when large values of R_F are used?

2.17 For the standard differential amplifier of Fig. 1.13 with $R_1 = R_2 = 10\ \text{k}\Omega$ and $R_F = R_3 = 200\ \text{k}\Omega$, find the typical and worst-case output offset limits due to V_{OS}, I_B, and I_{OS}, both positive and negative, using (a) a 741C and (b) an LF351 op amp. Find the value of $|T_0|$ for each circuit, using typical parameter vaues.

2.18 An HA2540 op amp (data shown in Appendix C) is used in the differentiator circuit of Fig. 1.7(b), with $R_F = 100\ \text{k}\Omega$, $R_1 = 200\ \Omega$ and $C = 1\ \mu\text{F}$.
(a) Find the worst-case output offset limits due to V_{OS}, I_B and I_{OS} for the circuit.
(b) Using asymptotes, sketch a Bode plot for the circuit (the plot of $|T|$ vs. frequency). Over what frequency range does this circuit form a useful differentiation function?

2.19 In the integrator circuit of Fig. 2.11, if a compensating resistor R is placed in series with the noninverting input of the op amp, find the equation for the output voltage of the integrator. If at time $t = 0$ there is to be no output, what should the value of R be?

2.20 A modification of the basic summing circuit is often used to adjust for dc offsets, as shown in Fig. P2.20. If the op amp is a 741C with $R_F = 200\ \text{k}\Omega$, $R_1 = 20\ \text{k}\Omega$, $R_2 = 10\ \text{k}\Omega$ and $R_3 = 510\ \text{k}\Omega$, choose values for R_A, R_B and R_x to allow for nulling the output voltage to zero, if the op amp is to work over a temperature range from 0 °C to 70 °C. What value should R be if it is used in the circuit?

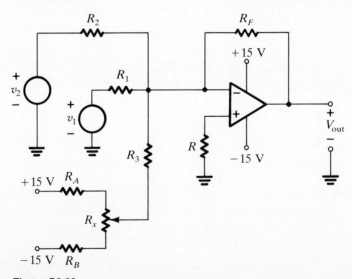

Figure P2.20

2.21 Repeat Example 2.6 using the circuit of Fig. 2.13, but compare results using a 741C versus an LF351.

2.22 For the unity-gain circuit of Fig. P2.22 construct a table for an error budget analysis if an FET op amp, the LF351 is used. Assume the power supplies may vary by $\pm 10\%$ and that the circuit is to work over a temperature range from 0 °C to 70 °C.

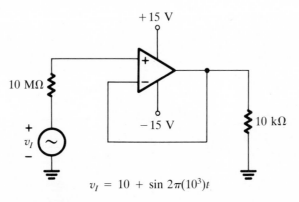

$$v_I = 10 + \sin 2\pi(10^3)t$$

Figure P2.22

2.23 If a 741 op amp were redesigned so that each transistor in the differential stage (see Fig. 2.14) was biased at $I_c = 100\ \mu A$, for $C_c = 30$ pF, how would this affect the values of SR, BWp, GB, V_{OS}, I_B, and I_{OS} for the circuit?

2.24 Compare anticipated values of V_{OS}, I_B, SR, and GB for two op amps that are biased for equal transconductance (g_m) in the input stage, and have equal compensation capacitance C_c. One is a bipolar-input stage and the other is an FET-input circuit.

2.25 Show that the circuits indicated in Fig. P2.25 are useful for measuring V_{OS} and I_B. What limitations exist in using these circuits? How would one of these circuits be adapted to measure I_{OS}?

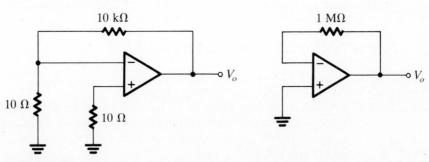

Figure P2.25

2.26 The circuit of Fig. P2.26 is a more elaborate, and also more useful, way to measure V_{OS}, I_B and I_{OS}, by appropriate choice of resistors R_s and R_F and closure of switches S_1 and S_2. Show (if S_1 and S_2 are open and $V_C = 0$ V) that the output voltage of this circuit is equal to

$$V_{out(2)} = \left(1 + \frac{R_F}{100}\right)V_{OS} + R_s\left(1 + \frac{R_F}{100}\right)(I_B^+ - I_B^-)$$

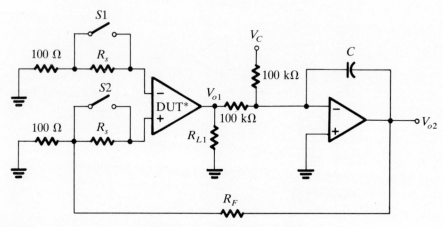

*DUT = Device Under Test

Figure P2.26 Basic test circuit for op amp parameters.

2.27 Using the circuit of P2.26, show that if $R_s \gg 100\ \Omega$, I_B^+, I_B^- and I_{OS} can be measured by appropriate operation of S_1 and $S_2(V_c = 0$ V$)$. By varying V_c over the range from -10 V to $+10$ V, with S_1 and S_2 shorted, show that the open-loop gain of the amplifier can be measured as the ratio

$$A_{OL} = \frac{\Delta V_C(-10 \text{ V to } +10 \text{ V})}{\Delta V_{in}} = \frac{\Delta V_C}{\Delta V_{O2}}\left(1 + \frac{R_F}{100}\right)$$

2.28 For the circuit of Fig. P2.28 estimate the output rise time for an input step function if (a) $V_{in} = 0.1$ V and (b) $V_{in} = 1.2$ V. Use typical data for a 741C op amp.

2.29 Repeat P2.28 using an LF351 op amp.

2.30 Repeat P2.28 using an HA2540 op amp.

2.31 The circuit of Fig. P2.28 is to be used as an amplifier that must give a reasonably low-distortion output for a 30 kHz input sinusoidal signal. What is the maximum peak amplitude permitted for V_{in} using (a) a 741C op amp and (b) an OP-27E op amp.

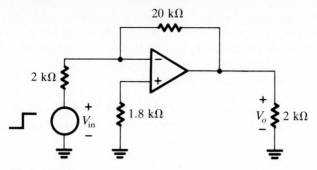

Figure P2.28

2.32 The circuit indicated in Fig. P2.32 is often used to increase the current output of an op amp. What requirements dictate the choice of R_1 and R_2? What controls the values of R_3 and R_4? Explain generally how the circuit works. Is it possible to have short-circuit protection?

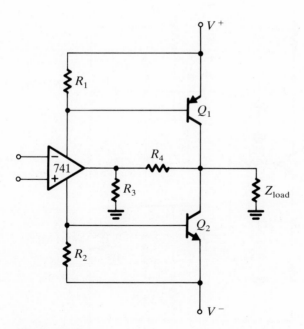

Figure P2.32

2.33 Comment on any problems anticipated using a power MOS output as indicated in Fig. 2.18(b). How would short-circuit protection by Q_5 and Q_6 work?

2.34 Using the circuit of Fig. 2.18(a) and a dual power supply of ± 30 V, specify component values in the circuit to provide at least 10 watts of output audio power to an 8-ohm load. Provide short-circuit protection for Q_3 and Q_4 at 2 amps. Use an LF351 for the op amp. Specify transistor types for Q_1–Q_4, and indicate whether heat sinks are required.

2.35 An alternative approach in using power MOS units is the circuit of Fig. P2.35, which utilizes a source-follower (common-drain) output connection for M_1 and M_2. Show how correct dc biasing can be obtained using the variable Zener diode Z_1. For use in a dc feedback loop, a dc continuous connection must be established from the output of the op amp back to the inverting input. Show how this could be accomplished in the circuit. Compare this circuit with the MOS output circuit of Problem 2.33 as to (a) ease of biasing (b) short-circuit protection and (c) output p-p voltage drive capability.

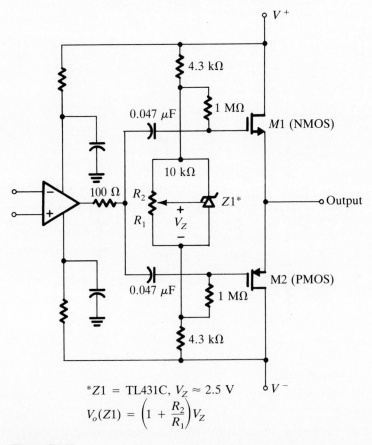

$$^*Z1 = \text{TL431C}, \; V_Z \approx 2.5 \text{ V}$$

$$V_o(Z1) = \left(1 + \frac{R_2}{R_1}\right)V_Z$$

Figure P2.35

2.36 The circuit in Fig. P2.36 was suggested by Robert Pease* of National Semiconductor for increasing the available power to a load by using a quad op amp. Comment generally on the principle that guarantees equal drive current from each op amp. If an MC34074 is used for the quad, what is the maximum current (positive and negative) that can be furnished to the load? What would be the power dissipation in the quad chip under these conditions?

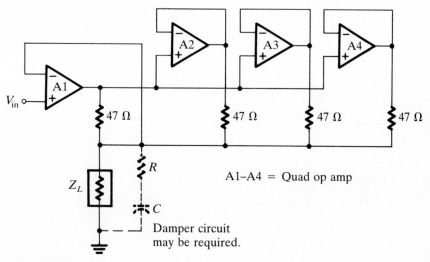

Figure P2.36

2.37 An automotive sensor circuit uses a circuit like that of Fig. 2.19 with an LF351 op amp and a power supply of $+12$ V. The reference signal at the noninverting input is $+6.2$ V, established by a Zener reference. If $R_1 = 1$ MΩ, $R_F = 10$ MΩ, $R_g = 100$ kΩ and the load is 10 kΩ with $C_2 = 10$ μF, what should C_1 be for a -3 dB f_{low} of 10 Hz? What is the midband gain?

If the heat of the engine causes the op amp to reach 70 °C, by how much could the dc output voltage of the op amp change? What type (ceramic, plastic, electrolytic, tantalum) capacitor should be used for C_1? Why should a 741 op amp not be used in this circuit?

2.38 Repeat the example of Section 2.6.3 for the two-op-amp circuit of Fig. P1.20. Assume LF351 op amps are used and $\pm 1\%$ resistors, with $V_{CM} = \pm 10$ V.

2.39 In the differential amplifer circuit of Fig. P2.39 the signal v_{diff} is a low-frequency signal of value 1 mV p-p, while the common-mode signal V_{CM} is due

* R. Pease, *Linear Brief 44*, National Semiconductor Corp. (April 1979).

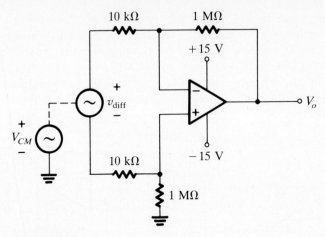

Figure P2.39

to 60 Hz pickup, and is 5 volts, rms. The power supply voltages may vary by ± 1 V, while the circuit operates at $25 \pm 10\,°C$. What should the precision of the resistors be, and which of the op amps in Appendix C should you use? Assume the resistors are stable with temperature.

2.40 The photographs shown in Fig. P2.40 were obtained for an LM10 op amp, connected to a Tektronix Model 577 curve tracer with a Model 178 Linear IC test fixture. This instrument is very useful for obtaining the dc characteristics of an op amp. The photographs indicate the parameters V_{OS}, I_B, I_{OS}, A_{OL}, CMRR, PSRR, and power-supply current. From the photographs find the parameter values for a power-supply voltage of ± 15 V. You may find it useful to refer back to the basic definitions in Section 2.4. Note the nonlinearities illustrated for $R_L = 50$ kΩ as compared to $R_L = 1$ kΩ. From the curves, what are the minimum power-supply voltages that the LM10 could employ and still remain linear? What is the input common-mode linear range (V_{ICMR}) for the op amp? What is the maximum output-voltage swing? By cooling the op amp in the test fixture it is observed that the offset voltage changes to -0.5 mV (at $T \approx -40\,°C$). Estimate the offset-voltage drift $\Delta V_{OS}/\Delta T$ in $\mu V/°C$.

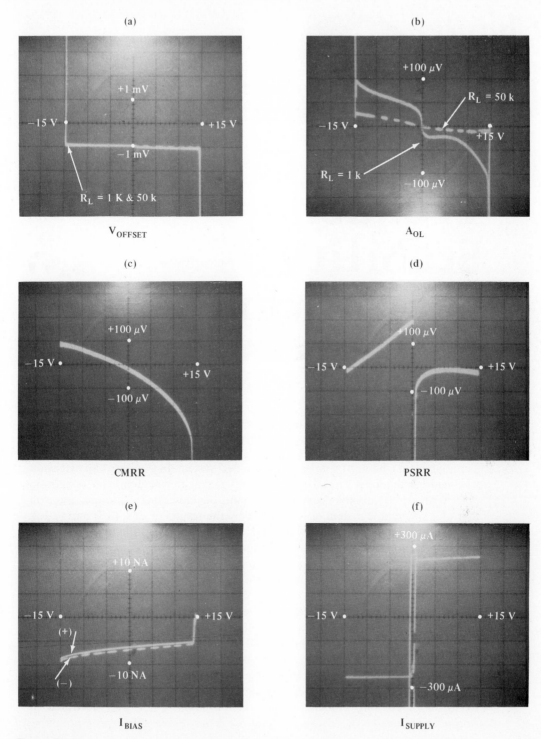

Figure P2.40

Chapter 3

Frequency Stability for Multiple-Pole Systems

The analysis in Chapter 1 was based on an ideal system. In Chapter 2 an extension was made to the more typical case of an op amp with one dominant open-loop pole. With purely resistive feedback we found the closed-loop response was still that of a single-pole system, as evidenced by the results of Eqs. (2.7) and (2.15). Thus, the maximum phase shift will be 90° and the basic inverting or noninverting amplifier is absolutely stable with frequency (cannot oscillate). However, in practice there is always stray capacitance (usually 1–10 pF, depending on circuit layout) at each node in the circuit, so there will be additional high-frequency poles in the system. Furthermore, the op amp itself seldom has a phase margin (ϕ_m) of 90°; i.e., additional poles are present in the open-loop op amp, even though these pole locations may be considerably beyond the unity-gain crossover frequency (or, beyond the gain-bandwidth product, GB). In this Chapter we will extend the analysis to include examples of circuits having more than one dominant pole in the response. Since analysis with multiple poles can be time consuming, it is helpful if the student has available either a programmable calculator or a computer. Examples of op amp modeling using the program SPICE are illustrated in Appendix D, together with several useful programs for the HP41 programmable calculator.

3.1 TRANSFER FUNCTIONS WITH TWO POLES

Perhaps the most prevalent example of an op amp circuit with a second important pole in the loop transmission is one where input capacitance between the inverting and noninverting terminals is important, as shown in Fig. 3.1(a). From Fig. 3.1(b)

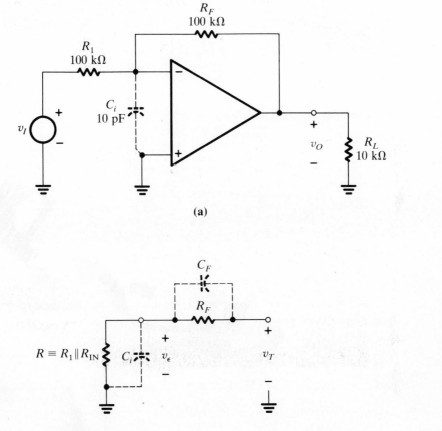

(a)

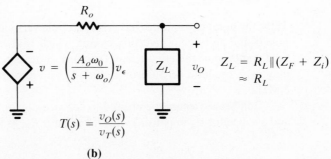

$$T(s) = \frac{v_O(s)}{v_T(s)}$$

(b)

Figure 3.1 (a) Op Amp with a second pole due to imput capacitance. (b) Loop transmission with compensation capacitance C_F added.

the loop transmission equations for this circuit are (ignore C_F for the present)

$$\left(\frac{v_\varepsilon}{v_T}\right)^* = \frac{\left(\dfrac{R}{1 + sRC_i}\right)}{\left(\dfrac{R}{1 + sRC_i}\right) + R_F}$$

or

$$\left(\frac{v_\varepsilon}{v_T}\right) = \left(\frac{R}{R + R_F}\right)\left[\frac{1}{1 + s(R\|R_F)C_i}\right]$$

and therefore the loop transmission becomes

$$T(s) = \frac{v_O(s)}{v_T(s)} \approx T_0 \left[\frac{1}{\left(1 + \dfrac{s}{\omega_0}\right)\left(1 + \dfrac{s}{\omega_i}\right)}\right] \tag{3.1}$$

where T_0 is the same as defined earlier in Eq. (2.5), namely

$$T_0 \approx -\left(\frac{R_L}{R_L + R_O}\right)\left(\frac{R}{R + R_F}\right)A_O \tag{2.5}$$

and

$$\omega_i = \frac{1}{(R_1\|R_{IN}\|R_F)C_i} \tag{3.2}$$

Using the parameter values of Fig. 3.1(a) with a 741 op amp the two poles in the loop transmission occur at frequencies

$$f_0 \approx \frac{1\ \text{MHz}}{2 \times 10^5} = 5\ \text{Hz}$$

and

$$f_i = [2\pi(100\ \text{k}\|100\ \text{k}\|2\ \text{M})(10\ \text{pF})]^{-1}$$
$$= 326\ \text{kHz}$$

Thus, the input capacitance has created a pole very close to the normal closed-loop pole of the unity-gain inverting circuit, which is at $(\frac{1}{2})$ (1 MHz), or 500 kHz. The time response of the circuit may therefore show considerable ringing, and in fact may even oscillate because of a second open-loop pole in the 741 op amp near 5 MHz.

The classic technique utilized to compensate for the input capacitance C_i is to add a capacitor C_F in parallel with the resistor R_F, as illustrated in Fig. 3.1(b). If C_F

---

* The ratio of the feedback signal v_ε at the input due to an applied output signal v_T is often referred to as the **feedback factor**, or **beta** (β) of the circuit.

is included the transfer function for v_ε/v_T becomes

$$\frac{v_\varepsilon}{v_T} = \frac{\left(\dfrac{R}{1 + sRC_i}\right)}{\left(\dfrac{R}{1 + sRC_i}\right) + \left(\dfrac{R_F}{1 + sR_F C_F}\right)} \tag{3.3}$$

and if we choose the time constants such that

$$RC_i = R_F C_F \tag{3.4}$$

then Eq. (3.3) becomes

$$\frac{v_\varepsilon}{v_T} = \frac{R}{R + R_F}$$

and the loop transmission is the same as for a basic inverting amplifier, namely

$$T(s) = \frac{v_o(s)}{v_T(s)} = -A_O \left(\frac{R_L}{R_L + R_O}\right)\left(\frac{R}{R + R_F}\right)\left(\frac{1}{1 + s/\omega_0}\right)$$

Thus, the zero introduced in the feedback path by C_F has cancelled the pole due to C_i. However, the closed-loop frequency response for the signal is not the same as without C_F. If C_F and C_i are not present the closed-loop response was given earlier by Eq. (2.8) as

$$\omega_{CL} = \omega_0(1 + |T_0|) \tag{2.8}$$

Now, however, (if $R_F C_F = RC_i$) the closed-loop gain from Fig. 3.1 becomes

$$A_{CL}^- \approx \frac{-\left(\dfrac{R_F}{R_1}\right)\left(\dfrac{|T_0|}{1 + |T_0|}\right)}{\left(1 + \dfrac{s}{\omega_F}\right)\left[1 + \dfrac{s}{\omega_0(1 + |T_0|)}\left(1 + |T_0|\omega_0\dfrac{R_O C_i}{A_O}\right) + s^2 \dfrac{|T_0|}{1 + |T_0|}\left(\dfrac{R_O C_i}{A_O \omega_0}\right)\right]} \tag{3.5}$$

where $\omega_F \equiv 1/R_F C_F$. Since typically $|T_0|$ is large and the time constant $R_O C_i$ is much less than $1/\omega_0$, Eq. (3.5) for the circuit of Fig. 3.1, reduces to a second-order function,

$$A_{CL}^-(s) \approx -\left(\frac{R_F}{R_1}\right)\left[\frac{1}{\left(1 + \dfrac{s}{\omega_F}\right)\left(1 + \dfrac{s}{\omega_0|T_0|}\right)}\right] \tag{3.6}$$

Using the circuit values shown in Fig. 3.1 and $C_F = RC_i/R_F \approx 9.52$ pF, the closed-loop poles are at

$$\omega_F = 2\pi(167 \text{ kHz})$$

and

$$\omega_0|T_0| = 2\pi(1 \text{ MHz} \times 0.48) = 2\pi(480 \text{ kHz})$$

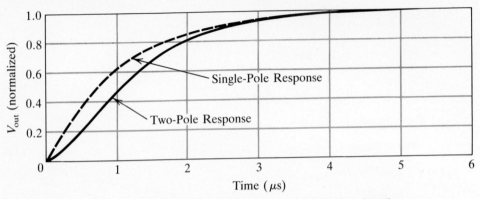

Figure 3.2 Actual and approximate small-signal response to a step function.

Thus, the -3 dB corner frequency can be approximated as*

$$f_{\text{high}}(-3 \text{ dB}) \approx \frac{1}{\left[\left(\frac{1}{167 \times 10^3}\right)^2 + \left(\frac{1}{480 \times 10^3}\right)^2\right]^{1/2}} = 158 \text{ kHz} \tag{3.7}$$

If an input step function were applied to the circuit of Fig. 3.1(b), the approximate output small-signal rise time from Eqs. (2.36) and (3.7) would be

$$\tau_r(10\text{–}90\%) \approx \frac{0.35}{158 \times 10^3} = 2.2 \ \mu\text{sec}$$

Since the circuit really has two significant poles, as shown by Eq. (3.6), the actual small-signal rise time will be slightly different, as indicated in Fig. 3.2. In this figure the actual two-pole response has a 10–90% rise time of 2.3 μsec, as compared with the single-pole approximation of 2.2 μsec. However, the single-pole approximation shown as Fig. 3.2 is a reasonable fit to the two-pole curve, and can be obtained with much less computational effort.

■ **Exercise 3.1**

Verify the step-function response shown in Fig. 3.2 using Eq. (3.6) and compare with the single-pole approximation of Eq. (3.7) so that

$$A_{CL}^-(s) \approx -\left(\frac{R_F}{R_1}\right)\left[\frac{1}{1 + \dfrac{s}{2\pi \times 158 \text{ kHz}}}\right] \tag{3.8}$$

---

* The approximation (that the overall -3 dB high frequency value is related to the square root of the sum of the squares of the reciprocals of the individual frequencies) is directly related to the validity of Eq. (2.39). Also, see Ghausi [Ref. 3.19], Chapter 8.

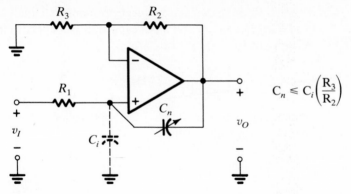

Figure 3.3 Input capacitance cancellation by a neutralizing capacitance C_n.

For circuits where the input capacitance is particularly objectionable, such as cases where R_1 is very large, it is possible to provide partial cancellation (in the literature this concept is often referred to as **neutralization**) of this capacitance by using positive feedback. Such a circuit is illustrated by the basic noninverting circuit of Fig. 3.3, with positive feedback obtained by C_n. Since the negative-feedback path due to R_3 and R_2 must dominate the positive feedback due to C_n, it is necessary that

$$\frac{R_3}{R_3 + R_2} \geq \left(\frac{C_n}{C_n + C_i}\right)$$

or that

$$C_n \leq C_i\left(\frac{R_3}{R_2}\right) \tag{3.9}$$

EXAMPLE 3.1

Compare the frequency response of the circuit of Fig. 3.3 with and without C_n for the case of $R_1 = 10\ \text{M}\Omega$, $C_i = 5\ \text{pF}$ (stray), and a closed-loop gain of 10 ($R_2 = 9\ \text{k}\Omega$ and $R_3 = 1\ \text{k}\Omega$). Use an LF351 op amp.

Solution

Assuming a single-pole open-loop resonse for the circuit of Fig. 3.3, the LF351 should have a closed-loop high-frequency pole at

$$f_{\text{high}}(-3\ \text{dB}) \approx \frac{4\ \text{MHz}}{10} = 400\ \text{kHz}$$

However, without neutralization the high-frequency response is actually controlled by R_1 and C_i. The LF351 has an internal input capacitance of approximately 3 pF, and an input resistance of 10^{12} ohms, thus

$$f_{input}(-3 \text{ dB}) \approx \frac{1}{2\pi(10 \text{ M}\Omega)(8 \text{ pF})} = 2 \text{ kHz}$$

and the overall circuit is therefore limited by the 2 kHz rolloff.

If C_n is employed, then with a value of

$$C_n \approx 8 \text{ pF}\left(\frac{1 \text{ k}\Omega}{9 \text{ k}\Omega}\right) = 0.89 \text{ pF}$$

the effect of C_i is predominately cancelled. However, the loop transmission for the circuit is now determined by a two-pole response, namely

$$T(s) = \left(\frac{-|T_0|}{1 + \dfrac{s}{\omega_0}}\right)\left[\frac{1}{1 + sR_1(C_i + C_n)}\right] \tag{3.10}$$

so that the circuit is only marginally stable. Usually, it is best to determine the value of C_n experimentally as a trade-off between neutralization and system response.

Ignoring R_O and R_{IN} of the op amp, the closed-loop gain of the circuit reduces to

$$\frac{v_O}{v_I}(s) = A_{CL}^+(s) = A_{CL}^+(\text{ideal})\left[\frac{-T(s)}{1 - T(s)}\right] \tag{3.11}$$

where

$$A_{CL}^+(\text{ideal}) = \frac{R_3 + R_2}{R_3}$$

and $T(s)$ was given by Eq. (3.10).

A limiting high-frequency pole can also be created if there is output load capacitance, since an added time constant results due to the product of the output resistance of the op amp and the load capacitance $R_O C_L$. For example, the circuit of Fig. 3.4 illustrates an inverting amplifier driving a load of R_L in parallel with C_L. The loop-transmission expression for this circuit reduces to a two-pole result

$$T(s) = T_0\left(\frac{1}{1 + \dfrac{s}{\omega_0}}\right)\left(\frac{1}{1 + s(R_O' \| R_L')C_L}\right) \tag{3.12}$$

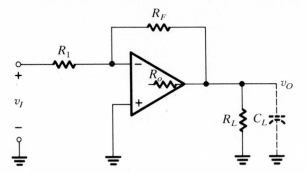

Figure 3.4 Stability problems due to load capacitance.

where, for Fig. 3.4

$$T_0 = -A_O\left(\frac{R_1'}{R_1' + R_F}\right)\left(\frac{R_L'}{R_L' + R_O}\right)$$

with

$$R_1' \equiv R_1 \| R_{\text{IN}}$$

$$R_L' \equiv R_L \| (R_F + R_1')$$

As an example, suppose $R_1 = 10$ kΩ, $R_F = 90$ kΩ, $R_L = 10$ kΩ and the total load capacitance is 100 pF. If a 741 op amp is used, the typical output resistance is 75 ohms. For $A_O = 200 \times 10^3$ and $GB = 1$ MHz, Eq. (3.12) thus becomes

$$T(s) \approx -19{,}750\left[\frac{1}{1 + \left(\dfrac{s}{2\pi \times 5 \text{ Hz}}\right)}\right]\left[\frac{1}{1 + \left(\dfrac{s}{2\pi \times 21.4 \text{ MHz}}\right)}\right]$$

Since the added pole is considerably beyond the unity-gain frequency of the amplifier (here, $f_{CL} \approx 100$ kHz) its effect on circuit performance is negligible. However, if a unity-gain configuration were used, particularly with an op amp having a high gain-bandwidth product, the effect of load capacitance could be significant.

The circuit shown in Fig. 3.5(a) is often used to compensate for the effect of large load capacitance. Here, a buffering resistance R_2 is inserted in series with the output of the op amp, but kept inside the dc feedback path to reduce its effect on dc gain. A compensation capacitance C_F is used to provide ac feedback to the inverting input and partially negate the effects of the $(R_2 + R_O)C_L$ lag network in the loop-transmission reponse. To understand how the frequency stability of the circuit is improved, let us obtain from Fig. 3.5(b) the equation for the loop

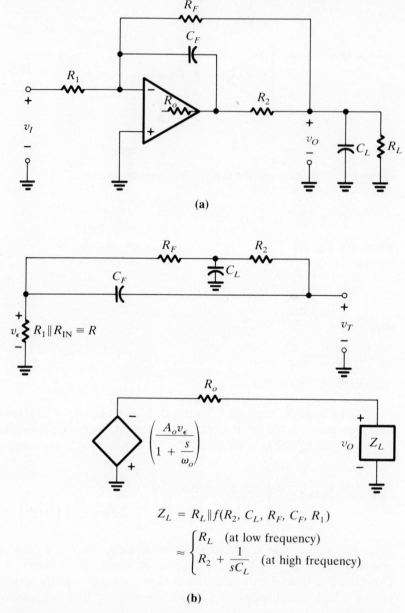

(a)

(b)

Figure 3.5 (a) Compensation circuit for load capacitance. (b) Model for loop transmission.

transmission. From the rather complex feedback path the the ratio v_ε/v_T is given by the determinant

$$\frac{v_\varepsilon}{v_T} = \frac{\begin{bmatrix} -\left(\dfrac{1}{R_F}\right) & (sC_F) \\[2ex] \left(\dfrac{1}{R_F}+\dfrac{1}{R_2}+sC_L\right) & \left(\dfrac{1}{R_2}\right) \end{bmatrix}}{\begin{bmatrix} -\left(\dfrac{1}{R_F}\right) & \left(\dfrac{1}{R_F}+\dfrac{1}{R_1}+sC_F\right) \\[2ex] \left(\dfrac{1}{R_F}+\dfrac{1}{R_2}+sC_L\right) & -\left(\dfrac{1}{R_F}\right) \end{bmatrix}} \tag{3.13}$$

where it is assumed that the reactance of C_L is much less than R_L. Thus, the loop-transmission equation for Fig. 3.5 becomes

$$T(s) = \frac{v_0(s)}{v_T(s)} = T_0\left[\frac{1+sa+s^2 b}{\left(1+\dfrac{s}{\omega_0}\right)(1+sc+s^2 d)}\right] \tag{3.14}$$

where the terms are

$$T_0 = \frac{-A_0 R}{R+R_2+R_F}$$

$$a = (R_F+R_2)C_F$$

$$b = R_F C_F R_2 C_L$$

$$c = \left[(R_F+R_2)C_F + R_2 C_L\left(1+\frac{R_F}{R_1}\right)\right] - (k)$$

$$d = bk$$

$$k = \left(\frac{R}{R+R_2+R_F}\right)$$

If we compare the equation for $T(s)$ for the basic circuit with load capacitance, as given earlier by Eq. (3.12), with the result for the compensated circuit, as given by Eq. (3.14), we see that as frequency becomes large (i.e., as $s \to \infty$) the loop transmission for the compensated case reduces to a single-pole response, whereas the original circuit ultimately gives a two-pole response. Hence, frequency compensation has indeed occured.

A further problem occurs when driving a large load capacitance, in that the amplifier's slew rate may be degraded. For example, a typical op amp can supply an output current only up to its short-circuit protection value, which for most general-purpose op amps is about 20 mA. If the load capacitance is 2000 pF, then the maximum slew rate for the circuit is

$$SR_{max} \approx \frac{I_0}{C_L} = \frac{20\text{ mA}}{2000\text{ pF}} = 10\text{ V}/\mu\text{sec}$$

regardless of the value of internal SR for the op amp. To reduce these load effects it is usually advisable to add a driver circuit inside the feedback loop, which can then supply much larger currents to charge the load capacitance. Circuits such as those indicated earlier in Table 2.2 or in Figs. 2.17 and 2.18 would be suitable.

An inverting integrator is another interesting case where a second pole can be important. The integrator circuit was shown earlier in Fig. 1.5, where we assumed an ideal op amp. If, however, we assume a single pole in the op amp open-loop response, then the equation for the closed-loop gain (where $GB = A_O\omega_0$ rad/sec) becomes

$$A_{CL}^-(s) \approx \frac{-\left(\dfrac{GB}{R_1 C}\right)[1 - f(R_O C)]}{s^2 + s\left[GB + \dfrac{1}{R_1 \| R_{IN} C}\right] + \dfrac{\omega_0}{R_1 \| R_{IN} C}} \tag{3.15}$$

if the output resistance R_O of the op amp is much less than $R_1 \| R_{IN}$. Also, the term $f(R_O C)$ is $\ll 1$, except for frequencies near the gain-bandwidth product GB.

The phase shift of Eq. (3.15) for frequencies past ω_0 is given by

$$\arg[A_{CL}^-(j\omega)] \approx \frac{\pi}{2} - \tan^{-1}\left(\frac{\omega}{GB}\right) \tag{3.16}$$

Thus, the additional phase shift beyond the normal value of 90° will be 26.6° at $\omega = GB/2$, and 45° at $\omega = GB$. The term in the numerator of Eq. (3.15) is due to the finite open-loop output resistance R_O of the op amp and in the frequency domain is

$$1 - f(R_O C) = \left[1 + \omega^2\left(\frac{R_O C}{GB}\right) - j\left(\frac{\omega}{A_O/R_O C}\right)\right] \tag{3.17}$$

This term adds an insignificant phase shift, but can increase the magnitude of the response near $\omega = GB$, depending on the $R_O C$ product. Hence, the integrator can show peaking in the output response.

EXAMPLE 3.2

Using a 741 op amp in the inverting integrator circuit of Fig. 3.6(a), sketch the frequency response for the circuit for frequencies $> \omega_0$.

Solution

For low to intermediate frequencies the response is dominated by the s term in the denominator of Eq. (3.15), giving the ideal gain of the integrator as

$$A_{CL}^-(j\omega)_{\text{Ideal}} = -\frac{1}{j\omega R_1 C} = \frac{1}{\omega R_1 C} \angle 90°$$

or inserting the parameter values of Fig. 3.6

$$A_{CL}^-(j\omega)_{\text{Ideal}} = \left(\frac{1}{f/16 \text{ kHz}}\right) \angle 90°$$

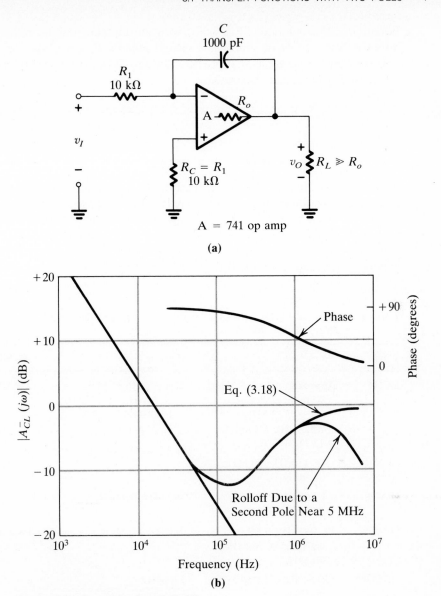

(a)

(b)

Figure 3.6 Circuit for Example 3.2.

Near the gain-bandwidth product of 1 MHz, however, we must use the complete gain expression of Eqs. (3.15) and (3.17), which with typical parameter values for a 741 reduces to

$$A_{CL}^{-}(j\omega) \approx \frac{\dfrac{j(16\ \text{kHz})}{f}\left[1 + \left(\dfrac{f}{1.3 \times 10^5}\right)^2\right]}{1.016 + j\left(\dfrac{f}{10^6}\right)} \tag{3.18}$$

Equation (3.18) is plotted in Fig. 3.6(b), with considerable peaking indicated in the response. Since a 741 op amp has a second pole in the open-loop response, the peaking is not as severe as that predicted by Eq. (3.18); the inclusion of a second pole near 5 MHz is also illustrated.

3.2 TRANSFER FUNCTIONS WITH MULTIPLE POLES

So far in this chapter we have concentrated on circuits with two poles and techniques for adding compensation to reduce the response to basically a one-pole system. However, many available op amps are not internally designed for a single-pole response. Most of these circuits fall in the category of high-frequency, and/or high-slew-rate op amps, which may be stable only for closed-loop gains of 5 or greater. For example, an OP-27 op amp has a typical value of gain-bandwidth

Table 3.1 APPROXIMATE OPEN-LOOP POLES AND ZEROES FOR VARIOUS OP AMPS

Type	Poles	Zeroes	A_{OL}(dc)Typ.
µA741	Approximately 5, 5 MHz; or more elaborately (4.4, 2.3 $\pm$ j5.13 MHz, 3.82 MHz, 6.33 MHz, 13.11 MHz)*	None; or (6.81 MHz, 10.2 MHz, 10.42 MHz, 10.88 MHz, 13.3 MHz, 21.76 MHz)*	2×10^5 (3.55×10^5)*
LF351	13.3, 15 MHz, 20 MHz, 75 MHz	—	3×10^5
OP-27	4.4, 800 kHz, 12 MHz, 20 MHz, 30 MHz	900 kHz, 6.5 MHz	1.8×10^6
OP-37†	30, 700 kHz, 9 MHz, 40 MHz(2), 50 MHz, 80 MHz	2 MHz, 7.5 MHz	1.8×10^6
NE5534†	1 kHz, 800 kHz, 50 MHz, 80 MHz	1.6 MHz	4×10^4
LM318†	140, 200 kHz, 40 MHz, 50 MHz(2)	500 kHz	3.2×10^5
MC34074	45, 3 MHz, 6.5 MHz, 12 MHz, 25 MHz, 52 MHz, 70 MHz	2 MHz, 7 MHz	1×10^5
HA2540	12 kHz, 60 MHz, 120 MHz, 200 MHz(2)	40 MHz	3.2×10^4

* From B. Wooley, et al., *IEEE J. S. S. Ckts*, Vol. SC-6, No. 6, pp. 357–66 (Dec. 1971).
† From W. Helms, *EDN*, pp. 279–89 (Oct. 27, 1983).

product (GB) of 8 MHz, with an SR of 2.8 V/μsec. However, the OP-37 is the same circuit, but with less internal compensation capacitance, and therefore has a larger GB of 63 MHz with an SR of 17 V/μsec, but because of its smaller capacitance, the OP-37 is stable only for gains greater than 5. Similarly, the HA2539 and HA2540 op amps have large GBs of 600 MHz and 400 MHz, and SRs of 600 V/μsec and 400 V/μsec, respectively, but are compensated only for closed-loop gains of 10 or greater. In Table 3.1 several widely used commercial op amps are listed, with best estimates of their open-loop poles (and zeroes) indicated. It is possible to consider the effects of all poles and zeroes in the system response, including the effects of input and load stray capacitance, but such analysis is not generally amenable to hand calculations. Instead, the use of a computer program, such as SPICE, is much preferred and several examples of such computer-aided analysis are shown in Appendix D. Another approach is to use a hand-held programmable calculator, such as the HP41 or TI59 units, and calculate the loop-transmission frequency response for programmed values of circuit poles and zeroes. Indeed, it is possible to purchase these programs ready for insertion into the calculator, with built-in capability for calculating gain and phase margins for an arbitrary function.*

---

* For example, program 41-01196-2 is available from the HP User's Library for use on the HP41CV (or CX), and will calculate gain and phase of a general mth order by nth order transfer function, and calculate gain and phase margin automatically.

EXAMPLE 3.3

For the unity-gain circuit of Fig. 3.7 plot the loop transmission vs frequency using an OP-27 with poles and zeroes as specified in Table 3.1. Estimate the phase margin, ϕ_m.

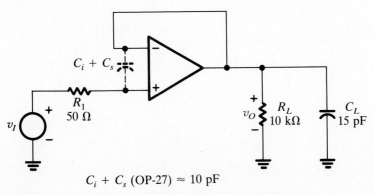

$$C_i + C_s \text{ (OP-27)} \approx 10 \text{ pF}$$

Figure 3.7   Circuit of Example 3.3 using an OP-27 op amp.

Solution

Using the poles and zeroes for the OP-27 as shown in Table 3.1, the loop transmission for Fig. 3.7 is

$$T(j\omega) \approx T_0 \left[\frac{\left(1 + j\dfrac{f}{0.9 \text{ MHz}}\right)\left(1 + j\dfrac{f}{6.5 \text{ MHz}}\right)}{\left(1 + j\dfrac{f}{4.4}\right)\left(1 + j\dfrac{f}{0.8 \text{ MHz}}\right)\left(1 + j\dfrac{f}{12 \text{ MHz}}\right)} \right] \quad \textbf{(3.19)}$$

$$\left(1 + j\dfrac{f}{20 \text{ MHz}}\right)\left(1 + j\dfrac{f}{30 \text{ MHz}}\right)\left(1 + j\dfrac{f}{f_L}\right)$$

where there is an added pole due to $R_0(C_L + C_i + C_s)$ at

$$f_L \approx \frac{1}{2\pi(70 \text{ }\Omega)(25 \text{ pF})} = 91 \text{ MHz}$$

and

$$T_0 \approx -1.8 \times 10^6$$

Both the asymptotic and calculated frequency response of Eq. (3.19) is shown in Fig. 3.8 near the unity-gain crossover frequency f_c, which is at approximately

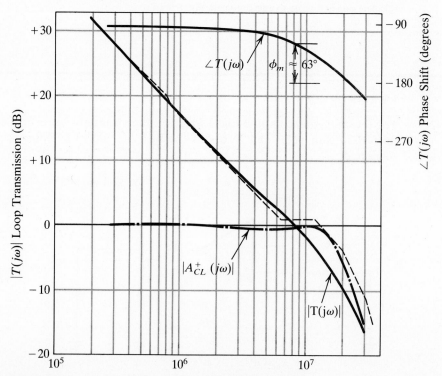

Figure 3.8 Loop transmission plot of Example 3.3 (OP-27).

8.2 MHz on the $T(j\omega)$ plot. Also indicated in Fig. 3.8 is the theoretical closed-loop gain magnitude $|A_{CL}^+(j\omega)|$, which is obtained from Eq. (3.19) as

$$A_{CL}^+(j\omega) = A_{CL}^+(\text{ideal})\left[\frac{-T(j\omega)}{1 - T(j\omega)}\right] \tag{3.20}$$

where (in this example) $A_{CL}^+(\text{ideal}) = 1.0$. It is apparent from the plot of $T(j\omega)$ that the phase margin is

$$\phi_m \approx 180° - 117° = 63°$$

and the gain margin is

$$GM \approx 12 \text{ dB}$$

Note also from the plot of $|A_{CL}^+(j\omega)|$ that there is negligible peaking, which indicates overshoot should be small in the step response of the amplifier.

Even though systems may have several poles and zeroes, as in Example 3.3, it is often sufficient to approximate both the frequency and time response by that of a two-pole (second-order) system (see Problem 3.4)

$$A_{CL}(s) \approx A_{CL}(\text{dc})\left[\frac{1}{1 + \left(\dfrac{2\zeta}{\omega_n}\right)s + \left(\dfrac{s}{\omega_n}\right)^2}\right] \tag{3.21}$$

where

$\xi =$ the **damping coefficient**

$\omega_n =$ the **undamped natural frequency**

Analysis of second-order systems is found in many texts and articles (see, for example, References 3.1–3.4 in Appendix A). It can be shown (see Problem 3.15) that the phase margin of the loop transmission $T(j\omega)$ of a second-order system is related to the damping coefficient ξ of the closed-loop system by

$$PM(\phi_m) = \tan^{-1}\frac{2\xi}{[(4\xi^4 + 1)^{1/2} - 2\xi^2]^{1/2}} \tag{3.22}$$

Similarly, the amount of peaking in the frequency response can be related to ξ by

$$\text{Peaking (in dB)} = 20\log_{10}\left|\frac{1}{2\xi(1 - \xi^2)^{1/2}}\right| \tag{3.23}$$

Peaking can then be related to ϕ_m by Eq. (3.22). The frequency ω_p at which maximum peaking occurs is given by

$$\omega_p = \omega_n(1 - 2\xi^2)^{1/2} \tag{3.24}$$

If the open-loop gain is very large, and the op-amp is dominated by a single-pole response over most of the frequency range of $T(j\omega)$, then one can relate the crossover frequency ω_c at which $|T(j\omega)| = 0$ dB to ω_n and ξ for the closed-loop system by

$$\omega_c = 2\pi f_c \approx \omega_n[(4\xi^4 + 1)^{1/2} - 2\xi^2]^{1/2} \tag{3.25}$$

See, for example, the text by Savant [Ref. 3.2], and Problem 3.15.

For a unit-step-function input, a second-order system has a normalized response dependent on ξ and ω_n as

$$v_o(t)_{\text{normalized}} = 1 - \frac{\exp(-\xi\omega_n t)}{(1 - \xi^2)^{1/2}} \sin\{\omega_n[(1 - \xi^2)^{1/2}t + \cos^{-1}\xi]\} \tag{3.26}$$

for $0 \leq \xi \leq 1$. Equation (3.26) is plotted in Fig. 3.9. The time t_p at which $v_o(t)$ has a peak overshoot can be obtained by differentiating $v_o(t)$ of Eq. (3.26) with respect to time, and setting the derivative equal to zero. This gives

$$t_p = \frac{\pi}{\omega_n(1 - \xi^2)^{1/2}} \tag{3.27}$$

Substituting Eq. (3.27) into Eq. (3.26), and solving gives the peak overshoot (OS) as

$$OS(\%) = 100 \exp\left[-\frac{\xi\pi}{(1 + \xi^2)^{1/2}}\right] \tag{3.28}$$

The results of Eqs. (3.22)–(3.28) are plotted in Fig. 3.10.

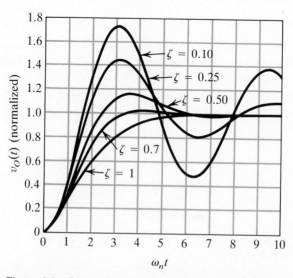

Figure 3.9 Step response of a second-order system.

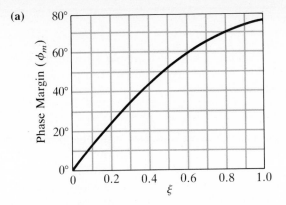

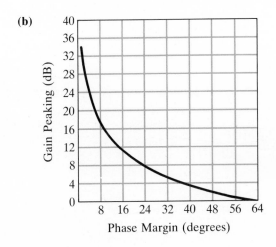

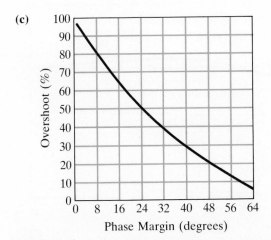

Figure 3.10 Relationships between phase margin and second-order system response.

EXAMPLE 3.4

Correlate the frequency response results of Example 3.3 with those of a second-order system approximation. Use the approximations to predict the small-signal step response of the amplifier.

Solution

The results of Example 3.3 and Fig. 3.8 indicated negligible peaking and a phase margin of $63°$ for $T(j\omega)$. Therefore, from Fig. 3.10(a), a value of ϕ_m of $63°$ would be equivalent to a closed-loop second-order system ξ of 0.7. Also, note from Fig. 3.10(b) that a $63°$ phase margin would be directly analogous to only 0.1 dB of peaking for a true second-order system. From Fig. 3.10(c) for a phase margin of $63°$ the step response of the closed-loop second-order system should have 6% overshoot, and from Eq. (3.26) the peak overshoot would therefore occur at

$$t_p = \frac{\pi}{\omega_n(1 - \xi^2)^{1/2}} \approx \frac{4.4}{\omega_n}$$

Since the crossover frequency f_c for Example 3.3 was 8.2 MHz then, from Eq. (3.25), we obtain for $\xi \approx 0.7$

$$\omega_n \approx \frac{2\pi \times 8.2 \text{ MHz}}{\{[4(0.7)^4 + 1]^{1/2} - 2(0.7)^2\}^{1/2}} = 2\pi(12.6 \text{ MHz})$$

and therefore

$$t_p \approx \frac{4.4}{2\pi(12.6 \text{ MHz})} = 56 \text{ nsec}$$

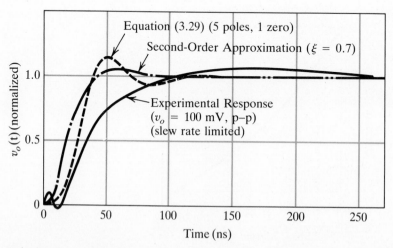

Figure 3.11 Comparisons of output response to a step-function input for the unity-gain circuit of Fig. 3.7

Using the value of ω_n of 2π (12.6 MHz) and $\xi = 0.7$, the second-order approximated step response of the OP-27 op amp circuit of Fig. 3.7 is plotted in Fig. 3.11, using Eq. (3.26) (or Fig. 3.9).

Figure 3.11 also shows a plot of the step response using the more exact relation for $A_{CL}^+(j\omega)$ from Eq. (3.20), which after substituting Eq. (3.19) reduces to*

$$A_{CL}^+(s) \approx \frac{\left(\dfrac{-T_0}{1-T_0}\right)\left(1+\dfrac{s}{s_z}\right)}{1+\left(\dfrac{s}{s_1}\right)+\left(\dfrac{s}{s_2}\right)^2+\cdots+\left(\dfrac{s}{s_5}\right)^5} \tag{3.29}$$

For this example the significant terms are

$$\left(\frac{-T_0}{1-T_0}\right) = \frac{1.8 \times 10^6}{1+1.8 \times 10^6} = 1.0$$

$$s_z = 2\pi(6.5 \text{ MHz})$$

$$s_1 = 2\pi\left(\frac{1}{\dfrac{1}{f_z}+\dfrac{1}{1-T_0}\displaystyle\sum_{i=1}^{5}\dfrac{1}{f_{pi}}}\right) \approx 2\pi\left(\frac{f_z GB}{f_z + GB}\right) \tag{3.30}$$

where GB = gain-bandwidth product = 8 MHz, and

$$s_2^2 = (2\pi)^2\left[\frac{(1-T_0)}{\dfrac{1}{f_{p1}}\displaystyle\sum_{n=2}^{5}\dfrac{1}{f_{pn}}+\dfrac{1}{f_{p2}}\displaystyle\sum_{n=3}^{5}\dfrac{1}{f_{pn}}+\dfrac{1}{f_{p3}}\displaystyle\sum_{n=4}^{5}\dfrac{1}{f_{pn}}+\dfrac{1}{f_{p4}f_{p5}}}\right] \tag{3.31}$$

or since there is one dominant pole at f_{p1},

$$s_2^2 \approx (2\pi)^2 GB\left[\frac{1}{\displaystyle\sum_{n=2}^{5}\dfrac{1}{f_{pn}}}\right] \tag{3.32}$$

By substituting the various poles and zeroes of Eq. (3.19) and reducing to the form of Eq. (3.29), the various terms reduce to

$$s_z = 2\pi(6.5 \text{ MHz})$$
$$s_1 = 2\pi(3.57 \text{ MHz})$$
$$s_2 = 2\pi(6.68 \text{ MHz})$$
$$s_3 = 2\pi(9.11 \text{ MHz})$$
$$s_4 = 2\pi(13.85 \text{ MHz})$$
$$s_5 = 2\pi(22.03 \text{ MHz})$$

---

* Since the zero at 0.9 MHz in Eq. (3.19) essentially cancels the pole at 0.8 MHz, these terms were removed in Eq. (3.29) for simplicity.

A comparison of the second-order approximation with the more exact Eq. (3.29) in Fig. 3.11 indicates very close correlation, with Eq. (3.29) having more overshoot. However, when compared to the actual experimental results for an OP-27 in the circuit of Fig. 3.7 it is apparent that slew-rate limiting is occuring, as well as other nonlinearities near $t = 0$. For the OP-27 op amp the minimum slew-rate limitation is 1.7 V/μsec; hence, for a 100 mV output signal the slew-rate-limited rise time can be as high as 60 nsec.

As stated earlier, op amps with very large values of gain-bandwidth product (GB) are usually not stable for a unity-gain connection. However, by artificially reducing the loop transmission through attenuation in the feedback path, we can use these high-frequency devices in either inverting or noninverting circuits, usually with improved high-frequency characteristics as compared to op amps that are stable for unity gain. For example, we can use the higher gain-bandwidth (and most importantly, higher slew-rate) OP-37 op amp in the unity-gain circuit of Fig. 3.7 with a slight modification so that the feedback factor is $\leq \frac{1}{5}$, to ensure frequency stability. The resulting circuit is shown in Fig. 3.12. The loop transmission for this circuit (for $R_O \ll R_L$) is

$$T(s) = -A_{OL}(s)\left[\frac{1 + sRC}{1 + s(R_1 + R + R_F)C}\right]\left[\frac{1}{1 + sR_OC_L}\right] \tag{3.33}$$

where the added pole and zero from the compensation network are at frequencies

$$\omega_p = \frac{1}{C(R_1 + R + R_F)}$$

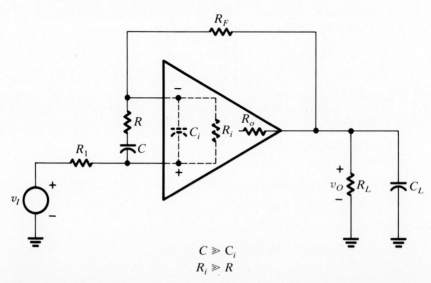

$$C \gg C_i$$
$$R_i \gg R$$

Figure 3.12 Modified noninverting unity-gain circuit for use with a high-frequency op amp.

and ω_z (which is $>\omega_p$) at

$$\omega_z = \frac{1}{RC} \tag{3.34}$$

If ω_p and ω_z are chosen much less than the crossover frequency ω_c [the frequency for which $|T(j\omega)| = 1$] then, in the frequency domain, the loop transmission reduces to

$$T(j\omega) \approx -A_{OL}(j\omega)\left(\frac{R}{R_1 + R + R_F}\right)\left[\frac{1}{1 + j\left(\dfrac{\omega}{\omega_L}\right)}\right]$$

where $\omega_L = 1/R_O C_L$. By choosing R_F and R appropriately the circuit can be designed for a given generator resistance R_1 to give adequate phase margin.

EXAMPLE 3.5

Using the unity-gain circuit of Fig. 3.12 and an OP-37 op amp choose values for R_F, R, and C to provide a stable amplifier with $\phi_m \geq 30°$. Assume the generator resistance R_1 is 50 ohms, $R_L = 10$ kΩ, $C_L = 15$ pF and the op amp input capacitance $C_i = 8$ pF. Sketch the loop transmission for the circuit vs frequency.

Solution
The data sheet for an OP-37 indicates typical parameter values of $GB = 63$ MHz, $SR = 17$ V/μsec and $R_O = 70$ Ω. For $A_{CL} = 5$ the phase margin (with no load capacitance) is 71° at a frequency of 6 MHz. Thus, a resistor ratio of

$$\frac{R}{R_1 + R + R_F} = \frac{1}{5}$$

should provide reasonable phase margin with good high-frequency bandwidth. We want to keep the value of resistor R small since it is in parallel with C_i of the op amp. So if we choose $R_F = 1$ kΩ, then for $R_1 = 50$ Ω we obtain $R \approx 270$ Ω, and indeed the time constant of RC_i is small ($RC_i \approx 2$ nsec). Since $\omega_z > \omega_p$, let us make a first choice of

$$\omega_z = 2\pi(2 \text{ MHz})$$

and therefore, from Eq. (3.34)

$$\omega_p = \omega_z\left(\frac{R}{R_1 + R + R_F}\right) \approx 2\pi(400 \text{ kHz})$$

So,

$$C = \frac{1}{R\omega_z} \approx 300 \text{ pF}$$

There is nothing absolutely critical about the chosen value of C. For improved phase margin one might in fact choose a value for C a factor of 2–4 times larger, which would ensure that the terms $|sRC|$ and $|s(R_1 + R + R_F)|$ would be truly greater than 1 in Eq. (3.33). With the values obtained for ω_p and ω_z, and using the open-loop pole and zero values indicated in Table 3.1, the loop transmission of Eq. (3.33) becomes, in the frequency domain

$$T(j\omega)_{\text{Fig. 3.12}} \approx \frac{-1.8 \times 10^6 \left[1 + j\left(\dfrac{f}{f_{Z1}}\right)\right] \displaystyle\prod_{\alpha=2}^{3} \left[1 + j\left(\dfrac{f}{f_{z\alpha}}\right)\right]}{\left[1 + j\left(\dfrac{f}{f_{p1}}\right)\right]\left[1 + j\left(\dfrac{f}{f_L}\right)\right]\left[1 + j\left(\dfrac{f}{f_{p2}}\right)\right]^2 \displaystyle\prod_{m=3}^{7} \left[1 + j\left(\dfrac{f}{f_{pm}}\right)\right]}$$

(3.35)

where

$$f_{z1} = f_{z2} = 2 \text{ MHz}$$

$$f_{z3} = 7.5 \text{ MHz}$$

$$f_L = \frac{1}{2\pi(70)(15 \text{ pF})} = 151 \text{ MHz (ignore)}$$

$$f_{p1} = 400 \text{ kHz}$$

$$f_{p2} = 40 \text{ MHz}$$

$$f_{p3} = 30 \text{ Hz}$$

$$f_{p4} = 700 \text{ kHz}$$

$$f_{p5} = 9 \text{ MHz}$$

$$f_{p6} = 50 \text{ MHz}$$

$$f_{p7} = 80 \text{ MHz}$$

(3.36)

If one uses either a programmable calculator or a computer, the parameter values of Eqs. (3.35) and (3.36) can easily be programmed to obtain magnitude and phase response for $T(j\omega)$. The results are indicated in the frequency-response plot of Fig. 3.13. Note that our first choice for ω_p and ω_z has produced a phase margin of 36°, with a peaking of +5 dB in the closed-loop response for $|A_{CL}^+(j\omega)|$. From Eq. (3.20)

$$A_{CL}^+(j\omega) = A_{CL}^+(\text{ideal})\left[\frac{-T(j\omega)}{1 - T(j\omega)}\right]$$

where, for the unity-gain noninverting circuit of Fig. 3.12, $A_{CL}^+(\text{ideal}) \approx 1.0$. If $T(j\omega)$ from Eq. (3.35) were approximated by a second-order system, then Fig. 3.10(c) indicates approximately 33% overshoot for a step-function input signal, corresponding to a value of $\xi \approx 0.3$. Also, with a crossover frequency of $f_c = 4.5$ MHz, Eq. (3.25) would result in

$$\omega_n \approx \frac{2\pi(4.5 \text{ MHz})}{\{[4(0.3)^4 + 1]^{1/2} - 2(0.3)^2\}^{1/2}} = 2\pi(4.9 \text{ MHz})$$

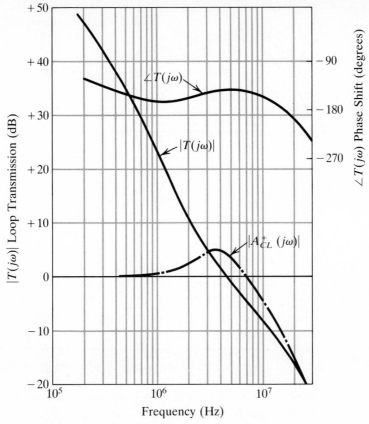

Figure 3.13 Loop transmission plot of Example 3.5 (OP-37).

and the peak overshoot would occur at

$$t_p \approx \frac{\pi}{2\pi(4.9 \text{ MHz})(1 - 0.09)^{1/2}} = 106 \text{ nsec}$$

■ **Exercise 3.2**

Show that an improved phase margin of $\phi_m = 45°$ results in Example 3.5 if ω_z is chosen as $2\pi(1 \text{ MHz})$ (or $C \approx 620 \text{ pF}$) and ω_p is therefore set at $2\pi(200 \text{ kHz})$. Sketch the Bode plot to verify your results. Show that this value of ϕ_m would correspond to a unity-gain closed-loop second-order system having $\xi \approx 0.4$, $\omega_n \approx 2\pi(5.3 \text{ MHz})$, and an overshoot of 23% for a unit-step input signal.

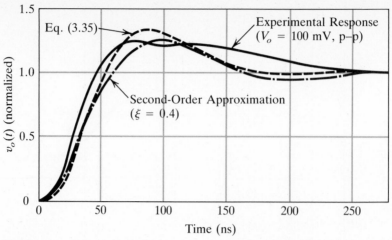

Figure 3.14 Output response comparisons for the circuit of Fig. 3.12 (OP-37).

If we compare the plots of $T(j\omega)$ and $|A_{CL}^{+}(j\omega)|$ for the OP-37 of Fig. 3.13 with those of Fig. 3.8 for the OP-27, we see similar plots with the OP-27 circuit indicating less overshoot and somewhat greater bandwidth. Further, for comparison the theoretical output time response for the OP-37 circuit of Fig. 3.12 is shown in Fig. 3.14, with the second-order approximation, as well as the more exact relation from Eq. (3.35), compared with an experimentally measured response. The calculated and measured responses were obtained for the parameter values of Exercise 3.2, giving a value of ϕ_m of 45°. It is apparent that the second-order approximation is very good when compared to the more exact relation of Eq. (3.35), and both provide a reasonable fit to the actual experimental curve for the OP-37. Since the value of SR for the OP-37 is much larger than that of the OP-27, there is no slew-rate limiting in the rise time, as was apparent for the OP-27 in Fig. 3.11.

The concept of reducing the loop transmission to ensure stability applies for inverting circuits as well as noninverting ones. For example, the circuit of Fig. 3.15 is a unity-gain inverting amplifier, with the same reduction of $T(j\omega)$ using the R and C network as in Fig. 3.12. Further, to illustrate the combination of compensation techniques the circuit of Fig. 3.15 uses C_F to help compensate for input stray capacitance, as detailed earlier in Section 3.1 and Fig. 3.1(a).

For the circuit of Fig. 3.15 the ratio of v_ε to v_O can be reduced to

$$\frac{v_\varepsilon}{v_O} \approx \left(\frac{R_A}{R_A + R_F}\right)\left[\frac{1 + sRC}{1 + sC(R + R_A\|R_F)}\right]\left(\frac{1 + sR_FC_F}{1 + sRC_{\text{in}}}\right) \tag{3.37}$$

where

$$C_{\text{in}} = C_s + C_i$$

$$C \gg C_{\text{in}}, C_F$$

$$R < R_A$$

$$R_A = R_1\|R_{\text{IN}}$$

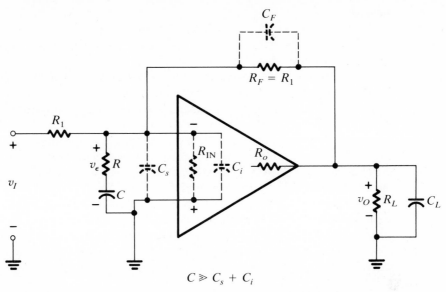

Figure 3.15 Modified inverting unity-gain circuit for use with high-frequency op amps.

Thus, the loop transmission is

$$T(s) = A_{OL}(s)\left[\frac{v_\varepsilon(s)}{v_O(s)}\right]\left(\frac{1}{1 + sR_OC_L}\right) \tag{3.38}$$

where it is assumed that $C_L \gg C_F$ and $R_O \ll R_L, R_F$.

■ **Exercise 3.3**

Using the circuit of Fig. 3.15, derive the circuit relation of Eq. (3.37). The denominator terms of Eq. (3.37) are not absolutely factorable, but can be reasonably approximated as indicated.

EXAMPLE 3.6

Use an HA2540 op amp in the inverting unity-gain circuit of Fig. 3.15, with $R_1 = R_F = 2\ k\Omega$, $R_L = 2\ k\Omega$, $C_L = 10\ pF$, and input stray capacitance $C_S = 3\ pF$. Choose values for R, C, and C_F to achieve a phase margin $> 30°$. Sketch $T(j\omega)$ vs frequency, and use the second-order approximation to indicate ξ and ω_n for the closed-loop system.

Solution

The HA2540 op amp (data sheet in Appendix C) is a very-wide-band, high-frequency amplifier with $GB = 400$ MHz and $SR = 400$ V/μsec. The circuit is stable for values of $A_{CL} \geq 10$. To achieve high-frequency performance the input bipolar-transistor stage of the op amp is biased at reasonably high collector currents (mA region), and therefore the input base currents are larger than those for general purpose op amps (μA versus ηA currents). Hence, it is necessary that the R_1 and R_F resistors be kept below 10 kΩ for good dc biasing and small output dc offsets. Furthermore, since input-stage currents are large, the input resistance R_{IN} of the HA2540 device is much lower than that of a general purpose op amp (10 kΩ for the HA2540 versus 2 MΩ for the 741). Thus, R_{IN} can be important in determining the loop transmission T_0 for the circuit.

We can see from the open-loop gain/phase vs frequency curve in the data sheet for the HA2540 that for $A_{OL} = 20$ dB, the phase is approximately $45°$ at 40 MHz, so if we let $\beta = \frac{1}{10}$ by proper choice of resistor R, we can then choose C_F to compensate for $C_s + C_i$ of the op amp. For $\beta = \frac{1}{10}$, near the crossover frequency f_c we desire that (assume the reactance of C is $\ll R$ at f_c), from Fig. 3.15,

$$\frac{(R_1 \| R_{IN} \| R)}{(R_1 \| R_{IN} \| R) + R_F} = \frac{1}{10}$$

or substituting values, $R = 294 \, \Omega$. Let us use the nearest $\pm 5\%$ resistor value $\leq 294 \, \Omega$, or 270 Ω. Let us then choose the value of C to position the location of the zero in Eq. (3.37) at least a factor of 5 away from the anticipated crossover frequency $f_c = 40$ MHz, or at 8 MHz. Thus

$$C \geq \frac{1}{2\pi(270 \, \Omega)(8 \text{ MHz})} \geq 73.6 \text{ pF}$$

Let us use $C = 100$ pF, so in reality the zero term is at $f_z = 5.9$ MHz. Now, to compensate for the total input capacitance of

$$C_{in} = C_i + C_s \approx 4 \text{ pF}$$

we can choose C_F, from Eq. (3.37), as*

$$C_F = \left(\frac{R}{R_F}\right) C_{in} \approx 0.5 \text{ pF}$$

Thus, in Eq. (3.37) we reduce to a pole-zero combination with values

$$\frac{v_\varepsilon}{v_O} \approx \left(\frac{1.667 \text{ k}\Omega}{3.667 \text{ k}\Omega}\right) \left[\frac{1 + \dfrac{s}{2\pi(5.9 \text{ MHz})}}{1 + \dfrac{s}{2\pi(1.32 \text{ MHz})}}\right] \tag{3.39}$$

---

* In practice, C_F is usually made variable and adjusted for best output-pulse response.

Therefore, the loop-transmission equation is

$$T(s) = A(s)\left[\frac{v_\varepsilon(s)}{v_O(s)}\right] \tag{3.40}$$

where $A(s)$ is the open-loop gain vs frequency specification for the op amp, including any output load effects.

The loop transmission of Eq. (3.40), using Eq. (3.39) and the data sheet gain-vs-frequency curve for the HA2540, is plotted in Fig. 3.16 for the cases of $C_F = 0.5$ pF and $C_F = 1$ pF. For $C_F = 0.5$ pF the crossover frequency is approximately 38 MHz, with a value of $\phi_m = 39°$, while for $C_F = 1$ pF we have an improved phase margin of 49° and a crossover frequency of 43 MHz. Using $C_F = 1$ pF, from Fig. 3.10 a value of ϕ_m of 49° would correspond to a second-order closed-loop system ξ of 0.46, while the value of ω_n would be $2\pi \times 53$ MHz from Eq. (3.25). In Fig. 3.17 the experimental step response for the circuit of Fig. 3.15 is compared with the second-order approximated response using Eq. (3.26). The comparison between the second-order approximation and the experimental response is not as good as for previous examples, partly due to the $R_F C_F$ time

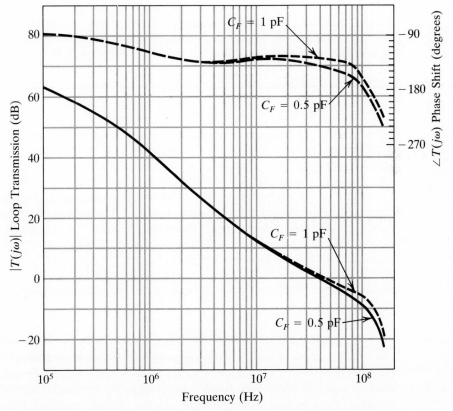

Figure 3.16 Loop transmission of Example 3.6 for an HA2540 op amp.

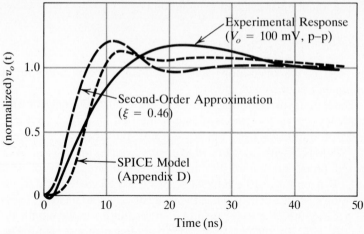

Figure 3.17 Output response comparisons for the circuit of Example 3.6 (HA2540).

constant which now appears in both $T(j\omega)$ and $A_{CL}(j\omega)$, but probably due more to the difficulty in adequately modeling very-high-frequency devices by only a two-pole response. The results from a SPICE model of the HA2540 (see Appendix D) are also compared in Fig. 3.17. Since the SPICE model more correctly models all the poles (and zeroes), as well as some nonlinear effects, the comparison with the experimental response is better.

■ **Exercise 3.4**

The gain- and phase-versus-frequency curves of an HA2539 op amp, which has somewhat improved characteristics of $SR = 600$ Vμ-sec and $GB = 600$ MHz (as compared to the HA2540) are shown in Fig. 3.18. Using values from the HA2539 curves, and the parameter values of Example 3.6, sketch the magnitude and phase response for $T(j\omega)$ for the circuit of Fig. 3.15. Find f_c and ϕ_m (for $C_F = 1$ pF) and compare with the results of the HA2540 circuit.

We could consider many other examples involving op amps with multiple poles (and zeroes) in the loop transmission, but the techniques employed in the previous illustrations are adaptable to most cases. It should also be apparent that detailed analysis is aided by either a programmable calculator, a small personal computer that is easily programmed, or the use of modeling techniques for computer-aided-design programs such as SPICE.

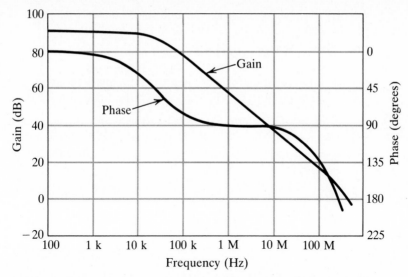

Figure 3.18 Open-loop gain and phase vs frequency for an HA2539 op amp. Source: Harris Semiconductor, Inc.

SUMMARY

Chapter 3 extended the Chapter 2 coverage of frequency response (and transient response) to the case for multiple open-loop poles (and zeroes). We found several classical techniques for eliminating the contributions of many of these extra poles, particularly when they were due to input or output capacitance in the circuit. Because of the complexity involved, the extensive use of computer-aided-design programs was indicated. Several examples demonstrated the use of SPICE, or programmable calculators, to help in solving for the dynamic response of the circuit. The reader is encouraged to study Appendix D on examples and helpful techniques for analyzing op amps using computer programs. These concepts will continue to be valuable, particularly when active filters are studied in Chapter 6.

PROBLEMS

3.1   For the example of Fig. 3.1 with $R_1 = R_F = 100$ kΩ, $C_i = 10$ pF, and C_F not present, and using a 741 op amp with an assumed second pole in the open-loop response at 5 MHz, verify if the circuit is stable, and find the phase margin, ϕ_m.

3.2   Derive Eq. (3.5) in the text for the circuit of Fig. 3.1. Ignore terms involving $R_O/R_F A_O$ in the numerator.

3.3 Verify Eq. (3.10) for Example 3.1 and the circuit of Fig. 3.3, if T_0 is

$$T_0 = -A_o\left(\frac{R_3}{R_3 + R_2}\right)$$

and the input resistance R_{IN} of the op amp is considered to be infinitely large. Using values given in Example 3.1 sketch the Bode plot for the circuit.

3.4 Substitute Eq. (3.10) into Eq. (3.11) and show for the compensated case of Example 3.1 with $C_n = C_i\ (R_3/R_2)$ that the gain expression reduces to a classic second-order system as given by Eq. (3.21) where the *undamped natural frequency* ω_n is

$$\omega_n = \left[\frac{\omega_0 T_0}{R_1(C_1 + C_n)}\right]^{1/2}$$

and the *damping coefficient* ξ is related by

$$\xi \approx \frac{1}{2[\omega_0 T_0 R_1(C_1 + C_n)]^{1/2}}$$

For the parameter values stated in Example 3.1 show that $\omega_n \approx 2\pi\ (26.8\ \text{kHz})$ and $\xi \approx 0.034$. For a step-function input show that the output of the amplifier should have 90% overshoot, with ringing at $\omega \approx \omega_n$.

3.5 Verify Eqs. (3.13) and (3.14) for the loop transmission of Fig. 3.5.

3.6 An LF351 op amp is used in an inverting unity-gain circuit to furnish an output signal to a 10 kΩ load, which is located 100 feet from the amplifier. To reduce interference and noise pickup an RG58 coaxial cable is used, which has a typical capacitance of 28 pF/ft. Use the circuit of Fig. 3.5 with $R_1 = R_F = 20\ \text{k}\Omega$ and $R_2 = 100$ ohms, and choose C_F to give the largest bandwidth consistent with a value of ϕ_m of $\geq 45°$. Sketch the Bode plot, (magnitude and phase) for the system.

3.7 In Problem 3.6, instead of using $R_2 = 100$ ohms inside the dc feedback loop, change the circuit to include R_2 outside the feedback path and equal to the characteristic impedance of the cable (i.e., $R_2 = Z_0 = 50$ ohms). Discuss the relative advantages and disadvantages of this circuit as compared with that of Problem 3.6.

3.8 In Problem 3.6 estimate the maximum output slew rate obtainable for the circuit. Show details for a circuit that would have its slew rate limited only by the LF351 op amp by using an added driver circuit, such as the one shown in Fig. 2.17(b).

3.9 Use the same circuit values as in Fig. 3.6, but use an OP-27 op amp instead of the 741 op amp, and sketch the gain (magnitude and phase) versus frequency as in Fig. 3.6(b).

3.10 The excess phase shift in an inverting integrator can be partially compensated by inserting a resistor R_a in series with the capacitor C, as illustrated in

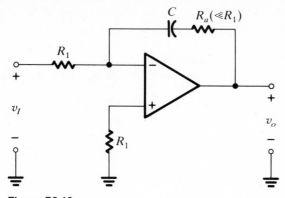

Figure P3.10

Fig. P3.10, where $R_a \ll R_1$. Show that a zero is introduced into the closed-loop gain expression by the addition of R_a. What value should one use for R_a to help correct the excess phase shift in Example 3.2?

3.11 The circuit of Fig. P3.11 is that of a high-frequency single-pole op amp with an open-loop gain given by

$$A_{OL}(s) = \frac{10^4}{1 + \dfrac{s}{2\pi \times 200 \text{ kHz}}}$$

and biased in a noninverting unity-gain configuration. Because of the circuit layout on the printed-circuit board there is a long path between the output and the inverting input of the op amp, which is modeled in Fig. P3.11 by a delay line of length L and characteristic impedance Z_O. It can be assumed the transfer function of the delay line is given by

$$\frac{v_F}{v_O} = \exp[-j\omega\tau L]$$

where $\tau \approx 2$ nsec/ft and $Z_O = 100$ ohms. Determine the maximum length of the line L if a stable system with 45° phase margin is desired.

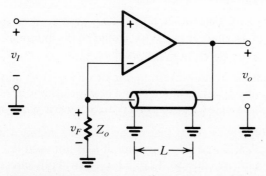

Figure P3.11

3.12 Using data available on any commercial op amp, other than those listed in Table 3.1, approximate the open-loop gain-versus-frequency curve in terms of A_{OL} and the various poles (and perhaps zeroes). Use data sheets available from any of the various manufacturers. Show an open-loop gain magnitude and phase plot comparing your approximation and the manufacturer's data.

3.13 Consider a general loop transmission characterized by three poles as

$$T(s) = \frac{T_0}{\left(1 + \dfrac{s}{\omega_1}\right)\left(1 + \dfrac{s}{\omega_2}\right)\left(1 + \dfrac{s}{\omega_3}\right)}$$

Show that a criterion for stability is that

$$T_0 < \left(2 + \frac{\omega_1 + \omega_3}{\omega_1} + \frac{\omega_1 + \omega_3}{\omega_2} + \frac{\omega_1 + \omega_2}{\omega_3}\right)$$

3.14 An early video op amp, the μA702, could be characterized by an open-loop gain of $A_O = 4000$ and pole locations as indicated in Problem 3.13 with $f_1 = 1$ MHz, $f_2 = 4$ MHz, and $f_3 = 40$ MHz. Show that a stable feedback circuit results if $T_0 < 57$, or that the inverting closed-loop gain must be $A_{CL}^- > 70$. Use the results of Problem 3.13.

3.15 For a second-order system described by the loop transmission

$$T(s) = \frac{T_0}{\left(1 + \dfrac{s}{s_1}\right)\left(1 + \dfrac{s}{s_2}\right)}$$

where the response is dominated by one pole (i.e., $s_2 \gg s_1$) and $T_0 \gg 1$, show that the damping coefficient ζ of the closed-loop system is related to ϕ_m of $T(j\omega)$ by Eq. (3.22). Similarly, show that the value of ζ and ω_n for the closed-loop system can be related to the crossover frequency ω_n of $T(j\omega)$ by Eq. (3.25). Use the basic definition of ζ and ω_n from Eq. (3.21).

3.16 Comment on what nonlinear effects in the OP-27 op amp could produce the very substantial differences in rise times between the theoretical and experimental time responses in Fig. 3.11.

3.17 Repeat Example 3.3 using an NE5534 op amp in the circuit of Fig. 3.7. Estimate the phase margin, ϕ_m. What would be the minimum value of $|T(j\omega)|$ for which the phase margin is greater than 45°?

3.18 Using the unity-gain non-inverting circuit of Fig. 3.12 and an HA2540 op amp, find parameter values of R_F, R and C, if the generator resistance R_1 is 75 ohms, $R_L = 2$ kΩ, and $C_L = 10$ pF. Try to achieve a phase-margin of $\geq 45°$.

3.19 It is not absolutely essential that capacitor C be included in the unity-gain circuits of Figs. 3.12 and 3.15; however, if C is not used the dc output offset voltage will increase, due to V_{OS} and I_B. For both circuits calculate the worst-case output offset voltages, due to V_{OS}, I_B, and I_{OS} with (a) C included and (b) C removed (shorted across C). Use parameter values specified in Examples 3.5 and 3.6.

3.20 Use the approximate data for pole locations for the HA2540 op amp from Table 3.1, and the circuit of Fig. 3.15, with values of $R_1 = R_F = 2$ kΩ, $C_F = 1$ pF, $R = 270$ Ω, $R_L = 2$ kΩ, $C = 100$ pF, $C_L = 10$ pF, $C_s + C_i = 4$ pF, and sketch $T(j\omega)$ versus frequency. Compare with Fig. 3.16.

3.21 The NE5539 is a high-frequency op amp manufactured by Signetics Corp. It has a GB value (measured at $A_{CL} = 7$) of 1200 MHz, with a slew rate of 600 V/μsec. The op amp has characteristics of $R_{IN} = 100$ kΩ, $R_{OUT} = 10$ Ω and $A_{VOL} = 53$ dB and can be approximated by open-loop poles at 5 MHz, 30 MHz, 200 MHz and 300 MHz and a zero at 60 MHz. If the amplifier is used in an inverting gain of 2 circuit, as indicated in Fig. P3.21, find values for R, C and C_F for stable operation with $\phi_m > 30°$. Assume $C_s + C_i$ of the circuit is 4 pF. Sketch the resulting Bode plot for the circuit.

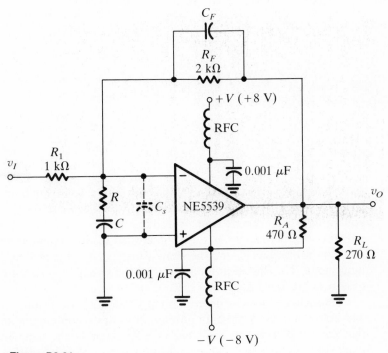

Figure P3.21

Chapter 4

Noise Analysis in Op Amp circuits

In this chapter we deal with one of the most fundamental limitations to amplifying an input signal, the noise of the amplifier itself. In practically every experimental apparatus where signals from transducers and sensors must be obtained, the scientist or experimenter is always interested in the minimum amplifiable signal that can be interpreted, and therefore is interested in the ratio of the signal to the input noise. This specification is given by the signal-to-noise ratio for the system, usually abbreviated SNR.

Noise is a statistical description of a random process inherent in all resistors and active devices. A measure of noise indicates the minimum amplifiable signal that can be detected in a system as a function of the temperature, frequency bandwidth, source impedance and/or bias on an active device. Although the designation noise may sometimes also include man-made environmental effects (such as hum, 60- or 120-Hz pickup, electromagnetic interference (EMI), intermodulation effects, etc.) these latter effects are not necessarily random in nature and for the present discussion are excluded from consideration. All semiconductor devices, as well as vacuum tubes, produce noise of one or several types.

One could spend an entire semester (or longer!) analyzing noise in devices and circuits. However, the intent of this chapter is merely to acquaint the student,

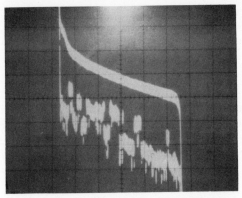

Figure 4.1 Gain of two op amps, obtained from the Tektronix Model 577 curve tracer. Vertical scale = 20 μV/div, horizontal scale = 5 V/div. Upper trace (first device) indicates typical low-frequency noise; lower trace (second device) indicates excessive burst ("popcorn") noise

and practicing engineer, with the basic types of noise, as well as methods for correctly predicting the effect of noise on various op amp circuits. The interested reader is referred to the many references listed in Appendix A for more detailed treatment and derivations of equations.

Operational amplifiers can exhibit wide deviations in electronic noise, both between different device types and even among devices of the same type and manufacturer. For example, in Fig. 4.1 we see a photograph indicating the open-loop gain of two op amps, obtained from the Tektronix Model 577 curve tracer, with the Model 178 Linear IC test fixture. Both devices were from the same manufacturer, and from the same production run. The first device (upper trace) indicates typical low-frequency noise for the op amp, but the second device (lower trace) indicates excessive low-frequency burst (or "popcorn") noise. Similarly, Fig. 4.2 indicates the amplification of a 10 μV, 100 Hz sinusoidal signal by (a) a 741 op

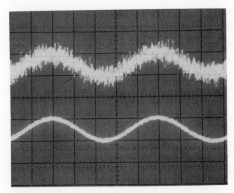

Figure 4.2 Amplification of a 10 μV, 100 Hz signal by a 741 op amp (upper trace) and an OP-27 amp (lower trace). Both circuits have identical gain (10^4) and bandwidth (20 Hz–10 kHz).

amp and (b) an OP-27 op amp. Both systems had identical gain and frequency bandwidth, yet it is obvious that the noise contamination of the signal with the 741 op amp is significantly greater than with the OP-27 op amp.

4.1 BASIC TYPES OF NOISE

This section presents a general description of the basic types of noise encountered in op amp circuits. No attempt is made to present the derivations of the particular noise equations; instead the reader is encouraged to pursue further study from the various references referred to in each case.

4.1.1 Thermal Noise

Thermal noise is also referred to as Johnson noise [Ref. 4.1] or Nyquist noise [Ref. 4.2]. The basic description of thermal noise originated from analysis by Nyquist, in 1928, involving a transmission line connecting two resistors. Using the Second Law of Thermodynamics, Nyquist showed that the noise power spectral density S_v of a resistor R in thermal equilibrium at absolute temperature T was equal to*

$$S_v(f) = \frac{4hfR}{\exp(hf/kT) - 1} \tag{4.1}$$

where h = Planck's constant = 6.624×10^{-34} joule-sec
$\quad k$ = Boltzmann's constant = 1.38×10^{-23} joule/°K
$\quad T$ = absolute temperature (°K)
$\quad f$ = frequency (Hertz)

If the frequency f is below 10^{11} Hertz, then the Nyquist equation reduces to the usually stated thermal-noise power spectral density, defined by S_v (or e_R^2) as†

$$S_v \equiv e_R^2 = 4kTR \text{(mean-square volts/Hertz)} \tag{4.2}$$

Thermal noise is due to the motion of free charge due to thermal energy, and is present in all resistors. Note also from Eq. (4.2) that the spectral density is constant as a function of frequency; a characteristic of constant power spectral density with frequency is often referred to as a **White noise** spectrum. We can also note from Eq. (4.2) that an electric field (i.e., a potential difference) does *not* have to be present for thermal noise to exist.

---

* Equation (4.1) can also be derived using black-body radiation with Planck's Law for quantized radiation. Further, if the quantum-mechanical correction of a residual ground-state energy ($T = 0$ °K) $E_0 = hf/2$ is included, the fundamental equation is [Ref. 4.3].

$$S_v(f) = 4hfR\left(\frac{1}{2} + \frac{1}{\exp(hf/kT) - 1}\right)$$

† In this text we will use the standard symbology for noise terms; lower-case symbols (e^2, i^2) refer to values of power spectral density (volts^2/Hz, amps^2/Hz), whereas upper-case symbols (E^2, I^2) refer to rms values (volts^2, amps^2).

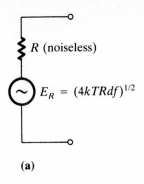

(a)

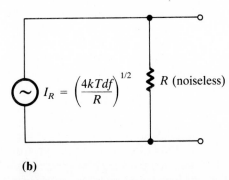

(b)

Figure 4.3 Equivalent circuits for thermal noise: (a) Thevénin circuit; (b) Norton circuit.

An equivalent-circuit representation of thermal noise is that of either a voltage source (Thevénin equivalent) or current source (Norton equivalent), as indicated in Fig. 4.3. In Fig. 4.3 the value of the noise is expressed as

$$E_R = (4kTR\Delta f)^{1/2}(\text{root-mean-square volts}) \tag{4.3}$$

or, for current

$$I_R = \left(\frac{4kT\Delta f}{R}\right)^{1/2} (\text{root-mean-square amperes}) \tag{4.4}$$

where Δf is defined as the noise bandwidth (Hz).

■ **Exercise 4.1**

By expansion of the series for $\exp(x)$, show that Eq. (4.2) results from (4.1).

■ **Exercise 4.2**

Show that the thermal noise of two resistors R_1 and R_2 in series is equivalent to the noise of a single resistor equal to the sum of R_1 and R_2.

■ **Exercise 4.3**

A resistor of value 100 kΩ has a noise bandwidth of 100 kHz. Find (a) the spectral density S_v and (b) the Thevénin equivalent source E_R if $T =$ room temperature (70 °F). If the resistor is immersed in liquid nitrogen ($T \approx -200$ °C), find E_R. Does this latter condition suggest possibilities for very-low-noise design techniques?

4.1.2 Shot Noise

Shot noise was first studied by Schottky [Ref. 4.4], who considered the fluctuations in the anode current of a temperature-limited thermionic vacuum-tube diode. He showed that the fluctuations in the instantaneous number of electrons in transit produced a noise current in the anode, whose spectral density is given by

$$S_s(f) \equiv i_s^2 = 2qI_{dc} \text{ (mean-square amperes/Hz)} \qquad (4.5)$$

where q is the electronic charge (1.6×10^{-19} coulombs) and I_{dc} is the mean anode current. In general, Eq. (4.5) will be a function of frequency. However, if $\omega \ll 1/\tau_r$, where τ_r is the transit-time of an electron from cathode to anode, the frequency correction to Eq. (4.5) is negligible. Equation (4.5) also holds for semiconductor diodes and transistors, since charge carriers (holes or electrons) cross a pn junction, and transit times are very short ($< 10^{-9}$ sec).

Since shot noise is due to the motion of charge carriers by a drift current, an electric field *must* be present for shot noise to exist. Like thermal noise, shot noise also has a White spectrum.

The equivalent-circuit representation for shot noise is that of a Norton current source, as indicated in Fig. 4.4 where the value of the noise current is

$$I_s = (2qI_{dc}\Delta f)^{1/2} \text{(root-mean-square amps)} \qquad (4.6)$$

■ **Exercise 4.4**

Compare the shot-noise current of a pn-junction diode (a) operating with a forward current of 1 mA, and (b) reverse biased with a reverse current of 1 nA.

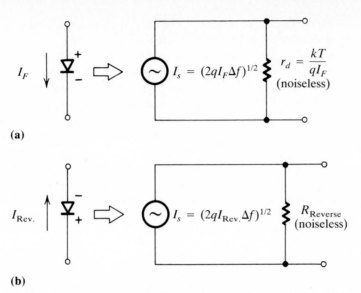

(a)

(b)

Figure 4.4 Equivalent circuits for shot noise in a pn diode: (a) forward bias; (b) reverse bias.

4.1.3 Low-Frequency Noise

Many devices show an excess noise spectral density at low frequencies, which is not predicted by standard noise equations. A characteristic of this type of noise is that a dc current I_{dc} must flow. This type of noise was first observed in vacuum tubes and given the name **flicker noise**. The spectral density is generally considered to be of the type

$$S_{LF}(f) = \frac{KI_{dc}^n}{f^\alpha} \text{ (mean-square amps/Hz)} \tag{4.7}$$

where K is a constant indicative of the material and manufacturing process, n is approximately 2, and α varies between 0.5 and 2. If $\alpha = 1$, flicker noise is often referred to as **1/f noise**, or **pink noise**. Flicker noise has been observed as low as 10^{-6} Hz, and in some MOS devices as high as 10 MHz. Many types of resistors can also exhibit excess noise at low frequencies, if a dc current flows through the resistor. The excess resistor-noise spectrum closely follows that of Eq. (4.7) with $n = 2$ and $\alpha = 1$. Carbon-composition resistors can exhibit a power-spectral-density value ten times that of the thermal-noise equation, for a frequency < 100 Hz, whereas metal-film and wirewound resistors usually indicate nearly pure thermal noise to frequencies as low as 1 Hz.

Another low-frequency noise spectrum often observed is in JFET circuits, where the spectral density varies as $1/f^2$. This noise is believed due to hole-electron recombinations via a trapping center, and is called generation-recombination noise. The spectral density equation is of the form

$$S_{GR}(f) = C\left(\frac{\tau_0}{1 + \omega^2 \tau_0^2}\right) \tag{4.8}$$

where τ_0 is the lifetime of charge carriers in the trapping center, and C is a constant involving the dc current and total number of charge carriers.

The noise observable in the photograph of Fig. 4.1(b) is another low-frequency type of noise, called **burst**, or **popcorn noise**. This phenomenon was particularly troublesome in early vintage type 709, 741, and LM101 op amps, where it was believed to be associated with the surface of the forward-biased emitter-base junctions of the input npn transistors [Refs. 4.6, 4.7]. Another theory suggested the existence of localized microplasmas in the reverse-biased base-collector junctions of the input bipolar devices [Ref. 4.7]. The most accepted approach to predict this effect is to include a parallel low-frequency noise current generator (between the emitter and base of the input transistors) whose mean-square value is given by

$$I_{BB}^2 = \frac{AI_B\Delta f}{1 + \left(\dfrac{\pi f}{2a}\right)^2} \text{ (mean-square amperes)} \tag{4.9}$$

where A is a constant and a is the average burst rate (typical values of a lie in the range of 50–500/sec). Burst noise is easily observable, if present, by the appearance of bursts of essentially constant-amplitude pulses having random pulse width and occurrance, at the ouput of a high-gain amplifier. Fortunately, today most high-quality op amps are screened against burst noise.

■ **Exercise 4.5**

Plot the noise spectra of an amplifier having both $1/f$ noise and burst noise. Assume the constants in Eqs. (4.7) and (4.9) are $n = 1$, $\alpha = 1$, $I_{dc} = I_B = 1\ \mu A$, $a = 100/sec$, $K = 2 \times 10^{-13}$, and $A = 2 \times 10^{-14}$, while the white noise level is 10^{-22} amps/Hz. The total power spectral density is thus given by (in mean-square amperes/Hz)

$$S_I(f) = 1 \times 10^{-22} + \frac{KI_B}{f} + \frac{AI_B}{1 + \left(\dfrac{\pi f}{2a}\right)^2}$$

Plot on log-log paper over a frequency range of 1 Hz to 10 kHz. Indicate the $1/f$ region, the burst-noise region, and the white-noise region.

4.1.4 Avalanche Noise

Noise due to avalanche breakdown can be particularly large. In regulator diodes (Zener diodes), an approximation to the noise spectral density has been suggested as [Ref. 4.8]

$$S_A = \frac{b^2 V_A^n}{I_A} \text{ (mean-square volts/Hz)} \tag{4.10}$$

where $b^2 \approx 5 \times 10^{-20}$ amp/Hz, $V_A =$ avalanche breakdown voltage, and I_A is the diode current. Eq. (4.10) would not be valid for regulator diodes operating below avalanche, in the Zener breakdown region (i.e., in the region $V_A < 5$ volts), where the noise is considerably less than that predicted by this equation. Further, recent measurements on regulator diodes with V_A in the range of 6–12 volts indicate that $4 \leq n \leq 6$.

4.1.5 Noise Bandwidth

The noise bandwidth Δf is not the same as the normal -3 dB bandwidth. The noise bandwidth is instead defined as the area under the power-transfer-function–versus–frequency curve, normalized by dividing by the peak value of the power transfer function, or basically

$$\Delta f \equiv \frac{1}{2\pi P_0} \int_0^\infty P(\omega)d\omega \qquad (4.11)$$

where

$\Delta f =$ noise bandwidth in Hertz

$P(\omega) = G_E^*(\omega) \cdot G_E(\omega)$, or $G_I^*(\omega) \cdot G_I(\omega)$†

$P_0 =$ peak value of $P(\omega)$

For example, if the voltage-gain–versus–frequency function $A_v(f)$ is known and the peak value is the mid-band gain A_O then Eq. (4.11) could be expressed as

$$\Delta f = \frac{1}{A_O^2} \int_0^\infty [A_v^2(f)]df \qquad (4.12)$$

---

† Note that $G_x^*(\omega) \cdot G_x(\omega)$ denotes the product of a function G_x with its complex conjugate G_x^*.

EXAMPLE 4.1

Calculate the noise bandwidth for a single-pole system having a transfer function

$$A_v(f) = \frac{v_O}{v_I} = \frac{A_O}{1 + j\left(\dfrac{f}{f_0}\right)}$$

where f_0 is the -3 dB bandwidth.

Solution

From Eq. (4.11) the power-transfer function is

$$[A_v^2(f)] = \left[\frac{A_O}{1 + j(f/f_0)}\right]\left[\frac{A_O}{1 - j(f/f_0)}\right] = \frac{A_O^2}{1 + (f/f_0)^2}$$

Therefore the noise bandwidth becomes

$$\Delta f = \frac{1}{A_O^2}\int_0^\infty \frac{A_O^2\, df}{1 + \left(\dfrac{f}{f_0}\right)^2}$$

Substituting $x = (f/f_0)$ leads to the standard form of the integral

$$\Delta f = f_0 \int_0^\infty \frac{dx}{1 + x^2}$$

The above equation can be integrated by substituting $x = \tan\varphi$, which gives for a single-pole system

$$\Delta f = \frac{\pi f_0}{2} = 1.57 f_0 \tag{4.13}$$

Hence, we see that the noise bandwidth of a single pole system is actually 57% *greater* than the -3 dB bandwidth.

For systems having a rolloff greater than -6 dB/octave, the noise bandwidth more closely approximates the -3 dB signal bandwidth. For example, a circuit having a response

$$A_v = \frac{A_O}{[1 + j(f/f_0)]^2}$$

has a noise bandwidth of $(\pi/4)f_0$, or $1.22 f_{-3\,\text{dB}}$.

4.2 SPECIFICATION OF AMPLIFIER NOISE

There are two distinct ways to analyze the noise effects in an amplifier. The most straightforward, but most time-consuming, way is to replace each resistor, transistor, diode, etc., in the amplifier by its noise model, and using the Superposition Principle calculate the noise produced at the output by each noise source.

Assuming there is no correlation* between the noise sources, the total output noise is obtained by adding the individual noise powers, or

$$E_0^2 = A_1^2 E_1^2 + A_2^2 E_2^2 + A_3^2 I_1^2 + \cdots \tag{4.14}$$

where A_1 is the gain for noise source E_1 and so on. It is easy to see that the output must be combined as the power, or the sum of the individual terms squared, since we know from circuit theory that two different frequency sinusoidal signals with rms amplitudes V_1 and V_2, if connected in series must produce a resultant rms amplitude equal to

$$V_{\text{resultant}}(\text{rms}) = (V_1^2 + V_2^2)^{1/2}$$

Since noise generators can be represented as a large number of component frequencies with random distribution of amplitudes and phases, then Eq. (4.14) must correspondingly hold.

4.2.1 Equivalent Noise Voltage (ENV) and Equivalent Noise Current (ENI)

The most accepted way to calculate noise in an amplifier, one that also offers a more logical circuits-oriented approach, is to express the total noise of an amplifier in terms of its **equivalent noise voltage (ENV)** and its **equivalent noise current (ENI)**. Really, the use of ENV and ENI concepts is based on a theorem due to Peterson (Stanford University, 1943), who showed that the noise characteristics of any linear two-port are sufficiently described by two external noise generators and the correlation between them. In fact, the two noise generators could be placed at the output, or one at the input and one and the output, but for ease of calculation it is usually more reasonable to place the generators at the input. The value of the ENV(e_n) is equal to the total equivalent input noise of the op amp, when the inputs of the op amp are *shorted*. It can be obtained by measuring the output noise and referring it back to the input by dividing by the voltage gain. Similarly, the value of the ENI(i_n) is obtained when the inputs to the op amp are *open-circuited*, by measuring the output noise and dividing by the current gain from input to output. A basic circuit representation of e_n and i_n is indicated in Fig. 4.5(a), with a form more suitable for op amp circuits shown in Fig. 4.5(b). The latter form is used for

---

* *Correlation* of noise sources implies that a noise pulse produced at one instant of time in one noise source physically causes a similar noise pulse to be produced in another source. Sometimes partial correlation of two noise sources E_1 and E_2 can occur. In this case the total noise would be [see Refs. 4.11 and 4.19]

$$E_{\text{total}}^2 = E_1^2 + E_2^2 + 2CE_1E_2$$

where C is the **correlation coefficient** and is theoretically bounded between $-1 \le C \le 1$. Fortunately, for almost all op amp situations correlation is negligible, so $C \approx 0$, and Eq. (4.14) holds.

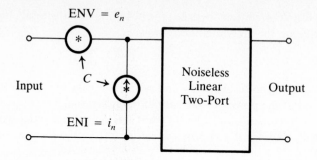

$ENV = e_n$

Input

C = Correlation Coefficient

$C \rightarrow$

$ENI = i_n$

Noiseless Linear Two-Port

Output

(a)

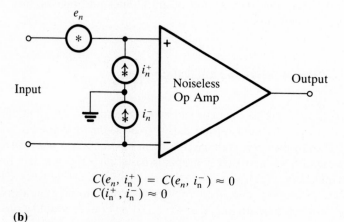

e_n

Input

i_n^+

i_n^-

Noiseless Op Amp

Output

$$C(e_n, i_n^+) = C(e_n, i_n^-) \approx 0$$
$$C(i_n^+, i_n^-) \approx 0$$

(b)

Figure 4.5 The ENV and ENI concept: (a) general representation for a linear two-port; (b) application to an op amp.

op amps since input bias current will produce shot noise in each half of the differential-input circuit.

For an op amp having a bipolar-transistor input differential stage, the value of the ENV for *each* transistor at midband is approximately [Refs. 4.9–4.11]

$$e_n\left(\frac{V}{\sqrt{Hz}}\right) \approx \left[4kT\left(r_b' + \frac{r_e}{2}\right)\right]^{1/2} \tag{4.15}$$

where r_b' is the internal base ohmic resistance and r_e is the incremental emitter resistance equal to kT/qI_E. Thus, the total value of ENV for a differential input (two transistors) becomes

$$e_{n(total)} \approx \left[8kT\left(r_b' + \frac{r_e}{2}\right)\right]^{1/2} \tag{4.16}$$

The ENI for a single bipolar transistor is predominantly due to shot noise and can be expressed as [Refs. 4.9–4.11]

$$i_n\left(\frac{A}{\sqrt{Hz}}\right) \approx \left\{2q\left[I_b + K_1 I_b^\gamma \left(\frac{f_b}{f}\right)^\alpha\right]\right\}^{1/2} \tag{4.17}$$

where generally $\gamma \approx \alpha \approx 1$, $K_1 \approx 1$, and thus Eq. (4.17) becomes

$$i_n \approx \left\{2qI_b\left[1 + \left(\frac{f_b}{f}\right)\right]\right\}^{1/2} \tag{4.18}$$

where f_b is defined as the **break frequency** between white noise and $1/f$ noise. Thus, in the circuit model of Fig. 4.5(b), if the dominant value of ENI is due to the input base current of each bipolar transistor in the input differential stage, then we have

$$i_n^+ = \left\{2qI_b^+\left[1 + \frac{f_b}{f}\right]\right\}^{1/2}$$

$$i_n^- = \left\{2qI_b^-\left[1 + \frac{f_b}{f}\right]\right\}^{1/2} \tag{4.19}$$

if the two break frequencies are the same.

If JFETs are used in the input stage of the op amp, the noise is predominantly due to the thermal noise of the channel of the JFET [Ref. 4.12] and any ohmic resistance in series with the source. This noise can be referred to the input gate of the JFET, resulting in an ENV of

$$e_n\left(\frac{V}{\sqrt{Hz}}\right) \approx \left[\frac{4kTK_2}{g_m}\left(1 + \frac{f_b}{f^x}\right)\right]^{1/2} \tag{4.20}$$

where g_m is the forward transconductance of the FET, which includes internal source ohmic resistance, $K_2 \approx 2/3$ if the channel is pinched off, f_b is the break frequency between low-frequency and white noise, and $(0.5 < x < 2)$. If a differential-input stage is used in the op amp, then the total ENV would be $\sqrt{2}$ times that of Eq. (4.20), provided that second-stage noise of the op amp is negligible. The ENI of a JFET is due to shot noise of the reverse-biased gate-to-channel, plus a high-frequency noise component due to Miller-effect feedback of noise in the channel by way of the gate-to-channel depletion-layer capacitance [Ref. 4.13], resulting in a value of

$$i_n\left(\frac{A}{\sqrt{Hz}}\right) \approx \left\{2qI_g + K_3\left(\frac{\omega^2 C_{gs}^2}{g_m}\right)\right\}^{1/2} \tag{4.21}$$

where C_{gs} is the gate-to-source capacitance of the JFET, and $K_3 \approx kT$.

If MOSFETs are utilized in the input stage of the op amp, the e_n value of Eq. (4.20) is still valid, except that the K_2 term may now be larger $(0.7 < K_2 < 2)$, and the break frequency f_b is also much larger than for JFETs. In general, since $I_g < 10^{-13}$ ampere and C_{gs} (MOSFET) $\ll C_{gs}$(JFET), the i_n generator of Eq. (4.21) can be ignored, except for very large source resistances. For MOSFETs the break frequency f_b is inversely proportional to gate area; hence, for low-noise requirements the input MOS devices must have large area, which implies a large channel-width-to-channel-length ratio [Refs. 4.14, 4.15].

4.2.2 Total Equivalent Input Noise

If a source resistance R_s is added to the basic circuit of Fig. 4.5(a) and a Thevénin input equivalent circuit formed to include the total noise due to the thermal noise of R_s, e_n, and i_n, we obtain a Thevénin open-circuited noise voltage e_{tni} of

$$e_{tni}\left(\frac{\text{volts}}{\sqrt{\text{Hz}}}\right) = [4kTR_s + e_n^2 + (i_n R_s)^2]^{1/2} \tag{4.22}$$

or

$$E_{tni}(\text{rms volts}) = e_{tni}\Delta f^{1/2} \tag{4.23}$$

It is illustrative to plot Eq. (4.22) as a function of the source resistance R_s, and indeed many op amp manufacturers include such a figure on data sheets.

EXAMPLE 4.2

Sketch e_{tni} (or, correspondingly, E_{tni} for a 1 Hz bandwidth) in the white noise region for a typical 741 op amp, for a range of R_s from 100 ohms to 100 kΩ. Estimate the value of $R_s(R_{opt})$ where e_{tni} is closest to the thermal noise of R_s. Show that this value is related by $R_{opt} = e_n/i_n$.

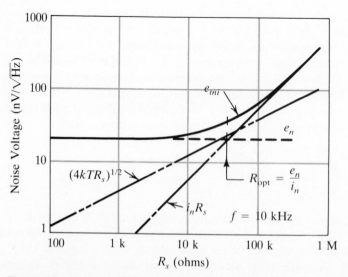

Figure 4.6 Noise plot for Example 4.2 for a 741 op amp.

Solution

From the data for the 741 op amp (Appendix C) the midband value of e_n is approximately $(4.5 \times 10^{-16})^{1/2}$, or 21 nV/$\sqrt{\text{Hz}}$, while i_n is $(3.2 \times 10^{-25})^{1/2}$, or 0.57 pA/$\sqrt{\text{Hz}}$. Thus Eq. (4.22) becomes

$$e_{tni}\left(\frac{\text{volts}}{\sqrt{\text{Hz}}}\right) = [4kTR_s + 4.5 \times 10^{-16} + 3.2 \times 10^{-25}R_s^2]^{1/2}$$

The relation for e_{tni} is sketched in Fig. 4.6, with each contributing part shown. From the sketch, and the data for e_n and i_n, the value of R_{opt} is $21 \times 10^{-9}/0.57 \times 10^{-12}$, or 36.8 kΩ.

■ **Exercise 4.6**

From the value for i_n for a 741 op amp, find the value for I_B^+ (or I_B^-) assuming i_n is due entirely to base-current shot noise of the input npn transistor. Compare your calculated value with the typical value of I_B shown on the data sheet. What does the comparison indicate about other noise sources?

A curve of e_{tni} as a function of source resistance R_s is often used to compare different types of op amps, as indicated in Fig. 4.7. Here, a comparison is made between a low-noise bipolar-transistor op amp (the OP-27) and a corresponding

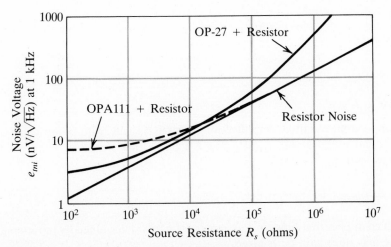

Figure 4.7 Comparison of total input-referred noise e_{tni} for a low-noise bipolar op amp (OP-27) vs a low-noise JFET op amp (OPA111).

low-noise JFET-transistor op amp (the OPA111). The OP-27 has a much lower value of e_n that does the OPA111, $3\text{nV}/\sqrt{\text{Hz}}$ as compared to $7\text{nV}/\sqrt{\text{Hz}}$, but the value of i_n is significantly less for the JFET, $0.4 \times 10^{-15}\,\text{A}/\sqrt{\text{Hz}}$ as opposed to $0.4\,\text{pA}/\sqrt{\text{Hz}}$ for the OP-27. Hence, as shown in Fig. 4.7, the total input-referred noise is less for the OP-27 for source resistances below 15 kΩ, but lower for the JFET op amp for $R_s > 15$ kΩ.

4.2.3 Noise Factor and Noise Figure

In early articles on op amp noise, the designations Noise Factor (F) or Noise Figure (NF) were occasionally used. The **Noise Factor** F is specified as the ratio of the available output-noise power per unit bandwidth to that portion of output noise caused by the source connected to the input, and measured at the standard temperature of 290 °K. In equation form this is given by

$$F \equiv \frac{\text{Total output-noise power}}{\text{Output-noise power due to thermal noise of } Z_S} \tag{4.24}$$

or in terms of the signal-to-noise ratio SNR

$$F \equiv \frac{\text{Input SNR}}{\text{Output SNR}} \tag{4.25}$$

The **noise figure** NF is then defined, in decibels, as

$$NF \text{ (dB)} \equiv 10 \log_{10} F \tag{4.26}$$

For example, in the basic circuit of Fig. 4.5(a) the noise factor F is related to the ENV and ENI by (assuming the correlation coefficient C is negligible)

$$F = \frac{e_n^2 + i_n^2 R_s^2 + e_s^2}{e_s^2} \tag{4.27}$$

where R_s is the source resistance connected to the input, and $e_s^2 = 4KTR_s(\text{volt}^2/\text{Hz})$.

■ **Exercise 4.7**

Suppose one has three amplification stages in cascade, with power gains G_1, G_2 and G_3, and noise factors F_1, F_2 and F_3. Show that the noise factor of the entire network F_{total} is given by

$$F_{\text{total}} = F_1 + \frac{F_2 - 1}{G_1} + \frac{F_3 - 1}{G_1 G_2}$$

which implies that noise in a system is primarily determined by input-stage noise, if the first-stage gain G_1 is large.

4.3 EXAMPLES OF NOISE CALCULATIONS

In this section we will consider several examples of noise calculations for both inverting and noninverting op amp circuits. The analysis will include quantitative examples employing equations for the spectral density, as well as approximation techniques for wide-band noise using graphical techniques. Finally the use of computer calculations employing SPICE will be illustrated.

4.3.1 Mathematical Analysis

The basic inverting, or noninverting, op amp circuit is shown in Fig. 4.8 with the various noise sources indicated. The various sources are

$$e_n = \text{ENV of op amp } (\text{V}/\sqrt{\text{Hz}})$$

$$i_n^-, i_n^+ = \text{ENI of op amp } (\text{A}/\sqrt{\text{Hz}})$$

$$e_1 = \text{thermal noise of } R_1 = (4kTR_1)^{1/2}(\text{V}/\sqrt{\text{Hz}})$$

$$e_2 = \text{thermal noise of } R_2 = (4kTR_2)^{1/2}(\text{V}/\sqrt{\text{Hz}})$$

$$e_F = \text{thermal noise of } R_F = (4kTR_F)^{1/2}(\text{V}/\sqrt{\text{Hz}})$$

$$e_L = \text{thermal noise of } R_L = (4kTR_L)^{1/2}(\text{V}/\sqrt{\text{Hz}})$$

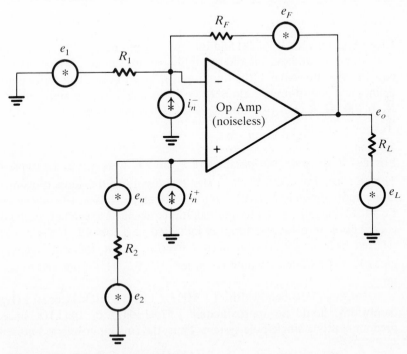

Figure 4.8 Op amp noise sources.

If the input signal is applied in series with e_1 the circuit is a standard inverting amplifier, whereas if the signal is applied in series with R_2 we have a basic noninverting amplifier.

By using superposition, we can calculate the gain to the output for each noise source, and then add as the square root of the sum of the squares to produce the total output noise in $V/\sqrt{Hz}$, as shown earlier in Eq. (4.14). Then, the total output noise (in rms volts) is obtained by multiplying by the square root of the noise bandwidth, $(\Delta f)^{1/2}$. Thus, by standard circuit analysis one can obtain, from Fig. 4.8,

$$
e_o^2(\text{V}^2/\text{Hz}) \approx e_n^2 \left(1 + \frac{R_F}{R_1} \right)^2 + e_2^2 \left(1 + \frac{R_F}{R_1} \right)^2 + e_1^2 \left(\frac{R_F}{R_1} \right)^2
$$

$$
+ e_F^2 + (i_n^-)^2 R_F^2 + (i_n^+)^2 R_2^2 \left(1 + \frac{R_F}{R_1} \right)^2
$$

$$
+ e_L^2 \left(\frac{1}{R_L} \right)^2 \left(\frac{R_o}{1 + T} \right)^2 \tag{4.28}
$$

where it is assumed that the loop transmission T is large.

EXAMPLE 4.3

Using Fig. 4.8 and Eq. (4.28) find the total output noise e_o, the total noise referred to the input e_{in} and the minimum amplifiable rms signal v_s, which occurs when v_s is equal to the rms value of the total input-referred noise. This latter condition also defines a signal-to-noise ratio SNR = 1. Assume a 741 op amp with $R_1 = 10\,\text{k}\Omega$, $R_F = 100\,\text{k}\Omega$, $R_2 = 9.1\,\text{k}\Omega$ and $R_L = 2\,\text{k}\Omega$. Temperature is 25 °C.

Solution

For a 741 op amp the parameters e_n and i_n were (from Example 4.2); $e_n \approx 21\,\text{nV}/\sqrt{\text{Hz}}$ and $i_n \approx 0.57\,\text{pA}/\sqrt{\text{Hz}}$. Furthermore, the loop transmission T_0 is large, approximately $2 \times 10^5 \times (10\,\text{k}\Omega/110\,\text{k}\Omega) = 1.87 \times 10^4$, so the last term in Eq. (4.28) due to R_L could be ignored. It is convenient to evaluate each noise source contribution in a tabular form as indicated in Table 4.1. If the output noise is referred back in series with the noninverting input, the value of e_{in} would be $28.2\,\text{nV}/\sqrt{\text{Hz}}$, while e_{in} would be larger ($31\,\text{nV}/\sqrt{\text{Hz}}$) if referred to the inverting input.

For a $-3\,\text{dB}$ bandwidth of 1 MHz $\times$ (10 kΩ/110 kΩ), or 91 kHz, the noise bandwidth should be approximately 1.57(91 kHz), or 143 kHz, since we have predominantly a single-pole system. Thus, the rms input-referred noise would be

$$
E_{\text{in}} \text{ (rms volts)} \approx (31 \times 10^{-9})(143\,\text{kHz})^{1/2} = 11.7\,\mu\text{V}
$$

Table 4.1 NOISE CALCULATIONS FOR EXAMPLE 4.3

Noise Source	Value	Gain Multiplying Factor	Output Noise Contribution $(nV/\sqrt{Hz})$
e_n	$21\ nV/\sqrt{Hz}$	11	231
i_n^+	$0.57\ pA/\sqrt{Hz}$	10^5	57
i_n^-	$0.57\ pA/\sqrt{Hz}$	10^5	57
e_2	$12.23\ nV/\sqrt{Hz}$	11	134.5
e_1	$12.83\ nV/\sqrt{Hz}$	10	128.3
e_F	$40.56\ nV/\sqrt{Hz}$	1	40.56
e_L	$5.74\ nV/\sqrt{Hz}$	*	negligible
Total e_o (root sum-of-squares)			$310\ nV/\sqrt{Hz}$
Total Input Referred Noise, e_{in}			$31 (or\ 28.2)\ nV/\sqrt{Hz}$

* The multiplying factor at dc is $(75\ \Omega/1 + T_0) \times (1/2\ k\Omega) = 2 \times 10^{-6}$; at high frequencies, as $T \to 0$, the factor approaches $(75\ \Omega/2.075\ k\Omega)$ or 3.6×10^{-2}. In either case, output noise due to R_L is negligible.

for an inverting amplifier, or for a noninverting amplifier

$$E_{in}\ (rms\ volts) = (28.2 \times 10^{-9})(143\ kHz)^{1/2} = 10.7\ \mu V$$

Hence, for a SNR of 1, v_s would be equal to E_{in}.

The previous example illustrated not only the importance of noise due to e_n, but also the significant effects of thermal noise in the input resistors R_1 and R_2. Often, the compensation resistor R_2 is not used in low-noise circuits, thereby eliminating its noise contribution.

The previous calculations considered only midband or white noise, and neglected both low- and high-frequency noise sources. Since the gain is decreasing at higher frequencies, it is reasonable to ignore any high-frequency effects, but we should justify the neglect of low-frequency noise in Example 4.3. From the 741 data sheet, if we approximate the low-noise region from the noise curves of e_n and i_n, we obtain

$$e_n^2 \approx \left(\frac{21\ nV}{\sqrt{Hz}}\right)^2 \left(1 + \frac{200\ Hz}{f}\right) \tag{4.29}$$

and

$$i_n^2 \approx \left(\frac{0.57\ pA}{\sqrt{Hz}}\right)^2 \left(1 + \frac{2\ kHz}{f}\right) \tag{4.30}$$

Thus, the correct output noise expression including e_n and i_n is, from Example 4.3 and Eq. (4.12),

$$E_0^2(\text{rms volts})^2 = \int_0^\infty (e_n^2) \left[\frac{A_{CL}^2 df}{1 + \left(\dfrac{f}{f_{CL}}\right)^2} \right]$$

$$+ \int_0^\infty (i_n^2) R_F^2 \left[\frac{df}{1 + \left(\dfrac{f}{f_{CL}}\right)^2} \right] + (\text{other noise sources}) \, \Delta f \quad \textbf{(4.31)}$$

where A_{CL} and f_{CL} are the closed-loop gain and bandwidth, respectively, which were defined in Example 4.3. Hence, if we substitute Eqs. (4.29) and (4.30) into Eq. (4.31), and separate the parts, we obtain

$$E_0^2(\text{rms volts})^2 = \left[\left(\frac{21 \text{ nV}}{\sqrt{\text{Hz}}}\right)^2 (11)^2 + (0.57 \text{ pA}/\sqrt{\text{Hz}})(10^5)^2 + \cdots \right](143 \text{ kHz})$$

$$+ 200 \left(\frac{21 \text{ nV}}{\sqrt{\text{Hz}}}\right)^2 (11)^2 \int_0^\infty \frac{df}{f\left[1 + \left(\dfrac{f}{f_{CL}}\right)^2\right]}$$

$$+ 2 \text{ kHz} \left(\frac{0.57 \text{ pA}}{\sqrt{\text{Hz}}}\right)^2 (10^5)^2 \int_0^\infty \frac{df}{f\left[1 + \left(\dfrac{f}{f_{CL}}\right)^2\right]} \quad \textbf{(4.32)}$$

or reducing Eq. (4.32),

$$E_0^2(\text{rms volts})^2 = (117 \ \mu v)^2 + (4.14 \ \mu v)^2 \int_0^\infty \frac{df}{f\left[1 + \left(\dfrac{f}{f_{CL}}\right)^2\right]} \quad \textbf{(4.33)}$$

Integration of Eq. (4.33) can be accomplished by expansion by parts, or from integral tables. The result is

$$E_0^2(\text{rms volts})^2 = (117 \ \mu\text{V})^2 + (4.14 \ \mu\text{V})^2 \left\{ \ln(f_{CL}) - \frac{1}{2} \lim_{y \to 0} [\ln(y)] \right\} \quad \textbf{(4.34)}$$

The function $\ln(y)$ is not defined at zero frequency. However, flicker noise cannot extend to zero frequency, since that would indicate infinite energy in zero bandwidth at dc! Thus, a practical limitation of low-frequency noise is reached when low-frequency noise is indiscernable from dc drift. A limit often imposed is 0.01 Hz (or equivalently, 100 sec). Hence, if we arbitrarily impose a 0.01 Hz value in Eq. (4.34), we obtain for total output noise

$$E_0^2(\text{rms volts})^2 = (117 \ \mu\text{V})^2 + (4.14 \ \mu\text{V})^2 [\ln(91 \text{ kHz}) + 2.3] \quad \textbf{(4.35)}$$

or

$$E_0^2(\text{rms volts})^2 = (117 \ \mu\text{V})^2 + (15.33 \ \mu\text{V})^2$$

hence

$$E_0^2(\text{rms volts})^2 = 118 \ \mu V$$

and therefore the total input-referred noise is now

$$E_{in}(\text{rms volts}) = 11.8 \ \mu V$$

for an inverting amplifier, or for a noninverting amplifier

$$E_{in}(\text{rms volts}) = 10.73 \ \mu V$$

Thus, it is evident that the contribution of low-frequency noise is negligible, since the amplifier bandwidth was reasonably large. However, for amplifiers whose bandwidth is in the low-frequency instrumentation region (dc–100 Hz), low-frequency noise may be the dominant noise effect.

4.3.2 Graphical Techniques*

Often, it is difficult to obtain theoretical equations for the noise power spectral density (NPSD) of an amplifier, particularly when one attempts to evaluate noise contributions from both low- and high-frequency regions. However, by using filters at several different frequencies it is possible to obtain experimentally the output NPSD over all practically useful frequencies. One can then divide the frequency spectrum into sufficiently narrow intervals so that an average value for e_{out}(or i_{out}) can be employed.

Consider the approximation to the output NPSD as measured on an amplifier and indicated in Fig. 4.9. This spectrum could also have been obtained by simple addition (on log paper) of e_n, i_n and the amplifier closed-loop gain, plus additions from other sources, such as resistors. For ease of computation the frequency spectrum is subdivided into six separate segments, as shown.

Region 1. In Region 1 the noise has a $1/f$ spectrum (pink noise or flicker noise), or $e_1 = K(1/f)^{1/2}$, where K is the value of e_1 at a frequency of 1 Hz. Now, in the frequency band between frequencies f_2 and f_1 we have noise of

$$E_{1(f_2 \text{ to } f_1)} = K\left[\int_{f_1}^{f_2} \frac{df}{f}\right]^{1/2} = K\left[\ln\left(\frac{f_2}{f_1}\right)\right]^{1/2} \tag{4.36}$$

or for one decade of frequency we have

$$E_1(1 \text{ decade}) = K[\ln(10)]^{1/2} = 1.52K \ (\text{rms volts}) \tag{4.37}$$

and for two decades

$$E_1(2 \text{ decades}) = \sqrt{2}(1.52K)(\text{rms volts}) \tag{4.38}$$

---

* This material is from two excellent articles on graphical analysis. One by L. Smith and D. Sheingold, "Noise And Op-Amp Circuits," *Analog Dialogue*, Vol. 3, No. 1 (1969), and the second by A. Ryan and T. Scranton, "DC Amplifier Noise Revisited," *Analog Dialogue*, Vol. 18, No. 1 (1984).

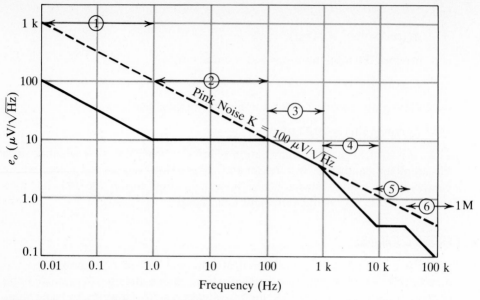

Figure 4.9 Output NPSD of an amplifier [Ref. 4.16].

Note that $1/f$ noise contributes *equal* increments over *each* decade of frequency. Thus, in Region 1, from Fig. 4.9 we have $K = 10~\mu V/\sqrt{Hz}$, and since Region 1 extends two decades

$$E_1(\text{total}) = \sqrt{2} \times 1.52 \times 10~\mu V/\sqrt{Hz} = 21.5~\mu v \tag{4.39}$$

Region 2. In Region 2 we have two decades of white noise. Therefore the noise contribution is

$$E_2(\text{total}) = 10~\mu V/\sqrt{Hz}[(100 - 1)]^{1/2} \approx 100~\mu V \tag{4.40}$$

Region 3. In Region 3 there is one decade of pink noise (from 100 Hz to 1 kHz) with $K = 100~\mu V/\sqrt{Hz}$, so the noise in this region is

$$E_3 = 100~\mu V/\sqrt{Hz}(1.52) = 152~\mu V \tag{4.41}$$

Region 4. The effect in this region is often called a **filter-skirt error**. In this region the NPSD is given by the function

$$e_4 = \frac{e_{o4}}{1 + j(f/f_c)}$$

or

$$e_4^2 = \frac{e_{o4}^2}{1 + (f/f_c)^2} \tag{4.42}$$

where f_c is the corner frequency. Thus, for a bandwidth from f_c to kf_c $(k > 1)$, we have

$$E_4^2 = e_o^2 \left[\int_{f_c}^{kf_c} \frac{df}{1 + (f/f_c)^2} \right] \tag{4.43}$$

which can be reduced to

$$E_4 = e_o \sqrt{f_c} \left[\int_1^k \frac{dx}{1 + x^2} \right]^{1/2} \tag{4.44}$$

or

$$E_4 = e_o \sqrt{f_c} \left[\tan^{-1}(k) - \frac{\pi}{4} \right]^{1/2} \tag{4.45}$$

which for one decade gives $E_{o4} \approx 0.8 e_o \sqrt{f_c}$. Thus, from the example of Fig. 4.9 in Region 4 we have

$$E_4 \approx (0.8)(3 \ \mu V/\sqrt{Hz})(1000)^{1/2} = 76 \ \mu V \tag{4.46}$$

Region 5. In this region there is white noise with a magnitude of $0.3 \ \mu V/\sqrt{Hz}$, and a bandwidth of approximately 20 kHz, so

$$E_5 \approx 0.3 \ \mu V/\sqrt{Hz}(20 \times 10^3)^{1/2} = 42 \ \mu V \tag{4.47}$$

Region 6. Here there is a -6 dB/octave skirt extending to infinity. Hence, Eq. 4.45 becomes

$$E_6 = 0.3 \ \mu V/\sqrt{Hz}(30 \ kHz)^{1/2} \left(\frac{\pi}{2} - \frac{\pi}{4} \right)^{1/2} = 46 \ \mu V \tag{4.48}$$

Total Output Noise. The total output noise is computed as the square root of the sum of the squares of Eqs. (4.39)–(4.48). Thus, the output noise that would be indicated by a true rms voltmeter would be $E_o(\text{total}) = 206 \ \mu V$.

The Pink-Noise Tangent. If a line of -3 dB/octave slope is lowered until it is tangent to the NPSD of Fig. 4.9 (as indicated by the dotted line in the figure), the main noise contributions should come only from those regions in the vicinity of this line. Any part of the NPSD more than 10 dB away from the line should contribute insignificant noise. Thus, in Fig. 4.9, only Regions 2, 3 and 4 should be important, and we could therefore approximate the total noise by summing noise from those regions, or

$$E_o(\text{total}) \approx [(E_2)^2 + (E_3)^2 + (E_4)^2]^{1/2} \tag{4.49}$$

or we obtain $E_o \approx 197 \ \mu v$, which is within 4% of the previous value.

4.3.3 Computer Analysis

Complex noise-analysis problems often require computer analysis to reduce the calculation time. Computer analysis can also provide more complete information on the total spectral density than can hand calculations. Several examples of computer modeling using the program SPICE are found in Appendix D. We will use the model there for the HA2540 op amp as well as a simpler model for the OP-27, to predict the system noise for a high-frequency video amplifier, indicated in Fig. 4.10. The circuit of Fig. 4.10 illustrates a useful concept for obtaining high-frequency performance, yet also very low dc output-voltage drift. The excellent dc performance of the OP-27 (OA1 in Fig. 4.10) determines the dc output offsets and drift of the total circuit, as well as ensuring excellent low-frequency noise performance. However, the bandwidth and high-frequency performance of the circuit is determined by the characteristics of the HA2540 device (OA2 in Fig. 4.10). The crossover frequency is set by equal time constants, $R_A C_A = R_2 C_2 = 10\ \mu\text{sec}$, or a crossover frequency of 16 kHz. Thus, the poor noise performance of the HA2540 op amp below 16 kHz does not limit the total noise of the circuit.

It is now necessary to model the OP-27 op amp to accurately predict circuit performance. A SPICE model that reasonably reproduces the important parameters of the OP-27 is indicated in Fig. 4.11. The details are left as an exercise for the student, however the important features produced by the circuit model of Fig. 4.11 are:

$$e_n = 3\ \text{nV}/\sqrt{\text{Hz}} \approx \left[8kT\left(r_b' + \frac{r_e}{2} + R_E \right) \right]^{1/2}$$

$$i_n^+ = i_n^- = 0.4\ \text{pA}/\sqrt{\text{Hz}} = 2q(0.5\ \mu\text{A})$$

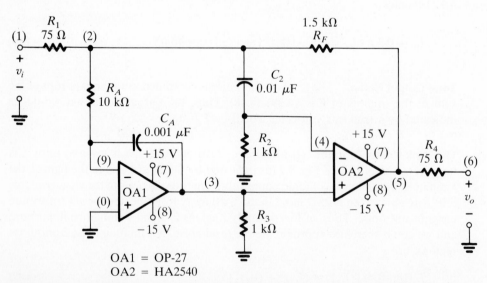

OA1 = OP-27
OA2 = HA2540

Figure 4.10 A video amplifier combining two op amps. Nodes used in SPICE analysis indicated in parenthesis.

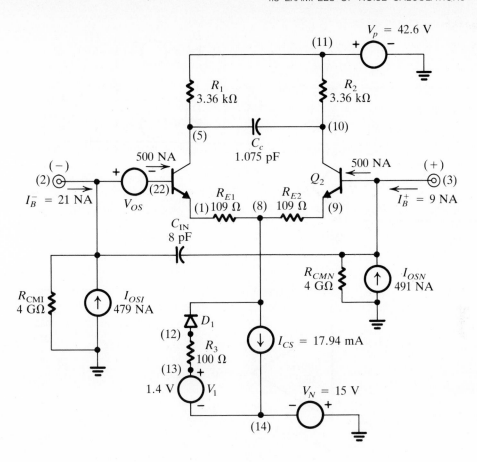

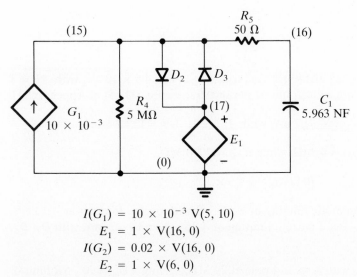

$$I(G_1) = 10 \times 10^{-3} \, V(5, 10)$$
$$E_1 = 1 \times V(16, 0)$$
$$I(G_2) = 0.02 \times V(16, 0)$$
$$E_2 = 1 \times V(6, 0)$$

Figure 4.11   A SPICE model for the OP-27 op amp.

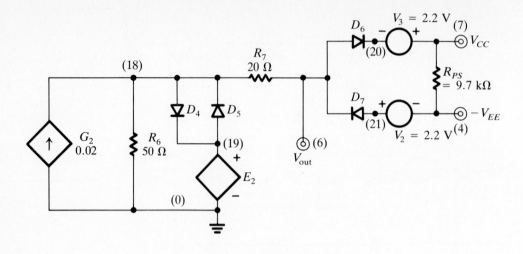

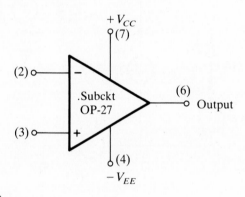

Figure 4.11 (continued)

i_n break frequency of 140 Hz, due to $KF = 2qf_b = 4.5 \times 10^{-17}$, with $AF = 1$ [KF and AF are SPICE model parameters; see Eq. (D.15) in Appendix D].

$I_B = 15$ nA $= (21 + 9)/2$ nA, while $I_{OS} = 21 - 9 = 12$ nA

R_{IN}(differential) $= 4$ MΩ, while $R_{CM} = 2000$ MΩ,

$C_{IN} = 8$ pF, $R_{OUT} = 70$ Ω, $A_{OL} = 1.5 \times 10^6$

Input common-mode limiting at ± 12.5 V, with output limiting at ± 13.5 V. Output short-circuit current limiting of $+35$ mA and -42 mA, with D_4, D_5, R_7 and E_2.

$GB = 8$ MHz, with a second pole at 22 MHz, giving a $\phi_m = 70°$, SR limit of ± 2.8 V/μsec, with D_2, D_3, R_5, E_1 and C_1.

■ **Exercise 4.8**

Using the circuit model of Fig. 4.11, and the example of the HA2540 model explained in Appendix D, verify each of the parameters above, and compare with quoted data sheet values for the OP-27 (Appendix C). The base ohmic resistance for Q_1 and Q_2 in Fig. 4.11 is 150 ohms (as stated by the manufacturer), while the current-gain (β or h_{FE}) is 1.79×10^4.

Thus, the complete description of the SPICE model subcircuit for the circuit of Fig. 4.11 is as follows:

```
.SUBCKT OP-27 2 3 4 6 7

*NODES: INV=2, NON-INV=3, PS+=7, PS-=4, VO=6.

* DEVICE CHAR: AOL=1.5E6, Z IN=4MEG/8PF, IB=15NA,

*IOS=12NA, RCM=2E9, RO=70, GB=8MHZ, SR=2 8V/US,

* VOS=30UV, VINCM=+-12.5V, VO=+-13.5V, IO LIMIT

* =+35MA, -42 MA, SEC.POLE AT 22 MHZ (PM=70°),

* EN=3NV/RTHZ, IN=0.4 PA/RTHZ. LAST NODE=22.

*

VOS    2  22  30U

IOSI   0   2  479NA

RCMI 2   0  4000MEG

CIN    2   3  8PF

RCMN 3   0  4000MEG

IOSN 0   3  491NA

VP   11   0  42.6

R1   11   5  3.36K

R2   11  10  3.36K

CC    5  10  1.075PF

Q1    5  22   1 N1

Q2   10   3   9 N1

RE1   1   8  109

RE2   8   9  109
```

```
ICS  8  14  17.94MA

VN  0  14  15

D1  12  8  DA

R3  12  13  100

V1  13  14  1.4

G1  0  15  5  10  10M

R4  15  0  5MEG

D2  15  17  DB

D3  17  15  DB

E1  17  0  16  0  1

R5  15  16  50

C1  16  0  5.963NF

G2  0  18  16  0  0.02

R6  18  0  50

D4  18  19  DA

D5  19  18  DC

E2  19  0  6  0  1

R7  18  6  20

D6  6  20  DA

D7  21  6  DA

V3  7  20  2.2

RPS  7  4  9.7K

V2  21  4  2.2

.MODEL  DA   D(IS = 5.73 E-14)

.MODEL  DB   D(IS = 1.47 E-16)

.MODEL  DC  D(IS = 3.07 E-16)

.MODEL N1  NPN (IS = 1FA, BF = 1.79 E4, RB = 150, KF = 4.5 E-17)

.ENDS OP-27
```

■ **Exercise 4.9**

Using the circuit of Problem 4.21 with $R = 1$ megohm, verify using the computer program SPICE that the total midband value of i_n for the model of the OP-27 is equal to $\sqrt{2}(0.4 \text{ pA}/\sqrt{\text{Hz}})$. Also, verify that the low-frequency noise corner for i_n is 140 Hz.

■ **Exercise 4.10**

Verify, using SPICE, that the value of ENV for the OP-27 model is indeed $3 \text{ nV}/\sqrt{\text{Hz}}$, with a noise corner between 2 and 3 Hz. Use the test circuit of Problem 4.21 with resistors R removed.

With the OP-27 model of Fig. 4.11 and the HA2540 model (Appendix D), the total input-referred noise spectral density e_{tni} was obtained using SPICE. The results are shown in Fig. 4.12 for two cases; (1) for $R_A = 10 \text{ k}\Omega$ and $C_A = 1 \text{ nF}$, and (2) for $R_A = 1 \text{ k}\Omega$ and $C_A = 10 \text{ nF}$. For the first case the input noise is primarily determined by the thermal noise of R_A, and the voltage produced by the product i_n (OP-27) $\times R_A$. By decreasing R_A to 1 kΩ, the thermal noise is lowered, as is the

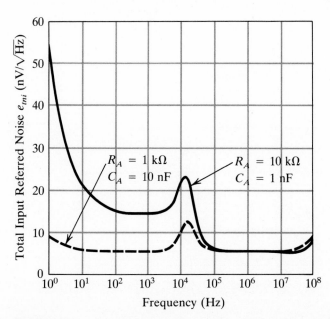

Figure 4.12 Total input-referred noise e_{tni} for the video amplifier of Fig. 4.10, using SPICE.

product $i_n R_A$. Hence, case (2) gives the best low-frequency-noise results. Past the crossover frequency of 16 kHz, the $5 \, \text{nV}/\sqrt{\text{Hz}}$ noise of e_n for the HA2540 op amp dominates the result.

The experimentally measured large-signal transient response of the video amplifier of Fig. 4.10 is compared in Fig. 4.13 with the SPICE analysis. The experimental results indicate more overshoot and ringing than that predicted by the computer model; this difference is due primarily to more phase shift in the actual circuit. To obtain the transient response it was necessary to drive the input from a 50-ohm pulse generator. Therefore, the circuit of Fig. 4.10 was modified by

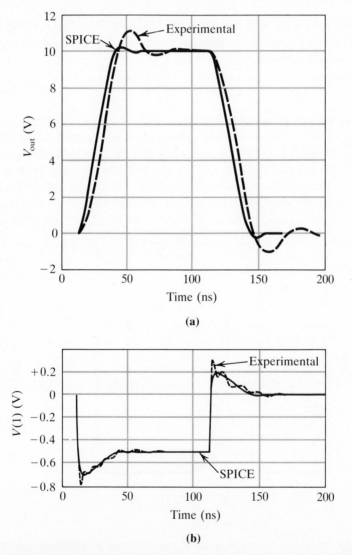

(a)

(b)

Figure 4.13 Transient response comparisons for the video amplifier.

connecting a 150-ohm resistor at node (1) to ground, thereby providing a 50-ohm input termination for the circuit. Also, resistor R_4 was changed to 50 ohms to allow an RG58 (50-ohm) coaxial cable connection to the output. Therefore, the pulse response at $V(1)$ in Fig. 4.13(b) indicates the mis-termination of the input in the nanosecond region.

4.4 NOISE MEASUREMENTS

There are several ways to measure noise. The most accurate technique is to employ a true-rms voltmeter which measures the rms heating effect of the applied noise, and converts this value to a dc-output reading. Such a circuit is indicated in Fig. 4.14, where R_1 and R_2 are resistive heaters and S_1 and S_2 are temperature sensors. The sensors could be thermocouples, thermistors, or any matched temperature-sensitive element. The true-rms voltmeter achieves excellent accuracy (to $\pm 0.1\%$) and can operate with any input waveform, including a dc signal. The circuit does suffer from overload problems, however, and limited low-frequency response.

A second, less costly technique for an rms-to-dc voltage-conversion system is to use analog-multiplier (or logarithmic-conversion) circuits to obtain explicitly the root-mean-square value of an input signal. Such a circuit is indicated, from a block diagram viewpoint, in Fig. 4.15. The accuracy of this circuit is limited (typically $>1\%$), and although the cost is considerably below that of a true-rms voltmeter, the circuit still requires two multipliers, as well as at least one op amp. The circuit is further limited in dynamic range, or to signals having a low **crest factor***. Also, the accuracy and frequency bandwidth of the explicit computation circuit is proportional to the amplitude of the input signal. For example, the

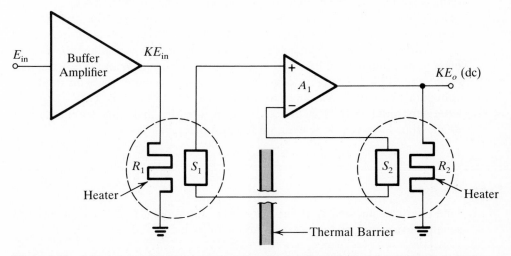

Figure 4.14 A true rms voltmeter based on the rms heating effect of the noise [Ref. 4.21].

---

* The *crest factor* of a signal is defined as the ratio of the peak value of the signal to its rms value.

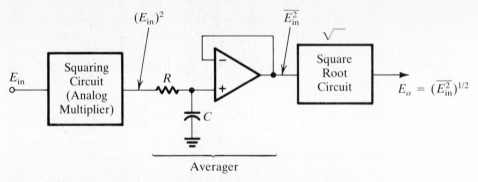

Figure 4.15 Direct computation of the rms value of an input signal.

AD637 offers an 8 MHz, -3 dB bandwidth with a 2 V rms input signal, but the bandwidth drops to 100 kHz for a 20 mV rms input signal.

One can also use the oscilloscope to measure wideband noise qualitatively by observing the peak-to-peak output-noise display. If the noise is predominantly Gaussian in amplitude distribution [i.e., the amplitude varies as $\exp(-x^2/2\sigma^2)$, where σ is the rms, or standard deviation], then the peak-to-peak value of the noise is equal to 6.6 times the rms value, within a factor of 99.9%, or 5 times the rms value would be the peak-peak value within 99% of the anticipated observation time. Usually, experimenters use a factor of 5 × rms noise to equal peak-peak noise, since the eye provides some visual integration of the observed noise trace on the oscilloscope. The real difficulty of the use of this latter technique is that measurements are not very repeatable because of variations due to oscilloscope intensity settings, and measurement time. A much more reliable alternative is to apply the noise signal to both channels of a two-channel oscilloscope (this technique is referred to as the "tangential method" in the literature; see Refs. 4.22 and 4.23 in Appendix A), with both channels identically calibrated. Then, adjust the voltage offset of one channel until the two bright traces just merge. With the noise signals removed the difference in the noise-free traces is approximately twice the rms noise voltage (actually the value can be within a range of 2–2.2 times σ). The value of this latter tangential method is that changes in intensity and time settings on the oscilloscope have very little effect on the measurement.

■ **Exercise 4.11**

Find the rms value and crest factor for (a) a sinusoidal signal, (b) a symmetrical square-wave signal, and (c) a pulse train with period T and duty cycle η.

■ **Exercise 4.12**

Verify that when two gaussian signals $f_1(x)$ and $f_2(x)$, [where $f(x) = \exp(-x^2/2\sigma^2)$] are added together, a resultant smooth curve—with no dips—is obtained when the two functions $f_1(x)$ and $f_2(x)$ are separated by exactly 2σ. This concept provides mathematical justification for the tangential method of measuring rms noise.

SUMMARY

This chapter has very briefly described the types of noise inherent in electronic circuits and shown how the limitations in op amp circuit performance due to noise can be calculated with simple models. Some examples demonstrating the advantages afforded with computer analysis of noise effects were included. The student should find several of the following problems helpful in deciding where to use FET-transistor op amps, as opposed to bipolar-transistor op amps, and how to tell whether a very-low-noise (usually expensive) op amp is required, or whether noise is unimportant and inexpensive devices can be used.

PROBLEMS

4.1 Verify Eq. (4.27) by the use of Thevénin's theorem and Fig. 4.5(a). Similarly, define the noise factor F for an op amp circuit having equal source resistance R_s in series with each input terminal.

4.2 Using the basic definition of the noise bandwidth, show that the noise bandwidth of a circuit having a voltage gain

$$A_V = \frac{A_o}{\left[1 + j\left(\dfrac{f}{f_0}\right)\right]^2}$$

is $\Delta f = (\pi/4)f_0$, or $1.22f_0$.

4.3 A simple bandpass filter can be constructed as indicated in Fig. P4.3. This is often called an RC–CR filter. Show that the noise bandwidth of the filter $\Delta f = 1/2\tau$, where $\tau = RC$. Does it matter whether the lowpass or the highpass circuit is first?

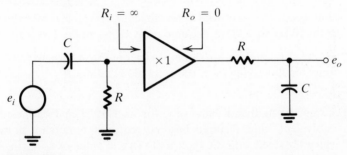

Figure P4.3

4.4 In Section 4.2 the correlation and correlation coefficient C were defined. Can you give an example where correlation could exist between two noise sources?

4.5 An amplifier, as indicated schematically in Fig. 4.5(a), has values of $e_n = 1$ nV/$\sqrt{\text{Hz}}$ and $i_n = 0.1$ pA/$\sqrt{\text{Hz}}$. If the source resistance R_s is 100 ohms find the noise figure NF for the circuit. If the values of e_n and i_n increase by a factor of 10, and R_s also changes to 500 kΩ, find the new NF. Can an observer therefore compare the two systems by comparing values of NF, without stating the value of R_s used?

4.6 Assume that Eqs. (4.15) and (4.18) are valid for a common-emitter (grounded emitter) bipolar transistor having a source resistance (resistor from base to ground) of R_s. Using Thevénin's Theorem, show that the total equivalent input noise for the circuit (noise voltage generator in series with R_s) is given by

$$e_{tni}\left(\frac{V}{\sqrt{\text{Hz}}}\right) = (e_n^2 + e_{R_s}^2 + i_n^2 R_s^2)^{1/2}$$

or, in the white-noise region,

$$e_{tni}\left(\frac{V}{\sqrt{\text{Hz}}}\right) = \left[4kT\left(R_s + \frac{r_e}{2} + r_b'\right) + 2qI_B R_s^2\right]^{1/2}$$

Show that the minimum value of e_{tni} occurs if the dc collector current I_c is chosen so that

$$I_c \approx \frac{kT(1 + h_{FE})^{1/2}}{qR_s}$$

4.7 Using the results of P4.6, find the optimum choice for I_c if (a) $R_s = 100$ ohms and (b) $R_s = 100$ kΩ. Find the total input noise e_{tni} in each case. Assume the current gain h_{FE} is 300 and the internal base ohmic resistance r_b' is 100 ohms.

4.8 In a JFET what should the dc value of the gate-to-source voltage (V_{gs}) be for minimum noise in the midband noise region?

4.9 A particular 2N4392 JFET has a maximum measured transconductance g_m of 20 millimhos, a gate current of 10 picoamps, and capacitance $C_{gs} = 10$ pF and $C_{gd} = 5$ pF. If the break frequency for e_n is $f_b = 100$ Hz sketch the noise voltage e_n (nV/$\sqrt{\text{Hz}}$) and noise current i_n (pA/$\sqrt{\text{Hz}}$) over the frequency range from 10 Hz to 1 MHz. Assume pure flicker noise. Use a log-log scale.

4.10 Sketch total input noise similar to that of Fig. 4.6 for an OP-27 (or OP-37) op amp, for R_s varying from 100 Ω to 100 kΩ. Find R_{opt} by using values of e_n and i_n at 1 kHz.

4.11 Using the midband value of i_n for an OP-27 in P4.10, estimate the noise-equivalent value of input base current, assuming shot noise. Compare the value obtained with the typical data sheet value of I_B for the OP-27. Explain why the noise-equivalent value of I_B is so much larger (Hint: observe the current-cancellation input scheme used for the OP-27). What fundamental principle involving addition of noise sources is involved?

4.12 The OPA111 JFET input op amp (manufactured by Burr-Brown Corp.), whose total input-referred noise was shown in Fig. 4.7, has white-noise-region values of $e_n = 6\,\text{nV}/\sqrt{\text{Hz}}$, $i_n = 4 \times 10^{-16}\,\text{A}/\sqrt{\text{Hz}}$, with a $1/f$ break frequency of $f_b = 200$ Hz for e_n, and high-frequency ω^2 noise with a corner frequency of 40 kHz. Estimate the values of input gate current I_g, g_m, and C_{gs} for each input transistor, assuming all noise is contributed by the input differential stage. Assume the junction operating temperature of the op amp is 40°C.

4.13 Verify Eq. (4.28) in the text.

4.14 Repeat Example 4.3 using an OP-27 op amp, and compare the values for total input-referred noise, in $\text{nV}/\sqrt{\text{Hz}}$.

4.15 Repeat Example 4.3 using an HA2540 op amp, and compare the values for total input-referred noise, in $\text{nV}/\sqrt{\text{Hz}}$, with the results for the 741 and OP-27 op amp (Problem 4.14).

4.16 Using an OP-37 op amp, design a circuit for a voltage gain of $|50|$, with a -3 dB bandwidth of 100 kHz. The signal is from a transducer with an internal impedance of $R + j\omega L$, where $R = 50$ ohms and $L = 1$ mH. Choose resistors to give the lowest possible value of input-referred noise, consistent with op amp output-load requirements. Should the amplifier be inverting or noninverting? The OP-37 is identical to the OP-27, except that $GB = 63$ MHz, $SR = 17$ V/μsec, and is stable for closed-loop gains ≥ 5.

4.17 A μA725 op amp has an open-loop gain of 3×10^6, a compensated gain-bandwidth product of 5 MHz (as measured at a gain of 100), with a second open-loop pole at 200 kHz. The values of e_n and i_n for the op amp are given by

$$e_n^2 = \left(\frac{9\,\text{nV}}{\sqrt{\text{Hz}}}\right)^2\left[1 + \left(\frac{f_{b1}}{f}\right)^{1/2}\right]$$

$$i_n^2 = \left(\frac{0.15\,\text{pA}}{\sqrt{\text{Hz}}}\right)^2\left[1 + \left(\frac{f_{b2}}{f}\right) + \left(\frac{f}{f_{b3}}\right)^{3/2}\right]$$

where $f_{b1} = 200$ Hz, $f_{b2} = 500$ Hz, and $f_{b3} = 10$ kHz. The op amp is used in the circuit indicated in Fig. P4.17.

(a) On a log-log graph sketch the output NPSD of e_o^2 vs frequency from 1 Hz to 1 MHz. Use asymptotes.

(b) Estimate the total output noise that would be indicated by a true-rms voltmeter. You may use asymptotic approximations.

(c) Using the pink-noise tangent principle estimate the output rms noise.

(d) Find the total input referred noise for the circuit, and estimate the equivalent noise resistance R_n for the circuit, defined by

$$R_n \equiv \frac{e_{\text{in}}^2\,(\text{total})}{4kT\Delta f}$$

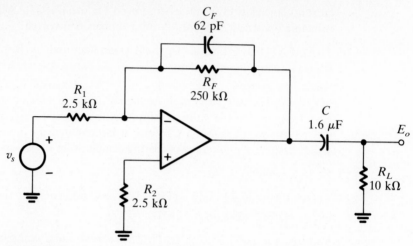

Figure P4.17

4.18 In Fig. P4.18 a circuit for measuring the temperature of an industrial process is shown, which uses a Type K (Chromel-Alumel) thermocouple as the sensor. The measuring thermocouple is compared to a reference junction of 0° Celsius, so that at 0 °C the dc signal V_i is zero. The process may vary over a temperature range of 0 °C to 100 °C, while the temperature of the resistors

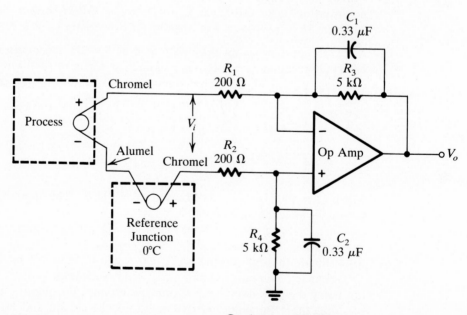

Op Amp = OP-27A
All resistors are metal film.
All capacitors are polypropylene.

Figure P4.18

and the op amp remain at $25\,°C \pm 10\,°C$. Using an OP-27A op amp, and assuming resistors R_1–R_4 are precision metal-film type (TC $= \pm 10$ ppm/$°C$), estimate the measurement accuracy of the circuit, in $°C$. You may assume any initial dc offsets have been trimmed to zero at 25°C. Include an estimate for total peak-peak noise in your sensivity calculations. You may assume the type K thermocouple potential varies as $40\ \mu V/°C$. What is the dc output voltage V_o at $25\,°C$? At $100\,°C$?

4.19 An MC34071 op amp (a single op amp, whose characteristics are identical to those of the MC34074) is used in a circuit having a single $+15$ V power supply, as indicated in Fig. P4.19. To set the dc output voltage at $+15\ V/2 = 7.5$ V, a 1N4100 voltage-reference diode is used, having a reference voltage of $V_Z = 7.5$ V, and dynamic resistance of $r_Z = 10$ ohms. The 1N4100 diode has avalanche noise as given by Eq. (4.10) with $n = 4$ and $b^2 = 5 \times 10^{-20}$. Estimate the total midband equivalent input noise (e_{in}) due to all noise sources, and the rms value E_{in}. What *percentage* of total input noise is due to the 1N4100 reference diode? What does this indicate about the use of reference diodes in low-noise circuits? Indicate how the circuit of Fig. P4.19 could be changed to eliminate most of the noise contribution from the reference diode.

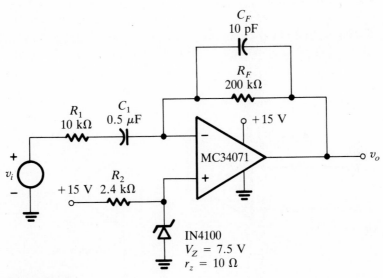

Figure P4.19

4.20 Using the SPICE model for the OP-27 op amp (Fig. 4.11), show that if $r_b' = 150$ ohms, $e_n = 3$ nV/$\sqrt{Hz}$, $i_n = 0.4$ pA/$\sqrt{Hz}$, $R_{IN} = 4$ megohms, and $I_B = 0.5\ \mu A$, that the collector current and β (h_{FE}) for Q_1 and Q_2 must be as indicated in Fig. 4.11, namely $\beta = 1.79 \times 10^4$ and $I_C = 8.97$ mA. From the schematic of the actual OP-27 device, shown in Appendix C, why is the shot noise of the bias-current-cancellation circuit (Q_6 on the data sheet) *not* included in the value for i_n (the equivalent noise current)?

4.21 An op amp manufacturer uses the circuit shown in Fig. P4.21 for measuring the equivalent noise current of an op amp, i_n^+ (or i_n^-). Show, if i_n^- and i_n^+ are equal, that the value of i_n is

$$i_n^+ = i_n^- \approx \frac{\left[\dfrac{e_{no}^2}{(100)^2} - \left(\dfrac{129 \text{ nV}}{\sqrt{\text{Hz}}}\right)^2\right]^{1/2}}{\sqrt{2}\,(500 \text{ k}\Omega)}$$

if resistor R is 500 kΩ. What frequency limitations are imposed by the input and stray capacitance of the op amp?

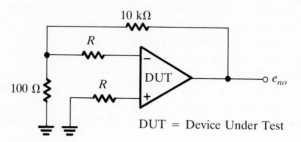

Figure P4.21

4.22 A general test circuit to obtain values of i_n and e_n for op amps is indicated in Fig. P4.22. What limitations are imposed by the circuit, particularly in

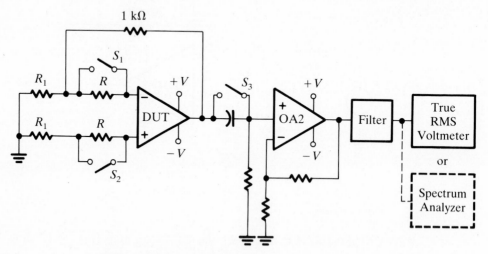

DUT = Device Under Test
OA2 = Low-Noise Op Amp (OP-27, OP-37, etc.)
R_1 = 100 Ω (or 10 Ω for low values of e_n)
To measure i_n, S_1 and S_2 are open.
To measure e_n, S_1 and S_2 are shorted.

Figure P4.22

measuring values of i_n for FET op amps? What is the purpose of switch S_3? What should be the characteristics of the filter? What limitations are imposed on the lowest frequency of noise measurement with this system. How could you automate the noise measurement for computer control?

4.23 Using SPICE, verify the plot of e_{tni} in Fig. 4.12, for $R_A = 1\,k\Omega$ and $C_A = 10\,nF$.

4.24 Using SPICE, verify the large-signal transient response of the video amplifier, as indicated in Fig. 4.13.

4.25 Using analysis similar to that indicated in modeling the OP-27, and the HA2540 of Appendix D, modify the SPICE model of Fig. D.1 for the LF351 to include noise due to e_n and i_n.

4.26 Obtain a SPICE model for the 741 op amp that includes accurate values of e_n, i_n, and the i_n corner frequency f_b.

4.27 Since uncorrelated noise adds as the square root of the sum of the squares, and gain adds directly, it is possible to improve the SNR of an op amp by paralleling devices, as illustrated in Fig. P4.27. If we have 9 identical OP-37

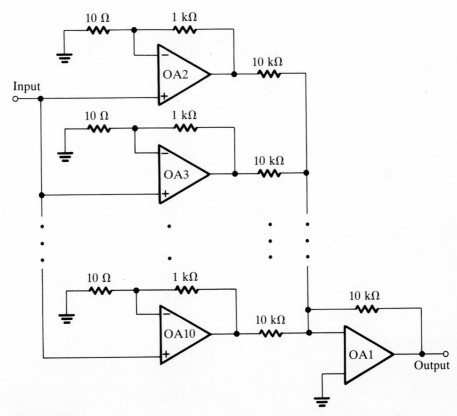

Figure P4.27

op amps in parallel (OA2–OA10), with OA1 an OP-27 device, find the gain, -3 dB bandwidth, and e_{tni} for the overall amplifier. Also, estimate probable values of V_{OS}, I_B and I_{OS} for the entire circuit, using typical values from the data sheet for the OP-27. The OP-37 units have parameters identical to the OP-27, except that the gain-bandwidth product is 63 MHz, with SR of 17 V/μsec. What are the main disadvantages to the use of this circuit?

4.28 Repeat Problem 4.27 using a FET-input op amp, the OPA111, for OA2–OA10. Parameters for the OPA111 were stated previously in P4.12 and Fig. 4.7. Compare input-referred noise e_{tni}, as well as i_n, for the two systems.

4.29 One can usually improve the noise specifications of an op amp by forming a composite amplifier, with a low-noise discrete-transistor input circuit connected to an op-amp. Such a circuit, as suggested by Tom Cate of Siliconix, Inc. (see Ref. 4.24) is shown in Fig. P4.29. The input circuit uses a dual monolithic JFET, the 2N5912, which has typical values of $I_{DSS} = 18$ mA, $V_p = -3$ V, $C_{iss} = 4$ pf and $C_{rss} = 1$ pf. The differential output voltage from J_1–J_2 is applied to the collector terminals (terminals 1 and 8) of the NE5534 op amp. The input npn transistors of the NE5534 are biased off by connecting terminals 2 and 3 to -15 V. Compensation capacitance (C_C) is added between terminals 5 and 8 of the op amp. The result is a composite op amp having input bias currents of 2 pA (typically, SR of 20–40 V/μsec, and low noise. Choose values for R_D, R_S, and C_C to provide unity-gain stability, as well as an input-stage gain of at least 5. With the values used, estimate the e_n

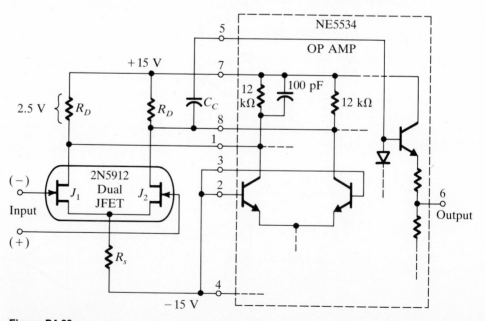

Figure P4.29

and i_n mid-frequency values for the composite op amp, and compare with typical values of $e_n = 4\,\text{nV}/\sqrt{\text{Hz}}$ and $i_n = 0.4\,\text{pA}/\sqrt{\text{Hz}}$ for the NE5534 op amp.

4.30 A composite amplifier circuit suggested by Precision Monolithics, Inc. (see Ref. 4.25), using paralleled low-noise bipolar transistors and the OP-27 op amp, is illustrated in Fig. P4.30. If the MAT-02 dual high-beta transistors

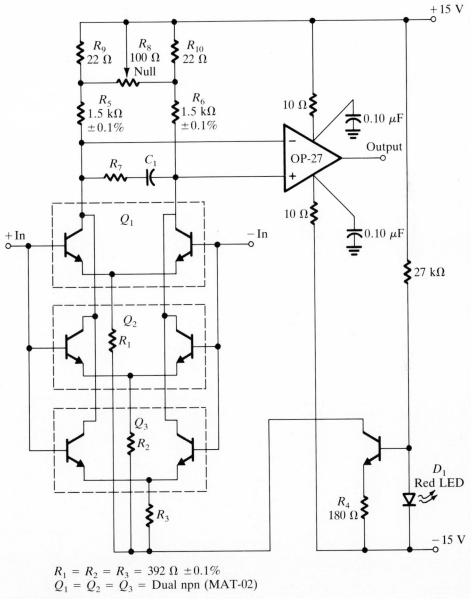

$R_1 = R_2 = R_3 = 392\ \Omega\ \pm 0.1\%$
$Q_1 = Q_2 = Q_3 = \text{Dual npn (MAT-02)}$

Figure P4.30

each have characteristics of $\beta = 900$, $r_b' = 10\,\Omega$, $f_T = 130\,\text{MHz}$ and C_μ (base-collector capacitance) $= 5\,\text{pF}$ at a collector current of $1\,\text{mA}$, estimate the values of e_n and i_n for the composite circuit. Show that the noise of the biasing circuit R_1–R_4, D_1, and Q_4 is negligible. Find values for R_7 and C_1 for a stable unity-gain amplifier. What are the values of A_{OL}, GB and SR for the composite circuit? What is the optimum source resistance R_{opt} for the amplifier?

Chapter 5

Other Linear Circuit Applications

We have already investigated many linear circuit applications in Chapters 1 and 2 that use a single op amp. Several important widely used circuits, however, with which the practicing engineer should be familiar, require more than one op amp, or are part of an overall system incorporating op amps. In this chapter we will analyze several of the more important circuits and demonstrate some practical applications involving their use.

5.1 INSTRUMENTATION AMPLIFIERS

An instrumentation amplifier (IA) is a precision differential amplifier intended for use in severe environments, where the signal to be amplified is accompanied by a large common-mode signal. Also, it is an improvement on the basic differential amplifier (discussed previously in Chapter 1, and in Problems 1.20 and 1.21), because it offers very high input impedance, low bias current, and a gain determined by one user-selected resistor. For example, the basic single-op-amp differential amplifier [refer to Fig. 1.13(a) and Eq. (1.26)] has a differential gain of

$$\frac{v_O}{v_{\text{diff}}} = -\frac{R_F}{R_1} \tag{1.26}$$

but a change in gain requires changing *two* resistors, usually R_1 and R_2 in Fig. 1.13(a).

Most commercial IA circuits are a modification of the classic three-op-amp circuit shown in Fig. 5.1(a), and often indicated symbolically as in Fig. 5.1(b). The terminals labeled "sense" and "reference" are externally accessible connections, so it is possible to add a current booster after A_3 with the sense terminal thus connected to the output of the booster, and also to refer the output of the IA to a reference other than ground. In the circuit, note that A_3 forms a standard differential amplifier if $R_3 = R'_3$ and $R_2 = R'_2$. Let us also assume that $R_F = R'_F$, and for the present that only a differential signal is available; i.e., $v_{in} = v_{diff}$. Since the input error signals of A_1 and A_2 approach zero, then the input signal v_{diff} must also appear across R_G, which therefore produces an output voltage

$$v_{O1} = v_{diff}\left(1 + \frac{R_F}{R_G} + \frac{R'_F}{R_G}\right) \tag{5.1}$$

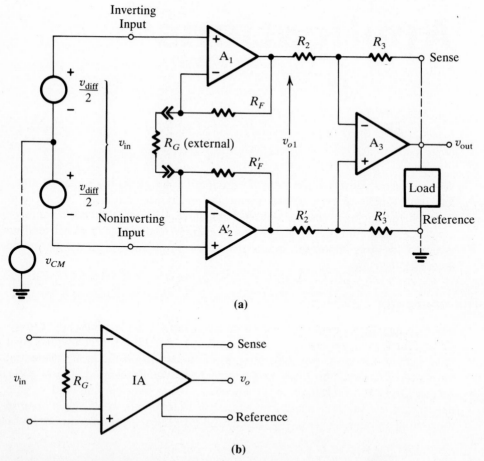

(a)

(b)

Figure 5.1 A 3-op-amp instrumentation amplifier circuit: (a) circuit diagram; (b) symbolic representation.

Since $R_F = R'_F$

$$v_{O1} = v_{\text{diff}}\left(1 + \frac{2R_F}{R_G}\right) \tag{5.2}$$

The standard differential amplifier connection of A_3 gives a gain $(v_{\text{out}}/v_{O1}) = -R_3/R_2$, hence the differential gain of the IA of Fig. 5.1 is

$$A_{\text{diff}} = \frac{v_{\text{out}}}{v_{\text{diff}}} = -\left(\frac{R_3}{R_2}\right)\left(1 + \frac{2R_F}{R_G}\right) \tag{5.3}$$

As stated earlier, it is apparent that the differential gain can be adjusted by merely changing R_G in Eq. (5.3).

Now, suppose we look at the common-mode gain of the basic IA circuit of Fig. 5.1. If v_{diff} is removed and a common-mode signal v_{CM} applied, then there will be no current flow through the R_G resistor, since an identical signal v_{CM} will be present at both ends of the resistor. Hence, no current will flow through the R_F or R'_F resistors either. Thus the output signal of both A_1 and A_2 will be v_{CM}, or ideally $v_{O1} = 0$. In Chapters 1 and 2 we established the relationship for the common-mode gain of the A_3 differential amplifier. If the common-mode rejection ratio of the A_3 amplifier itself is large [Eq. (2.40)], the common-mode gain for the circuit is

$$A_{CM} = \frac{v_{\text{out}}}{v_{CM}} = \left[\left(\frac{R'_3}{R'_3 + R'_2}\right)\left(\frac{R_3 + R_2}{R_2}\right) - \left(\frac{R_3}{R_2}\right)\right] \tag{5.4}$$

and the CMRR for the circuit becomes

$$\text{CMRR} = \left|\frac{A_{\text{diff}}}{A_{CM}}\right| = \left\{\frac{\dfrac{R_3}{R_2}\left(1 + \dfrac{2R_F}{R_G}\right)}{\dfrac{R_3}{R_2}\left[\dfrac{R'_3}{R_3}\left(\dfrac{R_3 + R_2}{R'_3 + R'_2}\right) - 1\right]}\right\} \tag{5.5}$$

If the stated conditions of $R_3 = R'_3$ and $R_2 = R'_2$ are met, then obviously CMRR $\rightarrow \infty$. However, the real advantage of the IA over the standard single-op-amp differential amplifier is apparent in the term $(1 + 2R_F/R_G)$ in the numerator of Eq. (5.5), as seen by the example below.

EXAMPLE 5.1

Compare the example of the basic single-op-amp differential amplifier of Section 2.7.3 and Fig. 2.20, where $R_F = R_3 = 100 \text{ k}\Omega$ and $R_1 = R_2 = 10 \text{ k}\Omega$, with the instrumentation amplifier of Fig. 5.1 having $R_G = 2.21 \text{ k}\Omega$, and all other resistors equal to 10 kΩ. Assume $\pm 1\%$ resistors, and that all op amps have large values of A_{OL} and CMRR.

Solution
For the previous circuit of Section 2.7.3 the differential gain was $A_{\text{diff}} = -10$, with a worst-case CMRR (due to the $\pm 1\%$ resistors) of 270.3 (or 48.6 dB). Also, the low-frequency differential-input resistance was 20 kΩ, while the common-mode input resistance was 55 kΩ.

For the IA circuit of Fig. 5.1, the differential gain is the same, or from Eq. (5.3)

$$A_{\text{diff}} = -(1)\left(1 + \frac{20 \text{ k}\Omega}{2.21 \text{ k}\Omega}\right) = -10.05$$

However, the low-frequency input resistance seen by either v_{diff} or v_{CM} approaches the common-mode input resistance, usually $\gg 10^7 \ \Omega$ for good op amps. Even with $\pm 1\%$ resistors the worst-case value for A_{CM} is, from Eq. (5.4),

$$\left(\frac{v_{\text{out}}}{v_{CM}}\right)_{\text{worst case}} = \left(\frac{R_3 + 1\%}{R_2 - 1\%}\right)\left\{\left(\frac{R_3' - 1\%}{R_3 + 1\%}\right)\left[\frac{(R_3 + 1\%) + (R_2 - 1\%)}{(R_3' - 1\%) + (R_2' + 1\%)}\right] - 1\right\}$$

Reducing, we have

$$\left(\frac{v_{\text{out}}}{v_{CM}}\right) = -2.02 \times 10^{-2}$$

Hence, the IA has a CMRR of $(10.05/2.02 \times 10^{-2})$, or 4.97×10^2 (54 dB), or a factor of 2 times larger than the basic single-op-amp differential circuit.

5.1.1 Frequency-Dependent CMRR

Although the dc CMRR of an instrumentation amplifier can be very large (> 100 dB in most cases), input capacitance from the inverting and noninverting inputs to ground can seriously degrade the high-frequency CMRR. For example, Fig. 5.2 illustrates a system with source resistances R_{S1} and R_{S2} and input capacitances (perhaps due to cable shields and stray capacitance) C_{i1} and C_{i2}. Unless $R_{S1}C_{i1} = R_{S2}C_{i2}$, the common-mode input signals to the IA will differ. This problem can be partially resolved by shielding the input signal leads and driving

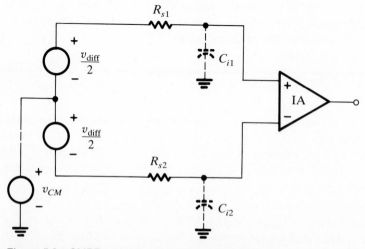

Figure 5.2 CMRR reduction due to imput capacitance.

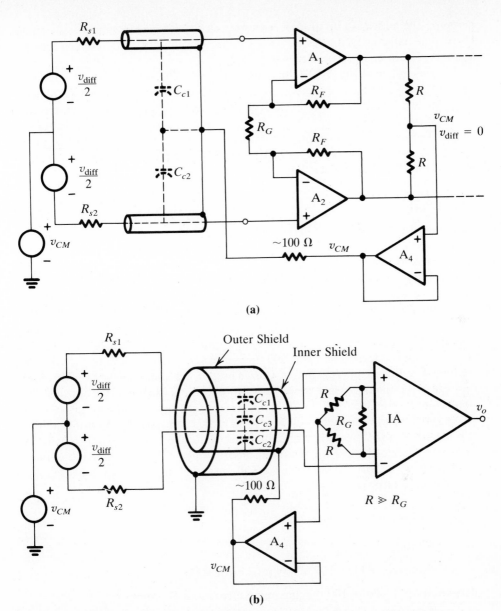

Figure 5.3 Using guarding (bootstrapping) to remove the effects of input capacitance.

the shield with a signal equal to v_{CM}.* Two examples are shown in Fig. 5.3. The first, shown in Fig. 5.3(a), is based on the premise that the common-mode gain of the A_1 and A_2 sections is unity. Thus, a signal derived from the midpoint of the two R resistors will be v_{CM}; however, for the differential signal v_{diff} the midpoint voltage

---

* This technique is referred to in the literature as **input guarding** or **bootstrapping**.

is zero. The added A_4 op amp is connected as a unity-gain noninverting circuit, hence the cable capacitances C_{c1} and C_{c2} are driven with equal common-mode signals at both ends, so neither is seen by v_{CM}.

The circuit of Fig. 5.3(b) illustrates a slightly different way to drive the C_{c1} and C_{c2} capacitances—obtaining the v_{CM} signal from R_G by the voltage divider with the two R resistors. As in Fig. 5.3(a) the C_{c1} and C_{c2} capacitors are not seen by the v_{CM} signal, and neither is C_{c3}, the capacitance between the differential-input leads. The use of a two-conductor, double-shielded cable in Fig. 5.3(b) is much preferred over the use of two individual single-shielded cables, particularly when interference from extraneous magnetic and electric fields is involved.

5.1.2 DC Offset Effects

Although IA circuits have differential inputs, they must provide a return path to ground for the bias currents. When the source involves transformer coupling, it is advantageous to return the center tap of the transformer to ground. However, for capacitively-coupled sources it is best to return both inputs of the IA to ground through identical biasing resistors.

The dc-offset voltage of an IA is divided into two components; input offset and output offset. Input-offset voltage is that part of the total dc-offset voltage that is directly proportional to gain; for example, input dc-offset voltage measured at the output for a dc gain of 100 is 100 times greater than for a gain of 1. However, output dc offset is independent of gain. Thus, at low gains the output dc-offset voltage is dominant, while at large gains the input dc-offset term would be important. For a given gain both dc-offset errors can be combined to give a total voltage-offset error referred to the input (RTI) or the output (RTO). For example, the AD624C instrumentation amplifier (see data sheet in Appendix C) has a maximum specified value for the input-offset voltage of 25 μV, while the output-offset voltage is 2 mV. Thus, for a gain of unity, the maximum (unnulled) input-offset voltage error is

$$\text{Offset error RTI} = \text{input offset} + \frac{\text{output offset}}{\text{gain}} \tag{5.6}$$

or, in this case,

$$\text{Offset error RTI} = 2.02 \, \text{mV} = \text{total error RTO}$$

However, for a gain of 100 the maximum error values become

$$\text{Offset error RTI} = 25 \, \mu\text{V} + \frac{2 \, \text{mV}}{100} = 45 \, \mu\text{V}$$

and

$$\text{Offset error RTO} = 25 \, \mu\text{V}(100) + 2 \, \text{mV} = 4.50 \, \text{mV}$$

In many precision instrumentation applications the above offsets are too large for accurate data processing. In these cases it is possible to correct automatically for dc drift and hold the output of the IA at zero volts dc (or some other reference, if desired). These circuits are called **auto-zero circuits** (an example is

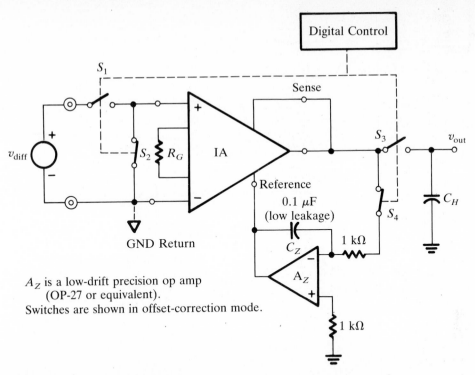

Figure 5.4 The auto-zero concept.

shown in Fig. 5.4). In this circuit when a control command is given to sample the output dc offset, switches S_1 and S_3 will open, while S_2 and S_4 will close. Thus, the signal V_{diff} is removed, and any offsets due to the IA will appear at the input of the error-correcting integrator A_Z; hence an inverting, corrective offset voltage is impressed at the reference input of the IA. This cancels the original output offset of the circuit. In the normal switch positions (S_1 and S_3 are closed, while S_2 and S_4 are open), the error signal remains on the C_Z integrator capacitor, providing automatic zeroing for the circuit. It is very important that C_Z be a low-leakage capacitor, such as polystyrene or polypropylene. The hold capacitor (C_H) is necessary to provide a continuous signal to the rest of the processing circuit when the IA is in the auto-zero corrective mode.

5.1.3 A Typical Monolithic IC Circuit

The AD624 instrumentation amplifier mentioned above is an excellent example of a single-chip (monolithic) design. The circuit is shown in abbreviated form in Fig. 5.5. With relation to the basic three-op-amp circuit, the A_1 and A_2 op amp functions of Fig. 5.1 are formed from Q_1, Q_3, A_1 and Q_2, Q_4, A_2, respectively, of Fig. 5.5. The A_3 amplifier function is repeated as A_3 in Fig. 5.5, with equal R_2, R'_2, R_3, and R'_3 resistors of 10 kΩ, each. The R_F and R'_F resistors of Fig. 5.1 are fixed (by R_{57} and R_{56}) by equal 20 kΩ resistors in the AD624. Also, on-chip resistors

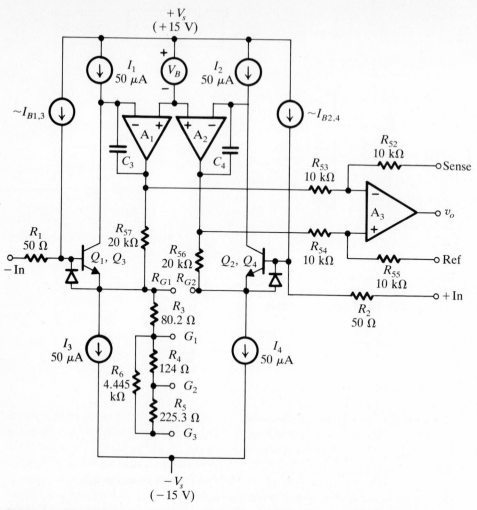

Figure 5.5 The AD624 monolithic instrumentation amplifier. source: Analog Devices, Inc., Norwood, MA 02062.

(R_3–R_6) provide some built-in control of the R_G resistor, with other gains set by an external resistor between the R_{G1} and R_{G2} terminals in the AD624. Input bias-current cancellation circuitry in Fig. 5.5 is also present to reduce typical input bias currents (I_B) to ±15 nA at 25 °C. The resistors used are silicon-chromium (on-chip) thin-film types, with low temperature coefficients. Laser trimming is used to adjust resistors to precise values. The AD624*, like similar IC instrumentation amplifiers, is capable of a CMRR of 120 dB for gains >500.

---

* Other monolithic IC instrumentation amplifiers similar to the AD624 are the AD524 (Analog Devices), AMP-01 (Precision Monolithics), INA101 (Burr-Brown), and LM363 (National Semiconductor).

■ **Exercise 5.1**

What fixed gains are available in the circuit of Fig. 5.5, by connecting the R_{G2} terminal to the G_1, G_2, and G_3 terminals, respectively? For a gain of 300 one can connect terminal R_{G2} to G_1 and then add an external resistor between R_{G2} and R_{G1} (i.e., in parallel with R_3 of Fig. 5.5); what value should this resistor have? What is the gain if the R_{G2} terminal is open circuited?

■ **Exercise 5.2**

Using the data sheet for the AD624 in Appendix C, estimate the -3 dB signal bandwidths for gains of 1, 10, and 100. Why is the gain-bandwidth product not constant, as it is for a typical op amp? Explain using the circuit of Fig. 5.5.

5.2 ISOLATION AMPLIFIERS

Isolation amplifiers (or isolators) are used primarily when an ohmic isolation between the input signal and the output signal is required. Isolation circuits usually have an input op amp, or IA, followed by a unity-gain isolation stage. Most applications of isolation amplifiers fall into one of three categories requiring signal and ground isolation; namely medical, industrial, and instrumentation. Whereas a standard instrumentation amplifier requires a ground return path for the input bias currents, an isolation amplifier does not. The input circuitry is fully floating; hence, if a bias current I_B flows out of one input lead, the same current will flow into the other input lead. The isolation amplifier concept can be illustrated by Fig. 5.6, which includes various error sources.

The offset voltage V_{OS} is referred to the input (RTI) and includes both a constant value and a gain-dependent term, just as was the case for the IA in Eq. (5.6). Similarly, the total input equivalent noise of the circuit is shown as E_{noise} in Fig. 5.6 (or E_{tni} of Chapter 4). There is the usual **common-mode rejection ratio** specification (CMRR), which indicates the ability of the input stage to reject the input voltage v_{CM}. However, we must also include the ability of the circuit to reject the voltage difference v_{ISO} between the input and output circuits; this specification is referred to as the **isolation-mode rejection ratio** (IMRR), although some manufacturers merely specify an overall common-mode rejection term to include both effects. The current leakage I_{LEAK} represents the maximum current that can flow between the input and output common terminals (across the isolation barrier) with a specified value for v_{ISO}. For medical applications the leakage current must be less than 10 μA rms for a 60 Hz, 120 V input. The impedance R_{ISO} in parallel with C_{ISO} represents the coupling between the two common terminals across the

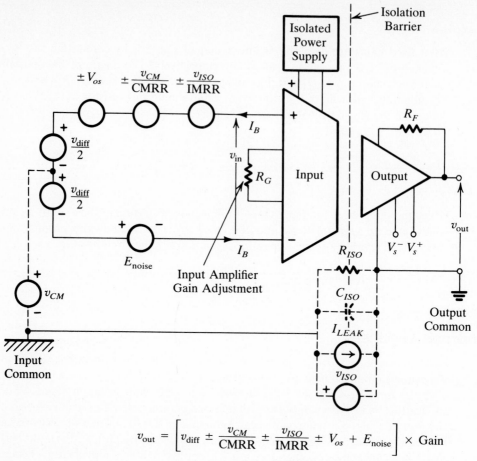

$$v_{out} = \left[v_{diff} \pm \frac{v_{CM}}{CMRR} \pm \frac{v_{ISO}}{IMRR} \pm V_{os} + E_{noise} \right] \times Gain$$

Figure 5.6 Isolation amplifier with error sources indicated.

isolation barrier; most isolation amplifiers have impedance values of $>10^{10}$ ohms in parallel with <10 pF.

Isolation of the input and output amplifiers is achieved using either (a) optical coupling, or (b) transformer coupling. Where frequency bandwidth is important, optical coupling is the best choice. However, if gain accuracy and linearity* is more significant, then transformer coupling is better. We will examine applications of each type of circuit in the following two sections.

---

* **Linearity,** or more significantly **nonlinearity,** terms have not specifically been encountered heretofore. In the context of amplifier usage nonlinearity is defined as the deviation from a straight line on the plot of output versus input. The magnitude of the **nonlinearity (NL) error** is calculated as

$$NL \ Error \ (\%) = \frac{[(Actual \ Output) - (Calculated \ Output)] \times 100\%}{Rated \ Full \ Scale \ (FS) \ Output}$$

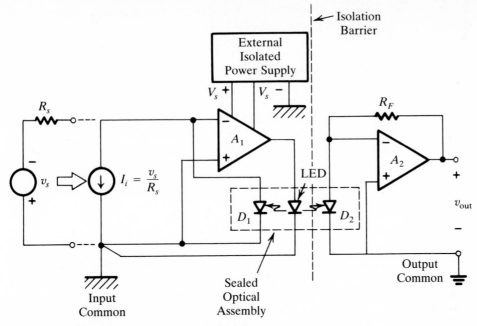

Figure 5.7 Optically coupled isolation amplifier.

5.2.1 Optically Coupled Isolation Amplifiers

With optical coupling between input and output it is possible to achieve a $-3\,\text{dB}$ frequency bandwidth approaching $100\,\text{kHz}$, yet still achieve isolation voltages (v_{ISO}) of $\pm 5000\,\text{V}$, peak. Also, isolation impedance coupling is better than that obtained with transformer coupling, with typical values of $10^{12}\,\Omega\|2.5\,\text{pF}$. Since a transformer is not part of the signal-transfer circuitry, an internal isolation power supply is not usually contained within the isolator, hence a separate isolated power supply has to be provided. One form of an optically-coupled circuit is illustrated in Fig. 5.7, which basically is a unity-gain current amplifier. The diodes D_1 and D_2 are optically coupled to the light-emitting diode (LED), with equal light output falling on each diode. Thus, the photocurrents generated by the light in D_1 and D_2 will be equal. Since D_1 is contained in the negative feedback loop of A_1, the LED, and D_1, nonlinearitiies are reduced by the loop transmission.

■ **Exercise 5.3**

Show that the output voltage in the circuit of Fig. 5.7 is $v_{\text{out}} = -I_i R_f$. Assume the input bias currents of A_1 and A_2 are negligible. The circuit indicated assumes unipolar input current; show how the circuit can operate in a bipolar mode (currents either into, or out of, the input). Hint: another current source is required.

DC errors in the optically coupled circuit are due to those indicated in Fig. 5.6, plus an error due to offset current. We can estimate an error budget for an isolator circuit, as indicated in Example 5.2.

EXAMPLE 5.2

The IS0100CP circuit (manufactured by Burr-Brown Corp.) is an optically-coupled isolation amplifier. The amplifier is used in the circuit of Fig. 5.8 to amplify a signal v_s having a 100 kΩ source resistance. Estimate the total error, both RTI and RTO, at 25 °C. The signal v_s being amplified is obtained as part of a 115 V ac distribution system.

Solution

The various error sources for the IS0100CP amplifier shown in Fig. 5.8 are, at 25 °C: $V_{OSI} = V_{OSO} = 200 \ \mu V$ (max); IMRR = 400 pA/V at 60 Hz; CMRR = 3 nA/V at 60 Hz; $I_{OS} = 10$ nA (max); Gain Error = 2% FS (max, adjustable to zero); nonlinearity = 0.07% (max); current noise (I_n) = 20 pA (p-p) for 0.01 Hz to 10 Hz, 1 pA/$\sqrt{\text{Hz}}$ at 10 Hz, and 0.7 pA/$\sqrt{\text{Hz}}$ for $f > 100$ Hz, at $I_{in} = 0.2 \ \mu A$. The range of I_{in} for unipolar operation is from -20 nA to $-20 \ \mu A$. The leakage current I_{LEAK} is specified as 0.3 μA (maximum) at 240 V, rms, 60 Hz. The maximum -3 dB bandwidth is 60 kHz.

The dc offsets, referred to the input, can be stated as

$$\text{dc error(RTI)} = \pm V_{OSI} + \frac{\pm V_{oso}}{\text{Gain}} \pm I_{os}R_s \tag{5.7}$$

or substituting values

$$\text{dc error(RTI)} = \pm 0.2 \text{ mV} \pm \frac{0.2 \text{ mV}}{10} \pm (0.01 \ \mu A)(0.1 \text{ M}\Omega)$$

$$= \pm 0.221 \text{ mV}$$

and referred to the output

$$\text{dc error(RTO)} = 10(\pm 0.221 \text{ mV}) = \pm 2.21 \text{ mV}.$$

At 60 Hz we have offset errors due to both common-mode and isolation-mode sources, or

$$|\text{ac error(RTI)}| = (1 \text{ V})(3 \text{ nA/V})(100 \text{ k}\Omega)$$
$$+ (\sqrt{2})(115 \text{ V})(0.4 \text{ nA/V})(100 \text{ k}\Omega) = 6.8 \text{ mV (peak)} \tag{5.8}$$

and

$$|\text{ac error(RTO)}| = 10(6.8 \text{ mV}) = 68 \text{ mV (peak)}$$

The rms noise in the circuit is due to shot noise of the reverse current of D_1 and D_2, and is therefore proportional to $(v_s/R_s)^{1/2}$. Even if the input current is equal to the maximum value of $-20 \ \mu A$, we would anticipate a worst-case rms

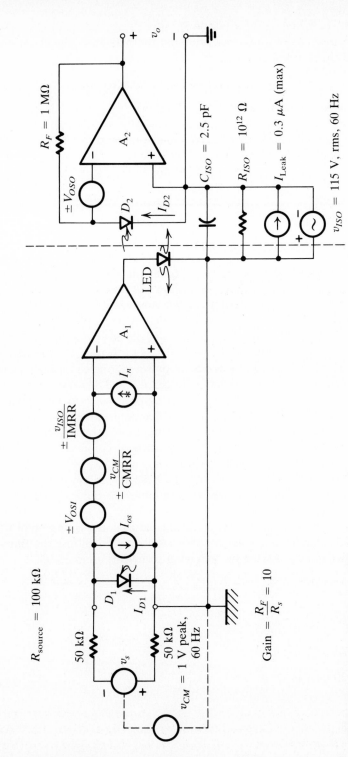

Figure 5.8 Circuit for Example 5.2.

noise current of $0.7 \text{ pA}/\sqrt{\text{Hz}} \times (20 \text{ }\mu\text{A}/0.2 \text{ }\mu\text{A})^{1/2}$, or $7 \text{ pA}/\sqrt{\text{Hz}}$. For the above circuit, the noise (RTI) would be, assuming the maximum signal bandwidth of 60 kHz, and the source is ohmic,

$$E^2_{\text{noise}} = \{[7 \text{ pA}/\sqrt{\text{Hz}}(100 \text{ k}\Omega)]^2 + [4kT(100 \text{ k}\Omega)]\}\Delta f_n \tag{5.9}$$

or with $\Delta f_n \approx \pi/2$ (60 kHz), then $E_{\text{noise}} = 0.22$ mV (rms), which is negligible with respect to the ac error of 6.8 mV. The gain error of 2% of full-scale output could be the dominating factor, however this error can be reduced to zero by trimming R_F. Thus, for this example it appears that both dc and noise errors are negligible compared to that caused by the isolation potential of 115 V, ac.

5.2.2 Transformer-Coupled Isolation Amplifiers

The significant error in the optically coupled circuit of Example 5.2 was due to the isolation voltage of 115 V, ac. For lower offset it is necessary to go to transformer coupling between input and output. However, the available frequency bandwidth is reduced, while the cost is increased over that of the optical isolator. Since a transformer is available, one can also obtain an isolated power supply for powering the input stage, as indicated in the general block diagram for the transformer-coupled isolator in Fig. 5.9. For this circuit, power is coupled through transformer T_1 to provide (by a dc/dc converter) voltages V^+ and V^- (typically ± 15 V) to power op amp A_1 in the input. The oscillator signal also acts as a carrier frequency to modulate the output signal of A_1 and then demodulate the transformer-coupled signal (removing the carrier frequency) at the input to A_2. In most circuits the input op amp A_1 can be connected in either an inverting or noninverting configuration. Similarly, the choice of feedback resistors (R_{FI} and R_{FO} in Fig. 5.9) is usually available to the user. It is also possible to have the common terminal for the oscillator circuit at a different potential than either the input or output common terminal.

Let us compare a transformer-coupled isolator in the same gain of 10 circuit of Example 5.2, having a 100 kΩ source resistance. We will use the Burr-Brown Model 3656B* isolator having the following specifications at 25 °C:

$$V_{OSI} = \pm 1 \text{ mV}$$

$$V_{OSO} = \pm 10 \text{ mV}$$

$$\text{IMRR} = 112 \text{ dB (min)}$$

$$I_B = 100 \text{ nA (max)}$$

$$I_{OS} = 20 \text{ nA (max)}$$

---

* Similar transformer-coupled isolators are the Analog Devices Models AD289, AD293, AD204, and the Burr-Brown Model 3450 series.

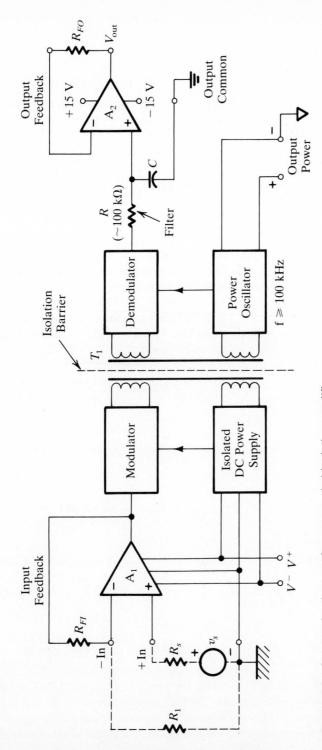

Figure 5.9 Concept for the transformer-coupled isolation amplifier.

Input Noise Voltage $= 5 \ \mu$V (p-p)(0.05 Hz to 100 Hz)

$\qquad\qquad\qquad\qquad = 5 \ \mu$V, rms (10 Hz to 10 kHz)

$f_{-3 \text{ dB}} = 30$ kHz

Output Noise Voltage $= [(5)^2 + (22/G_1)^2]^{1/2} \ \mu$V (p-p) (0.05 Hz to 100 Hz)

$\qquad\qquad\qquad\qquad = [(5)^2 + (11/G_1)^2]^{1/2} \ \mu$V, rms (10 Hz to 10 kHz)

Gain Error (adj. to zero) $= \pm 0.3 \%$ (max)

Nonlinearity $= \pm 0.05 \%$ (max)

$I_{\text{LEAK}} = 0.5 \ \mu$A (max) at 120 V, 60 Hz

$R_{ISO} = 10^{12} \ \Omega$

$C_{ISO} = 6$ pF

For a noninverting gain of 10 in Fig. 5.9, let us set the input-stage gain equal to 10, and the output gain equal to unity. To reduce bias-current errors, since $R_s = 100$ kΩ, a choice of $\pm 1\%$ resistors of value $R_1 = 110$ kΩ and $R_{FI} = 887$ kΩ will suffice. Further, a choice of $R_{FO} = 100$ kΩ will provide unity closed-loop gain for A_2, as well as bias-current compensation. Hence, the dc offsets (RTI) are, as in Example 5.2,

$$\text{dc error(RTI)} = \pm 1 \text{ mV} \pm \frac{10 \text{ mV}}{10} \pm (0.02 \ \mu\text{A})\left(\frac{887 \text{ k}\Omega}{10}\right)$$

$$= \pm 3.8 \text{ mV}$$

while referred to the output the error is ± 38 mV. At 60 Hz, with a 115 V (rms) value for v_{ISO} we have

$$|\text{ac error(RTI)}| = \sqrt{2}(115 \text{ V})\left(\frac{1}{\text{IMRR}}\right) = 0.41 \text{ mV (peak)}$$

or the error RTO is 4.1 mV.

The noise (RTI) can be estimated from the noise equations of Chapter 4 as

$$E_{\text{noise}}^2 \approx (5 \ \mu\text{V})^2 + \left(\frac{11 \ \mu\text{V}}{10}\right)^2$$

$$+ 4kT\left[100 \text{ k}\Omega + (0.81)(100 \text{ k}\Omega) + \frac{887 \text{ k}\Omega}{100} + \frac{200 \text{ k}\Omega}{100}\right]\Delta f \qquad \textbf{(5.10)}$$

For Δf assumed to be $(\pi/2)$ 30 kHz, the result is $E_{\text{noise}} \approx 13.3 \ \mu$V (rms). As in Example 5.2 the effect of noise is negligible in comparison to the dc and ac errors. A comparison with the results of Example 5.2 indicates much better rejection of the v_{ISO} potential by the transformer-coupled circuit, but larger offsets due to dc errors.

5.3 BRIDGE AMPLIFIERS

One of the most common uses of a differential amplifier is in amplifying output signals from a bridge* circuit. The bridge connection comprises four circuit elements, usually resistive, with one (or sometimes more) elements varying with the parameter under observation, whether it be temperature, force, or pressure. The basic bridge-amplifier circuit is shown in Fig. 5.10. The equations for the circuit of Fig. 5.10 are

$$v_1 = \frac{V_B}{2} \qquad v_2 = \frac{R(1+\delta)V_B}{R + R(1+\delta)} = V_B \frac{(1+\delta)}{(2+\delta)} \tag{5.11}$$

where $\delta \equiv \Delta R/R$. The input difference signal to the K amplifier is

$$v_1 - v_2 = V_B\left(\frac{1}{2} - \frac{1+\delta}{2+\delta}\right) = \frac{-\delta V_B}{2(2+\delta)} \approx -\frac{\delta V_B}{4} \tag{5.12}$$

if the deviation δ is $\ll 1$. Thus, the output of the circuit will be

$$v_O \approx -\left(\frac{K\delta}{4}\right)V_B \tag{5.13}$$

and the output voltage is therefore proportional to the deviation produced by the parameter. Note also, however, that any change in the bridge-excitation voltage V_B

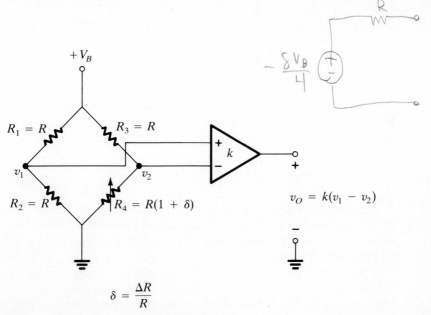

$$\delta = \frac{\Delta R}{R}$$

Figure 5.10 Basic bridge amplifier circuit.

---

* Also referred to as a **Wheatstone bridge**, attributed originally to S. H. Christie in 1833.

will also appear at the output with the same amplification as δ; hence, one of the significant problems with the basic bridge circuit of Fig. 5.10 is that it requires a very stable voltage V_B.

■ **Exercise 5.4**

If the resistor R_1 in Fig. 5.10 is also variable [i.e., $R_1 = R(1 + \delta)$], show that the output voltage is $v_O = -K\delta V_B/2$, if $\delta \ll 1$.

Two ways of implementing the amplifier gain K are shown in Fig. 5.11. In the first case of Fig. 5.11(a) a standard differential-amplifier connection produces an output voltage equal to

$$V_O \approx V_B\left(\frac{\delta}{2}\right)\frac{R_F}{R} \qquad = -\frac{V_B \delta}{4}\left(-\frac{2R_F}{R}\right) \tag{5.14}$$

provided that $\delta \ll 1$. The circuit of Fig. 5.11(b) uses a floating power supply, with the bridge resistors as part of the overall feedback loop. It can be shown (see Problem 5.20) that the output voltage is ($\delta \ll 1$)

$$v_O \approx V_B\left(\frac{\delta}{4}\right)\left(\frac{R_F + R_1}{R_1}\right) \tag{5.15}$$

The previous bridge-amplifier circuits have an output voltage proportional to the deviation δ only if δ is small ($\ll 1$). For many applications, however, the deviation may be significant. For example, a thermistor may have a change of resistance $\Delta R \gg R_O$, where R_O is the room temperature value. For such cases, the bridge circuit of Fig. 5.12 is useful. In this circuit the op amp feedback resistor *is part of the bridge*, with the result that the output voltage is equal to

$$v_O = -V_B\delta\left(\frac{R_F}{R + R_F}\right) \tag{5.16}$$

A disadvantage of the circuit of Fig. 5.12 is that the op amp must be very close to the bridge elements to reduce nonlinearities and frequency instability due to wiring capacitance. Also, calibration may be difficult due to the required adjustment of two resistors, R and R_F.

Instrumentation amplifiers offer significant advantages over op amps in bridge circuits due to improved CMRR, as well as better gain control. Consider the example of Fig. 5.13, where we are using the Analog Devices, Inc., AD624 IA, whose characteristics were shown earlier in Fig. 5.5. Since a constant bridge supply voltage is essential, the V_B voltage is obtained from a precision +10 V reference circuit (in this example the REF-01, although other equivalent references are available). Let us assume that the unbalance in the bridge (due perhaps, to strain) is between 0 and 5 Ω. Thus the dc signal presented to the IA varies from 0–25 mV, or

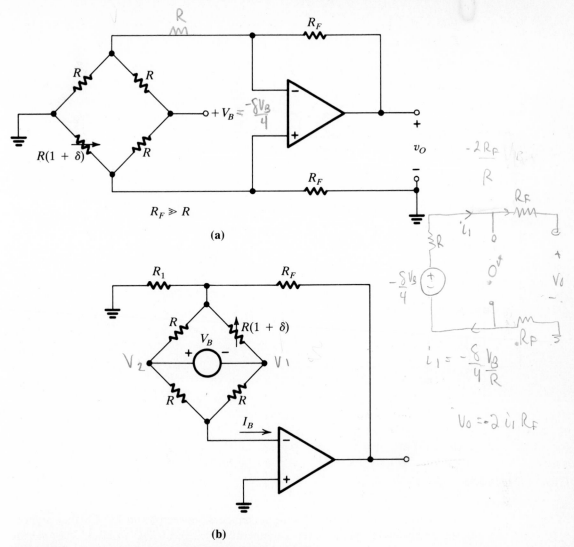

(a)

(b)

Figure 5.11 Two ways of implementing the bridge circuit.

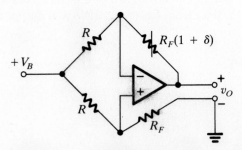

Figure 5.12 Bridge amplifier suitable for large deviations.

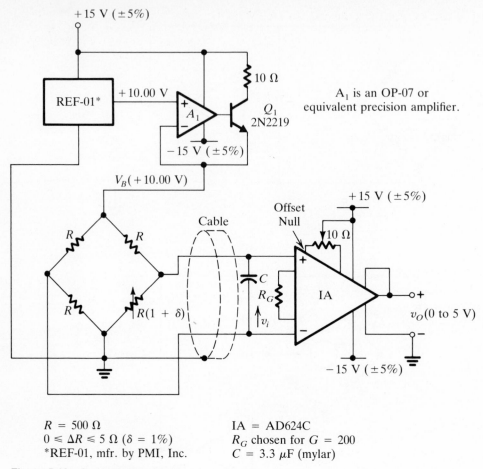

$R = 500\ \Omega$ IA = AD624C
$0 \leqslant \Delta R \leqslant 5\ \Omega\ (\delta = 1\%)$ R_G chosen for $G = 200$
*REF-01, mfr. by PMI, Inc. $C = 3.3\ \mu F$ (mylar)

Figure 5.13   An IA bridge circuit.

for a gain of 200 in the IA, the output change is between 0 and 5 V. Further suppose
the circuit must operate over a temperature range of 0 °C to 60 °C. Assume the
power supply voltages may vary by $\pm 5\%$ over this temperature range. The results
of an error budget analysis (see Section 2.4.3) for the circuit of Fig. 5.13 are shown
in Table 5.1. These results demonstrate that the most significant error is due to the
nonlinearity of the bridge itself, since from Eq. (5.12) the actual output voltage of
the circuit of Fig. 5.13 is

$$v_O = \frac{G\delta V_B}{4}\left(\frac{1}{1 + \dfrac{\delta}{4}}\right) \tag{5.17}$$

which can also be written as

$$v_O = \frac{G\delta V_B}{4}[1 - \varepsilon(\delta)] \tag{5.18}$$

Table 5.1 ERROR BUDGET ANALYSIS OF FIG. 5.13

Error Source	Specification	Error (RTI) (μV)	Error (RTO) (mV)	Resolution Error (RTO) (mV)
Gain (IA)	$\pm 0.25\%$	± 62.5	± 12.5	—
Δ Gain/ΔT(IA)	10 ppm/°C	± 8.75	± 1.75	± 1.75
Gain Nonlinearity (IA)	$\pm 0.001\%$	± 0.25	± 0.05	± 0.05
Gain Nonlinearity (Bridge)	*	-125	-25	-25
V_{OSI}(IA)	$\pm 25\ \mu$V	± 25	± 5	—
$\Delta V_{OSI}/\Delta T$(IA)	$\pm 0.25\ \mu$V/°C	± 8.75	± 1.75	± 1.75
V_{OSO}(IA)	± 2 mV	± 10	± 2	—
$\Delta V_{OSO}/\Delta T$(IA)	$\pm 10\ \mu$V/°C	± 1.75	± 0.35	± 0.35
I_B(5 Ω source unbalance)	± 15 nA	negl.	negl.	—
$\Delta I_B/\Delta T$ (5 Ω source unbalance)	± 50 pA/°C	negl.	negl.	—
I_{OS}(IA)	± 10 nA	± 2.5	± 0.5	—
$\Delta I_{OS}/\Delta T$(IA)	± 20 pA/°C	± 0.17	± 0.035	± 0.035
CMRR(IA)	110 dB	± 15.81	± 3.16	—
PSRR(IA)	110 dB	± 9.5	± 1.9	± 1.9
Resistor TC(IA)	(on same chip-compensated)			
Low-Freq. Noise (IA) (0.01–10 Hz)	0.2 μV (p-p)	0.2 (p-p)	0.04	0.04
V_B Errors (from REF-01) V_B Precision	± 30 mV	± 75	± 15	—
ΔV_B (Line Regulation)	$\pm 0.012\%$/V	± 4.5	± 0.9	± 0.9
$\Delta V_B/\Delta T$	± 8.5 ppm/°C	± 7.44	± 1.5	± 1.5
e_n(0.1–10 Hz)	30 μV (p-p)	0.075	0.015	0.015
Total Algebraic Worst-Case Error		360 μV	72 mV	33 mV
Percentage WC Error		1.43%	1.43%	0.66%
Probable RMS Error		163 μV (0.65%)	32.6 mV	25.3 mV (0.5%)

* See Eqs. (5.17)–(5.19).

where the **nonlinearity bridge error** between the assumed linear output and the actual output is

$$\varepsilon(\delta) = \frac{\delta}{2} - \frac{\delta^2}{4} + \frac{\delta^3}{8} \cdots \tag{5.19}$$

Since $\delta = 1\%$ in this example $\varepsilon(\delta) \approx 0.5\%$. Thus, since the calculated full-scale linear output is 5 V for the IA, the actual full-scale output due to the bridge will be low by $(5 \times 10^{-3})(5 \text{ V})$, or 25 mV. It would be much better, therefore, to use the bridge-amplifier connection of Fig. 5.12, thereby eliminating this bridge nonlinearity. The next most important contributions in limiting the resolution are temperature effects for the gain and V_{OS} for the IA, and for the reference source V_B. Still, by eliminating the 25 mV contribution of the bridge nonlinearity, one could achieve a probable resolution error (rms) for the circuit of 3.6 mV, which is only $\pm 0.7\%$ (715 ppm) of full-scale output. This is sufficient for better than 10-bit resolution in a digital conversion.

Before leaving the subject of bridge circuits, let us look at another two-amplifier circuit, one that has an output voltage directly proportional to the deviation δ, and thereby eliminates the nonlinearity problem in the standard bridge circuit of Figs. 5.11 and 5.13. The circuit, shown in Fig. 5.14, is suggested by J. Graeme of Burr-Brown Corp [Ref. 5.14]. A similar circuit using two standard op amps is also available (see Problem 5.25). The circuit of Fig. 5.14 basically establishes a constant current source, since the inverting input of the A_1 op amp must be at ground. The lower terminal of the bridge is then driven by the output of A_1, as in the single-op-amp circuit of Fig. 5.12. Nonlinearity correction occurs by obtaining a signal v_O from the output of the IA [which contains the nonlinear term

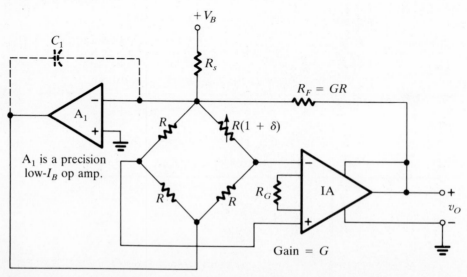

Figure 5.14 Two-amplifier bridge circuit that eliminates bridge nonlinearity.

in δ, as seen from Eq. (5.17)], and feeding back a scaled amount of v_O to correct for the nonlinearity. The resulting output voltage is then related linearly to δ by

$$v_O = \delta\left(\frac{GRV_B}{4R_s}\right) \tag{5.20}$$

5.4 CHOPPER-STABILIZED OP AMPS

Chopper-stabilized op amps are required when the application demands unusually low values of input dc-offset voltage and offset-voltage drift. The early concept of a chopper-stabilized amplifier (applicable only for an inverting op amp connection) is demonstrated in Fig. 5.15 [Ref. 5.15]. The high-frequency content of the error signal v_A is passed through the highpass filter ($\omega_2 \approx 1/R_2 C_1$) and amplified by A_2. Since A_2 is ac coupled, then R_2 can be chosen for small output dc drift due to I_B (or I_{OS}). The low-frequency and dc part of v_A is **modulated**,* and then amplified by the ac amplifier A_1 (the high-frequency content is removed by the $R_3 C_2$ lowpass filter). Since A_1 is ac coupled there is *no* dc-drift contribution for the overall amplifier. The ac output signal is then synchronously **demodulated**,* filtered by $R_7 C_3$ to remove switching spikes and noise, and then amplified by A_2. A typical open-loop gain-vs-frequency curve for the overall circuit is indicated in Fig. 5.15(b), where ω_1 is the bandwidth of the A_1 system, ω_2 is the highpass filter frequency of $R_2 C_1$, and ω_3 is the -3 dB high-frequency value for A_2. The overall dc gain is $G_O = G_1 G_2/4$† (although fullwave demodulation at v_D could produce $G_O = G_1 G_2/2$). Most chopper-stabilized circuits have values of $G_O > 10^6$, indeed $> 10^7$ in many instances.

It is very important that the switch S_1 not contribute a dc offset; for this reason a bipolar-transistor switch is not as suitable as an FET switch. In some very low dc-drift circuits manufacturers even use special mechanical vibrating-reed switches, and in other cases special low-leakage varactor diodes, or even light-modulated devices.

Since the dc gain [G_O of Fig. 5.15(b)] is much greater than the gain G_2, then the dc offsets contributed by A_2 are extremely small as an RTI signal. The equivalent input-offset voltage for the chopper amplifier becomes‡

$$V_{OS} = \frac{\pm V_{os2} \pm I_{os2} R_2}{(G_1/4)} + V_{os}^c \tag{5.21}$$

where $G_1/4$ is the gain of the chopper channel amplifier, and it is assumed that resistors are chosen so that $R_2 = R_7$. The remaining term in Eq. (5.21), V_{os}^c, is an

---

* *Modulation* of a signal basically means a conversion from one frequency domain to another, in this case from dc to ac. Similarly, *demodulation* means converting back to the original frequency domain; here, converting from ac to dc.

† In this analysis the gain of amplifier A_1 is G_1, while amplifier A_2 has a gain G_2, etc.

‡ Eq. (5.21) assumes that the condition $R_5 \gg R_4 \gg R_3$ holds in Fig. (5.15); hence the gain of the chopper circuit is $G_1/4$. For a modulator drive that is not a square wave, and for different resistor ratios, the chopper gain will decrease [Ref. 5.4].

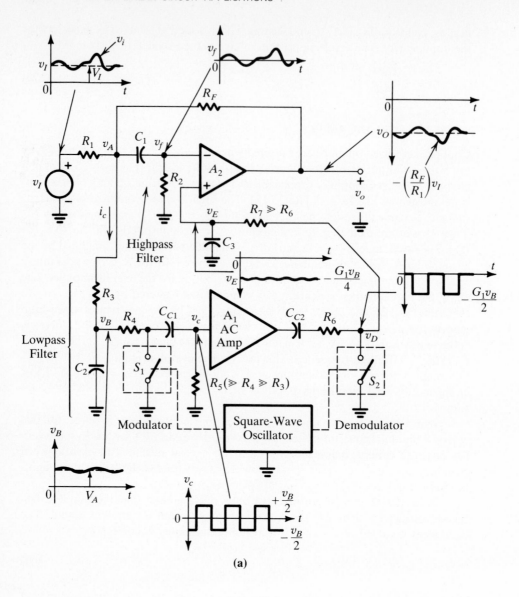

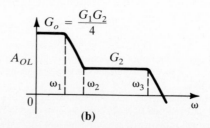

Figure 5.15 Early concept of a chopper-stabilized amplifier.

equivalent-input-offset term created by the sum of any error due to imperfect chopping, as well as thermal potentials at the input.

The essential disadvantage of the chopping amplifier concept of Fig. 5.15 is that only an inverting amplifier connection can be used. An entirely different concept for a chopper amplifier is available with a more recent complementary-MOS (CMOS) monolithic IC circuit, which uses MOS devices for the switching function. This circuit was originally developed by Intersil, Inc., but is now available from several other manufacturers. The circuit's basic operation is similar to the auto-zero concept, referred to earlier (see Fig. 5.14); a block diagram is shown in Fig. 5.16. As in the basic chopper circuit of Fig. 5.15, there are two amplifiers: A_1 is the main amplifier, which is connected continuously to the input signal v_I, while the nulling amplifier A_2 nulls alternately itself and then the main amplifier as well. The circuit requires two external low-leakage capacitors C_A and C_B which store the appropriate nulling potentials. These capacitors (nominally 0.1 μF each) should be high-quality film type, such as polystyrene, polypropylene, or mylar. The nulling arrangement of the circuit operates over the full common-mode and power-supply ranges, and is also not dependent on the output, hence the circuit can have very large values of CMRR, PSRR, and A_{OL}.

The circuit works as follows: with the A switches closed a dc voltage equal to the product $G_2 V_{OS2}$ is stored on C_A, with feedback to provide now a resulting **effective offset voltage** at the input of A_2 of $V_{OS2}/(1 + G_2)$. After A_2 is nulled, the A switches open and the B switches close; this supplies v_I to both A_1 and A_2, and also stores the output of A_2 on C_B. Hence, the overall output voltage of the circuit is

$$v_O = G_1\left[v_I + G_2 v_I + V_{OS1} + \left(\frac{1}{1 + G_2}\right)V_{OS2}\right] \tag{5.22}$$

or, since the nulling amplifier gain is large ($G_2 \gg 1$), then

$$v_O = G_1 G_2\left[v_I + \frac{V_{OS1} + V_{OS2}/G_2}{G_2}\right] \tag{5.23}$$

The amplifier also has correction feedback circuits to minimize chopper-frequency charge injection, and reduce output chopper spiking, as well as reducing intermodulation problems due to sum and difference frequencies ($f_c \pm f_I$). Further, optional use of an internal overload clamp allows a reduction in the recovery time of the amplifier, if the output stage should saturate. If the clamp terminal is connected to the inverting input terminal of the op amp, then the amplifier is prevented from saturating by reducing the gain of the circuit when the output voltage reaches about 1 V away from either the positive or negative supply value.

Two commercial types of chopper-stabilized circuits, similar to those of Figs. 5.15 and 5.16, are shown in Table 5.2, and compared with two precision op amps (one bipolar and one JFET input) and a varactor-bridge modulated circuit. It is very apparent that the monolithic IC chopper circuit offers the least value of V_{OS} and offset drift, while the varactor-bridge circuit has the lowest I_B current. The monolithic IC chopper also has the largest CMRR and PSRR, but suffers in comparison with other op amps regarding maximum power-supply voltage (this is

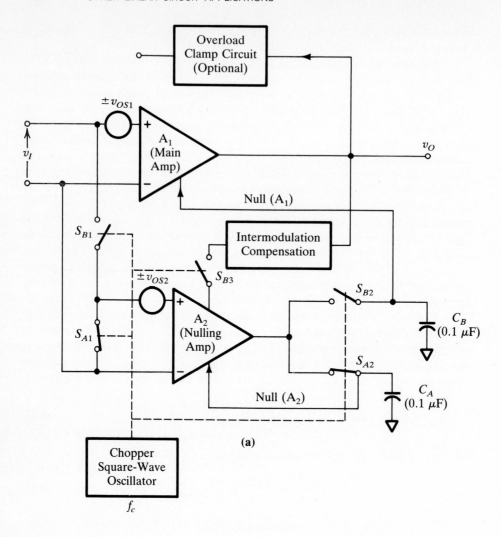

(a)

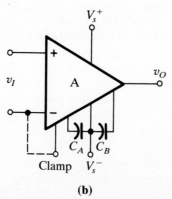

(b)

Figure 5.16 A monolithic CMOS IC chopper-stabilized amplifier.

Table 5.2 COMPARISON OF CHOPPER-STABILIZED AND PRECISION OP AMPS

Parameter	Precision Bipolar (OP-27A)	Precision JFET (OPA-111B)	Discrete Chopper Stabilized*	Monolithic Chopper Stabilized†	Discrete Varactor Bridge‡
$\pm V_{OS}(\mu V)$	25	250	20	5	—
$\Delta V_{OS}/\Delta T(\mu V/°C)$	0.6	1	0.1–0.3	0.05	30
Long-Term Drift (μV/month)	0.2	—	1–2	0.1–0.2	100
$I_B(pA)$	$\pm 40,000$	± 1	± 50	± 10 to 30	± 0.01
$I_{OS}(pA)$	$\pm 35,000$	± 0.75	NA	± 0.5 to 25	NA
$R_{IN}(\Omega)$	6 M	10^{13}	0.3 M–0.5 M	10^{12}	to 10^{14}
$A_{OL}(V/V)$	10^6	10^6	10^7	10^6	10^5
$V_{ICMR}(V)$	± 11	± 10	NA	-5 to 3.5	NA
CMRR (dB)	114	100	NA	110–120	NA
PSRR (dB)	100	100	—	110–120	—
$e_n(\mu V$, p-p)(0.1–10 Hz)	0.08	1.2	1.5–2	0.7–4	10(0.01–1 Hz)
$i_n(pA/Hz)$ @ 10 Hz	1.7	0.0075(p-p)	0.4–10(p-p)	0.01	0.001(p-p, 0.01–1 Hz)
GB(MHz)	8	2	3	0.45–2	0.002
SR(V/μs)	2.8	2	6–30	0.2–2.5	0.0004
Typ P.S. Voltage(V)	± 15	± 15	± 15	± 5	± 15
Max P.S. Voltage(V)	± 22	± 22	± 18	± 8	± 18
$I_{P.S.}$(mA)	3	2.5	5–10	0.2–2	± 15, -6
External C req'd?	no	no	no	2, 0.1 μF each	no
Technology	Mono. Bipolar	Mono. Bipolar-JFET	Modular	Mono. CMOS	modular
Cost	med	med	high	low	high

* Modular units equivalent to BB3291 and AD234-235. These units suitable for inverting gain only.

† Units cover types ICL7650, TSC7652, TSC7650A, TSC9007, LT1052.

‡ Units are typical of types BB3430, 3431. The 3430 is for inverting use, while the 3431 is for a non-inverting connection.

NA—not applicable.

due to the CMOS process, which allows only 16 V maximum total potential*) and the allowable input common-mode voltage range. The precision bipolar amplifier has the advantages of minimum e_n as well as largest GB value.

5.5 OPERATIONAL TRANSCONDUCTANCE AMPLIFIERS

The operational transconductance amplifier (OTA), a circuit somewhat similar to an op amp, has a forward characteristic described by transconductance (g_m) rather than voltage gain (A_v). Also, the output impedance of the OTA is best characterized by a dependent current source in parallel with a large impedance. The transconductance of the circuit is directly proportional to an injected (externally controlled) dc current; therefore the circuit has applications in gated, gain-controlled, instrumentation, and audio applications [Ref. 5.17].

A small-signal equivalent circuit for the OTA can be represented as in Fig. 5.17(a), with a simplified circuit diagram shown in Fig. 5.17(b). In the latter diagram an input control current I_{ABC} produces an equal current in transistor Q_3. So the collector currents for Q_1 and Q_2 as well as Q_4 and Q_6 will be $I_{ABC}/2$ (if all current gains h_{FE} are large). Moreover the current of Q_4 is mirrored in Q_5 (and Q_9), and therefore in Q_8 as well. Thus, for an input dc-bias current of I_{ABC}, the current drawn from the power supplies is approximately $2I_{ABC}$. Now suppose an input signal v_i is applied to unbalance the currents in Q_1 and Q_2. The collector current of a bipolar transistor is related exponentially to the base-emitter voltage as

$$I_C \approx I_s \exp\left(\frac{qV_{BE}}{mkT}\right) \tag{5.24}$$

where I_s is the reverse saturation current, $m \approx 1$, and kT/q is the usual thermal potential, equal to 26 mV at room temperature. Thus, for equal emitter-base areas for Q_1 and Q_2 in Fig. 5.17(b), the I_s values are equal and the voltage v_i is therefore related to the collector currents as

$$v_i = \frac{kT}{q} \ln\left(\frac{I_{C1}}{I_{C2}}\right) \tag{5.25}$$

If v_i is small (a few millivolts), then the ratio I_{C1}/I_{C2} is near unity, and the ln function above can be expanded to yield

$$v_i \approx \frac{kT}{q}\left(\frac{I_{C1} - I_{C2}}{I_{C2}}\right) = \frac{kT}{q}\left(\frac{I_{C1} - I_{C2}}{I_{ABC}/2}\right) \tag{5.26}$$

---

* Two recently introduced chopper-stabilized CMOS op amps, the Maxim MAX 420–423 series and the Teledyne TSC915, can now operate with ± 15 V power supplies. Further, the Teledyne TSC911 op amp has 150 pF self contained capacitors (C_A and C_B of Fig. 5.16) so that external capacitors are not required.

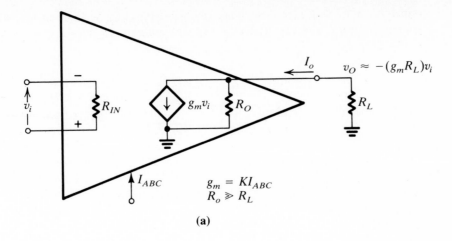

(a)

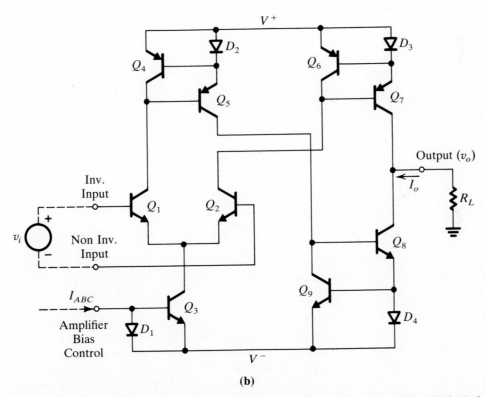

(b)

Figure 5.17 Operational transconductance amplifier (OTA). (a) Small-signal equivalent circuit. (b) A simplified circuit diagram.

since $I_{C2} \approx I_{C1} = I_{ABC}/2$. Also, since (with large h_{FE}) I_{C1} is equal to I_{C4}, which is mirrored by I_{C5} and eventually I_{C8}, and likewise for I_{C2} and I_{C7}, we obtain by substitution

$$v_i \approx \frac{2kT}{qI_{ABC}}(I_{C8} - I_{C7}) \tag{5.27}$$

or since the difference current $(I_{C8} - I_{C7})$ is equal to I_O, we have from Eq. (5.27) the relation

$$I_O \approx \frac{I_{ABC}v_i}{2(kT/q)} \equiv g_m v_i \tag{5.28}$$

Thus, the control of the amplifier bias current I_{ABC} provides a direct control of the transconductance, g_m.

■ **Exercise 5.5**

A manufacturer's data sheet specifies that an OTA (at 25 °C) has a transconductance

$$g_m = 19.2 I_{ABC}$$

an output resistance of

$$R_O = \frac{7.5\ \text{k}\Omega}{I_{ABC}}$$

and an input resistance of

$$R_{IN} = \frac{10}{I_{ABC}}$$

Are these values reasonable for the circuit of Fig. 5.17? What would be the value of h_{FE} for Q_1 and Q_2?

The linear operation of an OTA is predicated on a very small input voltage v_i. For example, from Eq. (5.25) a 10% difference in collector currents is achieved with only 2.5 mV signal. For large input signals several op amp manufacturers offer an OTA with linearizing diodes* added to the inputs of Q_1 and Q_2, as indicated in Fig. 5.18(b). Also shown in Fig. 5.18(a) is an output-buffer amplifier that is available on more recent OTAs; the connection of Q_{10} and Q_{11} to the high impedance current

---

* The concept of using diodes to improve both linearity, as well as reduce temperature sensitivity, is attributed to B. Gilbert, *IEEE J. Solid State Ckts.*, Vol. SC-3, No. 4, pp. 353–65, (Dec. 1968).

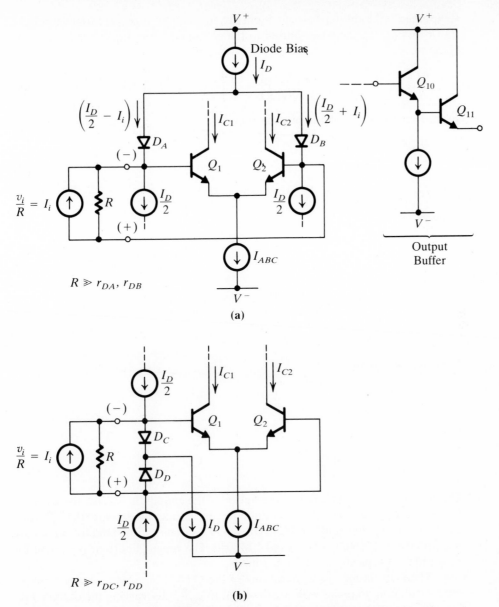

Figure 5.18 (a) Linearizing diodes D_A and D_B. (b) Similar circuit with D_C and D_D.

output of the OTA allows for the lower output impedance required of a more conventional op amp circuit.

To see how linearity is achieved, let us examine the circuit of Fig. 5.18(a). A Kirchhoff's Law voltage equation around the loop formed by D_A, Q_1, Q_2 and D_B gives

$$V_{DA} + V_{BE1} = V_{DB} + V_{BE2} \qquad (5.29)$$

If the areas of the emitter-base junctions are equal (D_A and D_B are formed from npn transistors having the base shorted to the collector), using Eq. (5.24) reduces Eq. (5.29) to,

$$\frac{kT}{q}\left[\ln\left(\frac{I_D/2 - I_i}{I_{SA}}\right) + \ln\left(\frac{I_{C1}}{I_{S1}}\right)\right] = \frac{kT}{q}\left[\ln\left(\frac{I_D/2 + I_i}{I_{SB}}\right) + \ln\left(\frac{I_{C2}}{I_{S2}}\right)\right] \qquad \textbf{(5.30)}$$

From Fig. 5.17(b) (ignoring base currents)

$$I_{C1} + I_{C2} = I_{ABC}$$

$$I_{C8} - I_{C7} = I_O$$

Now $I_{C1} = I_{C8}$ and $I_{C2} = I_{C7}$, so we can obtain

$$I_{C8} = \frac{1}{2}(I_{ABC} + I_O)$$

$$I_{C7} = \frac{1}{2}(I_{ABC} - I_O) \qquad \textbf{(5.31)}$$

which gives, by substitution into Eq. (5.30) and rearranging

$$\frac{kT}{q}\ln\left(\frac{I_D/2 + I_i}{I_D/2 - I_i}\right) = \frac{kT}{q}\ln\left(\frac{I_{ABC} + I_O}{I_{ABC} - I_O}\right)$$

Reducing, we obtain

$$I_O = I_i\left(\frac{2I_{ABC}}{I_D}\right) \qquad \textbf{(5.32)}$$

or in terms of voltage

$$v_O = -v_i\left(\frac{2I_{ABC}}{I_D}\right)\left(\frac{R_L}{R}\right) \qquad \textbf{(5.33)}$$

The equations above require no assumption of the amplitude of I_i (or therefore v_i). Commercially available OTAs containing linearizing diodes are the CA3280, LM13600, LM13700, and NE5517. Other OTA circuits with standard inputs are the CA3080, CA3060, CA3094, and LM3080. The range of current permitted for I_{ABC} and I_D is typically from 1 μA–1 mA.

There are numerous applications of the OTA. Fig. 5.19(a) shows a simple instrumentation amplifier with a gain equal to $g_m R_L$. By varying the current I_{ABC} the gain varies correspondingly. Part (b) of the figure shows a sample-and-hold circuit (the operation of which will be discussed later), which basically *samples* the input signal when the control input is *high* ($\sim$ +3.6V) and *holds* the signal at that level with the control input *low* (0–0.4V). The basic dc error in the circuit is due to the equivalent leakage current that removes charge from capacitor C during the hold cycle. Since the input to the MOS transistor M_1 is $> 10^{15}$ Ω, the only leakage is from the output of the OTA when the command signal is low ($I_{ABC} = 0$), which for most available OTAs is 200 pA. Since $dV/dt = I/C$, then for $C = 1000$ pF there is a *pulse tilt* of only 0.2 μV/μsec of hold time.

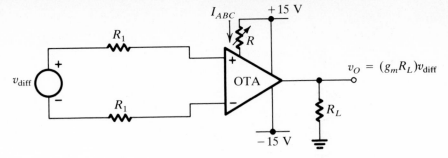

(a) Instrumentation Amplifier.

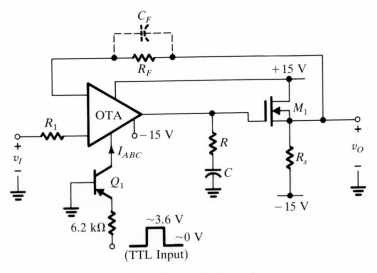

(b) Sample-and-hold circuit.

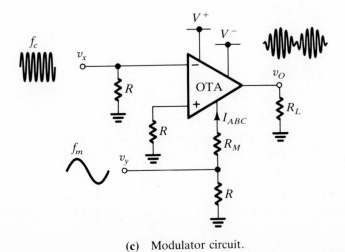

(c) Modulator circuit.

Figure 5.19 OTA application circuits.

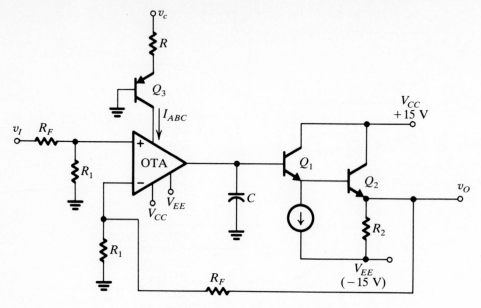

(d) Voltage-controlled low pass filter.

Figure 5.19 OTA application circuits.

The OTA can also form a simple modulation circuit, as indicated in Fig. 5.19(c). Since the output voltage from Eq. (5.28) is

$$v_O = -v_x \left(\frac{I_{ABC}}{2kT/q} \right) R_L$$

and since I_{ABC} is

$$I_{ABC} = \frac{v_y - V^-}{R_m}$$

the output becomes

$$v_O = -\text{const.} \times R_L(v_x \cdot v_y - v_x \cdot V^-) \tag{5.34}$$

A simple voltage-controlled lowpass filter circuit is formed using an OTA with the high-impedance input-buffer circuit (Q_1, Q_2) as shown in Fig. 5.19(d). It can be shown (see Problem 5.34) that the transfer function of the circuit is that of a single-pole response

$$\frac{v_O}{v_i} = \frac{K}{1 + \dfrac{s}{\omega_1}} \tag{5.35}$$

where $\omega_1 = g_m R_1/(R_1 + R_F)C$. Since g_m is directly proportional to I_{ABC} the filter response is directly varied by the control voltage V_C.

5.6 CURRENT-DIFFERENCING (NORTON) AMPLIFIERS

The current-differencing (or Norton) amplifier is a departure from the standard op amp design. In place of the usual differential, high-impedance input of the differential stage the Norton amplifier has a "current-mirror" input, with a transistor-connected diode for the noninverting input terminal, mirrored with an npn transistor connected to the inverting input. A schematic of a typical circuit design is shown in Fig. 5.20(a), with the symbol for a Norton amplifier shown in Fig. 5.20(b). Since the circuit is extremely simple, occupying a minimum of silicon area, most amplifiers are designed in the "quad" (4 amplifiers on one chip) configuration. The Norton amplifier is particularly advantageous for single-power-supply operation.

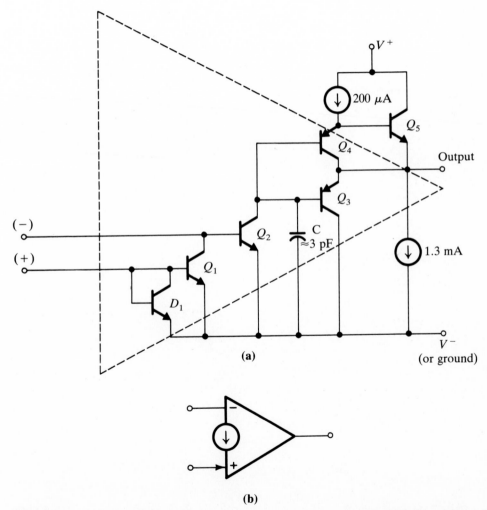

Figure 5.20 A current-differencing (Norton) amplifier: (a) circuit schematic; (b) symbol.

Circuit operation is determined by the current applied to the input diode D_1. This current is mirrored by the collector current of Q_1, therefore a known dc current is required by the inverting input terminal. Since the circuit is intended primarily for use with a single power supply, most standard configurations will require input- and perhaps output-coupling capacitors.

Typical biasing for the Norton amplifier is illustrated by the ac-coupled inverting circuit of Fig. 5.21(a), with the biasing equivalent circuit shown in Fig. 5.21(b). If we ignore the input bias current I_B [this is the base current for Q_2 of Fig.

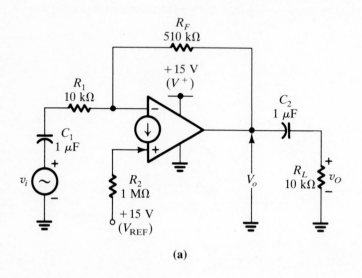

(a)

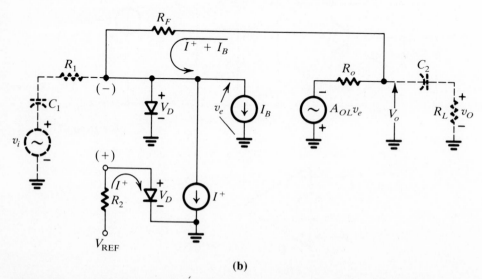

(b)

Figure 5.21 AC-coupled inverting amplifier: (a) Circuit; (b) Biasing equivalent circuit.

5.20(a)], the current through R_F is equal to the current into the noninverting input, which from Fig. 5.21 is (assume $V_D \approx 0.6$ V)

$$I^+ = \frac{15 \text{ V} - 0.6 \text{ V}}{1 \text{ M}\Omega} = 14.4 \text{ } \mu\text{A} \tag{5.36}$$

Thus, the output dc voltage V_O is approximately

$$V_O = 0.6 \text{ V} + 510 \text{ k}\Omega(14.4 \text{ } \mu\text{A}) = +7.9 \text{ V} \tag{5.37}$$

and the output is therefore biased approximately halfway between the power supply and ground.

■ **Exercise 5.6**

The LM3900 integrated circuit is a quad, current-differencing op amp with each amplifier having the following specifications:

$A_{OL} = 70$ dB = PSRR $\quad$ $I_{\text{supply}} = 1.6$ mA
Mirror gain = 0.9 to 1.1 (1.0, typ) $\quad$ $0.09 \text{ V} \leq V_O \leq 13.5 \text{ V}$ ($V_{\text{supply}} = +15$ V)
R_{IN} (inv.) = 1 MΩ $\quad$ $I_B = 30$ nA (200 nA, max)
$R_O = 8$ kΩ $\quad$ I_O (source) = 10 mA
$GB = 2.5$ MHz $\quad$ I_O (sink) = 5 mA ($V_O = 1$ V)
$SR^+ = 0.5$ V/μsec, $SR^- = 20$ V/μsec

With the above specifications, what is the range of dc output voltage V_O for Fig. 5.21(a)? What are the typical closed-loop values of gain, frequency bandwidth, and output impedance?

From the previous example, it is evident that the dc biasing is established by resistor R_2 and the reference dc voltage supply V_{REF} and that the choice of $R_F \approx 1/2$ R_2 will set the dc output voltage at 1/2 the power supply value if $V^+ = V_{\text{REF}}$. There is one disadvantage, however, in using the same voltage for V_{REF} and V^+, namely that low-frequency ripple on the power supply can be amplified by a "gain" of R_F/R_2 or 1/2.

The Norton amplifier can also be used in a noninverting gain configuration, as indicated in Fig. 5.22. Here, the circuit is biased from a filtered reference voltage V_{REF} to reduce ripple signals coupling to the output. Since V_{REF} is equal to $\frac{1}{2}$ the power-supply voltage a choice of $R_2 = R_F$ produces a $+7.5$ V dc output voltage. The ac midband voltage gain for the circut is

$$\frac{v_O}{v_i} = \frac{R_F}{R_1 + r_d} \tag{5.38}$$

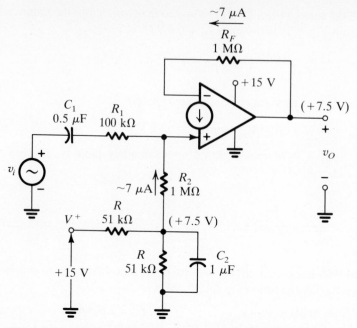

Figure 5.22 Norton amplifier in a noninverting circuit.

where the small-signal diode impedance is $r_d \approx 0.026/7 \ \mu A$, or 3.7 kΩ. With resistor values as indicated in Fig. 5.22 the gain is +9.64.

For lowest noise performance a different biasing technique may be used, referred to as N V_{BE} biasing and illustrated in Fig. 5.23. In Fig. 5.23(a) the input bias voltage at the inverting input [V_{BE} of Q_2 for Fig. 5.20(a)] establishes the current through resistor R_2. Since the noninverting input is returned to ground, diode D_1

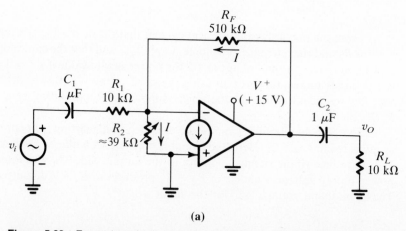

(a)

Figure 5.23 Examples of NV_{BE} biasing. (a) Basic single-power-supply bias.

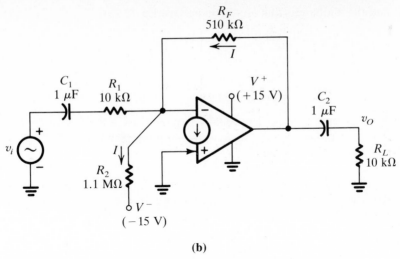

(b)

Figure 5.23 Examples of NV_{BE} biasing. (b) Using two power supplies.

(and therefore Q_1) of Fig. 5.20 is not conducting. Thus the current I must flow through R_F, fixing the output dc voltage at

$$V_O = V_{BE}\left(1 + \frac{R_F}{R_2}\right) \qquad (5.39)$$

Obviously, the output voltage will vary with temperature since V_{BE} changes by approximately $-2\ \text{mV/°C}$. If a negative power supply is available the circuit of Fig. 5.23(b) is preferred, as illustrated by the following example.

EXAMPLE 5.3

Compare the gain, biasing, and biasing temperature sensitivity for the two circuits of Fig. 5.23. Assume the characteristics of the LM3900 of Exercise 5.6.

Solution

From Exercise 5.6 the open-loop gain is 70 dB, or 3200. Thus, the loop transmission (at midband frequencies) for the circuit of Fig. 5.23(a) is

$$T_a = 3200\left(\frac{39\ \text{k}\Omega\|10\ \text{k}\Omega}{39\ \text{k}\Omega\|10\ \text{k}\Omega + 510\ \text{k}\Omega}\right)\left(\frac{10\ \text{k}\Omega}{10\ \text{k}\Omega + 8\ \text{k}\Omega}\right) = 27.3$$

and for Fig. 5.23(b) is

$$T_b = 3200\left(\frac{1.1\ \text{M}\Omega\|10\ \text{k}\Omega}{1.1\ \text{M}\Omega\|10\ \text{k}\Omega + 510\ \text{k}\Omega}\right)\left(\frac{10\ \text{k}\Omega}{10\ \text{k}\Omega + 8\ \text{k}\Omega}\right) = 33.9$$

and the midband gains are therefore [see Eq. (2.13)]

$$A_a = -\left(\frac{510 \text{ k}\Omega}{10 \text{ k}\Omega}\right)\left[1 - \frac{1}{28.3}\right] = -49.2$$

$$A_b = -\left(\frac{510 \text{ k}\Omega}{10 \text{ k}\Omega}\right)\left[1 - \frac{1}{34.9}\right] = -49.5$$

The V_{BE} input voltage is probably between 0.5 V and 0.6 V at 25 °C. Thus, in the first circuit, the output voltage is given by Eq. (5.39) as

$$V_O(\text{for } V_{BE} = 0.5 \text{ V}) = 7.04 \text{ V}$$

or (for $V_{BE} = 0.6$ V), $V_O = 8.45$ V, which is a 20% difference. However, the sensitivity to V_{BE} is removed in the (b) circuit, since V^- is much greater than V_{BE}; here, if $V_{BE} = 0.5$ V, $V_O = 7.69$ V, while $V_O = 7.83$ V if $V_{BE} = 0.6$ V. The difference is now only 1.8%.

The sensitivity is likewise improved by the circuit of Fig. 5.23(b). Let us assume a temperature coefficient of -2 mV/°C for V_{BE} and estimate the dc output voltage change for an ambient temperature change from 25 to 65 °C. The basic N V_{BE} bias circuit changes, from Eq. (5.39), as

$$\Delta V_O = \Delta V_{BE}\left(1 + \frac{R_F}{R_2}\right) = (-2 \text{ mV/°C})(40 \text{ °C})(14.08) = -1.13 \text{ V}$$

which is approximately a 15% decrease. However, for the circuit of Fig. 5.23(b) the output change is only 1%. The effects of changes in I_B are not important in this example, since I_B is typically only 30 nA (at 25 °C), decreasing to 20 nA at 65 °C.

If a differential input is desired, the Norton amplifier can be combined with a matched pnp pair of transistors (or, conversely, matched FETs) to obtain a true op amp circuit, as illustrated in Problem 5.38.

If higher frequency operation is necessary, the Norton amplifier is also available in a dual monolithic IC, the LM359. This amplifier is intended for higher bias currents (I_{supply} is typically 18.5 mA with a 12 V power supply, and $I_{\text{set}} = 0.5$ mA) that produce larger gain-bandwidth products and higher slew rates. The LM359 achieves values of $GB = 400$ MHz and $SR = 60$ V/μsec with a gain of 10. The ENV noise is also lower, (6 nV/$\sqrt{\text{Hz}}$ at a frequency of 1 kHz) with the circuit particularly adaptable to the N V_{BE} biasing technique. Both input- and output-stage currents are externally adjustable, so that the source and sink currents can be much larger than for the LM3900 circuit.

5.7 VOLTAGE AND CURRENT REGULATORS AND REFERENCES

One of the most useful applications of an op amp is in forming a voltage (or current) regulator, and precision reference. In Section 5.3, in the instrumentation bridge-amplifier example of Fig. 5.13, we saw that the reference voltage for the bridge V_B was a significant contribution to the error budget analysis. In the very important case of analog-to-digital (A/D) conversion, the accuracy of conversion is no better than the stability of the voltage reference; i.e., for $\pm\frac{1}{2}$ bit resolution in a 16-bit ($2^{16} = 65,536$) conversion the *total* allowed change in a 10 V reference over the full operating-temperature range would be $< 16\ \mu V$. There are similar requirements on the precision of a reference current. For example, many sensors are more linear in their response if driven by a constant current, rather than operating with a fixed voltage.

In this section we will look at only a few of the applications that require op amps to obtain a regulated voltage or current source. The interested reader is referred to Chapter 5 references in Appendix A for numerous other examples.

5.7.1 DC Voltage Regulators and Precision References

There is a subtle difference between a **regulator** and a **reference**. Both the voltage regulator and the precision reference use negative feedback to hold the output voltage constant against changes in temperature or load. However, the regulator usually has a raw* dc voltage input (a dc voltage with probably considerable ripple) and is concerned with rejecting the ripple, as well as furnishing an output current to a varying load (for example, the output-current requirement may be several amperes). Furthermore, the regulator usually must be protected against short circuits at the output as well. In fact, the precision, or absolute value, of the output dc voltage is usually not the main requirement in a regulator, but *it is in a reference*! The precision reference circuit usually has its input furnished by a reasonably regulated dc source with very low ripple. The output load of the reference is usually constant, or requires at most a variation in load current of a few milliamperes. Further, the requirement of *constancy* for the absolute value of output voltage is fundamental. In fact, the output voltage of a regulator can never be better than the precision of its internal reference.

Series Voltage Regulators. The basic principle of a series voltage regulator is illustrated in the simplified circuit of Fig. 5.24. Here the unregulated voltage V_I is applied to the collector of Q_1, which is in series with the signal (for this reason this type of circuit is referred to as a linear *series* voltage regulator). The output voltage V_O results from the inverting connection of the op amp, and is obviously

$$V_O = V_{REF}\left(\frac{R_F + R_1}{R_1}\right) \tag{5.40}$$

The basic circuit of Fig. 5.24 contains the minimum essential features of all series voltage regulators, which are (1) a **precision reference** V_{REF}; (2) a series **pass transistor** Q_1 that furnishes the current to the load; (3) an **op amp** A_1 whose purpose is to compare the reference V_{REF} to the feedback signal from V_O and

---

* In the literature an unregulated dc voltage, usually resulting at the output of a rectified ac voltage, is referred to as a "raw" dc voltage.

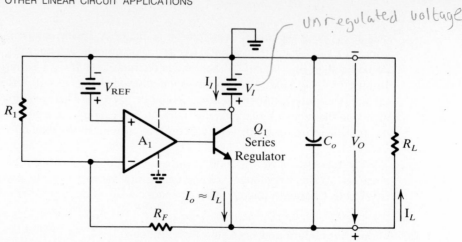

unregulated voltage

Figure 5.24 Basic concept of a series dc voltage regulator.

amplify the difference between the two; and (4) a precise **voltage divider** network (R_1 and R_F) that determines the dc value of the output voltage.

In addition to the output-voltage expression of Eq. (5.40), we can also obtain some other fundamental identities of the series regulator by utilizing the basic op amp relationships derived much earlier. For example, the open-loop output resistance R_O of Fig. 5.24 would be primarily due to the internal emitter resistance of Q_1 and the base resistance, or

$$R_O = \frac{mkT}{qI_o} + r_{\text{OHMIC}} + \frac{r_b' + R_O(A_1)}{1 + h_{FE1}} \tag{5.41}$$

where $m \approx 2$ if high-level injection is occuring in the bipolar transistor, $kT/q \approx 0.026$ V at room temperature, r_{OHMIC} includes any series ohmic resistance in the emitter of Q_1 as well as any wiring resistance, r_b' is the internal base resistance of Q_1 and $R_O(A_1)$ is the output (open-loop) resistance of the op amp A_1. From our earlier relationships [Eq. (2.12) and Fig. 2.5] we therefore obtain the closed-loop output resistance r_O as

$$r_O = \frac{R_O}{1 + T_0} \approx R_O\left(\frac{R_1 + R_F}{R_1 A_{OL}}\right) \tag{5.42}$$

if the gain of the emitter-follower–connected transistor Q_1 is unity. It is very important to note that the output resistance varies with the current supplied to the load.

We can also estimate the ability of the basic series voltage regulator to reject the ripple associated with V_I. The **ripple rejection** of a voltage regulator is defined as the ratio of the output ac voltage at the load (rms or peak-to-peak) to the input ac voltage, at a given frequency (usually 120 Hz). More often, it is specified in dB as

$$\text{ripple rejection} \equiv 20 \log_{10}\left|\frac{1}{(v_o/v_r)}\right| \tag{5.43}$$

where v_r is the ac ripple content of the input signal. In the circuit of Fig. 5.24 there are two components of output ac voltage, one due to the ac ripple fed to the output by virtue of the internal collector-to-emitter resistance (r_{ce}) of the bipolar transistor; the other term, which is usually more dominant, is due to the PSRR of the op amp A_1, since typically A_1 is biased from the V_I input. Hence, the output ripple is

$$v_O \approx v_r\left(\frac{r_o}{r_{ce}}\right) + v_r\left(\frac{R_1 + R_F}{R_1}\right)\left|\frac{1}{\text{PSRR}}\right| \tag{5.44}$$

We can also consider the line and load regulation of the regulator. The **line regulation** is defined as the (dc) change in output voltage due to a (dc) change in the input voltage, at a specified value of load current. Correspondingly, the **load regulation** is the change in dc output voltage produced by a change in dc load current, for a given value of input voltage. Usually the required load-current change is from no load (I_{NL}) to full load (I_{FL}).

Two other terms are often specified for voltage regulators. These are the **dropout voltage**, which is the minimum voltage difference permitted between V_I and V_O that will still achieve regulation; and the **quiescent current**, which is that part of the input current I_I not delivered to the load—in effect it is the current required by the regulator circuit for operation.

EXAMPLE 5.4

In Fig. 5.24 if $V_{\text{REF}} = 5$ V, $R_1 = 10$ kΩ, $R_F = 20$ kΩ, $V_I = 24$ V $\pm 20\%$ (with a ripple of 2 V, p-p), find V_O and the various characteristics of the regulator. Assume R_L may vary from 1 kΩ to 100 Ω. The op amp is a 741 device, and the bipolar transistor has h_{FE} (min) $= 50$, $r_{ce} = 100/I_C$, $r_b' = 50$ Ω, and $r_{\text{OHMIC}} = 0.5$ Ω.

Solution
From Eq. (5.40) the output voltage is equal to 5 V (30 kΩ/10 kΩ), or 15 V. For a load resistance change from 1 kΩ to 100 Ω the load current varies from 15 mA to 150 mA. If we use typical 741 parameters (note $V_{\text{supply}} = \pm 12$ V) of $A_{OL} = 1.4 \times 10^5(10^4$ at 120 Hz), $R_o = 75$ Ω and PSRR (120 Hz) ≈ 80 dB we obtain from Eq. (5.42) the open-loop output resistance as

$$R_O \approx \frac{0.052}{I_O} + 0.5\ \Omega + 2.5\ \Omega$$

and for an output current from 15 mA to 150 mA, we have $3.3\ \Omega \le R_O \le 6.4\ \Omega$. Thus, the closed-loop output impedance at dc is,

$$r_{O,\text{dc}} \approx R_O\left(\frac{3}{1.4 \times 10^5}\right) = 71\ \mu\Omega \text{ to } 136\ \mu\Omega$$

while at 120 Hz,

$$r_{O,120\,\text{Hz}} \approx R_O\left(\frac{3}{10^4}\right) = 1\ \text{m}\Omega \text{ to } 1.9\ \text{m}\Omega$$

Thus, from Eq. (5.44) for a load of 1 kΩ, the output ripple is

$$v_O = 2 \text{ V (p-p)} \left[\frac{1.9 \times 10^{-3} \ \Omega}{100 \text{ V}/15.5 \text{ mA}} + \frac{3}{10^4} \right] \approx 0.6 \text{ mV (p-p)}$$

while for a load of 150 mA we also obtain

$$v_O = 2 \text{ V (p-p)} \left[\frac{1 \times 10^{-3} \ \Omega}{100 \text{ V}/150.5 \text{ mA}} + \frac{3}{10^4} \right] \approx 0.6 \text{ mV (p-p)}$$

Therefore the ripple rejection is 2 V/0.6 mV, or 70 dB. To calculate the line regulation, we have an dc input-voltage variation of $\pm 20\%$, or V_I varies over the range 19 V $\leq V_I \leq$ 29 V, for a total $\Delta V_I = 10$ V. Let us assume a load current between the two extremes of 80 mA, but now for a dc change so that

$$\Delta V_O = 10 \text{ V} \left[\frac{80 \ \mu\Omega}{100 \text{ V}/80 \text{ mA}} + \frac{3}{1 \times 10^4} \right] \approx 3 \text{ mV}$$

where the assumption is made that the dc PSRR of the 741 reduced to 80 dB for a power supply voltage of 19 V and ground.

The load regulation, for a typical input voltage of 24 V, is obtained by the change in load current times the output resistance of the regulator, or

$$\Delta V_O \approx 150 \text{ mA } (71 \ \mu\Omega) - 15 \text{ mA } (136 \ \mu\Omega) = 9 \ \mu\text{V}$$

The above calculation, although theoretically correct, is not really reasonable in view of the fact that some ohmic wiring resistance obviously must exist between the regulation points in the circuit and the actual load. For example, if the load were one foot from the regulator, and a typical copper wire of size AWG 22 (American Wire Gauge No. 22) were used, the wire resistance would be 33 mΩ, and the output load regulation would be

$$\Delta V_O \approx (150 \text{ mA} - 15 \text{ mA})(33.1 \text{ m}\Omega) = 4.5 \text{ mV}$$

or $\Delta V_O/V_O = 0.03\%$. Thus, the load regulation for this as well as many other cases depends *entirely* on the wire resistance connecting the load.

The dropout voltage for this example is determined by the linear output range of the op amp. Since $V_O = 15$ V, the output voltage of the op amp is approximately 15.7 V. The 741 op amp circuit requires at least two V_{BE} voltage drops between its positive supply voltage and the output (see the 741 circuit diagram in Appendix C). Therefore, in the circuit of Fig. 5.24, the minimum value allowed for V_I is approximately 18 V. Thus the dropout voltage for this regulator is about 18 V − 15 V, or 3 V.

The quiescent current furnished by I_I to the regulator is the sum of the current through R_F and R_1 and the current drawn by A_1, or a total of 2 mA.

The voltage regulator is redrawn in Fig. 5.25 to indicate the more typical connection details. The output capacitor C_O is usually present but not absolutely required. Also indicated are the correct connections of the **sense** leads S^+ and S^- to

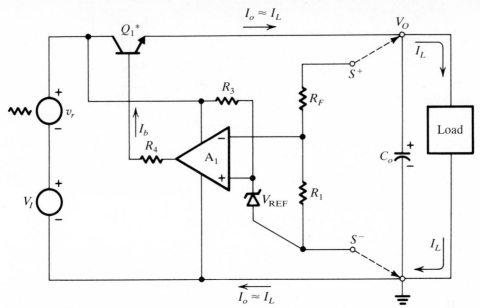

$^*Q_1$ may also be a Darlington transistor,
particularly for large I_o.

Figure 5.25 A simple dc-positive voltage series regulator.

the load. By connecting these terminals (note that in reality these are the feedback sensing points) as close to the load as possible the load regulation can be improved by eliminating the wiring resistance. The biasing of the reference potential V_{REF} is also shown. Typically the V_{REF} value is obtained from either a temperature-compensated voltage-reference (Zener) diode, or a monolithic IC band-gap reference ($V_{\text{REF}} = 1.2$ V). With the reference biased from the input voltage an extra source of output ripple is obtained, although this problem can be alleviated by added circuitry (see Problem 5.39).

The series regulator usually requires protection against a shorted-load condition, otherwise the feedback would attempt to provide maximum base-current drive to Q_1, thereby possibly destroying the transistor due to excessive power dissipation. Two ways to protect the series regulator against a shorted output are (1) limiting the maximum current that could be obtained from the Q_1 transistor at a constant value I_{SC} or (2) limiting the maximum power dissipation of Q_1 which requires **foldback current limiting** at a value I_{FB}, with final short circuit protection at a value I_{SC}. These concepts are illustrated by the circuits in Fig. 5.26. In (a) the diodes D_1 and D_2 and the transistor Q_2 are normally not conducting. However, if the voltage drop across R_{SC} reaches the turn-on voltage of a diode or the V_{BE} value for Q_2 the base current for the series pass transistor Q_1 is diverted to the load. The output characteristic of this short-circuit current-limiting approach is shown in the enclosed graph, where it is apparent that the pass transistor Q_1 would

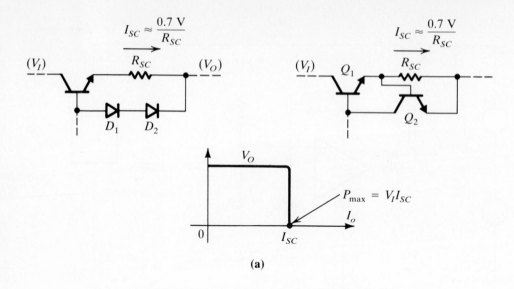

(a)

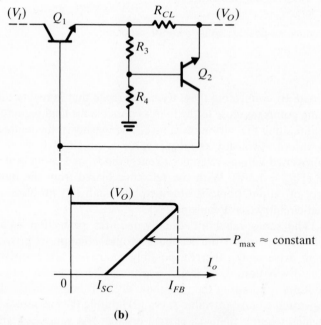

(b)

Figure 5.26 Regulator output protection circuits: (a) short-circuit current limiting; (b) foldback current limiting.

have to furnish a maximum current of I_{SC}, with a resulting maximum power dissipation of $V_I I_{SC}$.

However, in the second case of foldback current limiting it is possible to achieve essentially constant power dissipation in Q_1 along the **foldback line** of Fig. 5.26(b), with a maximum power dissipation in the transistor of

$$P_{\max} = I_{FB}(V_I - V_O) = I_{SC}V_I \tag{5.45}$$

provided that I_{SC} is

$$I_{SC} = I_{FB}\left(1 - \frac{V_O}{V_I}\right) \tag{5.46}$$

In general, the use of foldback current limiting is more efficient, as shown by Example 5.5.

EXAMPLE 5.5

Using the circuit parameters of Example 5.4 ($V_O = 15$ V) compare the maximum output current obtainable using (a) short-circuit current limiting and (b) foldback current-limiting, if the series transistor Q_1 can dissipate a maximum power of 10 watts.

Solution
With a value for V_I of 24 V $\pm$ 20%, the maximum power dissipation occurs with $V_I = 24$ V + 20%, or approximately 29 V. In the short-circuit current-limiting scheme, the maximum power dissipation occurs when $V_O = 0$ V, thus the maximum current available to the load would be slightly less than

$$I_L(\max) = \frac{10 \text{ W}}{29 \text{ V}} = 345 \text{ mA}$$

However, with foldback limiting, and I_{SC} chosen as in Eq. (5.46) by

$$I_{SC} = I_{FB}\left(1 - \frac{15 \text{ V}}{29 \text{ V}}\right) \approx 0.5 I_{FB}$$

the load current could be approximately equal to I_{FB} or

$$I_L(\max) = \frac{10 \text{ W}}{(29 \text{ V} - 15 \text{ V})} = 710 \text{ mA}$$

with I_{SC} therefore equal to 355 mA. Hence the foldback circuit is more efficient in supplying current to the load.

The values for resistors R_{CL}, R_3 and R_4 in the foldback circuit must satisfy two equations. At $V_O = 0$ V then $I_O = I_{SC}$ so

$$V_{BE2} = I_{SC} R_{CL} \left(\frac{R_4}{R_3 + R_4} \right) \tag{5.47}$$

and at $I_O = I_{FB}$

$$I_{FB} R_{CL} = \left(V_O + I_{FB} R_{CL} \right) \left(\frac{R_3}{R_3 + R_4} \right) + V_{BE2} \tag{5.48}$$

provided that the current through the resistive divider of R_3 and R_4 is at least 10 times the base current of Q_2. Solving the equations leads to a design criterion for R_{CL} and the resistive divider, namely

$$R_{CL} = \frac{V_O}{I_{SC} \left(1 + \dfrac{V_O}{V_{BE2}} \right) - I_{FB}} \tag{5.49}$$

and

$$\frac{R_3}{R_4} = \frac{I_{SC} R_{CL}}{V_{BE2}} - 1 \tag{5.50}$$

Shunt Voltage Regulators. Although most linear voltage regulators are of the series type, a shunt regulator (the pass transistor is in *shunt* with the output) is preferred in some applications. A typical example of a shunt regulator is shown in Fig. 5.27, where for diversification the bipolar pass transistor previously used is

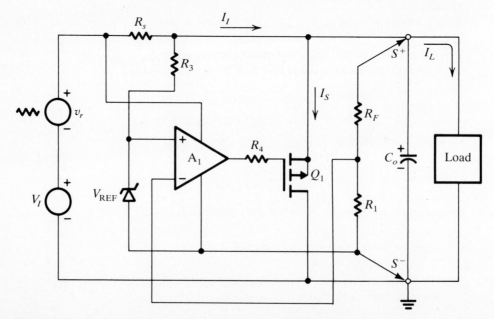

Figure 5.27 Shunt voltage regulator using a power MOS transistor.

now replaced by a PMOS power transistor. Obviously, a bipolar transistor could have been used for Q_1 as well, but the available output dc current requirement of the op amp would have to be considered in the design. For an MOS transistor the gate requires no input dc current, however the op amp A_1 must still supply the dynamic charging current for the gate capacitance, which may be > 1000 pF for a large area MOS transistor. Also, the MOS device has an internal pn-junction diode in parallel with the source and drain that will protect against reverse voltages at the output of the regulator.

The real advantage of the shunt regulator over the series regulator is that the shunt regulator does not necessarily require short-circuit protection. If the load is shorted, then Q_1 is shorted; also the reference-voltage circuit loses its supply voltage. Hence, Q_1 is protected and the output short-circuit current is limited to $I_{SC} = V_I/R_S$. This value would obviously require the element R_S to be a *power* resistor!

■ **Exercise 5.7**

Use the same parameter values of Example 5.4 to obtain a regulated output voltage of $+15$ V for the shunt regulator of Fig. 5.27. Find the required value (and power rating) of R_S. Assume Q_1 is a PMOS transistor having a threshold voltage of $V_T = -3$ V, $C_{gs} = 400$ pF, $C_{gd} = 100$ pF, and $C_{ds} = 300$ pF. Assume Q_1 obeys a relationship for drain current of

$$I_d = 0.5(V_{GS} - V_T)^2$$

Find $r_{O,dc}$, $r_{O,120\,Hz}$, the ripple rejection (in dB), the line regulation, the load regulation, and the dropout voltage. Compare with the results of Example 5.4.

Monolithic IC Regulators.   For most general-purpose applications the inexpensive three-terminal integrated-circuit voltage regulator is suitable. These devices are available, as either positive or negative regulators, from several manufacturers. Figure 5.28(a) shows the basic principle of a positive-voltage three-terminal regulator for an LM317 device. [For an excellent discussion of three-terminal IC regulators, see Ref. 5.31.] Basically, the op amp comparator A_1 is in parallel with the pass transistors Q_1 and Q_2. Thus, the quiescent current I_Q required by A_1 flows from the input to the output. Since the regulator is floating, all this quiescent current must be absorbed by the load. Fortunately, the 5 mA current through R_1 and R_2 in Fig. 5.28(b) is normally greater than I_Q. In the case of the LM317, the protection circuitry affords a shorted-output value of approximately 2.2 A. Also included with most three-terminal regulators is protection against an overvoltage at the input (a voltage exceeding the collector-to-emitter breakdown of Q_1 or Q_2), as well as a thermal-overload-protection circuit that senses the IC temperature and

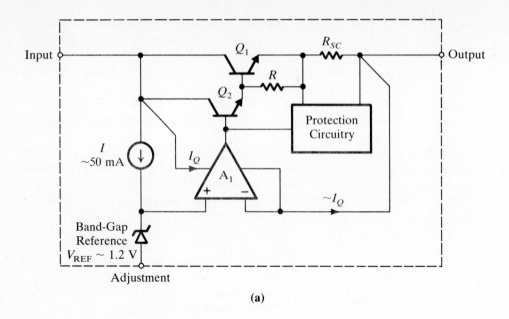

(a)

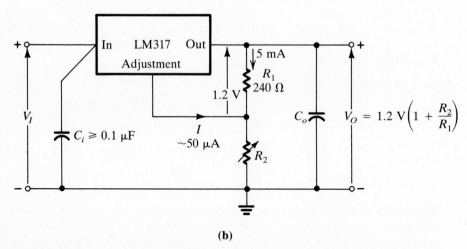

(b)

Figure 5.28 General circuit for the three-terminal LM317 IC positive voltage regulator.
(a) Circuit diagram. (b) Connection for variable output voltage.

removes base-current drive to Q_2 (and therefore Q_1) if the chip temperature exceeds 170 °C.

Line and load regulation with the monolithic IC circuit is not as good as can be achieved with a discrete design (values of 0.01 %/V and 0.1 %, respectively, are typical) but is more than adequate for most applications. Generally, the output voltage is adjustable from a minimum value equal to V_{REF} (or 1.2 V) to a maximum value determined by an input-to-output voltage limit of 40 V. Ripple rejection at 120 Hz is typically 60 dB while the dropout voltage value is 2 V. Output impedance (120 Hz) is typically 10 mΩ, for $I_O = 0.5$ A and $V_o = 10$ V. The output capacitor C_O is not required but does improve the load transient response, as well as reducing the output ripple. The real disadvantage to a three-terminal regulator is that no sense terminals exist, therefore wiring resistance degrades the load regulation directly.

Precision Voltage References.   As mentioned earlier, a voltage regulator has an output dc voltage that is only as stable as its voltage reference, V_{REF}. We utilized the 10 V, REF-01 precision reference in the bridge-circuit example of Fig. 5.13, where the error budget analysis indicated a significant dependence of the output voltage of the bridge amplifier on the precision of the reference voltage. For the basic series regulator, the output voltage varied directly with V_{REF}, as indicated by Eq. (5.40). Early references were usually achieved by biasing a Zener diode near its zero temperature-coefficient (TC) value, or adding a forward-biased pn-junction diode in series with the Zener diode, so that the two temperature coefficients cancelled; in fact, such is the case for the IN827A reference diode ($V_{REF} \approx 6.2$ V) used in Problem 5.39. The two difficulties with using a Zener diode as a reference are: (1) the zero TC is very dependent on holding the Zener current (I_Z) at an exact value, and (2) the dynamic impedance (r_Z) is seldom less than 5 ohms, so an unregulated input voltage used to bias the diode can contribute significantly to the output ripple.

More recent voltage references use either (a) a monolithic reference, usually based on the band gap of silicon ($V_{REF} \approx 1.2$ V), with internal negative feedback to lower the impedance of the reference, or (b) a Zener diode biased at its zero TC value with feedback circuitry to lower the dynamic impedance and hold the value of I_Z constant—at the appropriate value required for a zero TC. The circuitry for case (b) is often integrated along with a constant-temperature control loop on the same silicon chip, thereby holding the reference at a constant temperature and eliminating drift due to ambient temperature fluctuations. For example, the LM199AH device has a reference voltage of $V_{REF} = 6.95$ V with a dynamic resistance of 0.5 Ω, a TC of typically ± 0.2 ppm/°C (a change of only 2×10^{-7} parts per degree Celsius) and a long-term drift of 8 ppm/1000 hours. The circuitry is stabilized by an on-chip heater holding the temperature at approximately 135°C.

The TL431 device* is an inexpensive "programmable" band-gap reference that can be adjusted by a voltage-divider network to any value between 2.5 V and 36 V. The circuit is in reality a single-IC shunt regulator whose circuit concept is very similar to that of Fig. 5.27. The TL431 is not an extremely precise reference, since its maximum TC is 100 ppm/°C, for a 0 to 70 °C temperature change.

For actual use in a circuit other than a voltage regulator, the precision reference must usually be removed from input dc line-voltage changes, and a current buffer added to provide current to the load, particularly if the load requirement is greater than a few milliamperes. For example, in the circuit of the

---

* We utilized the TL431 earlier to bias an output driver stage using complementary MOSFETs; refer back to Problem 2.35, with Fig. P2.35.

LM317 [Fig. 5.28(a)], the band-gap reference is driven by a 50 μA current source (I); hence any change in V_I will have little effect on I. Further, the only current drawn from V_{REF} is the input bias current of the op amp A_1.

Two general precision-reference circuits are shown in Fig. 5.29. In Fig. 5.29(a) the op amp provides a buffer for the reference, and also increases the output voltage to +5 V. Unfortunately, the ripple rejection and line regulation are determined by

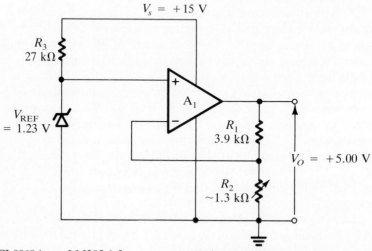

V_{REF} = ICL8069A, or LM385-1.2
$r_z \approx 1\ \Omega$

A_1 is a precision op amp.
R_1, R_2 are precision WW or MF resistors.

(a)

Z_1 = 1N827A (V_Z = 6.2 V)

(b)

Figure 5.29 Precision reference applications. (a) A simple +5 V buffered reference. (b) A circuit suitable for an A/D converter reference.

the dynamic impedance of V_{REF}, which is $1\,\Omega$. For a power-supply change of ΔV_S the output change in the 5 V reference will thus be

$$\Delta V_O = \left(\frac{1\,\Omega}{27\,k\Omega}\right)\left(\frac{5\,V}{1.23\,V}\right)\Delta V_S = (1.5 \times 10^{-4})\Delta V_S$$

or the rejection ratio will be 76 dB. The circuit of Fig. 5.29(b) uses a standard voltage-regulator diode unit, the IN827A, with $V_Z = 6.2\,V$, $r_Z = 10\,\Omega$, with a TC = 10 ppm/°C, *if I_Z is held constant at 7.5 mA*. In this circuit both positive and negative feedback are used (1) to provide a fixed 10.00 V output reference, and (2) to hold the Zener-diode current constant at the required value of 7.5 mA. The equation for the output voltage is

$$V_O = V_Z\left[1 + \frac{R_1}{R_2}\right] \tag{5.51}$$

while the current I_Z is

$$I_Z = \frac{V_O - V_Z}{R_F} \tag{5.52}$$

It is important in both circuits of Fig. 5.29 that the op amp is biased between the positive power supply and ground, so that the references could not forward bias at a value of 0.7 V (alternatively, if a diode is added between the output of the op amp and the rest of the feedback circuit, then the standard ± 15 V supply can be used).

Since the reference Z_1 in Fig. 5.29(b) is not directly connected to the power supply, the line regulation of the circuit is equal to the PSRR of the op amp, which is much larger than that of Fig. 5.29(a).

5.7.2 DC Current Regulators and References

With the use of an input control voltage v_I one can utilize op amps to form a current source, or a current sink.* The simplest connections for a current sink with a single op amp are illustrated in Fig. 5.30(a) and (b). An FET Q_1 is used with a bipolar transistor Q_2 to ensure that all of the sink current flows through the current-setting resistor R_1. For sink currents less than I_{DSS} of the FET the bipolar transistor Q_2 can be eliminated. If a constant dc current is required, than v_I could be replaced by a precision-reference or Zener diode.

For the output current to remain constant with changes in the load it is important that output impedance ("looking-back" impedance) of the current source be $\gg$ load impedance. In the circuit of Fig. 5.30(a) the impedance seen looking back into the current sink is

$$R_{LB} \approx R_O\left[1 + A_{OL}\left(\frac{R_1}{R_1 + \dfrac{r_{ds}}{1 + h_{FE}}}\right)\right] \tag{5.53}$$

---

* A current *source* supplies current to a load, while a current *sink* acts as a sink for the load current, i.e., the current flows from the load into the current sink.

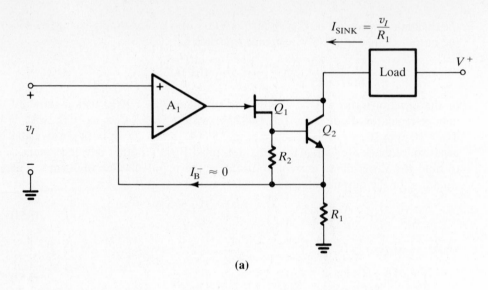

(a)

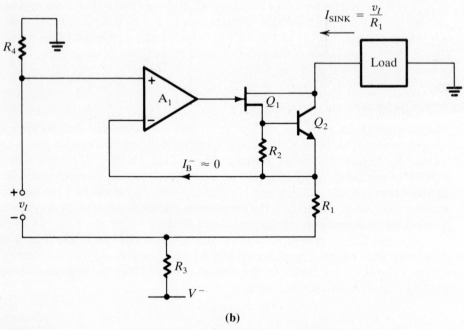

(b)

Figure 5.30 Two current sinks: (a) floating load; (b) grounded load.

where R_O is the open-loop looking-back resistance, which is approximately equal to $R_1 + r_{ds}/h_{FE}$, A_{OL} is the open-loop gain of the op amp, r_{ds} is the dynamic drain-to-source resistance of the FET, and h_{FE} is the current gain of the Q_2 bipolar transistor.

■ **Exercise 5.8**

Using the circuit of Fig. 5.30(b) design a current sink that will furnish a current of $-1\,\text{mA}$ to a 5 kΩ load. Assume v_1 is a precision band-gap reference ($v_I = 1.2\,\text{V}$). Use an LF351 op amp. The power supply available is $\pm 15\,\text{V}$.

By reversing the direction of current to the load, the circuits of Fig. 5.30 become current sources, as indicated in Fig. 5.31(a) and (b). Also shown in Fig. 5.31(c) is a simple current source obtained using a positive three-terminal IC voltage regulator, such as the LM317. Use is made of the fixed band-gap potential ($\sim 1.2\,\text{V}$) between the output and regulation terminals, so that the choice of resistor R produces a constant-output source current of value $I_{\text{source}} = 1.2V/R$. Similarly, a current sink of the same value is obtained with a negative regulator, such as the LM337 device.

All of the previous regulated-current circuits are purely unidirectional, current may only flow in one direction, either sinking or sourcing, but not both. However, a bilateral current source can be obtained using the same basic circuit we analyzed in Chapter 1 for a noninverting integrator (see Fig. 1.6), if the capacitor is removed and replaced by a load impedance. In fact, the application of this circuit as a current regulator is often referred to as either the Howland circuit, or the Howland current pump, named after Brad Howland of MIT who evidently originated the circuit concept in 1959 [Refs. 5.33–5.35].

The original Howland circuit is indicted in Fig. 5.32(a) and two improved versions in Fig. 5.32(b) and (c). The circuits use both positive and negative feedback to set the load current and increase the output impedance seen by the load. It is a good idea to use some small (10–100 pF) feedback capacitance C_F to stabilize the loop, although load capacitance to ground will also maintain stability. The basic circuit requires that $R_2/R_1 = R_4/R_3$, thus both positive and negative feedback would be equal if the load (and C_F) were removed. The load impedance forces negative feedback to be larger than positive feedback, which ensures stability in the absence of C_F. The operation of the circuit of Fig. 5.32(a) can best be analyzed by assuming that $V_1 = 0$ (R_1 is grounded) and only V_2 is present. Assuming an ideal op amp

$$\frac{V_2 - V_L}{R_2} + \frac{V_O - V_L}{R_4} = I_L \tag{5.54}$$

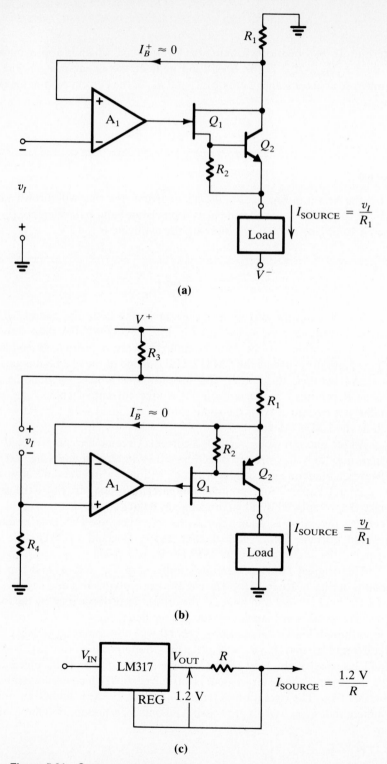

Figure 5.31 Some current sources.

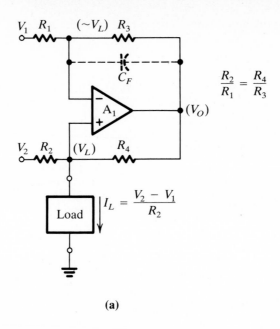

(a)

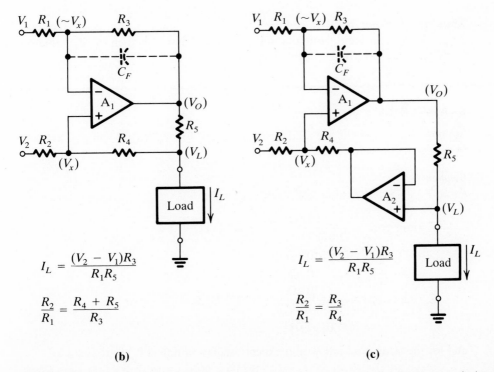

(b)   (c)

Figure 5.32   (a) The basic Howland bidirectional current pump; (b) and (c), improved circuits

and since the input error signal for A_1 approaches zero

$$\frac{V_L}{R_1} = \frac{V_O - V_L}{R_3} \qquad (5.55)$$

or $V_O = V_L(1 + R_3/R_1)$. Substituting, we obtain for the load current

$$I_L = \frac{V_2}{R_2} + \frac{V_L}{R_2}\left(\frac{R_2 R_3}{R_1 R_4} - 1\right) \qquad (5.56)$$

and if the condition $R_2/R_1 = R_4/R_3$ holds, Eq. (5.56) reduces to $I_L = V_2/R_2$. It can easily be shown that if $V_2 = 0$ and V_1 is applied, the load current would be $I_L = -V_1/R_2$. By superposition the total load current due to both V_2 and V_1 is

$$I_L = \frac{V_2 - V_1}{R_2} \qquad (5.57)$$

The most significant feature of the Howland circuit is the looking-back impedance seen by the load. If we short V_1 and V_2 to ground, replace the load by a test current source I_t and calculate the voltage v_t that appears at the noninverting terminal of A_1, the ratio is the looking-back impedance (or output impedance Z_O of the Howland circuit), which reduces to

$$Z_O \equiv \frac{v_t}{I_t} = \frac{R_2}{\left(\dfrac{R_2 R_3}{R_1 R_4} - 1\right)} \qquad (5.58)$$

Thus, the looking back impedance seen by the load is infinite if the ratio $R_2/R_1 = R_4/R_3$ is valid. Note that if the equality is not true, then the Z_O value will be finite, either positive or negative.

EXAMPLE 5.6

Suppose $\pm 1\%$ resistors are used for the circuit of Fig. 5.32(a), of value $10\,\text{k}\Omega$ each. What are the possible extremes of Z_O?

Solution
From Eq. (5.58), the value of Z_O can vary from

$$Z_O(\text{min pos.}) \approx \frac{10\,\text{k}\Omega}{\dfrac{(1.01)(1.01)}{(0.99)(0.99)} - 1} = +245\,\text{k}\Omega$$

to

$$Z_O(\text{max neg.}) \approx \frac{10\,\text{k}\Omega}{\dfrac{(0.99)(0.99)}{(1.01)(1.01)} - 1} = -255\,\text{k}\Omega$$

and for the latter case one would expect oscillation unless C_F were included.

Solving the equations of the basic Howland circuit for V_O with both V_1 and V_2 present, gives

$$V_O = (V_2 - V_1)\left(\frac{R_L}{R_2}\right)\left(1 + \frac{R_3}{R_1}\right) - V_1\left(\frac{R_4}{R_2}\right) \tag{5.59}$$

provided that $R_2/R_1 = R_4/R_3$.

The basic circuit is not very efficient in supplying power to a load. For example, suppose in Fig. 5.32(a) that V_1 is zero and V_2 is to supply $+ 1$ mA to a load of $R_L = 10$ kΩ. Thus, V_L must be $(1\text{ mA})(10\text{ k}\Omega) = + 10$ volts. If the value of V_2 is $+ 1$ V, then R_2 must be 1 kΩ, and the current through R_2 must be -9 mA, hence the current supplied from the output of the op amp through resistor R_4 must be 10 mA. Since the output linear-voltage range or **output voltage compliance** of most op amps is $\leq \pm 13$ V with a ± 15 V power supply, then the choice of resistor R_4 is limited to ≤ 3 V/10 mA, or 300 Ω. For this reason, it is typical to use a ratio of resistors R_4/R_2 (and therefore also R_3/R_1) equal to $\frac{1}{10}$. If we use $R_4 = 100$ Ω, the output of the op amp will then be $+ 11$ V. Now resistors R_1 and R_3 do not have to be equal to R_2 and R_4, but their ratio must match that of R_4/R_2 (equal to $\frac{1}{10}$). We could thus choose $R_1 = 100$ kΩ and $R_3 = 10$ kΩ, so that only an additional 0.1 mA would have to be supplied to R_1 and R_3. In this example, to obtain 1 mA into a load of 10 kΩ we require that 10.1 mA be furnished from the output of the op amp, for an efficiency of 1 mA/10.1 mA or only 10%.

The current efficiency can be improved by adding a resistor R_5 as shown in Fig. 5.32(b). For this circuit we require that $R_2/R_1 = (R_4 + R_5)/R_3$. The significant difference over the basic Howland circuit is that now R_5 can be much smaller than the other resistors. Solving for the load current in Fig. 5.32(b) we obtain

$$I_L = \frac{(V_2 - V_1)R_3}{R_1 R_5} \tag{5.60}$$

while the equation for the voltage at the V_x node is

$$V_x = (V_2 - V_1)\left[\frac{R_L\left(1 + \dfrac{R_4}{R_5}\right)}{R_2 + R_4}\right] + V_2\left(\frac{R_4}{R_2 + R_4}\right) \tag{5.61}$$

In the previous example, for an output current of 1 mA into a 10 kΩ load resistor, with $V_2 = 1$ V (and $V_1 = 0$ V), if we again choose a ratio $R_3/R_1 = \frac{1}{10}$ for good output-voltage compliance, from Eq. (5.60) we will need $R_5 = 100$ Ω. Since R_5 can now be very small with relation to R_4, let us choose $R_4 = 10$ kΩ; then R_2 must be 10(10.1 kΩ), or 101 kΩ.* The circuit, including component values and appropriate currents, is shown in Fig 5.33 where the op amp now only supplies a total output current of 1.17 mA for a 1 mA load current, for an efficiency of 86%.

---

* In reality, one would probably trim R_2 for the correct ratio $R_2/R_1 = (R_4 + R_5)/R_3$.

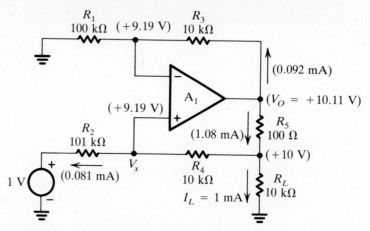

Figure 5.33 Example for the improved Howland circuit.

The circuit of Fig. 5.32(c) is similar in its operation to that of Fig. 5.32(b) except that the added buffer (A_2) increases the output impedance seen by the load.

SUMMARY

In this chapter we have examined several additional important types of linear circuits utilizing op amps. Today the instrumentation amplifier is certainly one of the most widely used circuits for very noisy environments, as is the isolation amplifier for situations where the input and output grounds must be isolated. Bridge circuits are a requirement not only for temperature measurement, but for strain measurement as well, as shown later in Chapter 8. The transconductance amplifier and Norton amplifiers are not widely used, but each type of circuit offers unique advantages as compared to standard op amp circuits, particularly for control-system applications, and also for automobile electronic systems having only one $+12$ V power supply. Since the chopper-stabilized op amp offers the lowest offset voltage and drift, several examples of circuit-design techniques and applications were presented.

The chapter closed with the standard series and shunt voltage-regulator circuits, and current regulators. Although voltage regulators using discrete devices are rapidly being supplanted by less costly monolithic IC regulators, several applications still require designs that use op amps and precision references. Since the availability of precision IC current references is limited, the discussion of the design of current sinks and sources using op amps is particularly important. As in previous chapters, the reader is encouraged to examine the chapter-end problems, which are designed to further cover the material by including several additional practical examples.

PROBLEMS

5.1 Show that the circuit of Fig. P5.1 can be considered a two-op-amp version of an instrumentation amplifier if $R_2/R_1 = R_4/R_3$ and that the gain is

$$\frac{V_O}{V_{in}} = -\left(1 + \frac{R_2}{R_1} + \frac{2R_2}{R_G}\right)$$

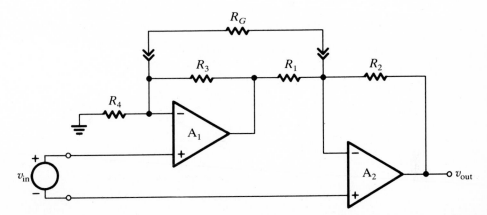

Figure P5.1

5.2 In the circuit of P5.1 if R_1-$R_4 = 10\,k\Omega$, and R_G is a series combination of $500\,\Omega$ and a $10\,k\Omega$ potentiometer, what is the range of gain available? For this range, what is the frequency bandwidth variation? Assume A_1 and A_2 are LF351 op amps.

5.3 In the circuit of Fig. 5.1, what would be a convenient way to adjust the CMRR? To adjust for dc offsets?

5.4 In the IA circuit of Fig. 5.1, what would be the effect on circuit performance by locating the gain-setting resistor R_G away from the rest of the circuit, with interconnection by shielded leads?

5.5 For the AD624 amplifier shown in Fig. 5.5, estimate the midband ENV for (a) a gain of 1 and (b) a gain of 100. Assume A_1-A_3 are noiseless, and each input transistor Q_1-Q_4 has $\beta = 300$ and $r'_b = 200$ ohms. Compare your answers with the typical data in Appendix C. Also, estimate the ENI for the IA and compare with that of the data sheet.

5.6 If the maximum input overload current permitted for the AD624 IA is $\pm 10\,mA$, what is the largest input overload voltage permitted, for a gain of 1000?

5.7 A circuit for increasing the gain of a differential amplifier is illustrated in Fig. P5.7(a). Show that the gain of this circuit reduces to [Ref. 5.4].

$$\frac{v_O}{v_{\text{diff}}} = -2\left(1 + \frac{1}{k}\right)\left(\frac{R_2}{R_1}\right)$$

if $R_1 = R'_1$ and $R_2 = R'_2$. Show that this same technique can be applied to an IA to increase the gain, as shown in Fig. P5.7(b). Find the gain of this circuit if the IA is configured as in Fig. 5.5, with R_{G2} connected to G_1.

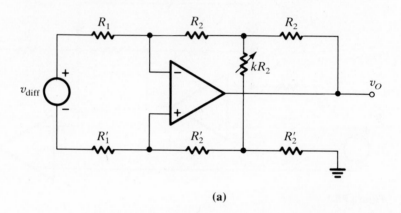

(a)

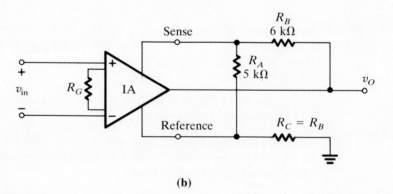

(b)

Figure P5.7

5.8 The circuit of Fig. P5.8 illustrated another technique for adjusting the gain in an instrumentation-amplifier circuit. For $R_1 = 1\,k\Omega$, $R = 10\,k\Omega$, and R_2 variable from $1\,k\Omega$ to $1\,M\Omega$, find the range of gain available. Are there any disadvantages to the use of this circuit, other than requiring an extra op amp (A_4)? What should be the characteristics of the A_4 op amp?

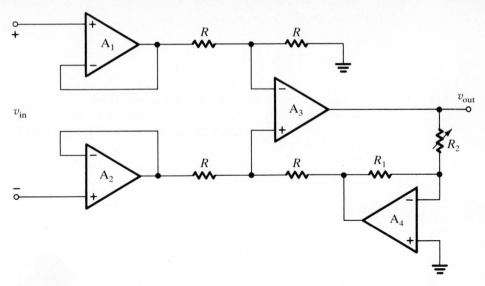

Figure P5.8

5.9 Why are most of the integrated-circuit IA circuits constructed using bipolar transistors for the input differential devices rather than FETs? A discrete version of an instrumentation amplifier using matched monolithic JFET transistors J_1 and J_2 is shown in Fig. P5.9.

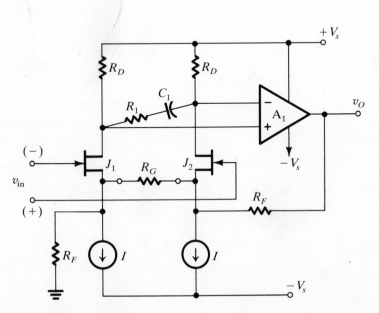

Figure P5.9

(a) Show that the gain of this circuit is

$$A = \left(1 + \frac{2R_F}{R_G}\right)$$

(b) If op amp A_1 is an OP-27E device, the JFETs have $I = 2\,\text{mA}$, with $g_m = 3\,\text{mmho}$, $C_{gs} = 4\,\text{pF}$, $C_{gd} = 1\,\text{pF}$, and the R_D resistors are chosen to satisfy the minimum input-voltage specification (V_{ICMR}) for the op amp, find values of R_1 and C_1 to provide frequency stability for gains from 1 to 1000. Assume resistor R_F is $100\,\text{k}\Omega$. You may wish to verify your results using SPICE (see Appendix D).

5.10 Instrumentation amplifiers are useful as the initial input stage of a phono-graph-cartridge preamplifier, as illustrated by the circuit of Fig. P5.10 [For additional details see Ref. 5.6]. The signal is obtained from a moving-magnet phono pickup coil, and thus represents a balanced differential input signal. For optimum damping the cartridge should see a load impedance of $47\,\text{k}\Omega$ ($R_1 + R_2$) in parallel with approximately 150 pF (C_1 and C_2 in series). Phonograph records require an RIAA (Record Industry Association of America) equalization network described by (approximately) a 1 kHz gain of 40 dB, poles at 50 Hz and 2 kHz and a zero at 500 Hz. The large CMRR of the AD624 can result in hum (60 Hz interference is referred to as "hum" in audio literature) rejection approaching 100 dB for the circuit. (a) Verify that the circuit of Fig. P5.10 indeed has the required gain and frequency response. (b)

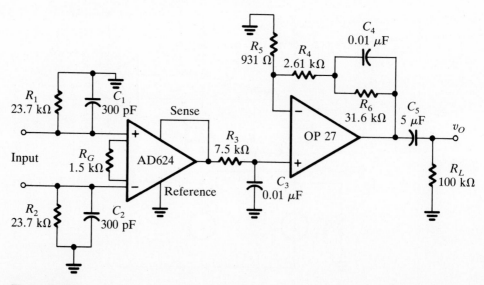

Figure P5.10

The high-frequency CMRR can be improved by making one of the input capacitors (C_1 or C_2) variable. Comment on the principle involved.

5.11 The circuit of Fig. P5.11 illustrates a different concept in obtaining a transfer of signal between a floating differential input and a ground-referred single-ended output. The circuit is basically an instrumentation amplifier using a monolithic, charge-balanced, dual switched-capacitor IC, the LTC1043 manufactured by Linear Technology Corporation [see this and other applications of switched capacitors in Ref. 5.7]. Explain the principles of operation for the circuit. What should be the requirements for op amp A_1? The author of the circuit indicates that CMRR values of 120 dB could be achievable to 10 kHz. What is the gain equation for the circuit? What fundamental limitations determine the bandwidth of the circuit?

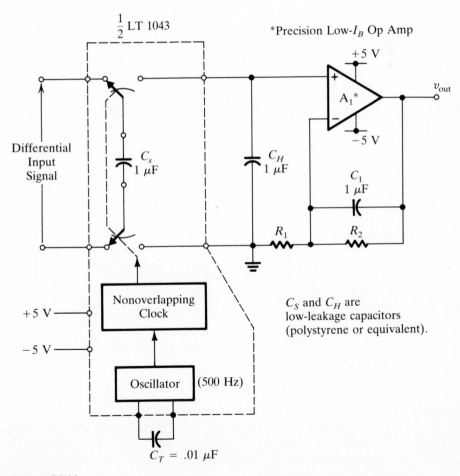

Figure P5.11

5.12 The circuit of Example 5.2 is revised to operate in the bipolar-input mode by using an internal reference-current source of $12\,\mu A$ [a reference source of $+12\,\mu A$ drives *each* inverting input of A_1 and A_2 of Fig. 5.8(a)]. If the allowable input-current range for linear operation is $-10\,\mu A$ to $+10\,\mu A$, what is the range of signal v_s? (b) Under bipolar operation the rms current noise is now $7\,pA/\sqrt{Hz}$ for $f > 100\,Hz$, compared to $0.7\,pA/\sqrt{Hz}$ with unipolar operation. Explain the difference.

5.13 In the circuit of Fig. 5.2 the $-3\,dB$ frequency bandwidth is to be reduced to $100\,Hz$. Show two ways to accomplish this.

5.14 Show a circuit that would provide an output voltage equal to the sum of three input currents, or

$$V_O = R_F[I_{in1} + I_{in2} + I_{in3}]$$

using three optical-coupled isolators, each similar to that of Fig. 5.7.

5.15 Explain the operation of the optical-coupled isolator circuit of Fig. P5.15. Show that the gain of the circuit is equal to R_F/R_1. What would determine the gain accuracy of the circuit?

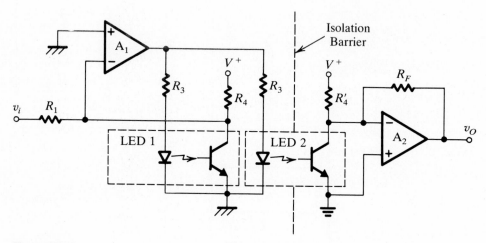

Figure P5.15

5.16 Show that the circuit of Fig. P5.16 is that of an optically coupled isolation multiplier, with an output equal to $K(v_1 \cdot v_2)$. If K is to be equal to $1/10$, what should be the value of R_F? Assume that the photoconductive cells R_x and R_y are matched, and the op amps are ideal.

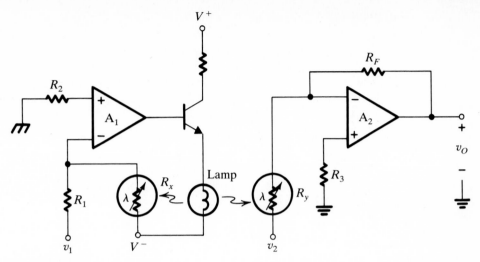

Figure P5.16

5.17 It is desired to monitor the efficiency of a utility company's power transformer by obtaining the primary-to-secondary transfer ratio. The typical voltages and currents anticipated are 2.2 kV and 1–10 amps on the primary. The transformer has a turns ratio of 10:1. Indicate how the circuit monitoring could be achieved using four isolation amplifiers. Assume the maximum linear output of each amplifier is 10 V.

5.18 One of the most demanding applications involving isolation amplifiers is an ECG (electrocardiogram) monitor for a patient. The patient must be protected from leakage currents and fault currents in excess of $10 \, \mu A$, rms. Further, the amplifier must not be damaged by a 5 kV defibrillator pulse. Use the basic transformer-coupled isolator circuit of Fig. 5.9 with the instrumentation-amplifier circuit of Fig. 5.3(a) to obtain an input IA monitor circuit. The guard amplifier [A_4 in Fig. 5.3(a)] is used to drive a right-leg electrode of the patient, thereby reducing pickup and providing a return path for the body's displacement current [Ref. 5.10].

5.19 Derive the output-voltage relation of Eq. (5.14) by obtaining the Thevénin equivalent circuit of the bridge amplifier of Fig. 5.11(a), seen looking back into the bridge from the input terminals of the op amp.

5.20 Derive Eq. (5.15) in the text for the circuit of Fig. 5.11(b). What are the advantages and disadvantages of this circuit as compared to that of Fig. 5.11(a).

5.21 Show that the output dc-offset voltage for the circuit of Fig. 5.11(a) is

$$V_{\text{out}} = \pm V_{OS}\left(1 + \frac{2R_F}{R}\right) \pm I_{OS}R_F$$

while the output dc offset for the circuit of Fig. 5.11(b) is

$$V_{\text{out}} = \pm V_{OS}\left(1 + \frac{R_F}{R_1}\right) + I_B\left[R_F + R\left(1 + \frac{R_F}{R_1}\right)\right]$$

5.22 Verify each of the terms in the error budget analysis of Table 5.1. Explain why terms like gain, initial offsets, etc., do not contribute to resolution. What is the small signal $f_{-3\,\text{dB}}$ for the circuit?

5.23 A two-op-amp bridge-amplifier circuit is shown in Fig. P5.23. Derive the expression for the output voltage in terms of δ and V_B, if $R_1/R_2 = R_3/R_4$. What advantages, and disadvantages, does this circuit have when compared to the single-op-amp circuit of Fig. 5.11(a), or 5.11(b)?

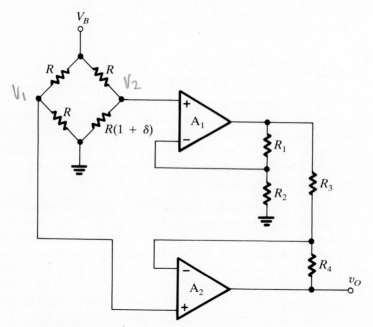

Figure P5.23

5.24 Derive the expression for the output voltage v_O in Fig. 5.14, including the dc-error terms V_{OS}, I_B and I_{OS} for both A_1 and the IA. Why might C_1 be required in the circuit?

5.25 A bridge circuit [Ref. 5.14] similar to that of Fig. 5.14, but using two op amps (instead of one op amp and one IA) is shown in Fig. P5.25. Show that the output voltage for this circuit is

$$v_O = \delta\left(\frac{V_B R_F}{R}\right)$$

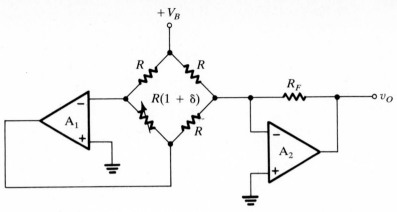

Figure P5.25

5.26 Discuss the factors that control the choice of the filter value for R_3C_2, R_7C_3 and R_2C_1 in the chopper-stabilized amplifier of Fig. 5.15. Explain the required polarity of the output signal at v_D. What should be the relation of the time constant $\tau = R_3C_2$ to the chopping frequency?

5.27 For the chopper-stabilized amplifier of Fig. 5.15, show that the input resistance of the chopper circuit (v_A/i_C) is equal to $2R_4$ if $R_5 \gg R_4 \gg R_3$ and the modulator is a square-wave signal.

5.28 A frequency response block diagram for the chopper-stabilized amplifier is indicated in Fig. P5.28. Find the relations for τ_A, τ_B and A_{oc}, using the circuit of Fig. 5.15.

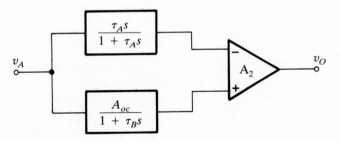

Figure P5.28

5.29 In the analysis of dc errors for the monolithic chopper circuit of Fig. 5.16, no mention was made regarding dc offsets due to I_B or I_{os}. Why are these terms not important?

5.30 For the OTA circuit of Fig. 5.17(b), show that the output voltage is really related to v_i by an expression

$$v_O = -R_L I_O = -\left[\frac{R_L I_{ABC} v_i}{2\left(\dfrac{kT}{q}\right)}\right](1 - a_1 v_i^2 + a_2 v_i^4 + \cdots)$$

Find the coefficients a_1 and a_2 [Hint: Express I_{C1} as αI_{ABC} and I_{C2} as $(1 - \alpha) I_{ABC}$, assuming h_{FE} is large]. Plot v_O vs v_i over a range $(-100\,\text{mV} \le v_i \le +100\,\text{mV})$, for $I_{ABC} = 650\,\mu\text{A}$, for $R_L = 1\,\text{k}\Omega$. Over what range of v_i would you consider the output linear?

5.31 Repeat the plot of P5.30 for the circuit of Fig. 5.18(a), with $I_{ABC} = 650\,\mu\text{A}$, $I_D = 200\,\mu\text{A}$, $R_L = 1\,\text{k}\Omega$, $R = 5.1\,\text{k}\Omega$ and $-1\,\text{V} \le v_i \le 1\,\text{V}$. Compare the two plots with respect to linearity and gain.

5.32 Using analysis similar to that for the circuit of Fig. 5.18(a), derive the equation for I_O for the linearizing circuit of Fig. 5.18(b).

5.33 Show that a four-quadrant multiplier can be obtained from the circuit of Fig. 5.19(c), by using a feedback resistor R_F between v_x and v_O. What value should R_F be to obtain

$$v_O = -KR_L(v_x \cdot v_y)$$

where K is a constant? What is the value of K? [Hint: Observe from Eq. (5.34) that one term must be cancelled to obtain $v_x \cdot v_y$]. Show how the basic circuit could be improved by using a pnp current source for I_{ABC}.

5.34 Derive Eq. (5.35) using the circuit of Fig. 5.19(d). If $R_1 = 100\,\Omega$, $R_F = 10\,\text{k}\Omega$, $R_2 = 5.1\,\text{k}\Omega$, $R = 20\,\text{k}\Omega$, $h_{FE1} = h_{FE2} = 100$, $C = 1000\,\text{pF}$ and the output resistance of the OTA is infinite, what is the range of filter frequencies available as V_c varies from $+1\,\text{V}$ to $+10\,\text{V}$?

5.35 In the circuit of Fig. 5.21(a), if the $+15\,\text{V}$ power supply has a ripple of $100\,\text{mV}$ (p-p), 120 Hz, what is the ac output p-p voltage at the $10\,\text{k}\Omega$ load? What would the output p-p ripple be for the circuit of Fig. 5.22?

5.36 Compare the Norton amplifier biasing circuits of Figs. 5.21, 5.23(a), and 5.23(b) regarding noise. Assume the input transistor has $h_{FE} = 150$ and $r_b' = 300\,\Omega$. Ignore the noise of the other transistors. Calculate the midband value of total equivalent input noise (in $\text{nV}/\sqrt{\text{Hz}}$) in series with v_i.

5.37 Using the basic temperature sensitivity of the NV_{BE} bias circuit of Fig. 5.23(a), eliminate R_1, and choose R_2 and R_F to produce an output voltage change of $10\,\text{mV}/^\circ\text{C}$, thereby obtaining a convenient temperature-sensing circuit.

5.38 A true op amp, with a low offset voltage and current can be obtained with a dual pnp input and the Norton amplifier, as indicated in Fig. P5.38. If $R_{cs} = 750\,\text{k}\Omega$, and the inputs of Q_1 and Q_2 are at ground, what would be the values of A_{OL}, GB and SR for the resultant circuit? Choose C_F for stable unity-gain operation. Use the LM3900 data in Exercise 5.6.

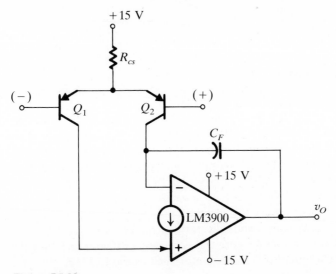

Figure P5.38

5.39 In the circuit of Fig. 5.25 the V_{REF} value is obtained with a temperature-compensated Zener diode, an IN827 unit, whose characteristics are $V_Z = 6.2\,\text{V}$ at $I_Z = 7.5\,\text{mA}$, with $r_Z = 10\,\Omega$ and TC = 10 ppm/°C. (a) Assuming the same values as Example 5.4 for the rest of the circuit, find the ripple rejection, line rejection, and load rejection. (b) Show a circuit that would permit a "starting current" for V_{REF} to be obtained from V_I and then have V_o provide the required 7.5 mA once the circuit reaches a steady-state output voltage. This would remove the degradation of ripple rejection from the original circuit.

5.40 In Fig. 5.26(b), show that the power dissipation in Q_1 is essentially constant along the foldback line from I_{FB} to I_{SC} provided that Eq. (5.46) holds.

5.41 Derive Equations (5.49) and (5.50). Combine with Eq. (5.46) to obtain a design criteria involving only I_{FB}. What value should R_{CL}, R_3 and R_4 be, using parameters from Example 5.5?

5.42 A simple dual power supply can be obtained from a single input voltage as shown in Fig. P5.42. Explain the principle of operation. What restrictions are placed on the op amp?

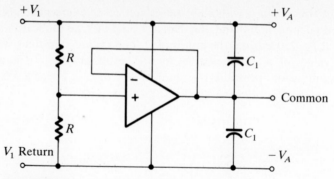

Figure P5.42

5.43 Design a linear series voltage regulator that can supply an output voltage that is adjustable from 0 V to +30 V, can supply 0.5 A to a load, and can sustain a short-circuit at the output. You have available an input transformer of rating 115 V ac (60 Hz) primary and 28 V (rms) secondary, at 28 VA rating. You have available a 2200 μF capacitor for filtering the output of the rectifier, and a 220 μF capacitor for the load. Specify *all* devices in your design using commerically available parts. Estimate your cost (for a lot of one) and compare with the cost and performance if your series regulator were replaced by a monolithic IC regulator such as the LM317.

5.44 A linear series voltage regulator with a much lower dropout voltage (and higher efficiency) than that of the standard circuit of Fig. 5.25, is indicated in Fig. P5.44, where the emitter-follower pass transistor is now replaced by a transistor connected as a common emitter. Using the rest of the circuit of Fig. 5.25 show the correct connection of all devices to achieve regulation. Are there any additional constraints on the type of op amp that must now be used? How does the frequency stability criterion for the two circuits compare? How would you incorporate short-circuit protection?

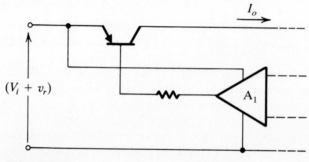

Figure P5.44

5.45 In the circuit of Fig. 5.27 and the problem of Exercise 5.7, if Q_1 were replaced by a pnp transistor having $h_{FE} = 50$, how would this affect the requirements for the op amp A_1?

5.46 Find the expression for the loop transmission $T(j\omega)$ for the basic series voltage regulator of Fig. 5.25 (Assume R_{sc} is present), and compare it with that for the shunt regulator of Fig. 5.27. Assume C_O is present in both circuits and V_I is a true voltage source (zero internal resistance).

5.47 An LM317 IC voltage regulator whose circuit is indicated in Fig. 5.28 is used to provide $+12$ V to a 24 Ω load resistance. If the wiring resistance is 0.1 Ω between the output terminal of the LM317 and the load, where should the R_1 resistor be connected, (a) at the output terminal of the IC, or (b) at the load terminal? Why?

5.48 A precision 10 V reference circuit, similar to that of Fig. 5.29(b), is shown in Fig. P5.48. Derive the equation for the output voltage V_O. Is this circuit in any way preferable to that of Fig. 5.29(b)? If the circuit of Fig. P5.48 is to be used as a reference for a 12-bit A/D converter that must operate over the temperature range from 0 to 70°C, with $V_s = 15$ V ($\pm 5\%$), and the resistors are wirewound with a TC of ± 10 ppm/°C, while the reference is a IN827A device, what is the accuracy permitted for an analog conversion?

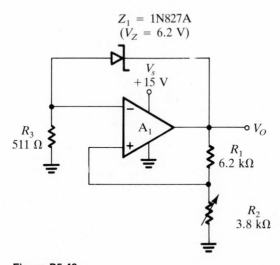

Figure P5.48

5.49 A simple adjustable output-voltage reference can be obtained using the LM10 integrated circuit, which contains an internal stable 200 mV reference, reference amplifier, and an op amp, all on the same monolithic chip [Ref. 5.32]. The pinouts for the 8-pin IC package are shown in Fig. P5.49(a). (1) In the circuit connection of Fig. P5.49(b), find the range of output adjustment for the

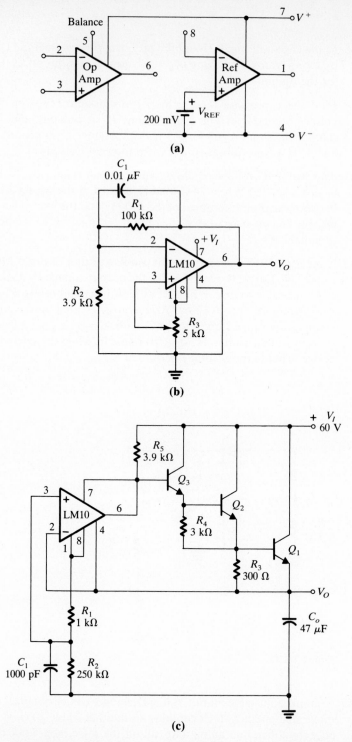

Figure P5.49 [Ref. 5.32] (a) The LM10 circuit. (b) An adjustable reference. (c) A voltage regulator.

reference circuit. (2) Find the output voltage of the series voltage regulator in Fig. P5.49(c). Note: The LM10 can operate with a mimimum total supply voltage $(V^+ - V^-)$ of 1.1V. Also, the common-mode linear input range includes V^- and the output can be shorted to V^+ and still remain linear.

5.50 A dual *tracking* voltage regulator can be formed using a LM317 three-terminal positive voltage regulator, and a discrete device negative regulator, as shown in Fig. P5.50. The output positive voltage (V_O^+) is used as a reference for the negative regulator. (a) What is the range of output voltages (V_O^+ and V_O^-) as the potentiometer R_2 is varied? (b) What is the main feature required of the op amp A_1? (c) If V_O^+ is shorted, what happens to V_O^-? Is V_O^- short-circuit protected against a short on its output?

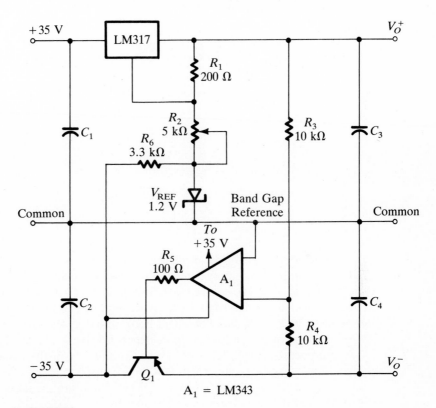

Figure P5.50

5.51 Derive Eq. (5.53) in the text. You may assume that $R_2 > (1 + h_{FE})r_e$ and that $r_{ds} \ll r_{ce}(1 + h_{FE})$.

5.52 Derive Eqs. (5.60) and (5.61) for the improved Howland circuit of Fig. 5.32(b). Assume an ideal op amp.

Chapter **6**

Active
RC Filters

RC filter theory is one of the most demanding, yet fascinating, practical applications of op amps, as is amply demonstrated by the number of texts and references devoted to the concept of active filters. In this chapter we will look at only a few of the most widely used types of RC active filters. The reader is encouraged to examine several of the many excellent books listed in Appendix A for other filter types and applications, as well as more details involving mathematical derivations. Our approach here will be to reduce the complexity of the equations to useful tables, graphs, and circuits, which can then be used in a "cookbook" fashion to achieve a particular design objective. When important, articles explaining the fundamentals of the derivations will be referenced.

The emphasis in this chapter is on resistor-capacitor (RC) filters, as opposed to resistor-inductor-capacitor (RLC) or inductor-capacitor (LC) types. Inductors are expensive, difficult to obtain in precision values, and nearly always change as a function of current and temperature. Further, an inductor of significant size has yet to be obtained in integrated-circuit (IC) form. By using a combination of resistors, capacitors, and op amps in linear feedback circuits, however, it is possible to obtain any reasonable frequency selectivity desired, at least for frequencies from sub-audio to the MHz region.

At the outset it is important to clarify some of the terms we will be using. Of course a **filter** is, in general, a frequency-selective network that allows a certain range of frequencies to be passed from input to output, while discriminating or attenuating other frequencies. The four most important types of filters are the **low pass (LP) filter**, the **highpass (HP) filter**, the **bandpass (BP) filter**, and the **band-rejection (BR) filter** (a BR filter is also called a **Notch filter**). Each of these filters is depicted graphically in Fig. 6.1.

The lowpass filter, indicated in Fig. 6.1(a), will pass frequencies from dc to a specified cutoff frequency ω_c and, ideally, provide no gain for (or stop) all frequencies beyond ω_c. In actuality there is a **transition band (TB)** between the **passband (PB)** and the **stopband (SB)**, defined by a width $TB = \omega_s - \omega_c$. Also

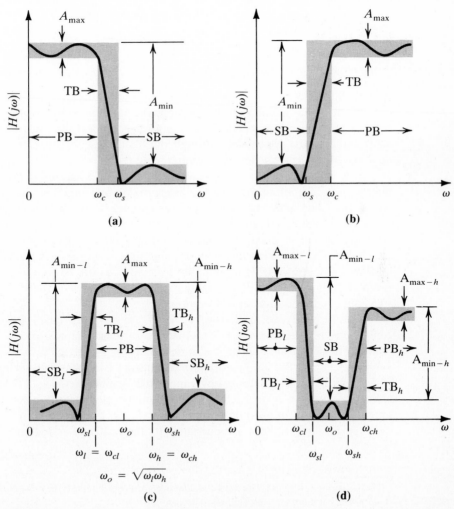

Figure 6.1 Basic filters: (a) lowpass; (b) highpass; (c) bandpass; (d) band rejection.

indicated in Fig. 6.1(a) is the fact that the gain function $|H(j\omega)|$ may not be absolutely constant over the range of frequencies from dc to ω_c but instead there may be some maximum variation, indicated as A_{max} (usually expressed in dB). Further, the SB attenuation is indicated as a gain loss of $\geq A_{min}$ (again, usually expressed in dB).

The highpass filter is the inverse of the LP filter, as shown in Fig. 6.1(b). Here, only frequencies *greater* than ω_c are passed, while frequencies from dc to ω_s are attenuated. The TB is now defined by $\omega_c - \omega_s$ and, as before, the passband may have an amplitude variation of A_{max}.

Figure 6.1(c) depicts a bandpass (BP) filter. The BP filter is centered at a frequency $\omega_0 = (\omega_l\omega_h)^{1/2}$ and the passband is now equal to $\omega_h - \omega_l$, usually taken as the -3 dB bandwidth of the filter. The stopbands are defined by frequencies such that $\omega_{sh} \leq \omega \leq \omega_{sl}$. The band-rejection filter, however, will pass all frequencies between dc and a cutoff frequency ω_{cl} as well as all frequencies greater than ω_{ch}, while attenuating frequencies in a stopband defined by $\omega_{sh} - \omega_{sl}$, as shown in Fig. 6.1(d).

6.1 APPROXIMATIONS TO FILTER RESPONSES

An *ideal* filter would have no deviation in amplitude in its passband ($A_{max} = 0$ dB), infinite amplitude attenuation in the stopband ($A_{min} = \infty$ dB), with a transition band of zero (for a lowpass filter $\omega_c = \omega_s$). Also, an ideal filter has a linear phase characteristic—the phase shift through the filter increases linearly as frequency increases. Actual filters can only approximate the ideal filter, choosing either an **amplitude approximation** or a **phase approximation** (also referred to as a **time-delay filter**). The most important amplitude-approximation functions are the Butterworth, the Chebyshev, and the Cauer (or elliptic), while the best known phase-approximation function uses Bessel functions, and is usually referred to as a linear-phase Thomson, or maximally flat time-delay function. Although the Thomson filter is inferior to others in terms of magnitude response, it nevertheless offers excellent pulse response with minimum overshoot, as will be seen later in Fig. 6.9. Another approximation filter offering good pulse response is the Parabolic filter, which can be found in several references.*

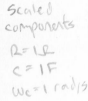

Nearly all active (and passive) filters are designed based on normalized components and frequencies. For example, resistors and capacitors are 1 ohm or 1 farad, while the cutoff frequency ω_c is designated as 1 rad/sec. To obtain a desired value of ω_c one multiplies the normalized frequency by a **frequency-scaling factor** k_f while multiplying all reactances by a **magnitude-scaling factor** k_m.† Since resistors are not a function of frequency (at least in the ideal sense) a resistor is only multiplied by the magnitude scaling factor k_m in the desired circuit. Since an inductor has a reactance proportional to the value of inductance it, too, is

---

* [See, for example, Ref. 6.4]. The parabolic filter offers less overshoot (for the same order n) than the Butterworth, but more than the Thomson filter.

† To be absolutely correct, one should really refer to k_f and k_m as the *de-normalizing* factors.

Table 6.1 FREQUENCY AND MAGNITUDE SCALING FOR NETWORK ELEMENTS

Normalized	Scaled (De-Normalized) Values
R (ohms)	$R' = k_m R$ (ohms)
C (farads)	$C' = C/k_m k_f$ (farads)
L (henries)	$L' = k_m L/k_f$ (henries)

K_f = frequency scaling factor

K_m = magnitude scaling factor

multiplied by k_m. However, since the reactance of a capacitor varies as $1/C$, a capacitor is transformed by *dividing* by k_m. The inductor and capacitor are transformed in frequency by dividing both the inductor and the capacitor by the frequency scaling factor k_f.* The effects of scaling are summarized in Table 6.1.

EXAMPLE 6.1

A network has a resistor, capacitor, and inductor of 1 Ω, 1 henry, and 1 farad. If scaling factors of $k_m = 1000$ and $k_f = 10^4$ are used, what are the new values of R, L_1 and C?

Solution
From Table 6.1 the new resistor is $R' = (10^3)\, 1\,\Omega = 1\,k\Omega$, while the inductor is now $L' = (10^3)(1/10^4)\, 1 = 100$ mH, and the capacitor is $C' = (1/10^3)(1/10^4)\, 1 = 0.1$ μF.

In addition to using normalized components with a cutoff frequency $\omega_c = 1$ rad/sec, it is also common practice to base all designs on that of a lowpass (LP) filter, and then transform the filter to a desired HP, BP, or BR if necessary. The LP to HP transform involves merely replacing the frequency variable s by a transformed variable, $s' = 1/s$,† which results in a passband from $\omega_c = 1$ to infinity, while the stopband is now from dc to $\omega_s < \omega_c$. Similarly, the transformation

$$s' = \left(\frac{s^2 + 1}{s}\right) = \left(s + \frac{1}{s}\right) \tag{6.1}$$

* For inductors, since $|Z_L| = \omega L$ must be constant both before and after frequency scaling; if ω increases by k_f, the L must correspondingly decrease by k_f. Similarly, since $|Z_c| = 1/\omega C$, then an increase of frequency by a factor k_f must require a multiplication of C by $1/k_f$. For a good discussion of scaling see Van Valkenburg [Ref. 6.2], Appendix A.
† Or, $s' = \omega_c/s$ if $\omega_c \neq 1.0$.

will transform the normalized lowpass passband (dc to $\omega_c = 1$) to a passband centered at $\omega_0 = 1$ with a bandwidth of unity. For a passband centered at a value of ω_0 other than unity and a bandwidth (the passband) defined by $BW = PB = \omega_h - \omega_l$ the transform variable is

$$s' = \frac{\omega_0}{BW}\left(\frac{s}{\omega_0} + \frac{\omega_0}{s}\right) \tag{6.2}$$

Wo = Centered at

BW = width

Correspondingly, a transformation from a lowpass to a band-reject (BR) filter is accomplished by defining

$$s' = BW\left(\frac{s}{s^2 + \omega_0^2}\right) \tag{6.3}$$

Associated with the transformation of the variable s is the transformation of any inductor and capacitor elements. For example, upon transformation to a highpass circuit an inductor of value L henries in a lowpass circuit must become

$$sL_{\text{lowpass}} \rightarrow \left(\frac{L}{s}\right)_{\text{highpass}} = \frac{1}{s\left(\frac{1}{L}\right)} = \frac{1}{sC_{\text{equiv}}}$$

and for the capacitor

$$\frac{1}{sC_{\text{lowpass}}} \rightarrow \left[\frac{1}{\left(\frac{1}{s}\right)C}\right]_{\text{highpass}} = s\left(\frac{1}{C}\right) = sL_{\text{equiv}}$$

Hence, for a lowpass to highpass transformation it is necessary to replace all capacitors by an inductor equal to $1/C$, and an inductor by a capacitor of value $1/L$. Similar relationships are obtained for lowpass to bandpass and lowpass to band-reject transformations. A summary of the various relationships is given in Table 6.2.

6.1.1 The Butterworth Approximation

If a normalized lowpass filter is approximated by a magnitude-squared function having as flat a characteristic as possible in the range from dc to ω_c, then a Taylor series approximation to the function must have as many derivatives as possible equal to zero near $\omega = 0$. Such a function was obtained by S. Butterworth in 1930[*] and is given by the magnitude-squared function

$$|H(j\omega)|^2 = \frac{N(\omega^2)}{D(\omega^2)} = \frac{H_0^2}{1 + \varepsilon^2\omega^{2n}} \tag{6.4}$$

---

[*] From S. Butterworth, "On the Theory of Filter Amplifiers," *Wireless Engineer*, Vol. 7, pp. 536–41 (1930).

Table 6.2 ELEMENT TRANSFORMATIONS FROM LOWPASS
TO OTHER FILTER TYPES*

Transformation	Replace s By	Network Element Changes

LP → HP $\dfrac{\omega_c}{s}$

$L \longrightarrow \dfrac{1}{\omega_c L}$

R stays the same

$C \longrightarrow \dfrac{1}{\omega_c C}$

LP → BP $\dfrac{\omega_0}{BW}\left(\dfrac{s}{\omega_0} + \dfrac{\omega_0}{s}\right)$

$L \longrightarrow \dfrac{L}{BW} \quad \dfrac{BW}{L\omega_o^2}$

$C \longrightarrow$ (parallel) $\dfrac{C}{BW}$; $\dfrac{BW}{\omega_o^2 C}$

LP → BR $BW\left(\dfrac{s}{s^2 + \omega_0^2}\right)$

$L \longrightarrow$ (parallel) $\dfrac{1}{L \times BW}$; $\dfrac{L \times BW}{\omega_o^2}$

$C \longrightarrow \dfrac{C \times BW}{\omega_o^2} \quad \dfrac{1}{C \times BW}$

* For normalized circuits ω_c and ω_0 are unity.

where $\varepsilon = 1$ satisfies the maximally flat condition and $N(\omega^2)$ and $D(\omega^2)$ represent the numerator and denominator terms, respectively. For $\varepsilon = 1$, note that at $\omega = \omega_c = 1$ the magnitude $|H(j\omega)|$ will be 3 dB below H_0 the value at dc. The pole locations of $H(s)$ can be determined from Eq. (6.4) by substituting $\omega = s/j$ and solving for the roots of the denominator (with $\varepsilon = 1$), or

$$D(s) \times D(-s) = 1 + \left(\frac{s}{j}\right)^{2n} = 1 + (-1)^n s^{2n} = 0 \qquad (6.5)$$

Let us take two cases. For $n = 1$ we have

$$1 - s^2 = (1 + s)(1 - s) = 0$$

and the roots are at $s = +1$ and -1 in the s plane. For $n = 2$, from Eq. (6.5) we have

$$1 + s^4 = 0, \qquad \text{or} \quad s_i = \sqrt[4]{-1}$$

or we can write in polar form

$$s_i = [1 \angle (180° + k360°)]^{1/4}$$

which reduces to root locations at

$$s_i = 1 \angle \frac{180° + k360°}{4}$$

or in rectangular coordinates at

$$s_i = -\frac{1}{\sqrt{2}} \pm j \frac{1}{\sqrt{2}}, \qquad +\frac{1}{\sqrt{2}} \pm j \frac{1}{\sqrt{2}}$$

Thus, for any n it is apparent that the roots (poles of the function) lie symmetrically on the unit circle in the s plane, as illustrated in Fig. 6.2(a). Since poles in the right half plane would lead to an unstable system, only the left-half poles are selected for synthesis. Thus, one obtains the class of functions known as **Butterworth polynomials** $B(s)$, which are for $n = 1$

$$B_1(s) = s + 1$$

and $n = 2$

$$B_2(s) = \left(s + \frac{1}{\sqrt{2}} + j \frac{1}{\sqrt{2}}\right)\left(s + \frac{1}{\sqrt{2}} - j \frac{1}{\sqrt{2}}\right)$$

or

$$B_2(s) = s^2 + \sqrt{2}s + 1$$

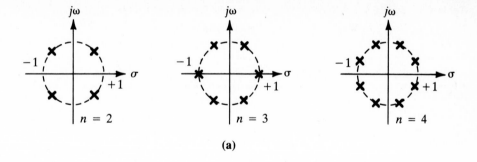

(a)

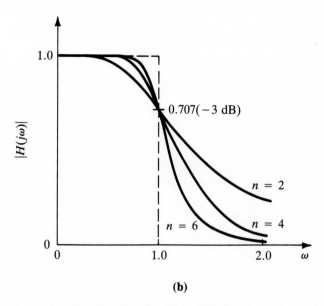

(b)

Figure 6.2 The Butterworth function. (a) pole locations in the complex plane. (b) Transfer function frequency response.

similarly, for $n = 3$ we have

$$B_3(s) = (s + 1)(s^2 + s + 1) = s^3 + 2s^2 + 2s + 1$$

and so on. A listing of the Butterworth polynomials and the quadratic factors (up to $n = 10$) is included in Table 6.3. Notice that for n odd, a pole must exist at $s = -1$. Also indicated in Fig. 6.2(b) is the frequency response of $|H(j\omega)|$ for several values of n. The response decreases past ω_c with a slope of $-n$ (20 dB/decade).

Let us look at one example illustrating the determination of the filter order n to meet a prescribed frequency response criteria.

Table 6.3 BUTTERWORTH POLYNOMIALS AND QUADRATIC FACTORS

(a) Polynomials

$$(s^n + a_{n-1}s^{n-1} + a_{n-2}s^{n-2} + \cdots + a_1s + 1)$$

n	a_1	a_2	a_3	a_4	a_5	a_6	a_7	a_8	a_9
1									
2	1.414								
3	2.000	2.000							
4	2.613	3.414	2.613						
5	3.236	5.236	5.236	3.236					
6	3.864	7.464	9.142	7.464	3.864				
7	4.494	10.098	14.592	14.592	10.098	4.494			
8	5.126	13.137	21.846	25.688	21.846	13.137	5.126		
9	5.759	16.582	31.163	41.986	41.986	31.163	16.582	5.759	
10	6.392	20.432	42.802	64.882	74.233	64.882	42.802	20.432	6.392

(b) Quadratic Factors

n	
1	$(s + 1)$
2	$(s^2 + 1.4142s + 1)$
3	$(s + 1)(s^2 + s + 1)$
4	$(s^2 + 0.7654s + 1)(s^2 + 1.8478s + 1)$
5	$(s + 1)(s^2 + 0.6180s + 1)(s^2 + 1.6180s + 1)$
6	$(s^2 + 0.5176s + 1)(s^2 + 1.4142s + 1)(s^2 + 1.9319)$
7	$(s + 1)(s^2 + 0.4450s + 1)(s^2 + 1.2470s + 1)(s^2 + 1.8019s + 1)$
8	$(s^2 + 0.3902s + 1)(s^2 + 1.1111s + 1)(s^2 + 1.6629s + 1)(s^2 + 1.9616s + 1)$
9	$(s + 1)(s^2 + 0.3473s + 1)(s^2 + s + 1)(s^2 + 1.5321s + 1)(s^2 + 1.8794s + 1)$
10	$(s^2 + 0.3129s + 1)(s^2 + 0.9080s + 1)(s^2 + 1.4142s + 1)(s^2 + 1.7820s + 1)(s^2 + 1.9754s + 1)$

EXAMPLE 6.2

It is desired to obtain a normalized Butterworth lowpass filter that is 3 dB below its value at dc at $\omega_c = 1$ rad/sec, and yet have an attenuation of ≥ 40 dB at $\omega_s = 2\omega_c$. Determine the filter order n required.

Solution

Since the magnitude response is -3 dB at $\omega = \omega_c$ the Butterworth characteristic for $\varepsilon = 1$ holds. Thus, from Eq. (6.4), at $\omega_s = 2$ rad/sec we must have

$$\left|\frac{H_0}{H(j2)}\right| \geq 40 \text{ dB} = 20 \log[1 + 2^{2n}]^{1/2}$$

or

$$[1 + 2^{2n}] \geq 10^4$$

or in general we must have, using the definitions from Fig. 6.1(a)

$$n \geq \frac{\log(10^{A_{min}/10} - 1)}{2 \log\left(\dfrac{\omega_s}{\omega_c}\right)} \tag{6.6}$$

With the values of this example $n \geq 6.64$. Since n must be an integer we take the next highest integral number, so we choose $n = 7$. Therefore, the actual attenuation (A_{min}) at $\omega_s = 2$ will be, from Eq. (6.4),

$$A_{min} = 10 \log\left[\frac{1}{(1 + 2^{14})}\right] = 42.1 \text{ dB}$$

6.1.2 The Chebyshev Approximation

The Chebyshev approximation achieves equal ripple in the passband by a magnitude-squared function

$$|H(j\omega)|^2 = \frac{H_0^2}{1 + \varepsilon^2 C_n^2(\omega)} \tag{6.7}$$

where the function $C_n(\omega)$ is defined by a polynomial*

$$C_n(\omega) \equiv \cos(n \cos^{-1}\omega) \qquad 0 \leq \omega \leq 1 \tag{6.8}$$

and

$$C_n(\omega) \equiv \cosh(n \cosh^{-1}\omega) \qquad \omega \geq 1 \tag{6.9}$$

Thus, the value of $C_n^2(\omega)$ is restricted to between 0 and 1 for $0 \leq \omega \leq \omega_c$ and must be > 1 for $\omega > \omega_c$. At $\omega = 1$, $C_n^2(1) = 1$, so the maximum deviation of the magnitude in the passband is defined by

$$A_{max}(\text{dB}) = 20 \log_{10}\left[\frac{1}{(1 + \varepsilon^2)^{1/2}}\right] \tag{6.10}$$

The pole locations are obtained, as per the Butterworth filter, by setting the denominator of Eq. (6.7) equal to zero, and solving for the roots, which requires that

$$C_n\left(\frac{s}{j}\right) = 0 \pm j\left(\frac{1}{\varepsilon}\right)$$

or from Eq. (6.8), for $\omega > 1$,

$$\cos\left[n \cos^{-1}\left(\frac{s}{j}\right)\right] = \pm j\left(\frac{1}{\varepsilon}\right) \tag{6.11}$$

---

* Chebyshev (also written as Tschebyscheff or Tchebysheff) polynomials evidently originated with a Russian mathematician, P. L. Chebyshev, in 1899.

The solution of Eq. (6.11) involves manipulations using trigonometric identities, leading to root locations s_k defined by [see particularly Refs. 6.1 and 6.2]

$$s_k = \sigma_k + j\omega_k$$

where (for $k = 1, 2, 3, \ldots, n$)

$$\sigma_k = \pm \sinh a \, \sin\left(\frac{2k + 1}{2n}\right)\pi \qquad (6.12a)$$

$$\omega_k = \cosh a \, \cos\left(\frac{2k + 1}{2n}\right)\pi \qquad (6.12b)$$

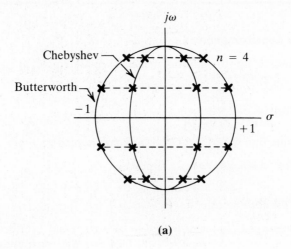

(a)

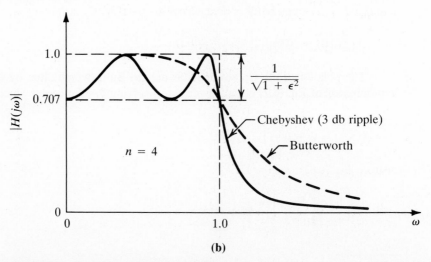

(b)

Figure 6.3 The Chebyshev function. (a) Pole locations for $n = 4$. (b) Magnitude response for $\varepsilon = 1$.

and

$$a \equiv \frac{1}{n} \sinh^{-1}\left(\frac{1}{\varepsilon}\right) \tag{6.12c}$$

The root locations for the Chebyshev function are along an ellipse, since Eq. (6.12) can be restated to give

$$\left(\frac{\sigma_k}{\sinh a}\right)^2 + \left(\frac{\omega_k}{\cosh a}\right)^2 = 1$$

which is the equation for an ellipse having a major semiaxis of $\cosh a$ and a minor semiaxis of $\sinh a$ with focal points at $\pm j\,1$. Shown in Fig. 6.3(a) are pole locations for both Chebyshev and Butterworth functions for the case $n = 4$. Although the Chebyshev function has ripple in the passband, while the Butterworth does not, still there is a much greater slope in the transition band for the Chebyshev.

EXAMPLE 6.3

Repeat Example 6.2 using a Chebyshev approximation for (a) 3 dB ripple in the passband, and (b) 0.5 dB ripple.

Solution

For the case of 3 dB ripple Eq. (6.10) requires a value $\varepsilon = 1$. For an attenuation of ≥ 40 dB at $\omega_s = 2\omega_c = 2$, Eq. (6.7) requires

$$\left|\frac{H_0}{H(j2)}\right| \geq 40 \text{ dB} = 20 \log[1 + C_n^2(2)]^{1/2}$$

Substituting Eq. (6.9) gives

$$[1 + \cosh^2(n \cosh^{-1} 2)]^{1/2} \geq 100$$

which is solved to yield

$$n \geq \frac{\cosh^{-1}(10^4 - 1)^{1/2}}{\cosh^{-1} 2} = 4.02$$

Thus, we could use $n \approx 4$, with an actual attenuation at $\omega_s = 2$ of

$$\left|\frac{H(j2)}{H_0}\right| = 20 \log_{10}[1 + C_4^2(2)]^{1/2} = 39.7 \text{ dB}$$

Note that the complexity of the filter has been considerably reduced, since $n = 4$ for the Chebyshev, whereas the requirement for the Butterworth was $n = 7$. However, if we require a ripple reduction within the passband to 0.5 dB, then from Eq. (6.10) we have

$$1 + \varepsilon^2 = 10^{0.05}$$

or $\varepsilon = 0.3493$. From Eq. (6.7), at $\omega_s = 2$

$$\left| \frac{H_0}{H(j2)} \right| \geq 40 \text{ dB} = 20 \log[1 + (0.3493)^2 C_n^2(2)]^{1/2}$$

which now yields

$$n \geq \frac{\cosh^{-1}[(10^4 - 1)/(0.3493)^2]^{1/2}}{\cosh^{-1}2} = 4.82$$

and therefore a choice of $n = 5$ must be made, with a resulting actual attenuation of 42 dB at $\omega_s = 2$ rad/sec.

We can calculate the pole locations using Eq. (6.12). For part (a), with 3 dB ripple and $n = 4$, the term a is equal to 0.2203, thus the $\sigma_k + j\omega_k$ roots are

$$\sigma_k = \pm\sinh(0.2203)\sin\left(\frac{2k + 1}{8}\right)\pi = 0.2221 \sin\left(\frac{2k + 1}{8}\right)\pi$$

and

$$\omega_k = \cosh(0.2203)\cos\left(\frac{2k + 1}{8}\right)\pi = 1.024 \cos\left(\frac{2k + 1}{8}\right)\pi$$

or the left-half-plane poles are at

$$s_i = -0.2056 \pm j0.3919, \quad -0.0850 \pm j0.9463$$

Similarly, for $n = 5$ and 0.5 dB ripple ($\varepsilon = 0.3493$) we have $a = 0.3548$ and roots at

$$\sigma_k = \pm\sinh(0.3548)\sin\left(\frac{2k + 1}{10}\right)\pi$$

$$\omega_k = \cosh(0.3548)\cos\left(\frac{2k + 1}{10}\right)\pi$$

with left-half-plane poles now at

$$s_i = -0.3623 + j0, \quad -0.2931 \pm j0.6252, \quad -0.1120 \pm j1.012$$

The location of the poles of the Chebyshev function for various ripple factors is indicated in Table 6.4, up to $n = 10$. Also, it is much easier to determine the order of a filter, given A_{max} and A_{min}, by using a nomograph. In Fig. 6.4 is a nomograph for determining the order n of a Butterworth lowpass filter (illustrated on the Figure are the three steps required to solve for n, given the data of Example 6.2). Similarly, the nomograph of Fig. 6.5 determines n for a Chebyshev lowpass filter.

Table 6.4 POLE LOCATIONS FOR THE CHEBYSHEV FUNCTION

n	$A_{max} = 0.5$ dB σ	$\pm j\omega$	$A_{max} = 1$ dB σ	$\pm j\omega$	$A_{max} = 3$ dB σ	$\pm j\omega$
1	2.8628	0	1.9652	0	1.0024	0
2	0.7128	1.0040	0.5489	0.8951	0.3224	0.7772
3	0.3132	1.0219	0.2471	0.9660	0.1493	0.9038
	0.6265	0	0.4942	0	0.2986	0
4	0.1754	1.0163	0.1395	0.9834	0.0852	0.9465
	0.4233	0.4209	0.3369	0.4073	0.2056	0.3920
5	0.1120	1.0116	0.0895	0.9901	0.0549	0.9659
	0.2931	0.6252	0.2342	0.6119	0.1436	0.5970
	0.3623	0	0.2895	0	0.1775	0
6	0.0777	1.0085	0.0622	0.9934	0.0382	0.9764
	0.2121	0.7382	0.1699	0.7272	0.1044	0.7148
	0.2898	0.2702	0.2321	0.2662	0.1427	0.2616
7	0.0570	1.0064	0.0457	0.9953	0.0281	0.9827
	0.1597	0.8071	0.1281	0.7982	0.0789	0.7881
	0.2308	0.4479	0.1851	0.4429	0.1140	0.4373
	0.2562	0	0.2054	0	0.1265	0
8	0.0436	1.0050	0.0350	0.9965	0.0216	0.9868
	0.1242	0.8520	0.0997	0.5448	0.0614	0.8365
	0.1859	0.5693	0.1492	0.5664	0.0920	0.5590
	0.2193	0.1999	0.1760	0.1982	0.1055	0.1962
9	0.0345	1.0040	0.0277	0.9972	0.0171	0.9896
	0.0992	0.8829	0.0797	0.8769	0.0491	0.8702
	0.1520	0.6553	0.1221	0.6509	0.0753	0.6459
	0.1864	0.3487	0.1497	0.3463	0.0923	0.3437
	0.1984	0	0.1593	0	0.0983	0
10	0.0279	1.0033	0.0224	0.9978	0.0138	0.9915
	0.0810	0.9051	0.1013	0.1743	0.0401	0.8945
	0.1261	0.7183	0.0650	0.9001	0.0625	0.7099
	0.1589	0.4612	0.1277	0.4586	0.0788	0.4558
	0.1761	0.1589	0.1415	0.1580	0.0873	0.1570

The quadratic factors are given by $s^2 + 2\sigma s + (\sigma^2 + \omega^2)$

6.1.3 The Elliptic (Cauer) Approximation

The elliptic (or Cauer*) filter is somewhat similar to the Chebyshev lowpass filter in that there exists equal ripple in the passband; however, it differs in that there is also equal ripple in the stopband. The ripple in the stopband is achieved with the introduction of transmission zeroes in $H(s)$. The elliptic filter offers a slope past the

---

* W. Cauer, *Synthesis of Linear Communication Networks*, (New York: 1958) McGraw-Hill.

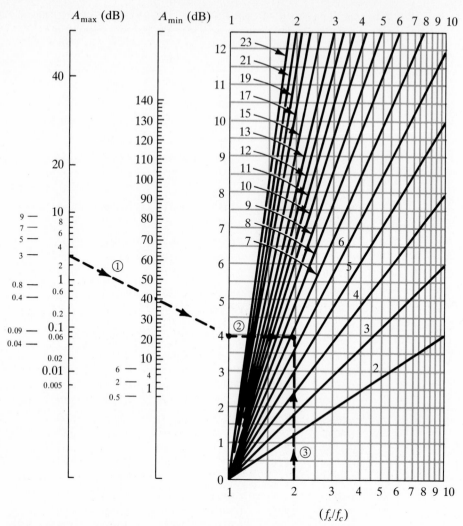

Figure 6.4 A nomograph for determining *n* for Butterworth lowpass filters.
Source: M Kawakami, ''Nomographs for Butterworth and Chebyshev Filters,'' *IEEE Trans. Circuit Theory,* vol. CT-10, pp. 288–89, June 1963.

cutoff frequency ω_c much steeper than that of Butterworth or Chebyshev filters. Stated another way, for prescribed values of ε and ω_s the elliptic filter will require the smallest value of *n*. However, one disadvantage of the filter is a very nonlinear phase response. Like Butterworth and Chebyshev filters, an elliptic filter can be specified by passband ripple (ε), stopband attenuation (ω_s/ω_c), and filter order (*n*). Since elliptic functions are quite complex, the determination of poles and zeroes is usually done by resorting to tables and nomographs, as well as using computer

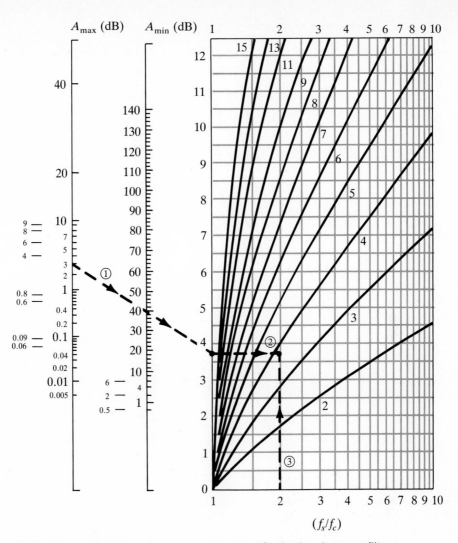

Figure 6.5 A nomograph for determining *n* for Chebyshev lowpass filters.
Source: M. Kawakami, *op. cit.*

programs.* For example, the nomograph of Fig. 6.6 would indicate that the design requirements of Examples 6.2 and 6.3 are essentially met by an elliptic filter with $n = 3$, whereas the Butterworth required $n = 7$, and the Chebyshev required $n = 4$.

---

* For example, see S. Darlington, "Simple Algorithms for Elliptic Filters and Generalizations Thereof," *IEEE Trans. Ckt. & Systems*, Vol. CAS-25, No. 12, pp. 975–80, (Dec. 1978) (A program for the HP 65 calculator); also, for the TI-59 calculator, see D. Báez-López and J. M. Ramirez-Cortés, "TI-59 Program Finds Elliptic Transfer Function For Low-Pass Filters," *Elect. Design*, Vol. 32, No. 26, pp. 234–40, (Dec. 27, 1984).

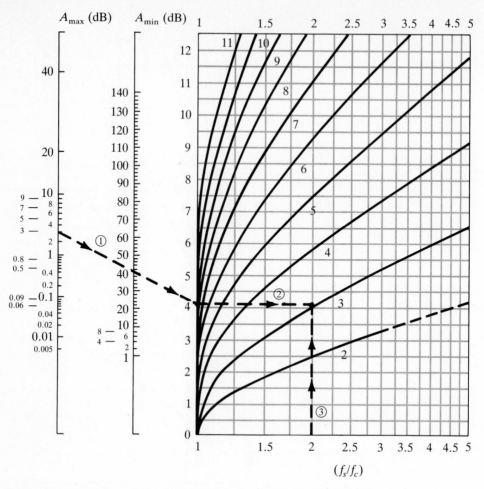

Figure 6.6 A nomograph for determining *n* for elliptic lowpass filters.
Source: M. Kawakami, *op. cit.* The curve for *n* = 2 was derived from other data.

The elliptic approximation is specified by the relationship

$$|H(j\omega)|^2 = \frac{H_0^2}{1 + \varepsilon^2 R_n^2(\omega)} \tag{6.13}$$

where the polynomial $R_n(\omega)$ is called the Chebyshev rational function. This function is defined in the *s*-domain (for *n* odd) by,

$$R_n(s) \atop {\scriptstyle [n \text{ odd}]} = \frac{K_n s(s^2 + \omega_{z1}^2) \cdots (s^2 + \omega_{z(n-1)/2}^2)}{(s^2 + \Omega_1^2) \cdots (s^2 + \Omega_{(n-1)/2}^2)} \tag{6.14}$$

and for *n* even by*

$$\underset{[n \text{ even}]}{R_n(s)} = \frac{K_n(s^2 + \omega_{z1}^2) \cdots (s^2 + \omega_{z/2}^2)}{(s^2 + \Omega_1^2) \cdots (s^2 + \Omega_{n/2}^2)} \tag{6.15}$$

It is also required that the coefficients and K_n be chosen for $R_n(\omega = 1) = 1$. Further, if Eqs. (6.14) and (6.15) are substituted into Eq. (6.13), the magnitude function for *n* odd (replacing ω by s/j), reduces to

$$H_a(s) = \frac{H_a \displaystyle\prod_{i=1}^{(n-1)/2} (s^2 + \Omega_i^2)}{a_0 + a_1 s + \cdots + a_{n-1} s^{n-1} + a_n s^n} \tag{6.16}$$

and we see that the order of the numerator is $(n-1)$ while the order of the denominator is *n*. For the case of *n* even we get

$$H_e(s) = \frac{H_e \displaystyle\prod_{i=1}^{n/2} (s^2 + \Omega_i^2)}{a_0 + a_1 s + \cdots + a_{n-1} s^{n-1} + a_n s^n} \tag{6.17}$$

and the order of *both* numerator and denominator are the same, equal to *n*.

Shown in Fig. 6.7 are the elliptic magnitude functions $|H(j\omega)|$ for representative cases of $n = 4$ and 5, as well as pole and zero locations. It is apparent that since $|H(j\omega)|$ must be equal to $(1/1 + \varepsilon^2)^{1/2} = A_{\max}$ at the normalized frequency $\omega_c = 1$, then $|H(0)| = 1$ for *n* odd, whereas $|H(0)| = A_{\max}$ if *n* is even.

Although a complete listing of tabulated values for elliptic filter parameters would be exhaustive, pole and zero locations for one example (a ripple of 0.5 dB $= A_{\max}$) and for filter order from $n = 2$ to 5 are shown in Table 6.5. Also, coefficient values for the second-order ($n = 2$) elliptic filter having ripple values from 0.01 dB to 3 dB are shown in Table 6.6. More extensive tables of elliptic filter parameters are available elsewhere.†

6.1.4 The Thomson Phase Approximation

The Thomson filter is the best known phase approximation that obtains a maximally flat time-delay response. This function is similar to the Butterworth and

---

* The form of Eqs. (6.15) or (6.17) is primarily used with active RC filters. There exist two other types of even-order cases that are more appropriate for passive RLC synthesis; one form is

$$H_1(s) = \frac{H_1 \displaystyle\prod_{i=2}^{n/2} (s^2 + \Omega_1^2)}{a_0 + a_1 s + \cdots + a_n s^n}$$

where the order of the numerator is now $(n-2)$ while that of the denominator is *n*. The second type is similar to that of $H_1(s)$ but with different coefficients so that $H_1(0)$ is the maximum passband value. The tables shown by Zverev [Ref. 6.16] are of the $H_1(s)$ type, rather than the $H_e(s)$ type of Eq. (6.17).

† For example, see Zhevrev [Ref. 6.16], and Christian and Eisenmann [Ref. 6.18].

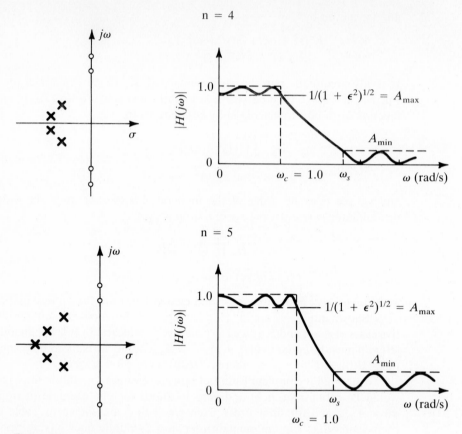

Figure 6.7   Examples of lowpass elliptic filters for $n = 4$ and $n = 5$.

Chebyshev approximations in that it is an all-pole (no zeroes) filter.* In the s-domain a transfer function producing time delay can be defined by

$$H(s) = \exp[-sT] \tag{6.18}$$

In the frequency domain the magnitude and phase is

$$|H(j\omega)| = 1 \angle -\omega T \tag{6.19}$$

and thus we have achieved the desired characteristic of an ideal filter—a linear phase relationship. Now, if the normalization $T = 1$ sec is imposed, then the exponential function in Eq. (6.18) becomes

$$H(s) = \frac{1}{\exp[s]} = \frac{1}{\cosh s + \sinh s} \tag{6.20}$$

---

* See W. E. Thomson, "Delay Networks Having Maximally Flat Frequency Characteristics," *Proc. IEEE* (Great Britain), Part 3, Vol. 96, pp. 487–90, (1949).

Table 6.5 ELLIPTIC MAGNITUDE FUNCTION $H(s)$ FOR THE CASE $A_{max} = 0.5$ dB*

$$H(s) = \frac{H(s^2 + \Omega_1^2)(s^2 + \Omega_2^2)\cdots}{a_0 + a_1 s + a_2 s^2 + \cdots}$$

n	A_{min}	Constant(H)	Numerator	Denominator
				$\omega_s/\omega_c = 1.5$
2	8.3	0.38540	$s^2 + 3.92705$	$s^2 + 1.03153s + 1.60319$
3	21.9	0.31410	$s^2 + 2.80601$	$(s^2 + 0.45286s + 1.14917)(s + 0.766952)$
4	36.3	0.015397	$(s^2 + 2.53555)(s^2 + 12.09931)$	$(s^2 + 0.25496s + 1.06044)(s^2 + 0.92001s + 0.47183)$
5	50.6	0.019197	$(s^2 + 2.42551)(s^2 + 5.43764)$	$(s^2 + 0.16346s + 1.03189)(s^2 + 0.57023s + 0.57601)(s + 0.42597)$
				$\omega_s/\omega_c = 2.0$
2	13.9	0.20133	$s^2 + 7.4641$	$s^2 + 1.24504s + 1.59179$
3	31.2	0.15424	$s^2 + 5.15321$	$(s^2 + 0.53787s + 1.14849)(s + 0.69212)$
4	48.6	0.0036987	$(s^2 + 4.59326)(s^2 + 24.22720)$	$(s^2 + 0.30116s + 1.06258)(s^2 + 0.88456s + 0.41032)$
5	66.1	0.0046205	$(s^2 + 4.36495)(s^2 + 10.56773)$	$(s^2 + 0.19255s + 1.03402)(s^2 + 0.58054s + 0.52500)(s + 0.392612)$
				$\omega_s/\omega_c = 3.0$
2	21.5	0.083974	$s^2 + 17.48528$	$s^2 + 1.35715s + 1.55532$
3	42.8	0.063211	$s^2 + 11.82781$	$(s^2 + 0.58942s + 1.14559)(s + 0.65263)$
4	64.1	0.00062046	$(s^2 + 10.4554)(s^2 + 58.471)$	$(s^2 + 0.32979s + 1.063281)(s^2 + 0.86258s + 0.37787)$
5	85.5	0.00077574	$(s^2 + 9.8955)(s^2 + 25.0769)$	$(s^2 + 0.21066s + 1.0351)(s^2 + 0.58441s + 0.496388)(s + 0.37452)$

*Adapted from M. E. Van Valkenburg, *Analog Filter Design*, p. 393, New York: (Holt, Rinehart and Winston, 1982).

Table 6.6 ELLIPTIC FUNCTION $H_e(s)$, FOR $n = 2^*$

$$H_e(s) = \frac{H_e^+(s^2 + \Omega_1^2)}{a_0 + a_1 s + s^2}$$

(^+H_e is equal to A_{min} at ω_s/ω_c)

ω_s/ω_c		A_{max} (dB)						
		3.10	2.50	1.94	1.41	0.92	0.45	0.09
2.0	a_1	0.597566	0.672335	0.761953	0.87093	1.03079	1.28475	1.70530
	a_0	0.748566	0.807532	0.889100	1.01055	1.21614	1.67671	3.39116
	Ω_1^2	7.46410	7.46393	7.46393	7.46393	7.46410	7.46394	7.46437
	H_e	0.070208	0.081143	0.095295	0.115081	0.146639	0.213409	0.449766
1.8		0.586497	0.658788	0.744765	0.852101	0.996903	1.22172	1.49664
		0.761473	0.821030	0.903240	1.02526	1.23061	1.68388	3.25137
		5.93375	5.93377	5.93375	5.93377	5.93399	5.93377	5.93385
		0.089828	0.103773	0.121775	0.146865	0.186645	0.269588	0.542449
1.6		0.568640	0.636848	0.716947	0.814969	0.942467	1.12264	1.21673
		0.780727	0.840896	0.923621	1.04564	1.24863	1.68414	3.01139
		4.55831	4.55832	4.55842	4.55832	4.55832	4.55832	4.55836
		0.119892	0.138356	0.162086	0.194981	0.246530	0.350990	0.654022
1.4		0.535956	0.596787	0.666375	0.747996	0.845981	0.956021	0.859430
		0.811695	0.872098	0.954382	1.07401	1.26798	1.65969	2.61881
		3.33173	3.33166	3.33173	3.33167	3.33172	3.33167	3.33171
		0.170533	0.196320	0.229155	0.274010	0.342509	0.473248	0.778164
1.2		0.461178	0.506162	0.553873	0.603117	0.647985	0.656811	0.450447
		0.867873	0.925546	1.00200	1.10866	1.26987	1.55118	2.02432
		2.23597	2.23595	2.23597	2.23595	2.23591	2.23595	2.23595
		0.271698	0.310453	0.358503	0.421457	0.511141	0.659054	0.896281

* Adapted from D. J. Sticht and L. P. Huelsman, "Direct Determination of Elliptic Network Functions," *Inter. J. of Computer and Elect. Engr.*, Vol. 1, pp. 277–80, (1973).

By dividing

$$H(s) = \frac{1/\sinh s}{1 + \cosh s/\sinh s} = \frac{1/\sinh s}{1 + \coth s} \qquad (6.21)$$

If a series expansion of the coth(s) function is used and truncated after selected values (depending upon n), one obtains a polymonial approximation to the $\exp(-s)$ function, which is for $n = 1$

$$H(s) = \frac{1}{s + 1}$$

for $n = 2$

$$H(s) = \frac{3}{s^2 + 3s + 3}$$

and for $n = 3$

$$H(s) = \frac{15}{s^3 + 6s^2 + 15s + 15}$$

Note that the numerator of $H(s)$ is chosen so that $H(\omega = 0) = 1$, similar to the Butterworth function. The polynominals defined above can be identified by a general class of functions called **Bessel polynomials** $B_n(s)$ having a recursion formula

$$B_n = (2n - 1)B_{n-1} + s^2 B_{n-2} \qquad (6.22)$$

The coefficients of $B_n(s)$ for $1 \leq n \leq 6$ are listed in Table 6.7 along with quadratic factors and root locations.

Table 6.7 BESSEL POLYNOMIALS FOR THOMSON LOWPASS FILTERS. NORMALIZED TIME DELAY $T = 1$ sec.

(a) Coefficients of $B_n(s) = a_0 + a_1 s + \cdots + a_{n-1}s^{n-1} + s^n$

n	a_0	a_1	a_2	a_3	a_4	a_5
1	1					
2	3	3				
3	15	15	6			
4	105	105	45	10		
5	945	945	420	105	15	
6	10,395	10,395	4,725	1,260	210	21

(b) Quadratic factors of $B_n(s)$ for n from 1 to 6

n	$B_n(s)$	$B_n(0)$
1	$s + 1$	1
2	$s^2 + 3s + 3$	3
3	$(s^2 + 3.67782s + 6.45944)(s + 2.32219)$	15
4	$(s^2 + 5.79242s + 9.14013)(s^2 + 4.20758s + 11.4878)$	105
5	$(s^2 + 6.70391s + 14.2725)(s^2 + 4.64934s + 18.15631)(s + 3.64674)$	945
6	$(s^2 + 8.4967s + 18.80113)(s^2 + 7.47142s + 20.85282)(s^2 + 5.03186s + 26.51402)$	10,395

(c) Roots of $B_n(s)$, for n from 1 to 6

n					
1	-1.0000000				
2	-1.5000000	$\pm j0.8660254$			
3	$-2.3221854;$	-1.8389073	$\pm j1.7543810$		
4	-2.8962106	$\pm j0.8672341;$	-2.1037894	$\pm j2.6574180$	
5	$-3.6467386;$	-3.3519564	$\pm j1.7426614;$	-2.3246743	$\pm j3.5710229$
6	-4.2483594	$\pm j0.8675097;$	-3.7357084	$\pm j2.6262723;$	-2.5159322	$\pm j4.4926730$

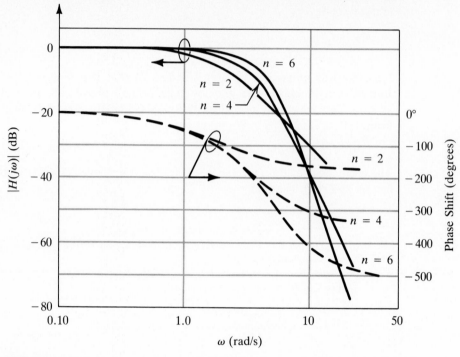

Figure 6.8 Magnitude and phase of $|H(j\omega)|$ for the Thomson filter, for T normalized to 1 sec.

The normalized magnitude and phase characteristics of the $H(j\omega)$ function for the Thomson filter for several cases of n are shown in Fig. 6.8. Compared with the Butterworth, Chebyshev, and elliptic filters:

(1) The Thomson filter is not down 3 dB at $\omega = 1$, rather the -3 dB frequency increases as the order n increases.
(2) There is much less attenuation than available with the other filters. Even for $n = 6$ an attenuation of 40 dB is not achieved until $\omega = 10$.
(3) The phase shift is changing much more uniformly in the Thomson filter, approaching the ideal case $d\theta/d\omega = -T$.

Since the Thomson filter is obviously inferior to other filters as far as attenuation for $\omega > \omega_c$ is concerned, why use it? The answer arises from considering item (3) above, particularly when one examines the time response of the various filters, as indicated in Fig. 6.9. This figure compares the step responses of the various filters for $n = 5$. It is obvious that the Thomson filter achieves nearly ideal response, whereas the Butterworth, Chebyshev, and elliptic filters exhibit considerable ringing with an accompanying long settling time. Even for $n = 10$, the Thomson

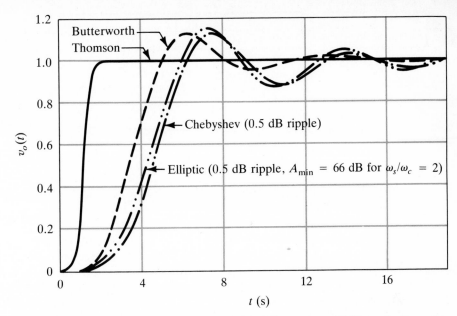

Figure 6.9 Step-function response comparisons for various LP filters, for the case $n = 5$, $\omega_c = 1$ rad/sec, and $T = 1$ sec.

maximally flat time-delay filter exhibits negligible overshoot [see Ref. 6.16 (p. 407)].

6.2 OP AMP LOWPASS FILTERS

In the preceeding section we looked at several types of magnitude approximation functions, and one phase approximation for lowpass filters. To meet a prescribed characteristic, the examples indicated a high-order (usually $n \geq 2$) filter requirement. Using passive components it is easy to obtain filters with prescribed values of A_{max}, A_{min} and ω_s/ω_c by consulting the many tables available for Butterworth, Chebyshev, and other types of filters. However, the requirements for passive synthesis usually demand inductors as well as capacitors, and obviously result in a gain ≤ 1. When we attempt synthesis by R and C elements and op amps, it becomes extremely difficult to achieve filter requirements for $n > 3$ using one op amp. Hence, the usual approach for higher-order active filters is to attempt only a second-order ($n = 2$) synthesis for each op amp, and then *cascade* the filters to achieve the desired overall transfer function $H(j\omega)$. Thus, if we were attempting to meet the requirements of the previous Example 6.2 for the Butterworth lowpass filter requiring $n = 7$, we could obtain an LP filter satisfying each of the quadratic factors of Table 6.3(b), and then cascade with a simple RC lowpass filter to satisfy the remaining first-order term $s + 1$. Such a synthesis might appear as indicated in Fig. 6.10, where each block would require at least one op amp.

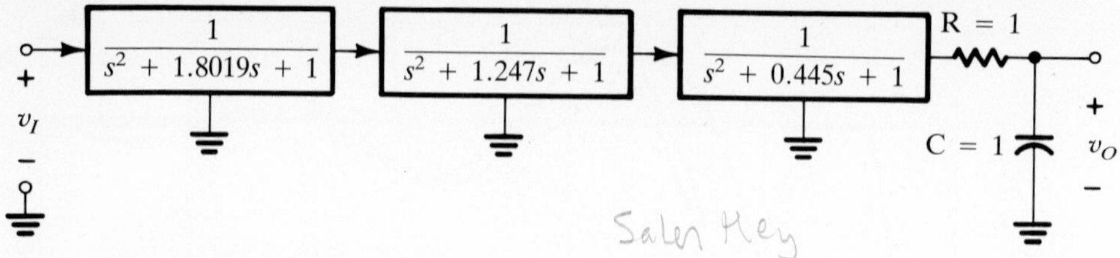

use op-Amps to simulate 2nd order filters

Salen Key

Figure 6.10 A cascade approach to realize the LP filter of Example 5.2, for a Butterworth normalized filter, $n = 7$.

We will initially concentrate on single-op-amp circuits used for active-filter requirements. The first circuit uses an op amp in a noninverting constant-gain (constant-K) configuration; it was originally presented by Sallen and Key using vacuum-tube amplifiers.* The second single-op-amp circuit uses the op amp in the inverting configuration, relying on the (ideally) infinite open-loop gain to produce a virtual ground at the inverting input terminal of the op amp (this filter is often called an **infinite-gain** type). For improved sensitivity, it may also be necessary to expand to multiple-op-amp circuits to obtain a prescribed filter requirement, particularly for high-Q networks.

6.2.1 The Single-Op-Amp Constant-K (Sallen and Key) Filter

The basic lowpass Sallen and Key filter is shown in Fig. 6.11, for a positive gain constant K. Here, since the op amp A_1 is connected in a noninverting configuration, the gain constant K is

$$K = 1 + \frac{R_B}{R_A} \tag{6.23}$$

The transfer function is readily obtained [Problem 6.11] as

$$H(s) = \frac{v_2}{v_1} = \frac{K\left(\dfrac{1}{R_1 R_2 C_1 C_2}\right)}{s^2 + \left[\dfrac{1}{R_1 C_1} + \dfrac{1}{R_2 C_1} + \dfrac{1}{R_2 C_2}(1 - K)\right]s + \dfrac{1}{R_1 R_2 C_1 C_2}} \tag{6.24}$$

which is the general form for a second-order lowpass filter, namely

$$H(s)_{LP} = \frac{N(s)}{D(s)} = \frac{H_0 \omega_c^2}{s^2 + \left(\dfrac{\omega_c}{Q}\right)s + \omega_c^2} \tag{6.25}$$

---

* R. P. Sallen and E. L. Key, "A Practical Method of Designing RC Active Filters," *IRE Trans. Ckt. Theory*, Vol. CT-2, pp. 74–85 (March 1955).

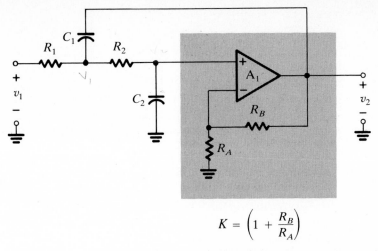

$$K = \left(1 + \frac{R_B}{R_A}\right)$$

Figure 6.11 A second-order ($n = 2$) constant-K lowpass filter (Sallen and Key filter).

where ω_c is the previously defined cutoff frequency and Q is the *quality factor** for the circuit. These are related from Eq. (6.24) as

$$H_0 = K = 1 + \frac{R_B}{R_A}$$

$$\omega_c = \left(\frac{1}{R_1 R_2 C_1 C_2}\right)^{1/2}$$

$$\frac{1}{Q} = \left[\left(\frac{R_2 C_2}{R_1 C_1}\right)^{1/2} + \left(\frac{R_1 C_2}{R_2 C_1}\right)^{1/2} + (1 - K)\left(\frac{R_1 C_1}{R_2 C_2}\right)^{1/2}\right] \tag{6.26}$$

Since there are five unknowns in the circuit (R_1, R_2, C_1, C_2, K) and only three parameters of interest (H_0, ω_c, Q), a designer has the choice of fixing two elements. There are several very obvious choices, the most important of which are:

(1) Let resistors and capacitors be equal:

$$R_1 = R_2 = R \text{ and } C_1 = C_2 = C.$$

From Eq. (6.26), we have

$$H_0 = K \qquad \omega_c = \frac{1}{RC} \qquad Q = \frac{1}{3 - K} \tag{6.27}$$

---

* The Q is probably familiar to the student from tuned circuits, where it was defined as $Q = f_0/BW$, with f_0 = center frequency, and BW = the bandwidth of the circuit. However, the Q of a lowpass or highpass circuit is also descriptive, since it indicates the closeness of the roots of $D(j\omega)$ to the $j\omega$-axis; i.e., the larger the Q, the smaller the real part of the roots. Therefore, a high-Q network will indicate more peaking in the frequency response, as well as more overshoot in the transient response.

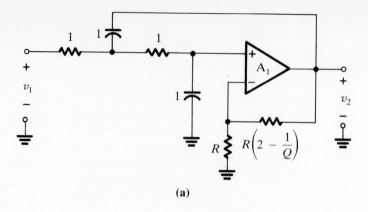

(a)

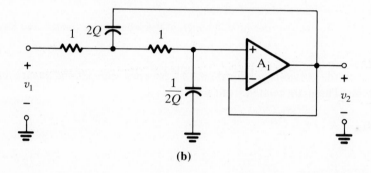

(b)

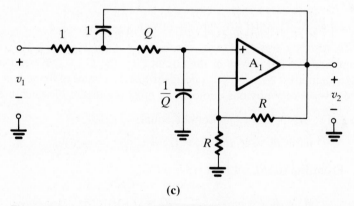

(c)

Figure 6.12 Various choices for a normalized LP Sallen and Key filter.

and since $K = 1 + (R_B/R_A)$ we can define resistors by

$$R_B = \left(2 - \frac{1}{Q}\right)R_A \tag{6.28}$$

This circuit is shown in Fig. 6.12(a), normalized for $\omega_c = 1$ rad/sec and $R = R_A$.

(2) Let the op amp achieve maximum frequency bandwidth, which occurs for unity gain, $K = 1$. Thus, if ω_c is normalized to unity and resistors are normalized to 1 Ω, then from Eq. (6.26) we have $\sqrt{C_1} = 1/\sqrt{C_2}$, or $C_1 = 2Q$ while $C_2 = 1/2Q$. This circuit is indicated in Fig. 6.12(b).

(3) Suppose that one chooses resistors R_A and R_B equal, so that $K = 2$, while also letting $R_1 = C_1 = 1$. We then require for $\omega_c = 1$ that $\sqrt{R_2} = 1/\sqrt{C_2}$ and to satisfy the requirement on Q we need $R_2 = Q$ and $C_2 = 1/Q$. This final circuit is shown in Fig. 6.12(c).

EXAMPLE 6.4

Using the equal-element Sallen and Key filter of Fig. 6.12(a), (a) implement the Butterworth lowpass filter of Example 6.2, as shown by the block diagram of Fig. 6.10, then, (b) using appropriate scaling factors design for a cutoff frequency of $\omega_c = 1000$ rad/sec.

Solution

From Table 6.3(a), or Fig. 6.10, for $n = 7$ the denominator polynomial for the Butterworth filter is

$$(s + 1)(s^2 + 1.8019s + 1)(s^2 + 1.247s + 1)(s^2 + 0.445s + 1)$$

The first term $s + 1$ is easily obtained with $R = 1$ and $C = 1$, as indicated in Fig. 6.10. The quadratic terms require Q values of $Q_1 = 1/1.8019$, $Q_2 = 1/1.247$ and $Q_3 = 1/0.445$ [from the normalized form of Eq. (6.25)]. Thus, the normalized version of the filters is as indicated in Fig. 6.13(a). We require a frequency-scaling factor $k_f = 1000$, and let us also use a magnitude-scaling factor of $k_m = 10,000$, so that the actual scaled circuit will be as indicated in Fig. 6.13(b).

One would probably wish to follow the v_2 output signal with a buffer amplifier, so that the output filter of 10 kΩ and 0.1 μF would not change due to loading. Further, the arrangement of the quadratic terms bears some explanation. Although one could implement the three quadratic terms in any order, practically it makes more sense to implement the lowest Q section first, proceeding toward finally the highest Q section. This procedure will realize the largest dynamic range for the set of amplifiers, since high-Q circuits produce ringing that could be attenuated if the low-Q sections were last in the sequence of gain.

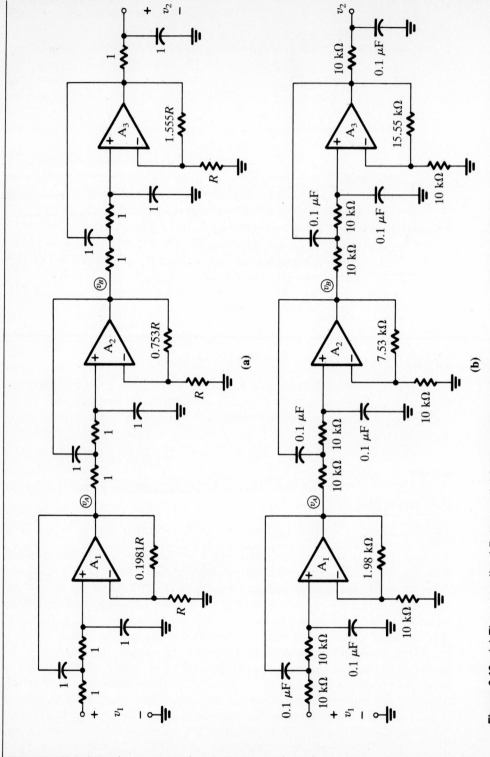

Figure 6.13 (a) The normalized Butterworth LP filter of Example 6.4, for $n = 7$. (b) Scaled with $k_f = 10^3$ and $k_m = 10^4$ to produce a cutoff frequency $\omega_c = 10^3$ rad/sec.

Although the Sallen and Key constant-K lowpass circuit will implement any all-pole function, such as the Butterworth, Chebyshev, or Thomson filters, it cannot be directly used to achieve a second-order elliptic-filter response, because of the existence of transmission zeroes (i.e., zeroes on the $j\omega$-axis). For the second-order elliptic filter the transfer function, from Eq. (6.17) or Table 6.6, was

$$H_e(s) = \frac{H_e(s^2 + \Omega_1^2)}{s^2 + a_1 s + a_0} \equiv \frac{H(s^2 + \omega_z^2)}{s^2 + (\omega_p/Q_p)s + \omega_p^2} \qquad (6.29)$$

A single-op-amp constant-K lowpass filter that will satisfy the requirements of the above transfer function is shown in Fig. 6.14,* where the zero-producing section is obtained by the input "twin-tee" RC network.† There are *two* possibilities for the element Y_4 in Fig. 6.14: (1) If the denominator term a_0 is greater than the numerator term Ω_1^2 (i.e., if $\omega_p > \omega_z$), then the location of the $j\omega$-axis zero is closest to the origin and $Y_4 = 1/R_4$. (2) If, however the poles are closest to the origin, then $\Omega_1^2 > a_0$ (i.e., $\omega_z > \omega_p$) and $Y_4 = s(aC)$. For elliptic filters, the poles are closest to the origin, so that case (2) holds and the Y_4 term is a capacitor aC. From Fig. 6.14,

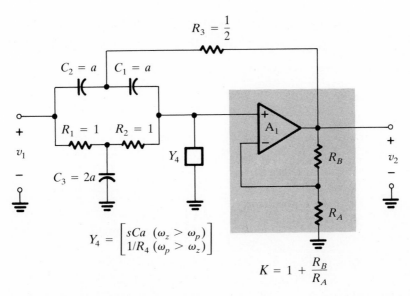

$$Y_4 = \begin{bmatrix} sCa \;\; (\omega_z > \omega_p) \\ 1/R_4 \;\; (\omega_p > \omega_z) \end{bmatrix}$$

$$K = 1 + \frac{R_B}{R_A}$$

Figure 6.14 A positive-gain (constant-K) realization for a normalized second-order LP filter with transmission zeroes.

---

* [See Ref. 6.1 (Section 4.4, p. 168) and Ref. 6.19 (pp. 299–303]. Also, W. J. Kerwin and L. P. Huelsman, *Proc. IEEE Inter. Conv. Record*, Part 10, pp. 74–80, (March 1966).
† See Problem 6.25.

the transfer function for $\omega_z > \omega_p$ reduces to

$$H_e(s) = \frac{v_2(s)}{v_1(s)} = \frac{H\left[s^2 + \dfrac{1}{R_1 R_2 C_3}\left(\dfrac{1}{C_1} + \dfrac{1}{C_2}\right)\right]\left[s + \dfrac{1}{C_3}\left(\dfrac{1}{R_1} + \dfrac{1}{R_2}\right)\right]}{\left(s^2 + \dfrac{\omega_p}{Q_p}s + \omega_p^2\right)\left[s + \dfrac{1}{C_3}\left(\dfrac{1}{R_1} + \dfrac{1}{R_2}\right)\right]} \qquad (6.30)$$

provided that R_3 is chosen as

$$R_3 = \left(\frac{C_3}{C_1 + C_2}\right)\left(\frac{1}{R_1} + \frac{1}{R_2}\right) \qquad (6.30a)$$

Thus, the common term in the numerator and denominator of Eq. (6.30) cancels, and the transfer function is identical to that of Eq. (6.29). The ω_p and Q_p terms in Eq. (6.30) are complicated functions of the elements as well as the gain K. However, by a judicious choice of the element ratios, (as indicated in Fig. 6.14), it is possible to reduce to the following equation for $H_e(s)$

$$H_e(s) = \frac{v_2(s)}{v_1(s)} = \frac{[K/(2C + 1)]\left(s^2 + \dfrac{1}{a^2}\right)}{s^2 + \left[\dfrac{2(C + 2 - K)}{a(2C + 1)}\right]s + \dfrac{1}{a^2(2C + 1)}} \qquad (6.31)$$

with the design parameters related to Eq. (6.29) by

$$a = \frac{1}{\omega_z}$$

$$R_3 = \frac{1}{2} \qquad R_1 = R_2 = 1$$

$$C_1 = C_2 = \frac{1}{\omega_z} \qquad C_3 = \frac{2}{\omega_z}$$

$$C = \frac{1}{2}\left[\left(\frac{\omega_z}{\omega_p}\right)^2 - 1\right] \qquad \text{so } C_4 = \frac{1}{2\omega_z}\left[\left(\frac{\omega_z}{\omega_p}\right)^2 - 1\right] \qquad (6.31a)$$

$$K = \frac{1}{2}\left[3 + \left(\frac{\omega_z}{\omega_p}\right)^2 - \frac{1}{Q_p}\left(\frac{\omega_z}{\omega_p}\right)\right]$$

$$H = K\left(\frac{\omega_p}{\omega_z}\right)^2$$

For the case $\omega_p > \omega_z$ the element $Y = 1/R_4$ and the transfer function (with the elements replaced by their normalized values) becomes

$$H_e(s) = \frac{v_2(s)}{v_1(s)} = \frac{K\left(s^2 + \dfrac{1}{a^2}\right)}{s^2 + \left[\dfrac{2(2 - K + 1/R_4)}{a}\right]s + \dfrac{(1 + 2/R_4)}{a^2}} \qquad (6.32)$$

with the appropriate design relationships for a, R_4 and K of

$$a = \frac{1}{\omega_z}$$

$$R_4 = \frac{2}{\left[\left(\frac{\omega_p}{\omega_z}\right)^2 - 1\right]}$$

$$K = \left[1.5 + \frac{1}{2}\left(\frac{\omega_p}{\omega_z}\right)\left(\frac{\omega_p}{\omega_z} - \frac{1}{Q_p}\right)\right]$$

$$H = K\left(\frac{\omega_p}{\omega_z}\right)^2$$

(6.33)

An elliptic-filter design based on the circuit of Fig. 6.14 is demonstrated in the following example.

EXAMPLE 6.5

The design requirements of Examples 6.2 and 6.3 were met by a Butterworth filter with $n = 7$, a Chebyshev filter with $n = 4$ (for -3 dB ripple) or $n = 5$ (for 0.5 dB ripple). For 0.5 dB ripple and $A_{min} \geq 40$ dB at $\omega_s/\omega_c = 2$, the nomograph of Fig. 6.6 indicates $n = 4$ for an elliptic-filter design, with an actual attenuation at $\omega_s/\omega_c = 2$ of approximately 49 dB. Using the data of Table 6.5 with the circuit of Fig. 6.14, design a lowpass filter with $\omega_c = 10^3$ rad/sec and compare the complexity of the circuit with that of the Butterworth design of Fig. 6.13.

Solution
From Table 6.5, for $n = 4$ and $\omega_s/\omega_c = 2$, the required transfer function $H_e(s)$ is

$$H(s) = \frac{(0.0036987)(s^2 + 4.59326)(s^2 + 24.2272)}{(s^2 + 0.30116s + 1.06258)(s^2 + 0.88456s + 0.41032)}$$

(6.34)

Now, although the poles and zeroes could be grouped in any order for synthesis, there is evidence [Ref. 6.1, Chap. 3] that a grouping giving the *largest* separation between poles and zeroes will produce the least sensitivity of the $H(s)$ function to changes in component values of the network. Hence, the grouping to be used will be

$$H(s) = H_1(s) \times H_2(s)$$

$$= \frac{H_1(s^2 + 4.59326)}{(s^2 + 0.88456s + 0.41032)} \times \frac{H_2(s^2 + 24.2272)}{(s^2 + 0.30116s + 1.06258)}$$

(6.34a)

where the product $H_1 \times H_2 = 0.0036987$. Since $\omega_z > \omega_p$ for both groupings, the network equations are those of Eqs. (6.30) and (6.31), where $Y_4 = sC_4$. Comparing Eq. (6.34) with the standard second-order form of Eq. (6.29) we can identify for

$H_1(s)$, $\omega_{z1} = 2.1432$, $\omega_{p1} = 0.6406$ and $Q_{p1} = 0.7242$. Similarly, for $H_2(s)$ we have $\omega_{z2} = 4.9221$, $\omega_{p2} = 1.0308$ and $Q_{p2} = 3.4228$. Since $Q_{p2} > Q_{p1}$ we will synthesize the $H_1(s)$ term first, with $H_2(s)$ cascaded as the second network. From Eq. (6.31) the various terms are for $H_1(s)$,

$$a = 0.4666$$

$$R_3 = 0.5 \qquad R_1 = R_2 = 1$$

$$C_1 = C_2 = 0.4666 \qquad C_3 = 0.9332 \tag{6.34b}$$

$$C_4 = 2.3783$$

$$K_1 = 4.7871 \qquad H_1 = 0.4276$$

and for $H_2(s)$,

$$a = 0.2032$$

$$C_3 = 0.4064 \qquad C_1 = C_2 = 0.2032$$

$$R_1 = R_2 = 1 \qquad R_3 = 0.5 \tag{6.34c}$$

$$C_4 = 2.2145$$

$$K_2 = 12.2025 \qquad H_2 = 0.5352$$

For the overall design, we are constrained by the requirement that, from Eq. (6.34), $H_1 \times H_2 = 0.0036987$, which obviously cannot be met since H_1 and H_2 are already defined. However, since additional gain (or attenuation, in this case) can easily be obtained from another op amp, we can arbitrarily add another op amp stage with an attenuation

$$K_3 = 0.0036987/(0.4276)(0.5352) = 0.01616 \tag{6.34d}$$

The resulting normalized networks for $H_1(s)$, $H_2(s)$ and K_3 are indicated in Fig. 6.15(a). The transformed circuit, with a frequency scaling factor $k_f = 10^3$ and with magnitude factors $k_{m1} = 9.332 \times 10^3$ for the first section H_1 and $k_{m2} = 4.064 \times 10^3$ for the H_2 section, is shown in Fig. 6.15(b).

If the elliptic circuit of Fig. 6.15(b) is compared to that of the Butterworth filter of Fig. 6.13(b), it is obvious that the Butterworth circuit is much easier to implement practically, even though $n = 7$ for the Butterworth as compared to $n = 4$ for the elliptic filter. The Butterworth circuit requires only 7 capacitors, all of *identical* values, whereas the elliptic circuit requires 8 capacitors, with varying values. The Butterworth requires 3 op amps and 13 resistors, (with 10 of these standard values) whereas the elliptic requires two op amps, and a third for gain control, as well as 12 resistors (with only 3 standard values). The frequency response for each section, $H_1(j\omega)$ and $H_2(j\omega)$, is shown in Fig. 6.16, as well as the overall filter response $H(j\omega)$.

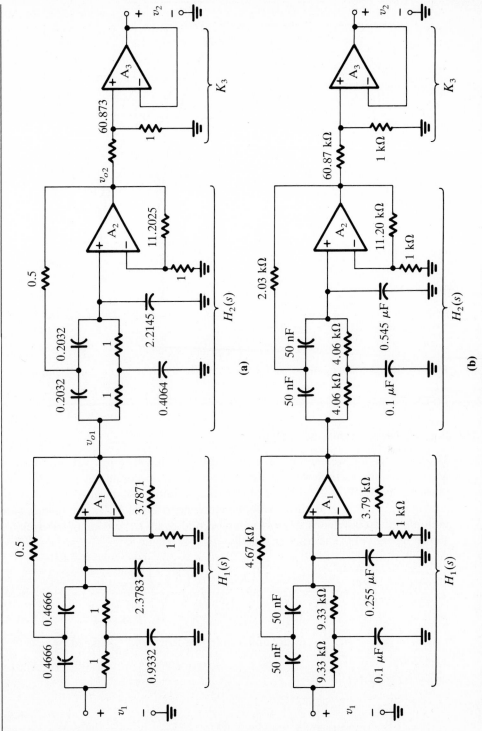

Figure 6.15 The elliptic lowpass filter of Example 6.5: (a) normalized; (b) scaled for $\omega_c = 10^3$ rad/sec, with magnitude scaling factors $k_{m1} = 9.332 \times 10^3$ and $k_{m2} = 4.064 \times 10^3$

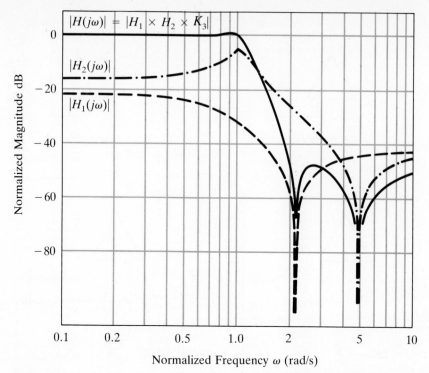

Figure 6.16 Frequency response for the normalized elliptic LP filter of Example 6.5.

6.2.2 The Single-Op-Amp Infinite-Gain Filter

In the last section we concentrated on an LP filter having a low value of positive gain K. In this section we will use a single op amp connected in the normal inverting-feedback connection, and use the condition of ideality $A_{OL} \to \infty$ to advantage. This type of filter will therefore be referred to as an infinite-gain multiple-feedback filter. A single-op-amp, second-order LP version of the circuit is shown in Fig. 6.17. The transfer function for this circuit is

$$H(s) = \frac{v_2(s)}{v_1(s)} = \frac{-\left(\dfrac{1}{R_3 R_2 C_1 C_2}\right)\left(\dfrac{R_3}{R_1}\right)}{s^2 + s\left(\dfrac{1}{R_1 C_1} + \dfrac{1}{R_2 C_1} + \dfrac{1}{R_3 C_1}\right) + \dfrac{1}{R_3 R_2 C_1 C_2}} \tag{6.35}$$

with a dc gain $-H_0 = -R_3/R_1$ and a pole frequency and Q defined by

$$\omega_c = \frac{1}{(R_2 R_3 C_1 C_2)^{1/2}}$$

$$\frac{1}{Q} = \left[R_2 R_3\left(\frac{C_2}{C_1}\right)\right]^{1/2}\left(\frac{1}{R_1} + \frac{1}{R_2} + \frac{1}{R_3}\right) \tag{6.36}$$

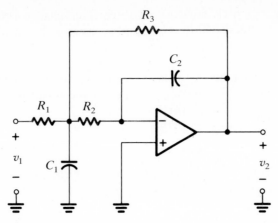

Figure 6.17 A second-order LP infinite-gain filter.

Various design procedures are possible. For example, if $H_0 = 1$ with $\omega_c = 1$, and all resistors are set to unity, then the conditions $C_1 = 3Q$ and $C_2 = 1/3Q$ will satisfy Eq. (6.36). If $H_0 \neq 1$, then another possibility would be to use H_0 as a design parameter with $R_1 = 1$, so that $R_3 = H_0$ and $R_2 = H_0/(1 - H_0)$, with the capacitors determined by

$$C_1 = 2Q\left[1 + \frac{1}{H_0}\right] \qquad C_2 = \frac{1}{2QH_0} \tag{6.37}$$

If standard capacitor values are desired, then a convenient choice is $C_1 = 1$, $C_2 = mC_1$, $R_1 = R_3/H_0$ and $R_2 = 1/R_3 m$, with

$$m \leq \frac{1}{4Q^2(1 + H_0)} \qquad \text{(Note } H_0 \text{ is positive)}$$

$$\tag{6.38}$$

$$R_3 = \frac{1}{2mQ}\{1 \pm [1 - 4mQ^2(1 + H_0)]^{1/2}\}$$

■ **Exercise 6.1**

Verify the design relationships of Eqs. (6.36)–(6.38) for the infinite-gain LP filter of Eq. (6.35) and Fig. 6.17.

6.2.3 Sensitivity Considerations

Before we proceed to other types of filters we need to consider the question, Which filter is the best choice for a particular requirement? The answer could obviously depend on such topics as (1) the number of resistors, capacitors, and op amps required, (2) the cost of one filter versus another, and (3) the ease of obtaining standard value components in the design. However, another primary consideration (and often the most important) is, how do the different filters change with respect to changes in component values? This last question is answered by considering the *sensitivity* of the filter.

Classical Sensitivity Functions. A filter's sensitivity to a change in some performance characteristic y because of a change in the nominal value of the element x is defined by Bode's **sensitivity function** S_x^y*

$$S_x^y \equiv \left(\frac{\partial y}{\partial x}\right)\frac{x}{y} = \frac{\partial y/y}{\partial x/x} = \frac{\partial(\ln y)}{\partial(\ln x)} \tag{6.39}$$

Thus, the sensitivity of a LP filter to a change in the cutoff frequency ω_c because of changes in a resistor R would be defined by

$$S_R^{\omega_c} = \left(\frac{\partial \omega_c}{\partial R}\right)\frac{R}{\omega_c}$$

whereas a change in the pole location, $p_0 = \sigma_0 + j\omega_0$ due to a change in gain K would correspondingly be defined by

$$S_k^{p_0} = \left(\frac{\partial \sigma_0}{\partial K}\right)\frac{K}{\sigma_0} + j\frac{\partial \omega_0}{\partial K}\left(\frac{K}{\omega_0}\right)$$

Further, if the parameter, (say ω_c) were a function of R_1, R_2 and C_1, then one would estimate the total percentage change in ω_c due to changes in the nominal values of R_1, R_2 and C_1 by computing

$$\frac{\Delta\omega_c}{\omega_c} \approx \left[S_{R1}^{\omega_c}\left(\frac{\Delta R_1}{R_1}\right) + S_{R2}^{\omega_c}\left(\frac{\Delta R_2}{R_2}\right) + S_{C1}^{\omega_c}\left(\frac{\Delta C_1}{C_1}\right)\right] \tag{6.40}$$

Some general properties of the sensitivity function are of particular interest in filter design. Suppose, for example, that we have a function characteristic y defined by a product of terms

$$y = x_1^m \cdot x_2^n \cdot x_3^p \tag{6.41}$$

Then, from the logarithmic definition of the sensitivity, since

$$\ln y = m \ln x_1 + n \ln x_2 + p \ln x_3$$

then the various individual sensitivities are

$$S_{x_1}^y = \frac{\partial(\ln y)}{\partial(\ln x_1)} = m \qquad S_{x_2}^y = n \qquad S_{x_3}^y = p \tag{6.42}$$

Also, if y is defined by the product of two functions $y = y_1 \cdot y_2$ then

$$S_{x_1}^y = \frac{\partial \ln(y_1 \cdot y_2)}{\partial \ln x} = \frac{\partial \ln y_1}{\partial \ln x} + \frac{\partial \ln y_2}{\partial \ln x}$$

---

* Originally defined by H. W. Bode in *Network Analysis and Feedback Amplifier Design*, (Princeton, N.J.: D. Van Nostrand, 1945). Bode was primarily interested in the change in the closed-loop transfer characteristics for an amplifier, due to changes in the vacuum-tube elements of the circuit.

or we have therefore

$$S_x^y = S_x^{y_1} + S_x^{y_2} \tag{6.43}$$

Obviously, if the performance characteristic y is defined by a ratio $y = y_1/y_2$ then

$$S_x^y = S_x^{y_1} - S_x^{y_2} \tag{6.44}$$

The sensitivity of the transfer function $H(j\omega)$ to a change in a parameter x may also be defined by (see Problem 6.20)

$$S_x^{H(j\omega)} = \frac{x}{|H(j\omega)|} \frac{\partial}{\partial x} |H(j\omega)| + jx \frac{\partial \theta(\omega)}{\partial x} \tag{6.45}$$

where $|H(j\omega)|$ is defined by

$$H(j\omega) = |H(j\omega)| \exp[j\theta(\omega)] \tag{6.46}$$

or from Eq. (6.45) we have both a *magnitude* and *phase sensitivity* defined by

$$S_x^{|H(j\omega)|} = \text{Re } S_x^{H(j\omega)}$$

$$S_x^{\theta(\omega)} = \frac{1}{\theta(\omega)} \text{Im } S_x^{H(j\omega)} \tag{6.47}$$

Now that we have obtained some basic identities regarding sensitivity, let us compare the various LP filters we have studied so far, to see if one filter offers a lower sensitivity when compared with the other types. For example, the LP Sallen and Key circuit of Fig. 6.11 and Eqs. (6.24)–(6.26) had the following parameter interrelationships:

$$K = H_0 = 1 + \frac{R_B}{R_A}$$

$$\omega_c = R_1^{-1/2} R_2^{-1/2} C_1^{-1/2} C_2^{-1/2} \tag{6.48}$$

$$\frac{1}{Q} = \left(\frac{R_2 C_2}{R_1 C_1}\right)^{1/2} + \left(\frac{R_1 C_2}{R_2 C_1}\right)^{1/2} + (1 - K)\left(\frac{R_1 C_1}{R_2 C_2}\right)^{1/2}$$

Using Eqs. (6.41) and (6.42), we have regarding sensitivity of ω_c to the parameters,

$$S_{R1}^{\omega_c} = S_{R2}^{\omega_c} = S_{C1}^{\omega_c} = S_{C2}^{\omega_c} = -\frac{1}{2} \qquad S_K^{\omega_c} = 0 \tag{6.49}$$

and since it can be easily shown that $S_x^{1/y} = -S_x^y$ the Q sensitivities are obtained as

$$S_K^Q = \frac{K}{(1 - K) + \left(\dfrac{C_2}{C_1}\right) + \left(\dfrac{R_2 C_2}{R_1 C_1}\right)} = KQ\left(\frac{R_1 C_1}{R_2 C_2}\right)^{1/2}$$

$$S_{R1}^Q = -\frac{1}{2} + Q\left(\frac{R_2 C_2}{R_1 C_1}\right)^{1/2} = -S_{R2}^Q \tag{6.50}$$

$$S_{C1}^Q = -\frac{1}{2} + Q\left[\left(\frac{R_1 C_2}{R_2 C_1}\right)^{1/2} + \left(\frac{R_2 C_2}{R_1 C_1}\right)^{1/2}\right] = -S_{C2}^Q$$

and for the gain-determining resistors, R_A and R_B of Fig. 6.11,

$$S_{R_B}^K = S_{R_B}^{H_0} = \frac{1}{1 + R_A/R_B}$$

$$S_{R_A}^K = S_{R_A}^{H_0} = S_{R_A}^{H_0} = \frac{-1}{1 + R_A/R_B}$$

(6.51)

which, if both resistors are fabricated from similar resistivity material and operate in the same environment, results in,

$$\frac{\Delta K}{K} \approx S_{R_B}^K \left(\frac{\Delta R_B}{R_B}\right) + S_{R_A}^K \left(\frac{\Delta R_A}{R_A}\right) = 0$$

(6.51a)

For comparison with the Sallen-Key LP filter, consider the infinite-gain filter of Fig. 6.17. From the results of Eqs. (6.36) we obtain

$$S_{R2}^{\omega_c} = S_{R3}^{\omega_c} = S_{C1}^{\omega_c} = S_{C2}^{\omega_c} = -\frac{1}{2} \qquad S_{R1}^{\omega_c} = 0$$

(6.52)

and for Q sensitivities we have

$$S_{R1}^Q = \frac{1}{1 + \dfrac{R_1}{R_2} + \dfrac{R_1}{R_3}}$$

$$S_{R2}^Q = S_{R3}^Q = \frac{-\left(1 - \dfrac{R_1}{R_2} + \dfrac{R_1}{R_3}\right)}{2\left(1 + \dfrac{R_1}{R_2} + \dfrac{R_1}{R_3}\right)}$$

(6.53)

$$S_{C2}^Q = -\frac{1}{2} \qquad S_{C1}^Q = \frac{1}{2}$$

■ **Exercise 6.2**

Verify each of the sensitivities of Eqs. (6.52) and (6.53) for the infinite-gain LP filter. Of particular interest is the latter condition for C_1 and C_2 of Eq. (6.53); i.e. $S_{C1}^Q = -S_{C2}^Q$. What would this say about changes in Q if C_1 and C_2 are fabricated from identical dielectric material?

EXAMPLE 6.6

Compare the various Sallen-Key LP filter circuits with those of the infinite-gain filter, for a normalized LP filter having $\omega_c = 1$, $Q = 5$ and appropriate design requirements for H_0.

Solution

For the Sallen-Key filter we will examine the sensitivities, defined now by Eqs. (6.49), (6.50), and (6.51), for the three circuits of Fig. 6.12. We have for the total change in ω_c (for small differential changes, *only*)

$$\frac{\Delta\omega_c}{\omega_c} \approx S^{\omega_c}_{R1}\left(\frac{\Delta R_1}{R_1}\right) + S^{\omega_c}_{R2}\left(\frac{\Delta R_2}{R_2}\right) + S^{\omega_c}_{C1}\left(\frac{\Delta C_1}{C_1}\right) + S^{\omega_c}_{C2}\left(\frac{\Delta C_2}{C_2}\right) + S^{\omega_c}_{K}\left(\frac{\Delta K}{K}\right)$$

(6.54)

or substituting values from Eq. (6.52),

$$\frac{\Delta\omega_c}{\omega_c} \approx -\frac{1}{2}\left[\left(\frac{\Delta R_1}{R_1}\right) + \left(\frac{\Delta R_2}{R_2}\right) + \left(\frac{\Delta C_1}{C_1}\right) + \left(\frac{\Delta C_2}{C_2}\right)\right]$$

(6.55)

Thus any increase in R or C values produces a decrease in the cutoff frequency ω_c. For changes in Q we have to look at the particular circuit involved. For circuit (a) of Fig. 6.12, and $Q = 5$ we have, from the relationship of Eqs. (6.50) and (6.51),

Sallen-Key, Circuit (a): $R_1 = R_2 = C_1 = C_2 = 1$

$$H_0 = K = 3 - \frac{1}{Q} = 2.8 \qquad R_B = 1.8R_A$$

$$S^Q_K = (2.8)(5)\sqrt{1} = 14$$

$$S^Q_{R1} = -\frac{1}{2} + 5\sqrt{1} = 4.5 = -S^Q_{R2}$$

(6.56)

$$S^Q_{C1} = 9.5 = -S^Q_{C2}$$

$$S^{H_0}_{R_B} = S^K_{R_B} = 9/14 = -S^K_{R_A} = -S^{H_0}_{R_A}$$

For the circuit of Fig. 6.12(b), however, the sensitive for Q are,

Sallen-Key, Circuit (b): $K = 1$, $R_1 = R_2 = 1$

$$H_0 = K = 1$$

$$S^Q_K = 2Q^2 = 50$$

$$S^Q_{R1} = -\frac{1}{2} + \frac{Q}{2Q} = 0 = -S^Q_{R2}$$

(6.57)

$$S^Q_{C1} = -\frac{1}{2} + \frac{2Q}{2Q} = \frac{1}{2} = -S^Q_{C2}$$

$$S^{H_0}_{R_B} = S^{H_0}_{R_A} = 0$$

For the circuit of Fig. 6.12(c), we have

Sallen-Key, Circuit (c): $R_1 = C_1 = 1$, $K = 2$

$$K = 2$$

$$S_K^Q = KQ\sqrt{1} = 10$$

$$S_{R1}^Q = -\frac{1}{2} + Q = 4.5 = -S_{R2}^Q \qquad (6.58)$$

$$S_{C1}^Q = -\frac{1}{2} + Q\left[1 + \frac{1}{Q}\right] = 5.5 = -S_{C2}^Q$$

$$S_{R_B}^K = \frac{1}{2} = -S_{R_A}^K$$

Now, let us look at the sensitivities for the infinite-gain LP filter, using Eqs. (6.52) and (6.53). The sensitivity function for ω_c is identical to that of the Sallen-Key circuit, so a total change could be approximated as in Eqs. (6.54) and (6.55). For the first circuit having $R_1 = R_2 = R_3 = 1$, $C_1 = 1/C_2 = 3Q$, we have for Q sensitivites:

Infinite-gain, Circuit A: $R_1 = R_2 = R_3 = 1$, $H_0 = 1$

$$H_0 = 1 = \frac{R_3}{R_1}$$

$$S_{R1}^Q = \frac{1}{3}$$

$$S_{R2}^Q = -\frac{1}{6} = -S_{R3}^Q \qquad (6.59)$$

$$S_{C2}^Q = -\frac{1}{2} = -S_{C1}^Q$$

$$S_{R3}^{H_0} = 1 = -S_{R1}^{H_0}$$

and for the case $R_1 = 1$, $R_3 = H_0$, $R_2 = H_0/1 + H_0$, with H_0 chosen as 2, we have from Eq. (6.37).

Infinite-gain, Circuit B: $R_1 = 1$, $R_3 = H_0$, $R_2 = H_0/1 + H_0$

$$H_0 = R_3 = 2 \qquad R_1 = 1 \qquad R_2 = \frac{H_0}{1 + H_0} = \frac{2}{3}$$

$$S_{R1}^Q = \frac{H_0}{2(1 + H_0)} = \frac{1}{3} \qquad S_{R3}^{H_0} = 1 \tag{6.60}$$

$$S_{R2}^Q = S_{R3}^Q = 0$$

$$S_{C2}^Q = -\frac{1}{2} = -S_{C1}^Q$$

For the standard capacitor design, $C_1 = 1$ and $C_2 = mC$, we have from Eq. (6.38),

Infinite-gain, Circuit C: $C_1 = 1$, $C_2 = mC_1$

$$C_1 = 1 \qquad C_2 = mC_1$$

$$R_1 = R_3/H_0 \qquad R_2 = 1/R_3 m$$

$$S_{R1}^Q = \frac{H_0}{H_0 + mR_3^2 + \dfrac{2mQR_3}{\{1 \pm [1 - 4mQ^2(1 + H_0)]^{1/2}\}}}$$

$$S_{R2}^Q = S_{R3}^Q = \frac{H_0 - mR_3^2 + \dfrac{2mQR_3}{\{1 \pm [1 - 4mQ^2(1 + H_0)]^{1/2}\}}}{2\left(H_0 + mR_3^2 + \dfrac{2mQR_3}{\{1 \pm [1 - 4mQ^2(1 + H_0)]^{1/2}\}}\right)} \tag{6.61}$$

$$S_{C2}^Q = -\frac{1}{2} = -S_{C1}^Q \qquad S_{R2}^{H_0} = 0 \qquad S_{R1}^{H_0} = 1 = -S_{R3}^{H_0}$$

where

$$m \leq \frac{1}{4Q^2(1 + H_0)} \tag{6.61a}$$

From above, let us again assume a gain $H_0 = 2$, and choose m as the equality in Eq. (6.61a), or

$$m = \frac{1}{4(5)^2(1 + 2)} = \frac{1}{300}$$

so that $C_1 = 1$, $C_2 = 0.0033C_1$ and R_3 is now equal to

$$R_3 = \frac{1}{2mQ} = \frac{300}{2(5)} = 30$$

Table 6.8 SENSITIVITY COMPARISON OF SINGLE OP AMP SALLEN-KEY AND INFINITE-GAIN LOW-PASS FILTERS, FOR EXAMPLE 6.6, FOR $\omega_c = 1$ rad/sec. AND $Q = 5$

	Sallen-Key ($K = H_0$)				Infinite-Gain		
	Circuit (a)	Circuit (b)	Circuit (c)		Circuit A	Circuit B	Circuit C
S^y_x	$K = 3 - 1/Q = 2.8$	$K = 1$	$K = 2$		$H_0 = 1$, Equal R	$H_0 = 2$, $R_1 = 1$	$H_0 = 2$, $C_1 = 1$, $C_2 = \dfrac{C_1}{300}$
$S^{\omega_c}_{x_i}$ *	$-\tfrac{1}{2}$	$-\tfrac{1}{2}$	$-\tfrac{1}{2}$		$-\tfrac{1}{2}$	$-\tfrac{1}{2}$	$-\tfrac{1}{2}$
S^Q_K	14	50	10				
S^Q_{R1}	4.5	0	4.5		$\tfrac{1}{3}$	$\tfrac{1}{3}$	$\tfrac{1}{3}$
S^Q_{R2}	-4.5	0	-4.5		$-\tfrac{1}{6}$	0	0
S^Q_{C1}	9.5	$\tfrac{1}{2}$	5.5		$\tfrac{1}{2}$	$\tfrac{1}{2}$	$\tfrac{1}{2}$
S^Q_{C2}	-9.5	$-\tfrac{1}{2}$	-5.5		$-\tfrac{1}{2}$	$-\tfrac{1}{2}$	$-\tfrac{1}{2}$
$S^{H_0}_{RA}$	$-\tfrac{9}{14}$		$-\tfrac{1}{2}$	$S^{H_0}_{R3}$	1	1	1
$S^{H_0}_{RB}$	$\tfrac{9}{14}$		$\tfrac{1}{2}$	$S^{H_0}_{R1}$	-1	-1	-1
				S^Q_{R3}	$-\tfrac{1}{6}$	0	0

* $x_i = R_1, R_2, C_1, C_2$ for Sallen-Key; $S^{\omega_0}_K = 0$.
 $x_i = R_2, R_3, C_1, C_2$ for Infinite-Gain; $S^{\omega_c}_{R1} = 0$.

so that $R_1 = 30/2 = 15$ and $R_2 = 300/30 = 10$. Thus, the sensitivities are, from Eq. (6.61),

$$S_{R1}^Q = \frac{1}{3} \qquad S_{R2}^Q = S_{R3}^Q = 0 \qquad S_{C2}^Q = -\frac{1}{2} = -S_{C1}^Q \tag{6.61b}$$

A sensitivity comparison among the various Sallen-Key and infinite-gain LP circuits is summarized in Table 6.8. For the Sallen and Key circuit, the unity-gain version (circuit b) gives the lowest sensitivities except for S_K^Q, which is generally not important since $K = A_{OL}/(1 + A_{OL})$ and open-loop gain changes would be insignificant if the closed-loop gain is unity. However, it is also very apparent that *any* of the three example circuits for the infinite-gain LP filter has a lower overall sensitivity to element changes than any of the three Sallen-Key circuits.

Before we leave the subject of sensitivity let us look at the sensitivities for the single-op-amp elliptic-filter design of Fig. 6.14. The calculations involved are identical to those presented earlier for the Sallen-Key and infinite-gain LP filters, although the mathematics is more detailed due to the complexity of the filter. The basic results are: (1) The sensitivities of the components to variations in the cutoff frequency $\omega_c = \omega_p$ and the transmission zero ω_z are all ≤ 1, and additionally $S_K^{\omega_z} = S_K^{\omega_p} = 0$. (2) The sensitivity of Q_p to component and gain changes is significantly larger. For example, from Eq. (6.31) the Q_p sensitivities due to changes in C_4 and K are

$$S_{C4}^{Q_p} = \frac{-2Q_p C(C - 1 + K)}{(2C + 1)^{3/2}} \tag{6.62a}$$

and

$$S_K^{Q_p} = \frac{2Q_p K}{(2C + 1)^{1/2}} = \frac{K}{(2 - K + C)} \tag{6.62b}$$

where the element C was defined earlier by $C_4 = aC$. If we use the design values of Example 6.54, we obtain for the $H_1(s)$ synthesis

$$S_{C4}^{Q_{p1}} = -1.75 \qquad S_{K1}^{Q_{p1}} = 2.07 \tag{6.62c}$$

whereas for the $H_2(s)$ synthesis we obtain, due to the larger Q,

$$S_{C4}^{Q_{p2}} = -15.2 \qquad S_{K2}^{Q_{p2}} = 17.6 \tag{6.62d}$$

When the values above are compared with sensitivity numbers for either Sallen-Key or infinite-gain LP filters in Table 6.8, it is evident that the single-op-amp circuit implementation of an elliptic filter has generally much higher sensitivities. For this reason, elliptic filters are usually designed using two or more op amps for each second-order section. Designs of this type are considered later, in Section 6.2.4.

Op Amp Gain-Bandwidth Limitations. Up to now we have assumed in all our LP filter circuits that the GB was infinitely large for the op amp, or that the value of GB was tremendously greater than ω_c for the filter. A logical follow-up question on the subject of sensitivity considerations is, how does ω_c (and Q) of the filter change due to a finite value of GB for the op amp? Stated another way, we could logically ask how much greater than ω_c must the GB of the op amp be, such that our pole locations move insignificantly from the locations obtained assuming that the GB is infinitely large.

This problem was considered by Budak and Petrela* by assuming a single pole in the open-loop gain for the op amp defined by [as per Eq. (2.1) of Chapt. 2]

$$A(s) = \frac{A_O \omega_0}{s + \omega_0} = \frac{GB}{s + \left(\dfrac{GB}{A_O}\right)}$$

Hence, the closed-loop gain expression for the amplifier K in the Sallen-Key filter of Fig. 6.11 is now defined by [as per Eqs. (2.15) and (3.11), previously]

$$K = A_{CL}^+(s) = A_{CL}^+(\text{ideal})\left[\frac{-T(s)}{1 - T(s)}\right]$$

$$= A_{CL}^+(\text{ideal})\left[\frac{1}{1 - \dfrac{1}{T(s)}}\right] \tag{6.63}$$

where $A_{CL}^+(\text{ideal}) = 1 + R_B/R_A$, and for the circuit of Fig. 6.11, assuming large R_{IN} and small R_O for the op amp,

$$T(s) = -\left(\frac{R_A}{R_A + R_B}\right)\left(\frac{GB}{s + \dfrac{GB}{A_O}}\right) \tag{6.64}$$

Substituting Eq. (6.64) into Eq. (6.63) and clearing, we now obtain for the gain K, (provided that the open-loop gain $A_O \gg K_O$),

$$K = \frac{GB}{s + \dfrac{GB}{K_O}} \tag{6.65}$$

where $GB = A_O \omega_0$ and $K_O = A_{CL}^+(\text{ideal}) = 1 + R_B/R_A$. If Eq. (6.65) is now substituted for the gain K in Eq. (6.24) one obtains, for the equal R, equal C case

---

* A. Budak and D. M. Petrela, "Frequency Limitations of Active Filters Using Operational Amplifiers," *IEEE Trans. Ckt. Theory*, Vol. CT-19, No. 4, pp. 322–328, (July 1972). [Also contained in Ref. 6.5].

$(R_1 = R_2, C_1 = C_2)$ of Eq. (6.27) and Fig. 6.12(a), a new transfer function

$$H(s) = \frac{v_2}{v_1} = \frac{GB_n}{s_n^3 + s_n^2\left(3 + \dfrac{GB_n}{3 - 1/Q}\right) + s_n\left(1 + \dfrac{GB_n}{3Q - 1}\right) + \left(\dfrac{GB_n}{3 - 1/Q}\right)} \qquad \text{(6.66a)}$$

where the normalized terms are defined by

$$s_n = \frac{s}{\omega_c} \qquad GB_n = \frac{GB}{\omega_c} \qquad\qquad \text{(6.66b)}$$

The effect of a finite value of gain-bandwidth product on the roots of the denominator of Eq. (6.66a) [the poles of the $H(s)$ function] is illustrated by a plot in the upper half s_n plane in Fig. 6.18(a), where each solid curve represents a constant value of Q, and the dotted lines represent values for the normalized GB_n value. For $GB_n = \infty$, the intersection of the constant Q lines represents pole locations for $H(s)$ for the previously assumed ideal case of an infinite gain-bandwidth product. Thus, as the ratio GB/ω_c becomes smaller (the cutoff frequency is closer to the value of GB for the op amp) the pole locations move closer to the origin of the s_n plane. Hence, the *actual* pole will have a *smaller* value of ω_c than the design value. Further, if the design Q is large ($Q \geq 3$) then as ω_c approaches the GB value, the actual Q becomes *less* than the design value for Q (the angle between the pole and the imaginary axis increases).

The curves indicated in Fig. 6.18(b) are for the unity-gain, equal resistance case of Fig. 6.12(b), for which the new transfer function is

$$H(s_n) = \frac{v_2}{v_1} = \frac{GB_n}{s_n^3 + s_n^2\left(2Q + \dfrac{1}{Q} + GB_n\right) + s_n\left(1 + \dfrac{GB_n}{Q}\right) + GB_n} \qquad \text{(6.67)}$$

Although the curves are similar to the equal R, equal C case of Fig. 6.18(a), it is apparent that the constant GB_n curves (dotted lines) are closer together for $Q \leq 3$ for the unity-gain case, which indicates *less* sensitivity to pole shifts because of finite GB.

Expressions for pole shifts due to changes in the GB value can be obtained by evaluating the derivative of the pole with respect to $1/GB$, with the result that for small shifts around the nominal values of ω_c and Q, one can obtained the actual values of ω_c and Q in terms of the design value as:

(1) Sallen-Key; equal R, equal C

$$\omega_c(\text{actual}) \approx \omega_c(\text{design})\left[1 - \frac{1}{2}\left(3 - \frac{1}{Q}\right)^2 \frac{\omega_c}{GB}\right] \qquad \text{(6.68a)}$$

$$Q(\text{actual}) \approx Q(\text{design})\left[1 + \frac{1}{2}\left(3 - \frac{1}{Q}\right)^2 \frac{\omega_c}{GB}\right] \qquad \text{(6.68b)}$$

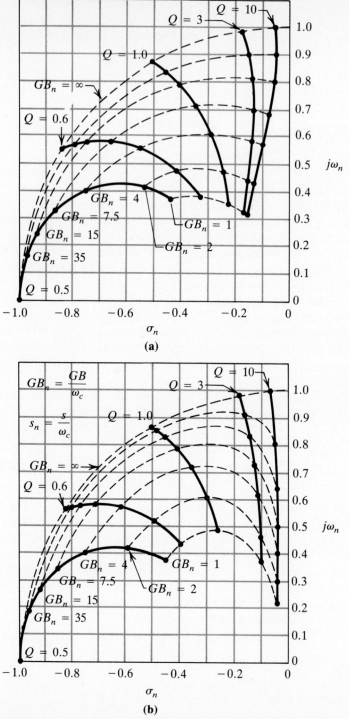

Figure 6.18 Sallen-Key LP filter sensitivity to finite *GB*: (a) equal *R*, equal *C*; (b) unity gain, equal *R*.

Source: A. Budak and D. M. Petrela, "Frequency Limitations of Active Filters Using Operational Amplifiers," *IEEE Tran. Circuit Theory*, vol. CT-19, no. 4, p. 324, July 1972.

and for a realization such that the percentage shifts $\Delta\omega_c/\omega_c = \Delta Q/Q \leq 10\%$, the requirement on the gain-bandwidth product is

$$GB \geq 45\left(1 - \frac{1}{3Q}\right)^2 \omega_c \tag{6.68c}$$

(2) Sallen-Key: equal R, unity-gain

$$\omega_c(\text{actual}) \approx \omega_c(\text{design})\left(1 - \frac{\omega_c Q}{GB}\right) \tag{6.69a}$$

$$Q(\text{actual}) \approx Q(\text{design})\left(1 + \frac{\omega_c Q}{GB}\right) \tag{6.69b}$$

and for small shifts so that $\Delta\omega_c/\omega_c = \Delta Q/Q \leq 10\%$, the requirement is

$$GB \geq 10Q\omega_c \tag{6.69c}$$

If the op amp indeed has only a single-pole open-loop response, it is possible to easily compensate the Sallen-Key lowpass filter by appropriately adding lead-lag compensation. This concept is indicated in Problem 6.26. A similar set of expressions arises from the infinite-gain filter of Fig. 6.17. For the case $H_0 = 1$, $R_1 = R_2 = R_3 = R$, and the open-loop gain defined by Eq. (2.1), the transfer function becomes

(3) Infinite-Gain: $H_0 = 1$, equal R

$$H(s_n) = \frac{v_2}{v_1} = \frac{GB_n}{s_n^3 + s_n^2\left[3Q + \dfrac{1}{Q} + GB_n\right] + s_n\left[2 + \dfrac{GB_n}{Q}\right] + GB_n} \tag{6.70}$$

with corresponding equations for the actual Q and ω_c

$$\omega_c(\text{actual}) \approx \omega_c(\text{design})\left(1 - \frac{3\omega_c Q}{2GB}\right) \tag{6.71a}$$

$$Q(\text{actual}) \approx Q(\text{design})\left(1 + \frac{\omega_c Q}{2GB}\right) \tag{6.71b}$$

and for small shifts the requrements on GB are

$$GB \geq 15\omega_c Q \qquad (\text{for } \Delta\omega_c/\omega_c \leq 10\%) \tag{6.71c}$$

$$GB \geq 5\omega_c Q \qquad (\text{for } \Delta Q/Q \leq 10\%) \tag{6.71d}$$

A plot of the pole locations of Eq. (6.70) for different values of Q and GB_n is shown in Fig. 6.19. In comparing this figure with that for the two Sallen and Key circuits it is apparent the constant Q lines, for Q between 0.6 and 3, lie along a nearly constant angle with the ω_n axis, indicating little shift of Q with a decrease in

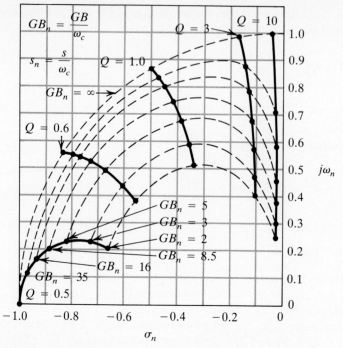

Figure 6.19 Pole locations for the infinite-gain LP filter for $H_o = 1$, equal R, as a function of the GB.
Source: Budak and Petrela, *op. cit.* p. 327.

GB_n. Also, since a single-op-amp circuit is seldom used for a $Q > 5$, then an analysis of Equations (6.68)–(6.70) would indicate that for minimum shift in $\Delta\omega_c$ the Sallen-Key unity-gain circuit is preferred, while for a minimum shift in ΔQ the infinite-gain circuit is better.

EXAMPLE 6.7

Using the data of Example 6.6, evaluate the pole shifts for each type of LP filter, assuming a 741 op amp is used, and ω_c is to be $2\pi \times 6.2 \times 10^4$ rad/sec.

Solution

For a 741 op amp the gain-bandwidth product is approximately 1 MHz, hence the normalized value of GB is $GB_n \approx 1\ \text{MHz}/62\ \text{kHz} = 16$. The *design value* of Q is 5, with ideal normalized ($GB = \infty$) pole locations at

$$s_n = -\frac{1}{10} \pm j\left(1 - \frac{1}{100}\right)^{1/2} = -0.1 \pm j0.995$$

For the various filters indicated in Figs. 6.18 and 6.19 we have *actual* complex pole (there is one real pole) locations* from the curves at

(Sallen-Key; equal R, equal C)

$$s_n \approx -0.08 \pm j0.81[Q_a \approx 5.1, f_{ca} \approx 0.81 \times 6.2 \times 10^4 = 50.5 \text{ kHz}]$$

(Sallen-Key; unity-gain, equal R)

$$s_n \approx -0.06 \pm j0.73[Q_a \approx 6.1, f_{ca} \approx 45.4 \text{ kHz}]$$

(Infinite-Gain; $H_0 = 1$, equal R)

$$s_n \approx -0.08 \pm j0.7[Q_a \approx 4.4 \ f_{ca} \approx 43.7 \text{ kHz}]$$

which compares with the analytical results (valid *only* for small changes) from Eqs. (6.68)–(6.71) (for Sallen-Key, equal R, equal C)

$$Q \approx 6.4 \qquad \omega_c \approx 45 \text{ kHz}$$

For Sallen-Key, unity-gain, equal R

$$Q \approx 6.6 \qquad \omega_c \approx 42.6 \text{ kHz}$$

and for infinite-gain, $H_0 = 1$, equal R

$$Q \approx 5.8 \qquad \omega_c \approx 33 \text{ kHz}$$

Since the $\Delta\omega$ and $\Delta\theta$ changes are large, the analytical results are evidently not in good agreement with values obtained from the curves.

---

* The actual pole locations, obtained by solving Eqs. (6.66a), (6.67), and (6.70) are: S-K, Equal R, Equal C: $s_n = -8.54$, $-0.086 \pm j0.8133$; with $Q_a = 4.74$, $f_{ca} = 50.7$ kHz
S-K, Unity-gain, Equal R: $s_n = -26.06$, $-0.0688 \pm j0.7805$; with $Q_a = 5.69$, $f_{ca} = 48.6$ kHz
Infinite-gain, $H_0 = 1$, Equal R: $s_n = -31.05$, $-0.0754 \pm j0.714$; with $Q_a = 4.76$, $f_{ca} = 44.5$ kHz

---

■ **Exercise 6.3**

From the results of Example 6.7, what should be the design values for Q and ω_c (normalized) to achieve* an actual Q and ω_c of 5 and 1, respectively? Assume a 741 op amp is used, as in the Example.

---

* The concept of changing design values to obtain a final design equal to that desired, is referred to as "predistortion." Basically, the poles of the function are "predistorted" on purpose so that, after shifting, their final locations are identical to those desired.

For additional comparison, the pole locations for the single-op-amp elliptic filter of Fig. 6.14 are shown in Fig. 6.20. The values $\omega_{z2} = 4.9221$ and $\omega_{p2} = 1.0308$ of Example 6.5 were used to obtain the graph. Including the effects of a finite gain-bandwidth product, the value for K of Eq. (6.65)

$$K = \frac{GB}{s + \frac{GB}{K_0}} \tag{6.65}$$

is now substituted into Eq. (6.31), the transfer function for $H_e(s)$, with the result that for normalized values $GB_n = GB/\omega_p$ and $s_n = s/\omega_p$ the equation now becomes

$$H_e(s_n) = \frac{v_2(s_n)}{v_1(s_n)} = \frac{GB_n(1/m^2)(s_n^2 + m^2)}{s_n^3 + a_2 s_n^2 + a_1 s_n + a_0} \tag{6.72a}$$

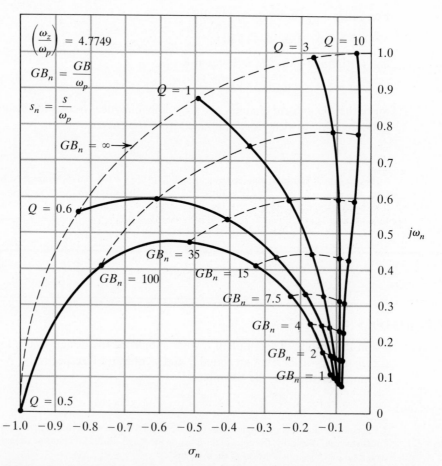

Figure 6.20 Pole locations for the H_2 ($j\omega$) elliptic LP filter of Example 6.5, for the case $(\omega_z/\omega_p) = 4.7749$, including the effects of a finite GB.

where

$$m = \left(\frac{\omega_z}{\omega_p}\right)$$

$$a_2 = \left(\frac{GB_n}{K_0} + \frac{3 + m^2}{m}\right)$$

$$a_1 = \left\{1 - GB_n\left[\frac{2}{m} - \frac{1}{K_0}\left(\frac{3 + m^2}{m}\right)\right]\right\} \tag{6.72b}$$

$$a_0 = \frac{GB_n}{K_0}$$

$$K_0 = \frac{1}{2}\left[3 + m^2 - \frac{m}{Q_P}\right]$$

If the graph of Fig. 6.20 is now compared with those of Fig. 6.19 (for the infinite-gain filter) or Fig. 6.18 (for the Sallen-Key filter), it is apparent that the elliptic-filter requires a *much greater* ratio of the *GB* of the op amp to the pole frequencies ω_p *even* for Q_p values less than unity.

6.2.4 Multiple-Op-Amp Filters

We have investigated several types of single-op-amp lowpass circuits, and have found that their sensitivities due to changes can be high. For lower sensitivities, and particularly for better tuning capabilities (the ability to *independently* adjust H_0, Q and ω_c) it is often necessary to use more than one op amp in the circuit. We will first look at a few examples of those circuits employing two op amps, and then expand to analyze the more common usage of three or four op amps.

Filters Using Two Op Amps. In the design of the elliptic LP filter of Example 6.5 shown in Fig., 6.15, we found that with a single op amp it was necessary to provide multiple feedback and therefore use many circuit elements to realize both transmission zeroes and poles. Further, an evaluation of the Q sensitivities using the design conditions of Example 6.5 gave much larger values for S_K^Q than we generally encountered in either the Sallen-Key or infinite-gain filters.

To lower the sensitivities for the elliptic design, the two-op-amp circuit of Fig. 6.21 is often used. This circuit is basically an infinite-gain LP, but using two op amps. For the general circuit of Fig. 6.21(a), the voltage-transfer function is

$$\frac{v_2(s)}{v_1(s)} = \frac{Y_1 - Y_2}{Y_3 - Y_4} \tag{6.73}$$

To obtain the values of the admittances Y_1 through Y_4 we divide the numerator and denominator by a common factor $s + a(a > 0)$ and then obtain a partial fraction expansion. Hence, from Eq. (6.73) we define for the numerator

$$Y_1 - Y_2 = \frac{H\left(s^2 + \frac{\omega_z}{Q_z}s + \omega_z^2\right)}{s + a} = c_1 s + c_2 + \frac{c_3 s}{s + a} \tag{6.74a}$$

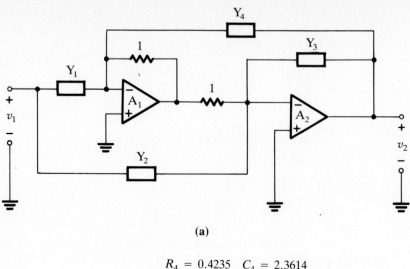

(a)

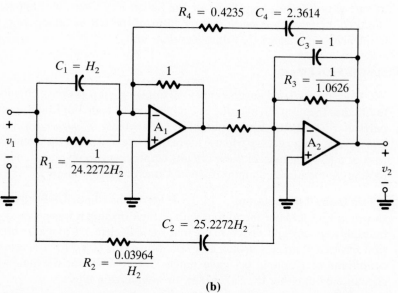

(b)

Figure 6.21 A two-op-amp general biquadratic filter: (a) basic concept; (b) implemented for the case $\omega_z > \omega_p$, suitable for the elliptic LP design of Example 6.5, for $H_2(s)$.

and similarly for the denominator

$$Y_3 - Y_4 = \frac{\left(s^2 + \dfrac{\omega_p}{Q_p}s + \omega_p^2\right)}{s + a} = d_1 s + d_2 + \frac{d_3 s}{s + a} \tag{6.74b}$$

Thus, if all coefficients are positive in either equation $Y_2 = 0 = Y_4$. However, if not all coefficients are positive the Y_1 and Y_3 admittances are set equal to the positive terms, while Y_2 and Y_4 are set equal to the negative terms. As an example, suppose we obtain the synthesis of $H_2(s)$ from Eq. (6.34a) defined in Example 6.5

$$H_2(s) = \frac{H_2(s^2 + 24.2272)}{(s^2 + 0.30116s + 1.06258)} = \frac{H_2(s^2 + \omega_z^2)}{s^2 + \left(\dfrac{\omega_p}{Q_p}\right)s + \omega_p^2}$$

with $\omega_z = 4.9221$, $\omega_p = 1.0308$, and $Q_p = 3.4228$. Thus, Eq. (6.74a) becomes

$$Y_1 - Y_2 = \frac{H_2(s^2 + \omega_z^2)}{s + a} = H_2\left[s + \frac{\omega_z^2}{a} + \frac{k_1 s}{s + a}\right] \tag{6.75a}$$

where for this example,

$$k_1 = -\left(\frac{\omega_z^2 + a^2}{a}\right) = -\left(\frac{24.2272 + a^2}{a}\right) \tag{6.75b}$$

Also, Eq. (6.74b) results in

$$Y_3 - Y_4 = s + \frac{\omega_p^2}{a} + \frac{k_2 s}{s + a} \tag{6.75c}$$

where now

$$k_2 = -\left[\frac{\omega_p^2 + a^2 - a(\omega_p/Q_p)}{a}\right]$$

$$= -\left[\frac{1.06258 - a(0.30116) + a^2}{a}\right] \tag{6.75d}$$

Since we have complete choice for the term a (except that $a > 0$) let us choose $a = 1$. Thus $k_2 = -2.3614$ and $k_1 = 25.2272$ while

$$Y_1 - Y_2 = H_2\left[s + 24.2272 - \frac{1}{0.03964 + 1/25.2272s}\right] \tag{6.75e}$$

or

$$Y_1 = H_2[s + 24.2272] \equiv C_1 s + \frac{1}{R_1}$$

and

$$Y_2 = \frac{H_2}{0.03964 + 1/25.2272s} \equiv \frac{1}{R_2 + 1/C_2 s}$$

Similarly, for the denominator terms we have

$$Y_3 = s + 1.0626 = C_3 s + 1/R_3$$

$$Y_4 = \frac{1}{0.4235 + 1/2.3614s} = \frac{1}{R_4 + 1/C_4 s}$$

The resulting normalized LP circuit is shown in Fig. 6.21(b), where the gain constant H_2 is now available as an independent parameter. The design suffers from the same problem as did the differentiation circuit of Fig. 1.7(a) in Chapter 1, namely the closed-loop gain of A_1 becomes very large as $s \to \infty$.

A two-op-amp circuit that is an improvement over the previous biquadratic filter is shown in Fig. 6.22. The circuit of Fig. 6.22(a) is for a second-order all-pole LP filter (such as a Butterworth, Chebyshev, or Thomson approximation), whereas the modified circuit of Fig. 6.22(b) will allow $j\omega$-axis zeroes, or is suitable for an

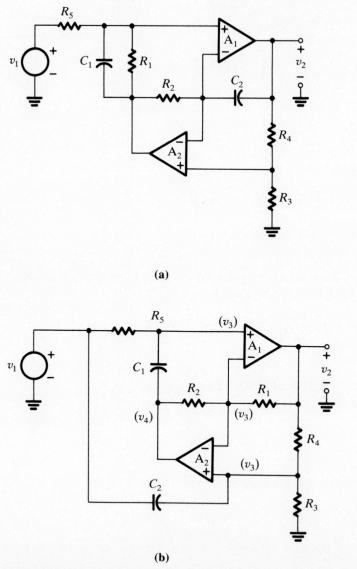

(a)

(b)

Figure 6.22 An improved two-op-amp LP filter: (a) an all-pole second-order LP; (b) a second-order LP with $j\omega$-axis zeroes, suitable for an elliptic filter design.

elliptic LP approximation, We will leave the derivation of the all-pole network as an exercise for the student, and concentrate on the elliptic realization of Fig. 6.22(b).

Exercise 6.4

Show that the transfer function for the LP filter circuit of Fig. 6.22(a) is

$$H(s) = \frac{v_2(s)}{v_1(s)} = \frac{H}{s^2 + a_1 s + a_0} \tag{6.76a}$$

where

$$H = \frac{1}{R_2 R_5 C_1 C_2}\left(1 + \frac{R_3}{R_4}\right)$$

$$a_1 = \frac{1}{R_1 C_1} \tag{6.76b}$$

$$a_0 = \frac{R_3}{R_2 R_4 R_5 C_1 C_2}$$

Find the gain at dc, $H(0)$.

To obtain the transfer function of Fig. 6.22(b), we assume an ideal op amp so that the voltage at the noninverting and inverting inputs of the op amps are equal. If we define that voltage to be v_3 and the voltage at the output of A_2 to be v_4 we obtain the following nodal equations:

$$\left(\frac{v_1 - v_3}{R_5}\right) - (v_3 - v_4)(sC_1) = 0$$

$$\left(\frac{v_4 - v_3}{R_2}\right) - \left(\frac{v_3 - v_2}{R_1}\right) = 0 \tag{6.77}$$

$$(sC_2)(v_1 - v_3) + \left(\frac{v_2 - v_3}{R_4}\right) - \left(\frac{v_3}{R_3}\right) = 0$$

Solving these above equations for $v_2(s)/v_1(s)$ leads to

$$H(s) = \frac{v_2(s)}{v_1(s)} = \frac{(s^2 + \omega_z^2)}{s^2 + \left(\dfrac{\omega_p}{Q_p}\right)s + \omega_p^2} \tag{6.78a}$$

where

$$\omega_z^2 = \frac{R_1}{R_2 R_5 C_1 C_2}\left(\frac{1}{R_3} + \frac{1}{R_4}\right)$$

$$\left(\frac{\omega_p}{Q_p}\right) = \frac{1}{R_3 C_2} \quad \text{or} \quad \frac{1}{Q_p} = \frac{1}{R_3}\left(\frac{R_2 R_4 R_5}{R_1}\right)^{1/2}\left(\frac{C_1}{C_2}\right)^{1/2}$$

(6.78b)

$$\omega_p^2 = \frac{R_1}{R_2 R_4 R_5 C_1 C_2} = \omega_z^2\left(\frac{R_3}{R_3 + R_4}\right)$$

Note also from Eq. (6.78b) that $\omega_z > \omega_p$, which is necessary for an elliptic LP design, and further that the gain at dc $H(0)$ is equal to $1 + R_4/R_3$.

The component sensitivities of the two-op-amp elliptic filter of Fig. 6.22(b) are low when compared with the previous single-op-amp filter of Fig. 6.14. From Eq. (6.78b) we obtain

$$S_{R1}^{\omega_z} = \frac{1}{2} \qquad S_{R2}^{\omega_z} = S_{R5}^{\omega_z} = S_{C1}^{\omega_z} = S_{C2}^{\omega_z} = -\frac{1}{2}$$

$$S_{R3}^{\omega_z} = \frac{-R_4}{R_4 + R_3} \qquad S_{R4}^{\omega_z} = \frac{-R_3}{R_4 + R_3}$$

(6.78c)

$$S_{R1}^{\omega_p} = \frac{1}{2} \qquad S_{R2}^{\omega_p} = S_{R4}^{\omega_p} = S_{R5}^{\omega_p} = S_{C1}^{\omega_p} = S_{C2}^{\omega_p} = -\frac{1}{2}$$

$$S_{C1}^{Q_p} = S_{R2}^{Q_p} = S_{R4}^{Q_p} = S_{R5}^{Q_p} = -\frac{1}{2} \qquad S_{C2}^{Q_p} = S_{R1}^{Q_p} = S_{R3}^{Q_p} = \frac{1}{2}$$

The Q_p sensitivities in particular are *much lower* than those obtained earlier for the single-op-amp LP filter of Example 6.5, and stated in Eq. (6.62c and d).

However, if we compare the effects of a finite gain-bandwidth product with the LP filter of Example 6.5, the two-op-amp circuit is more sensitive, since now there are *two* op amps inside the feedback loop, whereas previously there was one. Thus the limitations of a finite GB will produce much larger shifts in pole, and now zero, locations. If we substitute the single-pole approximation for the gain (where A_{OL} is the open-loop gain for op amps A_1 and A_2)

$$A_1 = A_2 = \frac{A_{OL}\omega_0}{s + \omega_0} = \frac{GB}{s + \left(\dfrac{GB}{A_{OL}}\right)} \approx \frac{GB^*}{s}$$

(6.79)

into the LP filter circuit of Fig. 6.22(b), and solve for the transfer function, with $GB_n \equiv GB/\omega_p$ and $s_n \equiv s/\omega_p$, we obtain

$$H(s_n) = \frac{v_2(s_n)}{v_1(s_n)} = \frac{b_2 s_n^2 + b_1 s_n + m^2}{a_4 s_n^4 + a_3 s_n^3 + a_2 s_n^2 + a_1 s + 1}$$

(6.80)

---

* The gain-bandwidth products of A_1 and A_2 in Fig. 6.22 are not necessarily equal. However, one would typically use a dual op amp (two op amps on the same substrate) for A_1 and A_2, and thus the two op amps would reasonably have the same GB values.

where

$$b_2 = 1 + \frac{Q_p\left(1 + \dfrac{R_2}{R_1}\right)[m^2 - 1]}{GB_n}$$

$$b_1 = \frac{m^2}{GB_n}\left(1 + \frac{R_2}{R_1}\right)$$

$$a_4 = \frac{1}{GB_n^2\left(1 + \dfrac{R_1}{R_2}\right)}$$

$$a_3 = a_4\left[\frac{1}{Q_p}\left(\frac{m^2}{m^2 - 1}\right) + GB_n + Q_p(m^2 - 1)\left(\frac{R_2}{R_1}\right)\right]$$

$$a_2 = 1 + \frac{\left(1 + \dfrac{R_1}{R_2}\right)}{GB_n}\left[\frac{1}{Q_p}\left(\frac{m^2}{m_2 - 1}\right) + Q_p\left(\frac{R_2}{R_1}\right)(m^2 - 1) + \frac{m^2\left(\dfrac{R_2}{R_1}\right)}{GB_n}\right]$$

$$a_1 = \frac{1}{Q_p} + \frac{m^2\left(1 + \dfrac{R_2}{R_1}\right)}{GB_n}$$

$$m^2 = \left(\frac{\omega_z}{\omega_p}\right)^2$$

Generally the a_4 coefficient is small, so the denominator of Eq. (6.80) can be approximated by a cubic equation. For this case the roots can be obtained using a programmable calculator, with the result plotted in Fig. 6.23 for the parameter values of the LP elliptic design of Example 6.5 and for the case $(\omega_z/\omega_p) = 4.7749$. Since the transmission zeroes are now a function of the gain-bandwidth product, the zeroes shift decidedly from the $j\omega_n$-axis for finite GB_n values. From Fig. 6.23(a), even for a gain-bandwidth product 100 times larger than the cutoff frequency, the shift of the zeroes is significant for Q_p values greater than one. In comparison with the single-op-amp circuit, whose pole locations were indicated in Fig. 6.20, we see that the shifting of the poles for the two-op-amp circuit is much more severe for $Q \geq 3$, and particularly for $GB_n < 35$. Hence, even though the sensitivity factors in Eq. (6.78c) are much less than those for the single-op-amp elliptic design, the use of the second op amp now demands a *much* larger gain-bandwidth product than did the single-op-amp design.

Before we leave the subject of LP filters using two op amps, let us look at one additional circuit suitable for realizing an all-pole LP filter. The circuit* is shown in Fig. 6.24, where it is assumed that the two op amps A_1 and A_2 are a dual

---

* A. S. Sedra and J. L. Espinoza, "Sensitivity and Frequency Limitations of Biquadratic Active Filters," originally published in *IEEE Trans. Ckts. Syst.*, Vol. CAS-22, pp. 122–30, (Feb. 1975) [also included in Ref. 6.8, pp. 86–94].

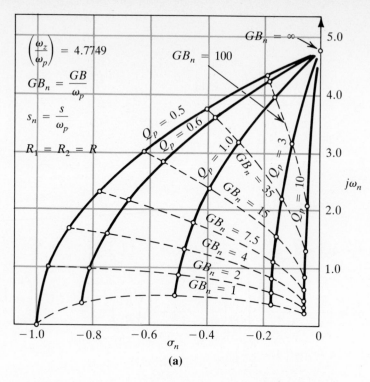

(a)

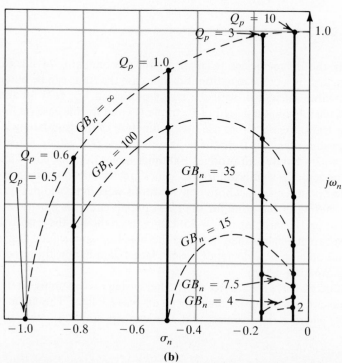

(b)

Figure 6.23 Effects of finite *GB* for the two-op-amp LP elliptic filter of Fig. 6.22 (b) for $(\omega_z/\omega_p) = 4.7749$, and with $R_1 = R_2 = R$: (a) zero shifts; (b) pole shifts.

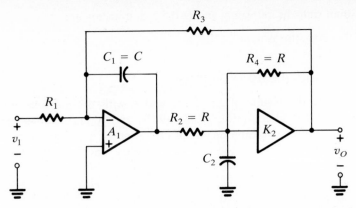

Figure 6.24 A two-op-amp, low-sensitivity circuit for obtaining an all-pole LP filter.

configuration on a single monolithic chip, and therefore have nearly identical GB values. The op amp A_1 employs an infinite-gain connection, while A_2 has a noninverting configuration. The transfer function for the circuit is that of a typical inverting LP

$$H(s) = \frac{v_o(s)}{v_1(s)} = \frac{-H}{s^2 + \left(\dfrac{\omega_c}{Q}\right)s + \omega_c^2} \tag{6.81}$$

where the design constraints are

$$\omega_c = \left(\frac{K_2}{R_3 RCC_2}\right)^{1/2} = \frac{1}{R_3 C}$$

$$H = K_2\left(\frac{1}{R_1 RCC_2}\right) \tag{6.81a}$$

$$C_2 = K_2 C\left(\frac{R_3}{R}\right)$$

$$K_2 = \frac{2Q}{Q+1}$$

Further, all element sensitivities $S_x^{\omega_c}$ and S_x^Q are low except for $S_{K_2}^Q$, which is equal to $(Q + 1)$. However, unlike the previous two-op-amp circuit of Fig. 6.22, which was very sensitive to changes in the gain-bandwidth product, the circuit of Fig. 6.24 has a frequency limitation (for $Q \gg 1$) that for identical op amps reduces to [Ref. 6.8, p. 92]

$$\frac{\Delta\omega_c}{\omega_c} \approx -2\left(\frac{\omega_c}{GB}\right) = -\frac{2}{GB_n} \tag{6.82a}$$

$$\frac{\Delta Q}{Q} \approx -\left[\frac{1}{\dfrac{GB}{3Q\omega_c} - 1}\right] = -\left[\frac{1}{\dfrac{GB_n}{3Q} - 1}\right] \tag{6.82b}$$

or, for small shifts in frequency and Q the requirements are

$$GB \geq 20\omega_c \text{ (for } \Delta\omega_c/\omega_c \leq 10\%) \tag{6.82c}$$

$$GB \geq 33\omega_c Q \text{ (for } \Delta Q/Q \leq 10\%) \tag{6.82d}$$

If we compare the results of Eq. 6.82c and d with the previous equations for single-op-amp LP filters, [Eqs. (6.68), (6.69) and (6.71)], we see that the GB requirements for the two-op-amp circuit are lower for $\Delta\omega_c$ changes, but higher (by a factor of 6.5 compared to the infinite-gain filter, and 3 for the unity-gain S-K filter) for ΔQ changes.

■ **Exercise 6.5**

Derive the transfer function of Eq. (6.81) for the two-op-amp LP filter of Fig. 6.24. Show that the design constraints of Eq. (6.81a) are a logical choice.

Filters Using Three or More Op Amps.   For greater versatility of design, and the ability to obtain not only LP, but HP and BP (and in some cases BR) filters as well, a three- or four-op-amp circuit is often used. The basic three-op-amp "biquad" active filter* is indicated in Fig. 6.25. The designation **biquad** refers to the ability of the circuit to realize a general *biquadratic* voltage-transfer function of the form

$$\frac{v_{\text{out}}}{v_{\text{in}}} = \frac{K\left[s^2 + \left(\dfrac{\omega_z}{Q_z}\right)s + \omega_z^2\right]}{s^2 + \left(\dfrac{\omega_p}{Q_p}\right)s + \omega_p^2} \tag{6.83}$$

by the use of simple op amp connections as integrators, "lossy" integrators† summers, and inverters. The circuit is also referred to as a *resonator* active filter. The basic three-op-amp circuit may be reduced to a two-op-amp design by the use of the "Howland circuit" (Fig. 5.32), connected as a noninverting integrator (Fig. 1.6).‡ This circuit is described in Problem 6.32. If a fourth op amp is added (A_4 in Fig. 6.25) it is possible to obtain either an HP output or an elliptic LP output at

---

* One of the best references to this general biquad structure is L. C. Thomas, "The Biquad: Part I—Some Practical Design Considerations," and "Part II—A Multipurpose Active Filtering System," in *IEEE Trans. Ckt. Theory*, Vol. CT-18, No. 3, pp. 350–61, (May, 1971).

† A "lossy" integrator is a basic inverting integrator, but with a resistor in parallel with the feedback capacitor.

‡ This connection is also called the "De Boo Integrator," after B. J. DeBoo, "A Novel Integrator Results by Grounding its Capacitor," *Electron. Des.*, Vol. 15 (June 7, 1967).

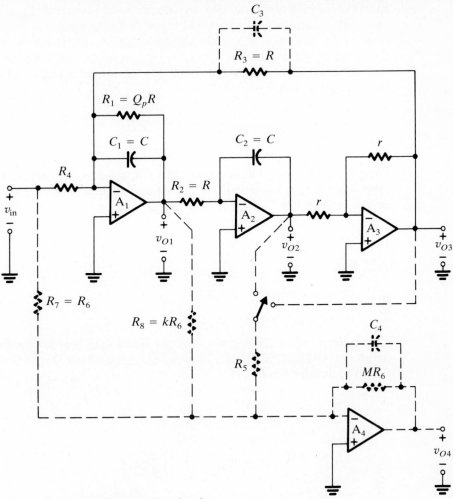

For tuning (in the order given):

1. R_3 adjusts ω_p.
2. R_1 adjusts Q_p.
3. R_5 adjusts ω_z.
4. R_8 adjusts Q_z.
5. R_6 (or R_4) adjusts overall gain.
6. $C_3 \approx \dfrac{4}{GB(\text{rad/s})R_3}$ compensates high-frequency Q enhancement.
7. C_4 can be chosen for an added (third-order) pole.

Figure 6.25 The biquad active filter (A_1–A_3). If A_4 is added, either an HP (v_{O3}-connected) or an elliptic LP (v_{O2}-connected) is obtained at v_{O4}.

v_{O4}. The versatility of the biquad circuit is demonstrated by the (relative) independent adjustments indicated in Fig. 6.25. The compensation capacitor C_3 is required if a large value of Q_p is needed, since the finite GB of the op amps will cause the actual Q_p value to increase at higher frequencies. In fact, Thomas* has shown that the actual Q_p for the biquad circuit as a function of the finite value of GB for the op amps is given by

$$Q_{\text{actual}} \approx \frac{Q_p}{1 - \dfrac{4Q_p}{GB_n}} \tag{6.84a}$$

where Q_p is the (ideal) design value and $GB_n = GB/\omega_p$, as before. Thus, as Q_p approaches $GB_n/4$, the actual Q_p for the circuit approaches infinity. Also, the change in frequency $\Delta\omega_c$ due to finite GB is given by

$$\frac{\Delta\omega_p}{\omega_p} \approx -\frac{3}{2GB_n} \tag{6.84b}$$

Thus, for small shifts in design values, one requires that

$$GB \geq 15\omega_p \text{ (for } \Delta\omega_p/\omega_p \leq 10\%) \tag{6.84c}$$

$$GB \geq 44\omega_p Q_p \text{ (for } \Delta Q_p/Q_p \leq 10\%) \tag{6.84d}$$

The requirement on GB for $\Delta\omega_p$ changes is less than that for the two-op-amp circuit [Eq. (6.82c)], but greater than the ΔQ_p requirement [Eq. (6.82d)].

The transfer functions for the various outputs in Fig. 6.25 are (see Problem 6.33)

$$H_1(s) = \frac{v_{O1}(s)}{v_{\text{in}}(s)} = \frac{-s\left(\dfrac{1}{R_4 C}\right)}{s^2 + s\left(\dfrac{1}{Q_p RC}\right) + \left(\dfrac{1}{R^2 C^2}\right)} \tag{6.85a}$$

which is a BP filter characteristic, and

$$H_2(s) = \frac{v_{O2}(s)}{v_{\text{in}}(s)} = -\frac{v_{O3}(s)}{v_{\text{in}}(s)} = \frac{\dfrac{1}{R_4}\left(\dfrac{1}{RC^2}\right)}{s^2 + s\left(\dfrac{1}{Q_p RC}\right) + \left(\dfrac{1}{R^2 C^2}\right)} \tag{6.85b}$$

which is an LP filter characteristic. If the additional op amp A_4 is added, with R_5 connected to the output of A_3, we have an HP filter described by (C_4 removed)

$$H_4(s) = \frac{v_{O4}(s)}{v_{\text{in}}(s)} = -M\left[\frac{s^2}{s^2 + s\left(\dfrac{1}{Q_p RC}\right) + \left(\dfrac{1}{R_2 C_2}\right)}\right] \tag{6.85c}$$

---

* Thomas, op. cit.

if R_4 and R_5 are chosen as

$$R_4 = \left(\frac{Q_p}{k}\right)R \qquad R_5 = R_6\left(\frac{k}{Q_p}\right) \tag{6.85d}$$

where k is an arbitrary constant that can be used to control the dynamic range.

If R_5 is connected to the output of A_2, then we have a LP with transmission zeroes at $\pm j\omega_z$, where $\omega_z > \omega_p$, or an elliptic LP design given by (C_4 included)

$$H_4(s)_{LP} = \frac{v_{o4}(s)}{v_{in}(s)} = \left(\frac{-1/R_6C_4}{s + \dfrac{1}{mR_6C_4}}\right)\left[\frac{s^2 + \omega_z^2}{s^2 + s\left(\dfrac{\omega_p}{Q_p}\right) + \omega_p^2}\right] \tag{6.85e}$$

where the dc gain is now $H_0 = -M(\omega_z/\omega_p)^2$, and resistors R_4 and R_5 are required to be

$$R_4 = \left(\frac{Q_p}{k}\right)R \qquad R_5 = \frac{kR_6}{Q_p\left[\left(\dfrac{\omega_z}{\omega_p}\right)^2 - 1\right]} \tag{6.85f}$$

Notice that including C_4 would permit an additional real pole, which would be required in a third-order elliptic LP design.

For the basic biquad the sensitivity functions $S_x^{\omega_p}$ and S_x^Q (where x represents the various R and C elements), are comparable to the values for the passive LC case,* which allows simple tuning and precise performance. Further, the sensitivity of Q_p to changes in open-loop gain (A_{OL}) is very small, with a typical value of $S_{A_{OL}}^{Q_p} \approx 2Q_p/A_{OL}$.†

There are other versions of the basic three-op-amp biquad circuit. For example, the circuit of Fig. 6.26(a) moves the lossy integrator to A_2, while the basic integrator is now A_1. The LP transfer function for this circuit (with $R_4 = R$) is

$$\frac{v_{o3}(s)}{v_{in}(s)} = \frac{-\left(\dfrac{1}{RC}\right)^2}{s^2 + s\left(\dfrac{1}{RCQ_p}\right) + \left(\dfrac{1}{RC}\right)^2} \tag{6.86a}$$

with frequency-limitation equations defined nearly identical to those of the standard biquad in Eqs. 6.84(a)–(d). The circuit of Fig. 6.26(b) uses high-Q integrators for the two input stages, and also a modified inverting circuit for A_3. Although the circuit requires two additional op amps, the actual Q_p obtained is much closer to the design Q_p than the standard biquad circuit.‡ In fact, assuming identical frequency characteristics for A_1 and A_4 (and A_2 and A_5) it is possible to obtain $S_{GB}^{Q_p} = 0$.

---

* J. Tow, "Active RC Filters—A State Space Realization," *Proc. IEEE* (*Letters*), Vol. 56, pp. 1137–39, (June 1968).

† L. C. Thomas, *op. cit.*, p. 352.

‡ See P. O. Brackett and A. S. Sedra, "Active Compensation for High-Frequency Effects in Op-Amp Circuits with Applications to Active RC Filters," *IEEE Trans. Ckts. Syst.*, Vol. CAS-23, pp. 68–72, (Feb. 1976).

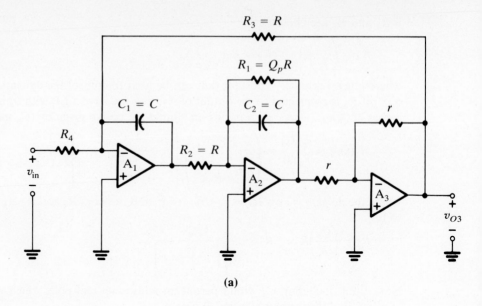

(a)

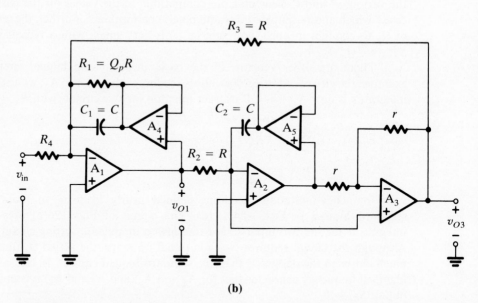

(b)

Figure 6.26 Two other forms of the 3-op-amp biquad filter: (a) interchanging A_1 and A_2; (b) use of high-Q integrators for A_1 and A_2.

EXAMPLE 6.8

Use the biquad circuit of Fig. 6.25 to realize the normalized $H_2(s)$ elliptic LP filter of Example 6.5, which was

$$H_2(s) = \frac{H_2(s^2 + 24.2272)}{s^2 + 0.30116s + 1.06258}$$

with $\omega_z = 4.9221$, $\omega_p = 1.0308$ and $Q_p = 3.4228$. Choose the parameter k to help equalize dynamic range in the filter.

Solution
With R and C normalized to unity, the basic biquad circuit of Fig. 6.25 has the elements R_4 and R_5 identified from Eq. (6.85f) as

$$R_4 = \frac{3.4228}{k} \qquad R_5 = \frac{kR_6}{74.6171}$$

The maximum output signal levels at v_{o1}, $v_{o2}(= |v_{o3}|)$ and v_{o4} are determined from Eqs. 6.85(a), 6.85(b), and 6.85(e), respectively, and are

$$\left|\frac{v_{o1}}{v_{in}}\right|_{max} = \frac{Q_p RC}{R_4 C} = k \qquad \left(\text{which occurs at } \omega = \omega_p = \frac{1}{RC}\right)$$

while we have for v_{o2}

$$\left|\frac{v_{o2}}{v_{in}}\right|_{dc} = \frac{1}{R_4} = \frac{k}{Q_p R} = \frac{k}{3.4228} \qquad \left|\frac{v_{o2}}{v_{in}}\right|_{\omega = \omega_p} = k$$

while for $v_{o4}(C_4$ is removed)

$$\left|\frac{v_{o4}}{v_{in}}\right|_{dc} = M\left(\frac{\omega_z}{\omega_p}\right)^2 \qquad \left|\frac{v_{o4}}{v_{in}}\right|_{\omega = \omega_p} = MQ_p\left[\left(\frac{\omega_z}{\omega_p}\right)^2 - 1\right]$$

Thus, if we choose the parameter k to be defined by

$$k = MQ_p\left[\left(\frac{\omega_z}{\omega_p}\right)^2 - 1\right] = 74.6171M \tag{6.87a}$$

then the maximum signal levels at v_{o1}, v_{o2}, v_{o3} and v_{o4} will be identical with amplitude kv_{in}. Also, R_4 and R_5 are now defined by

$$R_4 = \frac{1}{M\left[\left(\frac{\omega_z}{\omega_p}\right)^2 - 1\right]} = \frac{1}{21.8M} \tag{6.87b}$$

$$R_5 = MR_6 \tag{6.87c}$$

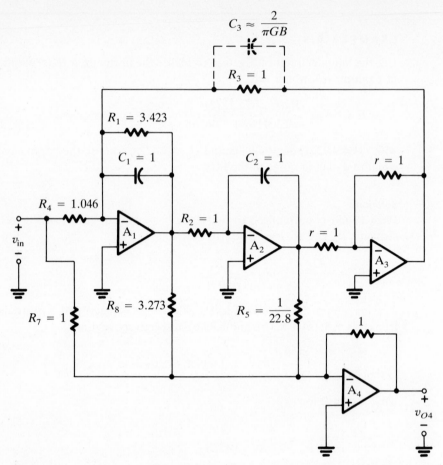

Figure 6.27 The biquad, elliptic LP circuit of Example 6.8, normalized for $R = C = 1$ and $\omega_p = 1$, with $Q_p = 3.423$, $M = 1/22.8$, and $k = 3.273$.

where M can now be chosen for overall system gain and output amplitude. Thus, if a gain at dc of unity is desired, then choose $M = (\omega_p/\omega_z)^2 = 1/22.8$, which gives $R_4 = 1.046$, $R_5 = R_6/22.8$ and $k = 3.273$. The resulting circuit normalized for $R = C = 1$ and $\omega_p = 1$ is shown in Fig. 6.27.

A circuit very similar to the biquad active filter is the **state-variable (SV) filter**, shown in Fig. 6.28. In fact, the state-variable filter has an advantage over the biquad, in that an HP function can be directly obtained without adding a fourth op amp. The state-variable circuit was so named due to its original analysis[*] based on

* W. J. Kerwin, L. P. Huelsman, and R. W. Newcomb, "State-Variable Synthesis for Insensitive Integrated Circuit Transfer Functions," *IEEE J. S.S. Ckts.*, Vol. SC-2, No. 3, pp. 87–92, (Sept. 1967).

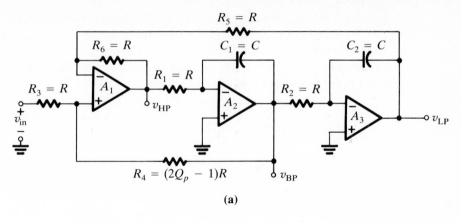

(a)

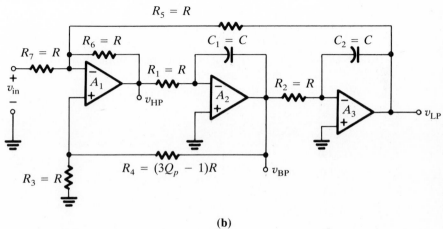

(b)

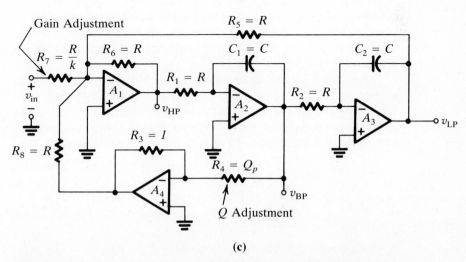

(c)

Figure 6.28 The state-variable (SV) filter. Circuits (a) and (b) differ by a gain constant and phaseshift. Circuit (c) allows independent adjustment of gain and Q_p.

state-variable equations and flow graphs. The (a) and (b) circuits in Fig. 6.28 differ only by the polarity of the output signals and the gain constants, with otherwise identical transfer functions, whereas the circuit in Fig. 6.28(c) allows an independent adjustment of both Q and the gain constant K. For the circuit of Fig. 6.28(a) the transfer functions at the various outputs are

$$\frac{v_{HP}(s)}{v_{in}(s)} = \frac{s^2\left(\dfrac{2Q_p - 1}{Q_p}\right)}{D(s)} \tag{6.88a}$$

$$\frac{v_{BP}(s)}{v_{in}(s)} = \frac{-s\omega_p\left(\dfrac{2Q_p - 1}{Q_p}\right)}{D(s)} \tag{6.88b}$$

$$\frac{v_{LP}(s)}{v_{in}(s)} = \frac{\omega_p^2\left(\dfrac{2Q_p - 1}{Q_p}\right)}{D(s)} \tag{6.88c}$$

where $D(s) = s^2 + (\omega_p/Q_p)s + \omega_p^2$. The maximum value of the gain is equal to $(2Q_p - 1)/Q_p$ for the HP and LP outputs, and $(1 - 2Q)$ for the BP output. The circuit of Fig. 6.28(b) has the following transfer functions:

$$\frac{v_{HP}(s)}{v_{in}(s)} = \frac{-s^2}{D(s)} \tag{6.89a}$$

$$\frac{v_{BP}(s)}{v_{in}(s)} = \frac{s\omega_p}{D(s)} \tag{6.89b}$$

$$\frac{v_{LP}(s)}{v_{in}(s)} = \frac{-\omega_p^2}{D(s)} \tag{6.89c}$$

where $D(s)$ is the same as in Eq. (6.88). Thus, the second circuit in Fig. 6.28 has an advantage of having unity gain for the HP and LP outputs, whereas the gain is equal to Q for the BP output. Further, for high-Q circuits one could form a voltage divider at the output of A_2, and thus reduce the required size of R_4 by the voltage divider ratio.

An elliptic LP filter is obtained, like the biquad circuit, by adding another op amp connected as a summer, as indicated in Fig. 6.29. Although the SV circuit of Fig. 6.28(b) is used, one could also utilize the circuits of Fig. 6.28(a) or (c) if desired. Basically, the HP and LP outputs are summed in a weighted fashion to obtain $j\omega$-axis zeroes. For the circuit of Fig. 6.29 the transfer function at v_{O4} is

$$\frac{v_{O4}(s)}{v_{in}(s)} = \frac{M\left[s^2 + \left(\dfrac{R_8}{R_9}\right)\omega_p^2\right]}{s^2 + s\left(\dfrac{\omega_p}{Q_p}\right) + \omega_p^2} \tag{6.90}$$

and for a given ω_z the choice of R_9 would be $R_9 = r(\omega_p/\omega_z)^2$. The parameter M can be used to adjust the gain of the circuit, just as for the biquad elliptic LP filter. Further, if a third-order pole is required, the capacitor C_4 may be added.

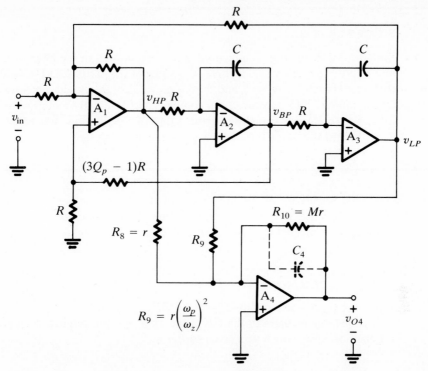

Figure 6.29 An elliptic LP filter using the SV concept.

The sensitivities of the SV filter are comparable to those of the biquad, with $S_x^{\omega_p}$ and $S_x^{Q_p}$ (where x represents the various R and C elements) being ≤ 1, while sensitivity to changes in the open-loop gain A_{OL} are proportional to Q_p/A_{OL}, just as for the biquad circuit. The Q enhancement effect is also present in the SV filter. Compensation can be achieved by adding leading phase (a capacitor C_3 in parallel with R_5 of Fig. 6.28); by replacing the integrators (A_2 and A_3 of Fig. 6.28) with high-Q integrators, as in Fig. 6.26; by adding a resistor in series with each integrator capacitor, thereby providing a leading phase shift (see Problem 3.10); or by replacing one of the inverting integrators with a noninverting integrator and interchanging the feedback to obtain a cancellation of the lagging phase due to finite GB [Ref. 6.1, p. 267].

For the basic SV circuit of Fig. 6.28, it can be shown that the actual Q is related to the design Q_p by an equation similar to that for the biquad filter [Eq. (6.84a)], which for small deviations is

$$Q_{\text{actual}} \approx \frac{Q_p + (2/GB_n)}{1 - (4Q_p/GB_n)} \qquad (6.91)$$

if $GB_n = GB/\omega_p$ and $GB_n \geq 4$. The results of Eqs. (6.84a) and (6.91) can be used to predistort the value of Q_p for a state-variable or biquad filter, as shown in the example below.

EXAMPLE 6.9

Suppose a 741 op amp is to be used in either a biquad or SV filter with a Q_p of 10 and a cutoff frequency $f_p = 20$ kHz. The value of GB_n is $10^6/20$ kHz $= 50$; thus, Eq. (6.91) reduces to Eq. (6.84a), and the design value of Q_p should therefore be 50/9, or approximately 5.15. However, if a compensated HA2540 op amp were used, then from Eq. (6.91) [or Eq. (6.84a)] the value of GB_n is now 400 MHz/20 kHz $= 2 \times 10^4$, and the predistorted Q_p is the same as the design Q_p.

The sensitivity of the movement of the dominant poles p_0 of the SV and biquad filters due to finite GB is approximately the same, for the choice of design elements as indicated in Figs. 6.25 and 6.28, and is for small changes [see Ref. 6.1, Section 5.6]

$$|S_{GB}^{p_0}| \approx \frac{5Q_p}{GB_n(4Q_p^2 - 1)^{1/2}} \tag{6.92}$$

which for $Q_p > 1$ reduces to $|S_{GB}^{p_0}| \approx 2.5/GB_n$.

For large changes in the GB of the op amps, the single-pole approximation for each op amp, which was given earlier as

$$A(\text{s}) = \frac{GB}{s + (\omega_0/A_O)}$$

can be substituted for A_1–A_3 for both the state-variable and biquad circuits, with resulting fifth-order denominator terms. However, a third-order approximation can be used without a great loss in accuracy, with the results indicated for the movement of one of the dominant quadratic roots in Fig. 6.30, as Q_p varies from 1 to 10. The instability and Q enhancement is evident in the figure as the roots move into the right half plane. It is also apparent that the biquad and SV filter have similar instabilities, with the biquad circuit of Fig. 6.25 offering perhaps slightly better stability than the SV filter of Fig. 6.28(a).

Many other filter circuits available in the literature will realize LP filters. We have examined only the more important ones that are particularly suitable for the synthesis of higher-order filters by *cascading* filter sections. However, it is also possible to *directly* obtain a high-order Butterworth, Chebyshev, or other approximation-function filter by starting with a passive RLC ladder circuit, and then using an active RC synthesis to simulate appropriate parts of the network. [The reader is particularly referred to References 6.1, 6.2, 6.9 and 6.20 for the analysis of the various direct synthesis techniques, and to References 6.16, 6.17, and 6.18 for extensive tables of RLC passive filters.] Most direct simulation techniques are based upon simulating an inductor by a special two-op-amp RC circuit called a **generalized impedance converter** (GIC), whose circuit is shown in Fig. 6.31. For this circuit the input impedance is equal to (see Problem 6.40)

$$Z_{\text{in}} = \frac{Z_1 Z_3 Z_5}{Z_2 Z_4} \tag{6.93a}$$

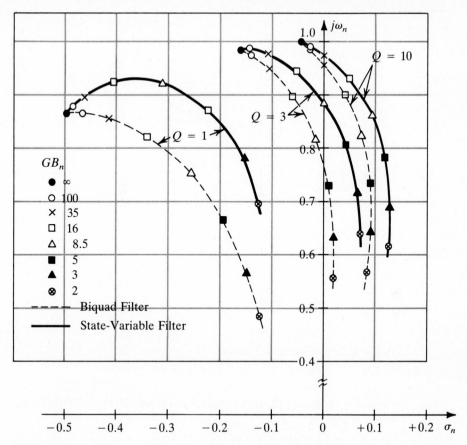

Figure 6.30 Sensitivity of biquad and state-variable filters to finite *GB*. The circuits compared are those of Fig. 6.24 (A$_4$ removed) and Fig. 6.28(a).

In particular, if we choose either Z_2 or Z_4 to be a capacitor C, and all other elements to be resistors, then the input impedance reduces to (for $Z_4 = 1/sC_4$)

$$Z_{\text{in}}(s) = sL_{\text{equiv.}} = s\left(\frac{R_1 R_3 R_5 C_4}{R_2}\right)$$ (6.93b)

which obviously is an inductor of value $R_1 R_3 R_5 C_4/R_2$ Henries. Similarly, if two capacitors are selected among the three values Z_1, Z_3, and Z_5 and the remaining elements chosen as resistors, then Eq. (6.93a) becomes (where D is a constant)

$$Z_{\text{in}}(s) = \frac{1}{Ds^2}$$ (6.93c)

Substituting $s = j\omega$ gives

$$Z_{\text{in}}(j\omega) = -\frac{1}{D\omega^2}$$ (6.93d)

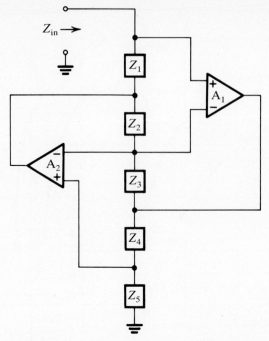

$Z_{in} \rightarrow$

Figure 6.31 A generalized impedance converter (GIC).

which is a **frequency-dependent negative resistor** (FDNR). With Z_1 and Z_5 chosen as capacitors

$$D = \frac{R_2 R_4 C_1 C_5}{R_3} \tag{6.93e}$$

or for Z_3 and Z_5 chosen as capacitors

$$D = \frac{R_2 R_4 C_1 C_5}{R_1} \tag{6.93f}$$

We know a filter's transfer function is not changed by multiplying by a magnitude scaling factor k_m so the FDNR becomes particularly useful in an LP filter by *choosing the magnitude scaling factor to be equal to* $1/s$. This technique is demonstrated by Example 6.10.

EXAMPLE 6.10

In Example 6.4 an $n = 7$ Butterworth LP filter was obtained by cascading Sallen-Key quadratic filters, as indicated in Fig. 6.13. The same filter in a resistive-terminated RLC ladder is shown in normalized form [from filter tables, such as Ref. 6.17, p. 605] in Fig. 6.32(a), with a transformation by $1/s$ in Fig. 6.32(b), where the

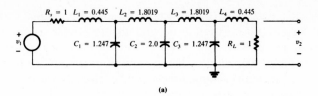

(a)

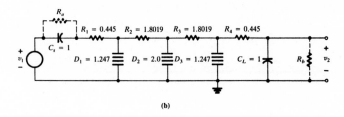

(b)

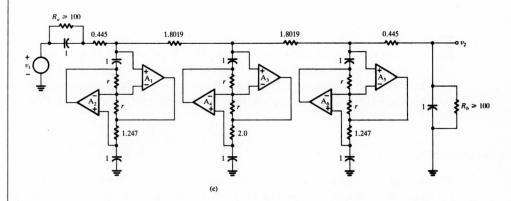

(c)

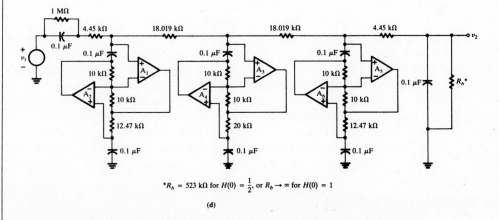

$^*R_b = 523$ kΩ for $H(0) = \frac{1}{2}$, or $R_b \to \infty$ for $H(0) = 1$

(d)

Figure 6.32 (a) An equal-termination seventh-order normalized LP of Example 6.4: (b) transformed to eliminate inductors; (c) normalized synthesis using FDNRs; (d) scaled for $\omega_c = 10^3$ rad/sec and $C = 0.1$ μF capacitors.

FDNR symbol is used. Resistors R_a and R_b must be added in parallel with C_s and C_L to ensure the correct transmission at dc, and also to furnish a return path to ground for the input bias current (I_B^+) of A_1, A_3 and A_5. For a scaled frequency of $\omega_c = 10^3$ and using 0.1 μF capacitors, the de-normalized circuit is shown in Fig. 6.32(d). Since $R_a(=1$ megohm) is large, one should preferably use FET-input op amps for A_1–A_6. Further, there is a significant advantage in using matched op amps for each FDNR section (i.e., a dual op amp), since analysis of GB effects would indicate a first-order cancellation in the numerator and denominator equation for $Z_{in}(j\omega)$ of Eq. 6.93(d) if the values of GB_1 and GB_2 (and GB_3 and GB_4, etc.) are equal.

A comparison of the ladder network of Example 6.10, formed using direct synthesis, and the cascade synthesis of Fig. 6.13(b) indicates that far fewer components are required for the cascade synthesis. The circuit of Fig. 6.13(b) requires three op amps, seven 0.1 μF capacitors, ten equal-value resistors (10 kΩ), and three nonstandard resistors, whereas the direct synthesis network using FDNRs requires six op amps, eight 0.1 μF capacitors, six 10 kΩ resistors and one 20 kΩ resistor, six nonstandard resistors, and two noncritical terminating resistors (~ 1 MΩ each). A practical comparison of the two circuits is obtained in Problem 6.41.

6.3 HIGHPASS FILTERS

We have spent what probably seems like an inordinate amount of time studying lowpass filters. In fact, by now the reader may have formed the opinion that LP filters are more extensively used than HP, BP, or other types. This latter statement is not necessarily true, however. The reason that so much study is spent on LP circuits is that all other types are obtainable from LP filters by a simple transformation. Further, because of this, filter tables are usually only given for the LP case, leaving the user to make the desired transformation. Moreover, when approximating an HP (or other) filter for special passband and stopband requirements, it is usually easier to transform the approximation requirements to an LP design, obtain the design, and then transform back to the HP (or other) circuit.

We will first concentrate on the transformations necessary to obtain a single-op-amp Sallen and Key and infinite-gain HP filter, and then briefly look at any further details necessary to obtain multiple-op-amp designs using biquad, state-variable, or other types.

6.3.1 Single-Op-Amp HP Circuits

As we discussed earlier in Section 6.1 (and Table 6.2), the transformation from a LP to a HP filter is accomplished by substituting $1/s$ for s. Thus, all resistors of value R are transformed to capacitors of value $1/R$, while capacitors of value C are

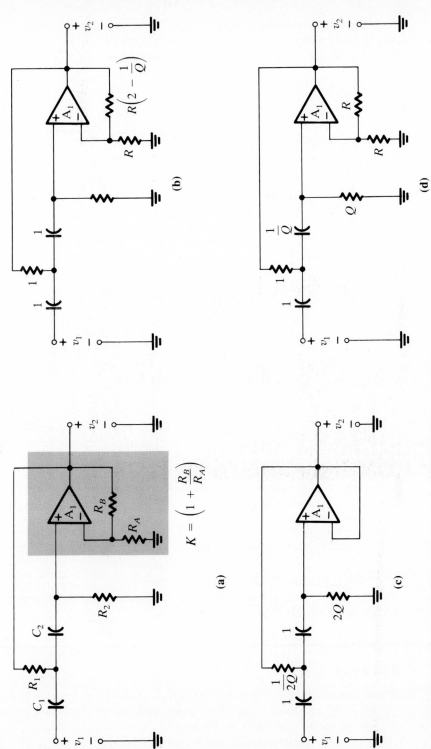

Figure 6.33 The Sallen and Key HP filter: (a) basic structure; (b) equal-R, equal-C case; (c) unity-gain case; (d) gain-of-two case.

307

transformed to resistors of value $1/C$.* The specifications for the op amp gain requirements are not changed. Thus, from the general Eq. (6.25) for a second-order LP filter, substituting $1/s$ for s obtains a general second-order HP filter

$$H(s)_{HP} = \frac{H_0 s^2}{s^2 + \left(\dfrac{\omega_c}{Q}\right)s + \omega_c^2} \tag{6.94}$$

with the identical Q as the LP network. Thus, the basic Sallen and Key LP filter of Fig. 6.11 is transformed to a HP filter as shown in Fig. 6.33(a), with the defining equations

$$H_0 = K = 1 + \frac{R_B}{R_A}$$

$$\omega_c = \left(\frac{1}{R_1 R_2 C_1 C_2}\right)^{1/2}$$

$$\frac{1}{Q} = \left[\left(\frac{R_1 C_1}{R_2 C_2}\right)^{1/2} + \left(\frac{R_1 C_2}{R_2 C_1}\right)^{1/2} + \left(\frac{R_2 C_2}{R_1 C_1}\right)^{1/2}(1 - K)\right] \tag{6.95}$$

Similarly, the three normalized standard LP circuits of Fig. 6.12 now appear as indicated in Fig. 6.33(b–d).

---

* This observation was first attributed to S. K. Mitra, "A Network Transformation for Active RC Networks," *Proc. IEEE*, Vol. 55, pp. 2021–22, (1967).

■ **Exercise 6.6**

Using the transformation $s \to 1/s$, $R \to 1/C$ and $C \to 1/R$ in the Sallen and Key LP filter of Fig. 6.11 and Eq. (6.25), show that Fig. 6.33(a) and the defining Eq. (6.95) results for a HP filter.

The transformations involved for a higher-order ($n > 2$) filter are indicated by Example 6.11, which is now based on the original design conditions of Examples 6.2 and 6.4 for a LP filter.

EXAMPLE 6.11

The design conditions of a general HP filter, as shown in Fig. 6.1(b), are that the -3 dB cutoff frequency ω_c be 1000 rad/sec, and that the filter have an attenuation of ≥ 40 dB in the stop-band for frequencies ≤ 500 rad/sec. Obtain a Butterworth HP filter using the constant-K Sallen and Key circuit.

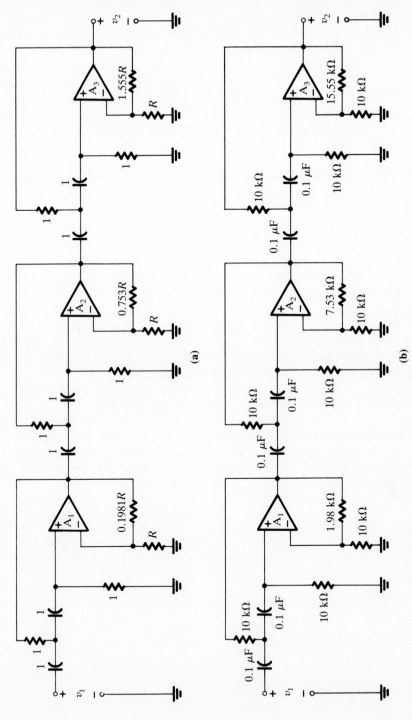

Figure 6.34 The HP filter of Example 6.11: (a) normalized circuit; (b) scaled for $\omega_c = 10^3$ rad/sec and $k_m = 10^4$.

Solution

The HP requirements demand that ω_c/ω_s be equal to 2 with an attenuation of ≥ 40 dB. The *equivalent* normalized LP filter requirement would thus be $\omega_c = 1$, with an attenuation ≥ 40 dB at $\omega_s = 2$. However, this requirement previously resulted in $n = 7$ for a Butterworth filter in Example 6.2, with the actual LP normalized circuit defined in Example 6.4 by Fig. 6.13(a). Since the equivalent LP circuit has been found, we can now transform back to the desired normalized HP circuit, as shown by the equal R equal C case in Fig. 6.34(a), with the final scaled circuit for $\omega_c = 10^3$ rad/sec, and using 0.1 μF capacitors, in Fig. 6.34(b).

To implement a single-op-amp highpass filter containing $j\omega$-axis zeroes, the circuit of Fig. 6.14 can be used with the element Y_4 now a resistor ($Y_4 = 1/R_4$) so that $\omega_p > \omega_z$. Alternatively, we can transform the HP requirements to an LP equivalent, realize the LP circuit, and then convert back to the required HP circuit. For example, the LP filter design of Example 6.5 realized an $n = 4$ elliptic filter having $\omega_s/\omega_c = 2$ and 0.5 dB ripple with $A_{\min} \geq 40$ dB. This same design is therefore suitable for an HP transformed to an LP, where the HP requirements are 0.5 dB ripple, $\omega_c/\omega_s = 2$ and $A_{\min} \geq 40$ dB. Thus, the normalized elliptic LP of Fig. 6.15 when transformed to an equivalent normalized HP circuit will appear as indicated in Fig. 6.35(a), with the circuit scaled for $\omega_c = 10^3$ rad/sec in Fig. 6.35(b). The output attenuation network formed by K_3 could be inserted at the input of the filter for an improved overall dynamic range, if desired.

The infinite-gain highpass filter is obtained from the lowpass circuit of Fig. 6.17 by again making the transformation $R \rightarrow C$ and $C \rightarrow R$, with the resulting HP circuit indicated in Fig. 6.36. The transfer function for this circuit is readily obtained by the LP $\rightarrow$ HP transformation of Eq. (6.35), or by direct calculation, giving

$$H(s) = \frac{v_2(s)}{v_1(s)} = \frac{-s^2\left(\dfrac{C_1}{C_3}\right)}{s^2 + s\dfrac{1}{R_2}\left(\dfrac{C_1}{C_2 C_3} + \dfrac{1}{C_3} + \dfrac{1}{C_2}\right) + \dfrac{1}{R_1 R_2 C_2 C_3}} \tag{6.96a}$$

with the relations

$$\omega_c = \left(\frac{1}{R_1 R_2 C_2 C_3}\right)^{1/2}$$

$$\frac{1}{Q} = \left(\frac{R_1}{R_2}\right)^{1/2}\left[\frac{C_1}{(C_2 C_3)^{1/2}} + \left(\frac{C_3}{C_2}\right)^{1/2} + \left(\frac{C_2}{C_3}\right)^{1/2}\right]$$

$$|H_0| = \frac{C_1}{C_3} \tag{6.96b}$$

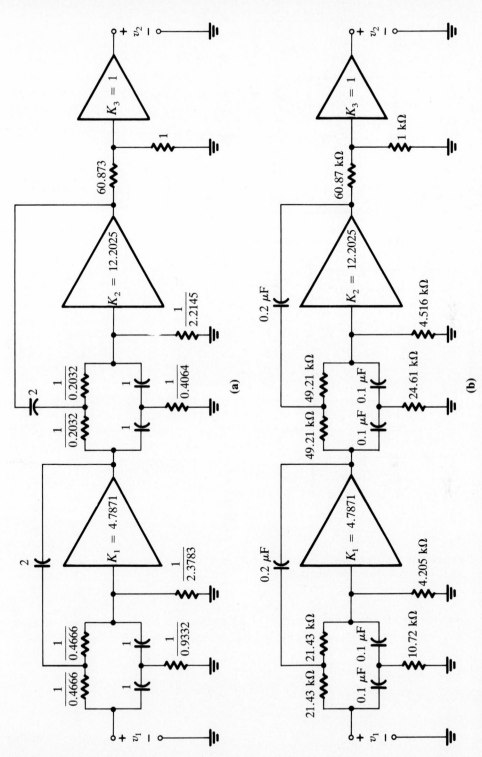

Figure 6.35 An elliptic HP filter, transformed from the LP filter of Example 6.5: (a) normalized; (b) scaled with $\omega_c = 10^3$ rad/sec and $k_m = 10^4$.

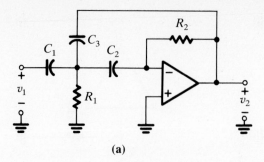

(a)

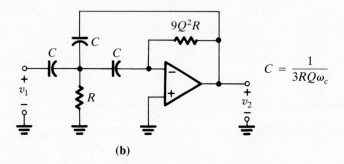

$$C = \frac{1}{3RQ\omega_c}$$

(b)

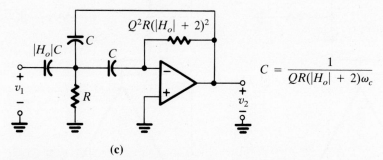

$$C = \frac{1}{QR(|H_o| + 2)\omega_c}$$

(c)

Figure 6.36 (a) The infinite-gain HP circuit. (b) The design for equal capacitors. (c) Choosing C_1 to adjust the gain.

As with the LP circuit a wide variety of design cases are possible. One obvious case is to let $C_1 = C_2 = C_3 = C$ in Fig. 6.36(a), which results in [see Fig. 6.36(b)]

$$C_1 = C_2 = C_3 = C = \frac{1}{3RQ\omega_c}$$

$$R_1 = R \qquad R_2 = 9Q^2R$$

$$\omega_c = \frac{1}{C(R_1R_2)^{1/2}} \qquad |H_0| = 1 \tag{6.97}$$

Another possibility would be to let $C_2 = C_3 = C$, and choose C_1 to adjust the gain. This would result in

$$C_2 = C_3 = C \qquad C_1 = |H_0|C$$
$$R_1 = R \qquad R_2 = Q^2R(|H_0| + 2)^2$$
$$C = \frac{1}{QR(|H_0| + 2)\omega_c} \qquad (6.98)$$

The sensitivity factors for the HP Sallen and Key and infinite-gain filters are all comparable to those obtained earlier for the LP cases, and shown in Table 6.8. Similarly, the sensitivity to finite gain-bandwidth product is similar to the equal R, equal C, highpass circuit having the identical requirement as the LP from Eq. (6.68c); i.e., for $\Delta\omega_c/\omega_c = \Delta Q/Q \le 10\%$, we require

$$GB \ge 45\left(1 - \frac{1}{3Q}\right)^2 \omega_c \qquad (6.99)$$

For the infinite-gain HP circuit with equal capacitors (Fig. 6.36b) the requirements for $\Delta\omega_c/\omega_c = \Delta Q/Q \le 10\%$ are slightly different than those for the infinite-gain LP circuit, and are [Ref. 6.5, p. 407]

$$GB \ge 7.5\omega_c Q\left(1 - \frac{1}{3Q^2}\right) \qquad \text{for } \Delta\omega_c/\omega_c \le 10\% \qquad (6.99a)$$

$$GB \ge 12.5\omega_c Q\left(1 - \frac{1}{25Q^2}\right) \qquad \text{for } \Delta Q/Q \le 10\% \qquad (6.99b)$$

■ **Exercise 6.7**

Using the infinite-gain filter, specify component values for a Chebyshev second-order HP filter having 0.5 dB ripple in the passband, a gain of unity, and a cutoff frequency $\omega_c = 10^5$ rad/sec. If a 741 op amp is used, by how much would the Q and ω_c change due to the finite GB?

6.3.2 Multiple-Op-Amp HP Circuits

The general two-op-amp biquadratic structure of Fig. 6.21 is very useful for implementing a highpass filter with $j\omega$-axis zeroes, using the same technique that was demonstrated in Fig. 6.35. Thus, a lowpass $n = 4$ elliptic filter having $\omega_s/\omega_c = 2$, 0.5 dB ripple in the passband, and with $A_{\min} \ge 40$ dB, is equivalent to a transformed HP with $\omega_c/\omega_s = 2$, and now with $\omega_p > \omega_z$. For example, the LP synthesis for the $H_2(s)$ function as defined by Eq. (6.34a) previously, now becomes with s replaced by $1/s$

$$H_2(s)_{HP} = \frac{H_2\left(\dfrac{24.2272}{1.0626}\right)\left(s^2 + \dfrac{1}{24.2272}\right)}{s^2 + s\left(\dfrac{0.30116}{1.0626}\right) + \dfrac{1}{1.0626}} \tag{6.100}$$

with the identities obtained as previously (for $a = 1$) of

$$Y_1 = \frac{1}{R_1} + C_1 s = H_2\left(\frac{24.2272}{1.0626}\right)s + \frac{H_2}{1.0626}$$

$$Y_2 = \frac{1}{R_2 + 1/C_2 s} = \frac{1}{1/H_2(23.7415) + 1/23.7415 H_2 s}$$

$$Y_3 = \frac{1}{R_3} + C_3 s = \frac{1}{1.0626} + s$$

$$Y_4 = \frac{1}{R_4 + 1/C_4 s} = \frac{1}{1/1.6577 + 1/1.6577 s} \tag{6.100a}$$

The resulting normalized two-op-amp circuit is shown in Fig. 6.37.

Similarly, the two-op-amp second-order LP filter of Fig. 6.22 is transformed into an all-pole HP, as shown in Fig. 6.38(a), or into a HP with $j\omega$-axis zeroes as

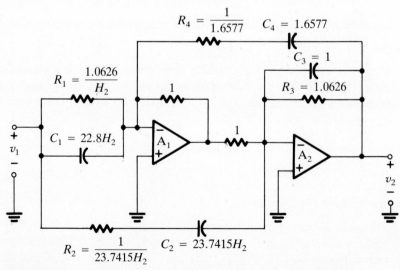

Figure 6.37 The two-op-amp biquadratic filter, suitable for the elliptic HP function of Eq. (6.100).

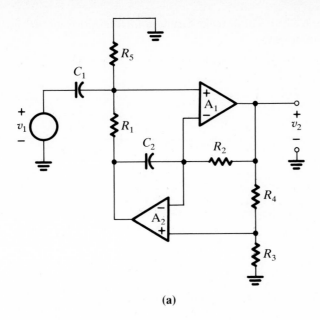

(a)

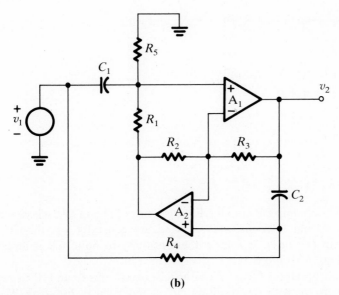

(b)

Figure 6.38 (a) A two-op-amp all-pole second-order HP. (b) A second-order HP with $j\omega$-axis zeroes.

shown in Fig. 6.38(b). The transfer function for these circuits are, for the all-pole network of Fig. 6.38(a)

$$\frac{v_2(s)}{v_1(s)} = \frac{H_0 s^2}{s^2 + s\left(\dfrac{\omega_c}{Q}\right) + \omega_c^2} \tag{6.101a}$$

with

$$H_0 = \left(\frac{R_4 + R_3}{R_3}\right)$$

$$\omega_c = \left(\frac{R_4/R_3}{R_1 R_2 C_1 C_2}\right)^{1/2}$$

$$\frac{1}{Q} = \frac{1}{R_5}\left(\frac{C_2}{C_1}\right)^{1/2}\left(\frac{R_3 R_1 R_2}{R_4}\right)^{1/2} \tag{6.101b}$$

and for the elliptic HP circuit of Fig. 6.38(b)

$$\frac{v_2(s)}{v_1(s)} = \frac{H_0(s^2 + \omega_z^2)}{s^2 + s(\omega_p/Q_p) + \omega_p^2} \tag{6.102a}$$

with the requirement that $R_5 R_2 > R_1 R_3$ and with

$$H_0 = 1$$

$$\omega_z = \left[\frac{1 - (R_1 R_3/R_5 R_2)}{R_1 R_3 C_1 C_2}\right]^{1/2}$$

$$\omega_p = \left(\frac{R_2/R_4}{R_1 R_3 C_1 C_2}\right)^{1/2}$$

$$\frac{1}{Q_p} = \frac{1}{R_5}\left(\frac{C_2}{C_1}\right)^{1/2}\left(\frac{R_3 R_1 R_4}{R_2}\right)^{1/2} \tag{6.102b}$$

As for the two-op-amp LP circuits the sensitivities $S_x^{\omega_p}$ and $S_x^{Q_p}$, where x represents the various R and C terms, are <1, and are generally less than those for a single-op-amp HP filter. However, the sensitivity to finite GB is large for both circuits of Figs. 6.38 and 6.22.

The two-op-amp LP circuit of Fig. 6.24 transforms to an HP by replacing R by C and C by R, with the resulting circuit indicated in Fig. 6.39. The transfer function for the circuit is now

$$\frac{v_2(s)}{v_1(s)} = \frac{-s^2\left(\dfrac{C_1}{C_3}\right)}{s^2 + \dfrac{s}{R_1 C_3 K_2}\left[1 + \dfrac{C_4}{C_2}(1 - K_2)\right] + \dfrac{1}{K_2 R_1 R_2 C_2 C_3}} \tag{6.103a}$$

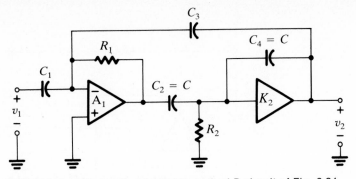

Figure 6.39 HP circuit obtained from the LP circuit of Fig. 6.24.

which with $C_2 = C_4 = C$ reduces to design criteria

$$\omega_c = \frac{1}{R_2 C}$$

$$C_3 = C\left(\frac{R_2}{R_1 K_2}\right)$$

$$|H_0| = \frac{C_1}{C_3}$$

$$K_2 = 2 - \frac{1}{Q} \tag{6.103b}$$

The sensitivity parameters $S_x^{\omega_c}$ and S_x^Q are low for this circuit, while the sensitivity to finite GB is comparable to the results stated earlier for the LP circuit, Eq. (6.82).

The three-op-amp state-variable circuit and the biquad with an added fourth op amp had available an HP filter response, as stated earlier by Eqs. (6.85c) and (6.88a). Thus, the analysis obtained earlier applies equally for HP considerations. If an HP with $j\omega$-axis zeroes is desired, then the biquad circuit of Fig. 6.25 or the SV filter of Fig. 6.29 are usable by correctly weighting the resistors in the summing amplifier, A_4.

We will close our discussion of HP filter circuits by looking at one example of the use of direct synthesis using the GIC to obtain an HP circuit. Earlier, from Eq. 6.93(b) we found that a simulated inductor was obtained from the general GIC circuit of Fig. 6.31 by choosing either Z_2 or Z_4 to be a capacitor, with all other elements a resistor. Thus, using the example of Fig. 6.32, an equal-termination seventh-order normalized HP circuit would appear as shown in Fig. 6.40(a), where the LP-circuit inductors now are capacitors of value $1/L$, while the LP circuit capacitors are now inductors of value $1/C$. The normalized circuit using GICs is shown in Fig. 6.40(b), where the selection $Z_4 = 1/sC_4$ is used, and since R_2 and R_3 cancel in Eq. (6.93b), then any convenient choice $R_2 = R_3 = r$ can be used. Also, the element $G_5(=1/R_5)$ is used to set the required value of simulated inductance, leaving R_1 and C_4 to be conveniently set at unity. The final circuit, scaled for

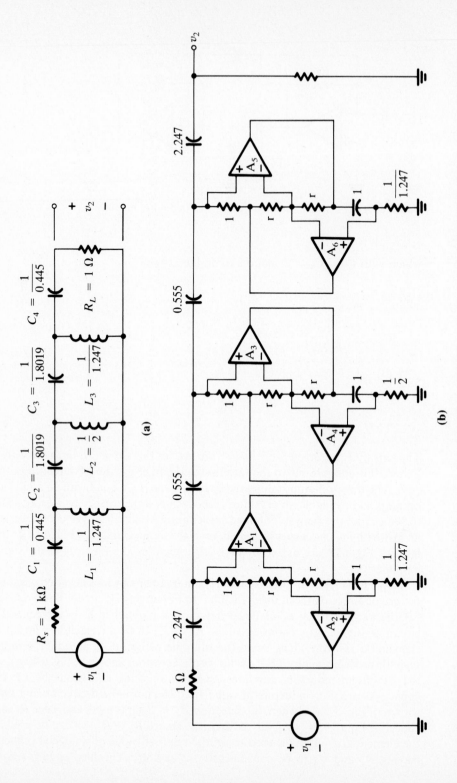

Figure 6.40 (a) An equal-termination seventh-order, normalized Butterworth HP filter: (b) transformed using the GIC to eliminate inductors;

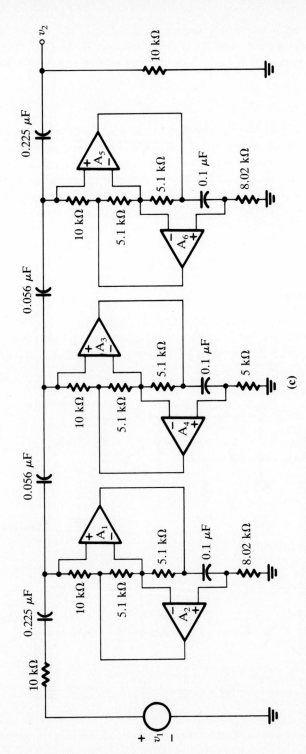

Figure 6.40 (c) scaled for $\omega_c = 10^3$ rad/sec and $k_m = 10^4$.

$\omega_c = 10^3$ rad/sec and a magnitude scaling factor of $k_m = 10^4$, is shown in Fig. 6.40(c). Since the elements Z_1 and Z_2 are both resistors in the GIC, there is a dc path for the input bias current I_B^+ to flow, without adding any other resistors.

6.4 BANDPASS FILTERS

For bandpass filters, there is not as simple a transformation as there was for an LP-to-HP, RC circuit. Hence, most of the active RC filters are obtained directly by circuit analysis, without resorting to transformations. However, for the passive case the transformation between L and C is well established, as indicated earlier in Table 6.2, and is certainly used by obtaining an LP design (normally from filter tables) and then transforming to the desired BP design.

As previously described for both the LP and HP circuits, we will concentrate first on single-op-amp BP realizations, and then look at several multiple-op-amp BP designs.

6.4.1 Single-Op-Amp BP Circuits

The Sallen-Key positive-gain bandpass filter is illustrated in Fig. 6.41(a). It is apparent that the filter includes components from both the previously considered LP and HP circuits, as $R_1 C_1$ forms an LP network, whereas $R_3 C_2$ obviously only

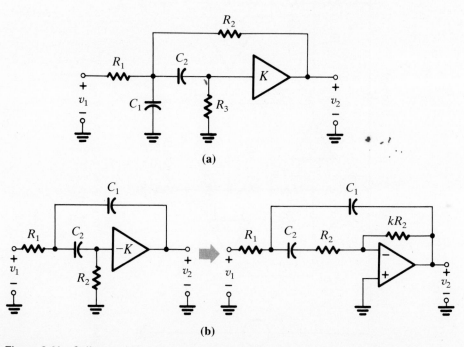

Figure 6.41 Sallen and Key bandpass filters: (a) positive-K network; (b) negative-K network.

permits higher frequencies to pass, and is therefore an HP network. For a positive-gain K the network has a transfer function

$$\frac{v_2(s)}{v_1(s)} = \frac{s\left(\dfrac{K}{R_1 C_1}\right)}{s^2 + s\left(\dfrac{1}{R_1 C_1} + \dfrac{1}{R_3 C_2} + \dfrac{1}{R_3 C_1} + \dfrac{1-K}{R_2 C_1}\right) + \dfrac{R_1 + R_2}{R_1 R_2 R_3 C_1 C_2}} \qquad (6.104a)$$

where the center frequency ω_0, Q and -3 dB bandwidth (BW) are obtained as

$$\omega_0 = \left(\frac{R_1 + R_2}{R_1 R_2 R_3 C_1 C_2}\right)^{1/2}$$

$$Q = \frac{\left(\dfrac{R_2 C_1}{R_3 C_2}\right)^{1/2}\left(1 + \dfrac{R_2}{R_1}\right)^{1/2}}{1 + \dfrac{R_2}{R_1} + \dfrac{R_2}{R_3}\left(1 + \dfrac{C_1}{C_2}\right) - K}$$

$$BW = \frac{\omega_0}{Q} = \left(\frac{1}{R_1 C_1} + \frac{1}{R_3 C_2} + \frac{1}{R_3 C_1} + \frac{1-K}{R_2 C_1}\right)$$

$$\text{Gain}_{(\omega = \omega_0)} = \frac{K}{\left[1 + \dfrac{R_1}{R_3} + \dfrac{R_1 C_1}{R_3 C_2} + \dfrac{R_1}{R_2}(1 - K)\right]} \qquad (6.104b)$$

The usual design approach for the SK positive-K BP filter is to utilize the amplifier gain K to set the Q (or bandwidth), since K is the only parameter that does not affect the center frequency ω_0. The most typical design conditions for the circuit are to let all capacitors be equal and all resistors be equal. For this case we have from Eq. (6.104)

$$R_1 = R_2 = R_3 = R, \; C_1 = C_2 = C$$

$$\omega_0 = \frac{\sqrt{2}}{RC}, Q = \frac{\sqrt{2}}{4 - K}$$

$$BW = \omega_0\left(\frac{4 - K}{\sqrt{2}}\right), \text{Gain}_{(\omega = \omega_0)} = \frac{K}{4 - K} = \frac{KQ}{\sqrt{2}} \qquad (6.105)$$

The sensitivities are obtainable from Eqs. (6.104b) and (6.105), and are, for equal R, equal C

$$S_{R1}^{\omega_0} = S_{R2}^{\omega_0} = \frac{1}{2} S_{R3}^{\omega_0} = \frac{1}{2} S_{C1}^{\omega_0} = \frac{1}{2} S_{C2}^{\omega_0} = -\frac{1}{4} \qquad S_K^{\omega_0} = 0$$

$$S_{C1}^{Q} = -S_{C2}^{Q} = \frac{1}{2} - \frac{Q}{\sqrt{2}} \qquad S_{R2}^{Q} = -3 S_{R1}^{Q} = \frac{3}{4} - \frac{3Q}{\sqrt{2}}$$

$$S_{R3}^{Q} = -\frac{1}{2} + Q\sqrt{2} \qquad S_K^{Q} = \frac{4Q}{\sqrt{2}} - 1 \qquad (6.106)$$

Although the ω_0 sensitivities are low, the Q sensitivities are *directly* proportional to the pole Q, so this circuit should be restricted to $Q < 10$ realizations.

The circuit of Fig. 6.41(b) realizes a BP circuit with a negative gain K. The circuit has the same number of components as the positive-K realization, because of the required resistor KR_2. The gain for the circuit is

$$\frac{v_2(s)}{v_1(s)} = \frac{-s\left(\frac{K}{K+1}\right)\left(\frac{1}{R_1 C_1}\right)}{s^2 + \frac{s}{K+1}\left(\frac{1}{R_1 C_1} + \frac{1}{R_2 C_2} + \frac{1}{R_2 C_1}\right) + \frac{1}{(1+K)R_1 R_2 C_1 C_2}} \quad (6.107a)$$

with the parameters defined by

$$\omega_0 = \frac{1}{[(1+K)R_1 R_2 C_1 C_2]^{1/2}}$$

$$Q = \frac{(1+K)^{1/2}}{\left(\frac{R_2 C_2}{R_1 C_1}\right)^{1/2} + \left(\frac{R_1 C_2}{R_2 C_1}\right)^{1/2} + \left(\frac{R_1 C_1}{R_2 C_2}\right)^{1/2}}$$

$$BW = \frac{1}{1+K}\left(\frac{1}{R_1 C_1} + \frac{1}{R_2 C_1} + \frac{1}{R_2 C_2}\right)$$

$$\text{Gain}_{(\omega = \omega_0)} = -K \bigg/ \left[1 + \frac{R_1}{R_2}\left(1 + \frac{C_1}{C_2}\right)\right] \quad (6.107b)$$

Note that, as opposed to the positive-K circuit, the center frequency ω_0 is a function of all elements, *including* the gain K. For equal R, equal C the parameters reduce to

$$R_1 = R_2 = R, C_1 = C_2 = C$$

$$\omega_0 = \frac{1}{RC(1+K)^{1/2}}, Q = \frac{(1+K)^{1/2}}{3}$$

$$BW = \frac{3\omega_0}{(1+K)^{1/2}}, \text{Gain}(\omega = \omega_0) = \frac{-K}{3} \quad (6.108a)$$

with the sensitivities defined by

$$S_{R1}^{\omega_0} = S_{R2}^{\omega_0} = S_{C1}^{\omega_0} = S_{C2}^{\omega_0} = -\frac{1}{2} \qquad S_K^{\omega_0} = -\frac{1}{2}\left(1 - \frac{1}{9Q^2}\right) = -S_K^Q$$

$$S_{R1}^Q = -S_{R2}^Q = -S_{C1}^Q = S_{C2}^Q = -\frac{1}{6} \quad (6.108b)$$

Thus, the sensitivities for the negative-K BP realization for S_x^Q are essentially *not* a function of Q. Hence the negative-K circuit would be better to use than the positive-K circuit to realize a high Q BP requirement.

The sensitivity of both circuits to a finite gain-bandwidth product has been obtained by Budak [Ref. 6.5, pp. 379, 382], assuming a single-pole op amp. The results for equal R, equal C are

Positive-K Circuit (Fig. 6.41a)

$$\frac{\Delta\omega_0}{\omega_0} \approx -4\sqrt{2}\left(1 - \frac{1}{2\sqrt{2}\,Q}\right)^2 \frac{\omega_0}{GB} = -\frac{\Delta Q}{Q}$$

so therefore

$$GB \geq 57\omega_0\left(1 - \frac{1}{3Q}\right)^2 \qquad \frac{\Delta\omega_0}{\omega_0} = \frac{\Delta Q}{Q} \leq 10\% \tag{6.109a}$$

and

$$GB \geq 113\omega_0\left(1 - \frac{1}{3Q}\right)^2 \qquad \frac{\Delta BW}{BW} \leq 10\% \tag{6.109b}$$

Negative-K Circuit (Fig. 6.41b)

$$\frac{\Delta\omega_0}{\omega_0} \approx -\frac{3Q}{2}\left(1 - \frac{1}{9Q^2}\right)\frac{\omega_0}{GB} = -\frac{\Delta Q}{Q}$$

so therefore

$$GB \geq 15\omega_0 Q\left(1 - \frac{1}{9Q^2}\right) \qquad \frac{\Delta\omega_0}{\omega_0} = \frac{\Delta Q}{Q} \leq 10\% \tag{6.110a}$$

and

$$GB \geq 30\omega_0 Q\left(1 - \frac{1}{9Q^2}\right) \qquad \frac{\Delta BW}{BW} \leq 10\% \tag{6.110b}$$

Just as for the Q sensitivity, the negative-K circuit is superior to the positive-K S-K circuit for shifts due to finite GB if Q is <4, but for large Q the positive-K circuit is superior.

The multiple-feedback infinite-gain bandpass filter is shown in Fig. 6.42, where the inclusion of the resistor R_3 is optional. The transfer function for the

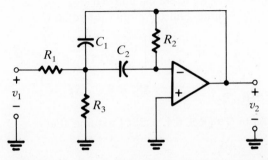

Figure 6.42 The multiple-feedback infinite-gain BP filter.

circuit with R_3 included, is

$$\frac{v_2(s)}{v_1(s)} = \frac{-s\left(\dfrac{1}{R_1 C_1}\right)}{s^2 + \dfrac{s}{R_2}\left(\dfrac{1}{C_1} + \dfrac{1}{C_2}\right) + \dfrac{1 + (R_1/R_3)}{R_1 R_2 C_1 C_2}} \qquad \text{(6.111a)}$$

with the parameter definitions

$$\omega_0 = \left[\frac{1 + (R_1/R_3)}{R_1 R_2 C_1 C_2}\right]^{1/2}$$

$$\frac{1}{Q} = \frac{1 + (C_1/C_2)}{[1 + (R_1/R_3)]^{1/2}}\left(\frac{R_1}{R_2}\right)^{1/2}\left(\frac{C_2}{C_1}\right)^{1/2}$$

$$BW = \frac{1}{R_2 C_1}\left(1 + \frac{C_1}{C_2}\right)$$

$$\text{Gain}_{(\omega = \omega_0)} = \frac{-R_2/R_1}{1 + (C_1/C_2)}$$

(6.111b)

Typically, an equal C design is used, with the result that now

$$C_1 = C_2 = C$$

$$\omega_0 = \frac{1}{C}\left(\frac{1 + (R_1/R_3)}{R_1 R_2}\right)^{1/2}$$

$$Q = \frac{1}{2}\left(\frac{R_2}{R_1}\right)^{1/2}\left(1 + \frac{R_1}{R_3}\right)^{1/2}$$

$$BW = \frac{2}{R_2 C}$$

$$\text{Gain}_{(\omega = \omega_0)} = -\frac{1}{2}\left(\frac{R_2}{R_1}\right)$$

(6.111c)

Notice that the elements R_1 and R_3 do *not* appear in the expression for the bandwidth, while the gain at resonance ($\omega = \omega_0$) is not a function of R_3. Therefore, tuning can be accomplished by adjusting R_1 for the gain of the circuit, and R_3 for the Q, while manipulating C and R_2 to set ω_0 and BW.

The sensitivities of the infinite-gain BP circuit for equal C are

$$S_{R2}^{\omega_0} = S_{C1}^{\omega_0} = S_{C2}^{\omega_0} = -\frac{1}{2} \qquad S_{R3}^{\omega_0} = -\frac{1}{2}\left[1 - \frac{1}{4Q^2(R_1/R_2)}\right] = S_{R3}^{Q}$$

$$S_{R1}^{Q} = S_{R1}^{\omega_0} = -\frac{1}{8Q^2(R_1/R_2)} \qquad S_{C1}^{Q} = S_{C2}^{Q} = 0 \qquad S_{R2}^{Q} = \frac{1}{2}$$

(6.111d)

while the sensitivity to finite GB [Ref. 6.5, p. 384] requires that

$$\frac{\Delta\omega_0}{\omega_0} \approx -Q\left(\frac{\omega_0}{GB}\right) = -\frac{\Delta Q}{Q}$$

or therefore

$$GB \geq 10Q\omega_0 \qquad \frac{\Delta\omega_0}{\omega_0} \text{ and } \frac{\Delta Q}{Q} \leq 10\%$$

and

$$GB \geq 20Q\omega_0 \qquad \text{for } \frac{\Delta BW}{BW} \leq 10\% \tag{6.111e}$$

From an observation of the results of sensitivities for the three single-op-amp BP circuits, it would appear that the circuit having the lowest sensitivity to overall element changes would be the infinite-gain circuit for $Q < 5$, with the negative-K Sallen-Key circuit next, and the positive-K Sallen-Key filter being last. The finite GB produces a decrease in ω_0 and BW and an increase in Q for all circuits.

EXAMPLE 6.12

Design a BP filter for a center frequency of 100 kHz, a Q of 5, and an input impedance ≥ 1 kΩ. Use standard values for components whenever possible. Use an LF351 op amp.

Solution
Let us compare each of the three filter circuits of Figs. 6.41(a), 6.41(b), and 6.42. We will assume the LF351 op amp has (from Appendix C) a 4 MHz gain-bandwidth product, an open-loop gain of 10^5, with a single pole in the open-loop response. We can predistort the poles by using the results for a finite GB. For the positive-K BP network of Fig. 6.41(a), from Eq. (6.109) the first-order shifts will be

$$\Delta f_0 \approx -f_0\left[5.7\left(1 - \frac{1}{3Q}\right)^2\left(\frac{1}{GB_n}\right)\right] = -0.12f_0$$

$$\Delta Q \approx +0.12Q \qquad \Delta BW \approx -0.24BW$$

Therefore, we should design for an actual Q, $Q_a \approx 0.88Q = 4.5$, while the value of f_0 should be approximately $1.12f_0$, or 112 kHz. Similarly, for the negative-K Sallen-Key BP circuit, the first-order shifts are

$$\Delta f_0 \approx -0.18f_0 \qquad \Delta Q \approx +0.18Q \qquad \Delta BW \approx -0.36BW$$

and the design should be $Q_a \approx 0.82Q = 4.1$, while $f_a \approx 118$ kHz. For the infinite-gain circuit, we have from Eq. (6.111e)

$$\Delta f_0 \approx -0.13f_0 \qquad \Delta Q \approx +0.13Q \qquad \Delta BW \approx -0.26BW$$

which obtains a predistortion design of $Q_a \approx 0.87Q = 4.4$, while $f_a \approx 113$ kHz.

For the positive-K BP filter the element values are found from Eq. (6.105), choosing a convenient value of $C_1 = C_2 = 1$ nF

$$K = 4 - \frac{\sqrt{2}}{Q_a} = 3.686 \qquad \text{Gain (at } f_0) = 11.7$$

$$R_1 = R_2 = R_3 = \frac{\sqrt{2}}{2\pi(1 \times 10^{-9})(112 \text{ kHz})} = 2.008 \text{ k}\Omega$$

For the negative-K BP filter the element values are found from Eq. (6.108a), choosing $C_1 = C_2 = 220$ pF

$$K = 9Q^2 - 1 = 150.3 \qquad R_1 = R_2 = 498\Omega \qquad \text{Gain (at } f_0) = -50.1$$

For the infinite-gain BP circuit the element values, from Eq. (6.111c) are, choosing $C_1 = C_2 = 1$ nF and $R_2 = 2R_1$,

$$R_1 = 6.19 \text{ k}\Omega$$

$$R_2 = 12.38 \text{ k}\Omega$$

$$R_3 = \frac{R_1}{37.72} = 164.14\Omega$$

$$\text{Gain (at } f_0) = -1.0$$

All three circuits are shown in Fig. 6.43, using the nearest available $\pm 1\%$ resistor values. Notice that the gain of the negative-K BP circuit is much greater than the other two filters, which could lead to dynamic range limitations in the filter response. The results of a SPICE analysis of the three BP filters using the component values of Fig. 6.43 and the SPICE model for the LF351 (see Appendix D) is shown in Table 6.9. From an observation of the results, it is apparent that the first-order $\Delta\omega_0$ shifts correctly produced $f_0 = 100$ kHz for all 3 filters. However,

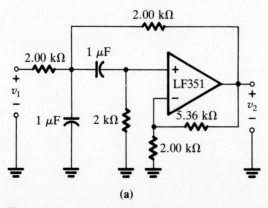

(a)

Figure 6.43 (a) The Sallen-Key positive-K BP filter;

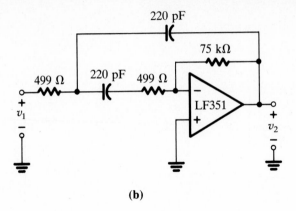

(b)

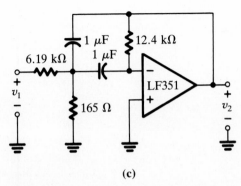

(c)

Figure 6.43 (b) the negative-*K* BP filter; (c) the infinite-gain BP filter (all for Example 6.12).

Table 6.9 RESULTS OF A SPICE ANALYSIS OF THE BP FILTERS OF FIGS. 6.43 AND 6.44

Type	f_0 (kHz)	−3 dB *BW* (kHz)	Q	Gain at f_0
Sallen-Key Positive-*K*	99.5	21.5	4.63	10.67
Sallen-Key Negative-*K*	100.2	21.0	4.77	−50.02
Infinite-Gain	100.2	20.2	4.96	−1.02
Two-Op-Amp [Fig. 6.44(b)]	99.5	20.2	4.93	1.97

Table 6.10 SENSITIVITY PARAMETERS FOR THE BANDPASS CIRCUITS OF EXAMPLES 6.12 AND 6.13

TYPE	$S_{R1}^{\omega_0}$	$S_{R2}^{\omega_0}$	$S_{R3}^{\omega_0}$	$S_{C1}^{\omega_0}$	$S_{C2}^{\omega_0}$	$S_K^{\omega_0}$	S_{R1}^{Q}	S_{R2}^{Q}	S_{R3}^{Q}	S_{C1}^{Q}	S_{C2}^{Q}	S_K^{Q}	$\frac{\Delta\omega_0}{\omega_0}$ (%)	$\frac{\Delta Q}{Q}$ (%)
Sallen-Key Positive K	$-\frac14$	$-\frac14$	$-\frac12$	$-\frac12$	$-\frac12$	0	3.3	-9.9	6.6	-3	3	13.1	-12	12
Sallen-Key Negative K	$-\frac12$	$-\frac12$	$-\frac12$	$-\frac12$	$-\frac12$	$-\frac12$	$-\frac16$	$\frac16$		$\frac16$	$-\frac16$	$\frac12$	-18	18
Infinite-Gain	$-\frac{1}{100}$	$-\frac12$	$-\frac12$	$-\frac12$	$-\frac12$		$-\frac{1}{100}$	$\frac12$	$-\frac12$	0	0		-13	13
Two-op-amp (Fig. 6.44)	0	$\frac12$	$-\frac12$	$-\frac12$	$-\frac12$		1	$\frac12$	$-\frac12$	$\frac12$	$-\frac12$		-5	2.5
Three-op-amp biquad (Fig. 6.25)	0	$-\frac12$	$-\frac12$	$-\frac12$	$-\frac12$		1	$-\frac12$	$-\frac12$	$\frac12$	$-\frac12$		-3.8	100
Three-op-amp SV (Fig. 6.28b)	$-\frac12$	$-\frac12$	0	$-\frac12$	$-\frac12$		$\frac12$	$-\frac12$		$\frac12$	$-\frac12$	$-\frac{14}{15}$	-3.8	102

the ΔQ shifts used were insufficient to obtain the desired Q of 5, except for the infinite-gain filter. The gain at the center frequency was within 2% of the design values for the S-K negative-K and infinite-gain filters. A comparison of the sensitivities $S_x^{\omega_0}$ and S_x^Q for the three circuits is presented in Table 6.10.

6.4.2 Multiple-Op-Amp BP Circuits

In a review of some 15 low-sensitivity two-op amp filters, Sedra and Espinoza [Ref 6.8, p. 90] found that the BP circuit of Fig. 6.44 offered exceptional performance at

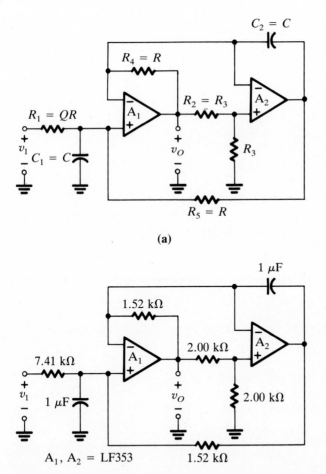

(a)

(b)

Figure 6.44 A two-op-amp low-sensitivity circuit for obtaining a BP function: (a) basic circuit; (b) circuit for a 100 kHz filter, having $Q = 5$, for Example 6.13.

the higher frequencies, and also had very low sensitivity parameters. The transfer function for the circuit is easily obtained as

$$
\frac{v_o(s)}{v_1(s)} = \frac{s\left(\dfrac{1}{R_1 C_1}\right)\left(1 + \dfrac{R_2}{R_3}\right)}{s^2 + s\left(\dfrac{1}{R_1 C_1}\right) + \dfrac{R_2/R_3}{R_4 R_5 C_1 C_2}}
\tag{6.112}
$$

which, with the values as indicated in Fig. 6.44, reduces to,

$$
\frac{v_o(s)}{v_1(s)} = \frac{s\left(\dfrac{2\omega_0}{Q}\right)}{s^2 + s\left(\dfrac{\omega_0}{Q}\right) + \omega_0^2}
\tag{6.112a}
$$

where $\omega_0 = 1/RC$. Further assuming identical op amps with the same GB the changes due to finite gain-bandwidth product for large Q, reduce to

$$
\frac{\Delta\omega_0}{\omega_0} \approx -2\left(\frac{\omega_0}{GB}\right)
\tag{6.113a}
$$

$$
\frac{\Delta Q}{Q} \approx 2\left(\frac{\omega_0}{GB}\right)\left[1 - 4Q\left(\frac{\omega_0}{GB}\right)\right]
\tag{6.113b}
$$

or for a 10% or less change in ω_0

$$
GB \geq 20\omega_0
\tag{6.113c}
$$

This circuit has an excellent adjustability for Q, since in Eq. (6.112) changing R_1 directly affects Q but *not* center frequency gain or ω_0.

EXAMPLE 6.13

Repeat Example 6.12 for the two-op-amp circuit of Fig. 6.44.

Solution

From Example 6.12, we desired a Q of 5, a center frequency of 100 kHz, and $R_{in} \geq 1\,k\Omega$ using a dual LF351 op amp (the LF353). With a 4 MHz gain-bandwidth product, from Eqs. (6.113c) and (6.113b) we have first-order shifts of

$$
\Delta f_0 \approx -2 f_0 \left(\frac{0.1\ \text{MHz}}{4\ \text{MHz}}\right) \approx -(0.05) f_0
$$

$$
\Delta Q \approx +0.025 Q
$$

The design should therefore be predistorted to $f_0 = 105\,kHz$, while the actual design Q should be $Q_a = 0.975 Q = 4.9$.

For $C_1 = C_2 = 1$ nF, the resistor values are all equal to 1,514.3Ω (1.52 kΩ is the nearest $\pm 1\%$ value) except R_1, which would be $4.9R$, or 7.382 kΩ (7.41 kΩ is the nearest $\pm 1\%$ value). The circuit is shown in Fig. 6.44(b), and the sensitivity parameters in Table 6.10. The results of a SPICE analysis of the circuit are included in Table 6.9, indicating excellent agreement with theory.

Since we are comparing different BP filter circuits, let us also include the biquad and state-variable circuits discussed earlier. The sensitivities of the two circuits are comparable, and are included in Table 6.10. From Eqs. 6.84(a) and (b), we obtain, assuming as in Example 6.12 an LF 351 op amp with $Q = 5$ and $f_0 = 10^5$ Hz, for the biquad circuit from Eqs. 6.84(a) and (b),

$$\Delta\omega_0 \approx -0.038\omega_0 \qquad \Delta Q \approx Q \qquad\qquad \textbf{(6.114a)}$$

whereas for the SV circuit, from Eqs. (6.84a) and (6.91)

$$\Delta\omega_0 \approx -0.038\omega_0 \qquad \Delta Q \sim 1.02Q \qquad\qquad \textbf{(6.114b)}$$

Hence, although the change in frequency is less than the other filters in Table 6.9, the ΔQ change is much greater. Therefore, if either the biquad or SV filter were used in this example one should add a phase-compensation capacitor in parallel with R_3 of the biquad (or R_5 of the SV circuit) or provide other means of adding a leading-phase correction.

One additional bandpass filter is worthy of attention, particularly for higher frequency applications. The basic single-op-amp, or even multiple-op-amp BP filters require that the gain-bandwidth product be much greater than f_0, conservatively at least a factor of 10 times the product Qf_0. Thus, if an inexpensive op amp such as the 741 device were used, the upper frequency limit for $Q = 10$ would be approximately 10 kHz. Even if a better op amp such as the LF356, OP-27, or MC 34081 were used, we are limited to a value of $Qf_0 \leq 80$ kHz. In fact, with large signal amplitudes slew-rate limitations could occur much below this latter value, particularly for an op amp such as the OP-27.

It is possible, however, to make use of the *GB* limitation by incorporating the effective single-pole response of the op amp as part of the filter itself. This type of filter is commonly referred to as an **active-R filter**, and is particularly suitable for BP applications having $f_0 \geq 50$ kHz; also, it is readily adaptable to monolithic IC fabrication, since no additional capacitors are required. We will look at one BP example of this type of circuit, that due to Schaumann,* although several other similar circuits exist in the literature, where it is theoretically possible to realize a BP having $\omega_0 \leq GB/2$.†

---

* Rolf Schaumann, "Low-Sensitivity High-Frequency Tunable Active Filter Without External Capacitors," *IEEE Trans. Circuits. & Syst.* Vol. CAS-22, No. 1, pp. 39–44, (Jan. 1975). [Also, see Ref. 6.1 (Chapt. 7), and Ref. 6.8 (Part V)].
† The active R approach is mostly of academic interest, since the gain-bandwidth product of a typical op amp will unfortunately shift with changes in temperature, as well as changes in power-supply voltage.

The basic circuit is shown in Fig. 6.45, where it is assumed that A_1 and A_2 are modeled by a single-pole response for the open-loop gain, as stated earlier from Eq. 2.1

$$A(s) = \frac{A_{OL}\omega_{OL}}{s + \omega_{OL}} = \frac{GB}{s + \dfrac{GB}{A_{OL}}} \approx \frac{GB}{s}$$

if the frequencies of concern are $\gg \omega_{OL}$. As compensated amplifiers A_1 and A_2 really can be used to realize integrators. Thus, a filter circuit using integrators (such as a biquad or SV type) could theoretically be configured by replacing each integrator with a single-pole compensated op amp.

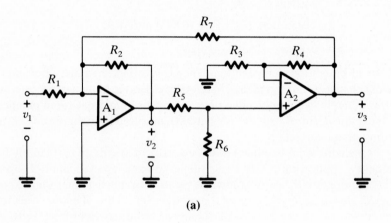

(a)

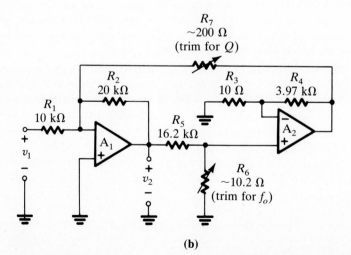

(b)

Figure 6.45 A high-frequency active-R filter: (a) basic circuit; (b) circuit for Example 6.14.

An analysis of the circuit for the transfer function v_2/v_1 obtains the response of a BP filter

$$\frac{v_2(s)}{v_1(s)} \approx \frac{-sK_0\left(\dfrac{\omega_0}{Q}\right)}{s^2 + s\left(\dfrac{\omega_0}{Q}\right) + \omega_0^2} \tag{6.115}$$

provided that the op amps have equal values $GB_1 = GB_2 = GB$, and that the condition holds

$$K_0 \ll 2Q^2\left[1 + \frac{1}{4Q^2}\right]^{1/2} \tag{6.115a}$$

with the following design constraints

$$\frac{R_2}{R_1} = 2K_0$$

$$\frac{R_4}{R_3} = \frac{2QGB}{\omega_0} - 1$$

$$\frac{R_2}{R_7} = 2\left[Q\left(\frac{GB}{\omega_0}\right) - K_0 - \frac{1}{2}\right] \tag{6.115b}$$

$$\frac{R_5}{R_6} = \left(\frac{GB}{\omega_0}\right)^2\left[1 + \frac{1}{4Q^2} - \frac{\omega_0}{GB}\left(\frac{K_0 + 0.5}{Q} + \frac{\omega_0}{GB}\right)\right]$$

and with somewhat involved relations for ω_0 and Q

$$\omega_0 \approx GB\left[\frac{R_6 R_1}{(R_6 + R_5)(R_1 + R_7)}\right]^{1/2} \tag{6.115c}$$

$$Q \approx \frac{\left[\left(\dfrac{R_2}{R_7}\right)\left(\dfrac{R_6}{R_6 + R_5}\right)\left(1 + \dfrac{R_2}{R_7} + \dfrac{R_2}{R_1}\right)\right]^{1/2}}{1 + \dfrac{\left(1 + \dfrac{R_2}{R_7} + \dfrac{R_2}{R_1}\right)}{(1 + R_4/R_3)}} \tag{6.115d}$$

Interestingly, the sensitivities $S_{R_i}^{\omega_0}$ and $S_{R_i}^{Q}$ (where i is equal to $1, 2, \ldots, 7$) are $< 1/2$ for a typical design; however, from Eq. (6.115c) we see that $S_{GB}^{\omega_0} = 1$. Thus, a change in the gain-bandwidth product (due to a change in either A_{OL} or ω_{OL} or both) would be reflected as a *direct change* in the center frequency ω_0. This is unfortunate, since a change in temperature or power-supply voltage usually produces a direct change in GB for an op amp.

EXAMPLE 6.14

Use an active R filter for the design of Example 6.12.

Solution

We required from Example 6.12 a Q of 5, $f_0 = 100$ kHz, $R_{in} \geq 1$ kΩ, and were using an LF351 (or an LF353, dual) op amp. Let us choose from Eq. (6.115b) a gain $K_0 = 1$. Thus, let $R_1 = 10$ kΩ and $R_2 = 20$ kΩ. Also, for $GB_1 = GB_2 = 4$ MHz we have

$$\frac{R_4}{R_3} = \frac{2(5)(4 \text{ MHz})}{100 \text{ kHz}} - 1 \approx 400$$

$$\frac{R_2}{R_7} = 2\left[5\left(\frac{4 \text{ MHz}}{100 \text{ kHz}}\right) - 1.5\right] \approx 199, \text{ so } R_7 \approx 200 \ \Omega$$

$$\frac{R_5}{R_6} = \left(\frac{4 \text{ MHz}}{0.1 \text{ MHz}}\right)^2\left[1 + \frac{1}{100} - \frac{0.1 \text{ MHz}}{4 \text{ MHz}}\left(\frac{1.5}{5} + \frac{0.1 \text{ MHz}}{4 \text{ MHz}}\right)\right]$$

$$\approx 1600$$

Notice that Eq. (6.115a) is satisfied, since

$$1 \ll 2(5)^2\left[1 + \frac{1}{100}\right]^{1/2}$$

The suggested procedure for turning the circuit is illustrated with the design values in Fig. 6.45(b), and is (1) vary the ratio R_6/R_5 to adjust the center frequency f_0, (2) adjust Q by varying R_7 and (3) adjust the gain at f_0 and K_0 by trimming R_1.

As the results of Example 6.14 indicated, the R_5/R_6 ratio was very large. This means that the larger bandwidth LF351 device was not necessary for the 100 kHz filter; the 741 op amp with 1/4 the *GB* value would have worked just as well. Or, phrased another way, it means that with the LF351 circuit we could expect to have formed a suitable active *R* BP filter to much higher frequencies than 100 kHz.

6.5 BAND-REJECTION FILTERS

It is often desirable to eliminate a contaminating frequency from a processed informational signal; for example, 60 Hz pickup may occur when processing the output signal of a transducer over long distances. Ideally, we would like to eliminate that one frequency, without disturbing the rest of the signal. A filter that best approximates this criterion is called a **band-rejection (BR) filter**, sometimes also referred to as a **notch filter**, **band-elimination filter**, or **bandstop filter**.

Most of the BR filters are based upon the use of the twin-tee network used earlier in the single-op-amp elliptic LP filter design of Fig. 6.14 (also, see Problem 6.14). A circuit using the twin-tee network with a constant positive gain (in some respect, we could consider this an addition to the class of Sallen and Key circuits) is one of the more often used BR filters, and is shown in Fig. 6.46(a). The feedback for the circuit could also be obtained from the output to the R_3 resistor, with the C_3 capacitor grounded (see Problem 6.53). The transfer function for Fig. 6.46(a) reduces to that of a standard band-rejection filter

$$H(s) = \frac{v_2(s)}{v_1(s)} = \frac{H(s^2 + \omega_0^2)}{s^2 + (\omega_0/Q)s + \omega_0^2}$$

(6.116a)

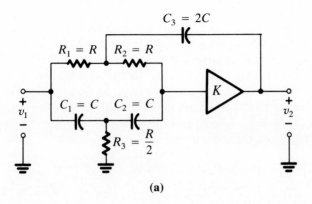

(a)

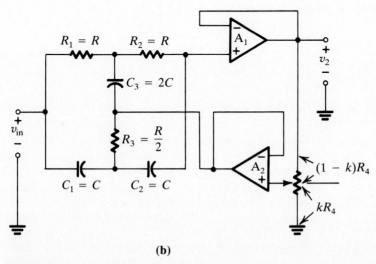

(b)

Figure 6.46 (a) Constant-K band-rejection filter. (b) Unity-gain version, with adjustable Q.

where for this circuit we have

$$\omega_0 = \frac{1}{RC}$$

$$Q = \frac{1}{4 - 2K} \tag{6.116b}$$

$$H = K$$

Budak [Ref. 6.5, p. 421] has calculated the sensitivities of the movement of the upper-half-plane $j\omega$-axis zero to variations of the elements, with the results

$$S_{R1}^Z = S_{R2}^Z = \frac{1}{8}(1 - j3) \qquad S_{R3}^Z = -\frac{1}{4}(1 + j)$$

$$S_{C1}^Z = S_{C2}^Z = -\frac{1}{8}(1 + j3) \qquad S_{C3}^Z = \frac{1}{4}(1 - j) \tag{6.116c}$$

Thus, minor tuning of the twin-tee circuit frequency ω_0 can be obtained by adjusting C_3 or R_3 while adjustment of the Q is obtained by varying the amplifier gain K. If the sensitivity of the circuit to finite GB is considered, the pole ω_0 will be reduced, while Q is increased; thus $\Delta\omega_0/\omega_0$ and $\Delta Q/Q$ shifts are similar to the case for the BP Sallen-Key circuit, being proportional to the product of Q and ω_0/GB.

Another use of the twin-tee circuit is demonstrated by the unity-gain circuit connection of Fig. 6.46(b), where the feedback signal now drives both R_3 and C_3. The transfer function for this circuit is

$$\frac{v_2(s)}{v_1(s)} = \frac{s^2 + \dfrac{1}{R^2C^2}}{s^2 + s(4/RC)(1 - k) + \dfrac{1}{R^2C^2}} \tag{6.117a}$$

with the parameter values

$$\omega_0 = \frac{1}{RC}$$

$$Q = \frac{1}{4(1 - k)} \tag{6.117b}$$

Thus, by adjusting the R_4 potentiometer ($0 \le k \le 1$) the Q of the unity-gain BR circuit is variable from $\frac{1}{4}$ to ∞. In actuality, the A_2 amplifier in Fig. 6.46(b) could be eliminated if at the notch frequency ω_0 the condition $R_3, X_{C3} \gg k(1 - k)R_4$ holds.

It is also possible to form a BR filter by appropriately summing a bandpass filter characteristic with the input signal, as shown by the circuits of Fig. 6.47(a) and (b). For the circuit of Fig. 6.47(a), if α is equal to zero we have a standard infinite-gain BP filter, with the transfer function given earlier by

$$H(s)_{\text{BP}} = \frac{-s\left(\dfrac{1}{R_1C}\right)}{s^2 + s\left(\dfrac{2}{R_2C}\right) + \dfrac{1}{R_1R_2C^2}} \tag{6.118a}$$

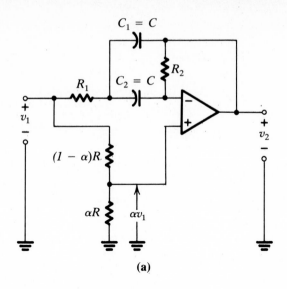

(a)

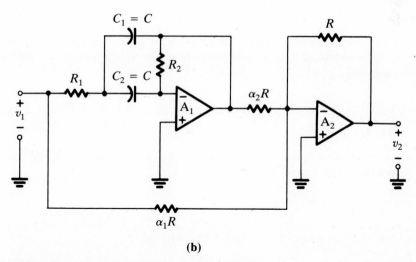

(b)

Figure 6.47   Forming a BR filter from a BP-filter function: (a) single-op-amp circuit; (b) summing using two op amps.

If $C_1 = C_2 = C$,

$$\omega_0 = \frac{1}{C(R_1 R_2)^{1/2}} \qquad Q = \frac{1}{2}\sqrt{\frac{R_2}{R_1}} \qquad\qquad \text{(6.118b)}$$

Now, using superposition, if $\alpha \neq 0$ we have the output voltage

$$v_2 = v_1 H(s)_{BP} + \alpha v_1 [1 - H(s)_{BP}] \qquad\qquad \text{(6.118c)}$$

or the total transfer function is obtained as

$$\frac{v_2(s)}{v_1(s)} = \alpha + (1 - \alpha)H(s)_{\mathrm{BP}}$$

$$= \alpha \left\{ \frac{s^2 + s\left(\dfrac{2}{R_2 C}\right)\left[1 - 2Q^2\left(\dfrac{1 - \alpha}{\alpha}\right)\right] + \omega_0^2}{s^2 + s\left(\dfrac{2}{R_2 C}\right) + \omega_0^2} \right\} \tag{6.118d}$$

where Q and ω_0 were defined above. Thus, for a BR filter we desire that

$$\alpha = \frac{2Q^2}{2Q^2 + 1} \tag{6.118e}$$

For the infinite-gain single-op-amp BR circuit, Budak [Ref. 6.5, p. 435] has shown the effect of a finite GB is to produce a pre-rejection peak in the output response, and a decrease in the post-rejection gain past ω_0.

■ **Exercise 6.8**

For the two-op-amp circuit of Fig. 6.47(b), show that a BR filter is obtained by a suitable choice of α_1 and α_2. Describe how you would tune the circuit for a desired ω_0 and Q.

■ **Exercise 6.9**

Show that the attenuation A of a BR filter at any bandwidth BW_x is given as a function of Q, f_0 and BW_x as

$$A_{\mathrm{dB}} = 10 \log\left[1 + \left(\frac{f_0}{QBW_x}\right)^2\right] \tag{6.119a}$$

and as a function of the -3 dB bandwidth as

$$A_{\mathrm{dB}} = 10 \log\left[1 + \left(\frac{BW_{-3\,\mathrm{dB}}}{BW_x}\right)^2\right] \tag{6.119b}$$

The biquad and state-variable filter circuits can be used to obtain a band-rejection characteristic by appropriately summing signals*, as shown in Fig. 6.48.

---

* The summing unfortunately must be perfect to remove a numerator term, resulting in Eq. (6.120). In practice both the biquad and state-variable circuits are difficult to tune for a good null in the output response, particularly if the null frequency $f_0 > 10\,\mathrm{kHz}$ and if $Q > 10$. Usually capacitor C_{comp} must be added to reduce Q enhancement.

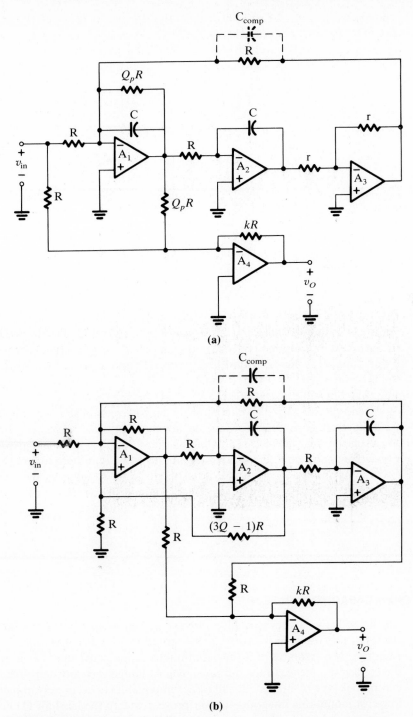

Figure 6.48 Multiple-op-amp band-rejection filters: (a) biquad circuit; (b) state-variable circuit.

The biquad circuit of Fig. 6.48(a) sums the BP output of A_1 with v_{in}, similar to circuits previously considered (Fig. 6.47). The state-variable circuit, however, adds the outputs of the HP and LP sections to obtain a transmission zero at $\pm j\omega_0$. The transfer function for the two circuits differs only in the polarity of the output, and is

$$\frac{v_O(s)}{v_{in}(s)} = \frac{\pm K\left[s^2 + \left(\dfrac{1}{RC}\right)^2\right]}{s^2 + s\left(\dfrac{1}{QRC}\right) + \left(\dfrac{1}{RC}\right)^2} \tag{6.120}$$

EXAMPLE 6.15

One desires to eliminate an interfering 60 Hz pickup signal by using a BR filter. A -3 dB bandwidth of 6 Hz is desired. Use as few components as feasible. Show how the circuit would be tuned.

Solution

Let us use the BR circuit of Fig. 6.47(a), which uses only one op amp and is easily adjusted for the correct bandwidth by varying the resistor R. The desired Q is equal to the center frequency divided by the bandwidth or $Q = 60/6 = 10$. Let us use $0.1\,\mu$F capacitors; hence, from Eq. 6.118(e) we desire $\alpha = 200/201$. Also, from Eq. (6.118b) we need $R_2 = 400\ R_1$ and thus $R_1 = (2\pi \times 0.1 \times 10^{-6} \times 1200)^{-1}$ or 1.325 kΩ. Therefore $R_2 = 530$ kΩ.

Since R_2 is large, to eliminate dc bias current offsets we should use an FET-input op amp. We have GB $\gg \omega_0$ for most any general-purpose op amp, so use as inexpensive a device as possible (perhaps the LF351, TL081, or equivalent). For tuning, one would first ground the noninverting input terminal of the op amp (i.e., $\alpha = 0$), and use R_1, R_2 and C adjustments to set f_0 and the bandwidth for the BP circuit. Then, the attenuation factor α is adjusted (perhaps using a potentiometer in series with two resistors) for the best obtainable notch at the desired 60 Hz.

6.6 SWITCHED-CAPACITOR FILTERS

The linear active and passive filter circuits studied so far have been continuous in time; i.e., no switching is involved that would lead to discontinuities in the time response. The response of a time-continuous input signal thus has a one-to-one direct correspondence to the output signal. Although certainly desirable, the time-continuous type of filter is difficult (if not impossible) to accurately implement in a low-cost monolithic integrated-circuit process, due to the need for (1) large-value capacitors and (2) very accurate ($< 1\,\%$) RC time constants. Of course, the use of an active R type of filter is possible in a monolithic IC form. However, we found the circuit was primarily useful for higher frequencies ($\geq 50\,\text{kHz}$), and also there was the necessity that the gain-bandwidth product be constant against power-supply, temperature, or other changes [see Eq. 6.115(c), where $S_{GB}^{\omega_0} = 1$].

Integrated-circuit manufacturers have refined the processing of metal-oxide-semiconductor (MOS) devices so that very precise width-to-length (W/L) ratios are obtainable for capacitors of very small value ($\geq 0.1\,\text{pF}$), and also these capacitors occupy a small area on the IC chip. Further, the *ratio* of two capacitors is obtained to *much* greater precision than the ratio of two resistors on a standard monolithic chip, approaching 0.1 percent for economical size geometries. Furthermore, with the extensive use of either NMOS or complementary-MOS (CMOS) transistors, it is possible to obtain an electronic switch that has a ratio of off-to-on resistance of greater than 10^5, with very low device capacitances (C_{gs} and C_{gd} can be made $< 0.05\,\text{pF}$). Thus, an active filter concept that uses MOS transistor switches and MOS capacitors (and MOS op amps, as well!) on the same monolithic IC substrate would be a viable alternative to the RC active-filter circuit.

Such a concept is indeed possible, with the introduction of the **switched-capacitor (SC) active filter** (also correctly referred to as an **analog sample-data filter**), first presented in 1972 by Fried* and furthered shortly after by workers at U. C. Berkeley† and others. The technique is based on the concept that a capacitor switched between two nodes at a rate much higher than the frequency of the signal is *equivalent* to a resistor connected between the same nodes. To illustrate this point, consider first the circuit of Fig. 6.49(a), where it is assumed that V_1 and V_2 are voltage sources with zero impedance, connected between ground and nodes 1 and 2, respectively. When the capacitor C_1 is switched to source V_1 then C_1 will charge to that voltage. Now, if the switch is thrown to position 2, then the amount of charge that flows into (or out of) V_2 is $C_1(V_1 - V_2)$. If the rate of switching is set by a clock of frequency $f_{cl} = 1/T$, with the clock frequency much greater than the signal frequency, then the average current into (or out of) V_2 is

$$I = \frac{C_1(V_1 - V_2)}{T} = f_{cl}C_1(V_1 - V_2) \tag{6.121a}$$

However, the above current is the same that we would have for a circuit comprising V_1, V_2 and a resistor, or

$$I = \frac{(V_1 - V_2)}{R_{eq}} \tag{6.121b}$$

Thus, the switched capacitor is *equivalent* to a resistor of value

$$R_{eq} \equiv \frac{1}{f_{cl}C_1} \tag{6.121c}$$

---

* D. L. Fried, "Analog Sample-Data Filters," *IEEE J. S.S. Ckts.*, Vol. SC-7, pp. 302–304, (Aug. 1972).
† R. W. Broderson, P. R. Gray, and D. A. Hodges, "MOS Switched-Capacitor Filters," *Proc. IEEE*, Vol. 67, pp. 61–75 (Jan. 1979). [This, and many other papers on SC filters can be found in Refs. 6.11 and 6.15.]

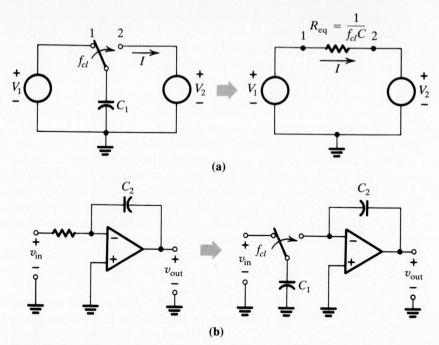

Figure 6.49 Basic concept of the switched-capacitor (SC) filter. (a) Equivalence of a resistor and the switched capacitor. (b) Equivalence of the RC integrator and the SC integrator.

where f_{cl} is the clock frequency. We can now replace a time-continuous system RC product by a switched-capacitor product

$$RC \equiv \frac{1}{f_{cl}}\left(\frac{C}{C_1}\right) = T\left(\frac{C}{C_1}\right) \tag{6.121d}$$

The last equation is very important practically, since the RC time-constant appears in SC form as the product of period T and the *ratio* of two capacitors; thus, an absolute value of capacitor is *not* important, which is an essential ingredient for good IC fabrication. The usefulness of the equivalent resistor concept is shown by the RC integrator circuit in Fig. 6.49(b), where for the RC continuous-time circuit we have in the frequency domain

$$H(j\omega) = \frac{v_{out}}{v_{in}} = -\left(\frac{1}{R_1 C_2}\right)\left(\frac{1}{j\omega}\right) \tag{6.122a}$$

and if one replaces R_1 by its switched-capacitor equivalence C_1 we have in the SC circuit

$$H(j\omega) \approx -\frac{f_{cl}}{j\omega}\left(\frac{C_1}{C_2}\right) \tag{6.122b}$$

Inherent in the above equations is the assumption that the switching frequency f_{cl} is much greater than any frequency of interest in the signal being switched. Since the action of the switch would involve a time delay of one period T between charging to v_{in} and transferance of charge to C_2, then a more accurate statement of the frequency response would include the time delay by multiplying by the factor $\exp(-j\omega T)$, with the result that Eq. (6.122b) is really*

$$\frac{v_{out}}{v_{in}}(j\omega) = -\left(\frac{C_1}{C_2}\right)\left(\frac{1}{e^{j\omega T}-1}\right) \tag{6.122c}$$

which, by using trigonometric identities can be reduced to

$$H(j\omega) = \frac{v_{out}}{v_{in}}(j\omega) = -\left(\frac{f_{cl}}{j\omega}\right)\left(\frac{C_1}{C_2}\right)\left[\frac{\omega T/2 e^{(-j\omega T/2)}}{\sin(\omega T/2)}\right] \tag{6.122d}$$

Thus for the case $\omega T/2 \ll 1$, we reduce to Eq. (6.122b).

---

* For a proof of this statement see any text on Fourier transforms, or sampled-data systems.

EXAMPLE 6.16

Estimate f_{cl} the upper frequency limit of the clock, if the phase error in Eq. (6.122d) is to be no more than 10 degrees. Further, what would be the maximum clock frequency if the MOS analog switch has a maximum ON resistance of 10 kΩ and the maximum capacitor value for C_1 or C_2 is 10 pF. If the capacitor has to be charged to within 1 % of the signal in 1/4 the period T, what are the requirements on the bandwidth and SR of the op amp, in a 5 V system?

Solution
The phase error in Eq. (6.122d) is contributed by the $\exp(-j\omega T/2)$ term. Thus, for an error $\leq 10°$ we have

$$\left(\frac{\pi f_{signal}}{f_{clock}}\right) \leq 10°\left(\frac{\pi}{180°}\right) = \frac{\pi}{18} \text{ (rad/sec)}$$

or we need a ratio $f_{clock}/f_{signal} \geq 18$. Also, for this ratio the amplitude error would be

$$\frac{\omega T/2}{\sin(\omega T/2)} = \frac{\pi/18}{\sin(\pi/18)} = 1.005$$

which is generally negligible. Further, the maximum charging-time constant would be 10 kΩ × 10 pf, or 100 ns. Since it would take approximately 5 time constants to charge a capacitor to within 1 % of its final value, and this is required to be accomplished in 1/4 T, we need

$$T/4 = \frac{1}{4f_c} \geq 5(100 \text{ ns}) = 500 \text{ ns}$$

or $f_c \leq 1/2000$ ns $= 500$ kHz, or $T = 2$ μs. Now, we have just found that for a phase error of $\leq 10°$, we need $f_{\text{clock}}/f_{\text{signal}} \geq 18$. Thus, this would impose an upper limit on the cutoff frequency limit of our SC filter, of approximately $f_c \leq 500$ kHz/18 $\approx$ 28 kHz. Thus, in general we would expect the switched-capacitor filters to be useful only in the audio range (Note: the audio range is considered to be from approximately 20 Hz to 20 kHz).

As far as the requirements on the op amps are concerned, we need a small-signal rise time of less than $T/4$, or 500 nsec, thus we need $f_{-3 \text{ dB}}$ for the op amp greater than $0.35/0.5$ μsec, or 0.7 MHz. For large-signal SR requirements, we would desire a maximum output 5 V change in $\leq T/4$, or 500 ns. Thus we need a SR of ≥ 5 V/0.5 μsec $= 10$ V/μsec. These requirements can be met with present state-of-the-art CMOS op amps.

In addition to the practical limitations of SC filters mentioned in Example 6.16, other limitations are imposed by their operation as discrete-time, or sampled-data filters. In theory, the maximum useful filter frequency is limited by the Nyquist criterion to 1/2 the clock frequency. Otherwise, any frequencies present in the input signal beyond this value will be *aliased* with the switching frequency, producing an output response of the filter at frequencies of $f_{cl} \pm f_{\text{in}}$. This effect will produce an increase in the output amplitude of a lowpass filter as shown by Fig. 6.50,[*] which is the response of a 1 kHz LP (Butterworth, second-order) filter as a function of the clock frequency f_{cl}. To prevent the magnitude increase past the cutoff frequency, one may have to limit the input-signal content to $\leq f_{cl}/2$ by using an analog LP filter in cascade with the SC discrete-time filter. Further, it is important to preserve clock phasing when replacing resistors by switched capacitors, otherwise considerable deviations will be observed in the filter response.

Another limitation of the SC filter is due to the channel noise of the MOS switches, and the high low-frequency voltage noise of the MOS op amps. Thus, the dynamic range and signal-to-noise ratio of the SC filter will be poorer than its analog counterpart. Moreover parasitic capacitances of the MOS transistors and capacitors may be important, as we will see in several later examples.

Before we proceed to some examples of actual SC filters let us look at some other interesting circuits using switches and capacitors that are also equivalent to analog functions. It is possible to form not only the basic inverting integrator of Fig. 6.49(b), but also a noninverting integrator by appropriate switching as indicated in Fig. 6.51(a), where the actual MOS switches are shown, as well as the stray capacitances associated with C_1 and C_2. The operation of the circuit of Fig. 6.51(a) occurs when (we assume for simplicity NMOS switches) the Φ_1 clock signal is high (Φ_2 is low) so that C_1 is connected to v_i; thus C_1 charges to v_i (as does also C_{S11}) through M_1 which is ON (as is also M_3). The stray capacitance C_{S12} does not

* R. W. Broderson et al, *op. cit.*, p.69.

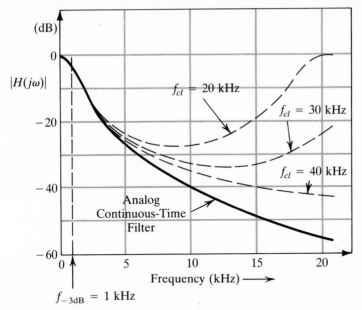

Figure 6.50 Frequency response of a second-order Butterworth LP filter having a cutoff frequency of 1 kHz, with varying clock frequencies f_{cl}.
Source: R. W. Broderson, *et al.*, "MOS Switched-Capacitance Filters," *Proc. IEEE*, vol. 67, pp. 61–75, Jan. 1979.

accumulate charge since it is shorted to ground by the ON resistance of M_3. Now, after the clock signal Φ_1 goes low, turning off M_1 and M_3, the *non-overlapping* clock signal Φ_2 goes to a high state, which removes the critical charge on C_{S11} through the ON resistance of M_2, and transfers the charge on C_1 to C_2. The stray capacitances of C_2 (C_{S21} and C_{S22}) are not important to the charge transfer, since C_{S21} is in parallel with the virtual ground of the op amp, while C_{S22} is in parallel with the output. Note that an inverting integrator is obtained by merely inter-changing the clock signals for M_1 and M_2.*

In Fig. 6.51(b) is an RC analog "lossy" integrator, and its corresponding SC counterpart. The capacitor C_1 charges to $Q_i = C_1 v_i$ on the Φ_1 clock cycle, while C_2 charges to the output voltage $Q_0 = C_2 v_0$. On the Φ_2 clock cycle the Q_i charge and the Q_0 charge balance to keep the input at a virtual ground. Using the resistor equivalence $R_2 = 1/f_{cl}C_2$, $R_1 = 1/f_{cl}C_1$ and $f_{-3\,dB} = 1/2\pi R_2 C_3 = f_{cl}C_2/2\pi C_3$, we obtain

$$\frac{v_O}{v_i}(j\omega) = \frac{-R_2/R_1}{1 + j\left(\dfrac{f}{f_{-3\,dB}}\right)} = \frac{-C_1/C_2}{1 + j\left(\dfrac{f}{f_{-3\,dB}}\right)} \tag{6.123}$$

* K. Martin, "Improved Circuits for the Realization of Switched-Capacitor Filters," *IEEE Trans. Ckts. and Syst.*, Vol. CAS-27, No. 4, pp. 237–44, (April 1980).

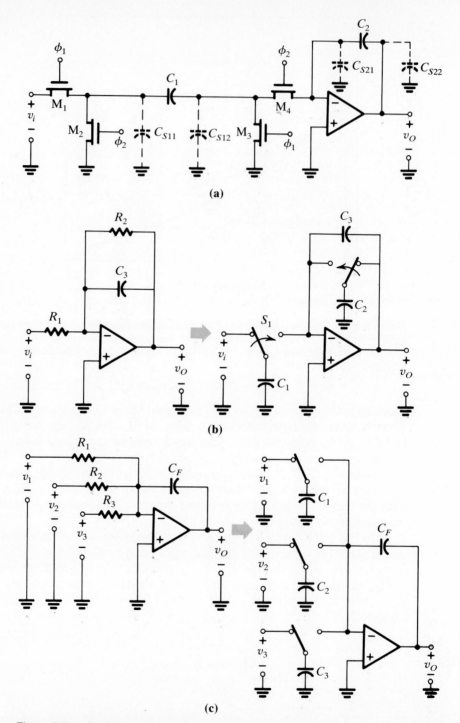

Figure 6.51 Additional SC functions. (a) Stray-insensitive non-inverting integrator. (b) Lossy integrator. (c) Summing integrator.

Similarly, in Fig. 6.51(c) the summing integrator has a transfer function in the s-domain of

$$v_O = -\frac{v_1}{R_1 C_F s} - \frac{v_2}{R_2 C_F s} - \frac{v_3}{R_3 C_F s} \tag{6.124a}$$

and correspondingly for the SC circuit we have

$$v_O = -\frac{f_{cl}}{s}\left(\frac{v_1 C_1}{C_F} + \frac{v_2 C_2}{C_F} + \frac{v_3 C_3}{C_F}\right) \tag{6.124b}$$

Most of the various continuous-time active filter circuits we have studied can be transformed to an SC equivalent, except for Sallen-Key circuits. The latter require a fixed dc gain-constant K, which is not directly amenable to SC design. However, the infinite-gain circuits are achievable—as indicated by the single-op-amp LP filter of Fig. 6.52(a) where the primed values refer to the replaced resistors

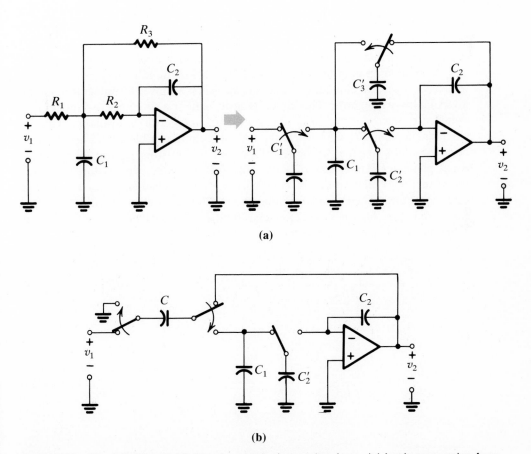

(a)

(b)

Figure 6.52 The infinite-gain LP filter in switched-capacitor form: (a) basic conversion from the RC circuit; (b) equivalent SC circuit with one less capacitor.

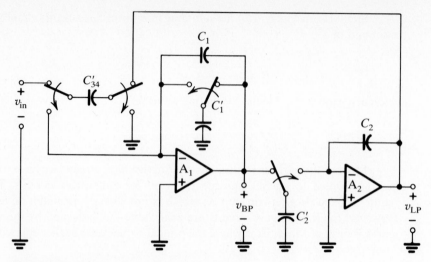

Figure 6.53 SC circuit for the biquad filter of Fig. 6.25.

in the analog counterpart. A reduced-component version of the SC circuit is shown in Fig. 6.52(b),* where there is charge sharing among all four capacitors.

The three-op-amp biquad circuit of Fig. 6.25 required a unity-gain inversion to achieve a general biquadratic function, as well as an inverting integrator and an inverting lossy integrator. This circuit is easily achieved with only two op amps in switched-capacitor form, since a noninverting integrator is available. The SC circuit is shown in Fig. 6.53, where the A_2 and A_3 amplifier blocks of Fig. 6.25 have been combined together in the A_2 block, and the resistors R_3 and R_4 are made equal, giving a LP filter gain of unity. Therefore, since the two resistors are equal, their functional relation can be combined in one switched-capacitor C'_{34} in Fig. 6.53, where the primed capacitors indicate a resistor replacement. As did the analog continuous-time filter of Fig. 6.25, there is both a LP and BP output for the biquad, which in the SC circuit reduce to

$$\frac{v_{LP}(s)}{v_{in}(s)} = \frac{f_{cl}^2\left(\dfrac{C'_2 C'_{34}}{C_1 C_2}\right)}{s^2 + s\left(\dfrac{f_{cl}C'_1}{C_1}\right) + f_{cl}^2\left(\dfrac{C'_2 C'_{34}}{C_1 C_2}\right)} \tag{6.125a}$$

and

$$\frac{v_{BP}(s)}{v_{in}(s)} = \frac{-s\left(\dfrac{f_{cl}C'_{34}}{C_1}\right)}{s^2 + s\left(\dfrac{f_{cl}C'_1}{C_1}\right) + f_{cl}^2\left(\dfrac{C'_2 C'_{34}}{C_1 C_2}\right)} \tag{6.125b}$$

---

* From Ref. 6.15, p. 253. The circuits of Fig. 6.52 validate the concept of conversion from analog to SC filters. SC circuits using two, or more, op amps are more important, practically.

The state-variable filter may also be realized using SC techniques, but eliminating the damped integrator (the elimination of resistor R_1 in Fig. 6.25) may lead to large dc offsets at the outputs of the op amps. A two-op-amp version with reduced sensitivities and lower offset is available from the literature [Ref. 6.15, p. 253]. The only real disadvantage to implementing either the biquad or SV filter in switched-capacitor form is that the capacitor ratios required may be unduly large, as indicated by the example below.

EXAMPLE 6.17

Use the biquad circuit of Fig. 6.53 to design a filter having $\omega_p = 2\pi(1\text{ kHz})$ and $Q_p = 10$. The clock frequency is $f_{cl} = 100\text{ kHz}$. Assume the smallest realizable capacitor value is 0.1 pF.

Solution
Since SC circuits are designed based on capacitor ratios, define $\alpha_1 = C_1'/C_1$ and $\alpha_2 = C_2'/C_2$. Also let us use an equal C design, $C_1' = C_2' = C_{34}'$. Thus, from Eq. (6.125),

$$\left(\frac{\omega_p}{Q_p}\right) = f_{cl}\left(\frac{C_1'}{C_1}\right) = f_{cl}\alpha_1 \qquad \text{or } \alpha_1 = \frac{2\pi}{Q_p}\left(\frac{f_p}{f_{cl}}\right)$$

$$\omega_p^2 = f_{cl}^2\alpha_1\alpha_2 \qquad \text{or } \alpha_2 = 2\pi Q_p\left(\frac{f_p}{f_{cl}}\right)$$

Solving gives the ratios $\alpha_1 = 2\pi \times 10^{-3} = 0.00628$, while $\alpha_2 = 2\pi \times 10^{-1} = 0.628$. Hence, the design would obtain $C_1' = C_2' = C_{34}' = 0.1$ pF, and $C_1 = (0.1/0.00628) = 15.92$ pF, while $C_2 = 0.159$ pF. Of course, if we reduce the ratio of f_{cl}/f_p the range of capacitor values is reduced, but then the effects indicated in Fig. 6.50 become more dominant.

The sensitivities of SC filters are the same as those of an analog continuous-time equivalent, as long as the clock frequency f_{cl} is much greater than the cutoff frequency of the filter, $f_p(f_c)$. However, as f_p approaches f_{cl} then the delay term exp $(j\omega T)$ in Eq. (6.122c) is no longer negligible, and one must resort to sampled-data analysis using z-transforms. Indeed, such an analysis [Ref. 6.1, p. 371-72] yields the following sensitivities for Example 6.17

$$S_{\alpha_1}^{f_p} \approx \frac{f_{cl}}{2\pi f_p}\sin\left(\frac{\pi f_p}{f_c}\right) = 0.5 \tag{6.126a}$$

$$S_{\alpha_2}^{f_p} \approx 0 \qquad S_{\alpha_1}^{Q_p} \approx 0 \tag{6.126b}$$

$$S_{\alpha_2}^{Q_p} \approx 2\pi Q_p\left(\frac{f_p}{f_{cl}}\right) = 0.63 \tag{6.126c}$$

all of which are certainly comparable to analog filters. In fact, many of the Q sensitivities vary as f_p/f_{cl}, hence making this ratio small is a necessity for low sensitivity.

The sensitivity of the SC filter to a finite GB of the op amp can be somewhat less than that of the active RC design. Martin and Sedra* have shown that for the stray-insensitive noninverting integrator of Fig. 6.51(a) the magnitude and phase errors due to the finite GB are approximately

$$M(\omega) \approx \left(\frac{-C_1}{C_1 + C_2}\right) \exp(-k_1) \tag{6.126d}$$

$$\theta(\omega) \approx 0 \tag{6.126e}$$

where $k_1 = \pi[C_2/(C_1 + C_2)](f_t/f_{cl})$, where the gain-bandwidth product is $GB = 2\pi f_t$. Similarly, for the inverting integrator [the clock signals Φ_1 and Φ_2 are interchanged for M_3 and M_4 of Fig. 6.51(a)] the errors are

$$M(\omega) \approx -\exp(-k_1)\left[1 - \left(\frac{C_2}{C_1 + C_2}\right)\cos\left(\frac{2\pi f}{f_{cl}}\right)\right] \tag{6.126f}$$

$$\theta(\omega) \approx -\exp(-k_1)\left[\left(\frac{C_2}{C_1 + C_2}\right)\sin\left(\frac{2\pi f}{f_{cl}}\right)\right] \tag{6.126g}$$

Notice that to minimize the effect of the finite GB on filter performance, the clock frequency should be chosen as low as possible, consistent with the necessity $f_p/f_{cl} \ll 1$.

Several commercially available second-order filters based on the biquad or SV switched-capacitor structure have LP, HP or BP outputs available. National Semiconductor offers the MF5 and MF10 universal filters, and also the MF4 and MF6 units configured as fourth- and sixth-order Butterworth LP filters to 20 kHz. The same company also offers a Switched-Capacitor Filter Handbook [see Ref. 6.12] with numerous filter tables and applications appropriate to SC implementation. Also available from EG&G Reticon are a series, R5604–R5606, synthesizing a six-pole Chebyshev BP filter with f_0 adjustable from 0.5 Hz to 10 kHz. Other R5600 filter series have f_0 adjustable to approximately 20 kHz, and can produce LP, HP and BR functions as well. Also, many manufacturers such as Intel, Motorola, AMI, TI and others, now offer SC ICs for one of the most demanding filter applications—telecommunications filter circuits.

Most of the higher-order SC filters are best implemented from an LC ladder-network circuit, where filter tables can be used. This implementation lets us use all the basic types of approximations (Butterworth, Chebyshev, Bessel, elliptic, etc.) plus the available transformations to HP, BP, or other filter types. We will close our discussion of SC circuits by looking at one example of a lowpass LC ladder circuit. First, let us concentrate on *one* section of an LC ladder, as shown

* K. Martin and A. S. Sedra, "Effects of the Op Amp Finite Gain and Bandwidth on the Performance of Switched-Capacitor Filters," *IEEE Trans. Ckts. & Syst.*, Vol. CAS-28, pp. 822–29, (Aug. 1981).

in Fig. 6.54(a) by the L_2–C_3 structure. The equations for this one section are

$$(V_1 - V_3)\frac{1}{sL_2} = I_2 \tag{6.127a}$$

$$V_3 = I_3\left(\frac{1}{sC_3}\right) = (I_2 - I_4)\frac{1}{sC_3} \tag{6.127b}$$

Now, our switched-capacitor circuits depend basically on op amps used as integrators (or lossy integrators). However, the op amp is a voltage-controlled device; hence, the use of currents is not conducive to a SC circuit. Let us therefore convert Eq. (6.127) to a voltage equation by multiplying both sides of the equation by an arbitrary scaling resistor R_x

$$(V_1 - V_3)\frac{R_x}{sL_2} = R_x I_2 \equiv V_2' \tag{6.128a}$$

$$V_3 = \frac{1}{sC_3 R_x}(I_2 R_x - I_4 R_x) \equiv \frac{1}{sC_3 R_x}(V_2' - V_4') \tag{6.128b}$$

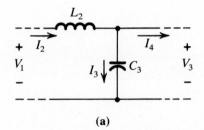

(a)

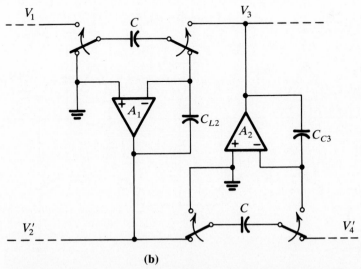

(b)

Figure 6.54 Switched-capacitor structure for an LC ladder: (a) one section of a lowpass LC ladder; (b) SC equivalent circuit.

where V_2' and V_4' are new defined variables equal to the respective current multiplied by the scaling resistor R_x. Eq. (6.128) is now in a suitable form for SC implementation using a difference integrator. The equivalent SC circuit for this one LC ladder section is shown in Fig. 6.54(b), where the switch phasing is now alternated between stages, thereby alleviating some of the excess phase shift. The capacitor ratios are chosen to reflect the appropriate integrator constants from Eqs. (6.128), namely

$$\frac{C_{L2}}{C} = \frac{L_2 f_{cl}}{R_x} \tag{6.129a}$$

$$\frac{C_{C3}}{C} = C_3 f_{cl} R_x \tag{6.129b}$$

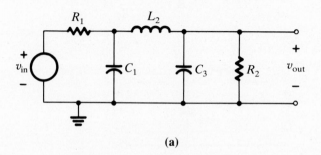

(a)

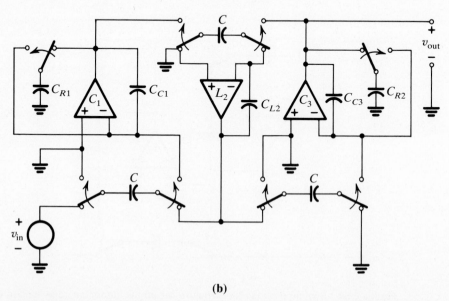

(b)

Figure 6.55 Third-order LC ladder filter: (a) RLC circuit; (b) SC equivalent circuit.

In Fig. 6.55 is an example of a third-order LP filter with resistive termination at each end, and its switched-capacitor equivalent.* The terminating resistor can be realized as part of the input (or output) op amp by using a lossy integrator in the appropriate position. The general design equations for each ith element (L_i, C_i, R_i) is now, from above,

$$\frac{C_{L_i}}{C} = L_i\left(\frac{f_{cl}}{R_x}\right) \tag{6.130a}$$

$$\frac{C_{C_i}}{C} = C_i(f_{cl}R_x) \tag{6.130b}$$

$$\frac{C_{R_i}}{C} = R_i\left(\frac{1}{R_x}\right) \tag{6.130c}$$

SUMMARY

In this chapter we have investigated some of the more useful active RC filter circuits. Our concentration has been on the four most important types of filters, the lowpass, highpass, bandpass, and band-rejection circuits. There are other less-used filter types, such as the all-pass filter (see Problem 6.55), that were not covered, and for this and other examples the reader is referred to the many texts available on filter theory [in particular, References 6.1–6.3, 6.5, and 6.20].

Further, this chapter does not cover some other useful concepts such as transformation techniques for LC ladder networks from LP to BP (and BR) specifications. To adequately cover this topic (and other ladder-network concepts such as "Leapfrog" filter techniques,†) would have added many additional pages to an already overlong chapter. Moreover, since the dominant goal of this text is the operational amplifier, and not the filter circuit per se, we have rightfully restricted our coverage to the more standard op amp filter applications.

The most important approximation techniques, and examples of their usage, were presented. It appears that currently there is increased interest, and use of the elliptic (Cauer) approximation, particularly since this approximation obtains the steepest rolloff past the cutoff frequency ω_c. Unfortunately, the elliptic filter

---

* For complex circuits in SC technology, the use of a computer program is recommended for complete analysis. Some of the more widely used SC analysis programs are DIANA, DINAP, ISCAP, SCANAL, SCAPN, and SWITCAP. References to these may be found in M. L. Liou, Y-L Kuo, and C. F. Lee, "A Tutorial on Computer-Aided Analysis of Switched-Capacitor Circuits," *Proc. IEEE*, Vol. 71, No. 8, pp. 987-1005, (Aug. 1983).

† The "Leapfrog" filter technique is a direct method of filter synthesis (as opposed to the cascade method), which uses negative feedback to simulate the voltage and current relations for a passive RLC filter. The original article was by F. E. J. Girling and E. F. Good, "Active Filters 12: The Leap-Frog or Active-Ladder Synthesis," *Wireless World*, Vol. 76, pp. 341–45, (July 1970). Although not directly analyzing this technique, the design of the third-order switched-capacitor LP filter of Fig. 6.55 utilizes this feedback concept.

equations are some of the most complex. However, numerous tables are available from Zhevrev [Ref. 6.16], Christian and Eisenmann [Ref. 6.18], and also from a National Semiconductor handbook [Ref. 6.12]. With the wide current availability of programmable calculators and personal computers, the serious filter user may even wish to program his or her own equations for the elliptic filter.

Our filter discussion ended with a new type of integrated circuit filter, the switched-capacitor (SC) filter. With the increased use of MOS circuits, and the continually decreasing silicon-chip area requirements, one would anticipate a rapid growth in the future for SC networks. In fact, evidence* would indicate that the present limitation of frequencies below 20 kHz is merely temporary, as LP filters operating to 1 MHz may be feasible.

PROBLEMS

6.1 Verify the element network transformations from a lowpass to a bandpass and band-reject filter in Table 6.2.

6.2 A normalized passive filter with termination resistors $R = 1\,\Omega$ is shown in Fig. P6.2. (a) Derive the transfer function (v_2/v_1), and show that this is a third-order $(n = 3)$ Butterworth lowpass filter, with gain $H_0 = \frac{1}{2}$ and $\omega_c = 1$ rad/sec. (b) Using Table 6.2, sketch the circuit for a highpass filter with $\omega_c = 1$ rad/sec. (c) Repeat (b) for a BP filter having $\omega_0 = 10^5$ rad/sec, a Q of 10, and a terminating resistor $R = 1\,k\Omega$.

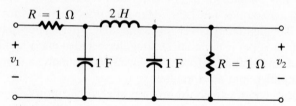

Figure P6.2

6.3 Show that the normalized Chebyshev function at $\omega = 0$, $|H(j0)/H_0|$, must be equal to 1 if n is odd, and equal to $1/(1 + \varepsilon^2)^{1/2}$ if n is even.

6.4 Show that the order n for a Chebyshev lowpass filter is given by

$$n = \frac{\ln[x + (x^2 - 1)^{1/2}]}{\ln[y + (y^2 - 1)^{1/2}]}$$

where

$$x = \left(\frac{10^{0.1 A_{min}} - 1}{10^{0.1 A_{max}} - 1}\right) \text{ and } y = \left(\frac{\omega_s}{\omega_c}\right)$$

---

* R. R. Schellenback, "Switched-Capacitor Filters—An Economical Approach to Critical Filtering," *Integrated Circuits Magazine*, pp. 30–38, (Oct. 1984).

6.5 Show that the attenuation (in dB) of a Chebyshev filter at any frequency f is obtained by

$$\text{Atten}(f)_{dB} = 10 \log_{10}\left\{1 + \left[(10^{0.1 \, A_{max}} - 1)^{1/2} \times \left(\frac{e^z + e^{-z}}{2}\right)\right]^2\right\}$$

where

$$z = n \ln\left\{\left(\frac{f}{f_c}\right) + \left[\left(\frac{f}{f_c}\right)^2 - 1\right]^{1/2}\right\}$$

6.6 Show that the frequency at which the Chebyshev lowpass filter is $-3\,dB$ below $|H(j\omega)| = 1$ is given by

$$\omega_{-3\,dB} = \cosh\left[\frac{1}{n}\cosh^{-1}\left(\frac{1}{\varepsilon}\right)\right]$$

6.7 Using the recursion formula Eq. (6.22) obtain the $B_4(s)$ polynomial of Table 6.7 from $B_3(s)$ and $B_2(s)$.

6.8 Plot on a *linear* graph the phase shift characteristic of the Thomson filter (for $n = 6$) of Fig. 6.8 and compare with the phase shift of a Butterworth filter (for the same $n = 6$). Comment on how well the ideal condition, $-d\theta/d\omega = T$ is achieved.

6.9 For a second-order ($n = 2$) Thomson filter the transfer function is of the form

$$H(s) = \frac{a_0}{s^2 + a_1 s + a_0}$$

with a resulting frequency response defined by

$$H(j\omega) = \frac{a_0}{(a_0 - \omega^2) + ja_1\omega} = |H(j\omega)| \angle \theta$$

where the phase function θ is obviously

$$\theta = -\tan^{-1}\left(\frac{a_1\omega}{a_0 - \omega^2}\right)$$

Since the time delay T is equal to $-d\theta/d\omega$, we have from the previous equation

$$T = -\frac{d\theta}{d\omega} = \left(\frac{a_1}{a_0}\right)\frac{\left(1 - \dfrac{\omega^2}{a_0}\right)}{1 + \omega^2\left(\dfrac{a_1^2}{a_0^2} - \dfrac{2}{a_0}\right) + \omega^4}$$

Using values for a_1 and a_0 from Table 6.7 plot T versus ω for $n = 2$. Similarly, find T for $n = 4$, plot it on the same graph, and compare the results of the two curves.

6.10 Another lowpass approximation function similar to the Thomson filter is the Gaussian function

$$|H(j\omega)|^2 = \exp(-\omega^2)$$

where a series expansion yields an all-pole function

$$|H(j\omega)|^2 = \frac{1}{1 + \omega^2 + \dfrac{\omega^4}{2!} + \dfrac{\omega^2}{3!} + \cdots}$$

such that an nth order filter is satisfied by the first $(n + 1)$ terms of the denominator. For the second-order case ($n = 2$) find the pole locations of $H(s)$ and compare with those of the Bessel filter from Table 6.7. Also, compare magnitude and phase characteristics with those for $n = 2$ in Fig. 6.8. On the same graph as in Problem 6.9, sketch the time delay T. What would you anticipate about the step function response?

6.11 Derive Eq. (6.24) for the circuit of Fig. 6.11. Assume an ideal op amp for A_1.

6.12 One might consider the case $K = 1$ and $C_1 = C_2 = 1$ F for the normalized Sallen and Key LP filter of Fig. 6.11. Show why this results in a non-realizable requirement for R_1 and R_2.

6.13 Use the simplified small-signal model for the 741 op amp (open-loop poles at 5 Hz and 5 MHz and $A_{OL} = 2 \times 10^5$) and obtain the transfer function v_2/v_1 for the LP circuit of Fig. 6.13(b) using SPICE, or any other CAD program. Verify that the dc gain is unity, with $\omega_c = 10^3$ rad/sec, and with $A_{min} > 40$ dB at $\omega_s = 2 \times 10^3$ rad/sec.

6.14 Show that the transfer function for the twin-tee network of Fig. P6.14 as $R_L \to \infty$ is

$$H(s) = \frac{v_2(s)}{v_1(s)} = \frac{H_e(s^2 + \omega_z^2)}{\left[s^2 + \left(\dfrac{\omega_p}{Q_p} \right)s + \omega_p^2 \right]}$$

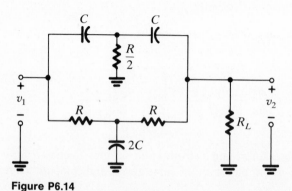

Figure P6.14

where

$$H_e = \frac{1}{3}$$

$$\omega_z = \frac{1}{RC}$$

$$\omega_p = \frac{1}{\sqrt{3}RC}$$

$$Q_p = \frac{\sqrt{3}}{4}$$

Also, show that $H(s) \to 1$ as $s \to 0$ (dc), and that $H(s) \to 1/3$ as $s \to \infty$.

6.15 Verify the complete design for the elliptic LP filter of Example 6.5, starting with Eq. (6.34). Verify each of the normalized element values, and the final transformed circuit of Fig. 6.15(b). Assuming that the LF351 op amp is used for A_1, A_2 and A_3 use the-pole SPICE model for the LF351 in Appendix D, Section D.1, and compare the transfer functions for $|H_1(j\omega)|$, $|H_2(j\omega)|$, and $|H(j\omega)|$ obtained from SPICE with those of Fig. 6.16.

6.16 Using the LP circuit of Fig. 6.17, specify component values for a dc gain $-H_0 = -5$, $f_c = 10$ kHz and a passband ripple of 1 dB (no ripple in the stopband). What will be the attenuation at $f = 20$ kHz?

6.17 Derive the transfer function for the elliptic second-order lowpass filter of Fig. 6.14, as shown in Eq. (6.30).

6.18 Using the data of Table 6.6, obtain the realization of a normalized second-order LP elliptic filter with $\omega_c = 1$ and an attentuation of ≥ 20 dB at $\omega_s = 2$. Use the circuit of Fig. 6.14 and sketch the magnitude and phase of your normalized circuit. Then, remove normalization and show all component values for $\omega_c = 10^4$ rad/sec, with the largest capacitor used being 0.1 μF.

6.19 Verify the component values of Fig. 6.15(b), using the scale factors $k_f = 10^3$, $k_{m1} = 9.332 \times 10^3$ and $k_{m2} = 4.064 \times 10^3$.

6.20 Show that the circuit of Fig. P6.20 is that of a third-order LP active RC filter having a transfer function

$$H(s) = \frac{H_0}{s^3 + a_2 s^2 + a_1 s + a_0}$$

Would this circuit be useful in designing an $n = 3$, LP filter for prescribed ω_c and ω_s/ω_c criteria?

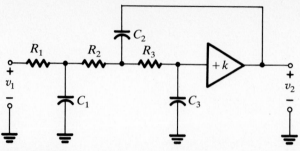

Figure P6.20

6.21 (a) Derive the sensitivity relationship of Eq. (6.45), with $H(j\omega)$ defined by Eq. (6.46). (b) Also show that

$$S_x^y = \frac{y_1 S_x^{y_1} + y_2 S_x^{y_2}}{y_1 + y_2}$$

if $y = y_1 + y_2$.

6.22 Verify the sensitivity functions S_{R2}^Q, S_{C1}^Q, and S_{C2}^Q in Eq. (6.50).

6.23 Specifiy component values for a Sallen-Key LP filter having $\omega_c = 2\pi \times 3 \times 10^5$ rad/sec, $H_0 = 1$ and $Q = 1$, if the largest capacitor and resistor to be used are 0.22 μF and 10 kΩ, respectively. If due to an increase in temperature all resistors change by $+5\%$, and capacitors by -10%, while the open-loop gain of the op amp decreases by 20%, estimate the change in ω_c and Q. Assume the op amp has characteristics similar to the LF351.

6.24 Repeat Problem 6.23 for an infinite-gain LP filter. Estimate the change in ω_c and Q and compare your results with that of Problem 6.23.

6.25 Derive Eqs. (6.65) and (6.66a) for the Sallen and Key LP filter having equal R and equal C.

6.26 It is possible to compensate the Sallen and Key LP filter circuit for a finite GB by adding a lead-lag network formed from R_2 and C_2 of Fig. 6.11, as indicated in Fig. P6.26. If the op amp has a single pole in the open-loop response, so that the gain constant K is given by Eq. (6.65), show that compensation is

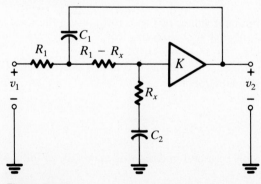

Figure P6.26

achieved if $R_x C_2 = K_0/GB$. Using the scaled circuit values of Fig. 6.13(b), what should the value of R_x be if a 741 op amp were used for A_1–A_3?

6.27 Estimate the actual ω_p, ω_z and Q_p for an elliptic design like that of Example 6.5 for $H_2(s)$ if (a) a 741 op amp is used, and (b) an HA2540 op amp is used. Use the data of Fig. 6.20 with ω_p (ideal) $= 2\pi$ (10 kHz).

6.28 Verify Eq. (6.73) for the two-op-amp filter circuit of Fig. 6.21(a). Show that the transfer function of Fig. 6.21(b) is indeed that of $H_2(s)$ of Eq. 6.34(a). For $\omega_p = \omega_c = 10^3$ rad/sec, scale the circuit element values so that the largest capacitor value is 0.47 μF. Compare the practicality of the resulting circuit with that of Fig. 6.15(b) for $H_2(s)$.

6.29 Repeat the Example of Fig. 6.21(b) and Equation (6.34a), using the general biquadratic two-op-amp circuit of Fig. 6.21(a), for the case $a = 1$. Show the normalized values for components, and compare with the circuit of Fig. 6.21(b).

6.30 Using the two-op-amp circuit of Fig. 6.21(b), repeat the design of Example 6.5 for an $n = 4$ elliptic LP filter. Compare your final circuit with that of Fig. 6.15(b) for $\omega_c = 10^3$ rad/sec. Let the largest capacitor value be 0.47 μF. Assume an ideal op amp.

6.31 Using the circuit of Problem 6.30, estimate the actual ω_p, ω_z and Q_p for the $H_2(s)$ circuit (a) if a 741 op amp is used, and (b) if an HA2540 device is used for both op amps. Use the data of Fig. 6.23, but assume ω_p (ideal) $= 2\pi$ (10 kHz).

6.32 Show that the circuit of Fig. P6.32 is a two-op-amp version of the basic biquad active filter of Fig. 6.25. Other than saving one op amp, is there any

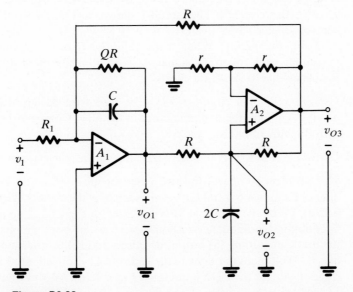

Figure P6.32

advantage to this circuit as compared with the basic biquad circuit of Fig. 6.25?

6.33 Verify the transfer functions for the biquad active filter of Fig. 6.25, as given in Eqs. 6.85(a)–(f).

6.34 Derive the transfer function (v_{O3}/v_{in}) for the biquad circuit of Fig. 6.26(b) and show that it is identical to the standard biquad circuit. Also, show that the op amp $A_4(A_5)$ provides a leading phase shift, which will compensate for the lagging phase shift of $A_1(A_2)$. Assume the open-loop gain of all op amps can be approximated by that of a single-pole system.

6.35 Using the normalized circuit of Fig. 6.27 for $\omega_p = 1$, find all component values for $\omega_p = 10^3$ rad/sec. Choose the resistor scaling factor so that each op amp drives a load ≥ 2 kΩ. Assume the MC34074 quad op amp (data in Appendix C) is used for A_1–A_4. If the maximum amplitude V_{O4} is 10 volts (peak), what is the maximum input value for V_{in} and the maximum frequency ω_p that is permitted?

6.36 In the SV filter circuit of Fig. 6.28(c), discuss how one could easily tune the circuit for changes in gain, frequency, and bandwidth. If one were to build a variable filter covering the frequency range from 0.1 Hz to 100 kHz, discuss the design details that might be involved.

6.37 Using the LM3900 Norton amplifier (data stated in Exercise 5.6), with a single power supply of $+15$ V, design an SV filter to give LP, HP and BP outputs for a second-order Butterworth response, a center frequency f_0 of 1 kHz, and a dc gain of unity for the LP output.

6.38 An electronically adjustable variable filter can be formed using the SV filter concept and an OTA (see Section 5.5), the CA3060 (a dual CA3080, data given in Exercise 5.5). The circuit is shown in Fig. P6.38. If the frequency-control voltage varies from 0 V to $+10$ V, what is the adjustable-frequency range for the circuit? What is the gain and Q of the circuit? What is the maximum value of input signal v_{in} permitted? Is there any limitation in frequency due to slew-rate effects?

6.39 Using the SV filter circuit of Fig. 6.29, repeat the design of Example 6.8. If possible, equalize the dynamic range in the filter. Compare the resulting filter with the biquad of Example 6.8.

6.40 Derive Eq. (6.93a) for the generalized impedance converter circuit of Fig. 6.31.

6.41 This problem compares the two cases for an $n = 7$ active Butterworth LP filter of Examples 6.4 and 6.10, as presented by the circuits of Figs. 6.13(b) and 6.32(d). Using the two-pole SPICE model for the LF351 op amp (Appendix D.1) obtain the frequency response printout for both circuits, and compare the results regarding (a) output dc offsets and (b) transfer-function accuracy of v_2/v_1. To obtain the same magnitude of v_2/v_1 you will need to add an extra stage of gain for the FDNR circuit of Fig. 6.32(d). Also, evaluate GB effects of

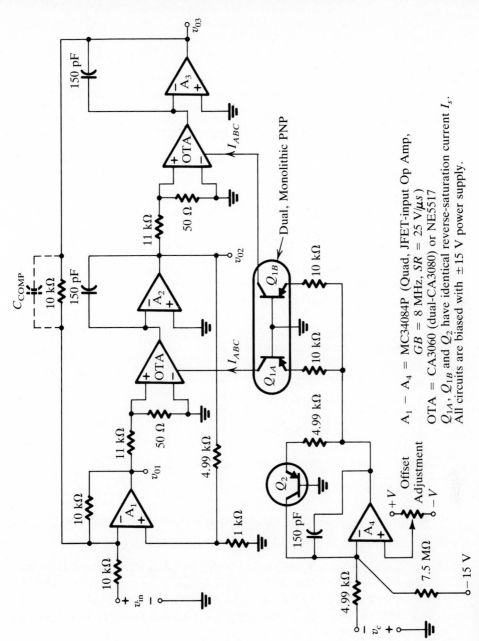

$A_1 - A_4 = $ MC34084P (Quad, JFET-input Op Amp, $GB = 8$ MHz, $SR = 25$ V/μs)

OTA = CA3060 (dual-CA3080) or NE5517

Q_{1A}, Q_{1B} and Q_2 have identical reverse-saturation current I_s.

All circuits are biased with ± 15 V power supply.

Figure P6.38

the op amps by assuming that $GB(A_2)$ is at its nominal value, while $GB(A_1) = 0.9\ GB(A_2)$ and $GB(A_3) = 1.1\ GB(A_2)$ for Fig. 6.13, while in Fig. 6.32 assume a similar random $\pm 10\%$ difference in GB among A_1–A_6.

6.42 Either using SPICE, or a programmable calculator, verify the transfer function $v_2(s)/v_1(s)$ for the highpass elliptic design of Fig. 6.35(b).

6.43 Obtain the sensitivities for the HP infinite-gain circuit of Fig. 6.36(b) and compare them with the LP equal R from Table 6.8.

6.44 Use the same specifications as in Exercise 6.7, and obtain a HP filter using the two-op-amp circuit of Fig. 6.38(a).

6.45 Derive the transfer function of Eq. (6.103a) for the HP circuit of Fig. 6.39, and show that the design conditions of Eq. (6.103b) are valid.

6.46 An $n = 4$ normalized elliptic LP filter is obtained from Zverev's tables [Ref. 6.16, p. 198] which has 0.28 dB ripple in the passband (A_{max}) and $A_{min} = 42.5$ dB at a stopband frequency $\omega_s = 1.96$. The circuit is shown in Fig. P6.46. Obtain an RC realization of the circuit, with a gain of unity, and an output impedance $<1\ \Omega$, with $\omega_c = 10^4$ rad/sec.

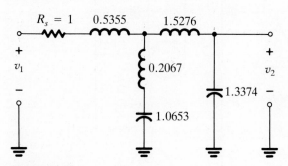

Figure P6.46

6.47 Repeat Problem 6.46 for a HP circuit with $\omega_c = 10^4$ rad/sec.

6.48 Repeat Example 6.12 for a BP filter, but use a 741 op amp.

6.49 It is possible to increase the Q of a BP filter by use of a Q enhancement circuit, shown in Fig. P6.49. The objective is to increase the Q of the overall circuit, while the infinite-gain BP circuit operates with a moderate value of Q. Show that with the parameter values indicated, the transfer function of the basic infinite-gain circuit remains at

$$\frac{v_2(s)}{v_{O1}(s)} = \frac{(1/Q)s}{s^2 + (1/Q)s + 1}$$

while the overall transfer function is

$$\frac{v_2(s)}{v_1(s)} = \frac{(1/Q)s}{s^2 + (1/Q_{total})s + 1}$$

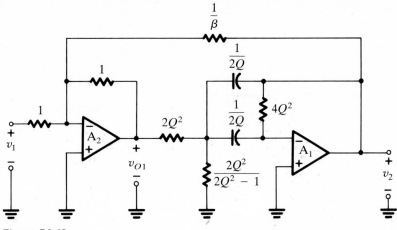

Figure P6.49

where the overall Q is $Q_{total} = Q/1 - \beta$. Show all element values for a design having $Q = 5$ and $f_0 = 50$ kHz but $Q_{total} = 50$, while the input impedance seen by the source v_1 is 10 kΩ. Use capacitors of value ≤ 1000 pF.

6.50 Using the transformation from LP to BP and the LP circuit of Fig. P6.2, obtain an $n = 3$ passive Butterworth BP filter with $\omega_0 = 10^5$ rad/sec. Comment on any problems that would arise when attempting an active filter synthesis of the resulting circuit.

6.51 Using the techniques suggested in Chapter 6 for adding leading phase to the circuit, show element values to realize either a biquad or SV BP filter meeting the design objectives of Example 6.12, but having $\Delta Q/Q < 10\%$.

6.52 For the active R circuit of Fig. 6.45(b), obtain the transfer function v_3/v_1. Is this a LP, HP, BP or BR circuit? What is the upper limit for f_0 for the basic BP circuit if an LF351 op amp were used? If an HA2539 op amp were used (data shown earlier in Exercise 3.4)?

6.53 Show that a band-rejection filter is also possible in the circuit of Fig. 6.46(a) by grounding the C_3 capacitor, and connecting from the output of the K amplifier to the R_3 resistor. Obtain the transfer function and equations for ω_0 and Q for this new circuit. Is there any preference of one circuit over the other?

6.54 A band-rejection filter can be obtained with the circuit of Fig. P6.54 by an appropriate choice of feedback elements. This circuit has been referred to as a Wein-bridge BR circuit.* Show that the transfer function reduces to that of a

---

* G. Darilek and O. Tranbarger, *Elect. Design*, pp. 80, 81, (Feb. 1, 1978).

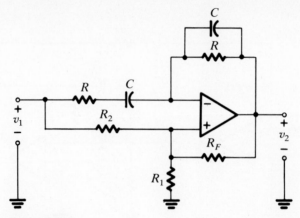

Figure P6.54

BR filter [Eq. (6.116a)] provided that $k_2 = 1/3$, where

$$k_2 = \frac{1/R_2}{\dfrac{1}{R_2} + \dfrac{1}{R_1} + \dfrac{1}{R_F}}$$

Also, show that with $k_2 = \frac{1}{3}$ the Q and ω_0 are

$$\omega_0 = \frac{1}{RC} \qquad Q = \left(\frac{1 - k_f}{2 - 3k_f}\right) \qquad \text{where } k_f = \frac{1/R_F}{\dfrac{1}{R_2} + \dfrac{1}{R_1} + \dfrac{1}{R_F}}$$

Design a filter having $f_0 = 60$ Hz and a $BW = 6$ Hz. Calculate all sensitivities for the circuit, $S_x^{\omega_0}$ and S_x^Q.

6.55 A second-order all-pass (AP) filter function has the general transfer function

$$\frac{v_2(s)}{v_1(s)} = \frac{\pm H\left[s^2 - s\left(\dfrac{\omega_o}{Q}\right) + \omega_0^2\right]}{s_2 + s\left(\dfrac{\omega_0}{Q}\right) + \omega_0^2}$$

(a) Sketch the normalized magnitude and phase of the AP function.

(b) The band-rejection filter circuits of Fig. 6.47 can realize the AP function by appropriate choice of α, α_1 and α_2. Find the correct choices for these parameters for both circuits of Fig. 6.47.

(c) What would be the correct choice of resistors for the biquad circuit of Fig. 6.48(a) to realize the AP filter?

(d) What would be the practical use of an AP filter?

6.56 In the switched-capacitor integrator of Fig. 6.49(b), assume the input signal is a sinusoid of amplitude 1 V and frequency f_0. If the clock frequency $f_c = 10 f_0$ and the integrator gain is unity, use Eq. 6.122(d) to sketch the output signal.

Let capacitor C_1 sample the input signal at the center of each clock cycle, and then transfer v_{in} to C_2 a half clock period later.

6.57 For the third-order passive lowpass filters of Problem 6.2, find capacitor values for the SC equivalent circuit (use the circuit of Fig. 6.55) if the smallest capacitor value is 0.2 pF. Use appropriate scaling factors to realize a cutoff frequency of $f_c = 3$ kHz and $f_{cl} = 128$ kHz, with a terminating load resistance of 1 kΩ. Choose the R_x scale-factor resistor to help minimize capacitor ratios. If the MOS op amps used have $A_{OL} = 2000$, $GB = 2\pi f_t = 2\pi(5 \text{ MHz})$ and $SR = 10$ V/μsec, what would be the magnitude and phase errors due to a finite GB for each integrator in the circuit?

Chapter **7**

Nonlinear and Other Functional Circuits

Heretofore we have analyzed mostly linear-circuit applications of operational amplifiers. Many requirements, however, demand some type of nonlinear function. One of these is a **comparator circuit**, which compares an input signal to a chosen reference voltage; its output voltage changes value when the input signal is greater than (or less than) the reference. Often applications require that the output voltage be **bounded**, or restricted between defined voltage levels; such an application would require a nonlinear circuit that would clamp the output once a required voltage level is achieved. Even more, we have already mentioned in earlier chapters the concept of analog-to-digital (A/D) conversion, which usually requires a preceding circuit that will sample the analog signal at some defined time and then hold that value for a prescribed time while the A/D conversion is performed. Several other conversion possibilities can require op amps, such as linear-to-logarithmic conversion (as well as an anti-log, or logarithmic-to-linear conversion), and ac-to-dc conversion, often accomplished with the aid of active op amp rectifier circuits. These and several other functional circuit applications using op amps will be discussed in this chapter.

7.1 COMPARATOR AND AMPLITUDE LIMITER CIRCUITS

Since the open-loop gain A_O of an op amp is large, a very small signal difference between the inverting and noninverting inputs can drive the output of the op amp to full saturation. This concept may be extended by including a reference voltage V_{REF} at one input of the op amp, and comparing an input signal v_I with the reference, as shown in Fig. 7.1(a). If the op amp were a 741 device with $A_O = 10^5$ and if $V_{REF} = +1$ V the output would switch to full saturation of approximately -14 V when the signal v_I becomes 0.3 mV more positive then V_{REF}; i.e., v_O goes from approximately $+14$ V to -14 V when v_I changes from $+1$ V to (1 V $+$ 28 V/10^5), or $+1.0003$ V. Hence, we have obtained a simple comparator circuit, whose output switches from one state to the other ($+14$ V to -14 V, or -14 V to $+14$ V) as the input signal becomes greater than, or less than, the V_{REF} value.

The simple circuit of Fig. 7.1(a) has some distinct disadvantages. The most important are: First, the op amp saturates at the output, and may also saturate at the input—this limits the recovery time of the op amp, and in the case of the 741 may result in several hundred microseconds required to go from saturation back to

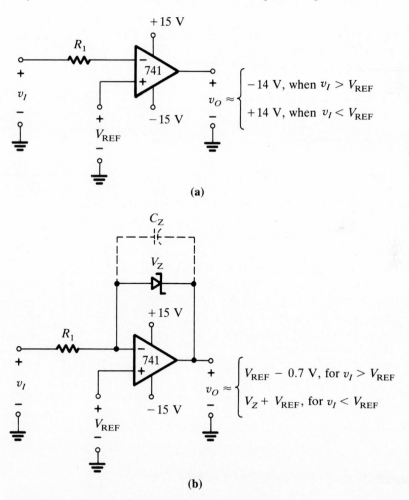

(a)

(b)

Figure 7.1 (a) simple comparator circuit using a 741 op amp. (b) Bounded comparator using a Zener diode for output amplitude limiting.

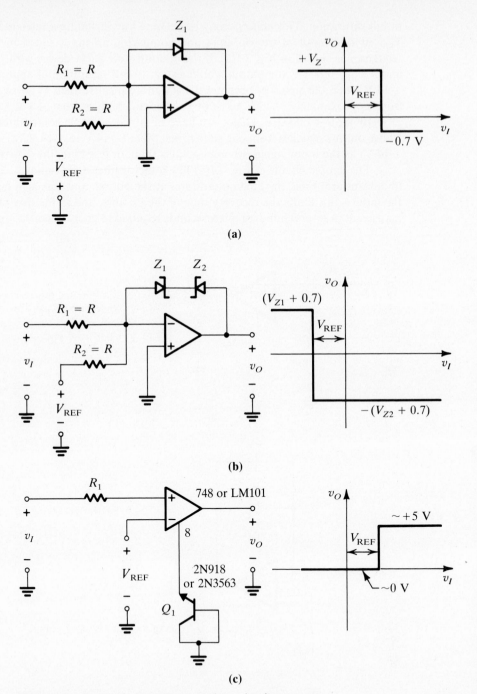

Figure 7.2 Amplitude-limited comparison circuits.

linear operation; Second, the signal levels at the output are large (± 14 V), which limits the speed of response due to slew-rate conditions—for a 741 with $SR = 0.5$ V/μsec, the time required for an output transition is 28 V/0.5 V/μsec = 56 μsec. Further, if we were driving from the op amp into a 5 V digital logic circuit, we would need to condition the signal to obtain a 0 to $+5$ V logic transition. Thus, some means of bounding (or amplitude limiting) the output is required, as well as a way to obtain a nonsaturation condition for the output of the op amp. One simple technique is to use a Zener diode in the feedback path, as shown in Fig. 7.1(b). For example, if $V_Z = +3.6$ V with $V_{\text{REF}} = +1$ V, then (assuming the diode has an impedance $\gg R_1$ during the offstate) the op amp output will remain linear, with an output voltage equal to approximately $1 - 0.7$ V, or 0.3 V when $V_I > V_{\text{REF}}$, since the Zener diode would conduct in the forward direction. However, when $V_I < V_{\text{REF}}$, the diode clamps the output at a value of $V_Z + V_{\text{REF}}$, or $+4.6$ V. One disadvantage to using the clamping diode in the feedback path, as indicated in Fig. 7.1(b), is the introduction of diode capacitance C_Z—which with R_1 forms an integrator until V_Z conducts, thereby instigating a slight time delay in the output response.

One can also place the reference voltage in the inverting input of the op amp using one of the circuits of Fig. 7.2(a) or (b). The resulting idealized transfer characteristics are also indicated in the figure. Note that since V_{REF} is now in the inverting input, the polarity must be opposite to that value used previously in the noninverting input. The circuit of Fig. 7.2(c) is particularly useful for conversion to an output $+5$ to 0 V logic swing; the key to its performance is using an op amp that has access to the base circuit of the output stage of the op amp (this is pin 8 for a μA748, or LM 101-201-301–type op amp). Also, using the low-capacitance Zener breakdown voltage of the emitter-base junction (BV_{EBO}) of an RF high-frequency transistor to limit the output-voltage amplitude is preferable to using a regular Zener diode.

■ **Exercise 7.1**

Design a simple comparator circuit using a 741 op amp that will produce an output signal as follows:

$V_O = +5$ V($\pm 10\%$), when $V_{\text{in}} > 0$ V.

$V_O = 0$ V (± 0.7 V), when $V_{\text{in}} < 0$ V.

This type of comparator is referred to as a **zero-crossing comparator**, since the reference voltage is ground.

A comparator with an easily adjustable threshold is shown in Fig. 7.3. This circuit is often called a **soft limiter**, since the output-voltage levels will increase slightly past the clamping value as the input signal changes. If the input signal is

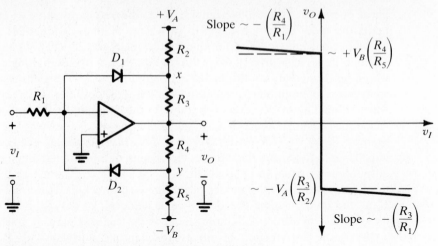

Figure 7.3 Adjustable voltage-limiting comparator.

positive then current flow through R_1 will cause D_1 to conduct (D_2 is off), thereby limiting the voltage at point x ideally to zero volts (actually, -0.5 to -0.7 V). Since the current through D_1 is initially small, the current through R_3 is that from R_2 and $+V_A$, or the negative output clamping level is $v_O \approx -V_A(R_3/R_2)$. Similarly, for negative v_I, D_2 will conduct (D_1 is now off) and point y will be at zero volts (again, really $+0.5$ to $+0.7$ V), and hence the positive-output clamping level is $v_O^+ \approx V_B(R_4/R_5)$. If the current through D_1 or D_2 is significant, then effectively the forward resistance of the appropriate diode is added to R_3 or R_4 and produces a linear inverting amplifier with a gain $v_O/v_I \approx -(R_3 + r_{D1})/R_1$ [or, $-(R_4 + r_{D2})/R_1$]. Typically, the resistors R_3 and R_4 are chosen greater than r_D and smaller than R_1, so that the slope of the curve past the clamping values is small.

EXAMPLE 7.1

Design a comparator using the circuit of Fig. 7.3 with ± 15 V power supplies, that will provide nominal output limiting at $+5$ V and -10 V. Also, for v_I between 0 and ± 15 V the output limits should change by less than 0.2 V. Assume typical diode parameters, and a 10 kΩ load resistor.

Solution
Let us choose $R_1 = 100$ kΩ in Fig. 7.3. Since we have a ± 15 V power supply, let $V_A = +15$ V and $-V_B = -15$ V. Thus, for small values of v_I we need (assume $V_D \approx 0.6$ V)

$$(5 - 0.6) \approx (15 + 0.6)\left(\frac{R_4}{R_5}\right)$$

$$-(10 - 0.6) \approx -(15 + 0.6)\left(\frac{R_3}{R_2}\right)$$

or $(R_4/R_5) = 0.28$ and $(R_3/R_2) = 0.60$. Once the diodes conduct, the slope of the transfer characteristic should be (R_3/R_1) [or (R_4/R_1)] ≤ 0.2 V/15 V $= 1.33 \times 10^{-2}$. Therefore, we need

$$R_3 = R_4 \leq 100 \text{ k}\Omega(1.33 \times 10^{-2}) = 1.33 \text{ k}\Omega$$

Let us use 1.3 kΩ for R_3 and R_4. From above we need $R_2 = 1.3$ kΩ/0.60 = 2.17 kΩ (use 2.2 kΩ) and $R_5 = 1.3$ kΩ/0.28 = 4.64 kΩ (use 4.7 kΩ). The op amp must be able to source and sink the required current and any load current. Thus, if we have a maximum input signal of ± 15 V, the maximum op amp output current will vary between -1.8 mA and -4.1 mA (sinking).

If the input signal contains significant noise contamination, then the open-loop comparator circuits of Figs 7.1–7.3 are not suitable because of possible "squegging" in the output signal—as shown in Fig. 7.4(a), where the output flips back and forth due to the noise present with the signal. For this situation one can add positive feedback by R_2 and R_F in Fig. 7.4(b), thereby establishing a hysteresis voltage

$$\Delta V_H \equiv V_U - V_L \approx \frac{R_2}{R_F}\left(V_O^+ - V_O^-\right) \tag{7.1a}$$

where it is assumed that $R_F \gg R_2$. If the hysteresis value is set greater than the peak-to-peak value of the noise, then the squegging in the output waveform is eliminated. The upper and lower threshold voltages are defined by the circuit of Fig. 7.4(b)* as

$$V_U = V_{\text{REF}} + \left| V_O^+\left(\frac{R_2}{R_2 + R_F}\right) \right| \tag{7.1b}$$

$$V_L = V_{\text{REF}} - \left| V_O^-\left(\frac{R_2}{R_2 - R_F}\right) \right| \tag{7.1c}$$

where V_O^+ and V_O^- are the output limiting voltages of the op amp. The circuit may also be implemented by summing the reference voltage V_{REF} through a resistor connected to the inverting input (as in Fig. 7.2), as well as interchanging the v_I and v_{REF} positions in Fig. 7.4(b).

A different comparison function is sometimes required to obtain an output-voltage transition if an input signal is *between* two defined levels, or within an input **window**. This circuit is called a **window comparator**,† and requires two comparator circuits along with a logical NOR function at the output, as indicated in Fig. 7.5.

---

* The positive-feedback comparator circuit is usually referred to as a Schmitt comparator, or Schmitt trigger circuit, after the originator of the concept.

† In nuclear instrumentation terminology, it is also referred to as a single-channel analyzer circuit.

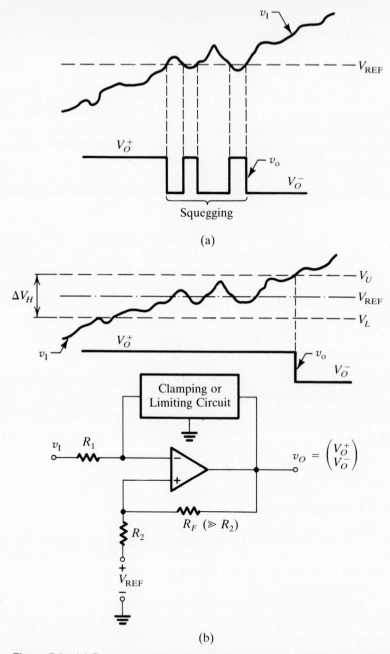

Figure 7.4 (a) Response of the open-loop comparator of Fig. 7.1 to a noisy input signal. (b) Response with positive feedback added, using a Schmitt comparator circuit.

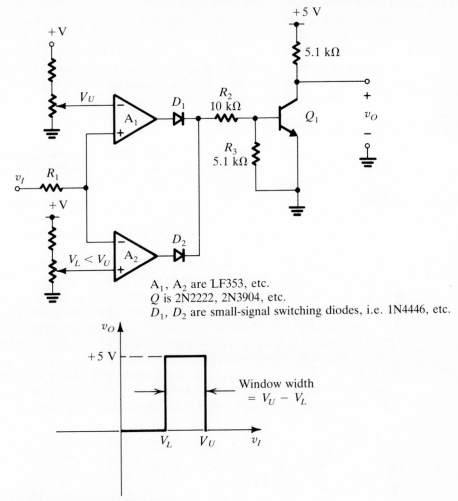

A_1, A_2 are LF353, etc.
Q is 2N2222, 2N3904, etc.
D_1, D_2 are small-signal switching diodes, i.e. 1N4446, etc.

Figure 7.5 Window comparator.

The circuit is most easily implemented with standard IC comparator chips* such as the LM311, or a quad comparator (such as the LM339), all of which have open-collector bipolar-transistor outputs that can be tied together for a NOR function. In the circuit of Fig. 7.5 the performance is as follows. The threshold limits for A_1 and A_2 are set at voltage limits V_U and V_L, where $V_U > V_L$. If the input signal amplitude is below V_L then $V_U > v_I$ and the output of A_1 is low. Similarly, with $V_L > v_I$ the output of A_2 is high. Hence, transistor Q_1 is turned on through D_2 (D_1 is off) and the output v_0 is low (Q_1 is saturated). Further, if v_I is larger than either V_L or V_U then the output of A_2 is low but the output of A_1 is high. Thus Q_1 will be

---

* In general, when output voltage levels of 0 and $+5$ V are required it may be more feasible to use standard logic comparators such as the LM311, or LM339, since these devices offer superior switching speed over op amps.

saturated and v_O is low. However, if v_I is greater than V_L but less than V_H, then the outputs of both A_1 and A_2 are low, and Q_1 will then be off (nonconducting), so v_O will be high. A window comparator is usually designed to have V_L and V_U voltages both be adjustable over a wide range. The design of the biasing circuits and the choice of R_1 may be important if dc-offset effects are considered, particularly if a bipolar-transistor op amp or IC comparator is used.

7.2 DIODE FUNCTION GENERATORS

We have already seen that diodes combined with op amps can form some very excellent clamping and amplitude limiting circuits. It should then be no surprise that, by a reorientation of diodes and resistors, an approximation to a nonlinear function such as $v_O = Kv_{in}^m$ (where $m \neq 1$) is possible. The diodes will basically act as a switch, allowing a piecewise-linear approximation to the desired nonlinear function. The accuracy of the approximation improves as more line segments are used.

The op amp piecewise-linear circuits used can generally be classified as either series limiters or shunt limiters, with both types symbolically represented in Fig. 7.6. In the series limiter circuit of Fig. 7.6(a) there will be no output until v_I is greater than the bias voltage V_{B1} (we assume here ideal diodes, and $V_{B3} > V_{B2} > V_{B1}$). Thus, the first breakpoint on the transfer characteristic curve is at $v_I = V_{B1}$. Over the range $V_{B1} \leq v_I \leq V_{B2}$ the gain is equal to $-R_F/R_1$. Similarly, when $v_I \geq V_{B2}$ then diode D_2 will conduct and the circuit gain is $-(R_F/R_1 \| R_2)$. When v_I reaches V_{B3} all three diodes are conducting and the gain increases to $-(R_F/R_1 \| R_2 \| R_3)$. Thus, the breakpoints are at $v_I = V_{B1}$, V_{B2} and V_{B3}. Also, we can equate the slope of the piecewise-linear segments of Fig. 7.6(a) as

$$S_1 = -\frac{R_F}{R_1}$$

$$S_2 = -\left(\frac{R_F}{R_1} + \frac{R_F}{R_2}\right)$$

$$S_3 = -\left(\frac{R_F}{R_1} + \frac{R_F}{R_2} + \frac{R_F}{R_3}\right)$$

(7.2)

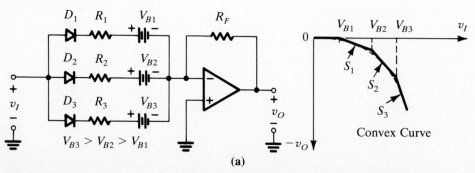

(a)

Figure 7.6 Diode piecewise-linear approximation circuits: (a) series limiting;

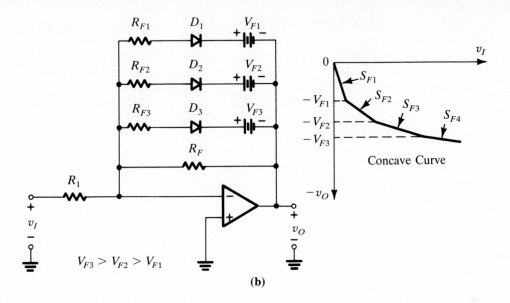

$V_{F3} > V_{F2} > V_{F1}$

(b)

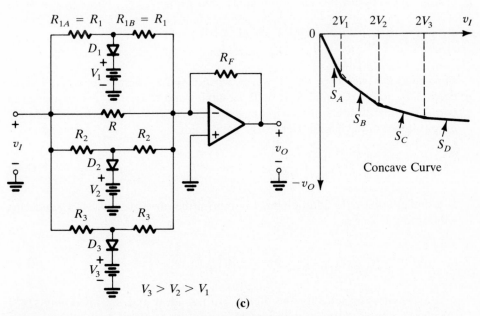

$V_3 > V_2 > V_1$

(c)

Figure 7.6 (b) shunt limiting with diodes in the feedback path; (c) shunt limiting with diodes in the input circuit. Ideal diodes are assumed.

Note that the slope of the curve continually *increases* as v_I increases (i.e., we have a convex curve).

To obtain a decreasing slope with increasing values of v_I (i.e., a concave curve) one can either place the diode network in shunt with the input and output, as indicated in Fig. 7.6(b), or use the diodes and voltage sources to shunt the input current as shown in Fig. 7.6(c). For the diodes in the feedback path of Fig. 7.6(b) the gain of the circuit will be $-R_F/R_1$ until the output voltage reaches the value $v_O = -V_{F1}$; at this point diode D_1 will conduct, placing R_{F1} in parallel with R_F and thereby decreasing the gain to $-(R_F\|R_{F1}/R_1)$. Similarly, when $v_O = -V_{F2}$ diode D_2 will conduct and the equivalent parallel resistance will be $R_F\|R_{F1}\|R_{F2}$. The slopes of the segments in Fig. 7.6(b) are therefore

$$S_{F1} = -\frac{R_F}{R_1} \qquad\qquad S_{F2} = -\frac{1}{R_1}(R_F\|R_{F1})$$

$$S_{F3} = -\frac{1}{R_1}(R_F\|R_{F1}\|R_{F2}) \qquad S_{F4} = -\frac{1}{R_1}(R_F\|R_{F1}\|R_{F2}R_{F3}) \tag{7.3}$$

The shunt-limiting circuit of Fig. 7.6(c) is usually somewhat simpler to implement than the feedback-limiting circuit above. For the case $v_I < V_1$ the circuit of Fig. 7.6(c) initially has an output slope (and gain)

$$S_A = -R_F\left(\frac{1}{R} + \frac{1}{2R_1} + \frac{1}{2R_2} + \frac{1}{2R_3}\right) \tag{7.4a}$$

since all diodes would be off. However, when $v_I = 2V_1$ there is an equal voltage drop of V_1 across R_{1A} and R_{1B}, so D_1 conducts and resistor R_{1B} is connected in parallel with the inputs of the op amp, thereby *not* contributing to the gain (or output slope) of the circuit. Hence, the gain is now

$$S_B = -R_F\left(\frac{1}{R} + \frac{1}{2R_2} + \frac{1}{2R_3}\right) \tag{7.4b}$$

In a similar fashion the addition breakpoints for the curve are at $v_I = 2V_2$ and $2V_3$, with output slopes of

$$S_C = -R_F\left(\frac{1}{R} + \frac{1}{2R_3}\right) \qquad S_D = -R_F\left(\frac{1}{R}\right) \tag{7.4c}$$

Of course, in actuality the diodes are not ideal and the breakpoints will therefore not be as abrupt as indicated. However, this nonideal diode characteristic really improves the curve accuracy, since the function being approximated is normally a continuous function. Also, in some instances a Zener diode could be substituted for the series combination of a diode and voltage source, thereby simplifying the circuit. Further, since all of the functions generated are inverting, one would have to add a unity-gain inverter circuit to obtain a positive-slope function.

EXAMPLE 7.2

The signal output of a 0–10 psig pressure transducer deviates from a linear response, starting at mid-scale, as indicated in the amplified signal response of Fig. 7.7 (the actual response curve). Correct the response by employing a correction curve, so that the final output is the desired linear response.

Solution

Let us use a two-diode piecewise-linear approximation function. Since the required correction curve* is convex we need to use the series limiting circuit of Fig. 7.6(a). We will use the slightly modified version, as shown in Fig. 7.7(b), which uses a compensating diode (D_C) to obviate the temperature sensitivity of the signal diodes D_1 and D_2, and obtains the required voltage sources by the potentiometers and resistors R_A and R_B. For this circuit, if $V_A < V_B$ then the first segment of the curve (D_1 and D_2 are off) is determined by R_F and R_3, or from Fig. 7.6(a)

$$S_1 = -\frac{R_F}{R_3} \tag{7.5a}$$

For D_1 to conduct it is necessary that point x in Fig. 7.7(b) be equal to the diode conduction voltage of D_1, or that current i_1 be given by

$$i_1 \approx \frac{v_I - 0.6 \text{ V}}{R_1} \approx \frac{0.6 \text{ V} - 0.6 \text{ V} + V_A}{R_A} \tag{7.5b}$$

so the first breakpoint V_{B1} will occur at

$$v_I = V_{B1} \approx V_A\left(\frac{R_1}{R_A}\right) + 0.6 \text{ V} \tag{7.5c}$$

with a slope of the transfer characteristic of

$$S_2 = -\left(\frac{R_F}{R_3} + \frac{R_F}{R_1}\right) \tag{7.5d}$$

Similarly, the next breakpoint and slope will be

$$v_I = V_{B2} \approx V_B\left(\frac{R_2}{R_B}\right) + 0.6 \text{ V} \tag{7.5e}$$

$$S_3 = -\left(\frac{R_F}{R_3} + \frac{R_F}{R_1} + \frac{R_F}{R_2}\right) \tag{7.5f}$$

The voltages V_A and V_B are typically obtained from a variable source, allowing a fine adjustment of the breakpoints.

---

* The correction curve is simply a function that, added to the actual response, produces the required linear output.

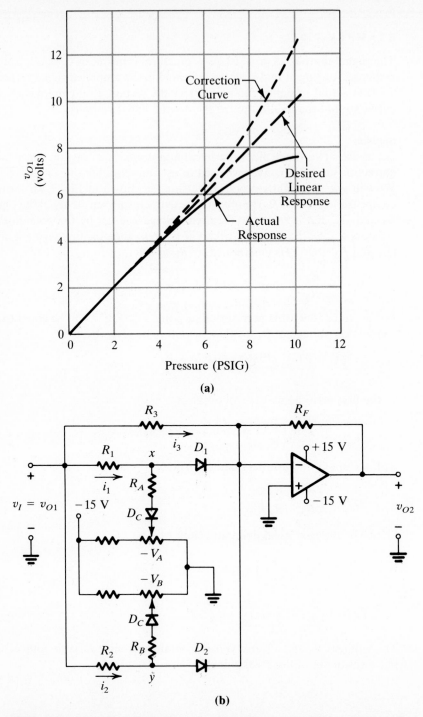

Figure 7.7 A practical illustration of a diode function generator. (a) Amplified pressure transducer output. (b) Modified series-limiter circuit.

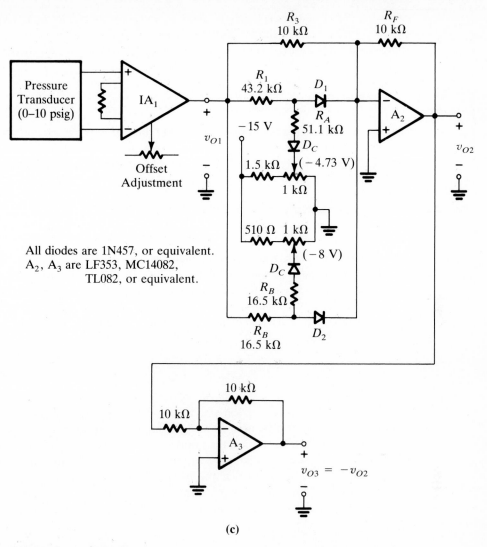

Figure 7.7 (c) Final circuit.

For this example, since the actual response is reasonably linear to $V_{O1} = 4$ volts, we can use a slope of $S_1 = -1$ in Eq. (7.5a), so we choose $R_F = R_3 = 10$ kΩ. Let us approximate the correction curve with the first breakpoint at $v_I = v_{O1} = 4.6$ V and a slope obtained from the curve of $S_2 \approx +1.23$ (since we are using an inverting amplifier, we will realize a slope of -1.23). Thus, from Eq. (7.5d) we need

$$-1.23 = -\left(1 + \frac{10 \text{ k}\Omega}{R_1}\right) \qquad R_1 = 43.2 \text{ k}\Omega \tag{7.6a}$$

From Eq. (7.5c) we obtain $V_A(R_1/R_A) = 4$ V, and if we choose $R_A = 51.1$ kΩ, then $-V_A = -4.73$ V. In a similar fashion, if we fit the second breakpoint to the approximation curve at $v_I = v_{O1} = 8.6$ V with a slope of $S_3 \approx +1.83$, then from Eq. (7.5f) we obtain

$$1.83 = 1.23 + \frac{10 \text{ k}\Omega}{R_2} \qquad R_2 = 16.5 \text{ k}\Omega \tag{7.6b}$$

and from Eq. (7.5e), if we choose $R_B = 16.5$ kΩ then we require $-V_B = -8$ V. The complete circuit including the required inverting unity-gain amplifier is shown in Fig. 7.7(c), along with typical design values that would be representative of the rest of the system.

The additional circuitry needed to achieve linearity correction may be rather extensive, as indicated previously in Fig. 7.7(c). In fact, if the amplified output signal v_{O1} were to be eventually digitized, then it would probably be advantageous to eliminate the diode function-generation circuit and directly store the needed correction curve in a *ROM* (*R*ead *O*nly *M*emory), thereby obtaining a better absolute correction.

7.3 LOGARITHMIC CIRCUITS

The diodes used in many of the previous function-generation and amplitude-limiting circuits can also be used as a logarithmic element to produce an output that is related to the logarithm of the input signal. For example, the circuit of Fig. 7.8(a) could be viewed as a clamping circuit that effectively clamps the output to approximately -0.6 to -0.7 V if the input is positive, and as a zero-crossing comparator circuit for negative input signals (if R_F is present, $v_O = -R_F/R_1$ for v_I negative). However, if we use the diode equation relating current and voltage

$$I_d = I_0\left[\exp\left(\frac{qV_d}{mkT}\right) - 1\right] \tag{7.7}$$

[where I_0 is the reverse saturation current $m \approx 1$ and kT/q is the thermal potential (~ 0.026 V at 25 °C)] then, since the input current is obtained as v_I/R_1 for v_I positive, the expression for the output voltage of the op amp is in reality a logarithmic function (for $V_d > 60$ mV)

$$v_O = -V_d = -\frac{mkT}{q}\ln\left(\frac{v_I}{R_1 I_0}\right) \qquad v_I > 0 \tag{7.8}$$

Thus, the output voltage is proportional to the *logarithm* of the input voltage. Now a diode is useful as a logarithmic element only over a restricted range of current; for currents below 10 nA the term m in Eqs. (7.7) and (7.8) typically changes to between 1.5 and 2 due to recombination of holes and electrons in the space-charge

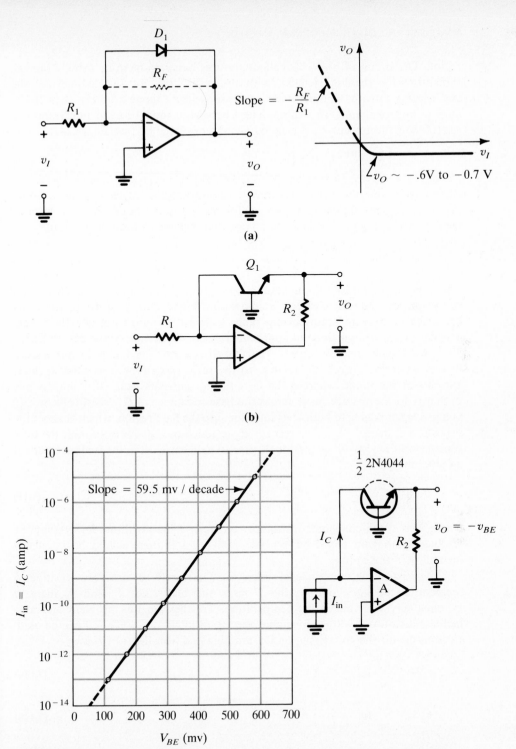

Figure 7.8 (a) A simple logarithmic circuit using a diode. (b) A more precise circuit using a bipolar circuit. (c) Actual experimental transfer characteristic using a 2N4044 npn transistor for Q_1 at $T = 27°C$.

region. The circuit of Fig. 7.8(b) eliminates this latter problem by using a bipolar transistor* for the log element, with the result that for selected devices the coefficient m remains at unity over a collector-current range from less than 10^{-12} amp to approximately 10^{-4} amp. The Ebers-Moll model for an npn transistor relates the collector current to the base-emitter voltage by [see Eq. (5.24)]

$$I_C = I_S\left[\exp\left(\frac{qV_{BE}}{mkT}\right) - 1\right] \tag{7.9}$$

where, as for the diode, I_S is the reverse saturation current, $m = 1$ and $kT/q \approx 0.026$ V at room temperature. Thus, for $V_O = V_{BE} > 60$ mV the -1 term is negligible, and Eq. (7.9) reduces to an equation similar to that for the diode,

$$v_O = -V_{BE} \approx -\frac{kT}{q}\ln\left(\frac{v_I}{R_1 I_S}\right) \tag{7.10}$$

The experimental plot of an actual logarithmic circuit using a 2N4044 npn transistor for the log element is shown in Fig. 7.8(c), indicating good log conformance over an input-current range from 10^{-13} amp to nearly 10^{-4} amp. The deviations from a slope of approximately 60 mV/decade (slope per decade at $27\,°C = kT/q \ln(10) \approx 59.5$ mV) for currents below 10^{-13} is due to the importance of the -1 term in Eq. (7.9) relative to the ratio I_C/I_S as well as other leakage currents at the input, whereas the deviation at currents near 10^{-4} amp is due primarily to the voltage drop across the base resistance of Q_1 (see Problem 7.9), and to a lesser degree to high-level injection into the base region, which changes the m coefficient from 1 to 2. The resistor R_2 is added in Fig. 7.8(b) to limit the loop transmission, since with transistor Q_1 present gain can exist in the feedback path of an amount

$$A_F = \frac{R_1}{R_2 + r_e} \tag{7.11}$$

where r_e is the incremental resistance $\approx kT/qI_C$. Thus, without R_2 present the feedback path gain could be $\gg 1$ for small r_e, and there would be frequency instability in the circuit.

The basic log equations of either Eq. (7.8) or (7.10) are very sensitive to temperature changes, due to the T term and also since I_0 and I_S increase exponentially with increasing temperature. To alleviate this problem and also increase the output voltage available, the log-ratio circuit of Fig. 7.9 can be used. For this circuit the voltages v_x and v_y are obtained from Eq. (7.10) as

$$v_x = -\frac{kT}{q}\ln\left(\frac{v_1}{R_1 I_{S1}}\right) \tag{7.12a}$$

$$v_y = -\frac{kT}{q}\ln\left(\frac{v_2}{R_3 I_{S2}}\right) \tag{7.12b}$$

---

* This circuit is attributed to W. L. Patterson, *Rev. Sci. Instr.*, Vol. 34, pp. 1311–16, (1963). The circuit is often referred to as a transdiode circuit.

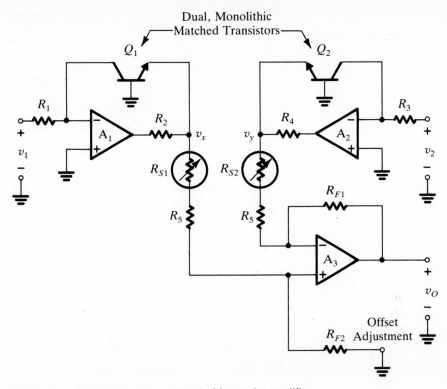

Figure 7.9 Temperature-compensated log ratio amplifier.

Thus, since the output voltage is (with $R_{S1} = R_{S2}$, $R_{F2} = R_{F1} = R_F$)

$$v_O = -\left(\frac{R_F}{R_5 + R_S}\right)(v_y - v_x) \tag{7.12c}$$

we obtain with equal transistors ($I_{S1} = I_{S2}$)

$$v_O = \left(\frac{R_F}{R_5 + R_S}\right)\left(\frac{kT}{q}\right)\ln\left(\frac{v_2 R_1}{v_1 R_3}\right) \tag{7.12d}$$

Hence, the output voltage is proportional to the logarithm of the *ratio* of v_2 and v_1. Thus this circuit could be used as a divider circuit, or if one input were a fixed reference we would have a standard logarithmic circuit with the I_S term removed. Temperature compensation is achieved by using either silicon resistors* or positive-temperature-coefficient (PTC) thermistors for the R_{S1} and R_{S2} resistors, as indicated in the example below.

---

* Silicon resistors are merely lightly doped silicon bars having a typical positive temperature coefficient of approximately +0.75%/°C. They are often referred to as a "sensistor" (trademark of Texas Instruments, Inc.), and are available in standard ±5% resistor values. The silicon resistors are available from either Texas Instruments or Amperex.

EXAMPLE 7.3

Using a 2N4044 dual npn transistor (characteristics in Problem 7.9), obtain a logarithmic output response of $+1$ V/decade for an input signal covering a 5 decade range from $+5$ mV to $+500$ V. Arrange the scale so that $V_O = +5$ V when $V_{in} = +500$ V. Since we have effectively compressed the input signal, this type of circuit is often referred to in the audio trade as a **compression amplifier**.

Solution

Since the output voltage is to be positive, let us apply the input signal to R_3 in Fig. 7.9 (i.e., $v_I = v_2$), and thus v_1 will be a reference voltage. For an output scale factor of 1 V/decade, from Eq. (7.12d) we need at 25 °C

$$\left(\frac{R_F}{R_5 + R_S}\right)(0.0257)\ln(10) = 1 \tag{7.13a}$$

or we must have the ratio $R_F/(R_5 + R_S) = 16.9$. For temperature compensation, we need from Eq. (7.12d)

$$\frac{dv_O}{dT} = 0 = \ln\left(\frac{v_2 R_1}{v_1 R_3}\right)\left[\frac{k}{q}\left(\frac{R_F}{R_5 + R_S}\right) - \left(\frac{kT}{q}\right)\frac{R_F\left(\frac{\partial R_5}{\partial T}\right)}{(R_5 + R_S)^2}\right] \tag{7.13b}$$

or we require that [at $T = T_0 = 25$ °C(298 °K)], using a PTC silicon resistor with $\Delta R_S/\Delta T \approx +0.75\%/°C$,

$$R_5 = T_0\left(\frac{\partial R_5}{\partial T}\right) - R_S \approx R_S[(298)(0.75 \times 10^{-2}) - 1] \tag{7.13c}$$

or $R_5 = 1.24 R_S$. Hence, if we use a nominal 1 kΩ value for R_S, then $R_5 = 1.24$ kΩ and $R_F = 37.8$ kΩ.

For the R_3 resistor, if we limit the maximum collector current of Q_2 to 100 μA [which would appear to be the largest value for good log conformance for the 2N4044 device, from Fig. 7.8(c)], then with a 500 V input we need $R_3 = 500$ V/100 μA = 5 MΩ. The R_1 resistor and the v_1 source will form a reference to set the output at $+5$ V when the input is at $+500$ V. From Eq. (7.12d), we therefore obtain

$$5 \text{ V} = (16.9)(0.0257)\ln\left(\frac{100 \text{ μA}}{v_1/R_1}\right) \tag{7.13d}$$

or we need $v_1/R_1 = 1$ nA. If we use a band-gap reference for v_1, then $v_1 \approx 1.24$ V, and we can use a potentiometer to obtain a variable reference. Using a 20 MΩ* resistor for R_1 would then require a $+20$ mV reference for v_1. This obviously demands an FET-input op amp for A_1 with a low offset voltage $V_{OS} \ll 20$ mV.

---

* This might be obtained with two 10-MΩ resistors in series. A value of 10 MΩ is about the largest precision stable resistor value we could use.

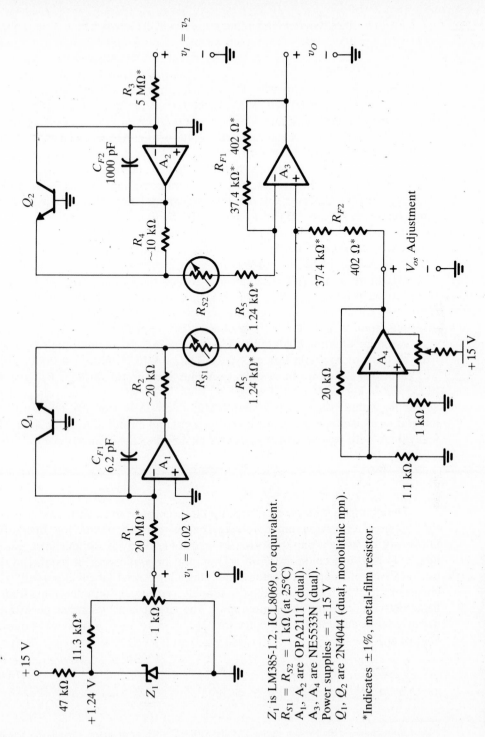

Z_1 is LM385-1.2, ICL8069, or equivalent.
$R_{S1} = R_{S2} = 1$ kΩ (at 25°C)
A_1, A_2 are OPA2111 (dual).
A_3, A_4 are NE5533N (dual).
Power supplies = ± 15 V
Q_1, Q_2 are 2N4044 (dual, monolithic npn).

*Indicates $\pm 1\%$, metal-film resistor.

Figure 7.10 Circuit for Example 7.3.

385

Further, since the minimum input current will occur when $v_2 = v_I = +5 \, \text{mV}$, or $I_i(\text{min}) = 5 \, \text{mV}/5 \, \text{M}\Omega = 1 \, \text{nA}$, then we must also use an FET-input op amp for A_2. Similarly, since the offset voltage of A_2 would add directly with the v_I value, we need an op amp for A_2 with a low V_{OS} value as well ($\ll 5 \, \text{mV}$). A good candidate would be the OPA111 op amp (mentioned earlier in Chapter 4), which has $I_B(\text{max}) = 1 \, \text{pA}$, $V_{OS}(\text{max}) = 0.25 \, \text{mV}$, or better yet the dual version (OPA2111) could be used for both A_1 and A_2. Another similar low V_{OS}, low I_B, FET op amp is the HA 5180. For fine tuning, the reference value of v_1 can be adjusted for $V_O = 0 \, \text{V}$ when $v_I = v_2 = +5 \, \text{mV}$. Then, for $v_I = v_2 = 500 \, \text{V}$ the R_{F2} resistor of Fig. 7.9 can be returned to an offset-adjustment potential that can be varied to set $V_O = +5 \, \text{V}$.

The normal technique of frequency compensation for A_2 would have $R_4 = R_3 = 5 \, \text{M}\Omega$. However, this requirement cannot be used here due to dynamic range limitations in A_2. When $v_2 = v_I = 500 \, \text{V}$, then $I_{\text{in}} = 100 \, \mu\text{A} = I_{C2}$. Also, since then $v_y = -0.0257 \ln(100 \, \mu\text{A}/10^{-15} \, \text{A}) = -0.651 \, \text{V}$, the A_2 op amp would be required to sink approximately $240 \, \mu\text{A}$. Since the maximum linear negative output voltage of A_2 would be $\sim -14 \, \text{V}$ (with $\pm 15 \, \text{V}$ supplies), then R_4 is limited to $13.4 \, \text{V}/0.24 \, \text{mA}$, or $56 \, \text{k}\Omega$. Hence, the gain around the feedback loop of A_2 would be approximately $r_{\text{out}}(Q_1) \| R_3/(r_{e2} + 56 \, \text{k}\Omega)$, or approximately 90. Thus, for this circuit one should add an integrating capacitor C_F between the output and the inverting input of A_2 to lower the gain at higher frequencies.

A similar situation holds for A_1. However, here the current through R_1 is held fixed at 1 nA, or v_x is constant at $-0.0257 \ln(1 \, \text{nA}/10^{-15} \, \text{A}) = -0.355 \, \text{V}$, so A_1 will have to sink a current of only 1 nA plus the current through R_{S1} and R_5 ($0.355 \, \text{V}/2.24 \, \text{k}\Omega = 158 \, \mu\text{A}$). If we set $R_2 = R_1 = 20 \, \text{M}\Omega$, then the voltage drop across R_2 would still be too large ($20 \, \text{M}\Omega \times 158 \, \mu\text{A} = 3160 \, \text{V!}$). Obviously an integrating capacitor between the inverting input and output of A_1 is required. The final circuit with representative values for all components is shown in Fig. 7.10.

The examples hitherto have used npn transistors as the logarithmic element; this requires a positive input voltage (or current) to obtain log operation. Obviously, by using a pnp transistor a logarithmic circuit is variable for negative inputs. In fact, one could use both an npn and pnp transistor in parallel in the feedback path of an op amp, thereby obtaining a log output for either polarity. The circuit of Fig. 7.11 is one often used to amplify very small output currents from a flame detector in a gas chromatograph.* The circuit converts either positive or negative input currents (in the range from $10^{-12} \, \text{A}$ to $10^{-6} \, \text{A}$) into a log output voltage at V_A

$$V_A = -\frac{kT}{q} \ln\left(\frac{+i_{\text{IN}}}{I_{SN1}}\right) \tag{7.14a}$$

---

* Used, for example, in the Hewlett Packard Model 5700A Gas Chromatograph. Circuits that amplify very small input currents are often referred to as *electrometers*.

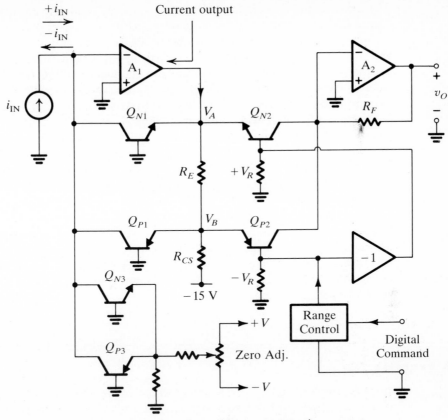

Q_{N3}, Q_{P3} allow a bias, or suppression current.
Q_{N1}, Q_{N2}; Q_{P1}, Q_{P2} are matched.

Figure 7.11 Logarithmic circuit suitable for amplifying small input currents of either polarity.

or for negative input currents

$$V_B = + \frac{kT}{q} \ln\left(\frac{-i_{IN}}{I_{SP1}}\right) \tag{7.14b}$$

Now, matching transistors Q_{N2} and Q_{P2} are connected in an antilogarithmic (or exponential) configuration, with the result that the output of A_2 for i_{IN} positive is

$$V_O = +I_{CN2}R_F = +R_F I_{SN2} \exp\left[\frac{q(V_R - V_A)}{kT}\right] \tag{7.14c}$$

Substituting Eq. (7.14a), with matched transistors so that $I_{SN1} = I_{SN2}$ gives

$$v_O = R_F i_{IN} \exp\left(\frac{qV_R}{kT}\right) \tag{7.14d}$$

The same equation holds for i_{IN} negative, since Q_{P1} and Q_{P2} are matched with $I_{SP1} = I_{SP2}$. The output response is therefore *linear* with respect to i_{IN}. If the Q_1 and Q_2 transistors are maintained at a constant temperature of 0 °C (by using, say, a thermoelectric cooler), then the q/kT term in Eq. (7.14d) would be constant. Further, if the op amps A_1 and A_2 were also maintained at 0 °C (i.e., if A_1 and A_2 were on the same substrate as the Q_1 and Q_2 transistors), then the input I_B error currents of these devices would be lowered by approximately $2^{(25/12)}$ (since input gate current of a JFET will double approximately every 12 °C), or a factor of 4.2. Also, there would be no offset-voltage drift with ambient temperature changes for A_1 and A_2.

The reference voltages ($+V_R$ and $-V_R$) in Fig. 7.11 can be used for range control of the circuit. By adjusting V_R in discrete steps of $(kT/q)\ln(10)$, or 54 mV, the current range for i_{IN} is changed by a factor of 10 (or, in effect the same output voltage is now applicable for input currents with a scale factor of $\times 1$, $\times 10$, $\times 100$, etc.) The advantage of this type of switching is that it allows switching at a low-impedance part of the circuit, which alleviates the typically large transients encountered with changing scale factors in a conventional linear electrometer circuit. Also, the range switching can be accomplished with a digital command to close, or open, an analog switch.

■ **Exercise 7.2**

If the A_1 amplifier of Fig. 7.11 is similar to one of the commercial low I_B op amps, such as an AD515, or BB3528, having $I_B(25 \text{ °C}) \approx 4 \times 10^{-14}$ A, what would be the value of I_B at 0 °C? Show that the equivalent noise voltage (e_{n1}) for A_1 is *not* important in determining circuit sensitivity, but that e_{n2} (for A_2) is. Why are the base-collector reverse currents (I_{CBO}) for Q_{N1} and Q_{P1} not important in the circuit?

An analog computational integrated circuit that will compute the output function

$$v_O = Y\left(\frac{Z}{X}\right)^m \tag{7.15}$$

where X, Y and Z can be inputs is also available from various manufacturers. This unit gives us the ability to multiply, divide, raise to a power m, take a square root ($m = \frac{1}{2}$), and perform logarithmic or antilogarithmic conversion. Typical ICs available are the AD538 from Analog Devices, Inc. and the 4302 from Burr-Brown Corp. Finally, there are also special IC modules, such as the Burr-Brown 4341 and the Analog Devices AD636, that utilize log and antilog circuitry to provide a true rms-to-dc conversion, based on the concept outlined previously in Chapter 4, (Fig. 4.15).

7.4 ACTIVE RECTIFIER CIRCUITS

7.4.1 Halfwave Rectifiers

The simple logarithmic circuit of Fig. 7.8(a) could be considered a halfwave rectifier circuit if $R_F = R_1$ since the output is effectively clamped at the diode voltage drop if the input is positive, and would equal $+v_I$ if v_I is negative. For a perfect rectifier, however, we would like the output voltage to be zero (rather than -0.6 to -0.7 V) for v_I positive. This is easily accomplished if the diode voltage is *made part of the open-loop circuit*, and thus placed *inside* the feedback path, as indicated in Fig. 7.12(a). The additional diode D_2 is normally added to keep the op amp from saturating when v_I is positive. Obviously, if the diodes D_1 and D_2 are reversed then v_O is equal to $-v_I$ when v_I is positive and zero when v_I is negative. From a circuits

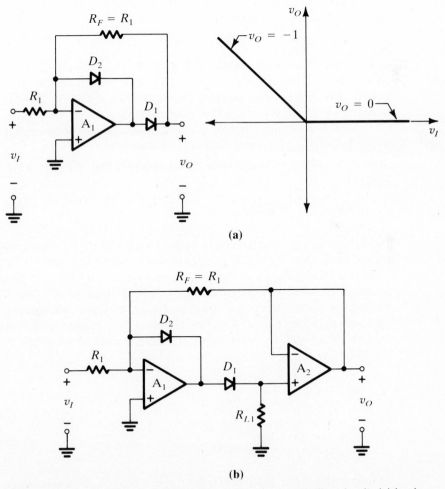

(a)

(b)

Figure 7.12 Precision halfwave rectifier, or zero-output limiter circuit: (a) basic inverting circuit; (b) additional op amp for low output impedance.

viewpoint, there is one disadvantage to the simple halfwave rectifier of Fig. 7.12(b). That is, the output impedance is near zero only when D_1 is conducting; otherwise, if D_1 is off then $r_{out} \approx R_F$. To alleviate this problem the circuit of Fig. 7.12(b), which uses A_2 as a unity-gain follower, can be employed, resulting in a uniform, very low output impedance. Active halfwave rectifiers are often used in simple ac voltmeter circuits, as shown in Example 7.3 below.

EXAMPLE 7.3

Use the halfwave rectifier circuit of Fig. 7.12(a) to design an ac voltmeter that will accept a sinusoidal input signal $v_I = V_m \sin \omega t$ and obtain a dc output voltage equal to the rms value of v_I. Design for an input impedance of ≥ 100 kΩ and for the maximum value $V_m = 10$ V. Examine the frequency and dc-offset limitations of the circuit. The minimum input frequency is 10 Hz.

Solution
If we specify $R_1 = R_F = 100$ kΩ in Fig. 7.12(a), we achieve the input resistance requirement of 100 kΩ. Also, if $V_m = 10$ V then the maximum required output voltage of A_1 will be approximately 10.7 V, which is within the linear output range of nearly all op amps using ± 15 V power supplies.

Now, the average value of a halfwave rectified sinusoidal signal is equal to V_m/π. However, the rms value of a sinusoid is equal to $V_m/\sqrt{2}$. Thus, we must follow the output voltage of the rectifier by an amplifier that will have a closed-loop dc gain of

$$|A_{CL2}| = \frac{\pi}{\sqrt{2}} = 2.22 \qquad (7.16a)$$

Further, to eliminate output ripple we need a parallel $R_{F2} C_{F2}$ time constant that is chosen such that $R_{F2} C_{F2} \gg 1/\omega_{min} = 1/2\pi(10 \text{ Hz}) = 15.9$ msec. If we therefore arbitrarily choose $R_{F2} C_{F2} \approx 50(1/\omega_{min})$, or $R_{F2} C_{F2} \approx 0.8$ sec, then by an arbitrary choice of $R_{F2} = 2.2$ MΩ we require $C_{F2} = 0.36$ μF (use 0.33 μF). This $R_{F2} C_{F2}$ time constant is somewhat large, since a change of input voltage would require approximately $5R_{F2} C_{F2}$, or 4 sec for the output dc voltage to settle to within 1% of the new value. With a time-constant of 0.8 sec, the actual maximum output ripple would be (for $f_{min} = 10$ Hz)

$$\Delta V_2 \approx \Delta t \left(\frac{I_{F2}}{C_{F2}} \right) \approx \frac{(100 \text{ msec})V_2}{R_{F2} C_{F2}} \qquad (7.16b)$$

or

$$\left(\frac{\Delta V_2}{V_2} \right) \approx \frac{100 \text{ msec}}{0.8 \text{ sec}} = 12.5\% \qquad (7.16c)$$

At frequencies larger than 10 Hz, the ripple would be correspondingly less.

The final design circuit for Example 7.3 is shown in Fig. 7.13. There is no frequency limitation on A_2, since it operates as a lowpass filter. Since the values of R_2 and R_{F2} are in the megohm range, one should use an FET-input op amp for A_2. Any dc offsets can be removed by the dc-offset adjustment network of R_3 and R_4.

The maximum frequency limitation for the circuit of Fig. 7.13 is determined by the bandwidth and SR limits of A_1. Since the GB of A_1 can easily be > 3 MHz, with $R_1 = R_{F1}$ (even including the attenuation between D_2 and R_{L2}) the loop transmission for A_1 would indicate a small-signal response to beyond 500 kHz. However, the SR limit is decidedly important, since with $V_m = 10$ V the output of A_1 must change rapidly from approximately -0.7 V (D_2 on) to $+10.7$ V (D_2 goes off, D_1 comes on), and the slew-rate-determined full-power bandwidth (BW_p) rating of the op amp is important. For example, if we were to use an LF353 (a dual LF351) op amp for A_1 and A_2, having $GB = 4$ MHz and $SR = 13$ V/μsec, then for an 11.4 V change at the output $f_{max} \approx 150$ kHz. Perhaps a better choice of op amps would be the dual FET op amp, the MC34082 having $GB = 8$ MHz and $SR = 25$ V/μsec, or the OPA606 with $GB = 12$ MHz, and $SR = 30$V/μsec. Either of the latter op amps should increase f_{max} to 300 kHz.

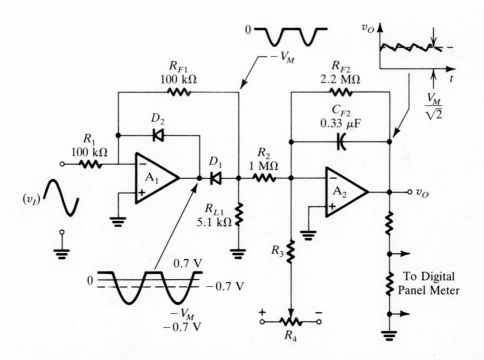

D_1, D_2 are small-signal switching diodes, i.e. 1N914, 1N4152.
A_2, A_2 are dual JFET-input Op Amps.

Figure 7.13 Circuit for the rms-to-dc voltmeter of Example 7.3.

7.4.2 Fullwave Rectifiers (Absolute-Value Circuits)

If full-wave rectification is desired, it is necessary to provide a signal path in the output of an op amp for both positive and negative cycles. Most of the fullwave rectifier circuits require two op amps, but there are a few ways to obtain the desired result with a single-op-amp circuit. A diode-bridge arrangement can be used inside the feedback loop, as indicated in Fig. 7.14(a), with the result that for a positive input signal the output of A_1 will be positive, causing D_1 and D_2 to conduct, while a

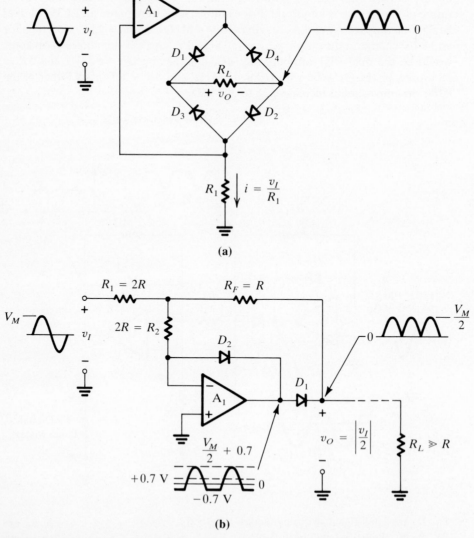

(a)

(b)

Figure 7.14 Single-op-amp fullwave rectifier circuits: (a) diode bridge circuit; (b) circuit suitable for $V_O = |v_I/2|$, if $R_L \gg R$.

negative input signal (and therefore negative output of A_1) will produce conduction of D_3 and D_4. Thus, the v_O voltage will provide the absolute value ($v_O = |iR_L| = |v_I|R_L/R_1$) or fullwave rectification of the input signal. By replacing the resistor R_L by a dc ammeter and parallel filter capacitor, one would have an output-meter movement that could be calibrated (by the choice of R_L, R_1 and the current scale factor) to indicate the rms value of v_I, the peak value of v_I, or some other indication. Further, for instrumentation applications the v_O voltage could be removed by using a differential amplifier to produce a ground-referred output.

The circuit of Fig. 7.14(b) will work as long as the load resistor R_L is $\gg R$. In this circuit if v_I is positive then D_2 conducts and D_1 is off. Thus the inverting input of A_1 is at ground and the output voltage is the voltage division between R_1 and R_2, or $v_O = |v_I/2|$. Similarly, if v_I is negative, then D_1 conducts (D_2 is off), and the output voltage is determined by the gain of $-R_F/R_1$, or $v_O = -|v_I| \times (-\frac{1}{2}) = |v_I/2|$. To ensure that R_L is large, one would probably add a unity-gain noninverting buffer at v_O.

If two op amps can be used, the fullwave rectifier circuit is much easier to implement, with a low output impedance for either input cycle. Two of the circuits used most often are shown in Fig. 7.15. The circuit of Fig. 7.15(a) relies on the basic precision halfwave circuit of Fig. 7.12(a), and requires summing the output at v_{O1} with the original input signal v_I. If v_I is positive, then $v_{O1} = -v_I$. Thus, the output v_{O2} will be

$$v_{O2} = -|v_I|\left(\frac{R_{F2}}{R_2}\right) - v_{O1}\left(\frac{R_{F2}}{R_2/2}\right) \tag{7.17a}$$

Since $v_{O1} = -v_I$

$$v_{O2} = |v_I|\left(\frac{R_{F2}}{R_2}\right) \tag{7.17b}$$

Similarly, when v_I is negative D_2 conducts and the output v_{O1} is zero, so the output voltage v_{O2} will then be equal to $-|v_I| \times (-R_{F2}/R_2)$, which is identical to Eq. (7.17b).

The circuit operation of the second circuit of the figure is somewhat different than that of the first circuit. If the input signal v_I is positive, diode D_1 conducts (D_2 will be off) and the output voltage v_A will be

$$v_A = -|v_I|\left(\frac{R_2}{R_1}\right) = -|v_I|\left(\frac{R}{R_1}\right) \tag{7.18a}$$

The output of A_2 will therefore be

$$v_O = -\left(\frac{R_5}{R_4}\right)v_A = +|v_I|\left(\frac{R}{R_I}\right) \tag{7.18b}$$

The voltage drop across R_3 will be zero, since the only currents flowing in R_3 are the input bias current I_B^+ of A_2 and the reverse leakage current of D_2. If the input signal v_I is negative diode D_2 conducts (and D_1 is off). But the voltage v_B must also

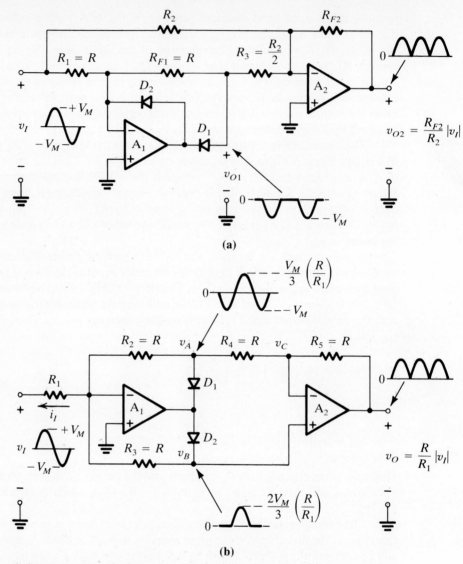

Figure 7.15 Two absolute-value (FW-rectifier) circuits using two op amps.

be equal to v_C, and therefore since R_2 and R_4 are equal, then $v_A = v_B/2$. Hence, the input current flowing in R_1 is now the sum of the currents in R_2 and R_3, or

$$i_I = \frac{v_I}{R_1} = \frac{v_B}{R_3} + \frac{v_A}{R_2} = v_B\left(\frac{1}{R} + \frac{1}{2R}\right) \tag{7.18c}$$

Solving for v_B (with v_I negative)

$$v_B = +|v_I|\left(\frac{2R}{3R_1}\right) \tag{7.18d}$$

The output voltage will now be

$$v_O = \frac{v_B}{2R_4}(R_5) + v_B = + |v_I|\left(\frac{R}{R_1}\right) \tag{7.18e}$$

It is obviously important that the appropriate resistors be matched in both circuits of Fig. 7.15.

The rectifier circuits examined heretofore have all relied on an inverting op amp connection, with the result that the input impedance was determined solely by the circuit input resistors used. It is possible, however, to form a precision fullwave rectifier with the input signal applied to the noninverting input, with the result that the circuit performance does not demand a low source impedance. The circuit of Fig. 7.16(a) is due to Graeme,* and uses two op amps with the signal v_I applied to the noninverting input of each. It is important that the resistors be well matched, with $R_1 = R_2 = R_3 = R_4/2$. In this circuit if v_I is positive then the output of A_1 is positive, so that D_1 will be off, D_2 will conduct, and current i_1 must be equal to v_I/R_1. Since A_2 is active $v_B = v_I$ and since D_1 is off the current flow through R_2 and R_3 must be

$$i_2 = \left(\frac{v_B - v_C}{2R}\right) = \frac{v_I - v_I}{2R} = 0 \tag{7.19a}$$

so the current i_1 must equal the diode current i_{D2} while the current i_F must be zero. Thus, the output voltage (for v_I positive) must be

$$v_O = |v_I| \tag{7.19b}$$

If v_I is negative, then D_1 conducts and D_2 will turn off. Thus $i_1 = -|v_I|/R_1 = i_2$, and the voltage v_A is

$$v_A = -|v_I|\left(\frac{R_2 + R_1}{R_1}\right) = -2|v_I| \tag{7.19c}$$

Since v_B must equal v_I the current through R_4 (and R_3) will be $v_I/R_3 = v_I/R$. The output voltage of A_2 is thus equal to that of Eq. (7.19b), namely

$$v_O = +i_F R_4 - |v_I| = |v_I|\left(\frac{2R}{R} - 1\right) = |v_I| \tag{7.19d}$$

The significant disadvantage of the circuit of Fig. 7.16(a) is that the required output dynamic range of A_1 is twice that for A_2. Hence, if the maximum linear output of A_1 is 10 volts, the overall circuit would only be useful for $v_O = 5$ volts.

The circuit of Fig. 7.16(b)† allows the gain of the precision rectifier to be varied by adjusting the potentiometer $R_1 = R$ but also has very high input impedance. When v_I is positive diode D_1 will conduct, which produces current

---

* J. G. Graeme, *Applications of Operational Amplifiers, Third-Generation Techniques*, p. 122, (New York: McGraw-Hill, 1973).
† J. Graeme, *op. cit.*, p. 134.

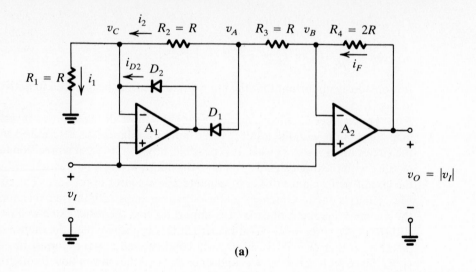

(a)

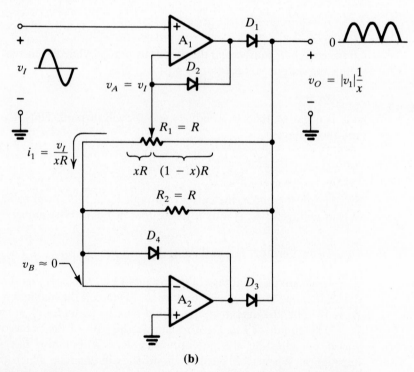

(b)

Figure 7.16 High input impedance fullwave rectifiers: (a) unity-gain circuit; (b) adjustable-gain circuit.

$i_1 = v_I/xR$, thereby causing D_4 to conduct. Hence, D_2 and D_3 are forced off. Thus, voltage v_B will be at ground potential and the output voltage is produced by A_1 connected as a noninverting amplifier, with

$$v_O = |v_I|\left[\frac{(1-x)R + xR}{xR}\right] = |v_I|\left(\frac{1}{x}\right) \tag{7.20a}$$

However, if the input signal is negative D_1 is reverse biased and D_2 will conduct with $v_A = -|v_I|$. The current i_1 will now reverse direction forcing D_3 into conduction (D_4 will go off), with the result that

$$v_O = -\left(\frac{R_2}{xR}\right)\left(-|v_I|\right) = \frac{|v_I|}{x} \tag{7.20b}$$

With the potentiometer control indicated, the gain of the circuit can be varied over a wide range from one to several hundred. Both circuits in Fig. 7.16 are particularly amenable to the use of a dual op amp, since equal V_{OS} values tend to cancel.

A word of caution should be noted when attempting to rectify high-frequency or fast changing waveforms. The inverting inputs [such as v_B in Fig. 7.16(b) or the inverting input of A_1 in Fig. 7.15(a)] will have considerable ringing that may offset overall network performance; in this case one may find that adding a low-capacitance Schottky diode between the inverting input terminal and ground will improve performance.

7.5 PEAK DETECTORS

Some applications require a circuit that will detect and store the maximum (or peak) value of an input waveform. Such circuits are referred to as **peak detectors** and in reality are circuits that are quite identical to the precision halfwave rectifier, except that a capacitor must be added to store the peak voltage. In principle, the circuit shown in Fig. 7.17 will detect the most positive value of the input signal v_I. As long as v_I is increasing in value the voltage v_C will be equal to v_I. However, when v_I decreases from its previous peak value the output voltage of A_1 will decrease from its previous value and, since the charge on C cannot change instantaneously, diode D_1 will reverse bias. Thus the capacitor C will hold the previous voltage it had acquired, which is the peak value of v_I. The unity-gain follower circuit merely unloads the capacitor C and provides a low output impedance with $v_O = v_C = v_I$ (peak). The peak voltage across C will decay due to leakage contributed by the diode D_1, the input bias current I_B^+ of A_2, the off-state leakage of the MOS switch M_1 (this device could also be a JFET transistor, an inverted-mode bipolar transistor, or a simple mechanical switch), and the equivalent parallel resistance of the capacitor. The change in the value of v_C from its peak value is called the **droop**, and if a good low-leakage capacitor is used for C (so that the equivalent parallel resistance of C is very large), then the droop per unit time is

$$\frac{\Delta v_C}{\Delta t} \approx \frac{\Delta v_O}{\Delta t} = \frac{\sum I_{\text{leakage}}}{C} \tag{7.21}$$

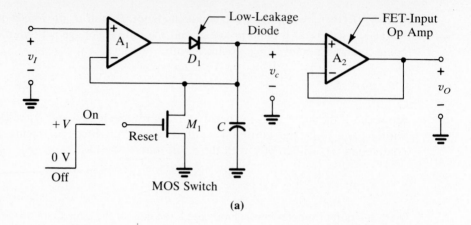

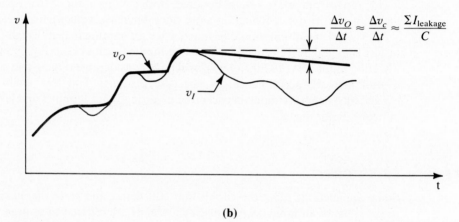

Figure 7.17   (a) Simple positive-peak-detector circuit. (b) Waveforms for v_I and v_O.

The circuit of Fig. 7.17(a) would have a lower dc offset if the output of A_2 were connected back to the inverting input terminal of A_1 (the capacitor C and switch M_1 would then be disconnected from the A_1 inverting terminal). The reset switch M_1 is not necessary if one desires v_O to always follow the $v_I(\max.)$ value.

One significant disadvantage to the simple peak detection circuit of Fig. 7.17(a) is that when D_1 turns off the v_I signal is less positive than the voltage v_C. Thus the error signal v_ε of A_1 becomes large, and the output of A_1 will drive to full negative saturation (~ -13.5 V for most op amps with $V_{\text{supply}} = \pm 15$ V). Hence, the recovery time of A_1 will be imposed on the waveform at v_C (and v_O), which means there will be a time delay before v_C can again follow the input signal. Obviously then, we need to ensure that the op amp does not saturate when the capacitor is holding the peak value of v_I. This can be accomplished with the more practical circuit of Fig. 7.18.

In the circuit of Fig. 7.18(a) the feedback has been obtained from the output of A_2 to the inverting input of A_1. The diode D_1 conducts as long as the output

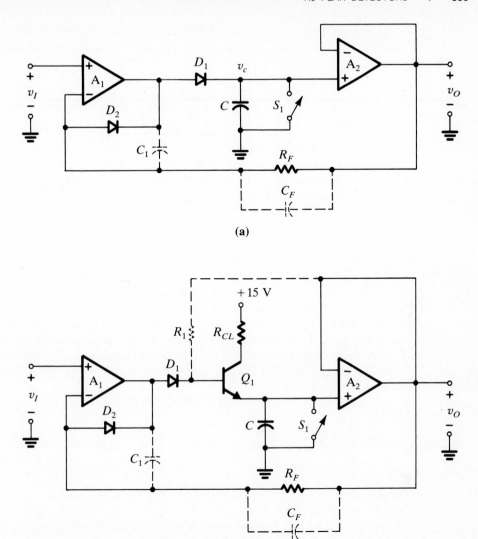

Figure 7.18 Nonsaturating peak-detector circuit: (a) basic circuit; (b) improved circuit for higher slew rate and lower leakage current.

voltage of A_1 is greater than v_C so, as before, $v_O = v_C = v_I$, but, when the input signal v_I drops below the value of v_C then D_1 turns off and v_O remains at the previous peak value of v_I. Thus, the error signal of A_1 drives the output of A_1 negative. However, the diode D_2 will now conduct, thus clamping the output voltage at A_1 at approximately 0.6–0.7 V below the value of v_I. Hence, A_1 remains in its linear region, thus eliminating the recovery time needed by the peak detector of Fig. 7.17. The value of R_F in Fig. 7.18(a) is usually several kΩ. The capacitors C_F and C_1 may be required for loop stability, and to prevent overshoot for a step input of v_I. The amplifier A_2 should be an FET-input device with low V_{OS} and drift. The greatest demand on performance is required of op amp A_1, as seen by the next example.

EXAMPLE 7.4

Suppose the input signal to the circuit of Fig. 7.18(a) is a fast signal that has a worst-case voltage change from 0 to 5 V in 25 nsec. What are the essential parameters required of the op amps A_1 and A_2 if the storage capacitor C is a 1000 pF polystyrene capacitor?

Solution

The op amp A_1 must have a slew rate (SR) of at least 5 V/25 nsec = 200 V/μsec. Further, to keep the small-signal bandwidth from limiting the response, the unity-gain bandwidth must be significantly greater than 0.35/25 nsec = 14 MHz [refer to Eq. (2.36)]. Further, A_1 must be stable for unity-gain, since when D_2 conducts then $A_{CL}(A_1) \approx 1$. Although these requirements are difficult to satisfy, they are not impossible for commercially available op amps. The most severe requirement for A_1 would occur if the 1000 pF capacitor had no initial charge and had to achieve 5 V in 25 nsec. Since the SR is proportional to the charging current I divided by the capacitor value C the peak current supplied through D_1 by A_1 must then be

$$I = C\left(\frac{\Delta V}{\Delta t}\right) = 1 \times 10^{-9}(200 \times 10^6) = 200 \text{ mA}$$

The last requirement of Example 7.4 would be exceedingly difficult to achieve with any relatively inexpensive op amp. However, by modifying the peak detector to that of Fig. 7.18(b), the peak-current requirement of 200 mA can be met. Here, a bipolar transistor Q_1 has been added between the diode D_1 and the capacitor. When D_1 conducts, the op amp A_1 now only has to supply the base current of Q_1 (i.e., if $h_{FE}(\beta)$ of Q_1 is ≥ 50 then the output current requirement of A_1 is ≤ 4 mA). The resistor R_{CL} in the collector of Q_1 will limit the maximum current through Q_1 when the reset switch S_1 is closed. The resistor R_1 has added another feature to the circuit of Fig. 7.18(b)—when D_1 turns off, Q_1 turns off and the output voltage remains equal to the capacitor voltage. Thus, R_1 will feed the same voltage back to the base of Q_1. Hence, the reverse voltage of Q_1 across the base to the emitter is held at zero volts, which effectively eliminates the leakage current that would be contributed by Q_1 if R_1 were not present.

As an example of a complete design, one might use the HA2540 or HA2539 op amps used earlier, which have an $SR \geq 400$ V/μsec. It would be necessary to reduce the loop transmission for these devices, as was shown in Fig. 3.12, since they are stable only for $A_{CL} \geq 10$. One could also use the HA2541 op amp, which is stable for unity gain and has an $SR = 280$ V/μsec with a $GB = 40$ MHz. For the A_2 op amp, an FET-input buffer would be suitable, such as the LH0033, LH0063, EL2004, BUF-03, or other similar unit—as indicated in Table 2.2. Also, it would be less expensive to merely add a two-transistor (FET-input and pnp output) unity-gain driver circuit in place of A_2.

For any of the aforementioned A_2 circuits, one could reasonably expect to achieve a total leakage current < 50 pA. Thus, for a 5 V maximum stored signal on C the longest hold time for a $\pm 0.1\%$ droop in capacitor voltage can be determined as

$$\Delta t = \Delta V \left(\frac{C}{I_{\text{leakage}}}\right) \leq \frac{(5\text{ V} \times 10^{-3})(1 \times 10^{-9})}{50 \times 10^{-12}} = 0.1\text{ sec}$$

7.6 SAMPLE-AND-HOLD AND TRACK-AND-HOLD CIRCUITS

In general, engineers tend to use the terms Sample-and-Hold (S/H) and Track-and-Hold (T/H) interchangeably. There is a significant difference between the two, however. An S/H circuit will *sample* the input signal and quickly return to the *hold* condition, as indicated in Fig. 7.19(a). A T/H circuit will *track* the signal for part of the time and *hold* it for the rest of the period, as shown in Fig. 7.19(b). Whereas an

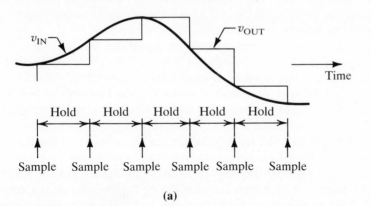

(a)

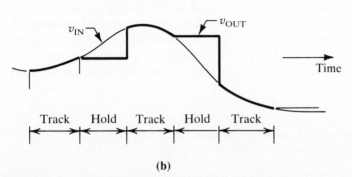

(b)

Figure 7.19 Difference between an S/H circuit and a T/H circuit: (a) S/H; (b) T/H.

S/H circuit cannot operate indefinitely in either mode, a T/H circuit can. A T/H circuit may be used as an S/H, but in general an S/H amplifier cannot be used in the T/H mode. Although used interchangeably, most of the circuits manufactured today are really T/H circuits. Both circuits operate with a digital logic-command input, with a logic '0' generally defining the hold mode and a logic '1' indicating the sample or track mode.

The most typical use of an S/H or T/H amplifier is in an analog-to-digital (A/D) conversion system, since the A/D converter usually requires a fixed stationary input signal for accurate processing. Other uses are in automatic-zero-correction circuits (auto-zero circuits), as well as in a "glitch-remover" circuit to follow a digital-to-analog (D/A) converter.

The operation of the T/H function is best described by observing the relation between the input and output signal in a typical circuit, as shown in Fig. 7.20.* When the digital command to track (sample) exists the output signal v_O should equal the input signal, except for possible dc offsets and nonlinearity in the op amps. The **aperture time** (t_{APER}) defines the time difference between when the hold command is initiated and the switch S_1 fully opens. This includes time delay in the switch and control circuits, as well as time jitter (uncertainty) in the input signal. The **droop** (in volts), or **droop rate** (in volts/sec) is identical to that defined earlier for the peak detector, and is determined by the leakage current flowing into (or out of) C_H when S_1 is open. The **acquisition time** t_{AQ} is the time required for the circuit to acquire the input signal (i.e., for $v_O = v_I$) to within some specified accuracy (for example, this term usually refers to the time required for the output signal to change, for a 0 to 10 V full-scale input signal, to within some defined error band–perhaps $\pm 0.1\%$ of v_I, which would be ± 10 mV). The **settling time** t_{SET} is the time required for the output to settle to within some defined error band, after the instigation of an S/H command transition. Note that the acquisition time as defined in Fig. 7.20(a) includes the settling time for a hold-to-track transition. Other terms of importance in an S/H circuit are indirectly indicated in Fig. 7.20(a). For example, during the hold period, when S_1 is off, the input signal may be injected via the interelectrode capacitance of the switch into A_2. If an FET is used for S_1 this injection would correspond to an output signal equal to $v_I C_{ds}/C_H$, where C_{ds} is the drain-to-source capacitance of the FET. This latter term is defined by the **feedthrough rejection ratio** (in dB) or simply feed through (in mV). There is also a **charge transfer** between the digital command signal and C_H that produces a **sample-to-hold offset**, or **hold step** (sometimes also called a **pedestal**) that occurs at the beginning of the hold period. This most likely would occur with an FET switch S_1 due to the drain-to-gate capacitance C_{dg} with an output step in voltage proportional to C_{dg}/C_H. There may also be an error between input and output

---

* The definitions indicated in Fig. 7.20(a) are not universally accepted by all manufacturers. However, the definitions and descriptions used here are those proposed by S. K. Tewksbury et al, "Terminology Related to the Performance of S/H, A/D, and D/A Circuits," *IEEE Trans. Ckts. and Syst.*, Vol. CAS-25, pp. 419–26, (July, 1978). Reprinted in *Data Conversion Integrated Circuits*, ed. D. J. Dooley, IEEE Press (1980).

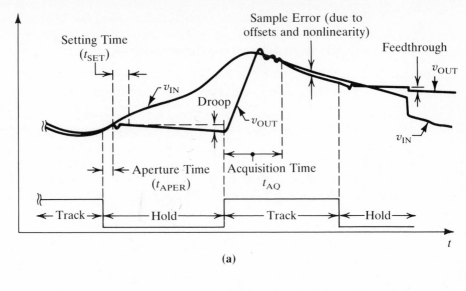

(a)

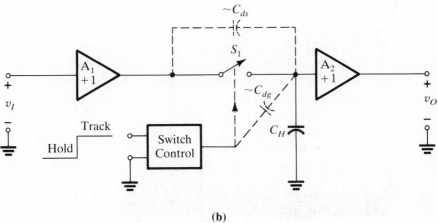

(b)

Figure 7.20 Signals in a T/H circuit: (a) defining parameters; (b) simplified T/H circuit.

signals after a hold-to-sample transition, due to **dielectric absorption** in the capacitor C_H. Basically, the dielectric material of the capacitor acts as a memory that remembers the previous value of v_I during the hold cycle and therefore produces a dc offset between v_I and v_O in the sample mode. Although the excess charge due to this memory effect will eventually decay, the time constant may take many seconds in very high resistivity capacitor material. The worst offenders are ceramic capacitors, with typical dielectric absorption of 0.1 % (an error of 10 mV for a 10 V stored signal), whereas the best capacitors, such as polypropylene and polystyrene, can have values as low as 0.001 % (a 100 μV error for a 10 V stored signal).

Since the Nyquist criterion requires the sampling rate to be at least twice the maximum signal frequency, in an A/D conversion system the characteristics of the S/H (or T/H) amplifier sets the maximum input-signal frequency as

$$f_{\max} = \frac{1}{2(t_{\mathrm{APER}} + t_{\mathrm{AQ}} + t_{\mathrm{CONV}})} \qquad (7.22)$$

where t_{CONV} is the conversion time of the A/D converter.

There are three main types of T/H (or S/H) amplifier circuits. For low-to-moderate-speed (3 μsec $< t_{\mathrm{AQ}} < 20$ μsec, for $C_{\mathrm{HOLD}} = 1$ nF) applications the previous circuit, described in Fig. 7.20(b) and shown more explicitly in Fig. 7.21(a), is used. The switch is generally a JFET (either N- or P-channel) with low gate-to-drain capacitance C_{gd}, a pinchoff-voltage $V_p(V_{GS\text{-OFF}}) < 5$ V and a low value of ON resistance (< 100 ohms). For this circuit the input signal v_I is generally in the range of ± 10 V, and the control signal at the gate must be a voltage equal to at least $(10 + |V_p|)$ volts so that S_1 can be turned off. When the control signal V_{Control} is high ($\sim +15$ V) then D_1 will be off and the JFET S_1 will operate with a gate-to-source bias of zero, hence the switch S_1 will be on with a resistance equal to the R_{ON} resistance. When the control signal goes low (~ -15 V) then D_1 conducts, bringing the gate voltage to approximately -14.4 V, turning off S_1 and leaving the previous value of v_I stored on the hold capacitor C_H. The worst-case pedestal feed through (hold step) would occur when v_I was at a maximum positive value of $+10$ V in the ON state, so that v_{GATE} was $+10$ V and the hold command to -15 V was initiated. Thus, the change in v_{GATE} is -25 V and the pedestal transferred to the noninverting input of A_2 (and therefore also the output of A_2) will be

$$v_{\mathrm{pedestal}} = -25\,\mathrm{V}\left(\frac{C_{gd}}{C_{gd} + C_H}\right) \approx -25\left(\frac{C_{gd}}{C_H}\right)(\text{volts}) \qquad (7.23)$$

or the worst-case charge transfer to the output will be 25 C_{gd} coulombs.

The other diodes in the basic circuit of Fig. 7.21(a) prevent saturation of A_1 when the circuit is in the hold mode. The compensation capacitors C_1 and C_F may be necessary for frequency stability, just as in the case of the peak-detector circuit of Fig. 7.18.

The basic T/H circuit of Fig. 7.21(a) can also be implemented with the operational transconductance amplifier (OTA) as shown earlier in Fig. 5.19(b) in Chapter 5. In that circuit the high output impedance and low leakage of the OTA in the OFF mode replaces the action of the JFET switch S_1 in Fig. 7.21(a). Since the maximum output current of a typical OTA is limited to 1 mA, the acquisition time is determined entirely by the value of C_H. For example, if C_H were 1 nF then the time required for C_H to charge to a 10 V step would be

$$\Delta t = \frac{C\Delta V}{I} = \frac{(1 \times 10^{-9})(10)}{1\,\mathrm{mA}} = 10\ \mu\mathrm{sec}$$

and, including the settling time of the A_1 and A_2 op amps, the acquisition time $t_{\mathrm{AQ}} > 10$ μsec. For larger values of C_H the value of t_{AQ} is even larger—i.e., if C_H is 10 nF then $t_{\mathrm{AQ}} > 100$ μsec.

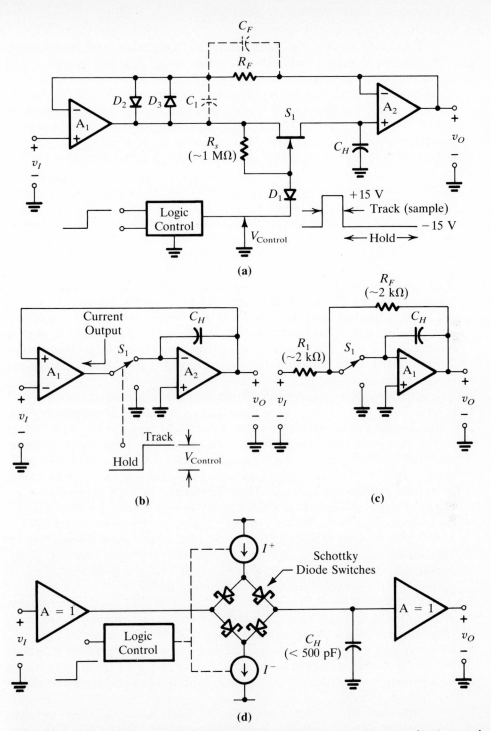

Figure 7.21 Three types of T/H (or S/H) amplifiers. (a) Basic closed-loop moderate-speed circuit. (b) Closed-loop integrator circuit. (c) Simple T/H integrator with lower input impedance, **suitable** for an acquisition time < 1 μsec. (d) A very high-speed open-loop S/H circuit.

The second circuit in Fig. 7.21(b) places the C_H capacitor in the feedback loop of A_2, thereby forming an integrator. Thus, the switch S_1 is looking at a virtual ground and a smaller amplitude control signal is required to drive the switch. Also, for large loop transmission for A_2 the output impedance of A_1 must be high (a current output), and thus an OTA would be useful for A_2. Notice that S_1 is an SPDT switch for improved feedthrough rejection. The same basic circuit is implemented in Fig. 7.21(c) with only one op amp. This circuit can have an acquisition time less than 1 μsec for small values of C_H (< 500 pF) and for a source capable of furnishing several milliamps to charge C_H. In some instances a Schottky-diode bridge switch replaces the JFET (or MOSFET) switch S_1, with a further decrease to $t_{AQ} < 200$ nsec.

For fastest operation, one cannot close the feedback loop around A_1 and A_2 in either Fig. 7.21(a) or (b), and even the feedback-integrator principle of Fig. 7.21(c) is not possible due to oscillation instability. Thus, the S/H circuit must work in an open-loop fashion, as indicated in Fig. 7.21(d), where the switch is now a Schottky-diode bridge, controlled by current-switching ECL (emitter-coupled-logic) components. The amplitudes permitted for v_I are usually also reduced to ± 2 V, while the hold capacitor is small ($C_H < 500$ pF). It is possible to achieve $t_{AQ} \leq 15$ nsec, S/R = 300 V/μsec, jitter ≤ 5 psec, $t_{SET} \leq 5$ nsec to 1mV, with a droop rate of 100 μV/μsec and a -3 dB bandwidth of > 50 MHz. These circuits are particularly useful in radar signal processing and in medical imaging applications.

It is possible to compensate for some of the errors inherent in the T/H process. For example, the circuit of Fig. 7.22(a) is the basic T/H integrator of Fig. 7.21(c), but with an identical FET switch S_2 and hold capacitor C_{H2} added to the noninverting input of op amp A_1. Now, as the gate voltage drives negative, turning off S_1 and producing a pedestal at the inverting input of A_1, there should also be an equal pedestal at the noninverting input of A_1, provided that the C_{gd} capacitances of the two switches are identical. Thus the pedestal becomes a common-mode voltage, which is reduced by the CMRR of the op amp. Similarly, adding an equal capacitance $C_{COMP} = C_{sd1}$ between the source of S_1 and the noninverting input of A_1 will provide equal charge injection to both the inverting and noninverting op amp inputs when S_1 (and S_2) is OFF, thereby providing rejection of the feedthrough charge. As shown in Fig. 7.22(a), it is also a good idea to clamp transients at the summing junction with Schottky diodes.

The circuit of Fig. 7.22(b) is useful in reducing the hold-state leakage current of S_2. In the sample mode both S_1 and S_2 are conducting, charging C_H to the v_I value. However, when the gate-control voltage goes to a low state then S_1 and S_2 are off, and since the output of A_2 is equal to the voltage on C_H resistor R_2 will fix the voltage at the source of S_2 to the same voltage on C_H. So the drain-to-source leakage current of S_2 reduces to zero and any feedthrough signal is reduced, due to two switches in series.

MOS transistor switches may also be used instead of JFET switches. Generally, the JFET is preferred since its ON resistance does not vary with signal amplitude, which is not the case for an MOS device. Also, the JFET switch has generally lower reverse-leakage current than its MOS counterpart. However, it is

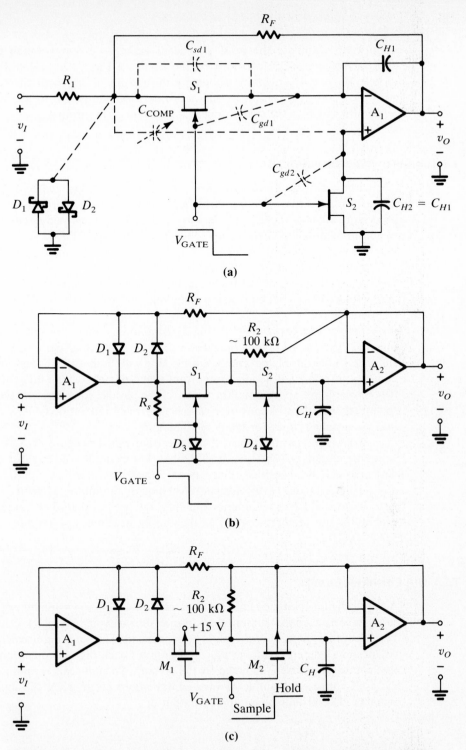

Figure 7.22 Some compensation circuits for T/H amplifiers. (a) Reduction of the pedestal and feedthrough. (b) and (c) Reduction of hold-mode leakage currents.

possible to eliminate the most significant leakage current between drain and substrate of the MOS transistor by the circuit of Fig. 7.22(c). Here the PMOS switch M_2 has its substrate driven by the output of A_2, with the resistor R_2 providing bootstrap action to maintain zero volts across M_2 in the hold mode while also isolating the substrate leakage current of M_1 from C_H.

7.7 D/A AND A/D CONVERSION

The current availability of inexpensive microprocessors has created a demand for data converters that will interface between the analog world and the digital processor. Most of these converters are available in integrated-circuit form. The digital-to-analog (D/A) converter (often referred to as a DAC) accepts a digital output word or data (either '1' or '0'), and converts it to an analog signal, using an op amp as either a current-summing or voltage amplifier, by appropriate choice of precision resistors or capacitors. Since the D/A converter is also the basis for other analog-to-digital (A/D) conversion techniques, we will study the D/A conversion technique first.

To interface between an analog signal and the digital input of the processor, one must use an A/D converter (also called an ADC) that employs op amps as summers, integrators, or comparators. We will limit our discussion of A/D conversion to four of the most important types, namely (a) the integrating ADC, (b) the successive-approximation ADC, (c) the parallel (or "flash") ADC, and (d) the switched-capacitor converter, which uses precision ratioed MOS capacitors like the switched-capacitor filters in Chapter 6.

It is important to inform the reader that our discussion of A/D and D/A converter circuits will be very brief. Only a few examples of the most important networks will be described. Since most universities devote a full semester (or quarter) to A/D and D/A conversion techniques, and many excellent articles and texts are available, we will merely highlight the use of op amp techniques (really, usually the use of comparators) as they apply to conversion requirements. [See Refs. 7.6–7.16.]

7.7.1 D/A Converter Circuits

A simple digital-to-analog conversion circuit can be formed using binary-weighted resistors connected to a summing op amp, as shown earlier in Fig. P1.12 and also in Fig. 7.23(a) for the case of a 4-bit D/A conversion. The basic requirements for the circuit are a reference voltage V_{REF}, a switch for each bit, and precision resistors that control the current summed by the op amp. The full-scale output voltage for the 4-bit converter example of Fig. 7.23(a) would occur when the input digital signal is 1111, producing an analog output of

$$v_O = -R \sum I_i$$

$$= -5 \, k\Omega (10 \, V) \left(\frac{1}{10 \, k\Omega} + \frac{1}{20 \, k\Omega} + \frac{1}{40 \, k\Omega} + \frac{1}{80 \, k\Omega} \right) \tag{7.24}$$

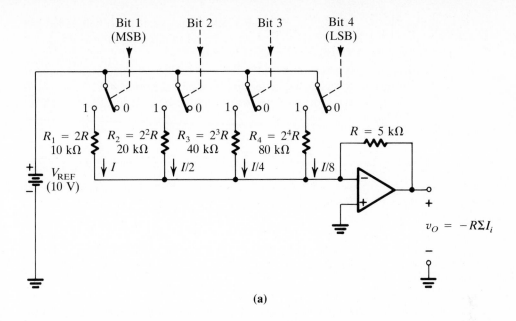

(a)

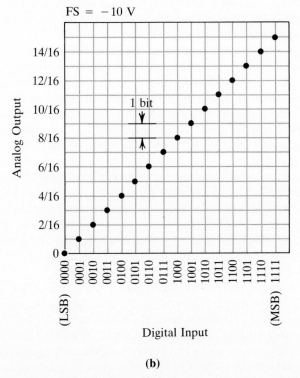

(b)

Figure 7.23 (a) A technique for digital-to-analog conversion using a summing op amp with binary-weighted resistors. (b) The conversion relationship.

or v_O (full scale) $= -10\,\text{V}\,(15/16) = -9.375\,\text{V}$. Thus, each bit (often called the least significant bit, LSB) for the 4-bit D/A conversion has a *resolution* of $V_{\text{REF}}/2^n$, or in this example $10\,\text{V}/16 = 0.625\,\text{V}$. Hence, the *accuracy* of conversion for a four-bit converter is no better than $(1/2^n)\,100\%$, or 6.25%. For better accuracy (or higher resolution) more bits would be required—for an accuracy of 0.1% we would need $2^{-n} = 0.001$, or $n = 10$ bits with a resulting resolution for $V_{\text{REF}} = 10\,\text{V}$ of $10\,\text{V}/2^{10} = 9.77\,\text{mV}$.

■ **Exercise 7.3**

Instead of a 0 to $-10\,\text{V}$ full-scale output one desires to have an output from $-5\,\text{V}$ (LSB) to $+5\,\text{V}$ (MSB). Using the circuit of Fig. 7.23(a) indicate what circuit changes would be necessary.

Several errors affect the accuracy of an D/A conversion [see Refs. 7.8 and 7.10]. There may be a **zero or dc-offset error** when the digital input is zero. This is usually due to the V_{OS} and I_B dc errors of the op amp, and can be trimmed out so that the output of the op amp reads a true zero volts. There can also be a deviation of the slope of the transfer curve (a **gain error**), which will affect all outputs by the same percent error; this static error can be trimmed (removed) by adjusting either the V_{REF} value, or more ideally, by adjusting the feedback resistor R in Fig. 7.23(a). However, two errors are not trimmable: a localized deviation of the transfer curve only in certain segments (a **linearity error**); and a **differential linearity** error, which is the difference between any two adjacent steps. This latter error can result in a nonmonotonic change in the transfer characteristic if the nonlinearity is ≥ 1 LSB. All of the above errors can also vary with temperature, which compounds the problem. Notice that the dc-offset error due to the bias current of the op amp in Fig. 7.23(a) cannot be entirely removed by adding a compensation resistor in series with the noninverting input, since the resistors R_1, R_2, etc. are changing with the digital input command. Additionally, there are dynamic errors in a DAC due to (a) the settling time t_{SET}, which is the time required for the output of the op amp to settle within a defined error band of $\pm\frac{1}{2}$ LSB; and (b) any additional time required to remove "glitches" in the output due to input switching (often, a sample-and-hold circuit follows the DAC to reduce this latter effect).

The binary-weighted resistor technique of Fig. 7.23(a) is not suitable for high-resolution integrated-circuit DACs due to the wide range of resistor values that are required. Fabrication techniques limit the matching of monolithic resistors to a maximum resistor ratio of approximately 20 to 1, thus if a 12-bit DAC were used the maximum ratio required for the binary-weighted circuit would be 2^{12} to 1, or 4096 to 1. Other divider circuits are possible, such as a connection of three 4-bit resistor quads, that would achieve a lower ratio requirement, but even so the ultimate practical accuracy is limited to about 10 bits. For this reason most

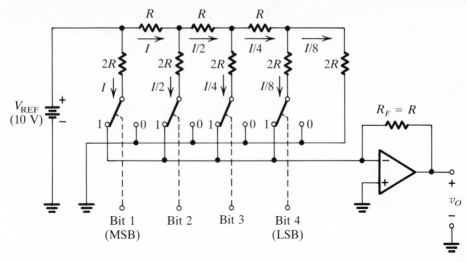

Figure 7.24 A 4-bit R-2R ladder DAC.

integrated-circuit D/A converters employ an R–$2R$ ladder network, where the maximum resistor ratio is $2:1$. Most of the monolithic IC converters use an inverted R–$2R$ circuit, as shown by the 4-bit ADC of Fig. 7.24. Just as for the binary-weighted DAC, the output voltage for the R–$2R$ circuit is (for a digital input of all 1's, 1111)

$$v_O = -R \sum I_i$$

$$= -\frac{V_{REF}}{2}\left[1 + \frac{1}{2} + \frac{1}{4} + \frac{1}{8}\right] \tag{7.25}$$

The ladder connection indicated in Fig. 7.24 has a significant advantage when compared to other types of R–$2R$ connections, in that the individual ladder currents are always switched against ground, either directly into ground for a digital '0' input, or into the op amp's virtual ground for a digital '1' input. Thus, voltage change across the switch is minimal, leading to very low charge injection. A practical illustration of a 4-bit R–$2R$ D/A converter using pnp current-steering switches is illustrated in Problem 7.26. However, the R–$2R$ ladder network has one significant disadvantage as compared with the binary-weighted circuit of Fig. 7.23(a). Note that the R–$2R$ circuit of Fig. 7.24 requires *twice* as many resistors. Conversely, a subtle advantage is achieved by the R–$2R$ ladder in that power dissipation in the resistors is more constant, allowing less drift than that achievable with the binary-weighted network.

7.7.2 A/D Converter Circuits

The analog-to-digital converter converts an input analog signal, either voltage or current, into an equivalent digital form. As with the D/A conversion process, essential characteristics of an A/D conversion are accuracy, linearity, stability, conversion speed (usually referred to as the conversion time t_{CONV}), and especially that there be no missing digital output codes. One can also use a relatively inexpensive technique to obtain A/D conversion, namely to use a voltage- or current-to-frequency conversion with a digital output counter; this technique will be discussed in Section 7.8.

One of the least expensive, and most precise, methods for A/D conversion is to employ an integrating-slope technique, usually referred to as an integrating ADC. These circuits are listed generically as single slope, dual slope, quad slope, and other types of integrating A/D converters, but all fall into the general category of analog conversion using an op amp integrator; an op amp comparator (usually a zero-crossing–detector configuration); some form of charge removal from the integrator capacitor; and a digital clock and counter, with the output count directly proportional to the input analog voltage (or current). In addition, most modern circuits include analog switches and an automatic-zero-correction (auto-zero) circuit that removes any dc offsets accumulating from the op amp integrator and comparator. Most of the commercial digital voltmeters employ an integrating A/D converter, with accuracies equivalent to a $6\frac{1}{2}$-digit conversion (essentially approaching a 20-bit conversion) possible. The main disadvantage of this technique is the long conversion time necessary for accurate integration, usually several hundred milliseconds.

Figure 7.25 illustrates a dual-slope integrating ADC with auto-zero correction. The circuitry is shown in Fig. 7.25(a), and a typical cycle of conversion in Fig. 7.25(b). The first part of the cycle (phase 1) begins with the input of the buffer amplifier A_1 shorted to ground (S_1 in position A) while switch S_2 closes to charge the auto-zero capacitor C_{AZ}. Thus, the sum of the accumulated dc-offset errors of A_1, A_2 and comparator A_3 is stored on C_{AZ}. Since the comparator A_3 is also included in the loop, the only limitation to automatic offset correction is the noise of the circuit, which normally is less than $10\,\mu V$. The time t_1 spent in auto-zero mode is fixed, but in any case is set larger than 20 charging-time constants to effectively integrate short-term drift. At the beginning of the second phase the auto-zero loop is opened (S_2 opened) and input switch S_1 is connected to point B (connected to V_{IN}). The integrator A_2 thus integrates the input signal for a fixed time t_2. Also, a counter may be triggered at the beginning of phase 2 and thereby count a fixed number of clock pulses. At the end of t_2 switch S_2 is positioned to point C, which is a fixed, precision reference voltage REF1, of opposite polarity to the input signal. Thus, during phase 2 a polarity determination of V_{IN} would have to be made to set REF1 to the correct polarity. Since the reference voltage is fixed, the slope of the output signal at A_2 is constant. Thus, the output of A_2 effectively de-integrates the input signal back through zero. It is therefore important that the value of V_{REF} be greater than the largest anticipated value of V_{IN}. The A_3 comparator will sense the zero crossing of the signal at its input, thereby ending phase 3 and stopping the digital counter, which had been reset at the start of phase 3. Thus the voltage changes at the output of A_2 are, at the end of time t_2

$$\Delta V_{O(A2)}(t = t_2) = -\left(\frac{V_{IN}}{R_{INT}\,C_{INT}}\right)t_2 \tag{7.26}$$

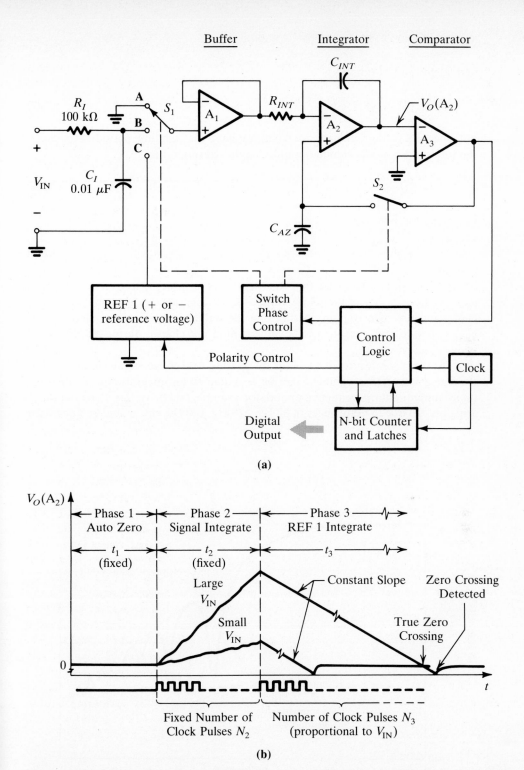

Figure 7.25 A dual-slope integrating A/D converter. (a) Basic circuit with auto-zero correction. (b) A typical output waveform at A_2 for a negative input voltage (V_{IN} is negative, V_{REF1} is positive).

and, at the end of time t_3

$$\Delta V_{O(A2)}(t = t_3) = -\left(\frac{V_{\text{REF1}}}{R_{\text{INT}} C_{\text{INT}}}\right) t_3 \tag{7.27}$$

but since the voltage changes are equal, we have that the time period t_3 (or N_3 — the total number of accumulated pulse counts during t_3) is

$$t_3 = V_{\text{IN}}\left(\frac{t_2}{V_{\text{REF1}}}\right) \tag{7.28a}$$

In terms of pulse counts

$$N_3 = V_{\text{IN}}\left(\frac{N_2}{V_{\text{REF1}}}\right) \tag{7.28b}$$

From these equations we see that the theoretical accuracy of conversion depends *only* on the accuracy of the REF1 value and the accuracy of the clock (which can easily be better than 10 ppm). Notice that the stability of the integration capacitor C_{INT} is not critical, except that its value should not change during an individual conversion cycle.

Another subtle advantage of the integrating A/D conversion technique is that the signal integration period t_2 can be set equal to an integral multiple of some input-contamination-frequency period, for example 60 Hz. In this case contaminating pickup due to frequencies of 60 Hz, 120 Hz, 180 Hz, etc., would be integrated

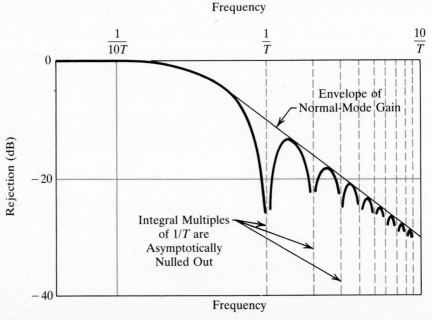

Figure 7.26 Normal-mode rejection in an integrating ADC, with $t_2 = T$.

for a complete cycle, thereby contributing an averaged value of zero at the output of the integrator. This rejection is called **normal-mode** or **line-frequency rejection** and is illustrated by the plot of Fig. 7.26. For the case of 60 Hz, the minimum signal integration time t_2 would be 1/60, or 16.7 msec; for 50 Hz, t_2 (min) = 20 msec.

■ Exercise 7.4

Because the signal integration time t_2 is only a part of the total conversion time, conversion rates for a dual-slope A/D converter are significantly less than $1/t_2$. (a) If a typical converter has an auto-zero phase of $t_1 = t_2$ and a maximum deintegrate period of $t_3 = 2t_2$, what is the maximum conversion time t_{CONV} for the circuit if 60 Hz normal-mode rejection is desired? It is possible to have rejection of both 50 Hz and 60 Hz? What would be the resulting t_{CONV}? (b) If a multiplexer with 10 analog inputs is connected to the A/D converter, what would be the minimum conversion time for the system, and still reject 60 Hz noise?

Although the integrating A/D converter offers excellent accuracy of conversion for low-frequency analog signals, some inherent errors are not compensated by the auto-zero loop. The switch S_2 may have a leakage current of ≤ 10 pA (CMOS, $T = 25\,°C$) which leads to a decrease of the voltage stored on C_{AZ} and C_{INT}. There may also be a problem on turning off (opening) both switches S_1 and S_2 due to charge injection through gate-to-drain capacitance of the switches (this is analogous to pedestal feedthrough in a S/H circuit). The op amps A_1 and A_2 also have nonlinearities associated with the level of output voltage, as well as slew-rate effects in A_1 as switch S_1 switches from V_{REF1} to ground. The capacitors C_{INT} and C_{AZ} also have dielectric absorption—but this can be alleviated by using polystyrene or polypropylene plastic capacitors. Further, there is a delay [illustrated in Fig. 7.25(a)] between the true zero crossing at the output of A_2, and the zero crossing detected by the control logic. The net result is that there is a difference in the number of counts N_3 as well as a residual error in the auto-zero command. It is essential to keep the combined effects of all errors mentioned above $< \frac{1}{2}$LSB for the converter output.

The successive-approximation A/D Converter is more widely used throughout the industry than any other type of ADC. Its basic operating principle consists of successively comparing the output of a D/A converter with the analog input signal and making a decision as to whether the D/A output is greater or less than the analog signal. The required components in a successive-approximation A/D converter are an op amp comparator, a D/A converter (with reference) and a successive-approximation register (SAR) as indicated in Fig. 7.27(a). The successive-approximation A/D operates by using the SAR to control the digital input to the D/A converter, by forming a bit-by-bit comparison starting with the most significant bit (MSB) and working toward the LSB, as indicated in Fig. 7.27(b) for

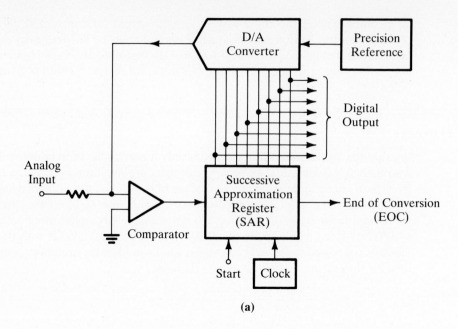

(a)

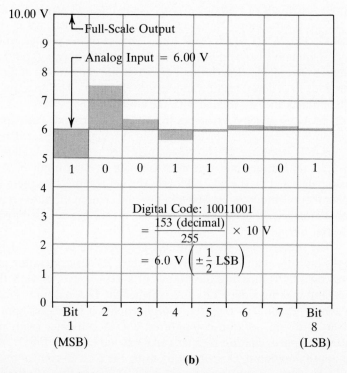

(b)

Figure 7.27 (a) Concept for the successive-approximation A/D converter. (b) SAR output for an analog input of +6.0 V, with $V_{REF} = 10.0$ V and an 8-bit comparison.

an analog input signal of 6.00 V and an 8-bit comparison. At the beginning of the cycle all SAR bits are reset to zero. When a start pulse is received the MSB of the SAR is set to a '1' (high output) and the output of the D/A converter is compared to the input analog signal. If the D/A output is less than the analog signal the MSB remains at '1'. If the output is greater than the analog signal, the SAR stores a '0' (low output) and makes the second MSB bit a '1'. This sequence is continued until all SAR bits (inputs to the D/A converter) are adjusted to make the D/A converter output as close as possible to the analog input signal. Thus, in Fig. 7.27(b) if the analog input signal is $+6.00$ V, the MSB output of the SAR would be 10 V (full scale) times 1/2 or 5.0 V; since 5 V < 6 V the MSB remains as a '1'. The second MSB will then go high, giving a DAC output of 10 V $(\frac{1}{2} + \frac{1}{4})$, or 7.5 V, which is greater than the analog input signal of 6 V; thus the second MSB remains low (a '0'). The third MSB is attempted as a '1', giving a DAC output of 10 V $(\frac{1}{2} + \frac{1}{8})$; we now have a DAC output of 6.25 V and 6.25 V > 6.00 V, so the third MSB remains at '0'. The process continues until we have a digital output code of the DAC of 10011001, or $+5.98$, which is within $\pm\frac{1}{2}$ LSB of the analog input signal of $+6.00$ V. At the completion of the comparison an end-of-conversion (EOC) signal is transmitted to the microprocessor, or whatever computational system is connected to the D/A converter.

Conversion time t_{CONV} in a successive-approximation register is directly proportional to the speed of the comparator and D/A converter, with values in the range of 1–10 μsec possible for 8-bit systems, and approaching 50–100 μsec for 16-bit circuits. Since the successive-approximation A/D converter offers t_{CONV} in the microsecond range, whereas the integrating ADC generally has conversion times in the several-hundred-millisecond domain, it is obvious the successive-approximation technique must be employed in higher bandwidth systems. The most important element limiting accuracy and linearity in the successive-approximation converter is the DAC used; the A/D conversion can be no better than the accuracy of the DAC itself.

EXAMPLE 7.5

For the 8-bit successive-approximation A/D converter example of Fig. 7.27, what general requirements are demanded for a conversion time of 1 μsec over a temperature range of 0 to 25 °C, and an accuracy of conversion of $\pm\frac{1}{2}$ LSB?

Solution
One bit (or $\pm\frac{1}{2}$ bit) in an 8-bit system is 1 part in 2^8 (or 256). For the 10 V reference we require a maximum of ≤ 1 bit error in 10 V for $\Delta T = 25$ °C. Hence we need an adjusted precision of V_{REF} to better than 10.00 V $\pm$ 10 V/2 (256) or 10.00 $\pm$ 0.02 V. Further, we need a temperature coefficient (TC) less than $\frac{1}{2}(\frac{1}{256})(\frac{1}{25}$ °C), or less than 78 ppm/°C. These requirements are not that severe, since commercial references of 10.00 V are available with a TC < 10 ppm/°C.

If we allow one clock period per bit precision, we would need 8 clock periods to reach the EOC, as well as one clock period to reset all bits and start conversion.

Hence, a minimum of 9 clock periods, or more probably 10 (allowing one after the EOC before the start pulse), are required for a complete data cycle. Hence if each complete cycle is to be ≤ 1 μsec a clock period of $1/10$ of t_{CONV} (or 100 nsec) is required. The settling time of the comparator must therefore be <100 nsec; furthermore the comparator must have a hysteresis $<\frac{1}{2}$ bit, or 20 mV, and a slew rate considerably greater than the output logic swing to the control portion of the SAR divided by 100 nsec. For example, if a 0 to 5 V output of the comparator is required in $\leq\frac{1}{5}$ clock period, the SR must be at least 5 V/20 nsec = 250 V/μsec. SR requirements apply to the D/A converter as well, but the output-voltage step of the DAC is only one LSB per decision, thereby decreasing the requirement to under 5 V/μsec.

In general, a successive-approximation A/D converter requires a preceding track-and-hold (T/H) circuit—to allow the input analog signal to be fixed during the conversion time. Acquisition time and uncertainties in the T/H circuit must thus be added to the t_{CONV} of the converter, thereby compounding the problems inherent in obtaining a total 1 μsec conversion. It can be shown* that without a T/H circuit the maximum sine-wave frequency that can be converted with $\pm\frac{1}{2}$ LSB resolution is

$$f_{\max} = \frac{1}{2^n t_{\text{CONV}} \pi} \tag{7.29}$$

or in this example $f_{\max} = 1.2$ kHz.

---

* See any of the general references for Chapter 7 in Appendix A.

The successive-approximation A/D converter can also be implemented in switched-capacitor (SC) technology, where ratioed capacitors replace the ratioed resistors in the D/A conversion. One of the simplest types of SC analog-to-digital converters is the charge-redistribution circuit of Fig. 7.28*, where binary-weighted capacitors are switched between ground, and either the input signal V_{IN} or a reference potential V_{REF}. In this circuit (illustrated for a 5-bit A/D conversion) the first cycle of operation connects switches S_1–S_6 to ground and switch S_8 to the input signal; switch S_7 is closed, so V_X the input to the comparator is equal to V_{OS} the offset voltage of the comparator and the total charge stored on all capacitors is $Q = 2CV_{OS}$. If S_1–S_6 are switched to V_{IN} the charge stored on the capacitors is now $Q = 2C(V_{OS} - V_{\text{IN}})$. In the hold mode of operation switch S_7 is opened and switches S_1–S_6 are grounded. Due to charge conservation the potential V_X must now go to $-V_{\text{IN}} + V_{OS}$ and the effect of V_{OS} is removed as an error source. The redistribution

---

* From J. L. McCreary and P. R. Gray, "All-MOS Charge Redistribution Analog-to-Digital Conversion Techniques—Part I," *IEEE J. S. S. Ckts.*, Vol. SC-10, No. 6, pp. 371–79 (Dec. 1975).

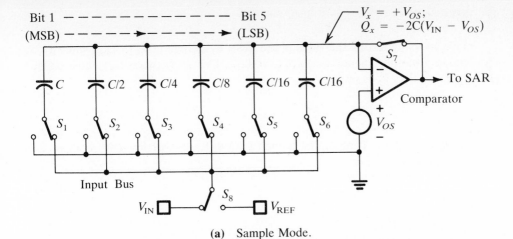

(a) Sample Mode.

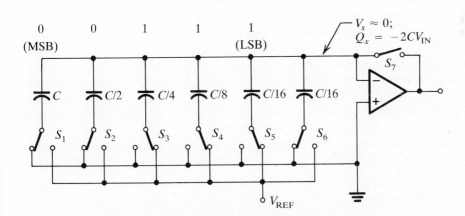

(b) Redistribution mode-checking bit 1.

(c) Final switch confiuration for an input $V_{IN} = 7\ V_{REF}/16$.

Figure 7.28 A switched-capacitor A/D conversion technique using charge redistribution. (a) Sample mode. (b) Redistribution mode-checking bit 1. (c) Final switch configuration for an input $V_{IN} = 7V_{REF}/16$.

419

mode starts by testing the value of the MSB by switching S_1 to V_{REF} while S_2-S_6 remain grounded; hence we have a voltage division between two equal capacitances, so that V_X is now

$$V_X = -V_{IN} + V_{OS} + \frac{V_{REF}}{2}$$

The output of the comparator is high ('1') if $V_X < 0$, or low ('0') if V_X is >0. Equivalently, we have

$$\text{MSB} = \begin{cases} \text{'1'} & \text{if } V_{IN} > \dfrac{V_{REF}}{2} \\[2ex] \text{'0'} & \text{if } V_{IN} < \dfrac{V_{REF}}{2} \end{cases} \tag{7.30}$$

and the output of the comparator is therefore the value (1 or 0) of the bit tested. If the MSB is zero, switch S_1 is connected to ground, otherwise it is left connected to the input bus. In an analogous fashion, the second bit is tested by connecting switch S_2 to V_{REF}. Now, however, the voltage division causes $V_{REF}/4$ to be added, so

$$V_X = -V_{IN} + V_{OS} + (\text{bit 1}) \frac{V_{REF}}{2} + (\text{bit 2}) \frac{V_{REF}}{4}$$

The conversion technique proceeds, testing each bit in sequence with the result

$$V_X = -V_{IN} + V_{OS} + (\text{bit 1}) \frac{V_{REF}}{2} + (\text{bit 2}) \frac{V_{REF}}{4} + (\text{bit 3}) \frac{V_{REF}}{8}$$

$$+ \cdots + (\text{bit } n)\left(\frac{V_{REF}}{2^n}\right) \tag{7.31}$$

where each bit is either a 1 or 0. A final switch configuration for a digital code 00111 is illustrated in Fig. 7.28(c).

Although the basic concept of Fig. 7.28 works quite well for low-accuracy conversion it is not practical for high resolution converters due to the large area required for the capacitors. For example, a 12-bit conversion would require a range of capacitors from 1 to 4096. By using two stages of capacitor ladders the range is reduced, as shown by the 13-bit binary example* of Fig. 7.29(a). In this figure one capacitor section contains the 7 most significant bits and the other the 6 least significant bits, with the two sections connected by a 64-to-1 divider. Thus a capacitor ratio of only 64 to 1 is required. The equivalent circuit of the two sections appears as indicated in Fig. 7.29(b), with the resultant output of the DAC equal to

$$V_{O(DAC)} = \frac{V_{REF}}{128} \left(\sum_{n=1}^{7} D_n C_n + \sum_{n=8}^{13} \frac{D_n C_n}{64} \right) \tag{7.32}$$

---

* From K. B. Ohri and M. J. Callahan, Jr., "Integrated PCM Codec," *IEEE J. S.S. Circuits*, Vol. SC-14, No. 1, pp. 38–46 (Feb. 1979). This circuit uses a dual-polarity V_{REF} and thus has bipolar capability. A disadvantage is the requirement for having a precision coupling capacitor, $C = 1.01587\ldots$

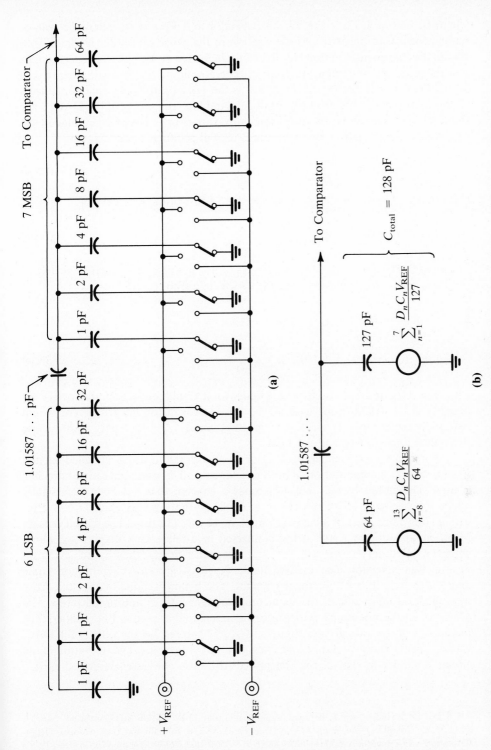

Figure 7.29 A 13-bit switched-capacitor DAC. (a) Circuit illustrating two stages of conversion. (b) DAC equivalent circuit.

421

where D_n is 0 or 1, C_n is the nth bit capacitor and V_{REF} is the reference voltage (either positive or negative). The operation of the capacitor ladder is identical to that of the charge-distribution circuit of Fig. 7.28, each bit being tested successively, and the sequence of comparator outputs corresponding to the analog equivalent signal. One critical element in the circuit is the 1.016 pF divider capacitor, since a change of this capacitor produces both gain and linearity errors in the DAC. Since the total equivalent capacitance of the entire capacitor is 128 pF, a change in the capacitor ratio of 1.016:1 by an amount ΔC will produce a gain error of

$$\text{Gain error} = 1 - \frac{\Delta C}{128} \tag{7.33a}$$

and a linearity error (which only affects the 6 LSBs of the network) of

$$\text{Linearity error} = \Delta C \sum_{n=8}^{13} \frac{D_n C_n}{64} \tag{7.33b}$$

Since typically capacitance ratios of $\pm 0.1\%$ are possible with current switched-capacitor technology, the errors in Eq. (7.33) reduce to

$$\text{Gain error} \approx 1 - \frac{1}{1.28 \times 10^5}$$

$$\text{Linearity error} \approx 1 - (10^{-3}) \sum_{n=8}^{13} \frac{D_n C_n}{64} \tag{7.34}$$

Although the gain error is entirely negligible for a 13-bit conversion, the worst-case linearity error would occur with all $D_n = 1$, for which the linearity error would reduce to essentially ΔC, or 1 part in 1000. Since $1/2^{13}$ is 1 part in 8192, the worst-case linearity error is >1 LSB.

For much higher accuracy A/D or D/A conversion using switched-capacitance networks a combination of both resistance- and capacitance-ratioed dividers is used. The circuit of Fig. 7.30 illustrates a concept that has been successfully applied* to achieve 15-bit resolution in a self-calibrating CMOS A/D converter with a conversion time of 80 μsec (15 bits), or 12 μsec (12 bits). The circuit uses an M-bit equal-ratioed resistor string connected to a reference voltage V_{REF}, along with a K-bit binary-ratioed (1, 2, 4, 8, ...) capacitor array, thereby achieving an $M + K$-bit conversion. The resistive divider $R_1 - R_{(2^M)}$ gives an inherent monotonic division of V_{REF} into 2^M identical voltages. The binary-weighted capacitor array then subdivides any one of the segmented voltages into 2^K additional levels. The offset-voltage-compensated comparator [identical to that used in Fig. 7.28(a)] thus requires a voltage gain greater than $V_O/V_{REF} 2^{M+K}$ to resolve the LSB of the DAC, where V_O is the output-voltage logic swing of the comparator. The operation of the circuit is similar to that of the charge-redistribution converter described earlier.

---

* H. S. Lee, D. A. Hodges, and P. R. Gray, "A Self-Calibrating 15-Bit CMOS A/D Converter," *IEEE J. S.S. Circuits*, Vol. SC-19, No. 6, pp. 813–19 (Dec. 1984). Also, B. Fotouhi and D. A. Hodges, "High-Resolution A/D Conversion in MOS/LSI," *IEEE J. S.S. Circuits*, Vol. SC-14, pp. 920–26 (Dec. 1979).

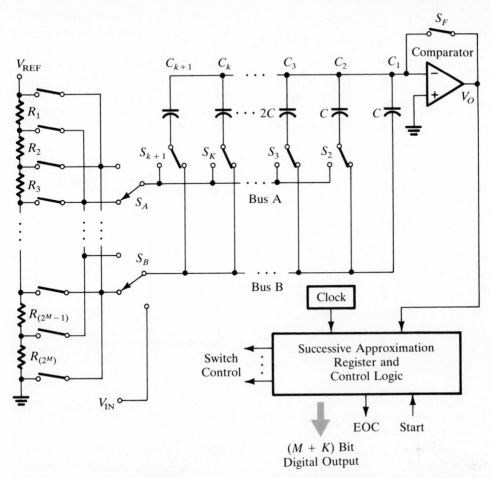

Figure 7.30 Simplified diagram of a combined resistive- and capacitive-switched A/D converter, which obtains high resolution.

With switch S_F closed all lower plates of capacitors C_2–C_{K+1} are connected to V_{IN} and thus store a voltage $V_{IN} - V_{OS}$, where V_{OS} is the offset voltage of the comparator. Switch S_F opens and a successive-approximation search is performed among the resistors R_1–$R_{(2M)}$ to find a voltage segment within which V_{IN} is contained. Then buses A and B are switched to each end of this voltage segment by contacting each end of the appropriate resistor in the string. The last phase is to switch the lower plates of the capacitor array in a successive-approximation sequence until the comparator input voltage reduces to the offset voltage. The comparator sequence is thus the digital code (within $\pm 1/2$ LSB) of the input analog signal. This technique is particularly insensitive to switch parasitic capacitance, since every node voltage is charged to its final value, thus eliminating any charge-sharing effects. Further, normal source- and drain-diffused resistors (typically, a sheet resistivity of 10–50 Ω/square) can be used for the R_1–$R_{(2M)}$ resistor string.

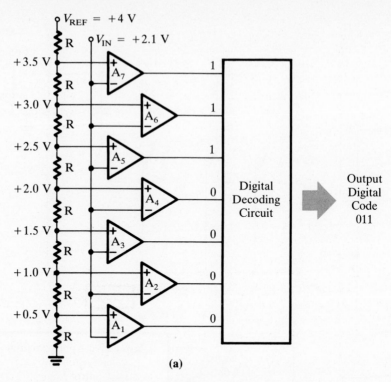

(a)

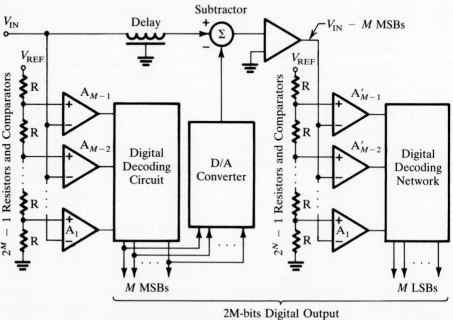

(b)

Figure 7.31 Parallel, or flash, ADC. (a) Example of a 3-bit conversion. (b) A two-step parallel converter with 2M-bit capability [Ref. 7.13].

The previous examples of A/D conversion sample the input signal, and then process each sampled increment before obtaining another sample. As we have noted earlier, in Eq. (7.29), the maximum input frequency that could be processed without an S/H (or T/H) circuit is limited to $(2^n t_{CONV} \pi)^{-1}$, or generally ≤ 1 kHz for an 8-bit converter with $t_{CONV} = 1$ μsec. Even with an S/H preceding the ADC, the maximum input frequency is less than $\frac{1}{2} t_{CONV}$ or < 500 kHz for the same values. For signals whose frequency content is in the MHz range a **parallel**, or **flash**, **ADC** must be used.

An example of a 3-bit parallel ADC is shown in Fig. 7.31(a). The reference voltage is subdivided into $2^n - 1$ equal segments, or in this example into 7 equal parts. A comparator compares the input signal V_{IN} with the particular reference-voltage segment. Thus in Fig. 7.31, with $V_{REF} = +4$ V each comparator has a reference voltage that differs from the next comparator by 4 V/8 or 0.5 V so the resolution is $V_{REF}/2^n$. In the example shown in Fig. 7.31(a), if V_{IN} is 2.1 V then the outputs of comparators A_1–A_4 will be low ('0'), while the outputs of A_5–A_7 will be high ('1'). The digital decoding network thus identifies its input and provides a digital output word of 011. The advantage in speed in the parallel converter occurs because the analog input signal is converted to a digital output in nearly one clock period. It is currently possible to obtain a 9-bit parallel ADC in bipolar technology with a conversion rate of 25 MHz, and a 6-bit conversion rate of 100 MHz. Some high-speed CMOS versions can achieve 25 MHz conversion rates.

The significant disadvantage of the parallel ADC technique is that it requires $2^n - 1$ comparators, which is currently impractical for $n > 8$. However, by processing the analog input signal in a two-step fashion, as shown in Fig. 7.31(b), it is possible to achieve 8-, 10-, or even 12-bit conversion, with only a 2:1 increase in conversion time. The conversion process first converts the M most significant bits, then reconverts these M MSBs to an analog signal which is subtracted from the original analog input signal, thereby leaving only the M least significant bits to process. The net digital output code is $2M$ bits, so a 12-bit parallel ADC can be obtained by using two 6-bit parallel A/D units. The two-step process obviously demands very careful timing between the input signal and the subtractor circuit. Typically, it would be expected that the worst-case linearity would occur around the transition point between the M MSBs and the M LSBs. Techniques exist, however, for eliminating much of these discontinuities by using digital correction logic [see, for example, Ref. 7.8, p. 427].

Many excellent examples of other types of A/D and D/A converters are available in the literature. Particularly good insights are available in Refs. 7.8, 7.11, and 7.16 in Appendix A.

7.8 V/F AND F/V CONVERTERS

In a voltage-to-frequency converter (referred to as either a V/F converter or a VFC) the input voltage is linearly related to an output frequency. Actually, we really could view the process as another type of ADC, since an analog input signal (voltage, or perhaps current) is converted to a frequency, which can then be counted by a binary counter for a fixed time period, resulting in an equivalent-output digital code. In many respects the VFC is quite similar to the integrating ADC discussed in the last section. Similarly, the frequency-to-voltage converter (F/V, or FVC) transforms a frequency input signal, such as the output of a digital counter, directly to an analog output signal. Perhaps the most distinuishing feature of either a VFC, or FVC, is a very low-cost inherently monotonic process of conversion.

A few of the many possible applications for these converters are shown in Fig. 7.32. The circuit of Fig. 7.32(a) illustrates a basic counting ADC by the addition of a few inexpensive components to a VFC. An analog signal in a noisy environment, particularly with a noisy ground system, can have a pulsed frequency output of a VFC optically coupled to another system, as shown in Fig. 7.32(b), thereby eliminating the direct interconnection of the two circuits. The optical coupling could also be obtained using a fiber-optic light pipe. Further, the transmission between the two systems could use either magnetic coupling (transformers), or RF signal transmission by AM or FM signal propagation. A direct temperature-to-frequency conversion is given in Fig. 7.32(c), where the temperature transducer could be as simple as a diode whose temperature varies approximately -2 mV/°C. Also available from several manufacturers (such as National Semiconductor, Motorola, and Analog Devices) are precision IC circuits that have a dc output voltage directly proportional to temperature, either in °Kelvin, °C or °F. One could also use a thermistor bridge and instrumentation amplifer (see Section 5.3) for temperature measurement. Similarly, a strain-gage bridge circuit with an IA affords an analog output voltage to a VFC, with the resulting output frequency directly proportional to stress, strain, or weight.

In Fig. 7.32(d) a motor-speed control circuit is easily obtained with a frequency-to-voltage conversion of the output pulses from a tachometer providing negative-feedback control for a motor. [These, and many other applications of V/F and F/V converters can be found in Refs. 7.8, 7.10, 7.11, and 7.17.]

The ideal response of a VFC is an output frequency directly proportional to the input voltage (or current). The constant of proportionality is determined by the full-scale input voltage V_{FS} and the full-scale output frequency f_{FS}. The relationship is

$$f_{\text{out}} = \left(\frac{f_{FS}}{V_{FS}}\right)V_{\text{IN}} \equiv GV_{\text{IN}} \tag{7.35}$$

where the gain constant G has units of pulses/sec/volt. As with other converters, the VFC has limitations to the ideal response of Eq. (7.35) due to offset and linearity errors, as well as dynamic range limitations. These errors are functions of temperature, power-supply, and input-signal changes.

Most of the V/F converters fall into two categories: either (a) a multivibrator type where a precision emitter-coupled astable multivibrator has a frequency output directly proportional to a current input, or (b) a charge- or current-balancing converter, with a controlled charge-rebalance loop obtained to null any input-current deviations provided by the analog input signal. Both types of VFCs have different advantages. The multivibrator-type converter can generally offer

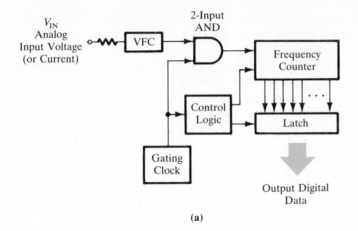

(a)

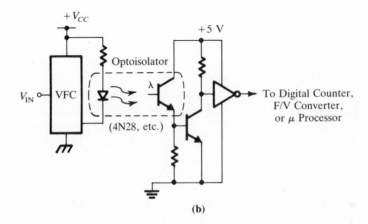

(b)

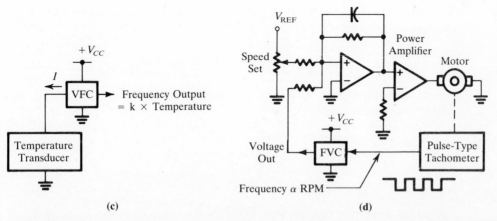

(c)

(d)

Figure 7.32 Some possible applications using V/F and F/V converters. (a) VFC used as a simple inexpensive ADC. (b) Noisy environment data link. (c) Temperature to frequency conversion. (d) Motor speed control circuit.

full-scale nonlinearity within 0.1 % to a full-scale frequency of 100 kHz, with low power dissipation. In addition, the output is usually a square-wave signal, which is superior for ac coupling without inducing dc-level shifts. Some monolithic ICs (such as the AD537) even include an internal band-gap reference with a calibrated temperature-dependent output voltage (1 mV/°Kelvin) that can be used for a temperature-to-frequency conversion. The basic construction of the AD537 V/F converter is shown in Fig. 7.33(a). The user supplies externally the resistor R and the oscillator capacitor C. The output frequency f_0 is related to the input voltage by

$$f_0 = \left(\frac{V_{IN}}{R}\right)\left(\frac{1}{10C}\right) = G_1 V_{IN} \tag{7.36}$$

Thus, the gain constant G_1 for the AD537 is equal to $\frac{1}{10}RC$ pulses/sec/volt.

The charge-balancing converter offers the highest resolution obtained in a VFC. Also, the advantages of the previous integrating-type ADC are inherently obtained, namely high linearity and good noise rejection. Further, by careful trimming a frequency range of 1 Hz to 30 MHz ($7\frac{1}{3}$ decades) with 0.08 % linearity has been reported using the charge-balancing technique, or 1 Hz to 10 MHz (7 decades) with 0.06 % linearity.* These latter circuits have a resolution capability exceeding a 16-bit conversion ADC.

An example of a typical circuit for a low- to medium-frequency range (1 Hz to 1 MHz) charge-balance VFC is shown in Fig. 7.33(b), where the balancing scheme is obtained by summing currents at the virtual-ground input of op amp A_1. The input voltage V_{IN} (which must be negative) produces a charging current for C_1 equal to V_{IN}/R. Thus the output voltage of A_1 ramps positive until the comparator's threshold voltage is reached, which then triggers the monostable, thereby producing a controlled output pulse of width t_x. The output pulse of the monostable then switches a reference current $I_{REF} > I_{IN}$ into the summing junction of A_1, thereby driving the output of A_1 negative. After time t_x the cycle repeats with I_{IN}, causing the output voltage of A_1 to again rise until the monostable is triggered. At steady state the total charge into and out of the summing junction of A_1 must balance, or

$$\left(\frac{V_{IN}}{R}\right)(T_0 - t_x) = \left(I_{REF} - \frac{V_{IN}}{R}\right)t_x \tag{7.37a}$$

Solving and substituting $T_0 = 1/f_0$ we obtain the relation between output frequency and input voltage

$$f_0 = \left(\frac{1}{I_{REF}Rt_x}\right)V_{IN} \tag{7.37b}$$

---

* See J. M. Williams, "V-F Converter Offers 120-dB Dynamic Range," *Electronic Design*, pp. 276–78 (Oct. 4, 1984). Also, by the same author, "Chopper Amplifier Improves Operation of Diverse Circuits," *EDN*, pp. 189–207 (March 7, 1985); and "Fast Comparator IC Speeds Converters and S/H Amplifiers," pp. 115–28, *EDN* (June 20, 1985).

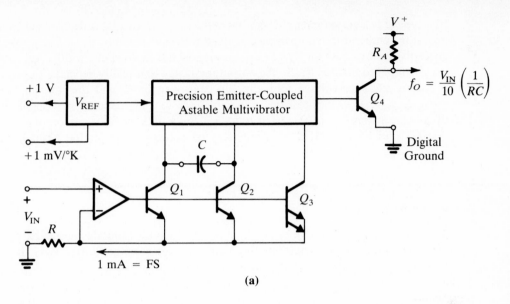

(a)

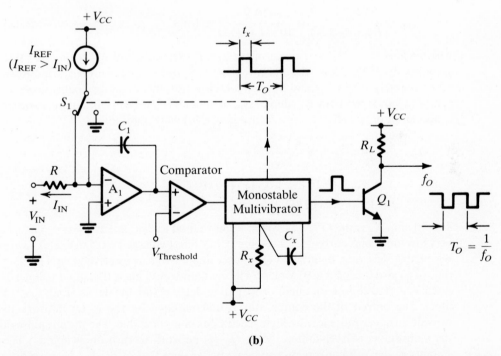

(b)

Figure 7.33 V/F converters: (a) typical multivibrator type, the AD537 (manufactured by Analog Devices, Inc.); (b) charge-balance converter using a current reference.

In a typical integrated-circuit design the reference current I_{REF} is determined by a precision temperature-compensated voltage reference (usually, a band-gap reference) divided by a resistor R_{REF}. Also, the monostable has its pulse width t_x directly proportional to resistor R_x. So the output frequency is in reality dependent upon a precision reference-voltage source, a precision resistor R, and the *ratio* of two resistors, R_{REF}/R_x. Since resistor ratios can track to a high degree, it is possile to obtain linearities to $\pm 0.002\%$ of full scale for a 10 kHz full-scale output, and $\pm 0.005\%$ of FS for 100 kHz output (see, for example, data for the AD650, the LM331 and the VFC320).

EXAMPLE 7.6

The circuit of Fig. 7.34 is an example of a V/F converter using the charge-balance principle of operation. Determine the output frequency range for $0 < V_{IN} \leq 10$ V, and explore dc-offset effects and linearity limitations.

Solution

The circuit of Fig. 7.34 provides a reference current of

$$I_{REF} = \frac{V_{REF1}}{R_2 + r_{ON}(J_3)} = \frac{10 \text{ V}}{10 \text{ k}\Omega + 35 \text{ }\Omega} \approx 1 \text{ mA} \tag{7.38a}$$

where r_{ON} is the 'ON' resistance of the JFET switch J_3 and has a typical value specified of 35 Ω. Thus, the variation of r_{ON} with temperature (r_{ON} increases approximately $1\%/°C$) would be an error. However, by adding two equivalent r_{ON} resistances in series with R_1 (due to r_{ON} of J_1 and J_2), we can obtain a first-order cancellation of r_{ON} effects, since from Eq. 7.37(b) we would have

$$f_0 = \frac{1}{t_x} \left(\frac{V_{IN}}{R_1 + 2r_{ON}} \right) \left(\frac{R_2 + r_{ON}}{V_{REF1}} \right)$$

$$= \frac{1}{t_x} \left(\frac{V_{IN}}{V_{REF1}} \right) \left[\frac{10 \text{ k}\Omega + 35 \text{ }\Omega}{2(10 \text{ k}\Omega + 35 \text{ }\Omega)} \right] = \frac{1}{2t_x} \left(\frac{V_{IN}}{V_{REF1}} \right) \tag{7.38b}$$

The op amp A_1 is the OPA111 which we have used earlier, in Chapters 4–6. It has very low input bias current (± 2 pA, max), low offset voltage (± 0.5 mV, max), with reasonable slew rate, bandwidth (2 V/μ-sec and 2 MHz, respectively), and settling time (6 μsec to 0.1% for a 10 V step). The comparator A_2 has a threshold voltage of -2.5 V, and is chosen for small propagation delay t_p (for the device used, $t_p \leq 14$ nsec). The output of the comparator is differentiated by the R_2C_2 network to provide a trigger pulse for the high-speed CMOS monostable. The output pulse of the monostable is level-shifted by the Q_1–Q_2 network to turn on switch J_3. The stability of the V/F conversion can be no better than that of R_1, R_2, V_{REF1} and t_x. So V_{REF1} is obtained using a precision Zener diode (Z_1) which has ± 10 ppm/$°C$ temperature coefficient, and op amp A_3 (refer to Problem P5.48 and Section 5.71). If a more precise reference were needed, once could use a commercial 10 V reference, such as the AD588 (1 ppm/$°C$ drift). The V_{REF2} threshold for comparator

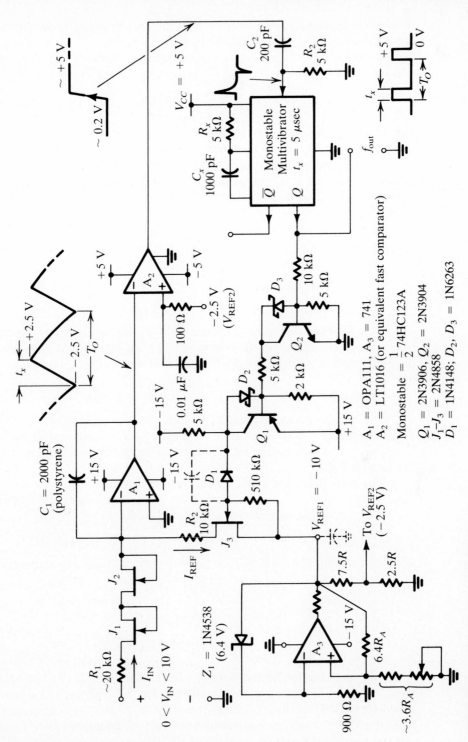

Figure 7.34 V/F converter of Example 7.6.

A_2 is derived from V_{REF1} by a simple voltage divider network. The stability of V_{REF2} is not important, since it is inside the loop.

From Eq. 7.38(b) the full-scale output frequency is obtained (with $t_x = 5\ \mu sec$, and $V_{IN} = +10\ V$) as

$$f_0\ (\text{full-scale}) = \frac{1}{2 \times 5\ \mu sec}\left(\frac{10\ V}{10\ V}\right) = 100\ kHz \tag{7.38c}$$

The minimum value of f_0 corresponds to the minimum input voltage V_{IN}. This is determined by offsets at the input and noise. For example, assume that R_1 or R_2 has been adjusted for the correct gain constant for the V/F converter to obtain exactly 100 kHz full-scale output with $V_{IN} = 10\ V$. Suppose that the circuit has to operate to 50 °C, or over a change in temperature of $\Delta T = 25$ °C. The input dc-offset current is due to that created by V_{OS} of A_1, as well as I_B^- of A_1, the cutoff channel-leakage current I_D (off) of J_3, as well as the gate current I_G of J_3. Assuming worst-case values from manufacturer's data, for $\Delta T = 25$ °C, we obtain

$$\Delta V_{OS1} \approx \pm 5\ \mu V/°C\ (25\ °C) = \pm 0.13\ \mu V$$

$$\Delta I_{B1} \approx \pm(10\ pA - 2\ pA) = 8\ pA$$

$$\Delta I_{D3}(\text{off}) = \Delta I_{G3} \approx (1\ nA - 0.2\ nA) = 0.8\ nA \tag{7.38d}$$

where it is assumed that leakage currents will double for every 10 °C increase in temperature. The change in the reference V_{REF1} can be expected to be no worse than ± 20 ppm/°C, or for $\Delta T = 25$ °C we have an equivalent-input-current change of

$$\Delta I_{REF} = [10\ V \times 20 \times 10^{-6}/°C \times 25\ °C]/R_2 = 500\ nA \tag{7.38e}$$

We can use resistors R_1 and R_2 that are precision metal-film type, with low TC (<50 ppm/°C). Since the output frequency f_0 is proportional to the *ratio* of these resistors, as indicated in Eq. 7.38(b), there should be no change in frequency due to their drift.

The noise limitation of the system can be described by a total equivalent-input-noise current. Assuming full shot noise for I_B^- of A_1 and I_{G3}, the input-noise current at the highest temperature of 50 °C is [see Eq. (4.5)]

$$i_{n1} = (2qI)^{1/2} = [2q(10\ pA + 1\ nA)]^{1/2} = 1.8 \times 10^{-14}\ amp/\sqrt{Hz} \tag{7.38f}$$

The thermal noise of R_1 and R_2 [See Eq. (4.4)] can be equated to an input current of

$$i_{n(R1)} = \left\{4kT\left[\frac{1}{R_1 + r_{ON}(J_1) + r_{ON}(J_2)}\right]\right\}^{1/2} = 0.9\ pA/\sqrt{Hz}$$

$$i_{n(R2)} = \left\{4kT\left[\frac{1}{R_2 + r_{ON}(J_3)}\right]\right\}^{1/2} = 1.3\ pA/\sqrt{Hz} \tag{7.38g}$$

where we again use the highest temperature $T = 50\ °C = 323\ °K$. The equivalent noise voltage of A_1 is given by the manufacturer as $\leq 3.3\ \mu V$ (p-p) for a bandwidth of 0.1 Hz to 10 Hz, and $\leq 1.2\ \mu V$ (rms) for a 10 Hz to 10 kHz bandwidth ($e_n \leq 10\ nV/Hz$). Thus, the equivalent noise current produced (J_3 off) would be $\leq 0.17\ nA$ (p-p) at $f \leq 10$ Hz, and $\leq 0.05\ pA/\sqrt{Hz}$ for broadband noise.

The highest noise is obtained from the -10 V reference, and is due mostly to avalanche noise of the Zener diode. Using a worst-case anticipated noise value of $500 \text{ nV}/\sqrt{\text{Hz}}$ (broadband) and $50 \mu V$ (p-p) for 0.1–10 Hz, the equivalent-input-noise current due to this source (which occurs only when J_3 is 'ON') is

$$I_{N3} \le 50 \mu V/10 \text{ k}\Omega = 5 \text{ nA (p-p)}(0.1\text{–}10 \text{ Hz})$$

$$i_{n3} \le 0.5 \mu V/\sqrt{\text{Hz}}/10 \text{ k}\Omega = 50 \text{ pA}/\sqrt{\text{Hz}} \text{ (broadband)} \tag{7.38h}$$

Thus the most significant component of input noise will be due to i_{n3}. However, this noise is *only effective* when J_3 is conducting (during time t_x).

The most significant parameter affecting overall accuracy will be the drift of the monostable period t_x, since Eq. 7.37(b) predicts a direct decrease in f_0 for an increase in t_x. The monostable used in Fig. 7.34 has (from manufacturer's data) a typical change of $\Delta t_x/t_x \approx -50$ ppm/°C, thus from Eq. 7.37(b) the change in f_0 would be (for small changes) for $\Delta T = 25$ °C,

$$\Delta f_0 = -f_0 \left(\frac{\Delta t_x}{t_x} \right) = -f_0(-50 \times 10^{-6} \times 25) = 1.25 \times 10^{-3} f_0 \tag{7.38j}$$

The results of the drift and noise analysis are summarized in Table 7.1, using a procedure analogous to that of the error budget analysis presented in Section 2.5.3. The analysis is indicated for $f_0 = 10$ Hz, corresponding to $V_{IN} = 1$ mV, and for the full-scale frequency of 100 kHz. It is apparent the dominant errors are those due to a shift in the multivibrator pulse width t_x and the reference V_{REF1}. The effect of noise is generally negligible, with the largest term due to the low-frequency (p-p, input voltage noise of the op amp A_1.

Noise transients produced by switching J_3 occur at both turn-on and turn-off of J_3.* These transients are due to the transient gate voltage producing charge injection at the drain of J_3 via the gate-to-drain capacitance C_{gd3} of J_3. For a typical value of C_{gs3} of 3 pF, and with a gate-voltage change of 5 volts, the charge injection would be 15 picojoules (pJ). In addition, the total propagation delay around the loop will provide an increase of the period T_0, particularly if the delay changes with temperature. For the devices used in Fig. 7.34 the propagation delays can be obtained from manufacturer's data as (maximum values) 16 nsec for A_2, 33 nsec for the monostable, 20 nsec for J_3 and ≤ 100 nsec for the Q_1–Q_2 network. Thus, a total propagation delay of <200 nsec between the output and input of A_1 could be expected. Since this represents only 0.2 μsec/10 μsec, or 2% of the minimum value of T_0 this dynamic error should be removed easily during initial calibration of the V/F converter by correct adjustment of the value of t_x. However, any change in the propagation delay due to temperature changes would produce a linearity error in the circuit. Since one could expect this latter temperature effect to be $\ll 2\%$ of full-scale frequency, a linearity error of $<0.1\%$ of full-scale frequency should be achievable.

---

* The transient can be decreased by adding a small capacitor at the node of R_2-J_3. However, this will increase recovery time.

Table 7.1 SUMMARY OF ERRORS FOR EXAMPLE 7.6
($I_{REF} = 1$ mA, $25°C \leq T \leq 50°C$)

Parameter	Input Equivalent Current $f_0 = 10$ Hz	Input Equivalent Current $f_0 = 100$ kHz
Input Bias and Offset Currents		
ΔI_{B1}	8 pA	8 pA
$\Delta I_{D3}(\text{off})$	0.8 nA	0.4 nA
ΔI_{G3}	0.8 nA	0.4 nA
$\Delta V_{os1}/R_1$	6.5 pA	13 pA
Drift in V_{REF1}		
$\Delta V_{REF1}/R_2$	± 500 nA	± 500 nA
Drift in R_1, R_2	~ 0	~ 0
Drift in $r_{ON}(J_1–J_3)$	~ 0	~ 0
Input Current Noise		
(a) *In White Noise Region*[1] (amperes, rms)		
Due to $i_n(A1)$, $i_{n(J3)}$, etc.	$< 10^{-13}$	$< 10^{-13}$
(b) *Low-Frequency Region* [0.1 Hz–10 Hz (amperes, p–p)] $I_n(A_1)$	negl.	negl.
$E_n(A_1/R_1)$	0.7 nA	0.33 nA
$(E_{n(REF1)}/R_2)D^2$	—	—
Algebraic Current Offset Error	± 502 nA	± 501 nA
Percentage Current Offset Error	$\dfrac{\pm 500 \text{ nA}}{1 \text{ mA}} = 0.05\%$	
Multivibrator Frequency Drift		
$\dfrac{\Delta f_0}{f_0}$	1.25×10^{-3}	1.25×10^{-3}
Total Percentage Algebraic Error	0.175%	0.175%

1. Assumes noise sources are not correlated.
2. The duty-cycle D is 5 μsec/100 msec = 5×10^{-5} at 10 Hz. At full scale (100 kHz), the value is $D = 5$ μsec/10 μsec = 0.5. The noise of REF1 is gated into the input of A_1 over a 5 μsec period. Thus, high-frequency noise of REF1 would predominantly appear at the output of A_1, with low-frequency noise components of REF1 appearing like a dc offset to A_1 over the sampling period T_0. For a good discussion of this effect, see Ref. 7.18.

The V/F converter can easily be configured for frequency-to-voltage conversion by applying an differentiated input pulse to either the comparator or the monostable of Fig. 7.33(b), thereby producing an output pulse t_x to switch S_1. The resistor R of Fig. 7.33(b) is connected across the integration capacitor C_1 as illustrated in Fig. 7.35(a), so the reference current injects a controlled charge $Q = I_{REF}t_x$ once every cycle ($T_0 = 1/f_{IN}$) into the input of A_1, or an average input current of

$$I_{average} = \frac{Q}{T_0} = (I_{REF}t_x)f_{IN} \tag{7.39a}$$

Thus the output voltage is

$$V_{out} = -(I_{REF}t_x R)f_{IN} \tag{7.39b}$$

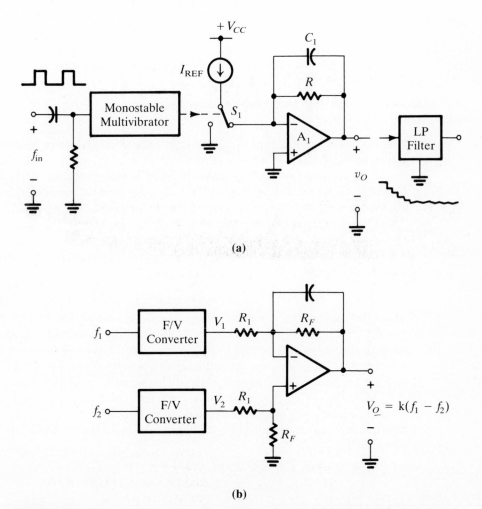

(a)

(b)

Figure 7.35 F/V converter: (a) configured from the charge-balance V/F converter of Fig. 7.33; (b) using an F/V converter to indicate the difference of two frequencies.

and therefore the input frequency has been converted to an output voltage. Since the ripple content at V_{out} is normally high, a lowpass filter usually follows the V/F conversion to smooth the signal. Of course, this filter will increase the conversion time of the overall F/V conversion process.

By using two F/V converters the output voltage of each can be summed using a differential amplifier, to produce an output voltage proportional to the difference of the input frequencies, as indicated in Fig. 7.35(b).

7.9 OP AMP MULTIVIBRATORS

The operational amplifier* can be used to obtain various pulse-generation circuits such as square-wave oscillators and single-pulse generators. The square-wave generator is in reality an astable multivibrator, often called a free-running multivibrator, whereas the single-pulse output circuit is a monostable multivibrator, often referred to as a 'one-shot' circuit. By careful control of the gain and frequency it is possible to shape the square-wave output of an astable multivibrator to obtain a sinusoidal oscillator. This technique will be explored in Section 7.10.

7.9.1 Astable (Free-Running) Multivibrators and Waveform Generators

Perhaps the most standard single-op-amp astable multivibrator circuit is that shown in Fig. 7.36(a). In its most basic form the output-amplitude-limiting Zener diodes are removed and the op amp is allowed to swing between its positive and negative output-saturation limits, but if a more precise amplitude control is required some form of output-signal limiting is demanded. The R_A resistors in Fig. 7.36(a) may be required if the differential input voltage exceeds the manufacturer's rating, otherwise they are not needed. The waveforms for the square-wave oscillator are indicated in Fig. 7.36(b). Assume that the output signal is clamped at its positive limit of

$$+V_Z = V_{Z2} + V_{D1} \tag{7.40a}$$

Thus the capacitor C_1 will be charging toward $+V_Z$ with a time constant $\tau = R_1 C_1$. When the voltage across C_1 exceeds the threshold voltage at the noninverting input of A_1, equal to βV_Z [where β is the positive feedback factor of $\beta = R_2/(R_2 + R_3)$], then the inverting input has become more positive than βV_Z and the output signal of A_1 will drive to its negative saturation limit of $V_O = -V_Z = -(V_{Z1} + V_{D2})$. The capacitor C_1 will now charge toward $-V_Z$, and once again the op amp will trigger when the negative threshold of $-\beta V_Z$ is crossed. The equation for v_1 can be obtained by starting at $v_1 = -\beta V_Z$ (at $t = 0$) so that over the period of $0 \leq t \leq T/2$

$$v_1(t) = -\beta V_Z + (1 + \beta)V_Z[1 - e^{-(t/R_1 C)}] \tag{7.40b}$$

---

* In the following multivibrator circuits one could use comparators (such as the LM311) as well, particularly if faster transition times between states are required.

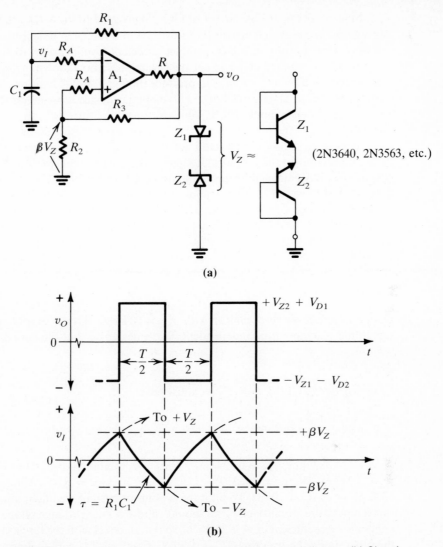

Figure 7.36 (a) A standard single-op-amp astable multivibrator. (b) Signal waveforms.

and since the half-cycle is completed when $v_1(t = T/2) = +\beta V_Z$,

$$+\beta V_Z = v_1\left(t = \frac{T}{2}\right) = -\beta V_Z + (1 + \beta)V_Z[1 - e^{-(T/2R_1C)}] \qquad \textbf{(7.40c)}$$

Solving for the period T gives the result

$$T = \frac{1}{f_{osc}} = 2R_1C \ln\left(\frac{1 + \beta}{1 - \beta}\right) = 2R_1C \ln\left[1 + 2\left(\frac{R_2}{R_3}\right)\right] \qquad \textbf{(7.40d)}$$

where the frequency of oscillation is $f_{osc} = 1/T$.

In general, the astable circuit of Fig. 7.36(a) is useful to $\sim GB/10$. For higher frequencies the op amp limitations of slew rate and recovery time from saturation will distort the output signal, or produce sufficient nonlinearities to stop oscillation. Usually, it is much better to use the emitter-base breakdown of a small-signal high-frequency bipolar transistor to produce the Zener-diode limiting circuit, since the total depletion-layer capacitance of the bipolar device is much less than that of a commercial Zener diode. An IC comparator with controlled output saturation can also be used to advantage in place of the op amp A_1. Further, the saturation of the output of A_1 can be eliminated if an op amp having available a compensation terminal previous to the output unity-gain stage is used; here, the Z_1–Z_2 clamping network can be connected between the compensation terminal and ground to limit the output-voltage swing. This technique was demonstrated earlier in the comparator circuit of Fig. 7.2(c) using an LM748 op amp. Other op amps such as the LM101, HA2625 and NE5534 may also be used with this technique.

EXAMPLE 7.7

Design a square-wave oscillator with $f_{\text{osc}} = 50$ kHz, and an output ± 10 V p-p signal that is temperature independent. Use a design so that the period $T = R_1 C$.

Solution
From Eq. 7.40(d) for $T = R_1 C_1$ we must have

$$2 \ln\left(\frac{1 + \beta}{1 - \beta}\right) = 2 \ln(e^{1/2}) = 2 \ln(1.6487)$$

or $\beta = 1/4.083$ and $R_2 = 0.3244 R_3$. Thus, we might choose $R_3 = 10$ kΩ and $R_2 = 3.24$ kΩ. We now need $T = 1/50$ kHz $= 20$ μsec $= R_1 C_1$. Choosing $C_1 = 1000$ pF gives $R_1 = 20$ kΩ. To limit the A_1 output current we might use $R = 1$ kΩ. For temperature stability of V_Z we should choose a Zener-diode voltage that has a temperature coefficient of $\sim +2$mV/°C, so that in series with the forward voltage of the other diode the resulting TC is $+2$mV/°C $- 2$mV/°C ≈ 0. A Zener voltage of 5.2–5.6 V is near the desired TC. Since RF transistors have reverse emitter-base breakdown voltages near 5–6 V, and in particular an inexpensive 2N3563 or 2N3640 device has $V_Z \approx 5.4$ V, either of these devices would be a good choice. Thus, the output clamping action would occur at approximately $\pm (5.4$ V $+ 0.6$ V$) = \pm 6$ V. To increase the output to ± 10 V we would need to follow the v_o voltage of ± 6 V by an op amp A_2 with a gain of 10 V/6 V or 1.67.

The choice of an op amp is determined by dc offsets and SR as well as GB. Since the voltage v_1 triggers at $\beta V_{O1} = \pm 1.47$ V, then dc offsets are not critically important since signal levels are high. We need an SR sufficient to permit an output voltage change for A_1 of $\pm V_O(\text{sat})$ in less than $T/2$ seconds, or less than 10 μsec. Hence, for A_1 we need $SR > 28$ V/10 μsec $= 2.8$ V/μsec. Also, the output saturation requirements for A_1 demand a recovery from saturation in much less than $T/2$, or

10 μsec. Some good choices for A_1 might be the LF357 (SR $= 40$ V/μsec), the MC34080 (SR $= 50$ V/μsec), the TL071 (SR $= 13$ V/μsec), the NE5534 (SR $= 13$ V/μsec), or the HA2540 (SR $= 400$ V/μsec). For the second op amp, similar SR conditions apply, except the op amp must be frequency stable for a feedback factor of $1/1.67$.

The astable multivibrator circuit of Fig. 7.36(a) could also be used as a triangular-wave generator if the voltage v_1 had a more constant linear slope. To obtain a constant slope it is necessary to charge (or discharge) the capacitor C_1 with a constant current. A circuit that will accomplish this is indicated in Fig. 7.37(a) and the associated waveforms in Fig. 7.37(b). When the output voltage of A_1 is at its positive saturation value, diode D_1 is reverse biased while D_2 is forward biased. Thus Q_1 will furnish a positive charging current of $\sim(V_{Z3} - V_{BE1})/R_4$ to C_1, while I_{C2} will be zero if R_8 is chosen to provide a reverse-bias voltage at the emitter of Q_2. When v_1 reaches the threshold voltage of $+\beta V_Z$ the output of A_1 switches low, reverse biasing D_2 (and forward biasing D_1) thus charging C_1 with a negative current of $\sim(V_{Z4} - V_{BE2})/R_5$. When the threshold voltage of $-\beta V_Z$ is reached the output voltage v_O switches back to its positive state, thus starting a new cycle. The pulse periods for each cycle are

$$T_1 = \frac{\Delta v_1 C_1}{I_{C1}} \qquad T_2 = \frac{\Delta v_1 C_1}{I_{C2}} \tag{7.41a}$$

and thus the total period T is given by

$$T = T_1 + T_2 = \Delta v_1 C_1 \left(\frac{1}{I_{C1}} + \frac{1}{I_{C2}} \right) \tag{7.41b}$$

Substituting expressions for I_{C1}, I_{C2}, Δv_1 and β

$$T \approx \frac{2V_Z R_2 C_1}{R_2 + R_3} \left(\frac{R_4}{V_{Z3} - V_{BE1}} + \frac{R_5}{V_{Z4} - V_{BE2}} \right) \tag{7.41c}$$

■ **Exercise 7.5**

If V_Z is chosen as ± 10 V, $R_2 = R_3 = 10$ kΩ, $R = 500$ Ω, $C_1 = 1000$ pF, $R_7 = R_8 = 13$ kΩ, $R_6 = 3.9$ kΩ, $R_4 = R_5 = 4.53$ kΩ, $Z_3 = Z_4 = 5.1$ V and $A_1 =$ LF351, sketch the voltage waveforms for v_1 and v_O of Fig. 7.37(b) and find the oscillation frequency f_{osc}. Assume Q_1 and Q_2, as well as D_1 and D_2, are standard small-signal devices.

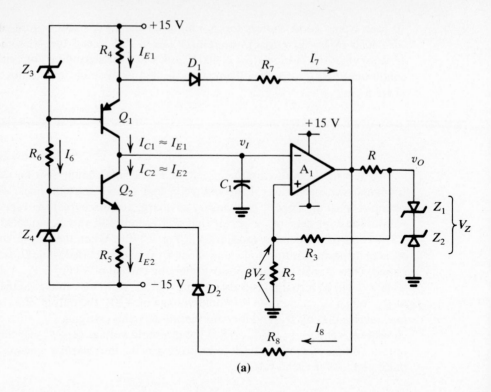

(a)

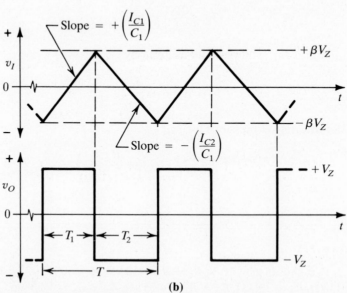

(b)

Figure 7.37 (a) A modification of the astable circuit to obtain a triangular-wave output. (b) Waveforms at v_1 and v_O.

A function-generation circuit with both square-wave and triangular-wave outputs can also be obtained using two op amps, thereby eliminating the Q_1-Q_2 current source of Fig. 7.37(a). The basic concept is illustrated by A_1 and A_2 in Fig. 7.38 [other versions can be found in Refs. 7.1 (Chapter 3), 7.2 (Chapter 10), and 7.4(a) (Chapter 9)]. The other elements (A_3-A_5) in Fig. 7.38(a) illustrate additional circuitry necessary to obtain a complete function generator having adjustable-output-amplitude sine, square-wave, and triangular-wave signals. The sine-shaping network (A_5) could be obtained using a diode function-generation circuit such as that of Fig. P7.8, or a commercial IC such as the AD639 or BB4302 function modules. Furthermore, it is possible to obtain a complete function-generator chip, operable over a frequency range from < 1 Hz to 100 kHz, using the XR-2206 or the ICL8038 integrated circuits.

The circuit of Fig. 7.38(a) has two essential components, A_1 connected as a Schmitt-comparator circuit and A_2 connected as an integrator. The output of A_1 is a square-wave pulse, which is integrated by A_2 to produce a constant-slope triangular wave. The signal v_{O1} is summed with the triangular waveform v_{O2} to produce a signal v_N that is compared against the 0 V (ground) reference at the inverting input of A_1. For example, suppose at some time $t = 0$ the signal v_{O1} has just switched to $+V_Z$. The attenuated voltage v_x, equal to αV_Z (where $0 < \alpha \le 1$), produces a constant current that is integrated by C to give an output voltage

$$v_{O2}(t) = -\frac{\alpha V_Z t}{R_4 C} + V_{O2}(t = 0) \tag{7.42a}$$

where $V_{O2}(t = 0)$ is the initial voltage across C at time $t = 0$. The signal at the noninverting input of A_1 by superposition, is therefore

$$v_N(t) = V_Z \left(\frac{R_1}{R_1 + R_2} \right) - \left[\frac{\alpha V_Z t}{R_4 C} - V_{O2}(t = 0) \right] \left(\frac{R_2}{R_1 + R_2} \right) \tag{7.42b}$$

Since $R_1 = R_2$ the equation reduces to

$$v_N(t) = \frac{V_Z}{2} \left(1 - \frac{\alpha t}{R_4 C} \right) + \frac{V_{O2}(t = 0)}{2} \tag{7.42c}$$

Now, when $v_N(t) = 0^+$ the A_1 comparator will change state, switching to $v_{O1} = -V_Z$. This will occur when $t = T/2$, or from Eq. 7.42(c) we can solve for $V_{O2}(t = 0)$, which is

$$V_{O2}(t = 0) = -V_Z \left[1 - \frac{\alpha T}{2 R_4 C} \right] \tag{7.42d}$$

Similarly, by substituting Eq. 7.42(d) into Eq. 7.42(a) we can obtain the value of v_{O2} at the end of the half-period

$$v_{O2}\left(t = \frac{T}{2} \right) = -V_Z \tag{7.42e}$$

Since we have a symmetrical square wave, the output voltage v_{O2} at $t = T$ must be $+V_Z$ volts, which also must be equal to $V_{O2}(t = 0)$, $V_{O2}(t = 2T)$, etc. The period T

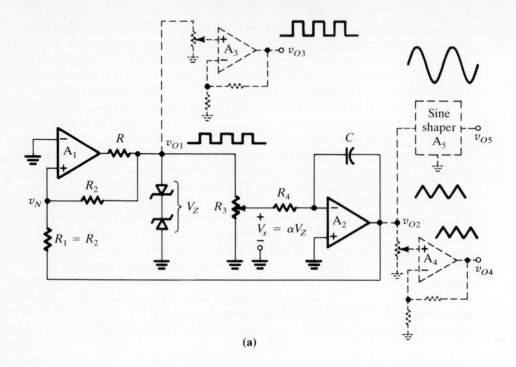

(a)

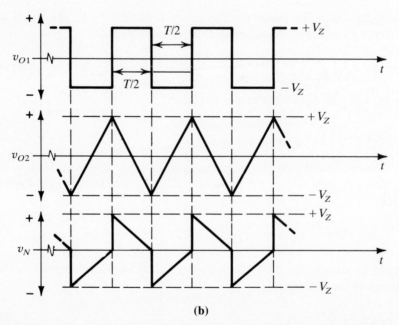

(b)

Figure 7.38 An op amp function generator: (a) circuit diagram; (b) waveforms.

can be obtained from the waveform for the triangular wave in Fig. 7.38(b). From Eq. 7.42(a), the slope must be

$$\frac{\Delta v_{O2}(t)}{\Delta t} = \left|\frac{\alpha V_Z}{R_4 C}\right| = \left|\frac{2V_Z}{T/2}\right|$$

So the period T is

$$T = \frac{4R_4 C}{\alpha} \tag{7.43a}$$

and the oscillation frequency is

$$f_{\text{osc}} = \frac{1}{T} = \frac{\alpha}{4R_4 C} \tag{7.43b}$$

Hence, the frequency of the signal generator can be adjusted very simply by the R_3 potentiometer. For a large range of adjustment, it is usually preferable to adjust R_4 and C as well, in decade steps, using the R_3 adjustment to change frequency within a decade.

7.9.2 Monostable (One-Shot) Circuits

A monostable multivibrator requires an input trigger pulse, and produces an output pulse with a precise pulse width T. One of the simplest possible configurations for such a circuit is shown in Fig. 7.39, with the associated waveforms. In the quiescent state the voltage v_1 at the inverting input of the op amp is made slightly positive ($\sim +0.5$ V for the circuit values indicated in the figure). Thus the output of A_1 will be at the negative limit of $-V_Z$ and v_N will be at ground potential. If a negative trigger pulse of amplitude $>v_1(>0.5$ V) is now applied at v_1 the output of A_1 will switch positive and the transition will couple through C driving v_N to $+2V_Z$. When the trigger pulse decays the positive v_N value will keep $v_O = +V_Z$. The voltage v_N will now decay exponentially toward ground with a time constant $\tau = RC$ as capacitor C charges toward $+V_Z$. When the voltage v_N reaches the threshold voltage of v_1 [$\sim +0.5$ V in Fig. 7.39(a)] the output voltage v_O will switch to $-V_Z$, bringing diode D_1 into conduction, rapidly charging C to the $-V_Z$ potential, and returning the circuit to its initial quiescent state. The equation for v_N during the pulse period from t_0 to $t_0 + T$ is

$$v_N(t) = 2V_Z e^{-(t-t_0/RC)} \tag{7.44a}$$

The voltage $v_N(t)$ is equal to V_1 at $t = t_0 + T$, hence the period of the one-shot circuit is

$$T = RC \ln\left(\frac{2V_Z}{V_1}\right) \tag{7.44b}$$

where $V_1 = V_B[R_1/(R_1 + R_2)]$ in Fig. 7.39(a). For the circuit values indicated in Fig. 7.39 the pulse width is equal to 37 μsec. There can be a problem with this circuit if the differential-input-voltage range of op amp A_1 is $<2V_Z = 20$ V. If this is

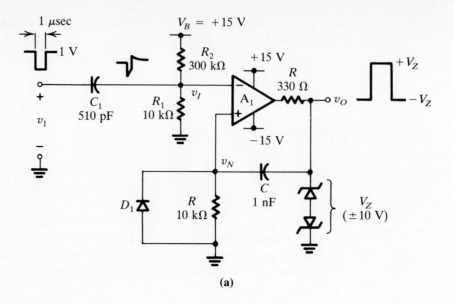

(a)

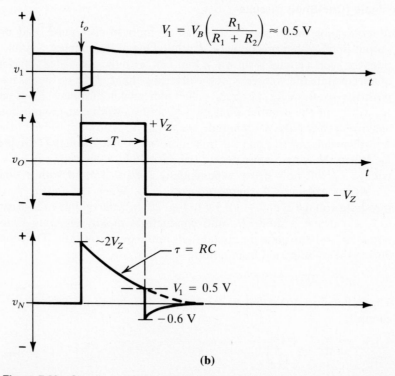

(b)

Figure 7.39 Simple op amp monostable multivibrator: (a) circuit; (b) waveforms.

the case one should add resistors in series with both input terminals, similar to those illustrated by R_A in Fig. 7.36(a). Further, one should choose R_1 and R_2 in Fig. 7.39(a) so that the time constant $R_1 \| R_2 C_1 \ll RC$. It is also important that the amplitude of $v_I < v_Z$ to prohibit false triggering.

Another monostable circuit is shown in Fig. 7.40 with its associated waveforms. In the quiescent state the output of A_1 is low $(-V_Z)$ since FET J_1 is not conducting. If a positive trigger pulse of amplitude $v_t \geq V_B$ is applied the FET switch J_1 will go ON, dumping the charge on capacitor C (it is important that the

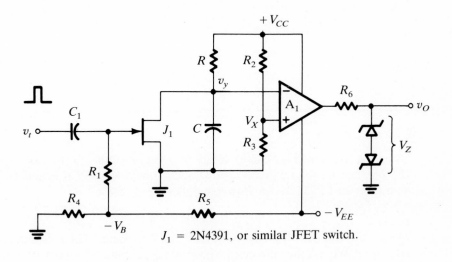

J_1 = 2N4391, or similar JFET switch.

(a)

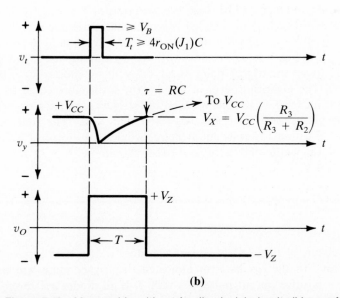

(b)

Figure 7.40 Monostable without feedback: (a) circuit; (b) waveforms.

trigger pulse have sufficient pulse width $T_t \geq 4r_{ON}C$ to allow complete discharge of C). The capacitor will now recharge toward V_{CC} until the threshold voltage $V_X = V_{CC} R_3/(R_3 + R_2)$ is reached. At this point v_O will switch back to its original state at $v_O = -V_Z$. Notice that no feedback is used in the circuit, although some Schmitt-feedback action could certainly be used to enhance transition time. The equation for v_Y during the recharge time is (assuming $r_{ON(J1)} \ll R$)

$$v_Y = V_{CC}[1 - e^{-(t/RC)}]$$ (7.45a)

and since the charging cycle ends when $v_Y = V_X$ at $t = T$, the pulse width T is

$$T = RC \ln\left(1 + \frac{R_3}{R_2}\right)$$ (7.45b)

Notice that changes in the power supply voltage V_{CC} have no effect on the pulse width T.

EXAMPLE 7.8

Using the circuit of Fig. 7.40(a) design for a pulse width $T = 10$ μsec. A 2N4861 JFET switch having $r_{ON}(\text{max}) = 60\ \Omega$ and $V_p(\text{max}) = -4$ V is available. The op amp A_1 is an LF357 device. Power supplies are ± 15 V.

Solution

The reverse voltage $-V_B$ must be at least -4 V to ensure that J_1 is initially in the OFF state. We will therefore need a positive trigger pulse of at least 4 V amplitude. The LF357 is a JFET input device, with bias currents of $I_B(\text{max}) = 50$ pA, hence resistors R_1, R_2 and R_3 could be large. We need resistor $R \gg r_{ON}(J_1)$. Therefore, let us choose $R > 10^3 r_{ON}(J_1)$, or > 60 kΩ. Since the differential-input voltage for A_1 is specified as ± 30 V (max) by the manufacturer, we will not need to add protection resistors R_A [see Fig. 7.36(a)] in series with the op amp inputs. Let us choose the ratio R_3/R_2 to set the trigger point V_X at $+5$ V; if we choose $R_3 = 10$ kΩ then $R_2 = 20$ kΩ. The logarithm term in Eq. 7.45(b) is therefore equal to $\ln(1.5)$, or 0.405. Therefore, for $T = 10$ μsec, we need $RC = 24.66$ μsec. If a convenient choice of $C = 240$ pF is used, then $R = 100$ kΩ should work. The time required to discharge C to within 1% of its initial charge would be $\tau = 5\ r_{ON}(J_1)\ C = 72$ nsec. Thus the pulse width of the trigger pulse should be $T_t \geq 70$ nsec, with the amplitude ≥ 4 V.

The circuit of Fig. 7.41 is one of the most widely used types of one-shot multivibrators. In the circuit form indicated the trigger pulse will be positive, producing a positive output pulse of width T. If all diodes are reversed, then a negative output pulse is produced requiring a negative input trigger pulse. The

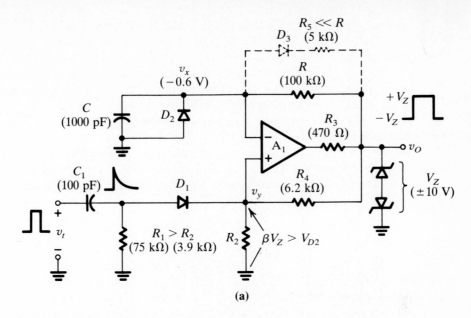

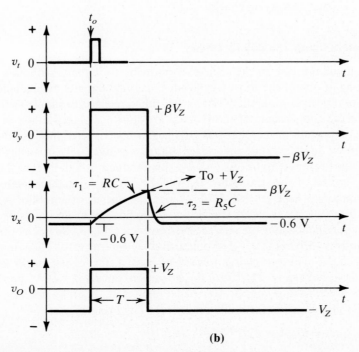

Figure 7.41 A widely used monostable circuit producing a positive output pulse: (a) circuit; (b) waveforms.

feedback factor β is such that βV_Z is $> V_{D2}$ or (with the values indicated in the circuit) $\beta V_Z \approx \pm 10$ V $(3.9$ k$\Omega/10.1$ k$\Omega) = \pm 3.9$ V in the quiescent state. Since the inverting input of A_1 is clamped at $v_X = V_{D2} \approx -0.6$ V the output of A_1 remains fixed at $-V_Z$. If a positive trigger pulse v_t of amplitude sufficient to raise v_Y above the v_X potential is applied [using the circuit values indicated in Fig. 7.41(a), we would need $V_t > 3.3$ V], then the output voltage will switch positive to $+V_Z$ and $v_Y = +\beta V_Z$. The capacitor C will now charge (through R) toward $+V_Z$. When the threshold voltage of $+\beta V_Z$ is reached the circuit flips back to its original state. If the D_3–R_5 network is added in parallel with R, when v_O swings back to $-V_Z$ diode D_3 will conduct, and the recovery time of C is decreased to approximately $5R_5 C$.

The equation for the charging time of C during the pulse period T is

$$v_X \approx -0.6 \text{ V} + (V_Z + 0.6 \text{ V})[1 - e^{-(t/RC)}] \tag{7.46a}$$

Since $v_X = \beta V_Z = V_Z R_2/(R_2 + R_4)$ at $t = T$ the pulse-width equation is

$$T = RC \ln\left[\left(1 + \frac{0.6 \text{ V}}{V_Z}\right)\left(1 + \frac{R_2}{R_4}\right)\right] \tag{7.46b}$$

Using circuit values specified in Fig. 7.41(a) the pulse width would be $T = 55$ μsec. The recovery time of the capacitor C at the end of the pulse period T would be approximately $5R_5 C$ or 25 μsec.

7.9.3 Multivibrators Using The 555 IC Timer

We should not dismiss the subject of multivibrator circuits without at least briefly looking at one of the most significant integrated circuits available for astable or monostable operation, the NE555 timer (often referred to simply as the **555 timer**). The basic components of the IC chip are shown within the box of Fig. 7.42(a), which illustrates the connections for a negatively triggered monostable multivibrator. In the quiescent state the trigger voltage v_t is high ($+V_{CC}$) causing the output of the comparator A_2 to be low (~ 0 V); this produces a high level at the $\bar{Q}$ output of the flip-flop. Thus, transistor Q_1 will be saturated and capacitor C will be discharged to near ground. With $\bar{Q}$ high the output of amplifier A_3 will be low (~ 0 V). Now, if a negative trigger pulse is applied of magnitude sufficient to drop the input signal below the reference value of $A_2(< V_{CC}/3)$, then the output of A_2 will go positive, driving $\bar{Q}$ low and unlatching the Q_1 transistor (also driving v_o high). Capacitor C will thus charge toward V_{CC} with a time constant $\tau = RC$. When the threshold voltage ($\sim 2V_{CC}/3$) of A_1 is reached, the output of A_1 goes high, which resets the flip-flop output ($\bar{Q}$) to a high state, thereby turning Q_1 on and discharging C. Since the equation for v_X is [ignoring V_{CE}(sat) of Q_1]

$$v_X(t) \approx V_{CC}[1 - e^{-(t/RC)}] \tag{7.47a}$$

and the pulse period T occurs when $v_X = 2V_{CC}/3$, the equation for T is obtained as

$$T \approx RC \ln 3 = 1.1 \, RC \tag{7.47b}$$

In the monostable configuration the practical range of pulse widths obtainable for the 555 is between 1 μsec and several seconds. The temperature stability of the

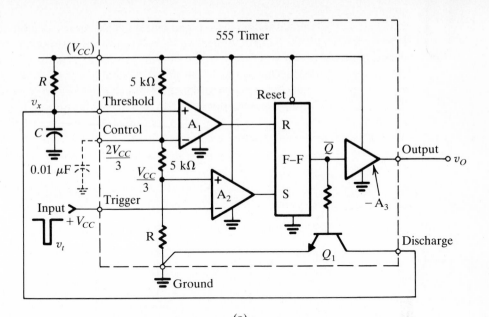

(a)

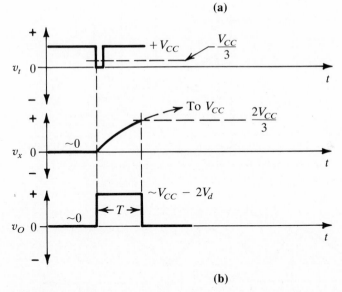

(b)

Figure 7.42 (a) The 555 timer connected as a monostable multivibrator.
(b) Waveforms.

pulse width T is excellent, typically 50 ppm/°C. The propagation delay between v_t and v_O is in the 100-200 nsec range.

The 555 circuit will operate with power-supply voltages between +4.5 V and +18 V, but was specifically designed for +5 V operation. For this latter case the output voltage levels are TTL compatible, with a low state of 0.25 V (max), and a high state of 3.3 V (typ), or 2.75 V (min). Furthermore, the output circuitry can either sink or source up to 200 mA of load current. This latter capability has also led to a problem with the basic design—a high-current transient pulse (> 300 mA) drawn from the power supply during an output transition. This problem requires close capacitive decoupling at the V_{CC} terminal. Several newer CMOS versions of the 555 timer circuit are also available; these circuits operate with significantly lower quiescent power, and furthermore do not have the output high-current transient.

The 555 timer may also be configured as an astable multivibrator, with the circuit connections indicated in Fig. 7.43. In this mode of operation the capacitor C

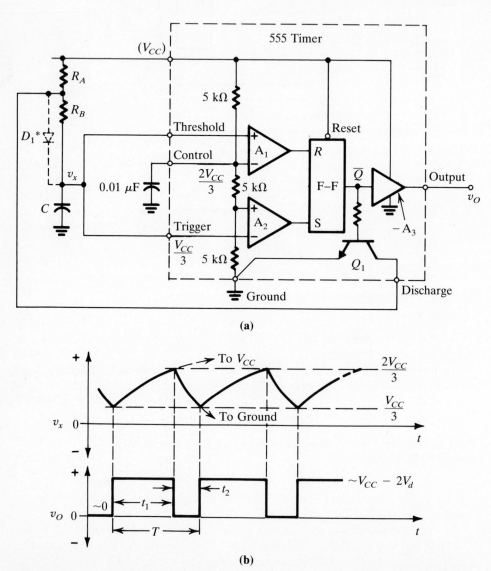

(a)

(b)

Figure 7.43 (a) The astable multivibrator connection for the 555 timer. (b) Waveforms.

charges toward V_{CC} with a time constant $\tau = (R_A + R_B)C$ until the threshold voltage of A_1 is reached ($\sim 2V_{CC}/3$). At this value comparator A_1 will switch, causing the output $\bar{Q}$ to go high, which then saturates Q_1 and discharges C back toward ground with a time constant [ignoring collector ohmic resistance and V_{CE}(sat) of Q_1] of $\tau_2 = R_B C$. Now comparator A_2 will trigger when the voltage v_X reaches the threshold level of $V_{CC}/3$. The output of the flip-flop will then drive low, turning off Q_1 and resulting in v_X again moving toward V_{CC}. The resulting timing equations for periods t_1, t_2 and T are*

$$t_1 = 0.69\,(R_A + R_B)C$$

$$t_2 = 0.69\,R_B C \qquad\qquad\qquad \text{(7.48a)}$$

$$T = t_1 + t_2 = 0.69\,(R_A + 2R_B)C$$

with the oscillation frequency equal to

$$f_{osc} = \frac{1}{T} = \frac{1.44}{(R_A + 2R_B)C} \qquad\qquad \text{(7.48b)}$$

The standard bipolar-transistor 555 timer is capable of $f_{osc} \le 500\,\text{kHz}$, with a temperature stability approaching 150 ppm/°C. A greatly improved version in CMOS design exists—the TLC555, manufactured by Texas Instruments, Inc.—that is capable of $f_{osc} \le 2\,\text{MHz}$, with significantly less propagation delay. Furthermore, due to the much higher input impedance, both astable and mono-stable configurations can use much larger timing resistors than the standard 555 bipolar circuit.

7.10 SINE-WAVE OSCILLATORS

The sinusoidal oscillator could have been considered along with the astable multivibrator, since both are free-running oscillators. However, the astable circuit produces an output square-wave (or triangular-wave) signal that is inherently limited by saturation of the output stage of the op amp. The sine-wave oscillator *must not* have output saturation limiting, otherwise the spectral purity of the sinusoid is poor. The basic principle that controls all sinusoidal oscillators is the **Barkhausen Criterion**, which can be simply stated as follows:

> The frequency at which a sinusoidal oscillator will operate is the frequency at which the total phase shift around the loop is zero (or $2\pi n$ radians, where $n = 0, 1, 2, \ldots$). Furthermore, oscillations will not be sustained if the magnitude of the loop gain is <1.

---

* As indicated in Fig. 7.43(a), if a 50% duty cycle is desired, add diode D_1 and choose $R_A = R_B = R$. Thus, diode D_1 will bypass R_B on the positive charging cycle so that $t_1 \approx 0.69\,RC$. When Q_1 saturates and pulls charge from C during t_2 the diode D_1 will reverse bias, so $t_2 = 0.69\,RC$ as well.

Stated in terms of the loop transmission we thus have the two conditions for oscillation

$$|-T(j\omega)| = 1 \qquad\qquad\qquad\qquad\qquad \textbf{(7.49a)}$$

$$\angle -T(j\omega) = 0° \qquad\qquad\qquad\qquad\qquad \textbf{(7.49b)}$$

We will examine three cases of a sinusoidal oscillator. The first case is a classic circuit that originated with vacuum-tube amplifiers more than 40 years ago, the Wein-bridge audio oscillator, whose basic circuit configuration, using a single op amp, is shown in Fig. 7.44(a). Basically, a bridge arrangement is formed between R_1, R_2 and the RC networks, with the op amp A_1 sampling the voltage at the

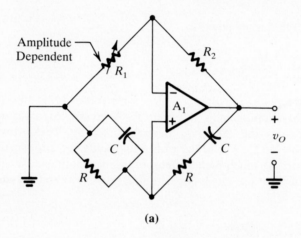

(a)

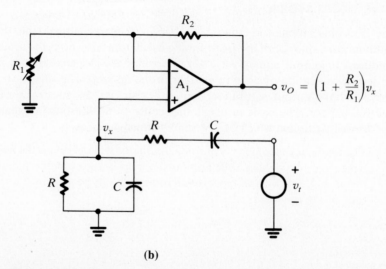

(b)

Figure 7.44 The Wein-bridge sinusoidal oscillator: (a) basic circuit; (b) circuit for obtaining $T(j\omega)$.

midpoints of the bridge. The crucial requirement is that the resistors and capacitors in the positive-feedback path to the noninverting input (point v_X) be equal. The equation for the loop transmission for the circuit of Fig. 7.44 is obtained by solving for v_X and v_O with the loop opened. Ignoring loading on the output we have, in the frequency domain,

$$v_X(j\omega) = \frac{\dfrac{R}{1 + j\omega RC}(v_t)}{\dfrac{R}{1 + j\omega RC} + R + \dfrac{1}{j\omega C}} \tag{7.50a}$$

and since $v_O = (1 + R_2/R_1)v_X$ the loop transmission is

$$-T(j\omega) = \frac{v_O}{v_t} = \left(1 + \frac{R_2}{R_1}\right)\left[\frac{1}{3 + j\left(\omega RC - \dfrac{1}{\omega RC}\right)}\right] \tag{7.50b}$$

Applying the two conditions of Eqs. (7.49) we obtain the oscillation frequency

$$\omega_{\text{osc}} = \frac{1}{RC} \tag{7.50c}$$

and the gain requirement that

$$\left(1 + \frac{R_2}{R_1}\right)\left(\frac{1}{3}\right) = 1 \tag{7.50d}$$

or that the closed-loop gain must be equal to 3, hence $R_2 = 2R_1$.

To vary the frequency it is necessary to change both resistors R and capacitors C simultaneously, as described in Fig. 7.45(a), which also shows the use of an incandescent lamp (L_1) to control the output amplitude, and therefore the frequency purity. The resistance of the lamp is inversely proportional to current through the lamp. Thus, if v_O increases in amplitude the lamp resistance decreases, which reduces the gain and output amplitude. It is also possible to use a PTC (positive-temperature-coefficient) resistor instead of L_1. The circuit in Fig. 7.45(b) uses a different technique to stabilize the output amplitude by utilizing a JFET in an automatic-gain-control (AGC) loop. When the circuit is turned on initially the JFET J_1 is operating with $V_{GS} = 0$ V, and has its channel resistance at a minimum value of $r_{ON} \leq 100 \ \Omega$. The overall loop transmission is thus > 1, since the gain from the output to the inverting input of the op amp is equal to 3.11. As the output oscillation builds up, a point is reached where the negative swing at v_O of the sine wave will cause $D_1 + V_z$ to conduct, thus driving the gate voltage of J_1 negative, increasing r_{ON} of the JFET and reducing the gain. A stable output amplitude is reached when the gain due to the R_1–R_2 network is exactly 3.0.

The previous analysis for the Wein-bridge oscillator circuit of Fig. 7.44 was based on an ideal op amp, with gain given by $v_O = (1 + R_2/R_1)v_X$. The effect of the finite gain-bandwidth product GB for the op amp can be determined in a way

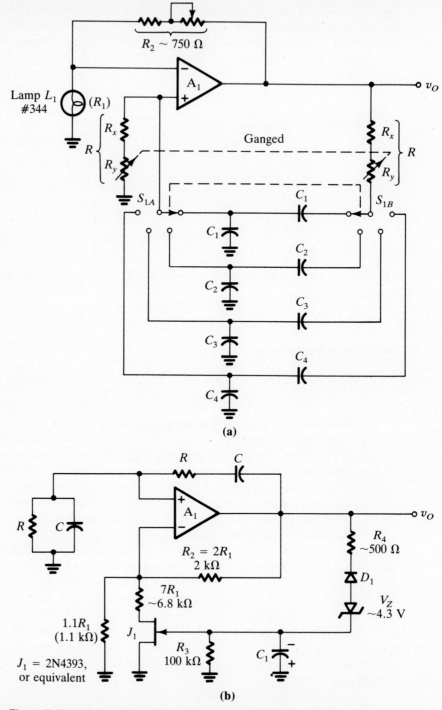

(a)

(b)

Figure 7.45 (a) A practical Wein bridge oscillator with amplitude control and frequency adjustment. (b) An AGC control using a JFET.

analogous to that used in active filters in Chapter 6, where the open-loop gain was assumed to be dominated by a single-pole response, as given earlier in Eq. (2.1)

$$A(s) = \frac{A_0\omega_0}{s + \omega_0} = \frac{GB}{s + \left(\dfrac{GB}{A_0}\right)}$$

For the noninverting gain connection of Fig. 7.44(b) the loop transmission of Eq. 7.50(b) now becomes [using Eq. (6.65)]

$$-T(j\omega) = \left(\frac{GB}{j\omega + \dfrac{GB}{K_0}}\right)\left[\frac{1}{3 + j\left(\omega RC - \dfrac{1}{\omega RC}\right)}\right] \qquad (7.50e)$$

where K_0 is equal to the ideal gain $(1 + R_2/R_1)$. Separating Eq. (7.50e) into real and imaginary parts and reducing gives

$$-T(j\omega) = \frac{K_0}{\left[3 + \dfrac{K_0}{GB}\left(\dfrac{1}{RC} - \omega^2 RC\right)\right] + j\left[\omega\left(RC + \dfrac{3K_0}{GB}\right) - \dfrac{1}{\omega RC}\right]} \qquad (7.50f)$$

Thus, applying the Barkhausen criterion of Eq. (7.49) we obtain the oscillation frequency now as

$$\omega_{\text{osc}} = \frac{1}{RC\left[1 + \dfrac{3K_0}{GB(RC)}\right]^{1/2}} \qquad (7.50g)$$

or if we define the *ideal* oscillation frequency as that of Eq. (7.50c), $\omega_{\text{osc}}(\text{ideal}) = 1/RC$, where the op amp is assumed ideal, then Eq. (7.50g) can then be written as

$$\omega_{\text{osc}} = \frac{\omega_{\text{osc}}(\text{ideal})}{\left[1 + \left(\dfrac{3K_0}{GB}\right)\omega_{\text{osc}}(\text{ideal})\right]^{1/2}} \qquad (7.50h)$$

Hence, the *actual* oscillation frequency will be *less* than the ideal value. Thus, for a shift in oscillation frequency of $\leq 10\%$ due to finite GB, the requirement is from Eq. (7.50h)

$$GB \geq 14.3\left(\frac{R_2}{R_1}\right)\omega_{\text{osc}}(\text{ideal}) \qquad (7.50j)$$

Similarly, the requirement that $|-T(j\omega)| = 1$ demands that the real part of Eq. (7.50f) has

$$\left[3 + \frac{K_0}{GB}\left(\frac{1}{RC} - \omega_{\text{osc}}^2 RC\right)\right] = K_0 = 1 + \frac{R_2}{R_1} \qquad (7.50k)$$

Substituting the defining Eq. (7.50c) for ω_{osc} and reducing to solve for the gain K_0 gives

$$K_0 = \left(1 + \frac{R_2}{R_1}\right) = \frac{3}{1 - \dfrac{\omega_{osc}(\text{ideal})}{GB}\left\{1 - \left[\dfrac{\omega_{osc}}{\omega_{os}(\text{ideal})}\right]^2\right\}} \tag{7.50l}$$

Therefore, we see that the required gain K_0 must be slightly *greater* than the ideal value of 3.0. For a shift in gain of $\leq 10\%$, Eq. (7.50l) would require that

$$GB \geq 6.4\omega_{osc}(\text{ideal}) \tag{7.50m}$$

Since the requirement of Eq. (7.50m) is not nearly as stringent as the oscillation frequency requirement of Eq. (7.50j), the determining result for $\leq 10\%$ shift in either the ideal oscillation frequency, or the ideal gain of 3 would be

$$GB \geq 43\omega_{osc}(\text{ideal}) \tag{7.50n}$$

The second sine-wave generator we shall consider is the phase-shift oscillator, shown in Fig. 7.46(a). Opening the circuit at v_0 and obtaining the loop transmission $T(s)$ around the loop gives

$$-T(s) = \frac{s^3 R_1 R^2 C^2}{1 + s4RC + s^2 3R^2 C^2} \tag{7.51a}$$

If we replace s by $j\omega$ in Eq. 7.51(a) and separate into real and imaginary parts, for oscillations to occur the imaginary part of the equation must be zero. This leads to an oscillation frequency

$$f_{osc} = \frac{1}{2\pi RC\sqrt{3}} \tag{7.51b}$$

and for $|T(j\omega)| = 1$, the resistor R_1 must be chosen as

$$R_1 = 12R \tag{7.51c}$$

An amplitude stabilization circuit [Ref. 7.4(a), p. 393] for the phase-shift oscillator is included in Fig. 7.46(b), where the "soft-limiter" circuit of Fig. 7.3 is used. Also shown in Fig. 7.46(b) is another output obtained from point v_X in the circuit. Since the gain relation between v_0 and v_X in Fig. 7.46(a) is

$$\frac{v_0}{v_X} = -sR_1C \tag{7.52a}$$

then in the frequency domain

$$v_x(j\omega) = -\frac{v_0(j\omega)}{j\omega R_1 C} \tag{7.52b}$$

or substituting the relations of Eqs. 7.51(b) and (c), in phasor notation at $\omega = \omega_{osc}$,

$$\hat{V}_X = V_0\left(\frac{\sqrt{3}}{12}\right)\angle 90° \tag{7.52c}$$

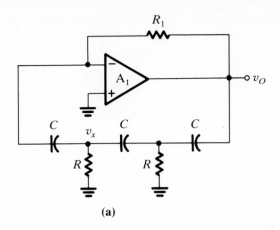

(a)

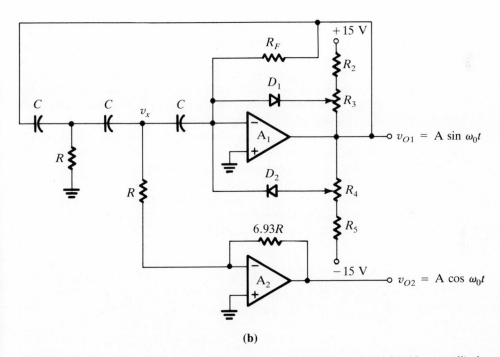

(b)

Figure 7.46 The phase-shift sinusoidal oscillator. (a) Basic circuit; (b) Limiting amplitude and alternative output.

Thus, if the feedback resistor for A_2 is set equal to $12/\sqrt{3}\, R$ (or $6.93R$), the output of A_2 will be out of phase by

$$\hat{V}_{O2} = -V_{O1} \angle 90° \qquad\qquad \textbf{(7.52d)}$$

A similar circuit that obtains a sine and cosine output is the quadrature oscillator (see Problem 7.45).

Both the Wein-bridge and phase-shift oscillators are useful for a fixed frequency oscillator. For a variable frequency oscillator the Wein-bridge circuit would be preferable, since the phase-shift circuit requires matching 3 resistors, as well as 3 capacitors.

■ **Exercise 7.6**

Derive Eq. 7.51(a), and the results for f_{osc} and R_1 in Eqs. 7.51(b) and (c).

The last oscillator we will analyze is one using three op amps, and in fact is based on the circuit of the state-variable (SV) filter, which was analyzed in Chapter 6 [see Fig. 6.28(b)]. The circuit is referred to as an SV sinusoidal oscillator, with the circuit diagram shown in Fig. 7.47. The changes from the SV filter circuit are (1) the Q determining network [R_3 and R_4 of Fig. 6.28(b)] is now replaced by the amplitude-limiting diode bridge of D_1–D_4, V_Z and resistors R_3 and R_4 and (2) positive feedback is added to start oscillations by including resistor R_7. Thus, the circuit behaves initially like a tuned filter with a very large Q. Oscillations build up until the conduction voltage of the bridge is reached (approximately 6.4 V in the circuit), at which point significant negative feedback from the output of A_2 to the input of A_1 is obtained, reducing the Q toward zero. A steady-state oscillation at v_{O2} will therefore occur with a peak-peak output amplitude equal to the bridge conduction voltage of approximately 12.8 V, p-p.

Ignoring the nonlinear amplitude-limiting bridge network, the loop transmission can be derived by opening the feedback path at the output of A_3 and applying a test generator v_t to R_5. The various equations are (in the s-domain)

$$v_{O3} = -\left(\frac{1}{sR_2C_2}\right)v_{O2} = -\left(\frac{1}{sRC}\right)v_{O2} \tag{7.53a}$$

$$v_{O2} = -\left(\frac{1}{sR_1C_1}\right)v_{O1} = -\left(\frac{1}{sRC}\right)v_{O1} \tag{7.53b}$$

$$v_{O1} = -R_6\left[\frac{v_t}{R_5} + \frac{v_{O2}}{R_7} - \frac{v_{O2}R_3}{R_3 + R_4}\left(1 + \frac{R_6}{R_5\|R_7}\right)\right]$$

$$\approx -v_t - v_{O2}\left(\frac{R_6}{R_7} - \frac{2R_3}{R_4}\right) \tag{7.53c}$$

The resulting loop transmission $T(s)$ is then equal to $T(s) = v_{O3}(s)/v_t(s)$, or from above Eq. 7.53(d) can be reduced in the frequency domain to

$$T(j\omega) \approx \frac{1}{\omega^2 R^2 C^2 + j\omega RC\left(\frac{R_6}{R_7} - 2\frac{R_3}{R_4}\right)} \tag{7.54a}$$

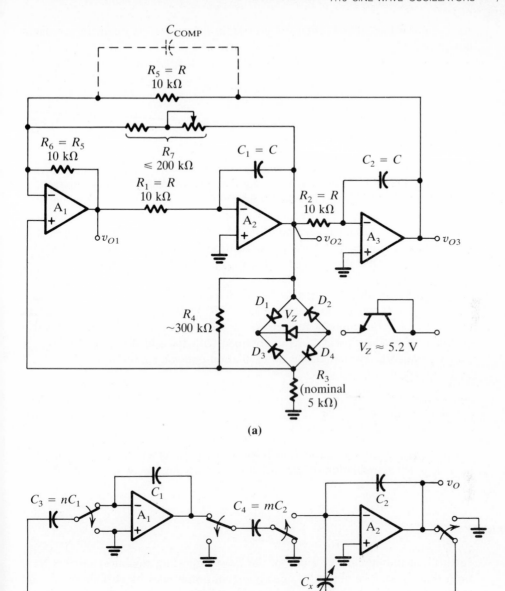

Figure 7.47 A sinusoidal oscillator using the state-variable filter: (a) basic circuit; (b) switched-capacitor equivalent.

Applying the Barkhausen criterion, we obtain the oscillation frequency and gain conditions

$$\omega_{osc} = \frac{1}{RC} \tag{7.54b}$$

$$R_7 \approx R_6 \left(\frac{R_4}{2R_3} \right) \tag{7.54c}$$

Actually, to start oscillations R_7 should be made less than the equality of Eq. 7.54(c), or slightly less than 200 kΩ using the values indicated in Fig. 7.47(a).

The SV oscillator can be easily adjusted for different frequencies by ganging the R_1 and R_2 resistors. The overall circuit suffers from the same basic problem as that of the SV filter, namely the finite GB of A_1–A_3 will introduce excess phase-shift in the loop, changing (lowering) the oscillation frequency. Partial compensation can be obtained with the addition of the C_{COMP} capacitor, thereby providing some leading phase.

The SV oscillator can also be implemented in switched-capacitor (SC) technology, as shown in the circuit* of Fig. 7.47(b), where the use of a noninverting integrator (A_2) functionally replaces both A_1 and A_3 in Fig. 7.47(a). Positive feedback to produce oscillations is obtained with the added switched capacitor pC_2-C_X network. The circuit has an oscillation frequency given by

$$f_{osc} \approx \frac{2f_{cl}}{\sin^{-1} \left[\frac{(nm)^{1/2}}{2} \right]} \tag{7.55}$$

where f_{cl} is the clock frequency, with the usual requirement for SC circuits that $f_{cl} \gg f_{osc}$. Thus, oscillation frequencies are generally limited to $f_{osc} < 10$ kHz.

SUMMARY

In this concluding chapter many of the most important nonlinear circuits have been illustrated. The ability to control signal amplitudes by various diode and transistor shaping networks has been explored in conjunction with active feedback using op amps. Active rectification was shown to be extremely useful, particularly in such applications as rms voltmeter circuits, peak detectors, and sample-hold (or track-hold) circuits. Combining the S/H function with analog-to-digital (and digital-to-analog) conversion was demonstrated by several of the most often used circuits; the reader is encouraged to examine the literature [particularly Ref. 7.8]

---

* R. P. Colbeck, "A CMOS Low-Distortion Switched Capacitor Oscillator with Instantaneous Start-Up," *IEEE J. S.S. Circuits*, Vol. SC-19, No. 6, pp. 996–98 (Dec. 1984).

for many other A/D techniques that were not covered. Another inexpensive technique for A/D conversion was explored by examining several of the voltage-to-frequency conversion circuits. Finally, square-wave, triangular-wave, and sinusoidal oscillators were presented in the form of many useful practical circuits.

PROBLEMS

7.1 For the amplitude-limited circuit of Fig. P7.1 sketch the output transfer characteristics (v_O vs v_I), if $V_{Z1} = V_{Z2} = 6.2$ V. If the capacitance of each Zener diode is 50 pF, what would be the frequency and transient response limitations for the circuit?

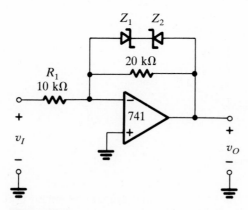

Figure P7.1

7.2 Sketch the transfer characteristic for the circuit of Example 7.1, indicating voltage clamping levels for v_I near zero and at $v_I = \pm15$ V.
   (a) Verify the maximum currents required to be sinked by the output of the op amp.
   (b) If the comparator transfer characteristic is to be changed from $v_I = 0$ V to $v_I = +5$ V, indicate the necessary additional circuit elements required. Use the ±15 V supplies for obtaining any necessary reference values.
   (c) In the original circuit of Example 7.1, if a resistor $R_F = 100$ kΩ is connected between the inverting input and the output of the op amp, how would this affect the transfer characteristics?

7.3 Sketch the transfer characteristics for the voltage limiter circuit of Fig. P7.3 if $V_{Z1} = V_{Z2} = 5.6$ V. Assume $V_{D1} = V_{D2} = 0.6$ V in forward conduction. If the diodes D_1 and D_2 have a junction capacitance of 2 pF ($V = 0$ V) while the Zener diodes have a junction capacitance of 50 pF, what would be the limiting frequency response for the circuit?

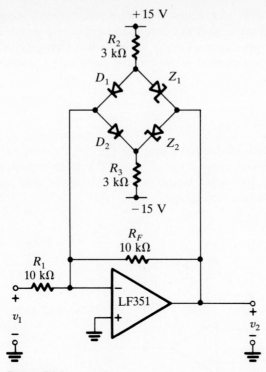

Figure P7.3

7.4 Indicate circuit values for a Schmitt comparator circuit that will switch to a positive output state ($V_O^+ = +10$ V) when the input signal v_I is greater than $+1$ V, and will remain at a low state ($V_O = 0 \pm 0.6$ V) for $v_I < 1$ V. What should the hysteresis, V_U and V_L voltages be if v_I has an interferance signal present of 10 mV, p-p? Use an OP-27 op amp with ± 15 V power supplies. Sketch the resulting transfer characteristic for the circuit.

7.5 In the circuit of Fig. P7.3, replace the Zener diodes Z_1 and Z_2 by small-signal diodes D_3 and D_4 (similar to D_1 and D_2) and change R_2 and R_3 to 30 kΩ each. Sketch the resulting transfer characteristic. Can you think of any practical use for the resulting circuit?

7.6 Using the diode function generator, approximate the function

$$v_O = -\sqrt{V_I}$$

over the range $0 \le v_I \le 5$ volts. Use a three-breakpoint approximation, and estimate the worst-case absolute error over the range of v_I.

7.7 For Example 7.2, the response of v_{o1} with pressure can be described by (this equation was obtained using the HP41 and the cubic regression program)

$$v_{o1} = 0.98p + 0.02p^2 - 3.96 \times 10^{-3}p^3$$

Use the SPICE program in Appendix D for the LF351 op amp, along with the circuit values from Fig. 7.7(c) and obtain the output response v_{O3}. Compare with the desired linear response of Fig. 7.7(a). Where do the curves deviate the most?

7.8 If the input signal v_I is a triangular waveform, show that the circuit of Fig. P7.8 will produce an output signal that is an approximation to a sine wave. Assume the divider network maintains a constant voltage (i.e., that currents through D_1–D_4 are $\ll I_S$). Show how using an op amp might improve circuit performance.

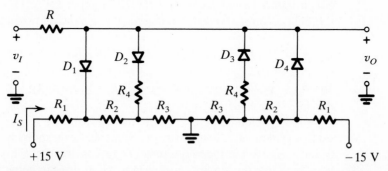

Figure P7.8

7.9 Assume that the deviation from log conformance in the simple log amplifier of Fig. 7.8(b) is caused by the voltage drop produced by base current I_B and the internal base resistance r_b' of Q_1.

(a) Show that adding a compensating voltage drop across R_4 in Fig. P7.9 can provide a first-order compensation for the $I_B r_b'$ effect. Why is this only a first-order correction? If $v_I = 10$ V, $R_1 = 10$ kΩ, $R_3 = 510$ kΩ, and the transistor has $\beta(h_{FE}) = 300$, $I_S = 10^{-15}$ amp, and $r_b' = 500$ ohms, what should the value of R_4 be for compensation?

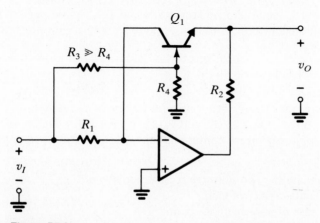

Figure P7.9

(b) If the dc loop transmission is to be equal to that of the op amp alone, what should the value of R_2 be? What would the maximum output voltage of the op amp be if the maximum input voltage is $v_I = +10$ V?

(c) What would be the output voltage if v_I is negative?

7.10 How would the offset voltage V_{OS} input bias current I_B and the equivalent noise parameters (e_n, i_n) for the op amp affect the output–input relationship for the basic log amplifier of Fig. 7.8(b)? How would the e_n and i_n values for the bipolar transistor Q_1 [see Eqs. (4.15) and (4.18)] affect performance?

7.11 Obtain the loop transmission $T(s)$ for the log amplifier (A_2) of Fig. 7.10, using circuit values as indicated. Use the JFET-input OPA2111 op amp (a dual OPA111), whose typical characteristics can be approximated by: $A_O = 1.8 \times 10^6$, dominant open-loop pole at 1.12 Hz, second pole at 3.5 MHz; R_{IN}, $C_{IN} = 10^{13}\,\Omega\|1\mathrm{pF}$; R_{CM}, $C_{CM} = 10^{14}\,\Omega\|3\mathrm{pF}$; $R_O = 100$ ohm; $V_{OS} = \pm 50\,\mu\mathrm{V}$ ($\pm 0.5\,\mu\mathrm{V}/°\mathrm{C}$); $I_B = \pm 0.5$ pA, $I_{OS} = \pm 0.25$ pA; $e_n \approx 6\ \mathrm{nV}/\sqrt{\mathrm{Hz}}$, $i_n \approx 4 \times 10^{-16}\mathrm{A}/\sqrt{\mathrm{Hz}}$; CMRR = 110 dB, PSRR = 110 dB; SR = 2 V/μsec. Assume the npn transistor Q_2 has $\beta(h_{FE}) = 300$, $r'_b = 500$ ohms, $C_{bc} = 1\mathrm{pF}$ and $r_{ce} \approx 100/I_C$. You can approximate the transistor by a simple common-base small-signal model. Assume stray capacitance at the inverting input of A_1 and A_2 of 3 pF. Sketch the magnitude $|T(j\omega)|$ vs. frequency for $v_I = 500$ V and $v_I = 5$ mV on the same semi-log plot. How does frequency response (and therefore output time response) vary with v_I for a log amplifier?

7.12 Explain how the offset adjustment required for the circuit of Fig. 7.10 is achieved by A_4. What advantage would this have over just a standard potentiometer adjustment?

7.13 The circuit of Fig. 7.9 obtains an output that is the logarithm of a division, v_2/v_1. Show how the circuit could be changed to obtain an output that is equal to the logarithm of $v_1 \times v_2$.

7.14 Change the circuit design for Example 7.3 (and Fig. 7.10) by making A_3 a unity-gain circuit with $R_{s1} + R_5 = R_{s2} + R_5 = 10\ \mathrm{k}\Omega$, $R_{F2} = R_{F1} = 10\ \mathrm{k}\Omega$, all $\pm 1\%$ metal-film resistors with low TCs (<100 ppm/°C). Then, add an additional op amp A_5 to the output of A_3, with a gain equal to that previously for A_3,

$$A = 16.9 = \left(1 + \frac{R_F}{R_s}\right)$$

where now only *one* temperature-sensitive resistor R_s is required. If $\Delta R_s/\Delta T \approx +0.75\%/°\mathrm{K}$, and $R_s(25\ °\mathrm{C}) = 1\ \mathrm{k}\Omega$, what should be the value of R_F for temperature compensation, with an output response for A_5 of $+1$ V/decade?

7.15 Compare the two fullwave rectifier circuits of Fig. 7.15 as to
(a) adjustability of gain,
(b) ease of implementation, and
(c) nonlinear effects.

7.16 Show that the circuit of Fig. P7.16 is an absolute-value circuit $v_O = |v_I|$. What is the main disadvantage of this circuit as compared with the circuits of Figs. 7.14–16?

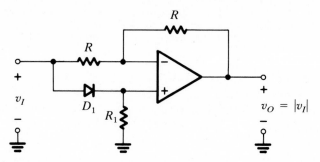

Figure P7.16

7.17 A possible full-wave rectifier circuit is shown in Fig. P7.17, with $R_A = R_B = R$. Show that the output is $v_O = |v_I|$. Explain the operation of the circuit for v_I positive and negative. What is a significant disadvantage of this circuit? How could you correct the problem?

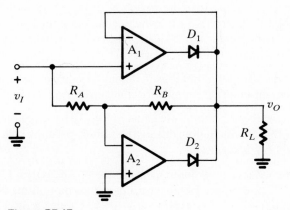

Figure P7.17

7.18 The circuit of Fig. P7.18 is suitable for an absolute-value circuit that requires only one power supply. The op amps could be a dual, ground-sensing op amp such as the bipolar input LM358 or MC34072 (a dual version of the quad MC34074; see data in Appendix C) or a PMOS-input op amp such as the CA3240 or CA3260. Explain the circuit operation for both positive and negative inputs, and show that $v_O = |v_I|$.

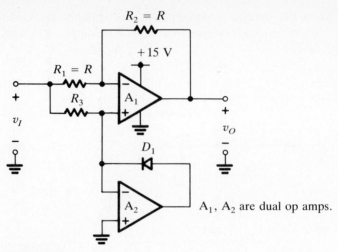

Figure P7.18

7.19 Indicate a circuit design that would provide a peak-to-peak detection; i.e., the output voltage will be equal to the peak-to-peak value of the input voltage.

7.20 Specify all components for the peak detector circuit of Fig. 7.18(b) if the input signal v_I is always between -10 V and $+10$ V, has a maximum anticipated voltage change of 10 V in 500 nsec, and has a required droop that is ≤ 10 mV/sec. Assume that the switch S_1 is an MOS switch with an OFF leakage of 10 pA (max), 5 pF switch capacitance, and an ON resistance of 100 ohms. How long will it take after the switch S_1 resets the capacitor until the circuit is again in normal operation?

7.21 The peak detector circuit of Figs. 7.17 and 7.18 detect the most positive peak. Show a circuit diagram suitable for a negative peak detector.

7.22 If current sources I^+ and I^- are equal in Fig. 7.21(d), and the logic command causes both currents to flow during the sample period, explain the operation of the T/H (or S/H) circuit.

7.23 Determine values for all components in the compensated T/H circuit of Fig. 7.22(a) if S_1 and S_2 are obtained using a dual monolithic N-channel JFET (2N5911) having $R_{on} = 100\ \Omega$, $V_P = -3.5$ V, $C_{dg} = 1.5$ pF, $C_{sd} = 0.2$ pF and an OFF leakage of 10 pA. The hold capacitor is 1000 pF, while the op amp is an LF351. Using typical device parameters estimate the acquisition time (t_{AQ}) for a 12-bit A/D converter having a conversion time of $t_{CONV} = 25\ \mu$sec. Estimate the maximum feedthrough signal (if v_I can vary between $+10$ V and -10 V), as well as the output pedestal error. What is the droop rate for the T/H circuit at 25 °C? If the aperture time (t_{APER}) is 20 nsec, what is the maximum input-signal frequency permitted? How does this value compare to the maximum signal frequency permitted without a S/H circuit, which is given by $f_{max} = (2\pi^{N+1} t_{CONV})^{-1}$, where N is the number of bits in the A/D conversion.

7.24 A monolithic IC S/H circuit developed by Signetics Corporation is conceptually illustrated* in Fig. P7.24. Amplifiers A_1 and A_2 are OTAs. A_3 is a high slew-rate amplifier, while A_4 and A_5 are unity-gain JFET-input op amps. Postulate a correct sequence of switching that would provide $v_O = v_I$ during the sample period, while obtaining zero volts across the switch S_2 during the hold mode.

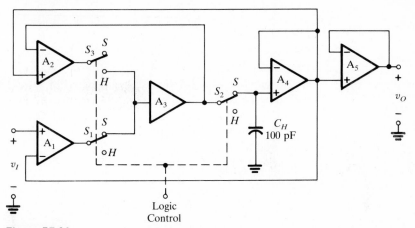

Figure P7.24

7.25 An R–$2R$ network connected as a voltage-switching DAC is depicted in Fig. P7.25. If V_{REF} is $+5$ V, show that the output voltage range is between ± 5 V.

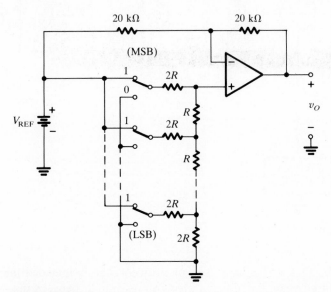

Figure P7.25

---

* *Electronic Design*, pp. 38, 40, (Jan. 23, 1986).

7.26 An actual schematic diagram of a D/A converter using an R-$2R$ resistor network and pnp current switches is shown in Fig. P7.26.

(a) If the digital input data is from TTL logic {$V_{OL} = 0.8$ V(max), $V_{OH} = 2.0$ V(min)], show that a low ('0') TTL input will produce cutoff of the pnp transistor and current flow into the TTL output, whereas a TTL high ('1') signal will turn off the diode, allowing current flow into the R-$2R$ summing network.

(b) Show that drift in the $+1.4$ V reference has no significant effect on the accuracy of the conversion.

(c) Suppose the reference is obtained using the 10 V reference, REF-01, whose characteristics were stated earlier in Fig. 5.13 and Table 5.1, the R-$2R$ network uses 10 kΩ and 20 kΩ precision $\pm 0.01\%$ resistors, with matching of 10 ppm and temperature coefficient of ± 20 ppm/°C (ratio TC of ± 5 ppm/°C), and the op amps are OP-27E units. If the circuit operates over the temperature range of 0–70 °C, how many bits could be converted for a $\pm 1/2$ LSB accuracy?

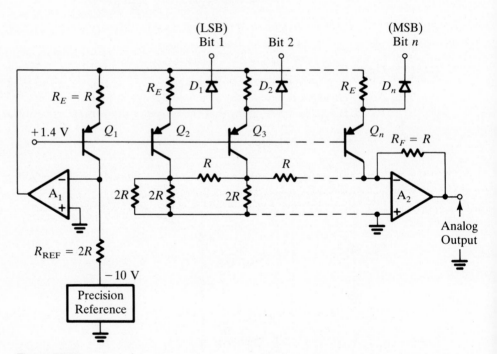

Figure P7.26

7.27 The D/A converter circuit of Problem 7.26 is intended for a 0 to -10 V output span. By adding a precision resistor R_s between the $-V_{REF}$ potential and the inverting input of A_2 the span can be shifted.

(a) What value should R_s be for a -5 V to $+5$ V span?

(b) What changes are necessary for a span from -10 V to $+10$ V?

7.28 This problem is intended for those students fully conversant with digital IC logic. Suppose V_{IN} in Fig. 7.25(a) is between 0 V and ± 1.99 V. Specify all components (using commercially available ICs) to provide a digital output, with an integration period of $t_2 = 1/60$ sec, and $t_1 = t_2 = \dfrac{t_3}{2}$ (max). Use CMOS analog switches for S_1 and S_2. Show a complete timing diagram for your circuit.

7.29 Another type of integrating A/D converter (auto-zero loop not shown) is shown in Fig. P7.29. Show that the output counts N_3 during the de-integrate phase is

$$N_3 = \frac{1}{2N_2}\left(\frac{V_{IN}}{V_{REF}} + 1\right)$$

Is there any advantage of this circuit as compared with that of Fig. 7.25(a)? What should N_3 be to achieve 3-digit (10-bit) resolution?

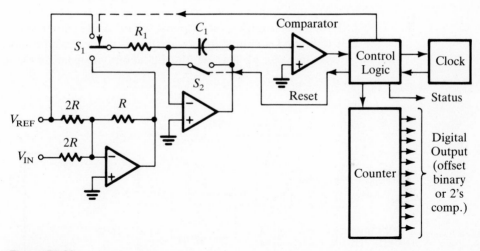

Figure P7.29

7.30 Suppose the successive-approximation A/D converter of Fig. 7.27(a) has a reference voltage of $+5$ V and the input analog signal is $+2$ V. Show the output of the SAR, similar to that of Fig. 7.27(b), and find the correct digital output code.

7.31 The 13-bit SC ladder network of Fig. 7.29 indicates the use of single-pole triple-throw (SP3T) switches. Since switches may only be implemented in CMOS technology with NMOS and PMOS devices, which are either on or off (a SPST switch), indicate how the switch requirements would actually be obtained with MOS switches. Also, indicate how the offset-correction comparator in Fig. 7.28 would be connected with the 13-bit ladder.

7.32 Suppose the combination RC-switched ADC circuit of Fig. 7.30 is to be used for a 12-bit converter. Let $M = 4$ bits and $K = 8$ bits. Let each resistor be 500 ohms, and the smallest capacitor be 1 pF. If the resistors are obtained from 20 ohms/square material, with a resistor width W of 10 microns, and the capacitors use a silicon-dioxide thickness of 500 Angstroms (the dielectric constant of silicon dioxide is 3.9), estimate the total amount of silicon chip area (die area) required for *just* the resistor and capacitor values.

7.33 This problem is concerned with correct grounding procedures and noise limitations for systems containing A/D converters. A typical data acquisition system might appear as indicated in Fig. P7.33, where the input 0–10 mV analog signal is connected to an AD624 instrumentation amplifier (IA), having a gain of 1000. The output of the IA is connected to a T/H amplifier, with the 0–10 V signal then processed by a 12-bit A/D converter.

   (a) Indicate in Fig. P7.33 the most logical connection of grounds, bypass capacitors and power supply connections to minimize any current coupling between the analog and digital circuitry.

   (b) What is the maximum value of the $f_{-3\,dB}$ bandwidth for the analog circuitry such that the total input equivalent noise of the system is $\leq 1/2$ LSB? Assume a single-pole response for the analog circuitry.

   (c) Due to printed circuit board layout there is a stray leakage impedance of 10^9 megohm $\|0.1$ pF between the digital output signals of the ADC and

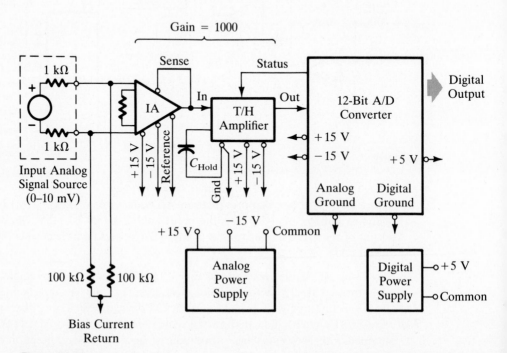

Figure P7.33

the input to the IA. What effects will this have on correct circuit operation. How could this problem be eliminated?

7.34 The multivibrator-type V/F converter circuit of Fig. 7.33(a) is intended for a positive V_{IN}. Show how the circuit connections would be configured for $-V_{IN}$.

7.35 The equivalent circuit for the LM131 (or LM231, LM331) V/F converter is shown in Fig. P7.35. The circuit is a charge-balance-converter. Explain the operation of the circuit and obtain the relation for $f_{out} = GV_{IN}$. Does this circuit offer any advantages when compared with that of Fig. 7.33(b)?

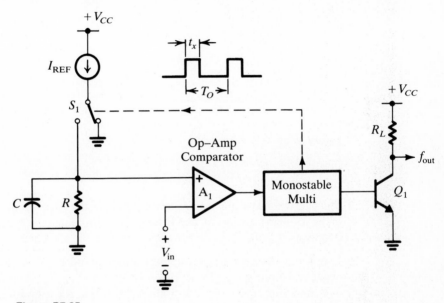

Figure P7.35

7.36 Using the single-op-amp astable multivibrator circuit of Fig. 7.36(a) design a 10 kHz oscillator with output limiting at ± 10 V. Design for an input threshold triggering at ± 2 V, and include additional circuitry to obtain a nonsymmetrical output square-wave with a duty cycle $D = \frac{1}{5}$. Sketch output waveforms at v_O and v_1. Discuss performance limitations of your circuit.

7.37 Using the circuits of either Fig. 7.37(a) or 7.38, design for a temperature-stable function generator having either a square-wave or a triangular-wave output, with frequency adjustable from 10 Hz to 100 kHz, and output amplitude adjustable from 1 V to 10 V, p-p.

7.38 Show that the circuit of Fig. P7.38 is a *bistable* (flip-flop) multivibrator with hysteresis. If $R_1 = 20$ kΩ, $R_2 = R_4 = 1$ kΩ, $R_3 = 3$ kΩ and $R_5 = 9$ kΩ sketch the transfer characteristic v_O versus v_I. Assume D_1 and D_2 are ideal diodes.

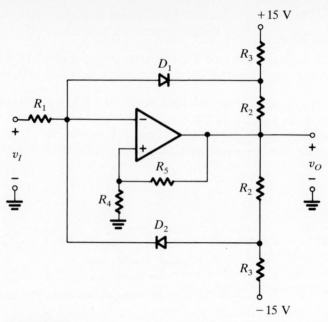

Figure P7.38

7.39 Show a switched-capacitor implementation of the basic astable multivibrator of Fig. 7.36(a), using all capacitors. Find the equation for the oscillation frequency f_{osc}. Hint: Only *one* capacitor need be switched.

7.40 Using the monostable multivibrator circuit of Fig. 7.41(a) design for a negative output pulse of width $T = 10$ μsec (i.e., v_O is in its quiescent state at $+V_Z$ and triggers to $-V_Z$) and an output-pulse p-p amplitude of 10 V. The input trigger pulse available is -3 V amplitude. Specify all components for the circuit.

7.41 Derive Eqs. (7.48a) for the 555 astable circuit of Fig. 7.43. Is it possible to achieve a 50% duty cycle (a symmetrical output square wave)? What would be the required ratio R_A/R_B to do so?

7.42 Specify all element values (including A_1) in Fig. 7.45(a) to obtain a sinusoidal oscillator covering a frequency range from 10 Hz to 100 kHz. Use standard resistor and capacitor values (Appendix E). Be sure A_1 can handle the SR requirements.

7.43 In the circuit of Fig. 7.45(b) if the JFET has typical values of $V_p = -2$ V, $I_{DSS} = 20$ mA, $r_{ON}(V_{gs} = 0) = 70$ Ω, find the peak-to-peak output steady-state oscillation magnitude.

7.44 A sinusoidal oscillator can be obtained using the twin-tee filter circuit (see Problem 6.14) and an op amp, as shown in Fig. P7.44.

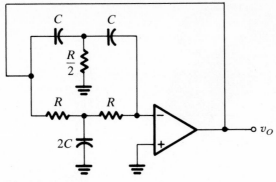

Figure P7.44

(a) Derive the equation for the oscillation frequency f_{osc} and the gain applying the Barkhausen criterion.

(b) Show how an AGC circuit could be implemented.

7.45 The circuit of Fig. P7.45 is a quadrature oscillator, with the signals v_{O1} and v_{O2} being in quadrature (i.e., if $v_{O1} = A \sin \omega_0 t$ then $v_{O2} = A \cos \omega_0 t$)

(a) If $R_1 = R_2 = R_3 = R$ and $C_1 = C_2 = C_3 = C$ derive the loop transmission $T(j\omega)$ and f_{osc} (ignore the nonlinear limiting).

(b) For amplitude stability the nonlinear limiting circuit is added, and resistor R is adjusted for output amplitude stability. Show a network that could be used for limiting.

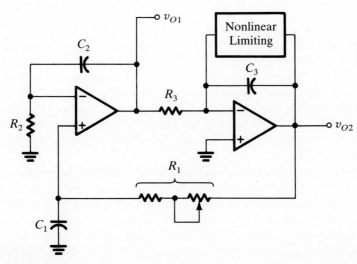

Figure P7.45

Chapter 8

Transducers, with Signal Processing Examples

One very important use of op amps is to process (or condition) the electrical signal from a transducer—whose ouput is proportional to some physical phenomenon such as temperature, pressure, force, flow, etc. Since nearly all transducers provide an analog output signal, the op amp becomes a very important element in amplifying (or perhaps dc-level shifting) the signal so that the output to an indicator is correctly linearly related to the phenomena being measured. It may also be necessary to filter the signal to remove objectionable pickup before final signal processing.

A transducer is a device that converts energy from one form to another. For example, a microphone converts sound energy (in the form of a pressure wave) into an output electrical signal. A thermistor is a nonlinear resistive element whose resistance is proportional to the temperature of the element; thus, a thermistor converts thermal energy to a resistive change, which is used to provide a voltage or current output signal. Further, one could consider a piezoelectric device, which converts mechanical stress into an electrostatic charge Q or a voltage V.

Several examples of the more widely used transducers and their signal processing circuitry are presented in this chapter. Significant topics include the measurement of temperature, force, pressure, and linear displacement, as well as a few other examples of air and fluid flow, moisture, and pH. The material presented is intended to be illustrative, but certainly not comprehensive since that would require another text at least the length of the present one. The reader is instead referred for further study to the many references for this chapter listed in Appendix A.

Finally it should be emphasized that students probably will not fully appreciate the intricacies involved in interfacing transducers with the processing circuits contained in this chapter and the references until they are practicing engineers in an industrial environment. There, in the realistic world of noise/RF contamination, stray magnetic fields, poor grounding,* ambient-temperature variation, variable power supplies, and cost/performance criteria the need for a library of good workable circuits will become abundantly clear!

8.1 TEMPERATURE MEASUREMENT

The most common transducers used for temperature measurement are shown in Table 8.1, where the advantages and disadvantages of each are compared.

8.1.1 Thermally-Sensitive Mechanical Switches

The thermoswitch is a temperature-sensitive mechanical switch fabricated by bonding together two strips of metal having widely different thermal coefficients of expansion. Thus, as heating (or cooling) occurs the strip will bend, either making (or breaking) a contact. This element is the basic sensor used for common thermostats, where the strip may be fabricated as a coil with one end fixed, so that when it expands a rotary action is obtained. Two examples of some simple circuits using a bimetallic thermoswitch are shown in Fig. 8.1. In Fig. 8.1(a) the oven is heated when the switch contact is made, and de-energized when the switch opens. The circuit of Fig. 8.1(b) uses a thermoswitch to monitor the interior temperature of an instrument. If the temperature exceeds the setpoint value of $60\,°C$ switch S_1 opens, which de-energizes the relay, thereby removing power to the instrument and turning on the over-temperature indicator light (S_2 opens and S_3 closes). Obviously, there are many applications where a requirement for a reasonably insensitive (± 2 to $\pm 4\,°C$) sensor could benefit from the use of the thermoswitch.

8.1.2 Thermocouples

A thermocouple is formed by the junction connection of two dissimilar metal wires. In 1821 Thomas Seebeck discovered that if the wires are joined at both ends and one end is heated, there will be a continuous flow of current in the circuit. Further, if the circuit is opened, the net open-circuit voltage (called the Seebeck voltage) is directly proportional to the junction temperature and the composition of the two

---

* For an enlightening treatment of grounding and shielding techniques, see Refs. 8.9–8.12 in Appendix A.

Table 8.1 COMMON TEMPERATURE TRANSDUCERS

Type	Characteristics	Advantages	Disadvantages
Thermoswitch	Bimetallic strip. Typically good for $\pm 2\,°C$ control. Range from $-20\,°C$ to $+250\,°C$.	Inexpensive. Can directly handle heater currents.	Not available for high temperatures. Considerable hysteresis.
Thermocouple	Low impedance ($<10\,\Omega$), EMF directly proportional to temperature, with dissimilar metals.	Self powered, simple, rugged, highly repeatable, inexpensive, very wide temperature range from $-250\,°C$ to $1800\,°C$. Fast response.	Nonlinear over some ranges. Very low voltages, typically from $20\,\mu V/°C$ to $60\,\mu V/°C$. Reference required.
Resistance Temperature Detector (RTD)	A resistor constructed from platinum, nickel, or nickel alloys. Positive temperature coefficient. Sensitivities from $+0.1\%/°C$ to $+0.7\%/°C$. Typical resistance ranges from $20\,\Omega$–$20\,k\Omega$.	Highly stable, low drift. Good linearity (better than thermocouples). Range of $-250\,°C$ to $+600\,°C$.	Expensive. Current source required. Low sensitivity. Self heating. Requires a bridge measurement. Slow response.
Thermistor	Generally, negative TC resistor with large nonlinear resistance change with temperature.	Highest temperature sensitivity. Low-cost. Available in wide range from $100\,\Omega$ to 1 megohm.	Limited temperature range, generally from $-100\,°C$ to $+150\,°C$. Very nonlinear. Somewhat fragile. Self heating.
Semiconductors	As simple as a pn junction ($\sim -2\,mV/°C$). Also available as precision Zener diode ($+10\,mV/°C$). ICs are generally two-terminal constant-current sources changing $+1\,\mu A/K$.	Very linear. Simple. Inexpensive.	Restricted temperature range ($<200\,°C$). Requires power supply. Limited availability.

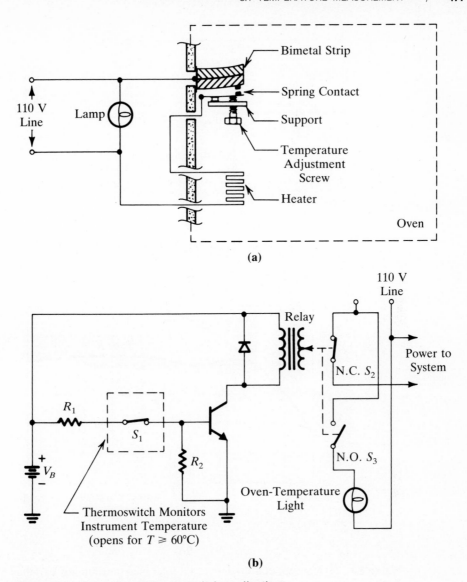

(a)

(b)

Figure 8.1 Some simple thermoswitch applications.

metals used. To correctly measure the junction temperature a **reference junction** (often called the cold junction) must be established (generally, the reference junction is chosen as $0\,°C$, which is $273.15\,°$ Kelvin), as indicated in Fig. 8.2(a) for the case of copper and constantan wires (this is called a type T thermocouple). The voltmeter will read the Seebeck voltage indicative of the difference between the two temperatures T_1 and T_2, or

$$V_S = V_1 - V_2 = \alpha(T_{J1} - T_{J2})$$
$$= \alpha(T_{J1} - 0) \tag{8.1}$$

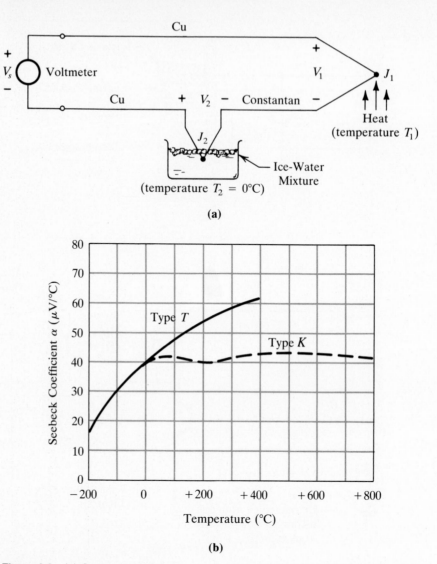

Figure 8.2 (a) Concept of a thermocouple reference junction. (b) Variation of the Seebeck coefficient with temperature for two different thermocouples.

where the proportionality constant α is referred to as the Seebeck coefficient. From a thermocouple table (these are widely available [see Ref. 8.3]) the value of α would be found to be approximately 40.7 μV/°C near room temperature. Thus, if T_{j1} were 50 °C the voltmeter reading should be 2.035 mV (from Ref. 8.3, the actual reading is indeed 2.035 mV). Unfortunately, the Seebeck coefficient α is not constant; instead, α generally increases with temperature as shown in Fig. 8.2(b) for the type T thermocouple. Yet for the type K (Chromel-Alumel) thermocouple α appears to be slowly varying near 40 μV/°C for the range $0° < T < 800$ °C. Some of the general

Table 8.2 CHARACTERISTICS OF VARIOUS THERMOCOUPLES

ANSI[1] Designation	Material[2]	Useful Temperature Range (°C)	Seebeck Voltage over Temperature Range (mV)	Seebeck Coefficient (Near 25°V) $\alpha(\mu V/°C)$
B	Platinum/30% Rhodium Platinum/6% Rhodium	0 to 1700	0 to 12.4	0.1
C[3]	Tungsten/5% Rhenium Tungsten/26% Rhenium	0 to 2300	0 to 37.0	7.3
E	Chromel-Constantan	−200 to 900	−8.8 to 68.8	60.9
J	Iron-Constantan	0 to 750	0 to 42.3	51.7
K	Chromel-Alumel	−200 to 1250	−6.0 to 50.6	40.5
R	Platinum/13% Rhodium Platinum	0 to 1450	0 to 16.7	6.0
S	Platinum/10% Rhodium Platinum	0 to 1450	0 to 15.0	6.0
T	Copper-Constantan	−200 to 350	−5.6 to 17.8	40.7

[1] ANSI—American National Standards Institute.
[2] The first material listed obtains the most positive potential at the junction.
[3] Not an ANSI symbol.

characteristics of the thermocouples most often used are indicated in Table 8.2. A plot of the output voltage (Seebeck voltage) available as a function of junction temperature is shown in Fig. 8.3 for several thermocouples. Most thermocouples are generally interchangeable from lot to lot within $\pm 2\,°C$ repeatability, and on special order within $\pm 1\,°C$.

In Chapter 4 (see Fig. P4.18) we considered an example of a typical thermocouple circuit using an ice-bath reference junction at $0\,°C$. In practice, it is obviously not very feasible to have an ice bath handy; hence an equivalent cold-junction reference must be obtained electronically. Some examples, as well as different gain configurations, are illustrated in Fig. 8.4. In Fig 8.4(a) the use of an instrumentation amplifier (here, the AD624 whose characteristics are included in Appendix C, although any equivalent IA such as the AMP-01, INA101, LM363, or the like could be used) provides excellent common-mode rejection, small drift, and low noise amplification. The cold-junction compensation for the type J (iron-constantan) junction J_1 is provided by the J_2 junction at the same temperature as integrated circuit IC1, an AD590 two-terminal temperature transducer* monitoring the ambient temperature ($15\,°C \leq T_{AMB} \leq 35\,°C$) and furnishing an output

---

* IC temperature transducers are discussed later. The temperature-dependent current of an LM334 current source could also be used in place of the AD590 device.

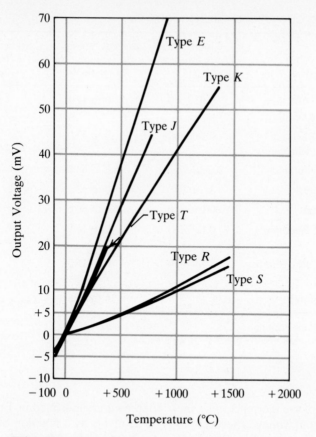

Figure 8.3 Thermocouple output voltage as a function of temperature (cold junction at 0°C).

current of 1 μA/°Kelvin. The equation for the input voltage to the IA is obtained as

$$V_i = V_{J1} - V_{J2} + \frac{I_1 R_1 - V_{\text{REF}}(R_1/R)}{1 + \dfrac{R_1}{R}} \tag{8.2}$$

The potential of the copper-constantan junction does not enter Eq. (8.2) since an equal thermocouple potential is formed at the constant-temperature isothermal block. In Eq. (8.2) are two variables, $-R_1$ and R. These can be obtained by referring to thermocouple tables to obtain the Seebeck coefficient (from Table 8.2, $\alpha \sim 51.7\ \mu$V/°C near ambient temperature) and the Seebeck voltage at ambient temperature (from Ref. 8.3, $V_{J2} = 1.277$ mV at 25 °C). Thus, from Eq. (8.2) we obtain for $V_i = V_{J1}$

$$\frac{dJ_2}{dT} = 51.7\ \mu\text{V/°C} = \frac{dI_1}{dT}(R_1) \bigg/ \left(1 + \frac{R_1}{R}\right) = 1\ \mu\text{A/°C}(R_1) \bigg/ \left(1 + \frac{R_1}{R}\right) \tag{8.3}$$

since the resistors R_1, R and R_G can be assumed to vary insignificantly with temperature, as well as the band-gap reference potential V_{REF}. The other equation is

$$1.277 \text{ mV} = \frac{298 \ \mu A(R_1) - 1.24\left(\dfrac{R_1}{R}\right)}{1 + \dfrac{R_1}{R}} \qquad (8.4)$$

Solving the two equations leads to $R_1 = 52.3 \ \Omega$ and $R = 4.537 \text{ k}\Omega$ (from Appendix E we might use $\pm 1\%$ precision resistors $R_1 = 52.3 \ \Omega$, and $4.32 \text{ k}\Omega$ in series with a $500 \ \Omega$ potentiometer for R).

The circuit* of Fig. 8.4(b) uses an inexpensive pn-junction diode having a typical temperature coefficient of $-2.1 \text{ mV}/°\text{C}$ to generate the relatively low $-6 \ \mu V/°\text{C}$ Seebeck coefficient for a type S thermocouple. The divider of R_1 and R_2 must therefore have a ratio $R_1/(R_1 + R_2) = 6/2100$, or $R_2 = 349R_1$. The dc-offset voltage at junction J_3 is removed by the zero adjustment of potentiometer R_5. Since the zero adjustment and the diode D_1 are biased from the same $+10 \text{ V}$ precision reference, there is no change in offsets or drift due to power supply changes. Also to be noted in Fig. 8.4(b) is that the thermocouple effect at reference junctions J_2 and J_3 are obtained with different metals; J_2 is formed by a platinum-copper couple while J_3 is formed by a platinum/10% rhodium and copper couple. However, since both J_2 and J_3 are at the *same temperature* the effect is exactly the same as if a couple of platinum to platinum/10% rhodium was first formed at ambient temperature T_2 and then connected to a second series junction of platinum/10% rhodium to copper at the same temperature.† From thermocouple tables the emf potential of J_1 is 9.585 mV at 1000 °C, so the closed-loop gain of the op amp should be, for a full-scale output voltage of 10 volts,

$$A_{CL}^- = \frac{10 \text{ V}}{9.585 \text{ mV}} = 1043 \approx \frac{R_9}{R_8 + R_1 \| R_2} \qquad (8.5)$$

or $R_9 \approx 1.15$ megohm. For all thermocouples operating over a wide temperature range, some type of linearization algorithm must be provided, either by analog breakpoint compensation circuits (as discussed earlier in Section 7.2) or, perhaps more efficiently, by computer or microprocessor storage in a ROM. The OP-77 precision op amp (manufactured by PMI) is particularly useful for thermocouple circuits, since it has $V_{OS} \leq 25 \ \mu V$, $A_{OL} \geq 5 \times 10^6$, $\Delta V_{OS}/\Delta T \leq 0.3 \ \mu V/°\text{C}$, excellent PSRR and CMRR (> 110 dB), and $0.35 \ \mu V$ p-p noise at low frequencies.

The lower noise versions of the chopper-stabilized op amps (see Table 5.2) are also good candidates for thermocouple circuits, as illustrated in the temperature measuring circuit of Fig. 8.4(c), where for illustration purposes an ICL7652

---

* See J. Wong, "Temperature Measurements Gain From Advances in High-Precision Op Amps," *Electronic Design*, pp. 167–71 (May 15, 1986).

† This is due to the empirical "law of intermediate metals," which states that a third metal (in this case platinum/10% rhodium) inserted between two dissimilar metals of a thermocouple junction will have *no* effect as long as the two junctions formed by the additional metal are at the *same* temperature.

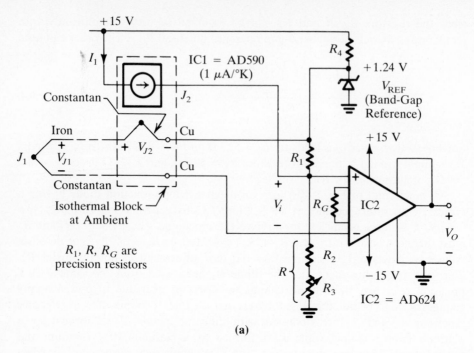

(a)

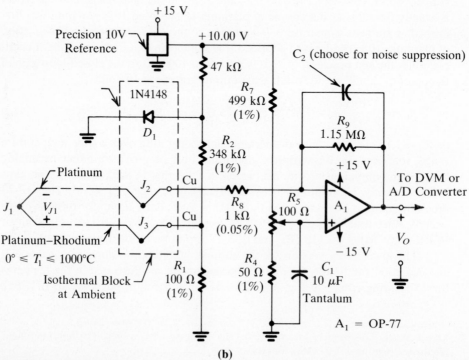

(b)

Figure 8.4 Several thermocouple circuits illustrating different techniques for obtaining a reference junction.

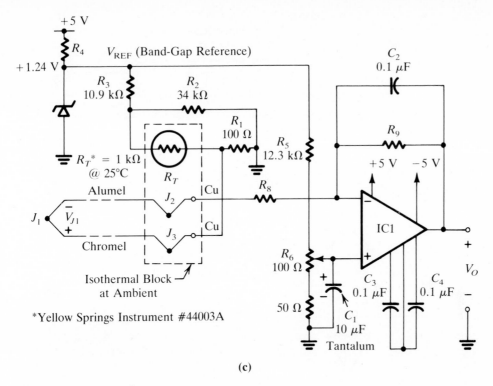

Figure 8.4 (continued)

device is used for IC1. The resistors R_8 and R_9 are chosen for full-scale temperature range, while R_6 allows a zero-offset adjustment. Here, the cold-junction compensation is provided by the R_1, R_2 and R_3 precision resistors and the thermistor R_T. Since a type K thermocouple (chromel-alumel) is used, the resistor combination is chosen to furnish a Seebeck coefficient of approximately $+40.5\ \mu V/°C$.

A complete IC thermocouple signal-conditioning circuit that contains the cold-junction compensation circuitry (and usually an input instrumentation amplifier, too) can be obtained commercially. Examples are the AD594/595 and the LT1025, as well as various modular units from several other manufacturers.

8.1.3 Resistance Temperature Detector (RTD)

The RTD is a wirewound resistance thermometer, typically wound using platinum wire (for this reason the designation **platinum resistance thermometer** is sometimes used), although for some applications nickel, nickel alloys, or even copper are used. Unlike thermocouples, the RTD element is usually encased in a protective sheath, or enclosed housing, as illustrated in Fig. 8.5(a). Contacts to the resistor are typically made with two wires at each end, thereby allowing a Kelvin bridge

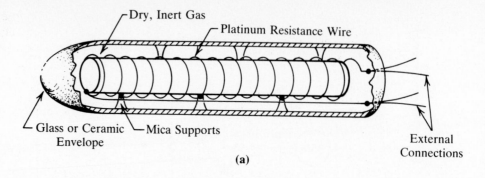

(a)

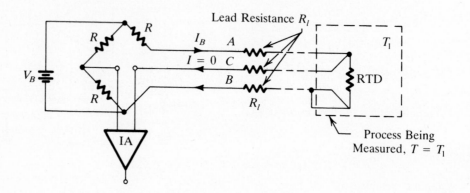

(b)

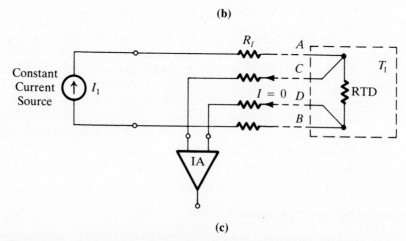

(c)

Figure 8.5 (a) Construction of an RTD. (b) Using a bridge connection for measurement. (c) A constant-current source excitation.

connection to eliminate lead resistance effects. As indicated in Table 8.1, the RTD is really the "standard" for temperature measurements, since the resistive element is highly stable, has very low drift (or aging), and generally good linearity. The RTD is expensive however, compared to thermocouples or other temperature sensors. Resistance values available range from 20 Ω to 20 kΩ, although most applications use values near 100 Ω (at 0 °C). Sensitivity to temperature changes is not very good, as platinum resistors have a temperature coefficient $\alpha \approx 0.00392$ ohms/ohm/°C, which for a 100 Ω resistance translates to $+0.392 \, \Omega/°C$ (or $+0.392\%/°C$). The value for α is actually the average slope of the R vs T curve over a temperature range from 0 to 100 °C. It is not unusual to achieve accuries of ± 0.1 °C using an RTD, provided the maximum temperature does not exceed 600 °C.

Because of the low sensitivity, and lead resistance effects, it is usually necessary either to use the RTD in a bridge configuration, or to drive the sensor from a constant-current source, as indicated in Fig. 8.5(b) and (c). In Fig. 8.5(b) since line C carries no current the lead resistance R_l contributes no error. Note that R_l does produce a voltage drop in lines A and B; as long as lines A and B are the same length, however, a cancellation effect is produced, The bridge resistors R are at ambient temperature, with very low temperature coefficients. Likewise, in Fig. 8.5(c) the constant-current-source excitation by I_1 eliminates lead-resistance effects in lines A and B and since lines C and D carry no current, lead effects are neglible here also. The advantage of the constant-current-source excitation is that now the length of lines A and B is immaterial. The current flow through the RTD will cause a self-heating error, with a typical value of 1/2 °C per milliwatt in free air. To reduce this error one should obviously use the smallest current consistent with the output voltage required, and use the largest physical size RTD possible. Another source of error is the nonlinearity of the temperature coefficient α, which is (for a 100-ohm RTD)$+0.39 \, \Omega/°C$ at 0 °C, but decreases to $+0.29 \, \Omega/°C$ near 800 °C. An approximation to the platinum RTD resistance is the Callendar–Van Dusen equation*

$$R(T) = R_o\left\{1 + \alpha\left[T - \delta\left(\frac{T}{100} - 1\right)\left(\frac{T}{100}\right) - \beta\left(\frac{T}{100} - 1\right)\left(\frac{T^3}{100}\right)\right]\right\} \qquad \textbf{(8.6a)}$$

where

R_o = resistance at $T = 0$ °C

α = Temperature coefficient at 0 °C, typically 0.00392 $\Omega/\Omega/°C$

$\delta \approx 1.49$

$\beta \approx 0 (T > 0)$, or $\approx 0.11 (T < 0)$

T = Temperature, in °C $\qquad \qquad \qquad \qquad \qquad \qquad \qquad \qquad \qquad$ **(8.6b)**

The exact values for the coefficients α, β, and δ are determined by finding $R(T)$ at four different temperatures over the range of interest and solving the resulting

---

* H. L. Callendar, *Phil. Trans. of the Royal Soc. England*, Vol. 178, p. 161 (1887) and M. S. Van Dusen, *J. Amer. Chem. Soc.*, Vol. 47, p. 326 (Feb. 1925).

equations. Although Eq. (8.6) appears formidable, the RTD element is actually more linear than the thermocouple.

Some measurement circuits using the RTD are shown in Fig. 8.6; in (a) is a circuit that will furnish a constant current of 2.5 mA to the RTD. Since the RTD is in the feedback loop of IC1 a potentiometric configuration is formed, and the impedance seen by the sensor approaches $R_{CM} \| R_{IN} (1 + T_0)$, where R_{CM} is the common-mode impedance of the op amp, R_{IN} is the dc open-loop input resistance and T_O is the loop transmission. Thus, an excellent high-impedance current source is seen by the RTD. The circuit connection of the op amp IC1 was presented earlier in Fig. 5.12, where it was shown that the nonlinearity term in the bridge configuration of R_1, R_2, R_3 and the RTD would be eliminated. Thus, the output voltage to the 8-bit ADC is (from Eq. 5.16, earlier)

$$v_O = 2.5 \text{ mA}[R(T) + 2R_l - R_3] \tag{8.7}$$

where $R(T)$ is the value of the RTD at temperature T, R_l is the lead resistance of the detector, and R_3 is balanced for 0 volts output at $0 \,°\text{C}$. The change of v_O with temperature is (if the temperature coefficient α is constant)

$$\frac{\Delta v_O}{\Delta T} = 2.5 \text{ mA}[\alpha R(T_0)] \approx (0.25 \text{ V})(0.004/°\text{C}) \tag{8.8}$$

or $\Delta V_O/\Delta T \approx +1\text{m V}/°\text{C}$. Thus, the most significant bit of the 8-bit converter is $1\,°\text{C}$, and the full-scale output measurement capability is $0\,°\text{C}$ to $255\,°\text{C}$.

The circuit of Fig. 8.6(b) utilizes a 100-ohm RTD with an inexpensive, $3\frac{1}{2}$ digit integrating A/D converter and liquid-crystal-display panel meter to indicate temperature over the range from $0\,°\text{C}$ to the maximum usable limit of $800\,°\text{C}$. Op amps A_1 and A_2 must be low-drift, low-offset units, with an input common-mode range that includes ground (the chopper-stabilized op amps such as the MAX420, LTC1052, ICL7560, TSC911 or dual-TSC913 might be used). The integrating A/D converter is connected in the ratiometric mode, so that the output display is equal to 1000 times the ratio (V_i/V_{REF}). Since V_i and V_{REF} are derived from the same 9 V power supply, changes in the power supply have negligible effect (hence, a 9 V battery could be used). At the lowest value of $0\,°\text{C}$ the imput signal v_i is zero, since A_2 has a gain of 2.0, and the resistance of both R_3 and the RTD are equal. If the lead resistance of the RTD is significant, resistor R_7 can be increased to compensate. At a maximum temperature of $800\,°\text{C}$ the output indication of the LCD would be $<800\,°\text{C}$ because the temperature coefficient of the RTD changes from $0.392\%/°\text{C}$ at $0\,°\text{C}$ to $0.29\%/°\text{C}$ at $800\,°\text{C}$. However, with resistor R_5 sampling the output of A_2, a first-order correction term is applied to reduce the V_{REF} value and provide a full-scale indication of $800\,°\text{C}$. In practice, the circuit would be calibrated by (i) adjusting either R_3 or R_7 to provide an LCD reading of 0 for $0\,°\text{C}$; (ii) adjusting R_2 to provide a correct display at some intermediate temperature (say $\sim 100\,°\text{C}$); and (iii) adjusting R_4 for a correct reading at the maximum temperature desired. Since these adjustments interact, the calibration procedure should be repeated until a correct display at the three reference values is repeatable. An overall resolution of $\pm 1\,°\text{C}$ is possible.

The circuit of Fig. 8.6(c) illustrates a more involved technique for providing compensation of the RTD nonlinearity. The RTD is connected to a 1 mA current source formed by a Howland circuit (see Section 5.7.2 and Fig. 5.32) composed of $R_3 = R_4 = R_6 = R_5 \| R_7$. Thus, (from Eq. 5.57, and Refs. 8.13, 8.14)

$$I = \frac{V_{\text{REF1}}}{R_3} - \frac{v_{O2}}{R_7} \tag{8.9}$$

The input voltage to the instrumentation amplifier A_1 is

$$v_I = IR_T \tag{8.10}$$

since the effects of lead resistance (R_l) are eliminated by the current source I and the four-wire connection to the RTD (Note; R_1, R_2 and C_2 is an input-noise filter and has no effect on v_I). If the IA has a gain of G, then $v_{O2} = -Gv_I + V_{\text{REF2}}$, or substituting Eqs. (8.9) and (8.10),

$$v_{O2} = -Gv_I + V_{\text{REF2}}$$

$$= -GR_T\left(\frac{V_{\text{REF1}}}{R_3} - \frac{v_{O2}}{R_7}\right) + V_{\text{REF2}} \tag{8.11}$$

or solving for v_{O2}

$$v_{O2} = V_{\text{REF1}}\left[\frac{\dfrac{-GR_T}{R_3} + \dfrac{V_{\text{REF2}}}{V_{\text{REF1}}}}{1 - \dfrac{GR_T}{R_7}}\right] \tag{8.12}$$

Also, from Fig. 8.6(c) the ratio $V_{\text{REF2}}/V_{\text{REF1}}$ is that of the summing amplifier gain of A_4, namely

$$\frac{V_{\text{REF2}}}{V_{\text{REF1}}} = \left(\frac{R_9}{R_9 + R_8}\right)\left(\frac{R_{11} + R_{10}}{R_{10}}\right) \tag{8.13}$$

From the Callendar–Van Dusen Eq. (8.6a) earlier, for $T > 0\,°C$ we can rewrite the equation as

$$R_T = R_0(1 + AT - BT^2) \tag{8.14a}$$

where

$$A = \alpha\left(1 + \frac{\delta}{100}\right) \approx 3.9784 \times 10^{-3}$$

$$B = \frac{\alpha\delta}{10^4} \approx 5.8408 \times 10^{-7} \tag{8.14b}$$

If Eqs. (8.14a) and (8.13) are substituted into Eq. (8.12) we obtain

$$v_{O2} = V_{\text{REF1}}\left[\frac{\dfrac{-GR_O}{R_3}(1 + AT - BT^2) + \dfrac{V_{\text{REF2}}}{V_{\text{REF1}}}}{1 - \dfrac{GR_O}{R_7}(1 + AT - BT^2)}\right] \tag{8.15}$$

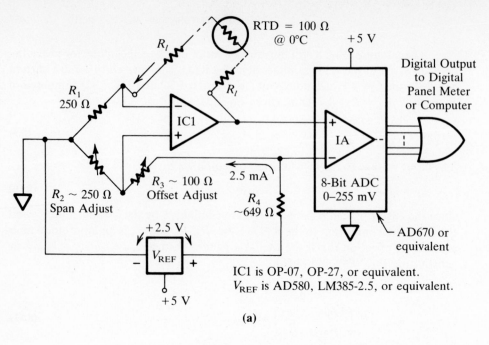

(a)

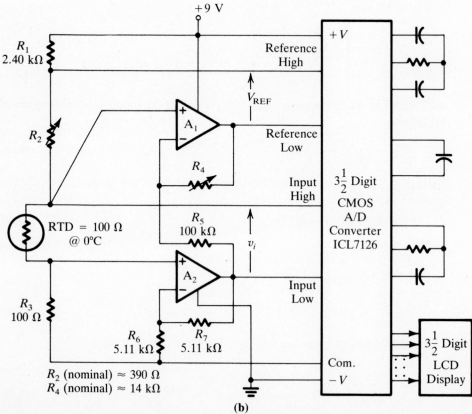

(b)

Figure 8.6 Temperature-measurement circuits using an RTD.

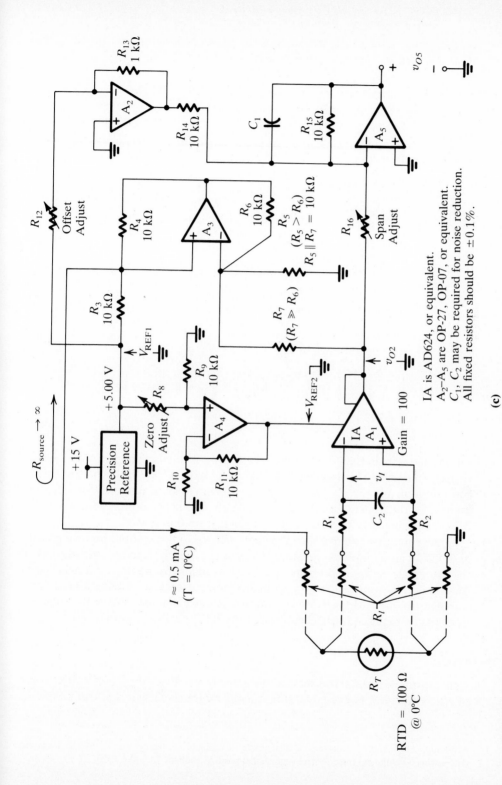

Figure 8.6 (continued)

489

In the actual circuit the second term in the denominator will be $\ll 1$, since $R_7 \gg R_0$. Hence, a series expansion gives

$$\frac{1}{1 - \dfrac{GR_0}{R_7}(1 + AT - BT^2)} = 1 + \frac{GR_0}{R_7}(1 + AT - BT^2) + \cdots \tag{8.16}$$

where the third and subsequent terms in the expansion are negligibly small. Thus, Eq. (8.15) reduces to

$$v_{O2} \approx V_{\text{REF1}}\left[-\frac{GR_0}{R_3}(1 + AT - BT^2) + \frac{V_{\text{REF2}}}{V_{\text{REF1}}} \right.$$

$$\left. -\frac{G^2 R_0^2}{R_3 R_7}(1 + AT - BT^2)^2 + \left(\frac{V_{\text{REF2}}}{V_{\text{REF1}}}\right)\frac{GR_0}{R_7}(1 + AT - BT^2) \right] \tag{8.17}$$

If Eq. (8.17) is rearranged to reflect the temperature-sensitive terms, one obtains

$$v_{O2} \approx V_{\text{REF1}}\left\{ \left(-\frac{GR_0}{R_3} + \frac{V_{\text{REF2}}}{V_{\text{REF1}}} \right)\left(1 + \frac{GR_0}{R_7} \right) \right.$$

$$+ \frac{GR_0 AT}{R_3}\left[-1 + \left(\frac{V_{\text{REF2}}}{V_{\text{REF1}}}\right)\left(\frac{R_3}{R_7}\right) - 2\left(\frac{GR_0}{R_7}\right) \right]$$

$$+ \frac{GR_0 BT^2}{R_3}\left[1 - \left(\frac{V_{\text{REF2}}}{V_{\text{REF1}}}\right)\left(\frac{R_3}{R_7}\right) - \left(\frac{GR_0}{R_7}\right)\left(\frac{A^2}{B} - 2\right) \right]$$

$$\left. + \frac{G^2 R_0^2 T^3}{R_3 R_7}(2AB) - \frac{G^2 R_0^2 T^4}{R_3 R_7}(B^2) \right\} \tag{8.18}$$

The desired term in Eq. (8.18) is that directly proportional to temperature. Thus, by correctly choosing the parameters ($V_{\text{REF2}}/V_{\text{REF1}}$), G and R_7 the coefficients of the constant term and the T^2 terms will be zero.* The choice of parameters is left as an exercise for the student (see Problem 8.8). With parameters optimized it is possible to achieve a linearity of $\pm 0.5\,°C$ over a range from 0 to $600\,°C$.

Several other circuits, which are not included in this section can be used with an RTD for measuring temperature. The student is encouraged to examine any of the many data books and application notes available from sensor manufacturers. Also available from some op amp manufacturers (such as Analog Devices and Burr-Brown) are various modules with the complete amplification and compensation circuits required for linearization of the RTD packaged in one unit.

8.1.4 Thermistors

A thermistor (a **thermal resistor**) has the greatest sensitivity to temperature changes of any of the sensors available, with a temperature coefficient that can be several

---

* Although the T^3 and T^4 terms remain, their effects are negligible for temperatures $< 600\,°C$. However, it is possible to eliminate these terms by additional positive feedback [see Ref. 8.13].

percent per degree Celsius, Thus, it is possible to detect very small changes in temperature ($\ll 1\,°C$) that would not be discernible if we were using a thermocouple or RTD. However, the thermistor resistance has a very nonlinear relationship with temperature, as indicated by the normalized curves for various thermistor materials in Fig. 8.7. Also indicated on the curve, for comparison, is the temperature response of a platinum RTD.

Thermistors are available with either a positive temperature coefficient (PTC) or a negative temperature coefficient (NTC), although most units used for temperature measurement are NTC devices with resistance-vs-temperature curves as indicated in Fig. 8.6. Such thermistors are fabricated from metal oxides of manganese, nickel, cobalt, iron, copper, and titanium. They are available in various sizes from very small beads (diameters to 0.02″), metallized surface-contact-type thermistors, and even small (0.05″ square) chips for hybrid IC construction.

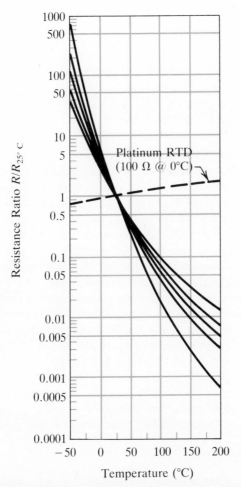

Figure 8.7 Typical thermistor resistance/temperature curves for NTC thermistors.

Temperature ranges include $-100\,°C$ to $+300\,°C$, although units operated continuously above $150\,°C$ may show long-term drift exceeding $2\,°C/\text{year}$. Over the temperature range from $-40\,°C$ to $+100\,°C$ thermistors are available with values (at $25\,°C$) between 100 ohms and 1 megohm, and interchangeable tolerances as good as $\pm0.2\,°C$. One must be careful when using thermistors to ensure low power dissipation in the device, since most units have self-heating thermal time constants of 1–$1.5\,\text{mW}/°C$ in still air.

A mathematical relationship that reasonably approximates the nonlinear curves of Fig. 8.7 is due to Steinhart and Hart*

$$\frac{1}{T} = a_0 + a_1(\ln R_T) + a_2(\ln R_T)^3 \tag{8.19a}$$

where

$$T = °K$$

$$R_T = \text{thermistor resistance}$$

$$a_i = \text{curve-fitting constants} \tag{8.19b}$$

If the temperature range is small, a somewhat simpler approximation is usually used

$$R_T = R_{T0} \exp\left[\beta\left(\frac{1}{T} - \frac{1}{T_0}\right)\right] \tag{8.20}$$

where R_{T0} is the resistance value at $25\,°C$.

It is possible to linearize the thermistor by adding fixed resistors (temperature-stable resistors such as wirewound or metal-film types) in parallel and/or series, as indicated by the circuits of Fig. 8.8(a–d). The circuit of Fig. 8.8(d) is particularly useful, in that operation from $-30\,°C$ to $105\,°C$ with accuracy and interchangeability of $\pm0.15\,°C$ is possible. This network is available from Yellow Springs Instrument Co. Of course, the linearized network now has a reduced sensitivity compared to the original NTC thermistor; however, the sensitivity is still as much as 400 times greater than that of a thermocouple.

The circuit of Fig. 8.9(a) uses a linearized thermistor network similar to that of Fig. 8.8(d) with an IA to obtain an output voltage that is linearly proportional to temperature. The composite network of R_1, R_2, R_{T1} and R_{T2}, is available from Yellow Springs Instrument Co. (Part No. 44201). In the circuit of Fig. 8.9(a), if $V_{\text{REF}} = 2.5\,\text{V}$, then the output voltage at V_1 is [Ref. 8.7, p. 14]

$$V_1 = (-0.0053483 V_{\text{REF}})T + 0.86507 V_{\text{REF}} \tag{8.21}$$

where T is in $°C$. Thus at $0\,°C$ the offset voltage V_2 should be adjusted to $V_2 = V_1 = 0.86507(2.5) = 2.1627$ volts. At $100\,°C$, the voltage V_1 will then be 0.8256

---

* J. S. Steinhart and S. R. Hart, "Calibration Curves for Thermistors," *Deep Sea Research*, Vol. 15, p. 497 (1968).

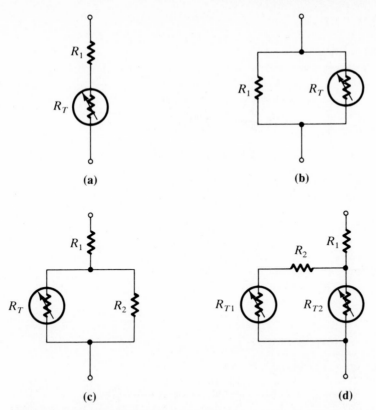

Figure 8.8 Some linearization networks for thermistors. Resistors R_1 and R_2 are wirewound or metal-film (TC $\approx$ 0) resistors.

volts, so the input signal to the IA will be $2.1627 - 0.8256 = 1.3371$ volts. If a full-scale output of 10 volts is desired, the gain of the IA should be set for 10/1.3371, or $G = 7.48$. The circuit is claimed to have a measurement accuracy within $\pm 0.2\,°C$ over the temperature range from 0 to 100 °C.

The circuit of Fig. 8.9(b) indirectly measures the temperature of R_{T1A}, which is produced by the rms heating effect of the input signal.* Thus, this circuit is an rms to dc converter (i.e., a true rms voltmeter) such as might be used for noise measurements. The two sets of thermistors (R_{T1} and R_{T2}) are each encased in a $0.08'' \times 0.150''$ bead enclosure by the manufacturer; each set must then be placed in an isothermal environment to remove outside ambient-heating effects (a sandwich of styrofoam is sufficient). An input signal v_{IN} will produce rms heating in R_{T1A}, with the temperature increase sensed by the thermally coupled R_{T1B} element (the resistance of R_{T1B} will therefore decrease). Thus, the input signal at the inverting input of the instrumentation amplifier will decrease, which in turn produces an amplified, positive output voltage which heats R_{T2B}, thereby heating R_{T2A} and

---

* This is a modified version of a circuit attributed to Jim Williams, *EDN*, p. 242, (June 28, 1984).

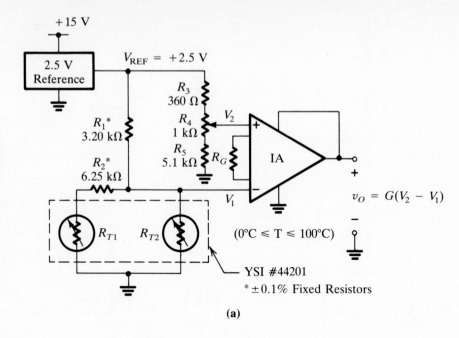

(a)

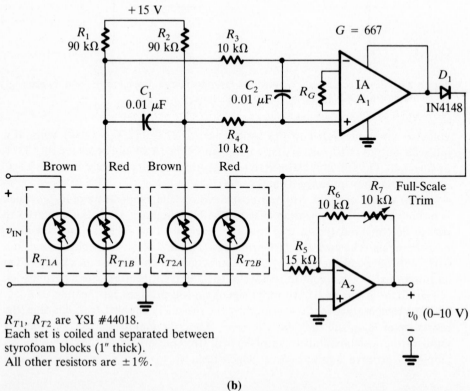

R_{T1}, R_{T2} are YSI #44018.
Each set is coiled and separated between
styrofoam blocks (1″ thick).
All other resistors are ±1%.

(b)

Figure 8.9 Temperature measurement circuits using linearized thermistors.

restoring balance in the input bridge when $R_{T2A} = R_{T1B}$. The circuit is capable of rms to dc conversion from dc to 50 MHz with $\pm 2\%$ accuracy, The crest factor of the input signal can also be as high as 100/1 without contributing significant error.

Individual thermistors can also be used as highly sensitive sensors to control heaters, as shown by the circuits of Fig. 8.10. Figure 8.10(a) shows a Bang-Bang controller (so called because the circuit never operates in a linear mode, instead the heater current is either fully on, or fully off; i.e., the heater "bangs on" or "bangs off"). Thermistors R_{T1} and R_{T2} are 2 kΩ at 25 °C (77 °F), and decrease to 480 Ω at the desired heater-control temperature of 150 °F (65.5 °C). The particular thermistors used (Thermometrics, Inc.) can be reasonably characterized by Eq. (8.20) with $\beta = 3548$. The control thermistor R_{T1} is fed from a 2 mA constant-current source. The control-temperature point is set by the Q_2 current-source value and the value of R_5, while hysteresis is determined by R_6. The LM311 comparator is used since it provides faster response than an op amp; also, since an on-off controller is used, overall control-system frequency stability is not primarily important. The output of Q_3 is optically coupled to the heater drive circuit by an optocoupler. This technique is often used in power circuits, since the relatively "dirty" ground of the heater circuit can be isolated from the "clean" ground of the sensitive input circuits.

In balancing, the circuit resistor R_3 would be adjusted so that the output of comparator A_1 would drive negative, turning off Q_3 and thereby providing heater current at just below the desired temperature of 150 °F. Resistor R_6 is then adjusted to set the hysteresis (for $\pm \frac{1}{2}$ °F hysteresis, $R_6 \approx 180$ kΩ). In the actual circuit thermal delays between the heater and the sensor would contribute to $> \pm \frac{1}{2}$ °F control.

The circuit of Fig. 8.10(b)* utilizes a linear servo-controlled loop with phase-angle firing of a silicon-controlled rectifier (SCR) to control a heater driven from the 110 V ac line. The set-point control allows heater operation from $+25$ °C to $+250$ °C, with a precision of better than ± 0.1 °C possible. When the temperature is below the set point the output of A_1 will be low, causing Q_1 to conduct and charge C_1 until the unijunction transistor (UJT) conducts. This produces a firing pulse for the SCR, thereby allowing ac current to flow through the heater. When the sensed temperature is above the set point, the output voltage of A_1 will be at a higher value, turning off Q_1 and removing drive voltage from T_1. The circuit will operate linearly around the set point with the UJT conduction synchronized to the 60 Hz line frequency by virtue of the fullwave rectified voltage at the emitter of Q_1. Since the servo loop now operates as a linear controller, thermal delays are very important and loop stability must be ensured. Typically, the closed-loop time constant is set by the product $R_F C_F$. The correct loop response can be obtained by switching in resistor R_4 (the thermistor R_T has a 25 °C sensitivity of 1.29 kΩ/°C, so this amounts to a 0.1 °C temperature change) and observing the output-voltage response of A_1. The value of C_F should then be chosen for critically damped response of the waveform.

---

* Again, a modified version of Jim Williams circuit, *EDN*, p. 89 (June 20, 1977). Mr. Williams is a premier designer of high-resolution circuits.

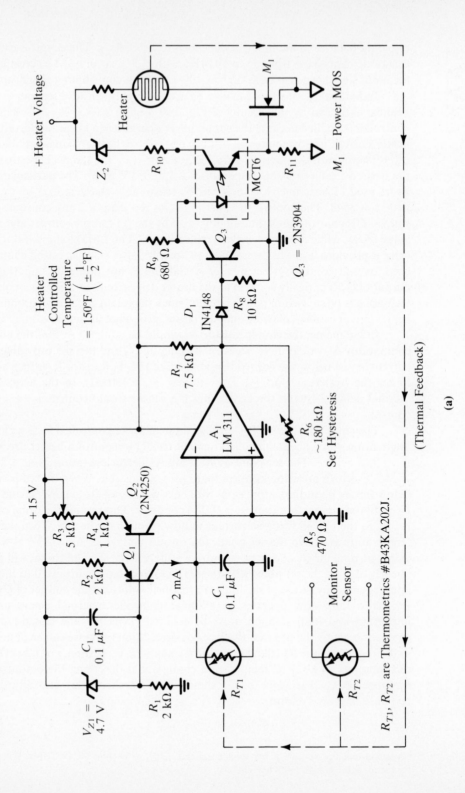

(a)

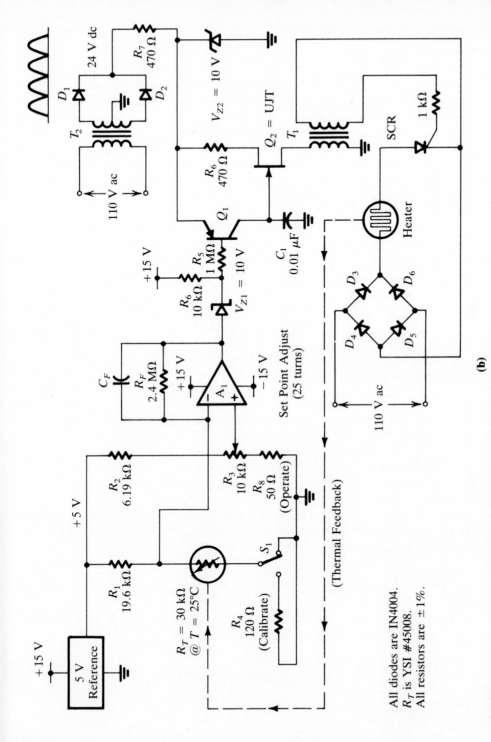

Figure 8.10 Measurement and control circuits using single thermistors.

(b)

All diodes are IN4004.
R_T is YSI #45008.
All resistors are ±1%.

8.1.5 Semiconductor Temperature Detectors

We have already seen how a simple pn-junction diode could use the $-2\,\text{mV}/°\text{C}$ temperature coefficient to compensate a thermocouple in Fig. 8.4(b). For better accuracy, however, one should use a diode sensor specifically designed, and guaranteed, to provide a standard temperature coefficient. Diodes such as the MTS 102–105 series guarantee temperature matching accuracy of $\pm 2\,°\text{C}$ to $\pm 5\,°\text{C}$ over a range of 0 to $100\,°\text{C}$, with linearity fixed at $-2.1\,\text{mV}/°\text{C}$. In addition, some integrated circuits (for example, the REF-02 reference) provide a temperature-sensitive output voltage with approximately $-2\,\text{mV}/°\text{C}$ change; hence, these circuits could be used as temperature transducers or to monitor the IC chip temperature in critical applications

A temperature detector much better than a single diode is the $\Delta V_{BE}/\Delta T$ change of a matched-monolithic (single-chip) transistor pair. For example, the circuit in Fig. 8.11(a) employs matched transistors Q_{1A} and Q_{1B} with the change in base-emitter voltages amplified by A_1. If the currents in Q_{1A} and Q_{1B} differ by a factor of 2, the equation for ΔV_{BE} is [from Eqs. (5.24) and (7.10)]

$$\Delta V_{BE} = V_{BE1A} - V_{BE1B} = \frac{kT}{q}\ln 2 \tag{8.22a}$$

or for a change in temperature

$$\frac{\Delta V_{BE}}{\Delta T} = \frac{k}{q}\ln 2 = +59.73\,\mu\text{V}/°\text{K} \tag{8.22b}$$

Thus, with gain $G = 167.4$ the output voltage changes by $+10\,\text{mV}/°\text{K}$. If the offset-voltage drift of the matched pair is $\leq 0.5\,\mu\text{V}/°\text{K}$ then an accuracy of better than $1\,°\text{C}$ is possible over a range of $100\,°\text{C}$.

The circuit of Fig. 8.11(b) also employs matched transistors, However, the basic difference between this and the preceding circuit is a precision ratio difference between the emitter-base junction areas of Q_1 and Q_2, namely $A_{EB2} = 8A_{EB1}$. Since the Q_1 and Q_2 transistors must have identical collector currents (if $\beta \gg 1$), because of the current-mirror arrangement of Q_3 and Q_4, the difference between the base-emitter voltages must be

$$V_{BE1} - V_{BE2} = \Delta V_{BE} = \frac{kT}{q}\left[\ln\left(\frac{I_{C1}}{I_{S1}}\right) - \ln\left(\frac{I_{C2}}{I_{S2}}\right)\right] \tag{8.23a}$$

or since $I_{C1} = I_{C2} = I/2$, and since the reverse saturation currents are related by $I_{S2} = 8I_S$ (since I_S is directly proportional to A_{EB}), we obtain

$$\Delta V_{BE} = \frac{kT}{q}\ln 8 \tag{8.23b}$$

and

$$I = 2\left(\frac{\Delta V_{BE}}{R}\right) = \left(\frac{2k\ln 8}{qR}\right)T \tag{8.23c}$$

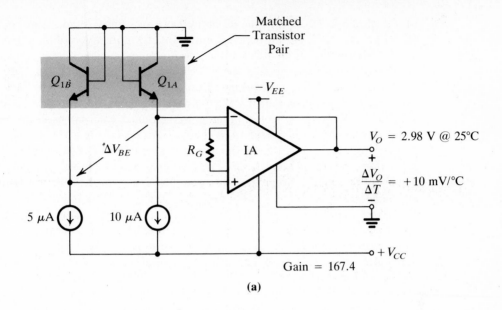

(a)

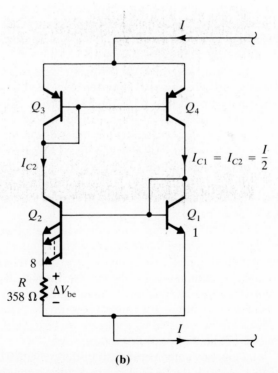

(b)

Figure 8.11 Temperature sensors using semiconductor elements: (a) Matched transistors: (b) Two-terminal current element.

If R is chosen as 358 Ω, then the IC circuit has a very linear temperature coefficient of $+1\ \mu A/^\circ K$. Although the actual circuit is slightly more involved than that of Fig. 8.11(b), the concept is identical to that used in many semiconductor temperature-to-current transducers, such as the AD590–592 and the LM 134, 234, 334 series.

The LM134–334 series differs from the circuit of Fig. 8.11(b), in that the equivalent ΔV_{BE} voltage is 68 mV (25 °C), and the change in the current I is equal to $(+227\ \mu V/^\circ K)/R_{SET}$, where R_{SET} is a user-supplied external precision resistor. Thus, current I (this is refered to as the I_{SET} current for the LM134–334 devices) can be programmed, as well as the temperature coefficient of the current.

Both the AD590 and LM134–334 series devices offer exceptionally simple temperature sensing circuitry. Two examples using the AD590 transducer are indicated in Fig. 8.12. The circuit of Fig. 8.12(a) allows direct interface to a $3\frac{1}{2}$-digit panel meter (199.9 mV, full scale). Resistor R_5 allows a zero adjustment, while R_1, R_2 and C_1 form a line filter to reduce interference and pickup. Since the two-terminal transducers are excellent high-impedance current sources, line-resistance or power-supply changes have no effect on accuracy. Similarly, the circuit of Fig. 8.12(b) offers a simple way to obtain a differential-temperature measurement, since the output voltage will be proportional to the difference of the temperatures sensed by $I(T_1)$ and $I(T_2)$. This circuit would also be a simple way to detect air flow if self-heating were allowed in IC1 and IC2, since one of the units could be encased in a shielded environment (no air flow) while the other could be inserted in an air stream; the resulting cooling effect would then be proportional to the difference of currents.

In Fig. 8.13(a) the LM334 three-terminal adjustable current source is used as a sensor with a band-gap voltage reference to obtain an output voltage that directly reads the temperature (°C) of the LM334. The R_{SET} resistor has the internal sense voltage of 68 mV (at 25 °C) across it so the current $I(T)$ is equal to 68 mV/2.3 kΩ, or 29.6 μA. If R_1 is adjusted to obtain 298.2 mV output $[R_1 = (298.2\ mV - 68\ mV)/29.6\ \mu A \approx 7.79\ k\Omega]$ while R_5 is adjusted to give a fixed voltage $V_2 = 273.2$ mV, then the output voltage $V_1 - V_2$ will directly reach 25 mV at 25 °C and will also change 1 mV/°C. This circuit is capable of $\pm 2\%$ linearity from 0 to 100 °C. The circuit is particularly useful in that it will operate for >1 year on a 1.5 V D-cell battery.

The LM334 current source is used in another simple temperature controller in Fig. 8.13(b), where the device senses the temperature of the process and provides an amplified signal to an inexpensive three-terminal voltage regulator via the adjustment terminal. Since the current through R_1 is constant at 1.2 V/1.2 kΩ = 1 mA (the three-terminal IC voltage regulator was discussed in Section 5.7.1) the difference of 1 mA $- I(T)$ must flow in R_2. The set-point temperature of the process can be adjusted by changing R_2 or R_3, although the larger R_3 is the more precise will be the controlled temperature.

A low-power temperature transducer* with a 0–100 μA analog meter readout is obtained with the LM334 in Fig. 8.13(c), using the LM10 op-amp and reference

---

* See this, and other applications of the LM10 in *Application Note AN211*, (December 1978), by R. C. Dobkin and M. Yamatake, National Semiconductor Corp., Santa Clara, CA.

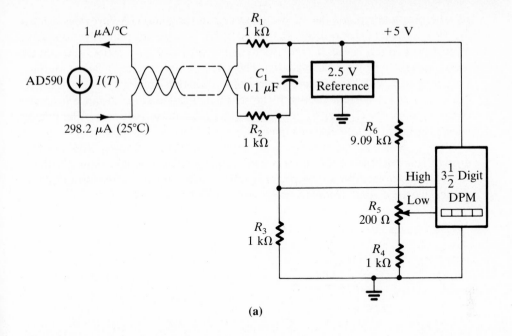

(a)

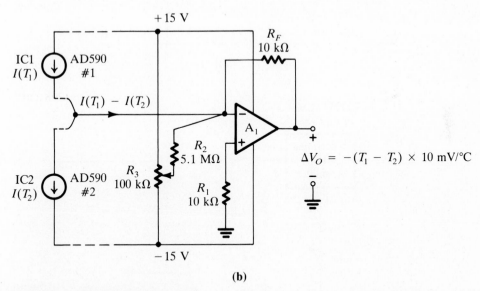

$$\Delta V_O = -(T_1 - T_2) \times 10 \text{ mV/°C}$$

(b)

Figure 8.12 Examples of applications for the AD590 current-source temperature transducer, useful from 0 °C to 100 °C.

IC (the pin numbers for the IC are identified in the figure). A_1 provides a fixed $+0.20\,\text{V}$ reference to resistor R_6. At $0\,°\text{C}$ the meter current is zero, hence $V(\text{pin2}) = V(\text{pin3}) = 0.20\,\text{V}$ (relative to pin 4 potential). At $100\,°\text{C}$ the $100\,\mu\text{A}$ meter current will flow through R_6. The circuit thus requires a linear output-voltage change with temperature at pin 3 of A_2, which is precisely what is obtained from the LM334 current source. If the sensor is located some distance from the circuit, capacitors C_1 and C_2 may be required for noise reduction. The analog current meter M_1 could also be replaced by a $1\,\text{k}\Omega$ resistor, obtaining an output of 0–$100\,\text{mV}$, which could then be read by a $199.9\,\text{mV}$ low-power liquid-crystal display. It is possible for the entire circuit to operate from one $1.5\,\text{V}$ D-cell battery.

Other semiconductor temperature sensors are available in the form of Zener diodes, whose output voltage varies linearly with temperature. For example, the

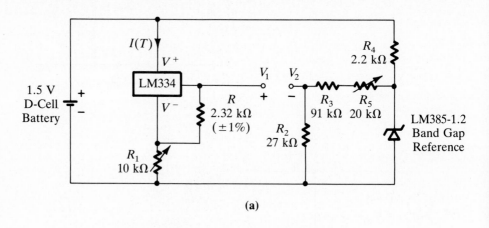

(a)

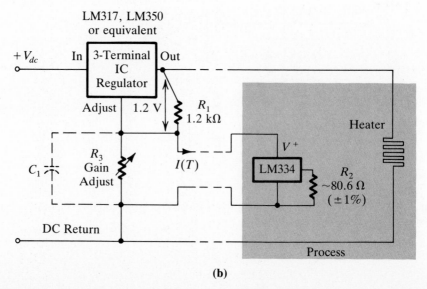

(b)

Figure 8.13 Some sensor applications for the LM334 three-terminal current source.

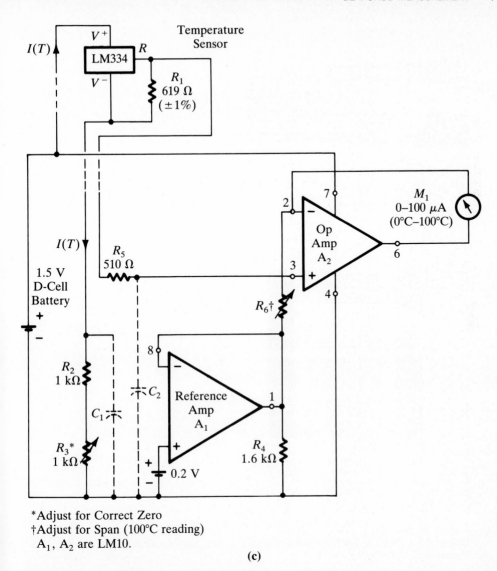

*Adjust for Correct Zero
†Adjust for Span (100°C reading)
A$_1$, A$_2$ are LM10.

(c)

Figure 8.13 (continued)

LM335 integrated circuit operates as a two-terminal Zener diode, with a break-down voltage directly proportional to temperature at $+10$ mV/°K. Further, by an optional adjustment terminal it is possible to set the output voltage precisely to a specified value (e.g., 2.982 volts at 25 °C = 298.2 °K).

8.2 FORCE MEASUREMENT

The element used most widely to measure force is the strain gage, which is constructed from thin resistive wires, typically arranged in a serpentine pattern as illustrated in Fig. 8.14(a) for force measurement in one direction and in Fig. 8.14(b)

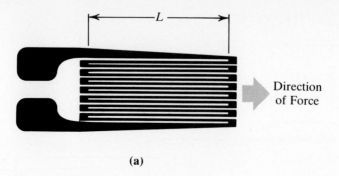

(a)

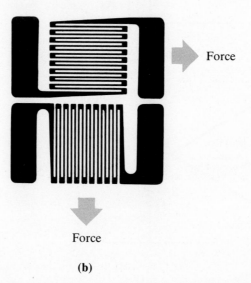

Force

(b)

Figure 8.14 Typical thin-film bonded strain gages. (a) One direction of force. (b) Two-degrees of force.

for force measurement in two directions. The strain gage is cemented or bonded to the structural member that experiences the force; as strain occurs the thin resistive wire elongates by an amount ΔL Since initial resistance is equal to $R_O = \rho L/A$ (typical values for R_O vary from 220 Ω to 1 kΩ), the resistance increase is

$$R_O + \Delta R = \rho \frac{(L_O + \Delta L)}{(A_O + \Delta A)} = R_O \left(\frac{1 + \dfrac{\Delta L}{L_O}}{1 - \left| \dfrac{\Delta A}{A_O} \right|} \right) \qquad \textbf{(8.24)}$$

since an increase in length produces a corresponding decrease in cross-section area, Since $\Delta L/L_O$ and $\Delta A/A_O$ are $\ll 1$, Eq. (8.24) can be expanded and only the first term of the expansion considered, leading to

$$\frac{\Delta R}{R_O} \approx \frac{\Delta L}{L_O}\left(1 + \frac{|\Delta A/A_O|}{\Delta L/L_O}\right) \approx 2\frac{\Delta L}{L_O} \qquad (8.25)$$

for the ideal case of an incompressible resistor material. The term in parenthesis is called the **gage factor** G_f, while **strain** ε is defined by $\Delta L/L_O$. So Eq. (8.25) reduces to

$$\frac{\Delta R}{R_O} = G_f\varepsilon \qquad (8.26)$$

For resistors constructed from platinum or other similar metals the gage factor varies from 2 to 4, while for semiconductor films the value of G_f can be >100 because the resistivity ρ of the semiconductor actually increases also.

Most of the circuits employing strain gages use a bridge connection and either a differential amplifier or an instrumentation amplifier. The circuit of Fig. 5.13 analyzed earlier is an excellent example of a strain-gage bridge attached to an instrumentation amplifier. For small deviations the output would be [see Eq. (5.18)]

$$v_O = \frac{GV_B}{4}(G_f\varepsilon) \qquad (8.27a)$$

where G_f and ε are the parameters previously defined, G is the gain of the IA and V_B is the bridge bias voltage. Since the resistance of the strain-gage element will also vary with temperature, it is common practice to include as one of the bridge elements a "dummy" gage with identical characteristics, but under no load. A typical half-bridge circuit is indicated in Fig. 8.15(a). As the active gage element experiences force the input dc signal at point A becomes greater than that at point B, thus V_{O1} increases. If the gage factor is 2 and the strain factor is $\varepsilon = 2\ \mu\text{inch/inch}$, then the bridge sensitivity is

$$\text{Sensitivity} = \frac{1}{4}(2 \times 2\ \mu\text{inch/inch}) = 1\ \mu\text{V/V} \qquad (8.27b)$$

For a bridge bias potential of $V_B = 10$ volts the sensitivity is 10 μV. If the gain of the IA is 1000, then an output voltage V_{O1} of 10 mV corresponds to 2 μinch/inch [or 2 $\mu\varepsilon$ (microstrains)]. Thus, for a 10 V full-scale output we have a full-scale measurement equivalent to 2000 $\mu\varepsilon$. We found in our previous error budget analysis for a similar bridge circuit (Table 5.1) that the worst-case resolution error (referred to the output for a temperature range of 0–60 °C) was 33 mV; thus, it would appear that a resolution approaching ± 10 mV (or $\pm 2\ \mu\varepsilon$) might be possible for a less limited operating-temperature range of ± 10 °C.

The sensitivity (and temperature stability) of a strain-gage circuit can be increased by using an active element in each of the four legs of the bridge circuit

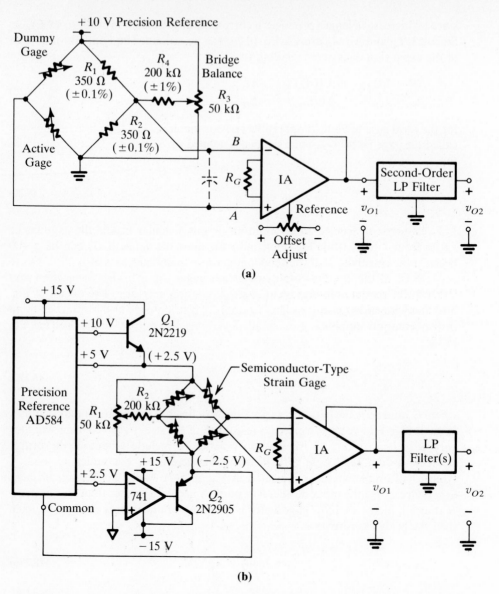

Figure 8.15 (a) Strain gage circuit with one active element. (b) Circuit with four active elements.

with the elements arranged so that two increase in resistance while two decrease. In this case the sensitivity is improved by a factor of 4. Such a circuit is shown in Fig. 8.15(b), where a semiconductor-type strain gage is used for increased sensitivity ($\varepsilon \gg 1$). Further, the bridge bias voltage is obtained with $+2.5$ V and -2.5 V, thus removing the common-mode voltage from the inputs of the IA and thereby eliminating offset errors due to the CMRR of the amplifier.

If a strain-gage bridge circuit has to operate over a wide temperature range, the circuit can have a much reduced resolution due to thermocouple-junction effects, dc drift of the IA, 60 Hz pickup, and $1/f$ noise. To eliminate most of these effects it is possible to use an ac sinusoidal bridge excitation, amplify, and then synchronously demodulate the output waveform. The ac phase and amplitude information available from the bridge is then converted to a proportional dc output signal. Any $1/f$ noise, dc drifts, and demodulator effects are mixed with the carrier frequency and can therefore be virtually eliminated by filtering. Further, the self-heating effect in the bridge elements is reduced by a factor of 2 with a sinusoidal excitation (i.e., with say 10 sin ωt rather than 10 V dc). Figure 8.16 shows a strain gage used as a weighting scale (a load cell) with a 1 kHz bridge excitation. The ultimate resolution of the circuit is determined by the amplitude stability of the sinusoidal generator.

In addition to strain-gage transducers (which probably account for 90% of the total usage), there are also piezoelectric-type force transducers, where the output signal is a change in charge directly proportional to the force applied. These transducers are typically of a ceramic-type material. The transducer output is strictly transient and a dynamic force change is needed to obtain a signal. In general, the linearity of such a system is inferior to that of one using strain gages, although the sensitivity of the transducer may be quite high. Since the output is a charge signal (ΔQ) and the static output impedance (R_{od}) is very large, one must use a charge amplifier to interface with the transducer. The circuit of Fig. 8.17 is typical of a piezoelectric transducer connected to a charge amplifier, Since the

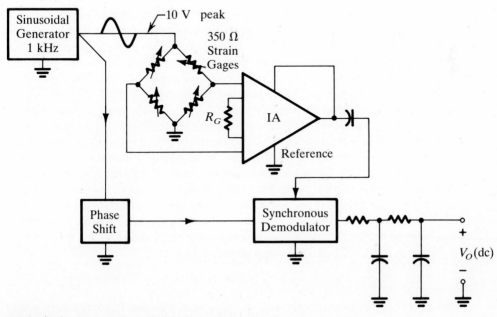

Figure 8.16   AC bridge excitation for a load cell.

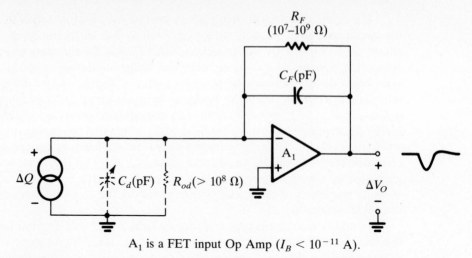

A₁ is a FET input Op Amp ($I_B < 10^{-11}$ A).

Figure 8.17 Force measuring system using a piezoelectric transducer and a charge amplifier.

Miller capacitance is large ($A_{OL} C_F \gg C_d$), then the change in charge is deposited on C_F, producing an output voltage change whose peak value is

$$v_O(\text{peak}) = -\frac{\Delta Q}{C_F} \qquad (8.28)$$

8.3 LINEAR DISPLACEMENT MEASUREMENT

Linear displacement transducers are used to precisely measure small displacements of an element from a reference position. Conversely, the transducer may also be used to measure how close one element is to another as the element is moved within the neighborhood of its reference position. Two important transducers are currently used for displacement (or proximity) detection—the linear-variable-differential transformer (LVDT), and the semiconductor Hall-effect device. A resistance potentiometer (or rheostat) can also be used for non-sensitive applications; the wiper arm of the potentiometer is attached to the moving member so that motion results in a position change, and therefore a proportional output-voltage change. Since the windings of the rheostat can be no closer than the wire diameter, this type of detector is limited in resolution to $>0.010''$. Another type of proximity detection is possible by monitoring the change in capacitance between two conductors, one fixed and one movable, with the capacitance change proportional to $\Delta l/l$, where l is the null (or zero) distance between the two surfaces. This type of detector can be more sensitive than a resistance potentiometer circuit, but is not as sensitive as the LVDT or Hall-effect sensors.

8.3.1 LVDT

The LVDT is the most widely used displacement transducer, particularly where very precise measurements ($<0.001''$) are required. Since a transformer is used, the excitation voltage must be an ac signal. A variable differential transformer was first used in 1906, as a motor reverser, although it was not until 1936 that its use as a transducer element was disclosed. The LVDT is constructed with two identical secondaries, symmetrically spaced from the primary, and connected in a series-opposition circuit. The movable element is a noncontacting cylindrical magnetic core connected to the element undergoing displacement. As the core moves relative to the two secondaries the induced voltage from the primary to each secondary will vary, thus varying the magnitude (and phase) of the total secondary output voltage. A sketch of the secondary output voltage vs core position is shown in Fig. 8.18. Obviously the core travel is limited, since when the core leaves the field area of one secondary the output voltage must reach a maximum, and then decrease. However, it is posible to continue the configuration of the secondary/primary

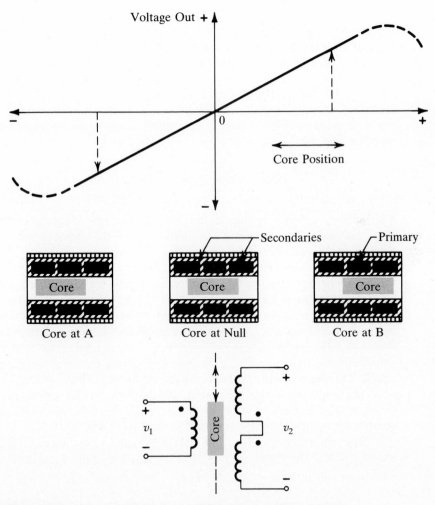

Figure 8.18 Output voltage of an LVDT as core position changes.

design of Fig. 8.18 by placing multiple windings along the length of the core and then appropriately connecting the secondaries and primaries to extend the useful linear range of a LVDT to several inches [Ref. 8.16, pp. 3–8].

The sensitivity of an LVDT is expressed in millivolts output per 0.001" displacement per volt excitation, or units of mV/mil/volt. Thus, the ideal output with infinite secondary load resistance should be the product of sensitivity × core displacement × primary input voltage. In actuality, the output voltage will depend on load resistance and excitation frequency, although for loads $> 50\,k\Omega$ (and if operated at the manufacturer's recommended frequency) the output voltage will be very close to the ideal value. Typical linearities of an LVDT are within $\pm 0.25\%$ of full-scale linear range. However, it is possible to achieve linearities of better than $\pm 0.05\%$ of full scale on special order. The resolution of a LVDT is infinite, thus the measurement capability of a position-sensing system will be determined by drift and noise in the electronics.

Since the LVDT requires an ac excitation signal, the output voltage from the secondary must be ac amplified, and then synchronously demodulated to obtain a dc output voltage proportional to displacement. However, just as for the ac bridge circuit of Fig. 8.16, it is absolutely essential that the primary sinusoidal generator have excellent amplitude stability. It is also possible (although with reduced sensitivity) to use a diode rectifier (discriminator) circuit connected to the LVDT secondary, thereby immediately obtaining a dc output. Other detection possibilities arise using an LVDT, since if the output signal v_1 is differentiated, then the resulting signal is

$$v_2 = \frac{dv_1}{dt} = \frac{d}{dt}(Kx) = K(\text{velocity}) \tag{8.29}$$

The signal v_2 is thus proportional to the velocity or rate of change of the movable core. Likewise, by processing the derivative of v_2, one obtains a signal v_3 proportional to acceleration ($\sim d^2x/dt^2$).

The basic signal-conditioning circuit for an LVDT is shown symbolically in Fig. 8.19. The input sinusoidal generator is typically set at a frequency designated by the manufacturer for minimum output null at zero position of the core (this frequency is usually between 100 Hz and 10 kHz). Obviously, a very precise sinusoidal input signal v_{pri} with excellent amplitude stability is required (usually, a circuit like the Wein-bridge oscillator, Fig. 7.45, is used). The preamplifier A_1 amplifies the output signal v_{sec}, thereby determining the noise limitations for the circuit. The phase-sensitive detector (synchronous demodulator) then performs an ac-to-dc conversion so that the resulting dc output v_o is now directly proportional to linear displacement. The phase-shift network (R, C) is normally required to account for additional phase shift due to the LVDT and A_1.

The entire circuit of Fig. 8.19 (except for the LVDT) is available in a single monolithic IC,* the Signetics Corp. NE5521, which contains a stabilized adjustable

---

* Z. Rahim, *EDN*, pp. 159–68 (May 29, 1986).

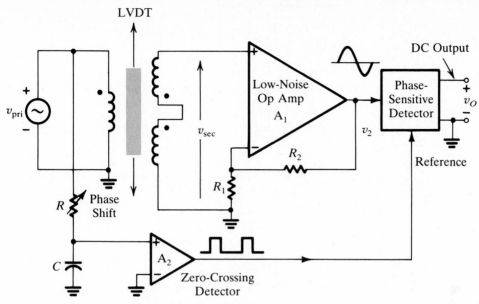

Figure 8.19 Standard LVDT signal-processing circuit.

oscillator, a demodulator, a comparator and an additional op amp that can be used as a second-order LP filter to remove ripple in the dc output signal. The IC can also be utilized to measure the phase difference between two equal-frequency signals.

In addition to oscillator amplitude drift, the standard LVDT processing circuitry of Fig. 8.19 may also suffer from phase shifts (between primary and secondary windings) that vary with temperature and core position; this considerably complicates obtaining high resolution. A significant increase in resolution can be gotten with a different type of circuit, a ratiometric converter. These converters* are virtually insensitive to drift in the oscillator amplitude, as well as phase-shift changes and drift. Figure 8.20 shows a block diagram of the system. The two precision resistors (R) form a stable voltage divider so that $V_{REF} = (V_1 + V_2)/2$, while the input signal to the differential amplifier A_1 is equal to the difference, $V_1 - V_2$. The output signal (V_{O1}) of A_1 is scaled by resistor R_G, and then multiplied by a voltage proportional to the digital value of position. The ratio bridge then compares V_{O2} with the scaled value of V_{O1} and produces an ac output proportional to the difference. The output signal V_{O3} is then amplified and converted to a dc output by a phase-sensitive detector and integrator. The resulting dc signal is then digitized by a wide-range voltage-controlled oscillator, which drives an up/down counter to null the error voltage. Thus, we have a closed-loop tracking feedback

---

* See D. Denaro, "Transducer Converters Ease Industrial Measurements," *Electronic Design*, pp. 118–24 (Sept. 4, 1986).

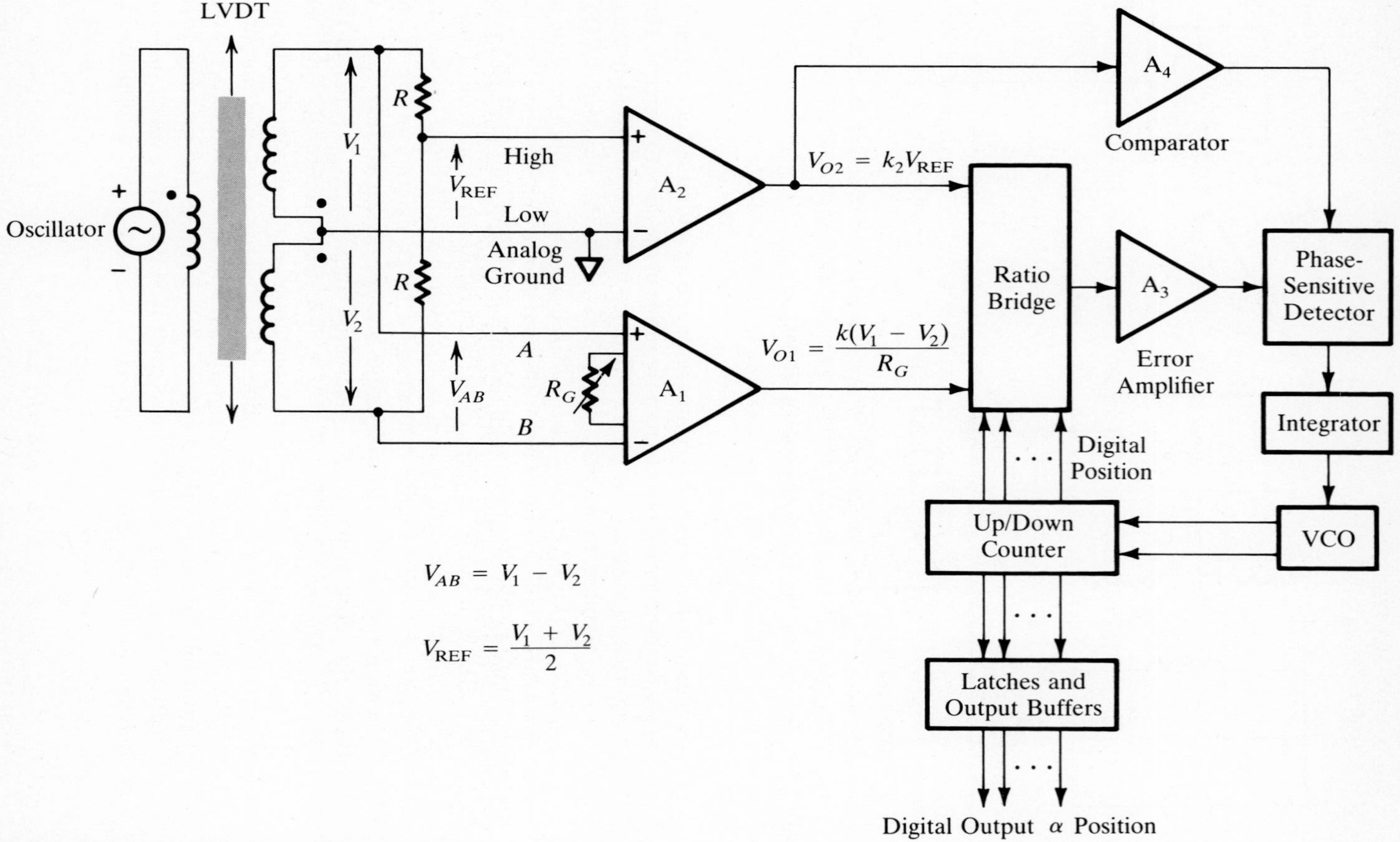

Figure 8.20 High-resolution LVDT circuit.

$$V_{AB} = V_1 - V_2$$

$$V_{REF} = \frac{V_1 + V_2}{2}$$

$$V_{O2} = k_2 V_{REF}$$

$$V_{O1} = \frac{k(V_1 - V_2)}{R_G}$$

system. Any changes in the primary oscillator amplitude have no effect on the circuit, since signals V_{REF} and V_{AB} are both affected equally. Similarly, internal gain changes have no significant effect, since they are divided by the overall loop transmission. The entire ratiometric converter can be obtained commercially as an integrated modular circuit, such as the Analog Devices 2S54 (14 bits) and 2S56 (16 bits), with guaranteed monotonicity and resolution capability to 8 nM. The secondary resistors (R) are also included in the package, and are precision ($\pm 0.02\%$), low TC (± 2 ppm/$^\circ$C matching) units.

8.3.2 Hall-Effect Circuits

A Hall-effect device is a semiconductor element that produces an output voltage proportional to a magnetic field.* The principle of operation is very simply indicated in Fig. 8.21(a), where the dc current I is passed through a semiconductor of length L, width W, and thickness t. If the current flow is perpendicular to a magnetic field B the force on the electrons (or holes) will cause a displacement of charge, and thereby induce a counterbalancing electric field. If contacts are placed perpendicular to the current flow an output voltage (the Hall Voltage V_H) will be obtained. It can be shown that the voltage is proportional to the current I and the field B as

$$V_H = \left| \frac{R_H I B}{10^8 t} \right| \tag{8.30}$$

where $R_H \approx 1.5/q \times$ concentration, I is in amperes, B is in Gauss, and t is in units of cm.

For displacement measurement, the Hall-effect sensor usually employs a fixed magnet, as illustrated in Fig. 8.21(b) and (c). In (b) the sensor is usually fixed, while a magnet is attached to the movable member. For better linear-displacement sensing, the Hall-effect device can be attached to a member that moves past a long bar magnet, as shown in (c). The linearity of output voltage vs displacement is generally inferior to that of a LVDT sensor, although it is possible to add additional magnets to help linearize the magnetic-field vs displacement contours.

The Hall-effect sensor is usually contained as part of an overall sensor/amplifier, current-source integrated circuit,† with typical output voltage sensitivities of 1–10 mV/gauss for a 0–1000 gauss variation. Although strongly dependent upon the arrangement of the magnetic field, these parameters can translate into output-voltage vs displacement sensitivities of ± 1 to ± 10 V/inch of displacement, for a total span of $< \pm 0.2''$.

---

* For a good discussion of the Hall-effect principle, see Ben Streetman, *Solid State Electronic Devices*, Second Edition, pp. 88–90 (Englewood Cliffs, NJ: Prentice-Hall, 1980).
† See Ref. 8.18 for characteristics and applications of several types of Hall-effect IC sensors.

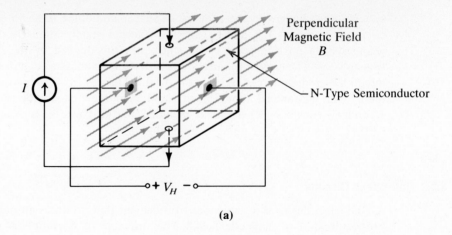

(a)

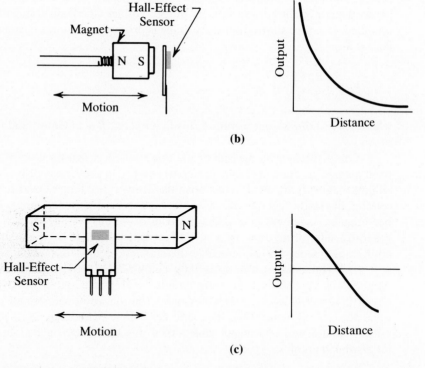

(b)

(c)

Figure 8.21   (a) The Hall effect principle. (b) Hall-effect proximity detector. (c) A linear displacement detector.

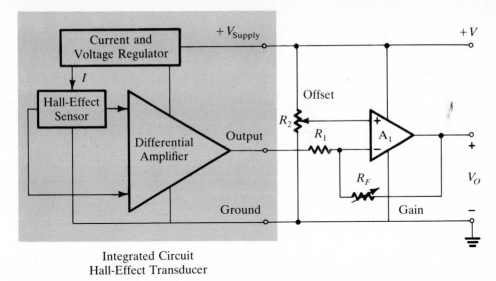

Figure 8.22 A representative interface circuit for Hall-Effect transducers.

Most of the Hall-effect transducers are designed to operate from a single power supply. Interfacing to the IC circuits requires both gain and offset-adjustment capability as shown in Fig. 8.22, where potentiometer R_2 is adjusted for offsets, while R_F is varied to obtain the desired output full-scale voltage. Further, if additional linearization of the transfer curve is desired, the output signal of A_1 could be processed by a diode curve-shaping network, as shown in Section 7.2.

8.4 PRESSURE MEASUREMENT

Pressure can be measured by a variety of transducers, some of which are shown in Fig. 8.23. In Fig. 8.23(a) a bellows expands and contracts with pressure, thereby changing a rheostat pickoff position and producing an output-voltage change. This type of sensor is widely used due to its simplicity, but lacks resolution due to the diameter of the resistance wire from which the rheostat is fabricated.

Similarly, a change in capacitance proportional to pressure change is obtained with the capacitive transducer of Fig. 8.23(b), where the force on a flexible metallic diaphragm produces a change of capacitance. If the capacitor is connected as part of an oscillator circuit, the output *frequency* will change in proportion to pressure. Alternatively, if the capacitor is used in a switched-capacitor amplifier with a fixed input voltage, the output *voltage* would change directly with pressure changes.

The LVDT, normally used for linear displacement measurement, is used with a C-tube–type Bourdon tube in Fig. 8.23(c) to indicate pressure. The Bourdon tube is made by bending a round tube into a noncircular cross-section and twisting the tube along its length. One end is solidly secured, while the other end of the tube is unrestrained and thus tends to flex back toward its original shape as pressure in the

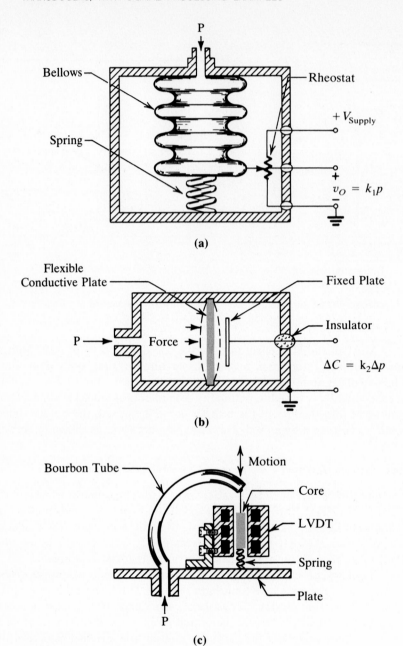

Figure 8.23 Several examples of pressure transducers.

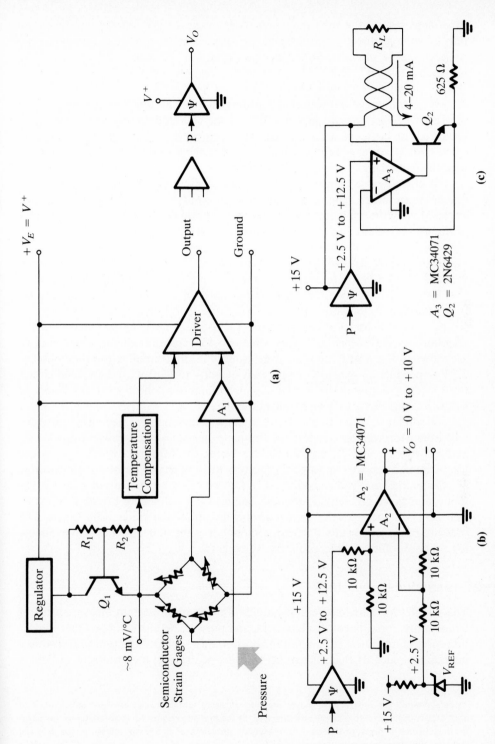

Figure 8.24 (a) The LX12-LX18 semiconductor pressure transducer and amplifier. (b) Obtaining a 0–10 VDC output. (c) A 4–20 mA current transmitter loop.

517

tube increases. As the tube moves the core of the LVDT follows, producing an output voltage directly proportional to displacement, and therefore indirectly proportional to pressure. Bourdon-tube transducers are extremely versatile, with full-scale ranges of from 0–15 psig* to as large as 0–10,000 psig. Typical linearity is ±0.2% of full scale using LVDTs.

The strain-gage transducer can also be used to measure very small changes in pressure by cementing the gage to a flexible member undergoing stress. The stress produced can be due to force exerted by the pressure of either a gas or a fluid. Any of the basic strain-gage bridge circuits shown earlier (in Figs. 8.15 or 8.16) could be used for interfacing.

A considerable increase in strain-gage sensitivity is obtained with semiconductor gages, which have a gage factor significantly larger than that of metallic gages. Most of the semiconductor gages are integrated into an IC chip along with a bridge excitation circuit and amplification circuitry, so that the output voltage is a high-level signal that requires very little additional gain. Although many manufacturers offer these sensors, we will examine only two of the more widely used versions. The LX line of pressure transducers available from National Semiconductor [Ref. 8.21], have a standardized output range of 2.5–12.5 V for an input range from minimum to maximum pressure. Available operating ranges are from -5 to $+5$ psi, to 0–300 psi. A diagram of the LX12–LX18 circuitry included with the transducer is shown in Fig. 8.24(a) while two convenient analog-interface circuits are shown in Fig. 8.24(b) and (c). The output of the first circuit requires an offset of 2.5 V to produce an output-voltage range of ~ 0 V to $+10$ V. In the second circuit the 2.5–12.5 V output at the emitter of Q_2 translates to a collector current change of 4 mA to 20 mA for a two wire transmitter.

A similar IC transducer/amplifier temperature-compensated circuit is available from Motorola Semiconductor Products. Instead of the bipolar transistor Q_1 and resistors R_1 and R_2 used in the LX series, the Motorola MPX devices use laser-trimmed resistors and two thermistors to compensate the strain-gage bridge against temperature shifts. Additionally, four op amps on the chip provide a high-input-impedance differential-amplifier connection to eliminate bridge loading, as well as a voltage reference and output-span (full-scale) range adjustment. The pressure range is typically 0–15 psi, although a range of 0–30 psi is also available for either absolute or differential measurements.

8.5 OTHER TRANSDUCER CIRCUITS

This chapter has shown several examples of the more important measurements of temperature, force, linear displacement, and pressure. Multitudinous other important cases of measurement are not included in this brief introduction to transducer interfacing—such as electrochemical measurements, level measurement of liquids

---

* psig ≡ pounds per square inch, gauge pressure. Pressure measurements are specified in units of absolute pressure (zero pressure at absolute zero, or the pressure *relative* to vacuum), gauge (or gage) pressure (which is pressure *relative* to atmospheric pressure), or differential pressure (which is the algebraic difference between two pressures).

and solids, vacuum measurement, fluid flow, humidity, and nuclear disintegration, to mention just a few. However, before ending this brief discussion of transducers we will include a few additional circuits, if for no other reason than to pique the reader's curiosity and desire to undertake additional study using the references listed in Appendix A. These final examples presented are very brief, and the circuits chosen to illustrate the rather unique and thought-provoking concepts of electronic measurement used.

8.5.1 Humidity

A measure of humidity indicates the amount of water vapor in the air, expressed as relative humidity (%) or absolute humidity. Relative humidity (RH) is generally defined as the percentage ratio of the vapor pressure of water in a gas (usually air) relative to the vapor pressure at full saturation at the same temperature. Absolute humidity is defined as the actual amount of water present in a given volume of gas (usually air), normally expressed in units of grams/m^3. Absolute humidity is normally not used in industrial work.

There are several very inexpensive sensors for measuring relative humidity. In the fifteenth century Leonardo da Vinci observed that a piece of wool or cotton increased in weight as it absorbed moisture from the atmosphere. Also, human hair (even horse hair!) will change its length depending on the air's moisture content. Instruments using hair are quite common for inexpensive domestic use.

Industrial circuits for humidity measurement involve many techniques. One of the more inexpensive sensors uses an Al_2O_3 capacitor-type detector,* where the capacitance of the sensor varies with the amount of moisture physically absorbed on the ceramic layer. An electrical equivalent circuit of the transducer is shown in Fig. 8.25(a). The detector can be made quite small (~ 60 mils, square), allowing the chip to be placed inside a sealed IC enclosure to monitor the moisture content of the IC environment; in this case moisture content as low as 1 ppm in air (at 1 atmosphere) is possible. The sensor is available in larger sizes for normal industrial use.

A switched-capacitor amplifier compliments the detector well as an interface circuit, as shown in Fig. 8.25(b)†. The switches (Linear Technology type LT1043) are driven by an internal clock which alternatively charges and discharges the humidity sensor. Since the charge voltage is fixed by the precision reference, the average current into the summing point of A_1 is determined by the sensor's capacitance, which is proportional to the relative humidity. The 22-megohm resistor prevents charge accumulation on the sensor. Since the capacitance transducer is nonlinear near 0% and 100% RH, the trim-potentiometers R_3 and R_5 must be included to define the overall span. Once calibrated, the overall accuracy is claimed to be within $\pm 2\%$ over a 5-90% RH range. The A_2 amplifier can be an

---

* A. D. Baranyi and S. K. Chang, *Hybrid Circuit Technology*, pp. 43–45 (Sept. 1986).
† Another design suggested by Jim Williams, "Monolithic CMOS-Switch IC Suits Diverse Applications," *EDN*, p. 188 (Oct. 4, 1984).

inexpensive device (741, or equivalent), since drift is established by A_1. The capacitor C_4 may be needed for additional lowpass filtering. The dual switch, LT1043, was also used previously, in Problem 5.11, to obtain an instrumentation amplifier.

Also available are resistance sensors whose conductive coating is sensitive to RH*, with the resistance value varying according to the relative humidity of the surrounding air. Unfortunately the RH is proportional to the logarithm of the resistor, hence a log amplifier circuit must be used to obtain a linear output.†

8.5.2 Fluid Flow

Many techniques exist for measuring the flow of fluids. We have paddlewheels and turbines whose rate of rotation is proportional to the fluid velocity, differential-pressure transducers that measure the pressure drop across two points in the stream, and even strain-gage bridge circuits that measure the force exerted on a member by the flowing medium, to mention only a few. A rather interesting thermal sensor can also be obtained by using wire that loses heat to the surrounding fluid. A measure of the heat loss is indicative of the flow.

Another example of a thermal flowmeter is diagrammed in Fig. 8.26. The temperature upstream is sensed by the temperature transducer T_1, while the temperature downstream is sensed by transducer T_2. Some inexpensive choices of transducers might be a semiconductor device like the AD590 or the LM393 [Ref.

---

* Phys-Chemical Research Corp., type PCRC-55.
† Several good circuit examples are shown in L. H. Sherman, "Sensors and Conditioning Circuits Simplify Humidity Measurement," *EDN*, pp. 179–88 (May 16, 1985). [Also see Ref. 8.8, pp. 161–64.]

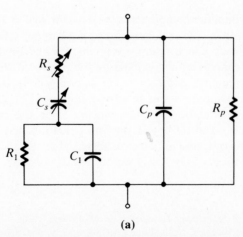

(a)

Figure 8.25 Relative humidity sensor and circuitry. (a) Sensor equivalent circuit.

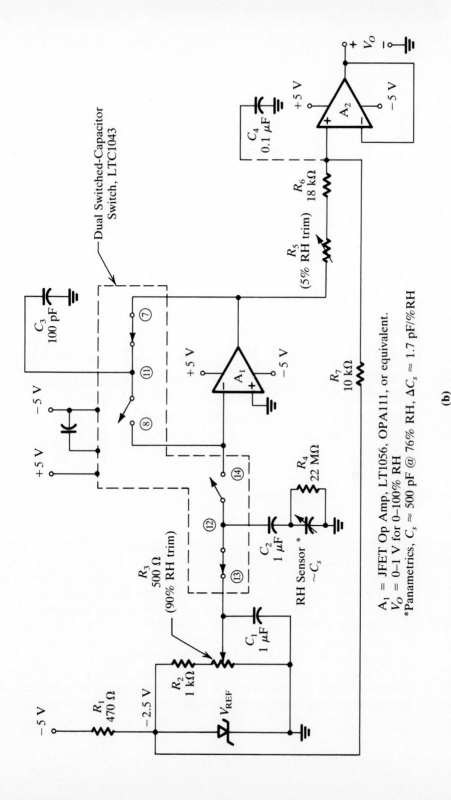

A_1 = JFET Op Amp, LT1056, OPA111, or equivalent.
V_O = 0–1 V for 0–100% RH
*Panametrics, $C_s \approx$ 500 pF @ 76% RH, $\Delta C_s \approx$ 1.7 pF/%RH

(b)

Figure 8.25 Relative humidity sensor and circuitry. (b) Signal processing switched-capacitor circuit.

521

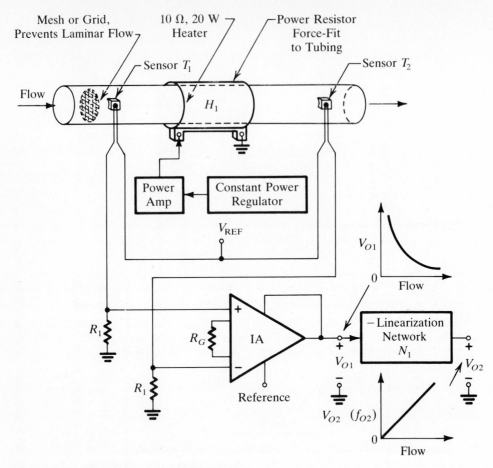

Figure 8.26 Temperature-sensing flowmeter.

8.1, p. 208] or, for higher resolution, a thermistor element*. The heater (H_1) should ideally be connected to a constant-power driver, but for reduced cost a fixed voltage could be applied to a vitreous resistor whose resistance remains relatively constant with temperature. At low flow rates the fluid temperature at T_2 is large compared to that at T_1, thus V_{O1} is high. However, at high flow rates very little heat is coupled to a given cross-section of the flowing medium, hence the difference $T_2 - T_1$ is small and V_{O1} will be low. Hence the relationship between V_{O1} and flow rate is approximately $V_{O1} \approx$ constant (1/flow). To linearize the output vs flow rate thus requires an inversion, and a linearization network N_1. It is sometimes desirable (for signal transmission) to perform a voltage-to-frequency conversion in N_1, thus obtaining a linear output-frequency change with flow at V_{O2}.

---

* J. Williams, *EDN*, p. 243 (June 28, 1984).

The sensors T_1 and T_2 should be placed relatively close to the heater, as should the mixing grid (for small tubing a distance of $1''$ apart is suggested). The correct distances obviously depend on full-scale flow rate, the type (and diameter) of piping, and the thermal characteristics of the fluid.

8.5.3 Air Flow (Anemometers)

The change-of-heat technique for measuring fluid flow can be easily extended to measure air flow as well. The circuit of Fig. 8.27(a) is suggested by Linear Technology as an inexpensive air-flow detector. With no air flow the sum of the Seebeck potentials of thermocouples TC1 and TC2 is greater than the voltage at the inverting input of A_1, thus the output voltage V_{O1} will be high (~ 5 V). When air flows past R_5, the cooling effect reduces the voltage at the noninverting input of A_1, and the output V_{O1} will drive low (~ 0 V). A chopper-stabilized op amp is required for A_1 since the error signal at the input of the comparator circuit is <1 mV. Resistor R_3 should be adjusted for the required sensitivity to flow.

The circuit of Fig. 8.27(b) can provide a linear dc-output-voltage change directly proportional to air flow*; i.e., a 0–10 V output for 0–1000 ft/min flow. The sensor is either a platinum filament (often called a hot-wire anemometer), or an inexpensive tungsten-lamp filament with its glass envelope removed ($\#328$, or equivalent). The lamp has a positive temperature coefficient. In the control loop of Fig. 8.27(b) the lamp is maintained at constant resistance (constant temperature) by the bridge connection of R_1–R_4, A_1 and the power transistor Q_1. Any tendency for the temperature of R_2 to decrease due to air flow would produce a decrease in the signal at the inverting input of A_1, thereby driving more current into the base of Q_1 and increasing the voltage output at the emitter of Q_1. Thus, the output voltage at the emitter of Q_1 is related to air flow. The circuit has higher sensitivity at low air flows, hence for a linear output at V_{O2} a linearization network N_1 is required. It is important to keep a small current constantly flowing in the filament, even at zero air flow, to ensure that the output at A_1 goes positive on turn on; a 2 kΩ resistor across the collector to emitter of Q_1 is usually sufficient. Resistor R_1 can be adjusted for sensitivity, while R_7 controls the full-scale output voltage at V_{O2}. The linearization network will also require an offset correction for the low end of the scale (near zero air flow). Finally, the power transistor Q_1 must be able to supply up to one ampere of current.

8.5.4 pH Measurement

Electrochemical measurements are needed for controlling many chemical, medical, and bacteriological processes. Some of the parameters sensed are electrical conductivity, dissolved oxygen (DO), oxidation-reduction potential (ORP, or

---

* J. Williams, *Ibid*, p. 244. [Also, see Ref. 8.1, p. 206.]

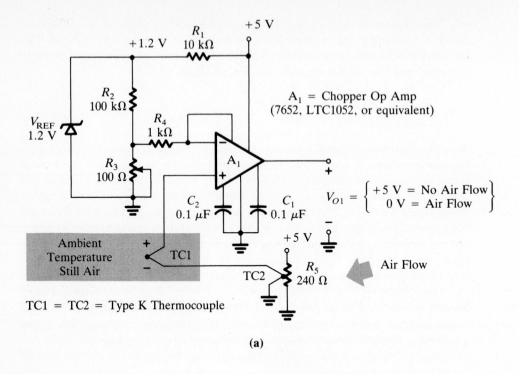

(a)

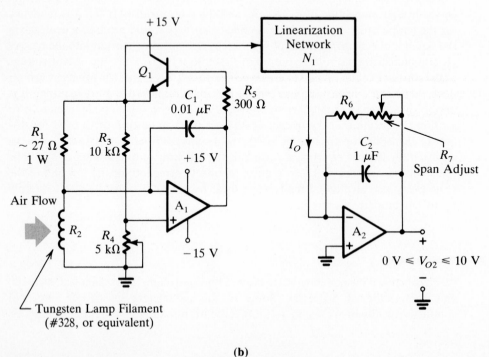

(b)

Figure 8.27 Air-flow detection by temperature sensing.

Redox), temperature, and pH. The pH* measurement indicates the degree of acidity or alkalinity of a solution, obtained by monitoring the hydrogen-ion concentration; the pH scale is logarithmic. Since in most solutions the hydrogen-ion concentration is a fraction, the pH value is really the negative of the logarithm (or the logarithm of the reciprocal) of the hydrogen-ion concentration. For example, pure water at 25 °C has a hydrogen-ion concentration of 1×10^{-7}, or a pH value of 7.0; likewise, the hydrogen-ion concentration of concentrated sodium hydroxide (very, very alkaline) is near 1×10^{-14} (pH = 14), while strong sulfuric acid has a pH near 1.0 (hydrogen-ion concentration $\approx 10^{-1}$).

For electrical measurement a solution containing hydrogen ions determines the potential of an electrode immersed in the solution, thus a measure of the potential directly determines the pH value. All pH measurements require a reference electrode in addition to the electrode measuring the pH of the solution in question. Since the pH is also a function of solution temperature, a temperature-compensation correction must also be made. One common sensing electrode has a glass tube and a silver–to–silver-chloride electrode immersed in a buffer solution and separated from the solution in question by a thin, porous, ion-selective glass bulb. The reference electrode is fabricated from a silver–to–silver-chloride electrode immersed in a potassium chloride (KCl) solution, and a permeable junction connection to the measuring solution. The potential difference between the sensing electrode and the reference electrode is given by the Nernst equation

$$\Delta V = V_{\text{sensor}} - V_{\text{REF}} = \frac{2.3RT}{ZF} \log A \qquad \textbf{(8.31)}$$

where V_x is a constant, dependent upon the reference electrode, RT/F is defined as the Nernst Factor, Z is the ion charge, and A is the activity of the ion (H^+ in this case). Thus, the potential ΔV is a direct measurement of the activity of the particular ion for which the membrane is sensitive. For the case of H^+ activity, the term 2.3 RT/ZF is equal to 59.16 mV at 298 °K. Thus, at any other temperature

$$V_{\text{sensor}} = V_{\text{REF}} - 1.985(T)(\text{pH}) \times 10^{-4} \qquad \textbf{(8.32)}$$

where T is in degrees Kelvin, and $\log A = -\text{pH}$. Since the ion-selective glass electrode has an electrical resistivity on the order of 10^9 ohms, special high-input-impedance (very low I_B) electrometer amplifiers must be used to interface with the pH electrode.

The graph in Fig. 8.28(a) shows the output potential of a typical pH sensor as a function of pH and temperature, where the reference potential is chosen for zero output at pH = 7 (distilled water). The pH sensor is buffered and amplified by the two-op-amp differential amplifier in Fig. 8.28(b) (this is the same circuit as in Problem 1.21). Since the output impedance of the glass pH electrode is so large ($\geq 10^9 \, \Omega$), special electrometer-type op amps must be used for A_1 and A_2. The

---

* The pH scale is attributed to Sven Sorenson, a Danish chemist, in 1909. The term **p** is from the French word *puissance* (meaning "power"), while **H** stands for the H^+ ion.

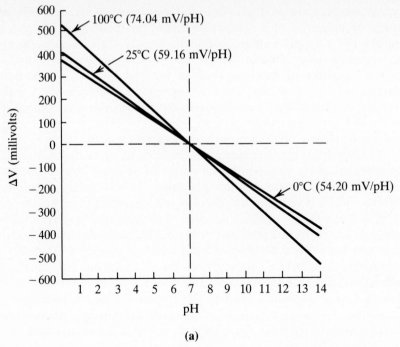

(a)

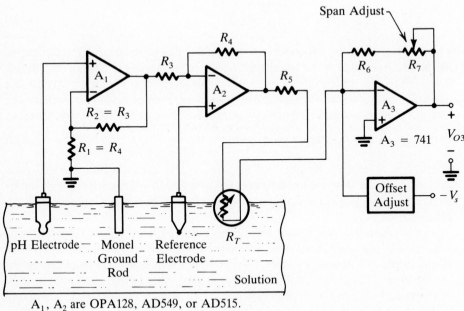

A$_1$, A$_2$ are OPA128, AD549, or AD515.

(b)

Figure 8.28 (a) Output potential of a typical glass pH electrode. (b) Op amp signal-conditioning circuit.

devices indicated in the figure have typical values of $I_B \approx 4 \times 10^{-14}$ amp, $V_{OS} \leq 0.5$ mV, $R_{IN} \geq 10^{13} \, \Omega$, and $C_{IN} \approx 1$ pF. The ground rod is often used to maintain the solution and the electronic circuit commons at the same potential. The temperature sensor (R_T) adjusts the gain of the circuit to compensate for the temperature sensitivity of the pH electrode.

SUMMARY

This chapter has been very brief. Our intent was only to consider a few of the more important measurement topics involving temperature, force, linear displacement, and pressure. In addition, some other examples of rather interesting circuit concepts have been included, to demonstrate how op amps can be integrated into a complete compensated-measurement system. The literature abounds with many, many other examples and circuit techniques. It is hoped that the student will grow to appreciate the panorama of possibilities offered by designing with operational amplifiers.

PROBLEMS

8.1 Suppose the ice-water mixture and junction J_2 were eliminated in Fig. 8.2(a), and that the voltmeter (V_S) is directly connected to the thermocouple monitoring temperature T_1. Sketch the equivalent electrical circuit formed and shown why the voltmeter will not read potential V_1.

8.2 Obtain the values for resistors R_1 and R in Fig. 8.4(a) if the thermocouple is a type K with an ambient Seebeck voltage of $V_{j2} = 1.000$ mV at 25 °C.

8.3 Estimate the accuracy possible for temperature measurement using the circuit of Fig. 8.4(a), if the ambient temperature is variable over the range $15 \,°C \leq T \leq 35 \,°C$. Use an error budget analysis approach. You may assume the TC of resistors R and R_1 is ± 50 ppm/°C, I_{C1} has a maximum nonlinearity of $\pm 0.1 \,°C$, and V_{REF} has a TC of ± 20 ppm/°C.

8.4 In the circuit of Fig. 8.4(c) verify that the temperature compensation circuit of V_{REF}, R_1, R_2, R_3 and R_T provides a Seebeck coefficient of approximately $+40.5 \,\mu V/°C$ over the temperature range from 15 to 35 °C. You may assume the thermistor can be characterized by the relation

$$R(T) = R(T_0) \exp\left[\beta\left(\frac{1}{T} - \frac{1}{T_0}\right) \right]$$

where $R(T_0) = 1 \, k\Omega$ at $T_0 = 25 \,°C$ (298 °K), and $\beta = 3260$.

8.5 Since the Seebeck coefficient is not constant for thermocouples [for example, see Fig. 8.2(b)], it is necessary for best accuracy to compare the measured Seebeck potential from the thermocouple against a computer-stored power series polynomial approximation for actual thermocouple output emf vs. temperature. For example, a type J thermocouple has the following approximation (obtained from the National Bureau of Standards, *Thermocouple Reference Tables*, NBS Monograph 125, NBS, Washington, D.C., 1979; also available in Ref. 8.3, p. T-12)

$$T = a_0 + a_1 v + a_2 v_2 + \ldots + a_n v^n$$

where v is the thermocouple output voltage, and the coefficients are

$$a_0 = -0.048868252$$

$$a_1 = 19873.14503$$

$$a_2 = -218614.5353$$

$$a_3 = 11569199.78$$

$$a_4 = -264917531.4$$

$$a_5 = 2018441314$$

Using the polynomial values above, compare the approximation with the curve of Fig. 8.3.

8.6 In the circuit of Fig. 8.6(a) compare the actual input reading to the ADC [using Eqs. 8.6(a) and (b)] at 255 °C, versus the theoretical reading assuming α is constant at $0.00392 \, \Omega/\Omega/°C$. Assume R_2 and R_3 have been correctly adjusted to the values indicated in the figure, and that $R_l = 0$.

8.7 Using the values specified in Eq. (8.6) and the circuit of Fig. 8.6(b), verify a correct LCD reading at 0 °C and 800 °C, using the nominal values specified for R_2 and R_4.

8.8 Using Eq. (8.18) and the RTD compensation circuit of Fig. 8.6(c), find values for all components to provide cancellation of the constant term and T^2 term in Eq. (8.18).

8.9 The circuit of Fig. P8.9 uses a silicon-based RTD manufactured by Micro Switch, Inc. The RTD is a thin-film resistor constructed of permalloy material sputtered (and then etched and laser-trimmed) onto a silicon substrate. The final chip size is 40 mils × 52 mils, with a resistance value of 2 kΩ at 20 °C, changing to 1584 Ω at −40 °C, and 3114 Ω at +150 °C. The TC is therefore positive (+6.5Ω/°C at −40 °C, +7.45 Ω/°C at 20 °C, and +9.5Ω/°C at 150 °C). The R_3 resistor is used in the circuit to improve the linearization of the sensor. The op amp/reference amp combination A_1, A_2 is the LM10 integrated circuit (data shown earlier in Problem 2.40), with IC package pin numbers as indicated. The overall circuit forms a half-bridge temperature

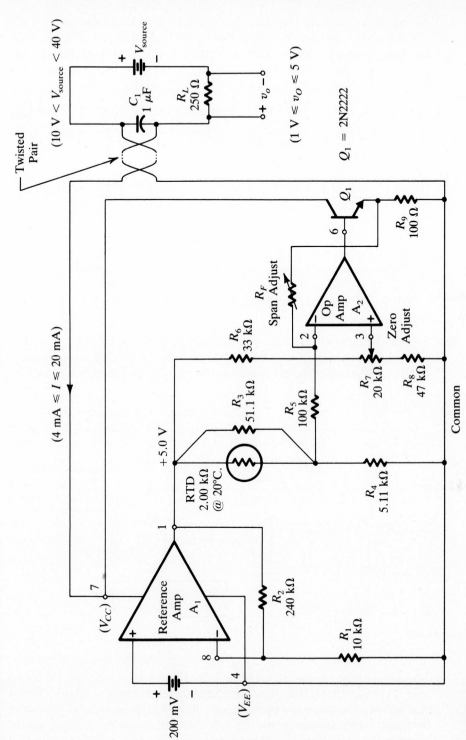

Figure P8.9

sensing circuit, with the output driving a 2-wire, 4–20 mA current loop. If the zero adjustment setting is made at $-40\,°C$ to obtain 4 mA in the loop, while the span adjustment (R_F) is made at $+150\,°C$ to furnish 20 mA, what are the correct values for R_F and V (pin 3) relative to the common terminal? With these settings, what is the accuracy of the $20\,°C$ reading?

8.10 For the thermistor data of Fig. 8.7, estimate the coefficient β for the two extreme curves, over the temperature range $0\,°C$ to $50\,°C$. Using your values for β find the error between actual resistance and that predicted by Eq. (8.20) at $150\,°C$.

8.11 For the circuit of Fig. 8.10(a) determine the correct value of R_6 and the collector current of Q_2 to provide $\pm\frac{1}{2}°F$ control at $150\,°F$. You may wish to express Eq. (8.20) in a series expansion, since the exponential term for $R_{T1}(T_1) - R_{T2}(T_2)$ is very small.

8.12 In the thermistor circuit of Fig. 8.10(b), what should be the output peak amplitude of the step-function response when R_4 is switched into the circuit (assume $25\,°C$)? If the thermistor has a coefficient of $24\,\Omega/°C$ at $250\,°C$, what would be the output step amplitude? At which temperature should the loop be compensated.

8.13 Assume the thermal-feedback loop of Fig. 8.10(b) can be modeled by an RC network as indicated in Fig. P8.13. What value of C_F would ensure system stability? What would be the crossover frequency f_C? Are there better ways to ensure stability and also increase f_C?

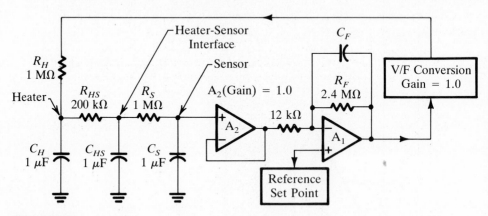

Figure P8.13

8.14 An inexpensive temperature probe is formed using a diode-connected transistor Q_1 in Fig. P8.14. If the diode temperature coefficient is $-2.1\,mV/°C$ at a current of $10\,\mu A$, determine the values for R_1 and R_2 to provide 0 V output at $0\,°C$ and $+10\,V$ output at $100\,°C$. What parameters of the op amp would result in linearity changes in the circuit?

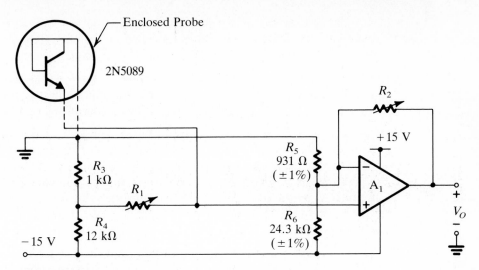

Figure P8.14

8.15 Suppose one wishes to obtain an output current proportional to the *average* of the temperature at each of four locations inside a chamber. The temperature may vary from 40 °C to 70 °C in the chamber. Using a semiconductor temperature transducer, indicate a simple circuit that would accomplish this. You have available a 5 V supply.

8.16 In the circuit of Fig. 8.13(c) ignore dc offsets of the op amp and reference. Assume $I(T)$ for the LM334 changes with temperature as

$$I(T) = \frac{(227\mu V/°K)T}{R_1}$$

and that the voltage drop across R_1 is 64 mV (298.2 °K), and changes linearly with temperature. What should the values be for R_3 and R_6 for correct circuit operation? If the LM10 has a dc supply current of 270μA, and both the LM334 and LM10 can operate with a total supply voltage of ≥ 1.0 V, how long would the circuit operate with one 1.5 V battery. Assume the battery has a 1500 mA-hour capacity.

8.17 In the circuit of Fig. 8.15(b), if the gage factor for each of the 4 gages is $G_f = 50$, while $\varepsilon = 1\mu\varepsilon$, what should the value of R_G be if an AD524 instrumentation amplifier is used to achieve an output full-scale sensitivity of 1000 $\mu\varepsilon$ for $V_{O1} = 10$ volts?

8.18 Show all components for each of the blocks indicated in Fig. 8.16. The sinusoidal generator should have good amplitude stability.

8.19 Show how one could use a quad CMOS analog switch connected to the secondary of the LVDT of Fig. 8.19, and clocked by the A_2 comparator output, to directly provide an ac-to-dc conversion without using the phase-sensitive detector.

8.20 A Hall-effect semiconductor device is fabricated on $10^{15}/cm^3$ doped n-type material, with an active region thickness of 20 micrometers. If the dc current I is 1 mA, estimate the Hall voltage produced by a 100 Gauss field.

8.21 Using the equations established in Chapter 6 (Section 6.6) for switched capacitance amplifiers, find the gain relation, and show that the output voltage span is 0–1 V for 0–100% RH for the circuit of Fig. 8.25(b).

8.22 Many gas detectors are thin-film resistive elements whose resistance varies with the concentration of gas in the air as $R \approx K/(\text{concentration})^{1/2}$. A particular methane gas sensor is found to have resistance of 4 kΩ at a methane concentration of 6000 ppm. Using the logarithmic amplifier principles of Chapter 7, and a voltage to frequency converter, design a circuit that will convert the sensor indication of 1000 ppm to 10,000 ppm to a frequency output of 100 Hz to 1 kHz.

8.23 Show a complete workable circuit for Fig. 8.26 that would produce an output frequency at V_{O2} of 0–300 Hz for a flow rate of 0–300 ml/min in the pipe. Assume a linearized thermistor network for sensors T_1 and T_2 (Eq. 8.21), a band-gap reference (V_{REF}), and the relation between V_{O1} and flow of

$$V_{O1} = \frac{3.3}{\text{FLOW}}$$

where units are volts and ml/min.

8.24 For the circuit of Fig. 8.28(b) find a compatible choice of resistors, and a temperature compensation circuit R_T, to obtain an output voltage at V_{O3} that is 0 V at pH = 0, increasing linearly to +14 V at pH = 14. Use power-supply voltages of +18 V and −12 V. The circuit should remain compensated for a solution temperature from 0 °C to 70 °C.

Appendix A

References

GENERAL

G.1   *Analogue Dialogue*, a magazine published 2–4 times a year by Analog Devices, Inc., Norwood, MA. (Available without charge to qualified engineers in industry).

G.2   *Applications Manual for Computing Amplifiers, Second Edition*, George A. Philbrick Researchers, Inc., Boston, MA, 1966. (currently out of print).

G.3   A. Barna, *Operational Amplifiers*, (New York: John Wiley & Sons, 1971).

G.4   Burr-Brown Electronics Series:

    (a) *Operational Amplifiers, Design and Applications*, Ed. J. G. Graeme, G. E. Tobey, and L. P. Huelsman, (New York: McGraw-Hill, 1971).

    (b) J. G. Graeme, *Applications of Operational Amplifiers, Third-Generation Techniques*, (New York: McGraw-Hill, 1973).

    (c) Y. J. Wong and W. E. Ott, *Function Circuits, Design and Applications*, (New York: McGraw-Hill, 1976).

    (d) J. G. Graeme, *Designing With Operational Amplifiers, Applications Alternatives*, (New York: McGraw-Hill, 1977).

G.5   *EDN*, a bi-weekly magazine, Cahners Publishing Co., Newton, MA. (Available without charge to qualified engineers in industry).

G.6   *Electronic Design*, a bi-weekly magazine, Hayden Publications, Hasbrouck Heights, NJ. (Available without charge to qualified engineers in industry).

G.7   *Electronics*, a bi-weekly magazine, McGraw-Hill, Inc.

G.8   T. M. Fredericksen, *Intuitive IC Op Amps*, National Semiconductor, Inc., Santa Clara, CA (1984).

G.9   R. G. Irvine, *Operational Amplifier Characteristics and Applications*, (Englewood Cliffs, NJ: Prentice-Hall, 1981).

G.10   W. G. Jung, *IC Op-Amp Cookbook*, *Second Ed.*, (Indianapolis, IN: Howard W. Sams & Co., 1980).

G.11   *Linear Applications*, Vol. I and Vol. II, National Semiconductor, Inc., Santa Clara, CA (1973 and 1976).

G.12   *Nonlinear Circuits Handbook*, Ed. D. H. Sheingold, Analog Devices, Inc., Norwood, MA (1974).

G.13   J. K. Roberge, *Operational Amplifiers*, *Theory and Practice*, (New York: John Wiley & Sons, 1975).

G.14   R. Seippel, *Operational Amplifers*, (Reston, VA: Reston Publ. Co., 1983).

G.15   J. V. Wait, L. P. Huelsman, and G. A. Korn, *Introduction to Operational Amplifier Theory and Applications*, (New York: McGraw-Hill, 1975).

G.16   C. F. Wojslaw and E. A. Moustakas, *Operational Amplifiers*, *The Devices and Their Applications*, (New York: John Wiley & Sons, 1986).

CHAPTER 2

2.1   G. E. Valley, Jr., and H. Wallman, *Vacuum Tube Amplifiers*, M.I.T. Radiation Lab Series, Ch. 2 (New York: McGraw-Hill, 1948).

2.2   W. C. Elmore, *J. Appl. Phy.*, Vol. 19, pp. 55–63 (Jan. 1948).

CHAPTER 3

3.1   J. J. D'Azzo and C. H. Houpis, *Feedback Control System Analysis and Synthesis*, (New York: McGraw-Hill, 1960).

3.2   C. J. Savant, Jr., *Basic Feedback Control System Design*, (New York: McGraw-Hill, 1958).

3.3   R. J. Barden and D. P. Braman, *EDN*, Vol. 26, No. 7, pp. 171–76 (April 1, 1981).

3.4   J. F. Pierce and T. J. Paulus, *Applied Electronics*, Ch. 11, (Columbus, Ohio: Charles E. Merrill Publs, Co., 1972).

3.5   A. Barna, *Operational Amplifiers*, (New York: John Wiley & Sons, 1971).

3.6   W. Helms, *EDN*, pp. 279–89 (Oct. 27, 1983).

3.7   R. A. Pease, *EDN*, pp. 93–94 (Feb. 20, 1979).

3.8   D. M. Weigland, *Electronic Design*, No. 15, pp. 64–66 (July 20, 1972).

3.9   R. J. Barden and D. P. Braman, *EDN*, Vol. 26, No. 6, pp. 151–62 (March 18, 1981).

3.10   N. Sevastopoulos, *Electronic Design*, No. 25, pp. 92–97 (Dec. 6, 1976).

3.11   G. Erdi, *IEEE J. S. S. Ckts.*, Vol. SC-16, No. 6, pp. 653–61 (Dec. 1981).

3.12   B. Wooley et al, *IEEE J. S. S. Ckts.*, Vol. SC-6, No. 6, pp. 357–66 (Dec. 1971).

3.13   J. K. Roberge, *Operational Amplifiers Theory and Practice*, (New York: John Wiley & Sons, 1975).

3.14   R. D. Thornton et al, *Multistage Transistor Circuits*, Chs. 1 and 8 (New York: John Wiley & Sons, 1965).

3.15   G. R. Boyle et al, *IEEE J. S. S. Ckts.*, Vol. SC-9, No. 6, pp. 353–63 (Dec. 1974).

3.16   G. Krajewska and F. E. Holmes, *IEEE J. S. S. Ckts.*, Vol. SC-14, No. 6, pp. 1083–87 (Dec. 1979).

3.17   P. R. Mukund and E. J. Kennedy, *The Use of SPICE2 for the Design of High Temperature Electronic Circuits*, M. S. Thesis, Univ. of Tenn., (July, 1981).

3.18 R. Sangsingkeow and J. M. Rochelle, *Analysis and Development of the High Frequency Common-Mode Rejection of an Instrumentation Amplifier*, M. S. Thesis, Univ. of Tenn., (Aug. 1984).

3.19 M. S. Ghausi, *Electronic Devices and Circuits: Discrete and Integrated*, (New York: Holt, Rinehart, and Winston, 1985).

CHAPTER 4

4.1 J. B. Johnson, *Phys. Rev.*, Vol. 32, pp. 97–109 (1928).

4.2 H. Nyquist, *Phys. Rev.*, Vol. 32, pp. 110–13 (1928).

4.3 H. Ekstein and N. Rostoker, *Phys. Rev.*, Vol. 100, p. 1023 (1955).

4.4 W. Schottky, *Ann. Phys.* (*Leipzig*), Vol. 57, pp. 541–67 (1918)

4.5 A. J. Broderson et al. *IEEE J. S. S. Ckts.*, Vol. SC-5, pp. 63–66 (April 1970)

4.6 R. C. Jaeger and A. J. Broderson, *IEEE Trans. Elec. Dev.*, Vol. ED-17, pp. 128–34 (Feb. 1970).

4.7 P. L. Leonard and S. V. Jaskolski, *Proc. IEEE*, Vol. 57, pp. 1787–88 (1969).

4.8 R. H. Haitz, *Electronic Communication*, Vol. 2, No. 2, pp. 18, 19 (Mar./April 1967).

4.9 E. R. Chenette, *Noise In Junction Transistors*, Ph.D. Thesis, Univ. of Minn., (July 30, 1959).

4.10 R. D. Thornton et al, *Characteristics and Limitations of Transistors*, Ch. 4 (New York: John Wiley & Sons, 1966).

4.11 C. D. Motchenbacher and F. C. Fitchen, *Low-Noise Electronic Design*, (New York: John Wiley & Sons, 1973).

4.12 A. van der Ziel, *Proc. IRE*, Vol. 50, pp. 1808–12 (Aug. 1962).

4.13 A. van der Ziel, *Proc. IRE*, Vol. 51, pp. 461–67 (March 1963).

4.14 C. T. Sah, *Proc. IEEE*, Vol. 52, pp. 795–814 (1964).

4.15 C. T. Sah et al, *IEEE Trans. Elec. Dev.*, Vol. ED-13, pp. 410–14 (1966).

4.16 L. R. Smith, "Noise and Operational Amplifier Circuits," *Analog Dialogue*, Vol. 3, No. 1 (1969).

4.17 A. Ryan and T. Scranton, "DC Amplifier Noise Revisited," *Analog Dialogue*, Vol. 18, No. 1 (1984).

4.18 M. J. Buckingham, *Noise In Electronic Devices and Systems*, Ellis Horwood Ltd, England, distributed by Halsted Press, a division of John Wiley & Sons, New York (1983).

4.19 *Electronic Noise: Fundamentals and Sources*, Ed. M. S. Gupta, (New York: IEEE Press, 1977).

4.20 *Low-Noise Microwave Transistors and Amplifiers*, Ed. H. Fukui, (New York: IEEE Press, 1981).

4.21 *Analog Circuit Design Seminar*, copyright by Analog Devices, Inc., Norwood, MA, (July 1984).

4.22 G. Franklin and T. Hatley, *Electronic Design*, Vol. 24, pp. 184–87, (Nov. 22, 1973).

4.23 M. E. Gruchalla, *EDN*, pp. 157–60 (June 5, 1980).

4.24 T. Cate, *EDN*, pp. 151–53 (May 27, 1981).

4.25 A. Jenkins and D. Bowers, *EDN*, pp. 323, 324, (May 3, 1984).

CHAPTER 5

5.1 *Analog Circuit Design Seminar*, copyright by Analog Devices, Inc., Norwood, MA (July 1984).

5.2 J. R. Riskin, *A User's Guide to IC Instrumentation Amplifiers*, Application Note, Analog Devices, Inc., Norwood, MA (January, 1978).

5.3   J. G. Graeme, *Applications of Operational Amplifiers: Third-Generation Techniques*, (New York: McGraw-Hill, 1973)

5.4   J. G. Graeme et al, *Operational Amplifiers: Design and Applications*, (New York: McGraw-Hill, 1971).

5.5   Y. J. Wong, W. E. Ott, *Function Circuits: Design and Applications*, (New York: McGraw-Hill, 1976).

5.6   S. Worcer and W. Jung, "Instrumentation Amplifiers Solve Unusual Design Problems," *EDN*, pp. 133–45 (Aug. 4, 1983).

5.7   J. Williams, "Application of a Switched-Capacitor Instrumentation Building Block," *Appl. Note 3*, Linear Technology, Inc., Malpitas, CA, (Dec. 1984).

5.8   *Transducer Interfacing Handbook*, D. H. Sheingold (Ed.), Analog Devices, Inc., Norwood, MA, (1980).

5.9   J. G. Graeme, *Designing With Operational Amplifiers; Applications Alternatives*, (New York: McGraw-Hill, 1977).

5.10   *Product Data Book*, Burr-Brown Corp., (July 1984).

5.11   *Isolation and Instrumentation Amplifiers Designers Guide*, Analog Devices, Inc., Norwood, MA, (Nov. 1978).

5.12   *Linear Applications Handbook*, National Semiconductor Corp., Santa Clara, CA, (1980).

5.13   L. L. Schick, "Linear Circuit Applications of Operational Amplifiers," *IEEE Spectrum*, pp. 36–50 (April 1971).

5.14   J. Graeme, "Tame Transducer Bridge Errors with Op-Amp Feedback Control," *EDN*, pp. 173–76 (May 26, 1982).

5.15   E. A. Goldberg, "Stabilization of Wide-Band Direct Current Amplifiers for Zero and Gain," *RCA Review*, Vol. II, No. 2, pp. 296–300 (June 1950).

5.16   J. K. Roberge, *Operational Amplifiers: Theory and Practice*, (New York: John Wiley & Sons, 1975).

5.17   "OTA-Operational Transconductance Amplifiers," *Publ. OTA-340*, RCA Corp. (1982).

5.18   "Applications of the CA3080 and CA3080A High Performance Operational Transconductance Amplifiers," *Appl. Note ICAN-6668*, RCA Corp. (Sept. 1971).

5.19   R. L. Geiger and E. Sanchez-Sinencio, "Active Filter Design Using Operational Transconductance Amplifiers: A Tutorial," *IEEE Ckts. & Devices*, Vol. 1, No. 2, pp. 20–32 (March 1985).

5.20   M. Giles, "On-Chip Stereo Filter Cuts Noise Without Preprocessing Signals," *Electronics*, pp. 104–08 (Aug. 11, 1981).

5.21   *Analog Data Manual, 1983*, NE5517 Data, Signetics Corp., pp. 10-66 through 10-77 (1983).

5.22   *Applications: Linear Integrated Circuits*, publ. *SSD245*, RCA Corp. (1983).

5.23   T. M. Frederiksen et al, *Appl. Note AN-72*, National Semiconductor Corp., Santa Clara, CA (Sept. 1972).

5.24   *DC Power Supply Handbook*, Hewlett Packard, Inc., Berkeley Heights, N.J. (1970).

5.25   P. Birman, *Power Supply Handbook*, Kepco, Inc., Flushing, N.Y. (1965).

5.26   *Voltage Regulator Handbook*, National Semiconductor, Inc., Santa Clara, CA (1981).

5.27   J. Alberkrack et al, *Linear/Switchmode Voltage Regulator Handbook*, Motorola, Inc., Phoenix, AZ (1982).

5.28   A. Adamian, *Voltage Regulator Handbook*, Fairchild Camera and Instrument Corp., Mountain View, CA (1978).

5.29   R. J. Haver, "Use Current Foldback to Protect Your Voltage Regulator," *EDN*, pp. 69–72 (Aug. 20, 1974).

5.30   R. C. Dobkin, "Designer's Guide to: IC Voltage Regulators," *EDN*, Part 1, pp. 93–98 (Aug. 20, 1979), Part 2, pp. 199–204 (Sept. 5, 1979).

5.31 R. C. Dobkin, "Break Loose From Fixed IC Regulators," *Elect. Design*, Vol. 8, pp. 118–22 (April 12, 1977).

5.32 R. J. Widlar, R. C. Dobkin, and M. Yamatake, "New Op Amp Ideas," Appl. Note *AN211*, National Semiconductor, Inc. (Dec. 1978).

5.33 R. A. Pease, "Improve Circuit Performance with a 1-Op-Amp Current Pump," *EDN*, Vol. 28, No. 2, pp. 85–90 (Jan. 20, 1983).

5.34 J. Williams, *A Designer's Guide to: Innovative Linear Circuits*, EDN (Cahners Publications), Newton, MA (1985).

5.35 T. M. Fredericksen, *Intuitive IC Op Amps*, National Semiconductor Technology Series, R. R. Donnelley & Sons (1984).

5.36 W. G. Jung, *IC Op-Amp Cookbook, 2nd Ed.*, Howard W. Sons & Co., Indianapolis, IN, 1980.

CHAPTER 6

6.1 L. P. Huelsman and P. E. Allen, *Introduction to The Theory and Design of Active Filters*, (New York: McGraw-Hill, 1980).

6.2 M. E. Van Valkenburg, *Analog Filter Design*, (New York: Holt, Rinehart and Winston, 1982).

6.3 Arthur B. Williams, *Electronic Filter Design Handbook*, (New York: McGraw-Hill, 1981).

6.4 C. S. Lindquist, *Active Network Design with Signal Filtering Applications*, Stewart and Sons, Long Beach, CA (1977).

6.5 Aram Budak, *Passive and Active Network Analysis and Synthesis*, (Boston, MA: Houghton Mifflin Co., 1974).

6.6 L. P. Huelsman, *Theory and Design of Active RC Circuits*, (New York: McGraw-Hill, 1968).

6.7 H. J. Blinchikoff and A. J. Zverev, *Filtering in the Time and Frequency Domains*, (New York: John Wiley & Sons, 1976).

6.8 *Modern Active Filter Design*, Rolf Schaumann et al, (New York: IEEE Press, 1981).

6.9 *Active Inductorless Filters*, S. K. Mitra, (New York: IEEE Press, 1971).

6.10 *Computer-Aided Filter Design*, Ed. G. Szentirmai, (New York: IEEE Press, 1973).

6.11 *MOS Switched-Capacitor Filters: Analysis and Design*, Ed. G. S. Moschytz, (New York: IEEE Press, 1984).

6.12 *Switched-Capacitor Filter Handbook*, Ed. K. Lacanette, National Semiconductor Corp., Santa Clara, CA (April 1985).

6.13 Don Lancaster, *Active Filter Cookbook*, Howard W. Sams and Co., Inc., Indianapolis, IN (1975).

6.14 A. B. Grebene, *Bipolar and MOS Analog Integrated Circuit Design*, Ch. 13, (New York: John Wiley & Sons, 1984).

6.15 *Analog MOS Integrated Circuits*, Ed. P. R. Gray et al, Part VI, (New York: IEEE Press, 1980).

6.16 Anatol J. Zverev, *Handbook of Filter Synthesis*, (New York: John Wiley & Sons, 1967).

6.17 L. Weinberg, *Network Analysis and Synthesis*, (New York: McGraw-Hill, 1962); reissued by Robert E. Krieger Publ., Inc., Melbourne, FL (1975).

6.18 E. Christian and E. Eisenmann, *Filter Design Tables and Graphs*, Transmission Networks International, Inc., Knightdale, NC (1977).

6.19 G. C. Temes and J. Lapatra, *Introduction to Circuit Synthesis and Design*, (New York: McGraw-Hill, 1977).

6.20 F. W. Stephenson (Ed.), *RC Active Filter Design Handbook*, (New York: John Wiley & Sons, 1985).

6.21 P. E. Allen and E. Sanchez-Sinencio, *Switched Capacitor Circuits*, (New York: Van Nostrand Reinhold, 1984).

6.22 R. Gregorian and G. C. Temes, *Analog MOS Integrated Circuits for Signal Processing*, (New York: John Wiley & Sons, 1986).

CHAPTER 7

7.1 J. W. Wait, L. P. Huelsman, and G. A. Korn, *Introduction to Operational Amplifier Theory and Applications*, Ch. 3, (New York: McGraw-Hill, 1975).

7.2 W. G. Jung, *IC Op-Amp Cookbook, Second Edition*, (Indianapolis, IN: Howard W. Sams & Co., Inc., 1983).

7.3 D. F. Stout and M. Kaufman, *Handbook of Operational Amplifier Circuit Design*, (New York: McGraw-Hill, 1976).

7.4 Burr-Brown Electronic Series [see Reference G.4]: (This series is particularly good for curve shaping, function generation, multivibrators, oscillators, and rectifiers).

7.5 S. Soclof, *Applications of Analog Integrated Circuits*, (Chapter 8), (Englewood Cliffs, NJ: Prentice-Hall, 1985).

7.6 "Track and Hold Amplifiers," from Micro-Networks Data Conversion Products Catalog, pp. 3-29 through 3-35 (1984).

7.7 *Linear Applications Handbook*, Vol. I and II, National Semiconductor, Inc., Santa Clara, CA (1973).

7.8 *Analog-Digital Conversion Handbook, 3rd Edition*, Ed. D. H. Sheingold (Englewood Cliffs, NJ: Prentice-Hall, 1986).

7.9 R. G. Irvine, Chapt. 8 [see Ref. G.9].

7.10 *Data Conversion Seminar*, Analog Devices, Inc., Norwood, MA (July 1984).

7.11 *Data Acquisition and Conversion Handbook*, Intersil, Inc. (1980).

7.12 G. Grandbois and W. Freeman, "Numerical Integration Techniques Speed Dual-Slope A/D Conversion," *Appl. Note 27.*, Oct. 1985, Teledyne Semiconductor, Inc., Mountain View, CA.

7.13 P. E. Allen & Edgar Sanchez-Sinencio, *Switched Capacitor Circuits*, Chapt. 7, (New York: Van Nostrand Reinhold, 1984).

7.14 *Analog MOS Integrated Circuits*, Ed. P. R. Gray et al, (New York: IEEE Press, 1980).

7.15 *Data Conversion Integrated Circuits*, Ed. D. J. Dooley, (New York: IEEE Press, 1980).

7.16 *Data Acquisition IC Handbook*, Teledyne Semiconductor (October 1985), Mountain View, CA, 94039-7267. Of particular interest is *Appl. Note 10*, "Voltage-to-Frequency Conversion," by M. O. Paiva, pp. 15-27 through 15-35.

7.17 R. Gregorian and G. C. Temes, Chapter 7 [see Ref. 6.22].

7.18 *Linear and Interface Circuits Applications*, Vol. I, Ed. D. E. Pippenger and E. J. Tobaben, Texas Instruments, Inc., Dallas, TX (1985).

CHAPTER 8

8.1 *Transducer Interfacing Handbook*, Ed. Daniel H. Shiengold, Analog Devices, Inc., Norwood, MA, 1980.

8.2 *Electronic Engineers' Handbook*, Ed. Donald G. Fink (New York: McGraw-Hill, 1975) (of particular interest are Sections 17 and 27).

8.3 *Temperature Measurement Handbook*, Omega Engineering, Inc., (1985).

8.4 *Thermistor Sensor Handbook*, Thermometrics, Inc., (1986).

8.5 P. J. O'Higgins, *Basic Instrumentation, Industrial Measurement*, (New York: McGraw-Hill, 1966).

8.6 Darold Wobschall, *Circuit Design for Electronic Instrumentation*, (New York: McGraw-Hill, 1979).

8.7 *Temperature Instruments and Sensors*, Yellow-Springs Instrument Co., Yellow Springs, OH (1985).

8.8 James M. Williams, *A Designer's Guide to: Innovative Linear Circuits*, Cahners Publishing Co. (1985) (a collection of articles authored by J. M. Williams in EDN magazine).

8.9 Ralph Morrison, *Grounding and Shielding Techniques in Instrumentation*, (New York: John Wiley & Sons, 1977)

8.10 Henry W. Ott, *Noise Reduction Techniques in Electronic Systems*, (New York: John Wiley & Sons, 1976).

8.11 A. Rich, "Shielding and Guarding," *Analog Dialogue*, Vol. 17, No. 1, pp. 8–13 (1983).

8.12 Paul Brokaw, "An I.C. Amplifier User's Guide to Decoupling, Grounding, and Making Things Go Right For a Change," Analog Dev. Appl. Note, Analog Devices, Inc., Norwood, MA (July 1979).

8.13 Robert A. Pease, "Improve Circuit Performance with a 1-Op-Amp Current Pump," *EDN*, Vol. 28, No. 2, pp. 85–90 (Jan. 20, 1983).

8.14 G. C. Pabon, "Development of a Circuit That Linearizes the Response of a Platinum Resistance Temperature Detector," M. S. Thesis, The University of Tennessee, Knoxville, TN, 37996-2100 (August 1985).

8.15 *Data Conversion Seminar*, Analog Devices, Inc., Norwood, MA (July 1984).

8.16 E. E. Herceg, *Handbook of Measurement and Control*, Schaevitz Engineering, Pennsauken, NJ (1972).

8.17 *Data-Acquisition Handbook*, Vols. I and II, Analog Devices, Inc., Norwood, MA (1984).

8.18 *Hall-Effect Transducers*, Micro Switch (a Honeywell Division), Freeport, IL (1982).

8.19 J. McDermott, "Sensors and Transducers," *EDN*, pp. 123–41 (March 20, 1980).

8.20 T. Ormond, "Pressure Sensors and Transducers," *EDN*, pp. 101–13 (May 1, 1986).

8.21 *Pressure Transducer Databooklet*, National Semiconductor Corp., Santa Clara, CA (1981).

8.22 M. Eleccion, "Sensors Tap IC Technology To Add More Functions," *Electronics*, Vol. 59, No. 22, pp. 26–30 (June 2, 1986).

8.23 *The Dehumidification Handbook*, Cargocaire Engr. Corp., Amesbury, MA (March 1982).

8.24 *pH and Conductivity Measurement Handbook*, Omega Engineering, Inc., Stamford, CT (1985).

APPENDIX D

D.1 L. W. Nagel, "SPICE2, A Computer Program to Simulate Semiconductor Circuits," ERL-M520, University of California, Berkeley, CA (May, 1975). SPICE is an acronym for *S*imulation *P*rogram with *I*ntegrated *C*ircuit *E*mphasis.

D.2 G. R. Boyle, et al, "Macromodeling of Integrated Circuit Operational Amplifiers," *IEEE J. S. S. Ckts.*, Vol. SC-9, No. 6, pp. 353–63 (Dec. 1974).

D.3 R. Sangsingkeow and J. M. Rochelle, "Analysis of the High Frequency Common-Mode Rejection of an Instrumentation Amplifier," M. S. Thesis, Univ. of Tenn., (August, 1984).

D.4 W. Helms, "Simple Compensation Program Optimizes Frequency Response," *EDN*, pp. 279–89 (Oct. 27, 1983).

D.5 *Hewlett Packard Series 40 Software Catalog, User's Library*, Hewlett Packard Corp., HP-User's Library, Dept. 39UL, 1000 N.E. Circle Blvd., Corvallis, Oregon 97330.

Appendix

Answers to Selected Problems

CHAPTER 1

1.3 $R_F = 1$ MΩ; 6×10^6; 1 kΩ; $f_b = 1$ kHz.

1.5 $v_O = -10v_1 - 5v_2$.

1.6 $v_O = [v_{N1} + v_{N2}] - [v_{I1} + v_{I2}]$; $r_{IN}\,(v_{I1}, v_{I2}) = 10$ kΩ; $r_{IN}\,(v_{N1}, v_{N2}) = 15$ kΩ.

1.8 $R_1 = 1$ MΩ, $R_F = 100$ MΩ; $R_T = 1$ MΩ, $R_2/R_3 = 99$ $(R_2, R_3 \ll R_F)$.

1.9   (a) If $R_F = 100$ kΩ, $R_1 = 33$ kΩ and $R_2 = 25$ kΩ.

1.10 If $C = 1$ μF, $R_1 = 100$ kΩ and $R_2 = 20$ kΩ.

1.17 From Ex. 1.4, the transfer function for Fig. 1.12(b) is

$$\frac{v_O}{v_I} = -\left(\frac{R_F + R}{R_1}\right)\left[\frac{1 + s(R\|R_F C)}{1 + s(RC)}\right]$$

Thus, if we choose $C = 1\,\mu$F, then for $\omega_2 = 10^2$ rad/sec, $R = 10$ kΩ. For $\omega_1 = 10^4$ rad/sec we need $R_F \approx 100$ Ω. We can thus choose R_1 to set the gain at -50, or $R_1 \approx 202$ Ω.

1.18 If the sensor's internal impedance is purely resistive, and is constant, we can use the internal sensor impedance as $R_1 = R_2 = 10$ kΩ, thus $R_F = R_3 = 100$ kΩ. If the sensor's impedance can vary we should use external resistors at least a factor of 100 times larger for R_1 and R_2.

1.19 $A_{\text{diff}} = -5$, $f_{3\,\text{dB}} = 318$ Hz.

1.21 The circuit has ∞ input resistance for both v_{diff} and v_{CM}.
1.22 $-10 \leq (v_O/v_I) \leq +10$.

CHAPTER 2

2.2 $T_O = -970.7$, $A_{CL}^-(\text{dc}) = -100[1 - 1/971.7] \approx -100$, Frac. Error $= 0.103\%$ $f_{CL} = 97.1$ kHz, $r_{\text{in}} = 10$ kΩ, $r_O = 0.103$ Ω (below ω_O).

2.3 Using typical 741C parameters from Appendix C: $T_O = -1951$, A_{CL}^- (dc) $= -100$, Frac. Error $= 0.051\%$, $f_{CL} = 9.76$ kHz, $r_{\text{in}} = 10$ kΩ, $r_O = 0.038$ Ω (below ω_O).

2.4 Using typical LF351 parameters from Appendix C: $T_O = -985$, $A_{CL}^- = -100$, Frac. Error $= 0.10\%$, $f_{CL} = 39.4$ kHz, $r_{\text{in}} = 10$ kΩ, $r_O = 0.05$ Ω (below ω_O).

2.6 $R_{CM} \sim 375$ MΩ.

2.7 $T_O = 9404$, $A_{CL}^+ = 21$, $r_{\text{in}} = 1000$ M$\Omega \| 1.88 \times 10^{10} = 950$ MΩ, $r_{\text{out}} = 0.008$ Ω, $f_{CL} = 47$ kHz. Ignoring any capacitance at the input, from Eq. (2.16) and Fig. 2.7

$$Z_{\text{in}}(s) \approx 2\,R_{CM} \| R_{\text{IN}} \left(\frac{1 + |T_O| + \dfrac{s}{\omega_O}}{1 + \dfrac{s}{\omega_O}} \right)$$

or for a 741

$$Z_{\text{in}} \approx 2\,R_{CM} \| R_{\text{IN}} (1 + |T_O|) \text{ to about } \omega = \omega_O \sqrt{\frac{0.19}{0.81}},$$

or $\omega \approx 0.48\,\omega_O (\sim 2.4$ Hz).

2.9 $|T_O| = 198,504$, $f_{CL} = 993$ kHz, $r_{\text{in}} \approx 2 \times 500$ M$\| 2$ M $(1 + |T_O|) \approx 1000$ M$\Omega = 2R_{CM}$ (at dc), $r_{\text{out}} = 0.38$ mΩ.

2.10 $T_O = 1/2$ that of P2.9, so $f_{CL} = 496$ kHz, $r_{\text{in}} = 10$ kΩ, $r_{\text{out}} = 0.76$ mΩ.

2.12 $r_{\text{in}}(v_1) = 20$ kΩ, $r_{\text{in}}(v_2) = r_{\text{in}}(v_3) = 10$ kΩ, $T_O = -7629$, $r_{\text{out}} = 9.75$ mΩ, $f_{CL} = 38.1$ kHz.

2.13 (b) $GB \geq 2$ MHz.

2.17 <u>741C</u>: $T_O = -9434$, $V_{\text{out}}(V_{OS}) = \pm 2$ mV(21) $= \pm 42$ mV(typ), or ± 157 mV(max). $V_{\text{out}}(I_{OS}) = \pm 20$ nA(200 kΩ) $= \pm 4$ mV(typ), or ± 60 mV(max).
<u>LF351</u>: $T_O = -4762$, $V_{\text{out}}(V_{OS}) = \pm 5$ mV(21) $= \pm 105$ mV(typ), or ± 273 mV(max). $V_{\text{out}}(I_{OS}) = \pm 25$ pA(200 kΩ) $= \pm 5$ μV(typ), or ± 0.8 mV(max).

2.18 (a) $V_O(\text{max}) = +2.52$ V; (b) useful to approximately 800 Hz.

2.19 $R = V_{OS}/I_B^+$.

2.20 $R = 6.37$ kΩ.

2.21 LF351 has total algebraic worst-case error of 78.3 mV vs. 71.2 mV for the 741C (if resistors have same TC), with higher offset-voltage error but lower current-offset errors.

2.22 Algebraic worst-case error $\approx \pm 99$ mV (or 0.99%), probable rms error $= \pm 81$ mV.

2.29 (a) τ_R(small-signal) ≈ 0.96 μsec, $\tau(SR) = 92$ nsec, $\tau_R \approx 0.96$ μsec; (b) $\tau_R \approx 1.3$ μsec.

2.30 (a) (Using data from Appendix C, 25 °C) τ_R (sm-sig) $\approx 0.35/26.7$ MHz $= 13.1$ nsec, SR limit $= 3$ nsec, so $\tau_R \approx 13.2$ nsec; (b) $\tau_R \approx 33$ nsec.

2.32 R_1 and R_2 are chosen to establish V_{BE} (for Q_1 and Q_2) to turn on Q_1 and Q_2 as the 741 approaches its limiting output current. Basically, the boosted voltage gain is $\sim (1 + R_4/R_3)$. Difficult to achieve good SC protection, due to the variability of $I(R_1)$ and $I(R_2)$.

2.35 (c) Poor p-p output voltage swing compared to P2.33.

2.36 The MC34074 output (max) is 30 mA (source), 45 mA (sink). So, it is theoretically possible to provide $+120$ mA, or -180 mA to the load. However, with even ± 20 mA output, the OA can only drive ± 13 V (Fig. 6 of MC34074 data), so at ± 30 mA output we would have $\sim \pm 12$ V output capability, and additionally a $47\,\Omega \times 30$ mA, or ~ 1.5 V drop across each 47 resistor, or $\sim \pm 10.5$ V across the load at ± 120 mA. Thus the minimum load resistor is $\sim 90\,\Omega$, with load power (max) of ~ 1.3 watts. Max power diss. per OA ≈ 180 mW, or 0.75 W/IC.

2.37 $C_1 = 0.015\ \mu\text{F}$, $\Delta V_O \approx 0.12$ V, ceramic preferred (due to heat). 741 has much too large I_B^-.

2.39 Precision $> 0.01\%$; OP-27A preferred.

CHAPTER 3

3.1 $\phi_M \approx 40°$

3.3 $\phi_M \approx 4.8°$

3.6 10 pF $< C_F <$ 100 pF, depending on ϕ_M desired

3.8 Due to I_{max} of the LF351, SR (max) ~ 5 V/μsec.

3.10 R_a not critical for this problem.

3.11 $L \approx 0.4''$

3.17 If $C_i + C_s = 10$ pF ($R_{\text{IN}} \sim 100$ kΩ), obtain $\phi_M \sim 51°$, $GM \approx 11$ dB, $f_c = 18$ MHz.

3.18 Many choices. Must have $\beta_0 \le 1/10$

3.19 For OP-37 $V_O = 0.6$ mV (with capacitor), 1.5 mV (without capacitor). Similarly, for the HA2540, the values are 40 mV and 190 mV.

3.21 Choose $\beta_O \le 1/10$ (many choices). Can approach $f_c = 100$ MHz.

CHAPTER 4

4.5 NF = 2.05 db, 0.05 dB

4.8 Want g_m max so $V_{gs} = 0$ V.

4.10 $R_{\text{opt}} = 7.5$ kΩ.

4.11 $I_B = 0.5\ \mu$A. Even though input dc currents may cancel, noise cannot.

4.12 $I_g = 0.5$ pA, $C_{gs} \approx 0.6$ pF

4.14 $e_{\text{in}} \approx 18.3$ nV/$\sqrt{\text{Hz}}$ (noninv. amplifier), $E_{\text{in}} \approx 19.6\ \mu$V (rms)

4.17 $E_O \approx 170\ \mu$V (rms), $R_n \approx 11$ kΩ.

4.18 $V_O = 25$ mV (25 °C); 102.5 mV (100 °C)

4.19 $e_{tni} = 240$ nV/$\sqrt{\text{Hz}}$, 94% due to V_Z.

4.27 $e_{tni} = 1$ nV/$\sqrt{\text{Hz}}$, $A_{\text{total}} = -909$, $V_{OS} < 10\ \mu$V.

4.28 $e_{tni} \approx 1.9$ nV/$\sqrt{\text{Hz}}$, $i_n \approx 2 \times 10^{-15}$ A/$\sqrt{\text{Hz}}$, $I_B = 10$ pA (max).

4.29 From Ref. 4.24: $e_n = 2$ nV/$\sqrt{\text{Hz}}$, $i_n = 10^{-15}$A/$\sqrt{\text{Hz}}$.

4.30 From Ref. 4.25: $e_n = 0.5$nV/$\sqrt{\text{Hz}}$, $i_n = 1.5$pA/$\sqrt{\text{Hz}}$, $A_{OL} = 30 \times 10^6$, $GB = 3$ MHz (at $A_{CL} = 10$), SR ≈ 2 V/μsec.

CHAPTER 5

5.2 $3.9 \le |A_{CL}| \le 42$, (84 kHz $\le BW \le$ 814 kHz)

5.6 $V_{\text{max}} \approx 2.8$ V

5.7 $A = 2000$

5.8 $-1 \le (v_O/v_{\text{in}}) \le -1000$

5.12 $-1 \text{ V} \leq V_s \leq 1 \text{ V}$

5.22 $f_{-3\,\text{dB}} \approx 100 \text{ Hz}$

5.30 $-15 \text{ mV} < v_i < +15 \text{ mV}$

5.33 $R_L = (2kT/q)(R_M/|V^-|)$

5.34 $500 \text{ Hz} \leq f \leq 15 \text{ kHz}$

5.35 v_O (worst-case) $\approx 53 \text{ mV}$, v_O (worst-case) $\approx 3 \text{ mV}$

5.36 Fig. 5.23(b) has lowest ENV; $e_{tni} \approx 15 \text{ nV}/\sqrt{\text{Hz}}$

5.38 $C_F \geq 24 \text{ pF}$ for $GB \leq 2.5 \text{ MHz}$, $SR \leq 0.5 \text{ V}/\mu\text{sec}$

5.39 Ripple rejection = 70 dB, line regulation = 0.02%, load regulation depends on line resistance.

5.48 $V_O = 10 \text{ V} = V_Z(1 + R_2/R_1)$

5.49 W.C. = 10 bit (± 1 bit); probable accuracy better than 11 bit (± 1 bit)

5.50 $0 \leq V_O \leq 5.33 \text{ V}$; 50 V

CHAPTER 6

6.10 $H(j\omega) = s^2 + 3s + 3$ for Bessel, versus $s^2 + 0.91 s + \sqrt{2}$ for Gaussian. Poles closer to $j\omega$ axis for Gaussian.

6.12 How about negative resistance?

6.16 (a) Requires a Chebyshev (Table 6.4) with (normalized) values of $\omega_c = 1.05$ $Q = 0.9565$. Many possibilities; for example choose $R_3 = 5 R_1$, $R_1 = R_2 = 1$. (b) From Fig. 6.5, $A_{\text{min}} \approx 15 \text{ dB}$.

6.18 For minimum ripple, and for $\geq 20 \text{ dB}$ attenuation at $\omega_s = 2$, choose $A_{\text{max}} = 1.94\text{dB}$, so $a_1 = 0.761953$, etc.

6.23 $\Delta\omega_c/\omega_c \approx +5\%$; $\Delta Q/Q \approx -7.9\%$. Due to finite GB, $\Delta\omega_c/\omega_c \approx +5\% - 7.5\% = -2.5\%$; $\Delta Q/Q \approx -7.9\% + 7.5\% = -0.4\%$.

6.24 $\Delta\omega_c/\omega_c \approx +5\%$; $\Delta Q/Q \approx +1.5\%$. Due to finite GB, $\Delta\omega_c/\omega_c \approx +5\% - 11.3\% = -6.3\%$; $\Delta Q/Q = +1.5\% + 3.8\% = +5.3\%$.

6.26 $R_x = 1.9\Omega, 2.8\Omega, 2.5\Omega$

6.27 For 741 op amp; $\Delta\omega_p \approx -24\%$, $\Delta Q_p \approx +15\%$

6.31 For 741 op amp: $\Delta\omega_p \approx -38\%$, $\Delta Q_p \approx -42\%$, $\Delta\omega_z = -39\%$

6.35 $R_1 = 6.85 \text{ k}\Omega$, $R_2 = 2 \text{ k}\Omega, \ldots$ $C_1 = C_2 = 0.5 \ \mu\text{F}$.

6.43 $S_{R_1}^{\omega_c} = S_{R_2}^{\omega_c} = S_{C_2}^{\omega_c} = S_{C_3}^{\omega_c} = -1/2$

6.54 $S_R^{\omega o} = S_C^{\omega o} = -1$, $S_{k_f}^Q = k_f Q/(1 - k_f)^2$, $S_{R_1}^Q = 1$, etc.

CHAPTER 7

7.1 $f_{-3\,\text{dB}}$ (before breakdown) $\approx 160 \text{ kHz}$, τ_R (small-signal) $\approx 2 \ \mu\text{sec}$. Due to larger-signal effects, maximum limit is 28 μsec.

7.2 At $V_{\text{in}} = \pm 15 \text{ V}$, $V_{\text{out}} = +4.35 \text{ V}$, -9.05 V.

7.3 $f_{3\,\text{dB}} < 2 \text{ MHz}$

7.9 $R_4 = 102 \ \Omega$, error = 0.23%, $R_2 = 10 \text{ k}\Omega$

7.10 V_O (due to V_{OS}) = $kT/q \ln (V_{OS}/R_1 I_s)$; similar effects for noise and currents.

7.11 $f_{CL}(A_1) \approx 1 \text{ kHz}$, $f_{CL}(A_2) \approx 6 \text{ Hz}(v_I = 5 \text{ mV})$ and $16 \text{ kHz}(v_I = 500 \text{ V})$

7.20 If $C = 0.015 \ \mu\text{F}$, at least 7.5 μsec.

7.23 Without S/H, $f_{\text{max}} = 3 \text{ Hz}$. Feedthrough $< 0.1 \text{ mV}$

7.27 (a) $R_S = 2R$

7.45 $\omega_{\text{osc}} = 1/RC$

Appendix C

Manufacturer's Data

Data for the following operational amplifiers is included with permission of the companies listed below:

μA741	Fairchild Camera and Instrument Corporation
LF351	National Semiconductor Corporation
HA2540	Harris Semiconductor
OP-27	Precision Monolithics, Inc.
MC34074	Motorola Semiconductor Products
AD624	Analog Devices, Inc.

A Schlumberger Company

µA741
Operational Amplifier

Linear Products

Description
The µA741 is a high performance Monolithic Operational Amplifier constructed using the Fairchild Planar epitaxial process. It is intended for a wide range of analog applications. High common mode voltage range and absence of latch-up tendencies make the µA741 ideal for use as a voltage follower. The high gain and wide range of operating voltage provides superior performance in integrator, summing amplifier, and general feedback applications.

- **NO FREQUENCY COMPENSATION REQUIRED**
- **SHORT-CIRCUIT PROTECTION**
- **OFFSET VOLTAGE NULL CAPABILITY**
- **LARGE COMMON MODE AND DIFFERENTIAL VOLTAGE RANGES**
- **LOW POWER CONSUMPTION**
- **NO LATCH-UP**

Connection Diagram
10-Pin Flatpak

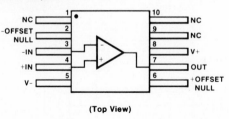

(Top View)

Order Information
Type	Package	Code	Part No.
µA741	Flatpak	3F	µA741FM
µA741A	Flatpak	3F	µA741AFM

Connection Diagram
8-Pin Metal Package

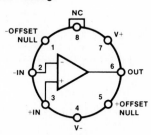

(Top View)

Pin 4 connected to case

Order Information
Type	Package	Code	Part No.
µA741	Metal	5W	µA741HM
µA741A	Metal	5W	µA741AHM
µA741C	Metal	5W	µA741HC
µA741E	Metal	5W	µA741EHC

Connection Diagram
8-Pin DIP

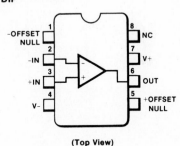

(Top View)

Order Information
Type	Package	Code	Part No.
µA741C	Molded DIP	9T	µA741TC
µA741C	Ceramic DIP	6T	µA741RC

µA741

Absolute Maximum Ratings

Supply Voltage	
µA741A, µA741, µA741E	± 22 V
µA741C	± 18 V
Internal Power Dissipation	
(Note 1)	
Metal Package	500 MW
DIP	310 mW
Flatpak	570 mW
Differential Input Voltage	± 30 V
Input Voltage (Note 2)	± 15 V
Storage Temperature Range	
Metal Package and Flatpak	−65°C to +150°C
DIP	−55°C to +125°C

Operating Temperature Range	
Military (µA741A, µA741)	−55°C to +125°C
Commercial (µA741E, µA741C)	0°C to +70°C
Pin Temperature (Soldering 60 s)	
Metal Package, Flatpak, and	
Ceramic DIP	300°C
Molded DIP (10 s)	260°C
Output Short Circuit Duration	
(Note 3)	Indefinite

Equivalent Circuit

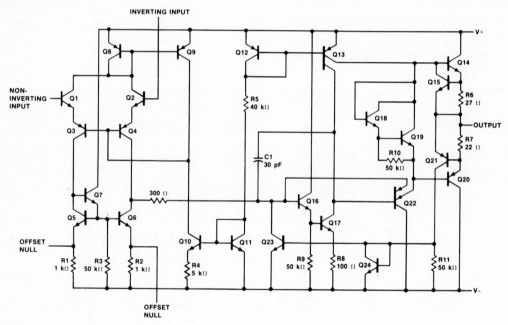

Notes

1. Rating applies to ambient temperatures up to 70°C. Above 70°C ambient derate linearly at 6.3 mW / °C for the metal package, 7.1 mW / °C for the flatpak, and 5.6 mW / °C for the DIP.

2. For supply voltages less than ± 15 V, the absolute maximum input voltage is equal to the supply voltage.

3. Short circuit may be to ground or either supply. Rating applies to +125°C case temperature or 75°C ambient temperature.

μA741

μA741 and μA741C
Electrical Characteristics $V_S = \pm 15$ V, $T_A = 25°C$ unless otherwise specified

Characteristic	Condition	μA741			μA741C			Unit
		Min	Typ	Max	Min	Typ	Max	
Input Offset Voltage	$R_S \leq 10$ kΩ		1.0	5.0		2.0	6.0	mV
Input Offset Current			20	200		20	200	nA
Input Bias Current			80	500		80	500	nA
Power Supply Rejection Ratio	$V_S = +10, -20$ $V_S = +20, -10$ V, $R_S = 50$ Ω		30	150		30	150	μV / V
Input Resistance		.3	2.0		.3	2.0		MΩ
Input Capacitance			1.4			1.4		pF
Offset Voltage Adjustment Range			± 15			± 15		mV
Input Voltage Range					± 12	± 13		V
Common Mode Rejection Ratio	$R_S \leq 10$ kΩ				70	90		dB
Output Short Circuit Current			25			25		mA
Large Signal Voltage Gain	$R_L \geq 2$ kΩ, $V_{OUT} = \pm 10$ V	50k	200k		20k	200k		
Output Resistance			75			75		Ω
Output Voltage Swing	$R_L \geq 10$ kΩ				± 12	± 14		V
	$R_L \geq 2$ kΩ				± 10	± 13		V
Supply Current			1.7	2.8		1.7	2.8	mA
Power Consumption			50	85		50	85	mW
Transient Response (Unity Gain) — Rise Time	$V_{IN} = 20$ mV, $R_L = 2$ kΩ, $C_L \leq 100$ pF		.3			.3		μs
Transient Response (Unity Gain) — Overshoot			5.0			5.0		%
Bandwidth (Note 4)			1.0			1.0		MHz
Slew Rate	$R_L \geq 2$ kΩ		.5			.5		V / μs

Notes

4. Calculated value from BW(MHz) = $\dfrac{0.35}{\text{Rise Time } (\mu s)}$

5. All $V_{CC} = 15$ V for μA741 and μA741C.

6. Maximum supply current for all devices
   25°C = 2.8 mA
   125°C = 2.5 mA
   −55°C = 3.3 mA

μA741

μA741 and μA741C
Electrical Characteristics (Cont.)   The following specifications apply over the range of $-55°C \leq T_A \leq 125°C$ for μA741, $0°C \leq T_A \leq 70°C$ for μA741C

Characteristic	Condition	μA741			μA741C			Unit
		Min	Typ	Max	Min	Typ	Max	
Input Offset Voltage							7.5	mV
	$R_S \leq 10$ kΩ		1.0	6.0				mV
Input Offset Current							300	nA
	$T_A = +125°C$		7.0	200				nA
	$T_A = -55°C$		85	500				nA
Input Bias Current							800	nA
	$T_A = +125°C$		.03	.5				μA
	$T_A = -55°C$		.3	1.5				μA
Input Voltage Range		± 12	± 13					V
Common Mode Rejection Ratio	$R_S \leq 10$ kΩ	70	90					dB
Adjustment for Input Offset Voltage			± 15			± 15		mV
Supply Voltage Rejection Ratio	$V_S = +10, -20;$ $V_S = +20, -10$ V, $R_S = 50$ Ω		30	150				μV/V
Output Voltage Swing	$R_L \geq 10$ kΩ	± 12	± 14					V
	$R_L \geq 2$ kΩ	± 10	± 13		± 10	± 13		V
Large Signal Voltage Gain	$R_L = 2$ kΩ, $V_{OUT} = \pm 10$ V	25k			15k			
Supply Current	$T_A = +125°C$		1.5	2.5				mA
	$T_A = -55°C$		2.0	3.3				mA
Power Consumption	$T_A = +125°C$		45	75				mW
	$T_A = -55°C$		60	100				mW

Notes
4. Calculated value from BW(MHz) = $\dfrac{0.35}{\text{Rise Time }(\mu s)}$

5. All $V_{CC} = 15$ V for μA741 and μA741C.
6. Maximum supply current for all devices
   25°C = 2.8 mA
   125°C = 2.5 mA
   −55°C = 3.3 mA

μA741

Typical Performance Curves for μA741E and μA741C (Cont.)

Frequency Characteristics as a Function of Supply Voltage

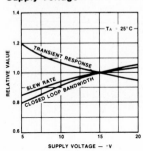

Voltage Offset Null Circuit

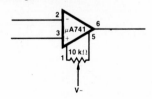

Voltage Follower Large Signal Pulse Response

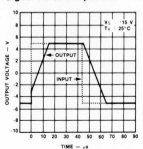

Typical Performance Curves for μA741A, μA741, μA741E and μA741C

Power Consumption as a Function of Supply Voltage

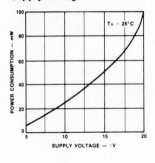

Open Loop Voltage Gain as a Function of Frequency

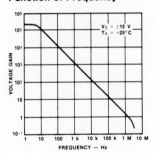

Open Loop Phase Response as a Function of Frequency

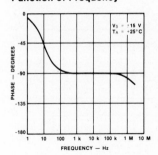

Input Offset Current as a Function of Supply Voltage

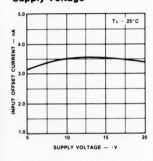

Input Resistance and Input Capacitance as a Function of Frequency

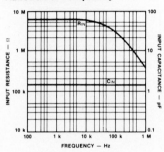

Output Resistance as a Function of Frequency

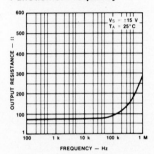

μA741

Typical Performance Curves for μA741A and μA741

Open Loop Voltage Gain as a Function of Supply Voltage

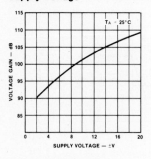

Output Voltage Swing as a Function of Supply Voltage

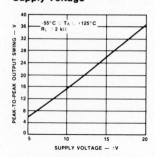

Input Common Mode Voltage as a Function of Supply Voltage

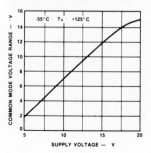

Typical Performance Curves for μA741E and μA741C

Open Loop Voltage Gain as a Function of Supply Voltage

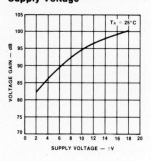

Output Voltage Swing as a Function of Supply Voltage

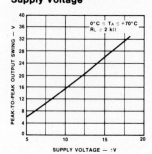

Input Common Mode Voltage Range as a Function of Supply Voltage

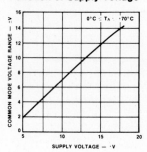

Transient Response

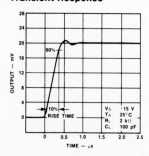

Transient Response Test Circuit

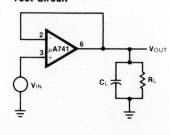

Common Mode Rejection Ratio as a Function of Frequency

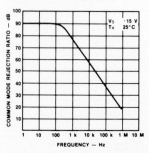

µA741

Typical Performance Curves for µA741A, µA741, µA741E and µA741C (Cont.)

Output Voltage Swing as a Function of Load Resistance

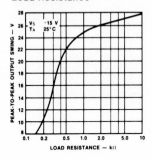

Output Voltage Swing as a Function of Frequency

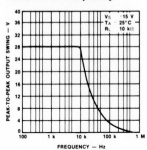

Absolute Maximum Power Dissipation as a Function of Ambient Temperature

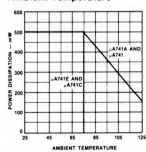

Input Noise Voltage as a Function of Frequency

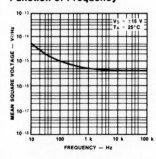

Input Noise Current as a Function of Frequency

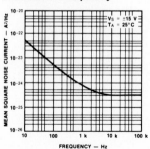

Broadband Noise for Various Bandwidths

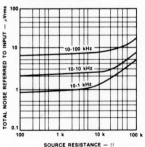

Typical Performance Curves for µA741A and µA741

Input Bias Current as a Function of Ambient Temperature

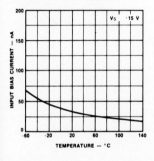

Input Resistance as a Function of Ambient Temperature

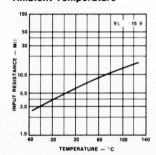

Output Short-Circuit Current as a Function of Ambient Temperature

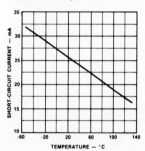

μA741

Typical Performance Curves for μA741A and μA741 (Cont.)

Input Offset Current as a Function of Ambient Temperature

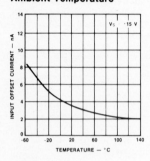

Power Consumption as a Function of Ambient Temperature

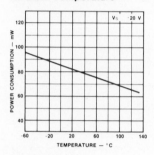

Frequency Characteristics as a Function of Ambient Temperature

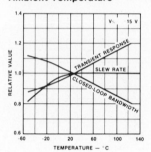

Typical Performance Curves for μA741E and μA741C

Input Bias Current as a Function of Ambient Temperature

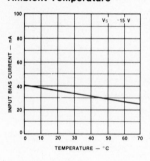

Input Resistance as a Function of Ambient Temperature

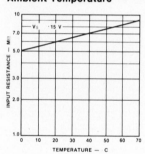

Input Offset Current as a Function of Ambient Temperature

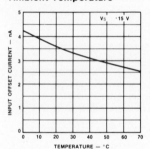

Power Consumption as a Function of Ambient Temperature

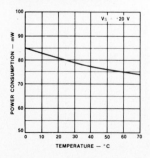

Output Short Circuit Current as a Function of Ambient Temperature

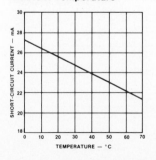

Frequency Characteristics as a Function of Ambient Temperature

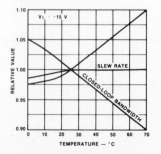

February 1985

LF351 Wide Bandwidth JFET Input Operational Amplifier

General Description

The LF351 is a low cost high speed JFET input operational amplifier with an internally trimmed input offset voltage (BI-FET II™ technology). The device requires a low supply current and yet maintains a large gain bandwidth product and a fast slew rate. In addition, well matched high voltage JFET input devices provide very low input bias and offset currents. The LF351 is pin compatible with the standard LM741 and uses the same offset voltage adjustment circuitry. This feature allows designers to immediately upgrade the overall performance of existing LM741 designs.

The LF351 may be used in applications such as high speed integrators, fast D/A converters, sample-and-hold circuits and many other circuits requiring low input offset voltage, low input bias current, high input impedance, high slew rate and wide bandwidth. The device has low noise and offset voltage drift, but for applications where these requirements are critical, the LF356 is recommended. If maximum supply current is important, however, the LF351 is the better choice.

Features

- Internally trimmed offset voltage   10 mV
- Low input bias current   50 pA
- Low input noise voltage   16 nV/$\sqrt{\text{Hz}}$
- Low input noise current   0.01 pA/$\sqrt{\text{Hz}}$
- Wide gain bandwidth   4 MHz
- High slew rate   13 V/μs
- Low supply current   1.8 mA
- High input impedance $10^{12}\Omega$
- Low total harmonic distortion $A_V = 10$,   <0.02%
  $R_L = 10k$, $V_O = 20$ Vp-p, BW = 20 Hz-20 kHz
- Low 1/f noise corner   50 Hz
- Fast settling time to 0.01%   2 μs

Typical Connection

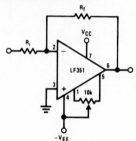

Simplified Schematic

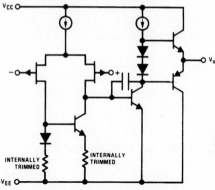

Connection Diagrams (Top Views)

Metal Can Package

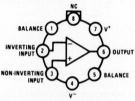

Note. Pin 4 connected to case.

Order Number LF351H
See NS Package H08C

Dual-In-Line Package

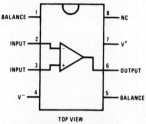

TOP VIEW

Order Number LF351N
See NS Package N08E

TL/H/5648–1

Absolute Maximum Ratings

Supply Voltage	± 18V	Input Voltage Range (Note 2)	± 15V
Power Dissipation (Note 1)	500 mW	Output Short Circuit Duration	Continuous
Operating Temperature Range	0°C to +70°C	Storage Temperature Range	-65°C to +150°C
$T_{j(MAX)}$	115°C	Lead Temp. (Soldering, 10 seconds)	300°C
Differential Input Voltage	± 30V		

DC Electrical Characteristics (Note 3)

Symbol	Parameter	Conditions	LF351			Units
			Min	Typ	Max	
V_{OS}	Input Offset Voltage	$R_S = 10$ kΩ, $T_A = 25$°C		5	10	mV
		Over Temperature			13	mV
$\Delta V_{OS}/\Delta T$	Average TC of Input Offset Voltage	$R_S = 10$ kΩ		10		μV/°C
I_{OS}	Input Offset Current	$T_j = 25$°C, (Notes 3, 4)		25	100	pA
		$T_j \leq 70$°C			4	nA
I_B	Input Bias Current	$T_j = 25$°C, (Notes 3, 4)		50	200	pA
		$T_j \leq \pm 70$°C			8	nA
R_{IN}	Input Resistance	$T_j = 25$°C		10^{12}		Ω
A_{VOL}	Large Signal Voltage Gain	$V_S = \pm 15$V, $T_A = 25$°C	25	100		V/mV
		$V_O = \pm 10$V, $R_L = 2$ kΩ				
		Over Temperature	15			V/mV
V_O	Output Voltage Swing	$V_S = \pm 15$V, $R_L = 10$ kΩ	± 12	± 13.5		V
V_{CM}	Input Common-Mode Voltage Range			$+15$		V
		$V_S = \pm 15$V	± 11			
				-12		V
CMRR	Common-Mode Rejection Ratio	$R_S \leq 10$ kΩ	70	100		dB
PSRR	Supply Voltage Rejection Ratio	(Note 5)	70	100		dB
I_S	Supply Current			1.8	3.4	mA

AC Electrical Characteristics (Note 3)

Symbol	Parameter	Conditions	LF351			Units
			Min	Typ	Max	
SR	Slew Rate	$V_S = \pm 15$V, $T_A = 25$°C		13		V/μs
GBW	Gain Bandwidth Product	$V_S = \pm 15$V, $T_A = 25$°C		4		MHz
e_n	Equivalent Input Noise Voltage	$T_A = 25$°C, $R_S = 100\Omega$, f = 1000 Hz		16		nV/$\sqrt{Hz}$
i_n	Equivalent Input Noise Current	$T_j = 25$°C, f = 1000 Hz		0.01		pA/$\sqrt{Hz}$

Note 1: For operating at elevated temperature, the device must be derated based on a thermal resistance of 150°C/W junction to ambient or 45°C/W junction to case.

Note 2: Unless otherwise specified the absolute maximum negative input voltage is equal to the negative power supply voltage.

Note 3: These specifications apply for $V_S = \pm 15$V and 0°C $\leq T_A \leq +70$°C. V_{OS}, I_B and I_{OS} are measured at $V_{CM} = 0$.

Note 4: The input bias currents are junction leakage currents which approximately double for every 10°C increase in the junction temperature, T_j. Due to the limited production test time, the input bias currents measured are correlated to junction temperature. In normal operation the junction temperature rises above the ambient temperature as a result of internal power dissipation, P_D. $T_j = T_A + \theta_{jA} P_D$ where θ_{jA} is the thermal resistance from junction to ambient. Use of a heat sink is recommended if input bias current is to be kept to a minimum.

Note 5: Supply voltage rejection ratio is measured for both supply magnitudes increasing or decreasing simultaneously in accordance with common practice.

Typical Performance Characteristics

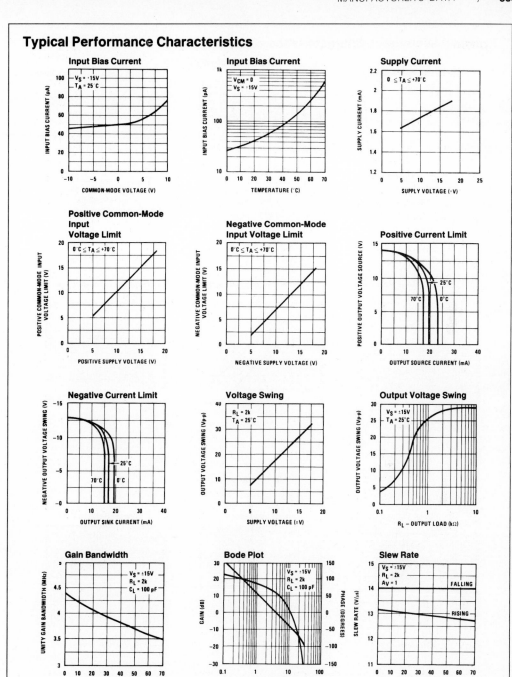

TL/H/5648–2

Typical Performance Characteristics (Continued)

Distortion vs Frequency

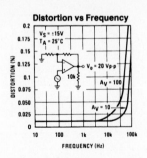

Undistorted Output Voltage Swing

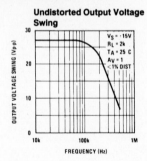

Open Loop Frequency Response

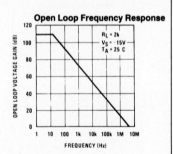

Common-Mode Rejection Ratio

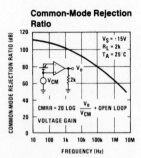

Power Supply Rejection Ratio

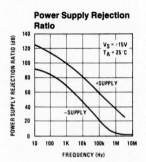

Equivalent Input Noise Voltage

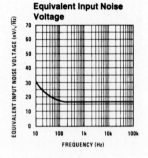

Open Loop Voltage Gain (V/V)

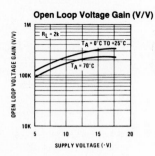

Output Impedance

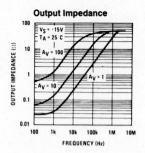

Inverter Settling Time

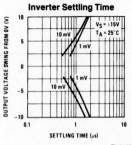

TL/H/5648–3

Pulse Response

Small Signal Inverting

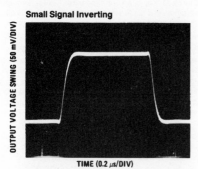

TL/H/5648-4

Small Signal Non-Inverting

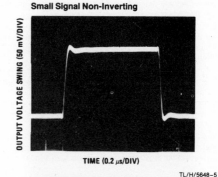

TL/H/5648-5

Large Signal Inverting

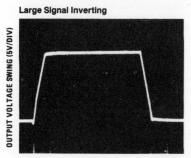

TL/H/5648-6

Large Signal Non-Inverting

TL/H/5648-7

Current Limit ($R_L = 100\Omega$)

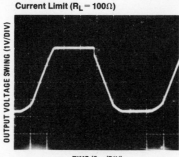

TL/H/5648-8

Application Hints

The LF351 is an op amp with an internally trimmed input offset voltage and JFET input devices (BI-FET II™). These JFETs have large reverse breakdown voltages from gate to source and drain eliminating the need for clamps across the inputs. Therefore, large differential input voltages can easily be accommodated without a large increase in input current. The maximum differential input voltage is independent of the supply voltages. However, neither of the input voltages should be allowed to exceed the negative supply as this will cause large currents to flow which can result in a destroyed unit.

Exceeding the negative common-mode limit on either input will cause a reversal of the phase to the output and force the amplifier output to the corresponding high or low state. Exceeding the negative common-mode limit on both inputs will force the amplifier output to a high state. In neither case

Application Hints (Continued)

does a latch occur since raising the input back within the common-mode range again puts the input stage and thus the amplifier in a normal operating mode.

Exceeding the positive common-mode limit on a single input will not change the phase of the output; however, if both inputs exceed the limit, the output of the amplifier will be forced to a high state.

The amplifier will operate with a common-mode input voltage equal to the positive supply; however, the gain bandwidth and slew rate may be decreased in this condition. When the negative common-mode voltage swings to within 3V of the negative supply, an increase in input offset voltage may occur.

The LF351 is biased by a zener reference which allows normal circuit operation on ±4V power supplies. Supply voltages less than these may result in lower gain bandwidth and slew rate.

The LF351 will drive a 2 kΩ load resistance to ±10V over the full temperature range of 0°C to +70°C. If the amplifier is forced to drive heavier load currents, however, an increase in input offset voltage may occur on the negative voltage swing and finally reach an active current limit on both positive and negative swings.

Precautions should be taken to ensure that the power supply for the integrated circuit never becomes reversed in polarity or that the unit is not inadvertently installed backwards in a socket as an unlimited current surge through the resulting forward diode within the IC could cause fusing of the internal conductors and result in a destroyed unit.

Because these amplifiers are JFET rather than MOSFET input op amps they do not require special handling.

As with most amplifiers, care should be taken with lead dress, component placement and supply decoupling in order to ensure stability. For example, resistors from the output to an input should be placed with the body close to the input to minimize "pick-up" and maximize the frequency of the feedback pole by minimizing the capacitance from the input to ground.

A feedback pole is created when the feedback around any amplifier is resistive. The parallel resistance and capacitance from the input of the device (usually the inverting input) to AC ground set the frequency of the pole. In many instances the frequency of this pole is much greater than the expected 3 dB frequency of the closed loop gain and consequently there is negligible effect on stability margin. However, if the feedback pole is less than approximately 6 times the expected 3 dB frequency a lead capacitor should be placed from the output to the input of the op amp. The value of the added capacitor should be such that the RC time constant of this capacitor and the resistance it parallels is greater than or equal to the original feedback pole time constant.

Detailed Schematic

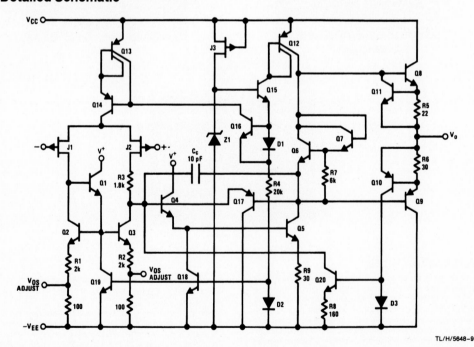

TL/H/5648–9

 **HARRIS**

HA-2540

Wideband, Fast Settling Operational Amplifiers

FEATURES

- VERY HIGH SLEW RATE   400V/μs
- FAST SETTLING TIME   200ns
- WIDE GAIN-BANDWIDTH   400MHz
- POWER BANDWIDTH   6MHz
- LOW OFFSET VOLTAGE   5mV
- INPUT VOLTAGE NOISE   6V/$\sqrt{Hz}$
- OUTPUT VOLTAGE SWING $\pm$10V
- MONOLITHIC BIPOLAR CONSTRUCTION

APPLICATIONS

- PULSE AND VIDEO AMPLIFIERS
- WIDEBAND AMPLIFIERS
- HIGH SPEED SAMPLE-HOLD CIRCUITS
- FAST, PRECISE D/A CONVERTERS

GENERAL DESCRIPTION

The Harris HA-2540 is a wideband, very high slew rate, mono-lithic operational amplifier featuring superior speed and band-width characteristics. Bipolar construction coupled with dielec-tric isolation allows this truly differential device to deliver out-standing performance in circuits where closed loop gain is 10 or greater. Additionally, the HA-2540 has a drive capability of $\pm$10V into a 1K ohm load. Other desirable characteristics in-clude low input voltage noise, low offset voltage, and fast settling time.

A 400V/μs slew rate ensures high performance in video and pulse amplification circuits, while the 400MHz gain-band-width-product is ideally suited for wideband signal amplifica-tion. A settling time of 250ns also makes the HA-2540 an ex-cellent selection for high speed Data Acquisition Systems.

The HA-2540-2 is specified over the -55ºC to +125ºC range while the HA-2540-5 is specified from 0ºC to +75ºC.

PINOUT

TOP VIEW

```
      ┌──┐ ┌──┐
   1 │      │ 14
   2 │      │ 13
   3 │      │ 12
IN- 4 │  -   │ 11 V+
IN+ 5 │  +   │ 10 OUTPUT
 V- 6 │      │ 9
   7 │      │ 8
      └──────┘
```

SCHEMATIC

SPECIFICATIONS

ABSOLUTE MAXIMUM RATINGS (Note 1)

Voltage between V+ and V– Terminals	35V
Differential Input Voltage	6V
Output Current	50mA (Peak)
Internal Power Dissipation (Note 2)	870mW (Cerdip)
Operating Temperature Range: (HA-2540-2)	$-55^oC \leq T_A \leq +125^oC$
(HA-2540-5)	$0^oC \leq T_A \leq +75^oC$
Storage Temperature Range	$-65^oC \leq T_A \leq +150^oC$

ELECTRICAL CHARACTERISTICS $V_{SUPPLY} = \pm 15$ Volts; R_L = 1K ohms, unless otherwise specified.

PARAMETER	TEMP	HA-2540-2 −55°C to +125°C			HA-2540-5 0°C to +75°C			UNITS
		MIN	TYP	MAX	MIN	TYP	MAX	
INPUT CHARACTERISTICS								
Offset Voltage	+25°C		3	5		3	15	mV
	FULL			10			20	mV
Average Offset Voltage Drift	FULL		20			20		µV/°C
Bias Current	+25°C		5	20		5	20	µA
	FULL			25			25	µA
Offset Current	+25°C		1	6		1	6	µA
	FULL			8			8	µA
Input Resistance	+25°C		10			10		Kohms
Input Capacitance	+25°C		1.0			1.0		pF
Common Mode Range	FULL	±10			±10			V
Input Noise Voltage (f = 1kHz, R_g = 0Ω)	+25°C		6			6		nV/$\sqrt{Hz}$
TRANSFER CHARACTERISTICS								
Large Signal Voltage Gain (Note 3)	+25°C	15K	30K		10K	30K		V/V
	FULL	5K			5K			V/V
Common-Mode Rejection Ratio (Note 4)	FULL	60			60			dB
Gain-Bandwidth-Product (Notes 5 & 6)	+25°C		400			400		MHz
OUTPUT CHARACTERISTICS								
Output Voltage Swing (Note 3)	FULL	±10			±10			V
Output Current (Note 3)	+25°C	10			10			mA
Output Resistance	+25°C		30			30		Ohms
Full Power Bandwidth (Note 3 & 7)	+25°C	5.5	6		5.5	6		MHz
TRANSIENT RESPONSE (Note 8)								
Rise Time	+25°C		14			14		ns
Overshoot	+25°C		5			5		%
Slew Rate	+25°C	350	400		350	400		V/µs
Settling Time: 10V Step to 0.1%	+25°C		200			200		ns
POWER REQUIREMENTS								
Supply Current	FULL		20	25		20	25	mA
Power Supply Rejection Ratio (Note 9)	FULL	60			60			dB

NOTES:

1. Absolute maximum ratings are limiting values, applied individually, beyond which the serviceability of the circuit may be impaired. Functional operability under any of these conditions is not necessarily implied.

2. Derate at 8.7mW/°C for operation at ambient temperatures above +75°c. Heat sinking required at temperatures above +75°c. T_{JA} = 115°C/W; T_{JC} = 35°C/W. Thermalloy model 6007 heat sink recommended.

3. R_L = 1KΩ, V_O = ±10V

4. V_{CM} = ±10V

5. V_O = 90mV.

6. A_V = 10.

7. Full power bandwidth guaranteed based on slew rate measurement using $FPBW = \dfrac{Slew\ Rate}{2\pi\ V_{peak}}$.

8. Refer to Test Circuits section of data sheet.

9. V_{SUPPLY} = ±5 VDC to ±15 VDC

TEST CIRCUITS

LARGE AND SMALL SIGNAL RESPONSE
TEST CIRCUIT*

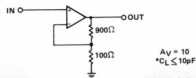

IN o   o OUT

900Ω

100Ω

A_V = 10
*$C_L \leq$ 10pF

LARGE SIGNAL RESPONSE
Vertical Scale: (Volts: A=0.5v/Div., B=5.0V/Div.)
Horizontal Scale: (Time: 50ns/Div.)

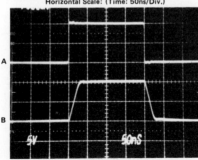

A

B

SMALL SIGNAL RESPONSE
Vertical Scale: Input=10mV/Div.; Output=50mV/Div.
Horizontal Scale: 20ns/Div.

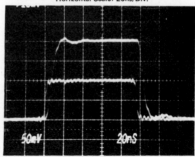

SETTLING TIME TEST CIRCUIT

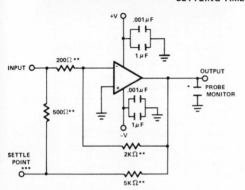

+V o   .001μF

1μF

INPUT o   200Ω**

OUTPUT

PROBE
MONITOR

.001μF

500Ω**

1μF

-V

SETTLE
POINT
***

2KΩ**

5KΩ**

* Load Capacitance should be less than 10pF.

** It is recommended that resistors be carbon composition and that feedback and summing network ratios be matched.

*** SETTLE POINT (Summing Node) capacitance should be less than 10pF. For optimum settling time results, it is recommended that the test circuit be constructed directly onto the device pins. A Tektronix 568 Sampling Oscilloscope with S-3A sampling heads is recommended as a settle point monitor.

PERFORMANCE CURVES (Continued)

CLOSED LOOP FREQUENCY RESPONSE

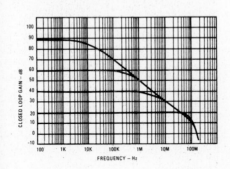

OUTPUT VOLTAGE SWING VS. FREQUENCY

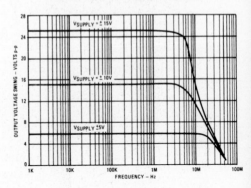

OUTPUT VOLTAGE SWING VS. LOAD RESISTANCE

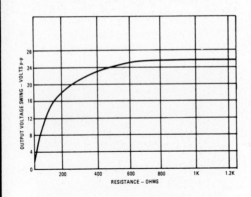

NORMALIZED AC PARAMETERS VS. TEMPERATURE

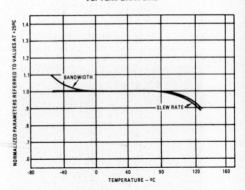

SETTLING TIME FOR VARIOUS OUTPUT STEP VOLTAGES

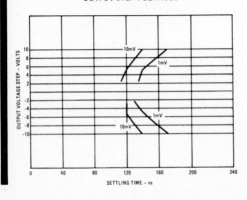

POWER SUPPLY CURRENT VS. TEMPERATURE AND SUPPLY VOLTAGE

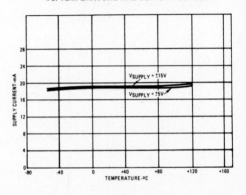

PERFORMANCE CURVES

INPUT OFFSET VOLTAGE AND BIAS CURRENT VS. TEMPERATURE

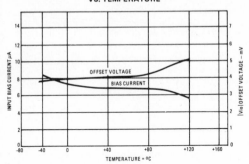

INPUT NOISE VOLTAGE AND NOISE CURRENT VS. FREQUENCY

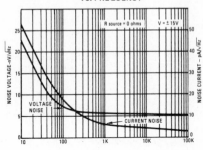

BROADBAND NOISE (0.1Hz TO 1MHz)
Vertical Scale: 10 μV/Div.
Horizontal Scale: 50ms/Div.

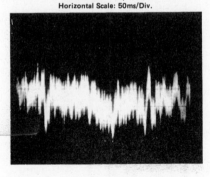

COMMON MODE REJECTION RATIO VS. FREQUENCY

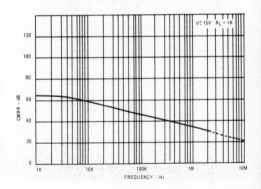

POWER SUPPLY REJECTION RATIO VS. FREQUENCY

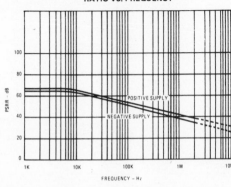

OPEN LOOP GAIN/PHASE VS. FREQUENCY HA-2540

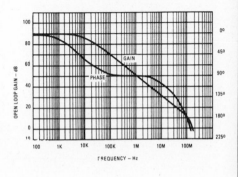

LOW-NOISE
PRECISION
OPERATIONAL AMPLIFIER

OP-27

PMI

FEATURES

- **Low Noise** .... $\begin{cases} \dots 80nV_{p-p} \ (0.1Hz \ to \ 10Hz) \\ \dots 3nV/\sqrt{Hz} \end{cases}$
- **Low Drift** .... $0.2\mu V/^\circ C$
- **High Speed** .... $\begin{cases} \dots 2.8V/\mu s \ Slew \ Rate \\ \dots 8MHz \ Gain \ Bandwidth \end{cases}$
- **Low V_{OS}** .... $10\mu V$
- **Excellent CMRR** .... 126dB at V_{CM} of $\pm 11V$
- **High Open-Loop Gain** .... 1.8 Million
- **Fits 725, OP-07, OP-05, AD510, AD517, 5534A sockets**

ORDERING INFORMATION†

$T_A = 25^\circ C$ V_{OS} MAX (μV)	PACKAGE			OPERATING TEMPERATURE RANGE
	HERMETIC TO-99 8-PIN	HERMETIC DIP 8-PIN	PLASTIC DIP 8-PIN	
25	OP27AJ*	OP27AZ*		MIL
25	OP27EJ	OP27EZ	OP27EP	IND/COM
60	OP27BJ*	OP27BZ*		MIL
60	OP27FJ	OP27FZ	OP27FP	IND/COM
100	OP27CJ*	OP27CZ*		MIL
100	OP27GJ	OP27GZ	OP27GP	IND/COM

* Also available with MIL-STD-883B processing. To order add /883 as a suffix to the part number. Screening Procedure: 1984 Data Book, Section 3.
† All commercial and industrial temperature range parts are available with burn-in per MIL-STD-883. Ordering Information: 1984 Data Book, Section 2.

GENERAL DESCRIPTION

The OP-27 precision operational amplifier combines the low offset and drift of the OP-07 with both high-speed and low-noise. Offsets down to $25\mu V$ and drift of $0.6\mu V/^\circ C$ maximum make the OP-27 ideal for precision instrumentation applications. Exceptionally low noise, $e_n = 3.5nV/\sqrt{Hz}$, at 10Hz, a low 1/f noise corner frequency of 2.7Hz, and high gain (1.8 million), allow accurate high-gain amplification of low-level signals. A gain-bandwidth product of 8MHz and a $2.8V/\mu sec$ slew rate provides excellent dynamic accuracy in high-speed data-acquisition systems.

A low input bias current of $\pm 10nA$ is achieved by use of a bias-current-cancellation circuit. Over the military temperature range, this circuit typically holds I_B and I_{OS} to $\pm 20nA$ and 15nA respectively.

The output stage has good load driving capability. A guaranteed swing of $\pm 10V$ into 600Ω and low output distortion make the OP-27 an excellent choice for professional audio applications.

PSRR and CMRR exceed 120dB. These characteristics, coupled with long-term drift of $0.2\mu V/month$, allow the circuit designer to achieve performance levels previously attained only by discrete designs.

Low cost, high-volume production of OP-27 is achieved by using an on-chip zener-zap trimming network. This reliable and stable offset trimming scheme has proved its effectiveness over many years of production history.

The OP-27 provides excellent performance in low-noise high-accuracy amplification of low-level signals. Applications include stable integrators, precision summing amplifiers, precision voltage-threshold detectors, comparators, and professional audio circuits such as tape-head and microphone preamplifiers.

The OP-27 is a direct replacement for 725, OP-06, OP-07 and OP-05 amplifiers; 741 types may be directly replaced by removing the 741's nulling potentiometer.

PIN CONNECTIONS

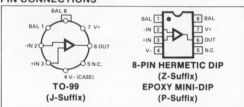

TO-99
(J-Suffix)

8-PIN HERMETIC DIP
(Z-Suffix)
EPOXY MINI-DIP
(P-Suffix)

SIMPLIFIED SCHEMATIC

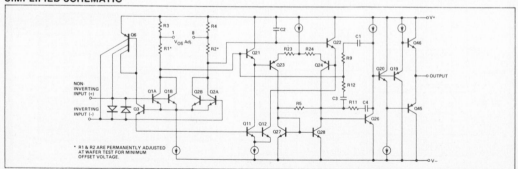

Precision Monolithics Incorporated

PMI — OP-27 LOW-NOISE PRECISION OPERATIONAL AMPLIFIER

ABSOLUTE MAXIMUM RATINGS (Note 4)

Supply Voltage .... ±22V
Internal Power Dissipation (Note 1) 500mW
Input Voltage (Note 3) .... ±22V
Output Short-Circuit Duration .... Indefinite
Differential Input Voltage (Note 2) .... ±0.7V
Differential Input Current (Note 2) .... ±25mA
Storage Temperature Range .... −65°C to +150°C
Operating Temperature Range
OP-27A, OP-27B, OP-27C (J, Z) ..... −55°C to +125°C
OP-27E, OP-27F, OP-27G (J, Z) ...... −25°C to +85°C
OP-27E, OP-27F, OP-27G (P) .... 0°C to +70°C
Lead Temperature Range (Soldering, 60 sec) ...... 300°C
DICE Junction Temperature .... −65°C to +150°C

NOTES:
1. See table for maximum ambient temperature rating and derating factor.

PACKAGE TYPE	MAXIMUM AMBIENT TEMPERATURE FOR RATING	DERATE ABOVE MAXIMUM AMBIENT TEMPERATURE
TO-99 (J)	80°C	7.1mW/°C
8-Pin Hermetic DIP (Z)	75°C	6.7mW/°C
8-Pin Plastic DIP (P)	62°C	5.6mW/°C

2. The OP-27's inputs are protected by back-to-back diodes. Current limiting resistors are not used in order to achieve low noise. If differential input voltage exceeds ±0.7V, the input current should be limited to 25mA.
3. For supply voltages less than ±22V, the absolute maximum input voltage is equal to the supply voltage.
4. Absolute maximum ratings apply to both DICE and packaged parts, unless otherwise noted.

ELECTRICAL CHARACTERISTICS at $V_S = \pm15V$, $T_A = 25°C$, unless otherwise noted.

PARAMETER	SYMBOL	CONDITIONS	OP-27A/E MIN	TYP	MAX	OP-27B/F MIN	TYP	MAX	OP-27C/G MIN	TYP	MAX	UNITS
Input Offset Voltage	V_{OS}	(Note 1)	—	10	25	—	20	60	—	30	100	µV
Long-Term V_{OS} Stability	V_{OS}/Time	(Note 2)	—	0.2	1.0	—	0.3	1.5	—	0.4	2.0	µV/Mo
Input Offset Current	I_{OS}		—	7	35	—	9	50	—	12	75	nA
Input Bias Current	I_B		—	±10	±40	—	±12	±55	—	±15	±80	nA
Input Noise Voltage	e_{np-p}	0.1Hz to 10Hz (Notes 3, 5)	—	0.08	0.18	—	0.08	0.18	—	0.09	0.25	µVp-p
Input Noise Voltage Density	e_n	f_O = 10Hz (Note 3)	—	3.5	5.5	—	3.5	5.5	—	3.8	8.0	nV/$\sqrt{Hz}$
		f_O = 30Hz (Note 3)	—	3.1	4.5	—	3.1	4.5	—	3.3	5.6	
		f_O = 1000Hz (Note 3)	—	3.0	3.8	—	3.0	3.8	—	3.2	4.5	
Input Noise Current Density	i_n	f_O = 10Hz (Notes 3,6)	—	1.7	4.0	—	1.7	4.0	—	1.7	—	pA/$\sqrt{Hz}$
		f_O = 30Hz (Notes 3,6)	—	1.0	2.3	—	1.0	2.3	—	1.0	—	
		f_O = 1000Hz (Notes 3, 6)	—	0.4	0.6	—	0.4	0.6	—	0.4	0.6	
Input Resistance — Differential-Mode	R_{IN}	(Note 4)	1.5	6	—	1.2	5	—	0.8	4	—	MΩ
Input Resistance — Common-Mode	R_{INCM}		—	3	—	—	2.5	—	—	2	—	GΩ
Input Voltage Range	IVR		±11.0	±12.3		±11.0	±12.3		±11.0	±12.3	—	V
Common-Mode Rejection Ratio	CMRR	$V_{CM} = \pm11V$	114	126		106	123	—	100	120	—	dB
Power Supply Rejection Ratio	PSRR	$V_S = \pm4V$ to $\pm18V$	—	1	10	—	1	10	—	2	20	µV/V
Large-Signal Voltage Gain	A_{VO}	$R_L \geq 2k\Omega$, $V_O = \pm10V$	1000	1800	—	1000	1800	—	700	1500	—	V/mV
		$R_L \geq 600\Omega$, $V_O = \pm10V$	800	1500	—	800	1500	—	600	1500	—	
Output Voltage Swing	V_O	$R_L \geq 2k\Omega$	±12.0	±13.8	—	±12.0	±13.8	—	±11.5	±13.5	—	V
		$R_L \geq 600\Omega$	±10.0	±11.5	—	±10.0	±11.5	—	±10.0	±11.5	—	
Slew Rate	SR	$R_L \geq 2k\Omega$ (Note 4)	1.7	2.8	—	1.7	2.8	—	1.7	2.8	—	V/µs
Gain Bandwidth Prod.	GBW	(Note 4)	5.0	8.0	—	5.0	8.0	—	5.0	8.0	—	MHz
Open-Loop Output Resistance	R_O	$V_O = 0$, $I_O = 0$	—	70	—	—	70	—	—	70	—	Ω
Power Consumption	P_d	V_O	—	90	140	—	90	140	—	100	170	mW
Offset Adjustment Range		$R_P = 10k\Omega$	—	±4.0	—	—	±4.0	—	—	±4.0	—	mV

NOTES:
1. Input offset voltage measurements are performed ~ 0.5 seconds after application of power. A/E grades guaranteed fully warmed-up.
2. Long-term input offset voltage stability refers to the average trend line of V_{OS} vs. Time over extended periods after the first 30 days of operation. Excluding the initial hour of operation, changes in V_{OS} during the first 30 days are typically 2.5µV — refer to typical performance curve.
3. Sample tested.
4. Guaranteed by design.
5. See test circuit and frequency response curve for 0.1Hz to 10Hz tester.
6. See test circuit for current noise measurement.

PMI — OP-27 LOW-NOISE PRECISION OPERATIONAL AMPLIFIER

ELECTRICAL CHARACTERISTICS for $V_S = \pm 15V$, $-55°C \leq T_A \leq +125°C$, unless otherwise noted.

PARAMETER	SYMBOL	CONDITIONS	OP-27A			OP-27B			OP-27C			UNITS
			MIN	TYP	MAX	MIN	TYP	MAX	MIN	TYP	MAX	
Input Offset Voltage	V_{OS}	(Note 1)	—	30	60	—	50	200	—	70	300	μV
Average Input Offset Drift	TCV_{OS} TCV_{OSn}	(Note 2)	—	0.2	0.6	—	0.3	1.3	—	0.4	1.8	μV/°C
Input Offset Current	I_{OS}		—	15	50	—	22	85	—	30	135	nA
Input Bias Current	I_B		—	$\pm$20	$\pm$60	—	$\pm$28	$\pm$95	—	$\pm$35	$\pm$150	nA
Input Voltage Range	IVR		$\pm$10.3	$\pm$11.5	—	$\pm$10.3	$\pm$11.5	—	$\pm$10.2	$\pm$11.5	—	V
Common-Mode Rejection Ratio	CMRR	$V_{CM} = \pm 10V$	108	122	—	100	119	—	94	116	—	dB
Power Supply Rejection Ratio	PSRR	$V_S = \pm 4.5V$ to $\pm 18V$	—	2	16	—	2	20	—	4	51	μV/V
Large-Signal Voltage Gain	A_{VO}	$R_L \geq 2k\Omega$, $V_O = \pm 10V$	600	1200	—	500	1000	—	300	800	—	V/mV
Output Voltage Swing	V_O	$R_L \geq 2k\Omega$	$\pm$11.5	$\pm$13.5	—	$\pm$11.0	$\pm$13.2	—	$\pm$10.5	$\pm$13.0	—	V

ELECTRICAL CHARACTERISTICS for $V_S = \pm 15V$, $-25°C \leq T_A \leq +85°C$ for OP-27J and OP-27Z, $0°C \leq T_A \leq +70°C$ for OP-27P, unless otherwise noted.

PARAMETER	SYMBOL	CONDITIONS	OP-27E			OP-27F			OP-27G			UNITS
			MIN	TYP	MAX	MIN	TYP	MAX	MIN	TYP	MAX	
Input Offset Voltage	V_{OS}		—	20	50	—	40	140	—	55	220	μV
Average Input Offset Drift	TCV_{OS} TCV_{OSn}	(Note 2)	—	0.2	0.6	—	0.3	1.3	—	0.4	1.8	μV/°C
Input Offset Current	I_{OS}		—	10	50	—	14	85	—	20	135	nA
Input Bias Current	I_B		—	$\pm$14	$\pm$60	—	$\pm$18	$\pm$95	—	$\pm$25	$\pm$150	nA
Input Voltage Range	IVR		$\pm$10.5	$\pm$11.8	—	$\pm$10.5	$\pm$11.8	—	$\pm$10.5	$\pm$11.8	—	V
Common-Mode Rejection Ratio	CMRR	$V_{CM} = \pm 10V$	110	124	—	102	121	—	96	118	—	dB
Power Supply Rejection Ratio	PSRR	$V_S = \pm 4.5V$ to $\pm 18V$	—	2	15	—	2	16	—	2	32	μV/V
Large-Signal Voltage Gain	A_{VO}	$R_L \geq 2k\Omega$, $V_O = \pm 10V$	750	1500	—	700	1300	—	450	1000	—	V/mV
Output Voltage Swing	V_O	$R_L \geq 2k\Omega$	$\pm$11.7	$\pm$13.6	—	$\pm$11.4	$\pm$13.5	—	$\pm$11.0	$\pm$13.3	—	V

NOTES:

1. Input offset voltage measurements are performed by automated test equipment approximately 0.5 seconds after application of power. A/E grades guaranteed fully warmed-up.
2. The TCV_{OS} performance is within the specifications unnulled or when nulled with $R_P = 8k\Omega$ to $20k\Omega$.

PMI — OP-27 LOW-NOISE PRECISION OPERATIONAL AMPLIFIER

DICE CHARACTERISTICS

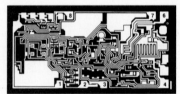

DIE SIZE 0.054 × 0.108 inch, 5832 sq. mils
(1.37 × 2.74mm, 3.76 sq. mm)

1. NULL
2. (−) INPUT
3. (+) INPUT
4. V−
6. OUTPUT
7. V+
8. NULL

For additional DICE information refer to
1984 Data Book, Section 2.

WAFER TEST LIMITS at $V_S = \pm 15V$, $T_A = 25°C$ for OP-27N, OP-27G, and OP-27GR devices; $T_A = 125°C$ for OP-27NT and OP-27GT devices, unless otherwise noted.

PARAMETER	SYMBOL	CONDITIONS	OP-27NT LIMIT	OP-27N LIMIT	OP-27GT LIMIT	OP-27G LIMIT	OP-27GR LIMIT	UNITS
Input Offset Voltage	V_{OS}	(Note 1)	60	35	200	60	100	μV MAX
Input Offset Current	I_{OS}		50	35	85	50	75	nA MAX
Input Bias Current	I_B		±60	±40	±95	±55	±80	nA MAX
Input Voltage Range	IVR		±10.3	±11	±10.3	±11	±11	V MIN
Common-Mode Rejection Ratio	CMRR	V_{CM} = IVR	108	114	100	106	100	dB MIN
Power Supply Rejection Ratio	PSRR	$V_S = \pm 4V$ to $\pm 18V$	—	10	—	10	20	μV/V MAX
Large-Signal Voltage Gain	A_{VO}	$R_L \geq 2k\Omega$, $V_O = \pm 10V$	600	1000	500	1000	700	V/mV MIN
		$R_L \geq 600\Omega$, $V_O = \pm 10V$	—	800	—	800	600	
Output Voltage Swing	V_O	$R_L \geq 2k\Omega$	±11.5	±12.0	±11.0	±12.0	±11.5	V MIN
		$R_L \geq 600\Omega$	—	±10.0	—	±10.0	±10.0	
Power Consumption	P_d	$V_O = 0$	—	140	—	140	170	mW MAX

NOTE:
Electrical tests are performed at wafer probe to the limits shown. Due to variations in assembly methods and normal yield loss, yield after packaging is not guaranteed for standard product dice. Consult factory to negotiate specifications based on dice lot qualification through sample lot assembly and testing.

TYPICAL ELECTRICAL CHARACTERISTICS at $V_S = \pm 15V$, $T_A = +25°C$, unless otherwise noted.

PARAMETER	SYMBOL	CONDITIONS	OP-27N TYPICAL	OP-27G TYPICAL	OP-27GR TYPICAL	UNITS
Average Input Offset Voltage Drift	TCV_{OS} or TCV_{OSn}	Nulled or Unnulled $R_P = 8k\Omega$ to $20k\Omega$	0.2	0.3	0.4	μV/°C
Average Input Offset Current Drift	TCI_{OS}		80	130	180	pA/°C
Average Input Bias Current Drift	TCI_B		100	160	200	pA/°C
Input Noise Voltage Density	e_n	$f_O = 10Hz$	3.5	3.5	3.8	nV/$\sqrt{Hz}$
		$f_O = 30Hz$	3.1	3.1	3.3	
		$f_O = 1000Hz$	3.0	3.0	3.2	
Input Noise Current Density	i_n	$f_O = 10Hz$	1.7	1.7	1.7	pA/$\sqrt{Hz}$
		$f_O = 30Hz$	1.0	1.0	1.0	
		$f_O = 1000Hz$	0.4	0.4	0.4	
Input Noise Voltage	e_{np-p}	0.1Hz to 10Hz	0.08	0.08	0.09	μVp-p
Slew Rate	SR	$R_L \geq 2k\Omega$	2.8	2.8	2.8	V/μs
Gain Bandwidth Product	GBW		8	8	8	MHz

NOTE:
1. Input offset voltage measurements are performed by automated test equipment approximately 0.5 seconds after application of power.

TYPICAL PERFORMANCE CHARACTERISTICS

0.1Hz TO 10Hz$_{p-p}$ NOISE TESTER FREQUENCY RESPONSE

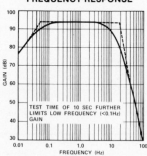

VOLTAGE NOISE DENSITY vs FREQUENCY

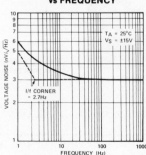

A COMPARISON OF OP AMP VOLTAGE NOISE SPECTRA

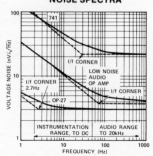

INPUT WIDEBAND VOLTAGE NOISE vs BANDWIDTH (0.1Hz TO FREQUENCY INDICATED)

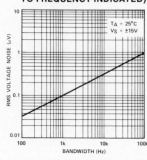

TOTAL NOISE vs SOURCE RESISTANCE

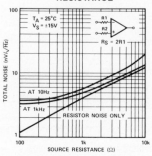

VOLTAGE NOISE DENSITY vs TEMPERATURE

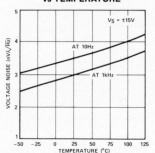

VOLTAGE NOISE DENSITY vs SUPPLY VOLTAGE

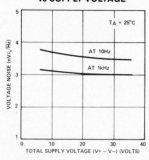

CURRENT NOISE DENSITY vs FREQUENCY

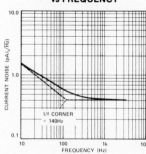

SUPPLY CURRENT vs SUPPLY VOLTAGE

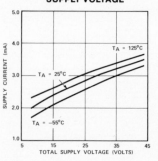

PMI — OP-27 LOW-NOISE PRECISION OPERATIONAL AMPLIFIER

TYPICAL PERFORMANCE CHARACTERISTICS

OFFSET VOLTAGE DRIFT OF EIGHT REPRESENTATIVE UNITS vs TEMPERATURE

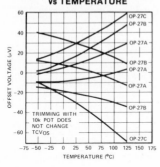

LONG-TERM OFFSET VOLTAGE DRIFT OF SIX REPRESENTATIVE UNITS

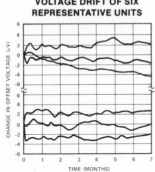

WARM-UP OFFSET VOLTAGE DRIFT

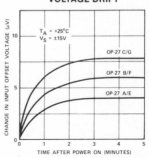

OFFSET VOLTAGE CHANGE DUE TO THERMAL SHOCK

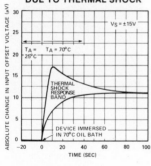

INPUT BIAS CURRENT vs TEMPERATURE

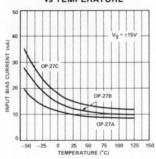

INPUT OFFSET CURRENT vs TEMPERATURE

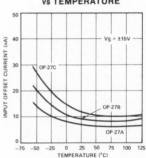

OPEN-LOOP GAIN vs FREQUENCY

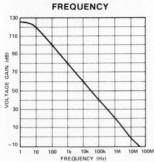

SLEW RATE, GAIN-BANDWIDTH PRODUCT, PHASE MARGIN vs TEMPERATURE

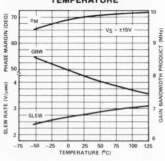

GAIN, PHASE SHIFT vs FREQUENCY

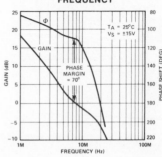

TYPICAL PERFORMANCE CHARACTERISTICS

OPEN-LOOP VOLTAGE GAIN vs SUPPLY VOLTAGE

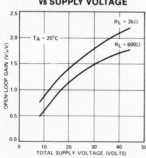

MAXIMUM OUTPUT SWING vs FREQUENCY

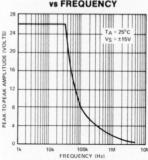

MAXIMUM OUTPUT VOLTAGE vs LOAD RESISTANCE

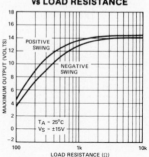

SMALL-SIGNAL OVERSHOOT vs CAPACITIVE LOAD

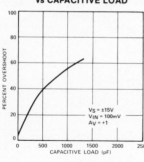

SMALL-SIGNAL TRANSIENT RESPONSE

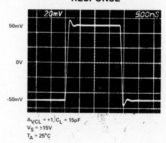

LARGE-SIGNAL TRANSIENT RESPONSE

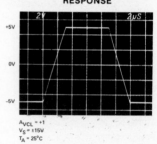

SHORT-CIRCUIT CURRENT vs TIME

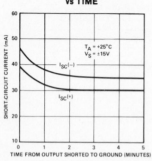

CMRR vs FREQUENCY

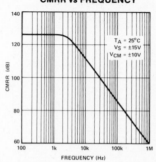

COMMON-MODE INPUT RANGE vs SUPPLY VOLTAGE

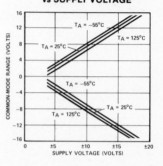

TYPICAL PERFORMANCE CHARACTERISTICS

VOLTAGE NOISE TEST CIRCUIT (0.1Hz-TO-10Hz)

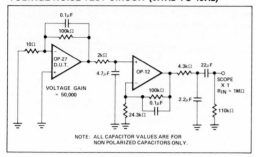

NOTE: ALL CAPACITOR VALUES ARE FOR NON POLARIZED CAPACITORS ONLY.

LOW-FREQUENCY NOISE

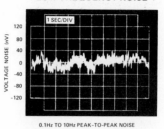

0.1Hz TO 10Hz PEAK-TO-PEAK NOISE

NOTE:
Observation time limited to 10 seconds.

OPEN-LOOP VOLTAGE GAIN vs LOAD RESISTANCE

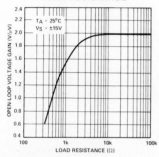

PSRR vs FREQUENCY

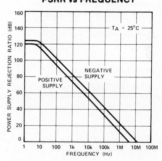

APPLICATIONS INFORMATION

OP-27 Series units may be inserted directly into 725, OP-06, OP-07 and OP-05 sockets with or without removal of external compensation or nulling components. Additionally, the OP-27 may be fitted to unnulled 741-type sockets; however, if conventional 741 nulling circuitry is in use, it should be modified or removed to ensure correct OP-27 operation. OP-27 offset voltage may be nulled to zero (or other desired setting) using a potentiometer (see Offset Nulling Circuit).

The OP-27 provides stable operation with load capacitances of up to 2000pF and ± 10V swings; larger capacitances should be decoupled with a 50Ω resistor inside the feedback loop. The OP-27 is unity-gain stable.

Thermoelectric voltages generated by dissimilar metals at the input terminal contacts can degrade the drift performance. Best operation will be obtained when both input contacts are maintained at the same temperature.

OFFSET VOLTAGE ADJUSTMENT

The input offset voltage of the OP-27 is trimmed at wafer level. However, if further adjustment of V_{OS} is necessary, a 10kΩ trim potentiometer may be used. TCV_{OS} is not degraded

(see Offset Nulling Circuit). Other potentiometer values from 1kΩ to 1MΩ can be used with a slight degradation (0.1 to 0.2μV/°C) of TCV_{OS}. Trimming to a value other than zero creates a drift of approximately $(V_{OS}/300) \mu V/°C$. For example, the change in TCV_{OS} will be 0.33μV/°C if V_{OS} is adjusted to 100μV. The offset-voltage adjustment range with a 10kΩ potentiometer is ±4mV. If smaller adjustment range is required, the nulling sensitivity can be reduced by using a smaller pot in conjuction with fixed resistors. For example, the network below will have a ±280μV adjustment range.

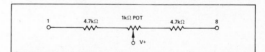

NOISE MEASUREMENTS

To measure the 80nV peak-to-peak noise specification of the OP-27 in the 0.1Hz to 10Hz range, the following precautions must be observed:

(1) The device has to be warmed-up for at least five minutes. As shown in the warm-up drift curve, the offset voltage

PMi — OP-27 LOW-NOISE PRECISION OPERATIONAL AMPLIFIER

typically changes $4\mu V$ due to increasing chip temperature after power-up. In the 10-second measurement interval, these temperature-induced effects can exceed tens-of-nanovolts.

(2) For similar reasons, the device has to be well-shielded from air currents. Shielding minimizes thermocouple effects.

(3) Sudden motion in the vicinity of the device can also "feedthrough" to increase the observed noise.

(4) The test time to measure 0.1Hz-to-10Hz noise should not exceed 10 seconds. As shown in the noise-tester frequency-response curve, the 0.1Hz corner is defined by only one zero. The test time of 10 seconds acts as an additional zero to eliminate noise contributions from the frequency band below 0.1Hz.

(5) A noise-voltage-density test is recommended when measuring noise on a large number of units. A 10Hz noise-voltage-density measurement will correlate well with a 0.1Hz-to-10Hz peak-to-peak noise reading, since both results are determined by the white noise and the location of the 1/f corner frequency.

UNITY-GAIN BUFFER APPLICATIONS

When $R_f \leq 100\Omega$ and the input is driven with a fast, large signal pulse ($>1V$), the output waveform will look as shown in the pulsed operation diagram below.

During the fast feedthrough-like portion of the output, the input protection diodes effectively short the output to the input and a current, limited only by the output short-circuit protection, will be drawn by the signal generator. With $R_f \geq 500\Omega$, the output is capable of handling the current requirements ($I_L \leq 20mA$ at $10V$); the amplifier will stay in its active mode and a smooth transition will occur.

When $R_f > 2k\Omega$, a pole will be created with R_f and the amplifier's input capacitance (8pF) that creates additional phase shift and reduces phase margin. A small capacitor (20 to 50pF) in parallel with R_f will eliminate this problem.

PULSED OPERATION

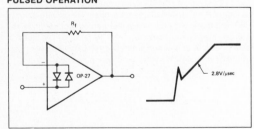

COMMENTS ON NOISE

The OP-27 is a very low-noise monolithic op amp. The outstanding input voltage noise characteristics of the OP-27 are achieved mainly by operating the input stage at a high quiescent current. The input bias and offset currents, which would normally increase, are held to reasonable values by the input-

bias-current cancellation circuit. The OP-27A/E has I_B and I_{OS} of only $\pm 40nA$ and $35nA$ respectively at $25°C$. This is particularly important when the input has a high source-resistance. In addition, many audio amplifier designers prefer to use direct coupling. The high I_B, V_{OS}, TCV_{OS} of previous designs have made direct coupling difficult, if not impossible, to use.

Voltage noise is inversely proportional to the square-root of bias current, but current noise is proportional to the square-root of bias current. The OP-27's noise advantage disappears when high source-resistors are used. Figures 1, 2, and 3 compare OP-27 observed total noise with the noise performance of other devices in different circuit applications.

Total noise = $[(\text{Voltage noise})^2 + (\text{current noise} \times R_S)^2 + (\text{resistor noise})^2]^{1/2}$

Figure 1 shows noise-versus-source-resistance at 1000Hz. The same plot applies to wideband noise. To use this plot, just multiply the vertical scale by the square-root of the bandwidth.

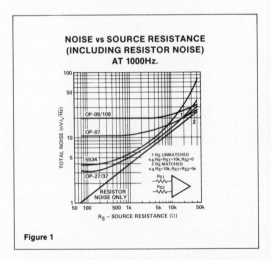

NOISE vs SOURCE RESISTANCE (INCLUDING RESISTOR NOISE) AT 1000Hz.

Figure 1

At $R_S < 1k\Omega$, the OP-27's low voltage noise is maintained. With $R_S > 1k\Omega$, total noise increases, but is dominated by the resistor noise rather than current or voltage noise. It is only beyond R_S of $20k\Omega$ that current noise starts to dominate. The argument can be made that current noise is not important for applications with low-to-moderate source resistances. The crossover between the OP-27 and OP-07 and OP-08 noise occurs in the 15-to-40kΩ region.

Figure 2 shows the 0.1Hz-to-10Hz peak-to-peak noise. Here the picture is less favorable; resistor noise is negligible, current noise becomes important because it is inversely proportional to the square-root of frequency. The crossover with the OP-07 occurs in the 3-to-5kΩ range depending on whether balanced or unbalanced source resistors are used (at 3kΩ the I_B, I_{OS} error also can be three times the V_{OS} spec.).

PMI — OP-27 LOW-NOISE PRECISION OPERATIONAL AMPLIFIER

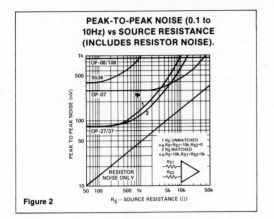

Figure 2

PEAK-TO-PEAK NOISE (0.1 to 10Hz) vs SOURCE RESISTANCE (INCLUDES RESISTOR NOISE).

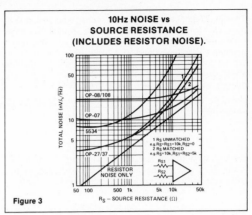

Figure 3

10Hz NOISE vs SOURCE RESISTANCE (INCLUDES RESISTOR NOISE).

Therefore, for low-frequency applications, the OP-07 is better than the OP-27/37 when $R_S > 3k\Omega$. The only exception is when gain error is important. Figure 3 illustrates the 10Hz noise. As expected, the results are between the previous two figures.

For reference, typical source resistances of some signal sources are listed in Table 1.

Table 1

DEVICE	SOURCE IMPEDANCE	COMMENTS
Strain gauge	<500Ω	Typically used in low-frequency applications.
Magnetic tapehead	<1500Ω	Low I_B very important to reduce self-magnetization problems when direct coupling is used. OP-27 I_B can be neglected.
Magnetic phonograph cartridges	<1500Ω	Similar need for low I_B in direct coupled applications. OP-27 will not introduce any self-magnetization problem.
Linear variable differential transformer	<1500Ω	Used in rugged servo-feedback applications. Bandwidth of interest is 400Hz to 5kHz.

OPEN-LOOP GAIN

FREQUENCY AT:	OP-07	OP-27	OP-37
3Hz	100dB	124dB	125dB
10Hz	100dB	120dB	125dB
30Hz	90dB	110dB	124dB

For further information regarding noise calculations, see "Minimization of Noise in Op-Amp Applications", Application Note AN-15.

AUDIO APPLICATIONS

The following applications information has been abstracted from a PMI article in the 12/20/80 issue of Electronic Design magazine and updated.

Figure 4 is an example of a phono pre-amplifier circuit using the OP-27 for A_1; R_1-R_2-C_1-C_2 form a very accurate RIAA network with standard component values. The popular method to accomplish RIAA phono equalization is to employ frequency-dependent feedback around a high-quality gain block. Properly chosen, an RC network can provide the three necessary time constants of 3180, 318, and 75µs.[1]

For initial equalization accuracy and stability, precision metal-film resistors and film capacitors of polystyrene or polypropylene are recommended since they have low voltage coefficients, dissipation factors, and dielectric absorption.[4] (High-K ceramic capacitors should be avoided here, though low-K ceramics—such as NPO types, which have excellent dissipation factors, and somewhat lower dielectric absorption—can be considered for small values.)

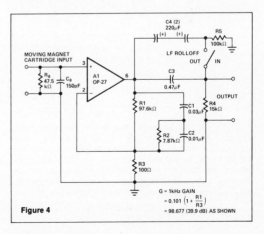

Figure 4

PMI — OP-27 LOW-NOISE PRECISION OPERATIONAL AMPLIFIER

The OP-27 brings a $3.2nV/\sqrt{Hz}$ voltage noise and 0.45 $pA/\sqrt{Hz}$ current noise to this circuit. To minimize noise from other sources, R_3 is set to a value of 100Ω, which generates a voltage noise of $1.3nV/\sqrt{Hz}$. The noise increases the $3.2nV/\sqrt{Hz}$ of the amplifier by only 0.7dB. With a $1k\Omega$ source, the circuit noise measures 63dB below a 1mV reference level, unweighted, in a 20kHz noise bandwidth.

Gain (G) of the circuit at 1kHz can be calculated by the expression:

$$G = 0.101 \left(1 + \frac{R_1}{R_3}\right)$$

For the values shown, the gain is just under 100 (or 40dB). Lower gains can be accommodated by increasing R_3, but gains higher than 40dB will show more equalization errors because of the 8MHz gain-bandwidth of the OP-27.

This circuit is capable of very low distortion over its entire range, generally below 0.01% at levels up to 7V rms. At 3V output levels, it will produce less than 0.03% total harmonic distortion at frequencies up to 20kHz.

Capacitor C_3 and resistor R_4 form a simple −6dB-per-octave rumble filter, with a corner at 22Hz. As an option, the switch-selected shunt capacitor C_4, a nonpolarized electrolytic, bypasses the low-frequency rolloff. Placing the rumble filter's high-pass action after the preamp has the desirable result of discriminating against the RIAA-amplified low-frequency noise components and pickup-produced low-frequency disturbances.

A preamplifier for NAB tape playback is similar to an RIAA phono preamp, though more gain is typically demanded, along with equalization requiring a heavy low-frequency boost. The circuit in Fig. 4 can be readily modified for tape use, as shown by Fig. 5.

The network values of the configuration yield a 50dB gain at 1kHz, and the dc gain is greater than 70dB. Thus, the worst-case output offset is just over 500mV. A single $0.47\mu F$ output capacitor can block this level without affecting the dynamic range.

The tape head can be coupled directly to the amplifier input, since the worst-case bias current of 80nA with a 400mH, 100 μin. head (such as the PRB2H7K) will not be troublesome.

One potential tape-head problem is presented by amplifier bias-current transients which can magnetize a head. The OP-27 and OP-37 are free of bias-current transients upon power up or power down. However, it is always advantageous to control the speed of power supply rise and fall, to eliminate transients.

In addition, the dc resistance of the head should be carefully controlled, and preferably below $1k\Omega$. For this configuration, the bias-current-induced offset voltage can be greater than the $100\mu V$ maximum offset if the head resistance is not sufficiently controlled.

A simple, but effective, fixed-gain transformerless microphone preamp (Fig. 6) amplifies differential signals from low-impedance microphones by 50dB, and has an input impedance of $2k\Omega$. Because of the high working gain of the circuit, an OP-37 helps to preserve bandwidth, which will be 110kHz. As the OP-37 is a decompensated device (minimum stable gain of 5), a dummy resistor, R_p, may be necessary, if the microphone is to be unplugged. Otherwise the 100% feedback from the open input may cause the amplifier to oscillate.

Common-mode input-noise rejection will depend upon the match of the bridge-resistor ratios. Either close-tolerance (0.1%) types should be used, or R_4 should be trimmed for best CMRR. All resistors should be metal-film types for best stability and low noise.

Noise performance of this circuit is limited more by the input resistors R_1 and R_2 than by the op amp, as R_1 and R_2 each generate a $4nV/\sqrt{Hz}$ noise, while the op amp generates a $3.2nV/\sqrt{Hz}$ noise. The rms sum of these predominant noise sources will be about $6nV/\sqrt{Hz}$, equivalent to $0.9\mu V$ in a 20kHz noise bandwidth, or nearly 61dB below a 1mV input signal. Measurements confirm this predicted performance.

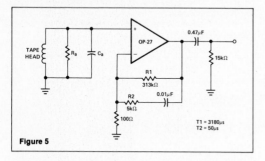

Figure 5

While the tape-equalization requirement has a flat high-frequency gain above 3kHz ($T_2 = 50\mu s$), the amplifier need not be stabilized for unity gain. The decompensated OP-37 provides a greater bandwidth and slew rate. For many applications, the idealized time constants shown may require trimming of R_1 and R_2 to optimize frequency response for nonideal tape-head performance and other factors.[5]

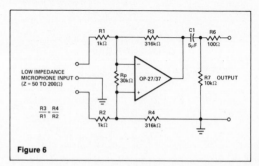

Figure 6

PMI — OP-27 LOW-NOISE PRECISION OPERATIONAL AMPLIFIER

For applications demanding appreciably lower noise, a high-quality microphone-transformer-coupled preamp (Fig. 7) incorporates the internally-compensated OP-27. T_1 is a JE-115K-E 150Ω/15kΩ transformer which provides an optimum source resistance for the OP-27 device. The circuit has an overall gain of 40dB, the product of the transformer's voltage setup and the op amp's voltage gain.

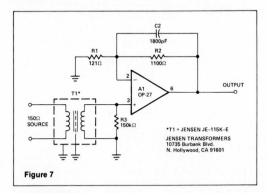

Figure 7

Gain may be trimmed to other levels, if desired, by adjusting R_2 or R_1. Because of the low offset voltage of the OP-27, the output offset of this circuit will be very low, 1.7mV or less, for a 40dB gain. The typical output blocking capacitor can be eliminated in such cases, but is desirable for higher gains to eliminate switching transients.

Capacitor C_2 and resistor R_2 form a 2μs time constant in this circuit, as recommended for optimum transient response by the transformer manufacturer. With C_2 in use, A_1 must have unity-gain stability. For situations where the 2μs time constant is not necessary, C_2 can be deleted, allowing the faster OP-37 to be employed.

Some comment on noise is appropriate to understand the capability of this circuit. A 150Ω resistor and R_1 and R_2 gain resistors connected to a noiseless amplifier will generate 220 nV of noise in a 20kHz bandwidth, or 73dB below a 1mV reference level. Any practical amplifier can only approach this noise level; it can never exceed it. With the OP-27 and T_1 specified, the additional noise degradation will be close to 3.6dB (or −69.5 referenced to 1mV).

References

1. Lipshitz, S.P., "On RIAA Equalization Networks," *JAES*, Vol. 27, June 1979, p. 458-481.

2. Jung, W.G., *IC Op Amp Cookbook*, 2nd Ed., H.W. Sams and Company, 1980.

3. Jung, W.G., *Audio IC Op Amp Applications*, 2nd Ed., H.W. Sams and Company, 1978.

4. Jung, W.G., and Marsh, R.M., "Picking Capacitors," *Audio*, February & March, 1980.

5. Otala, M., "Feedback-Generated Phase Nonlinearity in Audio Amplifiers," London AES Convention, March 1980, preprint 1976.

6. Stout, D.F., and Kaufman, M., *Handbook of Operational Amplifier Circuit Design*, New York, McGraw Hill, 1976.

BURN-IN CIRCUIT

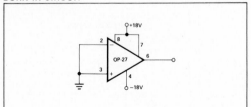

OFFSET NULLING CIRCUIT

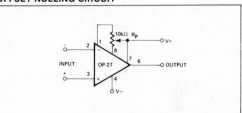

PMI® **Precision Monolithics Incorporated** A Bourns Subsidiary
® **1500 SPACE PARK DR., SANTA CLARA, CA 95050** • **TEL (408) 727-9222** • **TWX 910-338-0218** • **TLX 172 070**
06840137G5M PRINTED IN USA

MOTOROLA

SEMICONDUCTORS

P.O. BOX 20912 • PHOENIX, ARIZONA 85036

Advance Information

HIGH SLEW RATE, WIDE BANDWIDTH, SINGLE SUPPLY QUAD OPERATIONAL AMPLIFIER

A standard low-cost Bipolar technology with innovative design concepts is employed for the MC34074 series of monolithic quad operational amplifiers. These devices offer 4.5 MHz of gain bandwidth product, 13 V/μs slew rate, and fast settling time without the use of JFET device technology. In addition, low input offset voltage can economically be achieved. Although these devices can be operated from split supplies, they are particularly suited for single supply operation, since the common mode input voltage range includes ground potential (V_{EE}). The all NPN output stage, characterized by no deadband crossover distortion and large output voltage swing, also provides high capacitive drive capability, excellent phase and gain margins, low open-loop high frequency output impedance and symmetrical source/sink ac frequency response.

The MC34074/33074/35074 series of devices are available in standard or prime performance (A Suffix) grades and specified over commercial, industrial/vehicular or military temperature ranges.

- Wide Bandwidth: 4.5 MHz
- High Slew Rate: 13 V/μs
- Fast Settling Time: 1.1 μs to 0.10%
- Wide Single Supply Operating Range: 3.0 to 44 Volts
- Wide Input Common Mode Range Including Ground (V_{EE})
- Low Input Offset Voltage: 2.0 mV Maximum (A Suffix)
- Large Output Voltage Swing: −14.7 V to + 14.0 V for V_S = ± 15 V
- Large Capacitance Drive Capability: 0 to 10,000 pF
- Low T.H.D. Distortion: 0.02%
- Excellent Phase Margins: 60°
- Excellent Gain Margin: 12 dB

MC34074,A
MC35074,A
MC33074,A

QUAD HIGH PERFORMANCE SINGLE SUPPLY OPERATIONAL AMPLIFIERS

SILICON MONOLITHIC INTEGRATED CIRCUIT

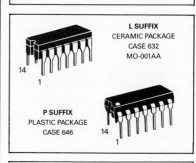

L SUFFIX
CERAMIC PACKAGE
CASE 632
MO-001AA

P SUFFIX
PLASTIC PACKAGE
CASE 646

PIN CONNECTIONS

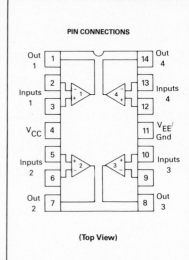

Out 1	1		14	Out 4
Inputs 1	2		13	Inputs 4
	3		12	
V_{CC}	4		11	V_{EE}/Gnd
Inputs 2	5		10	Inputs 3
	6		9	
Out 2	7		8	Out 3

(Top View)

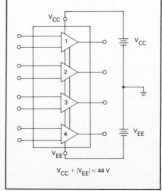

SINGLE SUPPLY

3.0 V to 44 V

V_{CC}

V_{EE}

SPLIT SUPPLIES

V_{CC}

V_{CC}

V_{EE}

V_{EE}

V_{CC} + |V_{EE}| ≤ 44 V

ORDERING INFORMATION

Device	Temperature Range	Package
MC35074L, AL	−55 to + 125°C	Ceramic DIP
MC33074L, AL	−40 to + 85°C	Ceramic DIP
MC33074P, AP	−40 to + 85°C	Plastic DIP
MC34074L, AL	0 to + 70°C	Ceramic DIP
MC34074P, AP	0 to + 70°C	Plastic DIP

ADI-770

MC34074 Series

MAXIMUM RATINGS

Rating	Symbol	Value	Unit
Supply Voltage (from V_{CC} to V_{EE})	V_S	+44	Volts
Input Differential Voltage Range	V_{IDR}	Note 1	Volts
Input Voltage Range	V_{IR}	Note 1	Volts
Output Short-Circuit Duration (Note 2)	t_S	Indefinite	Seconds
Operating Ambient Temperature Range MC35074,A MC33074,A MC34074,A	T_A	 −55 to +125 −40 to +85 0 to +70	°C
Operating Junction Temperature	T_J	+150	°C
Storage Temperature Range Ceramic Package Plastic Package	T_{stg}	 −65 to +150 −55 to +125	°C

MAXIMUM DEVICE POWER DISSIPATION

Ambient Temperature	+25°C	+70°C	+85°C	+125°C	°C
Power Dissipation	1250	800	650	250	mW

NOTES:
1. Either or both input voltages must not exceed the magnitude of V_{CC} or V_{EE}.
2. Power dissipation must be considered to ensure maximum junction temperature (T_J) is not exceeded.

EQUIVALENT CIRCUIT SCHEMATIC   (EACH AMPLIFIER)

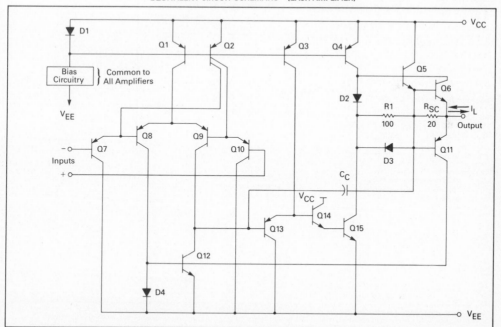

 MOTOROLA *Semiconductor Products Inc.*

MC34074 Series

DC ELECTRICAL CHARACTERISTICS (V_{CC} = + 15 V, V_{EE} = −15 V, R_L connected to ground, T_A = T_{low} to T_{high} [Note 3] unless otherwise noted)

Characteristic	Symbol	MC35074A/34074A/33074A			MC35074/34074/33074			Unit
		Min	Typ	Max	Min	Typ	Max	
Input Offset Voltage (V_{CM} = 0)	V_{IO}							mV
V_{CC} = + 15 V, V_{EE} = −15 V, T_A = + 25°C		—	0.5	2.0	—	2.0	4.5	
V_{CC} = + 5.0 V, V_{EE} = 0 V, T_A = + 25°C		—	0.5	2.5	—	2.5	5.0	
V_{CC} = + 15 V, V_{EE} = −15 V, T_A = T_{low} to T_{high}		—	—	4.0	—	—	6.5	
Average Temperature Coefficient of Offset Voltage	$\Delta V_{IO}/\Delta T$	—	10	—	—	10	—	$\mu V/°C$
Input Bias Current (V_{CM} = 0)	I_{IB}							nA
T_A = + 25°C		—	100	500	—	100	500	
T_A = T_{low} to T_{high}		—	—	700	—	—	700	
Input Offset Current (V_{CM} = 0)	I_{IO}							nA
T_A = + 25°C		—	6.0	50	—	6.0	75	
T_A = T_{low} to T_{high}		—	—	300	—	—	300	
Large Signal Voltage Gain V_O = ± 10 V, R_L = 2.0 k	A_{VOL}	50	100	—	25	100	—	V/mV
Output Voltage Swing	V_{OH}							V
V_{CC} = + 5.0 V, V_{EE} = 0 V, R_L = 2.0 k, T_A = + 25°C		3.7	4.0	—	3.7	4.0	—	
V_{CC} = + 15 V, V_{EE} = −15 V, R_L = 10 k, T_A = + 25°C		13.7	14	—	13.7	14	—	
V_{CC} = + 15 V, V_{EE} −15 V, R_L = 2.0 k, T_A = T_{low} to T_{high}		13.5	—	—	13.5	—	—	
V_{CC} = + 5.0 V, V_{EE} = 0 V, R_L = 2.0 k, T_A = + 25°C	V_{OL}	—	0.1	0.2	—	0.1	0.2	
V_{CC} = + 15 V, V_{EE} + −15 V, R_L = 10 k, T_A = + 25°C		—	−14.7	−14.4	—	−14.7	−14.4	
V_{CC} = + 15 V, V_{EE} = −15 V, R_L = 2.0 k, T_A = T_{low} to T_{high}		—	—	−13.8	—	—	−13.8	
Output Short-Circuit Current (T_A = + 25°C) Input Overdrive = 1.0 V, Output to Ground	I_{SC}							mA
Source		10	30	—	10	30	—	
Sink		20	47	—	20	47	—	
Input Common Mode Voltage Range	V_{ICR}							V
T_A = + 25°C		V_{EE} to (V_{CC} − 1.8)			V_{EE} to (V_{CC} − 1.8)			
T_A = T_{low} to T_{high}		V_{EE} to (V_{CC} − 2.2)			V_{EE} to (V_{CC} − 2.2)			
Common Mode Rejection Ratio (R_S ≤ 10 k)	CMRR	80	97	—	70	97	—	dB
Power Supply Rejection Ratio (R_S = 100 Ω)	PSRR	80	97	—	70	97	—	dB
Power Supply Current	I_D							mA
V_{CC} = + 5.0 V, V_{EE} = 0 V, T_A = + 25°C		—	6.5	8.0	—	6.5	8.0	
V_{CC} = + 15 V, V_{EE} = −15 V, T_A = + 25°C		—	7.5	10	—	7.5	10	
V_{CC} = + 15 V, V_{EE} = −15 V, T_A = T_{low} to T_{high}		—	—	11	—	—	11	

NOTES: (continued)

3. T_{low} = −55°C for MC35074, MC35074A T_{high} = + 125°C for MC35074, MC35074A
      = −40°C for MC33074, MC33074A   = + 85°C for MC33074, MC33074A
      = 0°C for MC34074, MC34074A   = + 70°C for MC34074, MC34074A

 MOTOROLA *Semiconductor Products Inc.*

MC34074 Series

AC ELECTRICAL CHARACTERISTICS (V_{CC} = + 15 V, V_{EE} = −15 V, R_L connected to ground, T_A = + 25 C unless otherwise noted)

Characteristic	Symbol	MC35074A/34074A/33074A			MC35074/34074/33074			Unit
		Min	Typ	Max	Min	Typ	Max	
Slew Rate (V_{in} = −10 V to + 10 V, R_L = 2.0 k, C_L = 500 pF)	SR							V/μs
A_V + 1		8.0	10	—	—	10	—	
A_V −1		—	13	—	—	13	—	
Settling Time (10 V Step, A_V = −1.0)	t_s							μs
To 0.10% (± ½ LSB of 9-Bits)		—	1.1	—	—	1.1	—	
To 0.01% (± ½ LSB of 12-Bits)		—	2.2	—	—	2.2	—	
Gain Bandwidth Product (f = 100 kHz)	GBW	3.5	4.5	—	—	4.5	—	MHz
Power Bandwidth (A_V = + 1.0, R_L = 2.0 k, V_O = 20 V_{P-P}, THD = 5.0%)	BWp	—	200	—	—	200	—	kHz
Phase Margin	ϕm							Degrees
R_L = 2.0 k		—	60	—	—	60	—	
R_L = 2.0 k, C_L = 300 pF		—	40	—	—	40	—	
Gain Margin	A_m							dB
R_L = 2.0 k		—	12	—	—	12	—	
R_L = 2.0 k, C_L = 300 pF		—	4.0	—	—	4.0	—	
Equivalent Input Noise Voltage R_S = 100 Ω, f = 1.0 kHz	e_n	—	32	—	—	32	—	nV/$\sqrt{Hz}$
Equivalent Input Noise Current (f = 1.0 kHz)	I_n	—	0.22	—	—	0.22	—	pA/$\sqrt{Hz}$
Input Capacitance	C_i	—	0.8	—	—	0.8	—	pF
Total Harmonic Distortion A_V = + 10, R_L = 2.0 k, 2.0 ≤ V_O ≤ 20 V_{P-P}, f = 10 kHz	THD	—	0.02	—	—	0.02	—	%
Channel Separation (f = 10 kHz)	—	—	120	—	—	120	—	dB
Open-Loop Output Impedance (f = 1.0 MHz)	z_o	—	30	—	—	30	—	Ω

TYPICAL PERFORMANCE CURVES

FIGURE 1—INPUT OFFSET VOLTAGE versus TEMPERATURE FOR REPRESENTATIVE UNITS

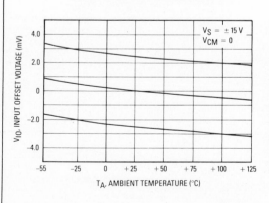

FIGURE 2—INPUT COMMON-MODE VOLTAGE RANGE versus TEMPERATURE

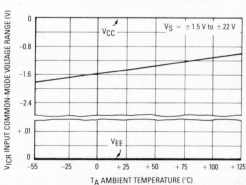

 MOTOROLA *Semiconductor Products Inc.*

MC34074 Series

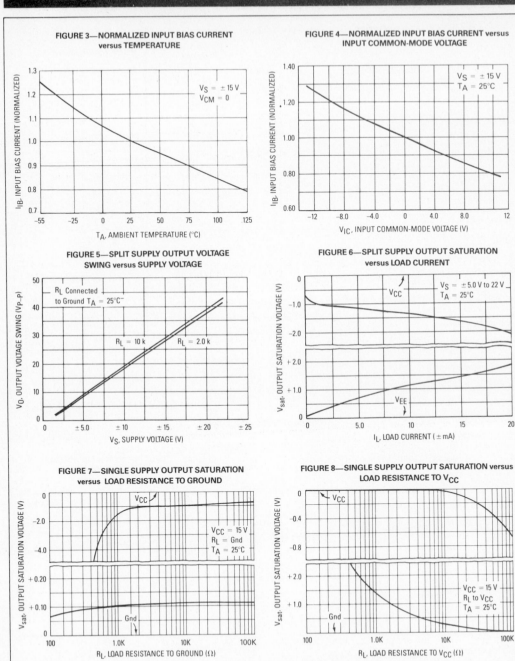

FIGURE 3—NORMALIZED INPUT BIAS CURRENT
versus TEMPERATURE

FIGURE 4—NORMALIZED INPUT BIAS CURRENT versus
INPUT COMMON-MODE VOLTAGE

FIGURE 5—SPLIT SUPPLY OUTPUT VOLTAGE
SWING versus SUPPLY VOLTAGE

FIGURE 6—SPLIT SUPPLY OUTPUT SATURATION
versus LOAD CURRENT

FIGURE 7—SINGLE SUPPLY OUTPUT SATURATION
versus LOAD RESISTANCE TO GROUND

FIGURE 8—SINGLE SUPPLY OUTPUT SATURATION versus
LOAD RESISTANCE TO V_{CC}

 MOTOROLA *Semiconductor Products Inc.*

MC34074 Series

FIGURE 9—OUTPUT SHORT CIRCUIT CURRENT
versus TEMPERATURE

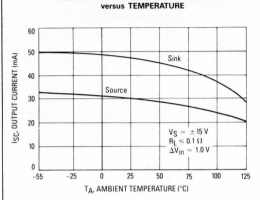

FIGURE 10—OUTPUT IMPEDANCE versus FREQUENCY

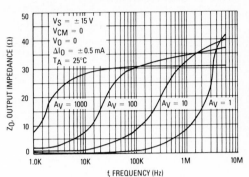

FIGURE 11—OUTPUT VOLTAGE SWING versus FREQUENCY

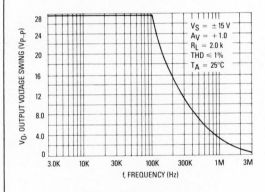

FIGURE 12—OUTPUT DISTORTION versus FREQUENCY

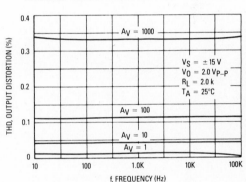

FIGURE 13—OUTPUT DISTORTION versus
OUTPUT VOLTAGE SWING

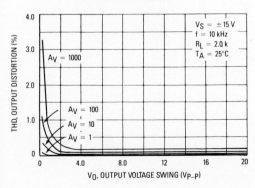

FIGURE 14—OPEN-LOOP VOLTAGE GAIN versus TEMPERATURE

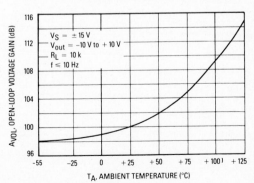

 MOTOROLA *Semiconductor Products Inc.*

MC34074 Series

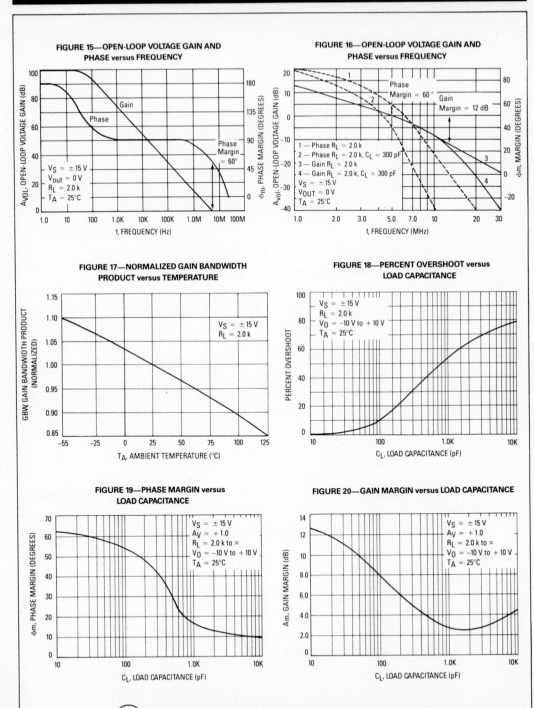

FIGURE 15—OPEN-LOOP VOLTAGE GAIN AND PHASE versus FREQUENCY

FIGURE 16—OPEN-LOOP VOLTAGE GAIN AND PHASE versus FREQUENCY

FIGURE 17—NORMALIZED GAIN BANDWIDTH PRODUCT versus TEMPERATURE

FIGURE 18—PERCENT OVERSHOOT versus LOAD CAPACITANCE

FIGURE 19—PHASE MARGIN versus LOAD CAPACITANCE

FIGURE 20—GAIN MARGIN versus LOAD CAPACITANCE

(M) MOTOROLA *Semiconductor Products Inc.*

MC34074 Series

FIGURE 21—PHASE MARGIN versus TEMPERATURE

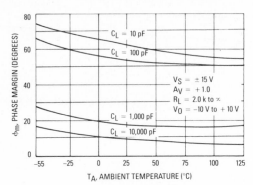

FIGURE 22—GAIN MARGIN versus TEMPERATURE

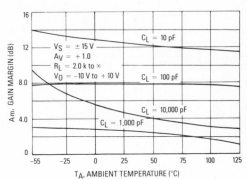

FIGURE 23—NORMALIZED SLEW RATE versus TEMPERATURE

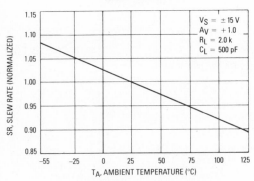

FIGURE 24—OUTPUT SETTLING TIME

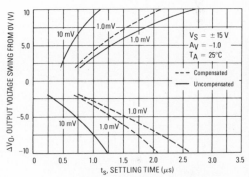

FIGURE 25—SMALL-SIGNAL TRANSIENT RESPONSE

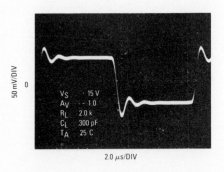

FIGURE 26—LARGE-SIGNAL TRANSIENT RESPONSE

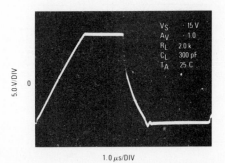

MOTOROLA *Semiconductor Products Inc.*

MC34074 Series

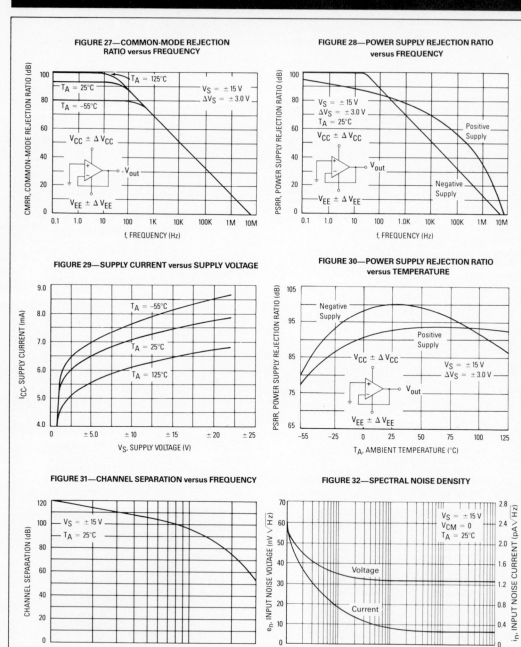

FIGURE 27—COMMON-MODE REJECTION RATIO versus FREQUENCY

FIGURE 28—POWER SUPPLY REJECTION RATIO versus FREQUENCY

FIGURE 29—SUPPLY CURRENT versus SUPPLY VOLTAGE

FIGURE 30—POWER SUPPLY REJECTION RATIO versus TEMPERATURE

FIGURE 31—CHANNEL SEPARATION versus FREQUENCY

FIGURE 32—SPECTRAL NOISE DENSITY

 MOTOROLA *Semiconductor Products Inc.*

APPLICATIONS INFORMATION
CIRCUIT DESCRIPTION/PERFORMANCE FEATURES OF THE MC34074 FAMILY

Although the bandwidth, slew rate, and settling time of the MC34074 amplifier family is similar to op amp products utilizing JFET input devices, these amplifiers offer other additional distinct advantages as a result of the PNP transistor differential input stage and an all NPN transistor output stage.

Since the input common mode voltage range of this input stage includes the V_{EE} potential, single supply operation is feasible to as low as 3.0 volts with the common mode input voltage at ground potential.

The input stage also allows differential input voltages up to ± 44 volts, provided the maximum input voltage range is not exceeded. Specifically, the input voltages must range between V_{EE} and V_{CC} supply voltages as shown by the maximum rating table. In practice, although not recommended, the input voltages can exceed the V_{CC} voltage by approximately 3.0 volts and decrease below the V_{EE} voltage by 0.3 volts without causing product damage, although output phase reversal may occur. It is also possible to source up to approximately 5.0 mA of current from V_{EE} through either input's clamping diode without damage or latching, although phase reversal may again occur.

If at least one input is within the common mode input voltage range and the other input is within the maximum input voltage range, no phase reversal will occur. If both inputs exceed the upper common mode input voltage limit, the output will be forced to its lowest voltage state.

Since the input capacitance associated with the small geometry input device is substantially lower (0.8 pF) than the typical JFET input gate capacitance (3.0 pF), better frequency response for a given input source resistance can be achieved using the MC34074 amplifiers. This performance feature becomes evident, for example, in fast settling D-to-A current to voltage conversion applications where the feedback resistance can form an input pole with the input capacitance of the op amp. This input pole creates a 2nd order system with the single pole op amp and is therefore detrimental to its settling time. In this context, lower input capacitance is desirable especially for higher values of feedback resistances (lower current DAC's). This input pole can be compensated for by creating a feedback zero with a capacitance across the feedback resistance, if necessary, to reduce overshoot. For 2.0 kΩ of feedback resistance, the MC34074 family can typically settle to within 1/2 LSB of 8 bits in 1.0 μs, and within 1/2 LSB of 12 bits in 2.2 μs for a 10 volt step. In a typical inverting unity gain fast settling configuration, the typical symmetrical slew rate is ± 13 volts/μs. In the classic non-inverting unity gain configuration the typical output positive slew rate is + 10 volts/μs, and the corresponding negative slew rate will typically exceed the positive slew rate as a function of the fall time of the input waveform.

Since the bipolar input device matching characteristics are typically superior to that of JFETs, a low untrimmed maximum offset voltage of 2.0 mV prime and 4.5 mV downgrade can be economically offered with high frequency performance characteristics. This combination is ideal for low-cost precision, high-speed quad op amp applications.

The all NPN output stage, shown in its basic form on the equivalent circuit schematic, offers unique advantages over the more conventional NPN/PNP transistor Class AB output stage. A 10 kΩ load resistance can typically swing within 1.0 volt of the positive rail (V_{CC}), and within 0.3 volts of the negative rail (V_{EE}), providing a 28.7 Vp-p swing from ± 15 volt supplies. This large output swing becomes most noticable at lower supply voltages.

The positive swing is limited by the saturation voltage of the current source transistor Q4, and V_{BE} of the NPN pull up transistor Q5, and the voltage drop associated with the short circuit resistance, R_{SC}. The negative swing is limited by the saturation voltage of the pull-down transistor Q15, the voltage drop $I_L R_1$, and the voltage drop associated with resistance R_{SC}, where I_L is the sink load current. For small valued sink currents, the above voltage drops are negligible, allowing the negative swing voltage to approach within millivolts of V_{EE}. For large valued sink currents (>5.0 mA), diode D3 clamps the voltage across R_1, thus limiting the negative swing to the saturation voltage of Q15, plus the forward diode drop of D3 ($\approx V_{EE} + 1.0$ V). Thus for a given supply voltage, unprecedented peak-to-peak output voltage swing is possible as indicated by the output swing specifications.

If the load resistance is referenced to V_{CC} instead of ground for single supply applications, the maximum possible output swing can be achieved for a given supply voltage. For light load currents, the load resistance will pull the output to V_{CC} during the positive swing and the output will pull the load resistance near ground during the negative swing. The load resistance value should be much less than that of the feedback resistance to maximize pull up capability.

Because the PNP output emitter-follower transistor has been eliminated, the MC34074 family offers a 20 mA minimum current sink capability, typically to an output voltage of ($V_{EE} + 1.8$ V). In single supply applications the output can directly source or sink base current from a common emitter NPN transistor for fast high current switching applications.

In addition, the all NPN transistor output stage is inherently fast, contributing to the bipolar amplifier's high gain-bandwidth product and fast settling capability. The associated high frequency low output impedance (30 Ω typ @ 1.0 MHz) allows capacitive drive capability from 0 to 10,000 pF without oscillation in the unity closed loop gain configuration. The 60° phase margin and 12 dB gain margin as well as the general gain and phase characteristics are virtually independent of the source/sink output swing conditions. This allows

 MOTOROLA *Semiconductor Products Inc.*

ANALOG DEVICES

Precision Instrumentation Amplifier

AD624

FEATURES
Low Noise: 0.2μV p-p 0.1Hz to 10Hz
Low Gain TC: 5ppm max (G = 1)
Low Nonlinearity: 0.001% max (G = 1 to 200)
High CMRR: 130dB max (G = 500 to 1000)
Low Input Offset Voltage: 25μV, max
Low Input Offset Voltage Drift: 0.25μV/°C max
Gain Bandwidth Product: 25MHz
Pin Programmable Gains of 1, 100, 200, 500, 1000
No External Components Required
Internally Compensated

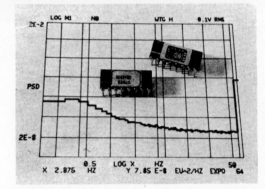

PRODUCT DESCRIPTION
The AD624 is a high precision low noise instrumentation amplifier designed primarily for use with low level transducers, including load cells, strain gauges and pressure transducers. An outstanding combination of low noise, high gain accuracy, low gain temperature coefficient and high linearity make the AD624 ideal for use in high resolution data acquisition systems.

The AD624C has an input offset voltage drift of less than 0.25μV/°C, output offset voltage drift of less than 10μV/°C, CMRR above 80dB at unity gain (130dB at G = 500) and a maximum nonlinearity of 0.001% at G = 1. In addition to these outstanding dc specifications the AD624 exhibits superior ac performance as well. A 25MHz gain bandwidth product, 5V/μs slew rate and 15μs settling time permit the use of the AD624 in high speed data acquisition applications.

The AD624 does not need any external components for pre-trimmed gains of 1, 100, 200, 500 and 1000. Additional gains such as 250 and 333 can be programmed within one percent accuracy with external jumpers. A single external resistor can also be used to set the 624's gain to any value in the range of 1 to 10,000.

PRODUCT HIGHLIGHTS
1. The AD624 offers outstanding noise performance. Input noise is typically less than 4nV/√Hz at 1kHz.
2. The AD624 is a functionally complete instrumentation amplifier. Pin programmable gains of 1, 100, 200, 500 and 1000 are provided on the chip. Other gains are achieved through the use of a single external resistor.
3. The offset voltage, offset voltage drift, gain accuracy and gain temperature coefficients are guaranteed for all pre-trimmed gains.
4. The AD624 provides totally independent input and output offset nulling terminals for high precision applications. This minimizes the effect of offset voltage in gain ranging applications.
5. A sense terminal is provided to enable the user to minimize the errors induced through long leads. A reference terminal is also provided to permit level shifting at the output.

Route 1 Industrial Park; P.O. Box 280; Norwood, Mass. 02062
Tel: 617/329-4700   TWX: 710/394-6577
 West Coast   **Mid-West**   **Texas**
714/842-1717   **312/653-5000**   **214/231-5094**

SPECIFICATIONS (typical @ $V_S = \pm 15V$, $R_L = 2k\Omega$ and $T_A = +25°C$ unless otherwise specified)

Model	AD624A	AD624B	AD624C	AD624S
GAIN				
Gain Equation				
(External Resistor Gain Programming)	$\left[\dfrac{40,000}{R_G} + 1\right] \pm 20\%$	*	*	*
Gain Range	1 to 1000	*	*	*
(Pin Programmable, see Table I)				
Gain Error, Max				
G = 1	± 0.05%	± 0.03%	± 0.02%	*
G = 100	± 0.25%	± 0.15%	± 0.1%	*
G = 200	± 0.5%	± 0.35%	± 0.25%	*
G = 500	± 0.5%	± 0.35%	± 0.25%	*
G = 1000	± 1%	*	*	*
Nonlinearity, max				
G = 1	± 0.005%	± 0.003%	± 0.001%	*
G = 100	± 0.005%	± 0.003%	± 0.001%	*
G = 200	± 0.005%	± 0.003%	± 0.001%	*
G = 500, 1000	± 0.005%	*	*	*
Gain vs. Temperature, max				
G = 1	5ppm/°C	*	*	*
G = 100	10ppm/°C	*	*	*
G = 200	10ppm/°C	*	*	*
G = 500, 1000	25ppm/°C	15ppm/°C	**	**
VOLTAGE OFFSET (May be Nulled)				
Input Offset Voltage, max	200μV	75μV	25μV	**
vs. Temperature, max	2μV/°C	0.5μV/°C	0.25μV/°C	2μV/°C
Output Offset Voltage, max	5mV	3mV	2mV	**
vs. Temperature, max	50μV/°C	25μV/°C	10μV/°C	50μV/°C
Total Offset Voltage RTI				
G = 100	250μV	105μV	45μV	130μV
G = 200	225μV	90μV	35μV	115μV
G = 500	210μV	80μV	30μV	105μV
Offset Referred to the				
Input vs. Supply				
G = 1	70dB	75dB	80dB	**
G = 100	95dB	105dB	110dB	**
G = 200	95dB	105dB	110dB	**
G = 500, 1000	100dB	110dB	115dB	**
INPUT CURRENT				
Input Bias Current, max	± 50nA	± 25nA	± 15nA	*
vs. Temperature	± 50pA/°C	*	*	*
Input Offset Current, max	± 35nA	± 15nA	± 10nA	*
vs. Temperature	± 20pA/°C	*	*	*
INPUT				
Input Impedance				
Differential Resistance	$10^9\Omega$	*	*	*
Differential Capacitance	10pF	*	*	*
Common Mode Resistance	$10^9\Omega$	*	*	*
Common Mode Capacitance	10pF	*	*	*
Input Voltage Range				
Max Differ. Input Linear (V_D)	± 10V	*	*	*
Max Common Mode Linear (V_{CM})	$12V - \left(\dfrac{G}{2} \times V_D\right)$	*	*	*
Common Mode Rejection dc				
to 60Hz with 1kΩ Source Imbalance, min				
G = 1	70dB	75dB	80dB	*
G = 100	100dB	105dB	110dB	*
G = 200	100dB	105dB	110dB	*
G = 500, 1000	110dB	120dB	130dB	*
OUTPUT RATING	± 10V @ 5mA	*	*	*
DYNAMIC RESPONSE				
Small Signal − 3dB				
G = 1	1MHz	*	*	*
G = 100	150kHz	*	*	*
G = 200	100kHz	*	*	*
G = 500	50kHz	*	*	*
G = 1000	25kHz	*	*	*

``odel	**AD624A**	**AD624B**	**AD624C**	**AD624S**
Slew Rate	5.0V/μs	*	*	*
Settling Time to 0.01%, 20V Step				
G = 1 to 200	15μs	*	*	*
G = 500	35μs	*	*	*
G = 1000	75μs	*	*	*
NOISE				
Voltage Noise, 1kHz				
R.T.I.	4nV/√Hz	*	*	*
R.T.O.	75nV/√Hz	*	*	*
R.T.I., 0.1 to 10Hz				
G = 1	10μV p-p	*	*	*
G = 100	0.3μV p-p	*	*	*
G = 200	0.2μV p-p	*	*	*
G = 500, 1000	0.2μV p-p	*	*	*
Current Noise				
0.1Hz to 10Hz	60pA p-p	*	*	*
SENSE INPUT				
R_{IN}	10kΩ ± 20%	*	*	*
I_{IN}	30μA	*	*	*
Voltage Range	± 10V min	*	*	*
Gain to Output	1 ± 0.01% typ	*	*	*
REFERENCE INPUT				
R_{IN}	20kΩ ± 20%	*	*	*
I_{IN}	30μA	*	*	*
Voltage Range	± 10V min	*	*	*
Gain to Output	1 ± 0.01% typ	*	*	*
TEMPERATURE RANGE				
Specified Performance	− 25°C to + 85°C	*	*	− 55°C to + 125°C
Storage	− 65°C to + 150°C	*	*	*
POWER SUPPLY				
Power Supply Range	± 5V to ± 18V	*	*	*
Quiescent Current	3.5mA (5mA max)	*	*	*
PRICE				
100s	$11.90	$15.55	$23.35	$25.95

NOTES
*Specifications same as AD624A.
**Specifications same as AD624B.   Specifications subject to change without notice.

FUNCTIONAL BLOCK DIAGRAM

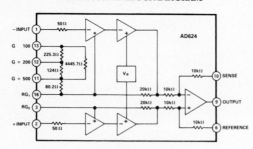

PIN CONFIGURATION

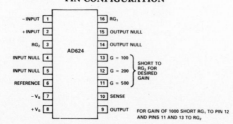

OUTLINE DIMENSIONS
Dimensions shown in inches and (mm).

16-PIN CERAMIC DIP PACKAGE

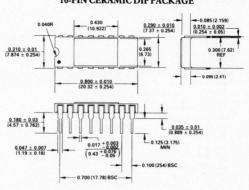

Typical Characteristics

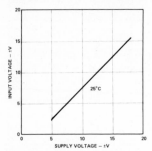

Figure 1. Input Voltage Range vs. Supply Voltage, G = 1

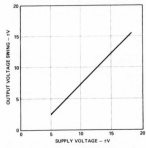

Figure 2. Output Voltage Swing vs. Supply Voltage

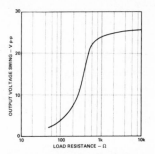

Figure 3. Output Voltage Swing vs. Resistive Load

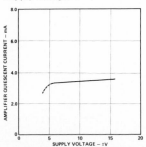

Figure 4. Quiescent Current vs. Supply Voltage

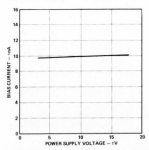

Figure 5. Input Bias Current vs. Supply Voltage

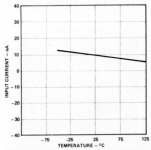

Figure 6. Input Bias Current vs. Temperature

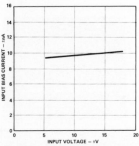

Figure 7. Input Bias Current vs. CMV

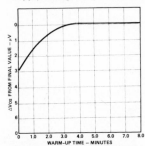

Figure 8. Offset Voltage, RTI, Turn On Drift

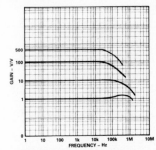

Figure 9. Gain vs. Frequency

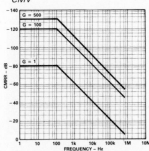

Figure 10. CMRR vs. Frequency RTI, Zero to 1k Source Imbalance

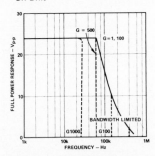

Figure 11. Large Signal Frequency Response

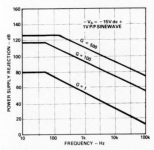

Figure 12. Positive PSRR vs. Frequency

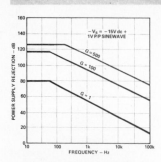

Figure 13. Negative PSRR vs. Frequency

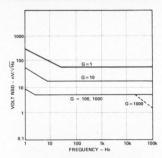

Figure 14. RTI Noise Spectral Density vs. Gain

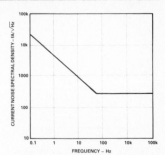

Figure 15. Input Current Noise

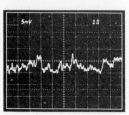

Figure 16. Low Frequency Voltage Noise – G = 1 (System Gain = 1000)

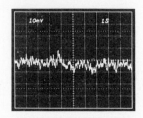

Figure 17. Low Frequency Voltage Noise – G = 1000 (System Gain = 100,000)

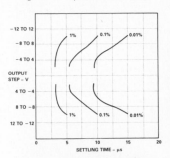

Figure 18. Settling Time Gain = 1

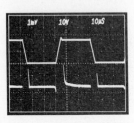

Figure 19. Large Signal Pulse Response and Settling Time – G = 1

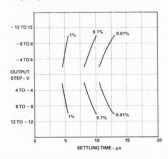

Figure 20. Settling Time Gain = 100

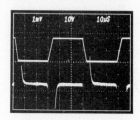

Figure 21. Large Signal Pulse Response and Settling Time G = 100

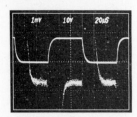

Figure 22. Range Signal Pulse Response and Settling Time G = 500

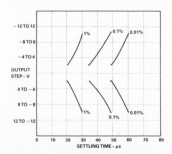

Figure 23. Settling Time Gain = 1000

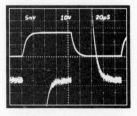

Figure 24. Large Signal Pulse Response and Settling Time G = 1000

Appendix 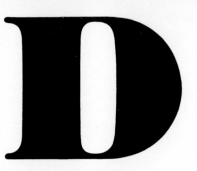 **D**

Computer Modeling of Op Amps

This appendix presents several examples of computer-aided modeling of op amp circuits. The intent of any computer analysis is always (a) to reduce the calculation time for a particular problem and/or (b) to allow a closer correlation with experimental results than could be obtained by simple hand calculations. Any model for a physical system can at best approximate the real world within a small error; for this reason any computer analysis should always be checked against an actual circuit performance.

Since the computer-aided analysis program SPICE [Ref. D1] is currently the most widely used program in electronic circuit analysis and is available for use with many different computer systems including the personal computer (PC), the illustrations shown are stated in SPICE format (the version used by the author was 2G.3). Fortunately most colleges, universities, and industries have easy access to the program.

In addition to analysis by SPICE, several program examples are also illustrated for use with a hand-held programmable calculator, the HP41 from Hewlett-Packard Corporation. Although it lacks the memory available on a large computer, the programmable calculator offers portability and less expense, while still tremendously reducing calculation time for repetitive operations. The programmable calculator was used extensively for calculations in Chapters 3 and 6.

D.1 Op Amp Modeling with SPICE

Two examples will be shown. The first case illustrates a simplified two-pole model of the LF351 op amp. The typical parameter data for the LF351 is obtained from the data sheet in Appendix C and is as follows:

$$A_{OL} = 110 \text{ dB} \qquad V_{OS} = \pm 5 \text{ mV}$$
$$\text{CMRR} = 100 \text{ dB} \qquad GB = 4 \text{ MHz}$$
$$\text{PSRR}(-) = 90 \text{ dB} \qquad \phi_M = 60°$$
$$\text{PSRR}(+) = 120 \text{ dB} \qquad SR = +13, -14 \text{ V/}\mu\text{sec}$$
$$Z_{IN} = 10^{12} \Omega \| 3 \text{ pF} \qquad V_{ICMR} = +15, -12 \text{ V}$$
$$I_B = (+) 50 \text{ pA} \qquad V_O(\text{max}) = \pm 13.5 \text{ V}$$
$$I_{OS} = \pm 25 \text{ pA} \qquad I_{SC} = +20, -17 \text{ mA}$$
$$R_{\text{out}} = 50 \Omega \qquad \text{Power-Supply Current} = 1.8 \text{ mA (at } \pm 15\text{V)}$$

A SPICE model that satisfies the above parameters is shown in Fig. D.1. The input dc offsets and Z_{IN} are modeled similar to the circuit of Fig. 2.12 by the voltage source V_{OS}, the current sources I_{BI} and I_{BN}, R_{IN} and C_{IN}, and the voltage-controlled voltage sources (VCVSes) ECMRR and EPSRR. Since we desire to have (from Fig. 2.12)

$$\text{ECMRR} = \frac{V_{IN}(\text{common-mode})}{\text{CMRR}} = \frac{1}{10^5}\left[\frac{V(8,0)^* + V(3,0)^*}{2}\right]$$

we can define ECMRR by a polynomial of order two, where

$$\text{ECMRR} = [P_{0c} + P_{1c}V(8,0) + P_{2c}V(3,0)] \tag{D.1}$$

and the required coefficients are

$$P_{0c} = 0$$

$$P_{1c} = P_{2c} = \frac{1}{2 \times 10^5} = 5 \times 10^{-6}$$

Similarly, since the PSRR is modeled by an input voltage source

$$\text{EPSRR} = \frac{\Delta V_{\text{supply}}}{\text{PSRR}}$$

we now have due to both power supplies

$$\frac{\Delta V_{\text{supply}}}{\text{PSRR}} = \frac{\Delta V_{CC}}{\text{PSRR}(+)} + \frac{\Delta V_{EE}}{\text{PSRR}(-)}$$

where V_{CC} and V_{EE} are nominally $+15$ V and -15 V. Changes from the nominal values require that a second-degree polynomial again be defined by

$$\frac{\Delta V_{\text{supply}}}{\text{PSRR}} = \text{EPSRR} = \frac{[+15 \text{ V} - V(7,0)]}{\text{PSRR}(+)} - \frac{[-15 \text{ V} - V(4,0)]}{\text{PSRR}(-)} \tag{D.2}$$

Substituting and reducing

$$\text{EPSRR} = P_{0p} + P_{1p}V(7,0) + P_{2p}V(4,0)$$

---

* In SPICE notation, the voltage between two nodes a and b is referred to as $V(a, b)$.

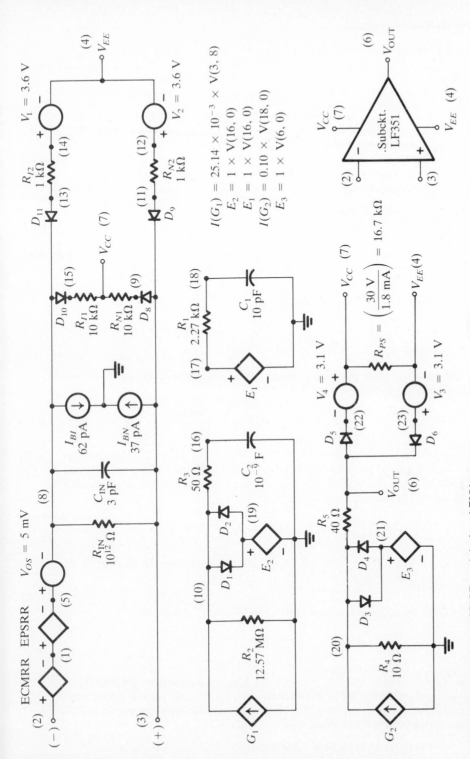

Figure D.1 Simplified SPICE model of an LF351 op amp.

where now the coefficients are

$$P_{0p} = 4.8934 \times 10^{-4}$$

$$P_{1p} = -1 \times 10^{-6}$$

$$P_{2p} = 3.1623 \times 10^{-5}$$

The limitation of the maximum input potential of $V_{ICMR} = +15$ V and -12 V is modeled by the diode limiter networks in Fig. D.1, comprising D_8-D_{11}, V_1, V_2, R_{N1}, R_{N2}, R_{I1} and R_{I2}. If either input terminal (nodes 8 and 3) exceeds $+15$ V then diode D_{10} (or D_8) would conduct; whereas diode D_{11} (or D_9) will conduct if the input voltage is less than -12 V. The resistors merely limit the currents if the inputs are overdriven.

The dominant pole for the LF351 occurs at a frequency f_{p1} of

$$f_{p1} = \frac{GB}{A_{OL}} = \frac{4 \text{ MHz}}{110 \text{ dB}} = 12.65 \text{ Hz}$$

The pole at f_{p1} and the gain A_{OL} are modeled by the current source G_1 and the R_2C_2 time-constant–that is

$$f_{p1} = \frac{1}{2\pi R_2 C_2} = \frac{1}{2\pi(12.57 \text{ M}\Omega)(1 \text{ }\eta\text{F})} = 12.65 \text{ Hz}$$

and

$$A_{OL} = G_1 R_2 = (25.14 \times 10^{-3})(12.57 \text{ M}\Omega) = 3.16 \times 10^5$$

The phase margin of 60° can be included by a second pole in the open-loop response at a frequency f_{p2} given by

$$90° - \phi_M = \tan^{-1}\left(\frac{GB}{f_{p2}}\right) \tag{D.3}$$

or $f_{p2} = 7$ MHz. This pole at 7 MHz is included in Fig. D1 by the $R_1 C_1$ network. The R_3 resistor is part of the slew-rate limiting network composed of R_3, D_1, D_2, and E_2. The positive output slew rate of $+13$ V/μsec is due to the maximum available current that can charge C_2, or in effect

$$SR(+) = \frac{\Delta V_{out}(+)}{\Delta t} \approx \frac{I_{max}^+}{C_2} = 13 \text{ V/μsec}$$

or $I_{max}^+ = 13 \times 10^6 \times 1 \times 10^{-9} = 13$ mA. The forward voltage across D_1 must therefore be

$$V(D_1) = 13 \text{ mA} \times 50 \text{ }\Omega = 0.65 \text{ V}$$

and thus the required reverse saturation current of D_1 is given by

$$V(D_1) = 0.65 \text{ V} = \frac{kT}{q} \ln\left[\frac{13 \text{ mA}}{I_S(D_1)}\right] \tag{D.4}$$

or $I_S(D_1) = 1.48 \times 10^{-13}$ A. Similarly, for negative-output slew-rate limiting, at -14 V/μsec, $I_S(D_2) = 2.29 \times 10^{-14}$ A. In actuality, D_1 and D_2 only provide partial limiting of the maximum current to C_2, since for a 10 V input overdrive signal (between terminals 2 and 3) the maximum transient current from G_1 would be

$$I = (25.14 \times 10^{-3}) \text{ 10 V} = 251.4 \text{ mA}$$

which would divide between D_1 and R_3, or with $I_S(D_1) = 1.48 \times 10^{-13}$ A, the actual peak current charging C_2 would be 14.5 mA instead of 13 mA.

The maximum output of ± 12.5 V is obtained with the diode limiting network of D_5, D_6, V_3 and V_4. The output resistance of 50 ohms is obtained with the sum of R_4 and R_5. The R_5 resistor, along with D_3, D_4, and E_3, also provides output short-circuit current limiting [Ref. D.2] at $I_{SC}(+) = 20$ mA and $I_{SC}(-) = 17$ mA. The required values of I_S are, similar to the calculations shown previously,

$$V(D_3) = 20 \text{ mA } (40 \text{ }\Omega) = \frac{kT}{q} \ln \left[\frac{20 \text{ mA}}{I_S(D_3)} \right]$$

and

$$V(D_4) = 17 \text{ mA } (40 \text{ }\Omega) = \frac{kT}{q} \ln \left[\frac{17 \text{ mA}}{I_S(D_4)} \right]$$

These equations result in

$$I_S(D_3) = 6.78 \times 10^{-16} \text{ A}$$

$$I_S(D_4) = 6.05 \times 10^{-14} \text{ A}$$

To assess the validity of the SPICE model the open-loop gain versus frequency curve was obtained using the circuit of Fig. D.2. This circuit allows the loop to be closed for dc stability, but open for gain modeling, since the feedback is shorted by the capacitor C of 100 farads, and the feedback pole due to $L \times C$ occurs at

$$f = \frac{1}{2\pi(LC)^{1/2}} = 1.6 \times 10^{-5} \text{ Hz}$$

The gain versus frequency comparison is shown in Fig. D.3. Although the gain magnitude versus frequency is modeled well, the phase response does not agree with the manufacturer's data past 5 MHz, since a two-pole model is inadequate for good phase response representation.

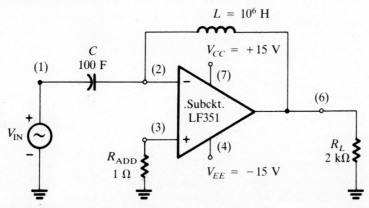

Figure D.2 Circuit for checking A_{OL} vs frequency.

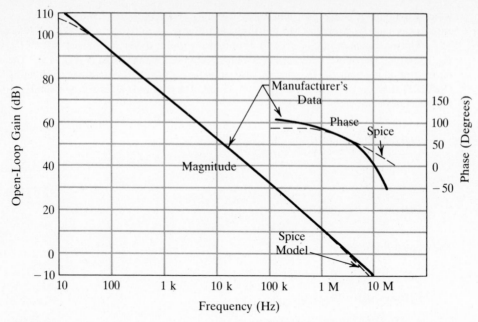

Figure D.3 Comparison of open-loop gain for the SPICE model with the actual LF351 op amp.

The complete SPICE input data required for the ac frequency response of the circuit of Fig. D.2 follows:

AC ANALYSIS --- AOL(S) VS FREQUENCY

****   INPUT LISTING   TEMPERATURE

                                                 = 27.000 DEG C

```
************************************************************************
 AC DEC 10  1  100MEGHZ
RADD  3  0  1
VIN  1  0  AC
C  2  1  1E2
L  2  6  1E6
VCC  7  0  +15
VEE  4  0  -15
RL  6  0  2K
X1  2  3  4  6  7  LF351
.SUBCKT  LF351  2 3 4 6 7
*
*NODES: INV=2, NON-INV=3, PS+ =7, PS-=4, VO=6.
*DEVICE CHARACTERISTICS:  AOL=110DB(3.16E5), CMRR=100DB,
* PSRR(-)=90DB, PSRR(+)=120DB, ZIN=10E12/3PF, IB=50PA,
```

```
* IOS=25PA, VOS=5MV, GB=4MHZ, ROUT=50; SR=+13, -14V/US, CM INPUT
* LIMIT=+15V, -12V; OUTPUT LIMIT=+ -13.5V; ISC=+20MA, -17MA. LAST
*NODE=23.


ECMR            2 1 POLY(2) 8 0 3 0 0 5U 5U
EPSRR           1 5 POLY(2) 7 0 4 0 489.3416U -1U 31.62277U
VOS             5 8 5MV
RIN             8 3 1E12
CIN             8 3 3PF
IBI             8 0 62PA
IBN             3 0 37PA
D10             8 15 DA
D11            13  8 DA
RI1            15  7 10K
RI2            13 14 1K
V1             14  4 3.6
D8              3 9 DA
D9             11 3 DA
RN1             9 7 10K
RN2            12 11 1K
V2             12  4 3.6
G1              0 10 3 8 25.14M
R2             10  0 12.57MEG
C2             16  0 1NF
E1             17  0 16 0 1
R3             10 16 50
R1             17 18 2.27K
C1             18  0 10PF
E2             19  0 16 0 1.0
D1             10 19 DSP
D2             19 10 DSN
G2              0 20 18 0 0.1
R4             20  0 10
D3             20 21 DB
D4             21 20 DA
E3             21  0 6 0 1.0
R5             20  6 40
D5              6 22 DA
D6             23  6 DA
V3             23  4 3.1
V4              7 22 3.1
RPS             7  4 16.67K
.MODEL DA D(IS=6.05E-14)
.MODEL DB D(IS=6.786E-16)
.MODEL DSP D(IS=1.5E-13)
.MODEL DSN D(IS=2.3E-14)
.ENDS LF351
.PRINT AC VM(6) VP(6) VDB(6)
.PLOT  AC VDB(6) VP(6)
.END
```

In Fig. D.4 the unity-gain small-signal, as well as large-signal slew-rate limited pulse response for the SPICE model is compared with the manufacturer's data. The correlation is reasonably good, except for input overdrive and feedthrough spikes in the large-signal transient response. The slopes of the large-signal rise and fall times are approximately the same as the manufacturer's data, which indicates that the network of D_1 and D_2 in Fig. D.1 is a reasonably effective model for slew-rate effects.

The second circuit example to be modeled with SPICE is the high-frequency HA2540 op amp. The modeling used in this example will illustrate a more exact approximation to the actual op amp, and will include variation of CMRR and PSRR with frequency, as well as characterization of the noise of the op amp by the equivalent noise voltage (ENV) and equivalent noise current (ENI). To include the latter effects, it is necessary to more adequately simulate the input circuit of the op amp.

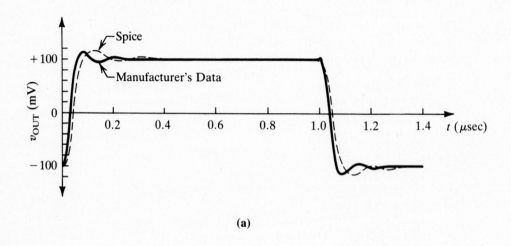

(a)

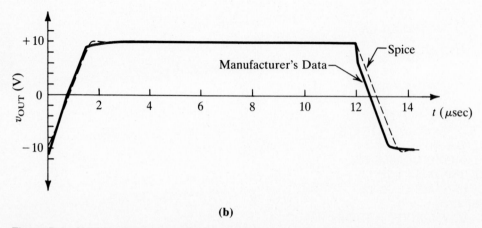

(b)

Figure D.4 Noninverting unity-gain pulse-response comparison for the LF351 op amp: (a) small signal. (b) large signal (slew rate limited).

The SPICE model for the HA2540 is indicated in Fig. D.5. The typical parameters for the op amp are obtained from the data sheet of Appendix C and are:

$A_{OL} = 90$ dB $\qquad\qquad\qquad V_{OS} = \pm 3$ mV

$CMRR_{dc} = 65$ dB $\qquad\qquad GB = 400$ MHz

$PSRR(-)_{dc} = 64$ dB $\qquad\qquad \phi_M = $ (no spec.) stable for $A \geq 10$

$PSRR(+)_{dc} = 66$ dB $\qquad\qquad SR = \pm 400$ V/μsec

$Z_{IN} = 10$ k$\Omega \| 1$ pF $\qquad\qquad V_{ICMR} = \pm 12$ V (typ)*

$I_B = 5$ μA $\qquad\qquad\qquad\quad V_O(\text{max}) = +12, -13$ V*

$I_{OS} = \pm 1$ μA $\qquad\qquad\qquad I_{SC} = +40, -30$ mA*

$R_{out} = 30$ Ω $\qquad\qquad\qquad$ ENV $= 5$ nV/$\sqrt{\text{Hz}}$ (at 10^5Hz)

Power Supply Current $= 20$ mA (at ± 15 V) $\qquad$ ENI $= 3$ pA/$\sqrt{\text{Hz}}$ (at 10^5 Hz)

In Fig. D.5 the open-loop differential gain is obtained by the gain of the input complementary stage (which very closely approximates the actual HA2540 input circuit) of Q_{N1}, Q_{N2}, Q_{P1}, and Q_{P2}, and the gain obtained by the G_N, G_P, and R_{D1} network. The dc input base currents of Q_{N1} and Q_{N2} are partially cancelled by the pnp base currents of Q_{P1} and Q_{P2}. There are several mutually constraining factors that govern the characteristics, and dc biasing of, the input stage. Chief among these factors are the following:

(1) The midband equivalent noise current ENI is specified as 3 PA/$\sqrt{\text{Hz}}$, which can be related to [see Eq. (4.18)]

$$\text{ENI} = 2qI_B(\text{total}) = 3 \times 10^{-12}$$

or

$$I_B(\text{total}) = 28 \ \mu\text{A} = |I_{BN1}| + |I_{BN2}| + |I_{PN1}| + |I_{PN2}|.$$

(2) The slew rate is ± 400 V/μ-sec; given a nominal value of 5 pF for C_{D1}, we must have a charging current of

$$I = 5 \text{ pF} (400 \times 10^6) = \pm 2 \text{ mA}$$

Hence, in Fig. D.5 the maximum available current for a positive input overdrive signal $[V(5, 4) = \text{positive}]$ will be 0 mA from the G_N source and 2 mA from the G_P source. Similarly, for a negative input overdrive signal $[V(5, 4) = \text{negative}]$ 2 mA will be supplied by G_N while 0 mA is furnished by G_P. Thus, the I_{CSN} and I_{CSP} current sources must be approximately 2 mA each. Note that, for simplicity, the conductance of G_N and G_P is chosen as the reciprocal of the R_{CN}, or R_{CP}, collector resistors.

(3) The current-gain (β, or h_{FE}) of the input transistors can be chosen to unbalance the base currents to meet the I_B and I_{OS} values, or in Fig. D.5 we have

$$I_B^+ = 4.55 - 10 = -5.45 \ \mu\text{A}$$

$$I_B^- = 5.55 - 9 = -3.45 \ \mu\text{A}$$

and therefore

$$I_B = \frac{I_B^+ + I_B^-}{2} = -4.45 \ \mu\text{A}$$

while $I_{OS} = |I_B^+ - I_B^-| = 1$ μA. These values closely correlate with the typical values $I_B = 5$ μA and $I_{OS} = 1$ μA.

---

* Data obtained experimentally; typically data not specified by the manufacturer. Short-circuit current values are typical output drive capability before distortion.

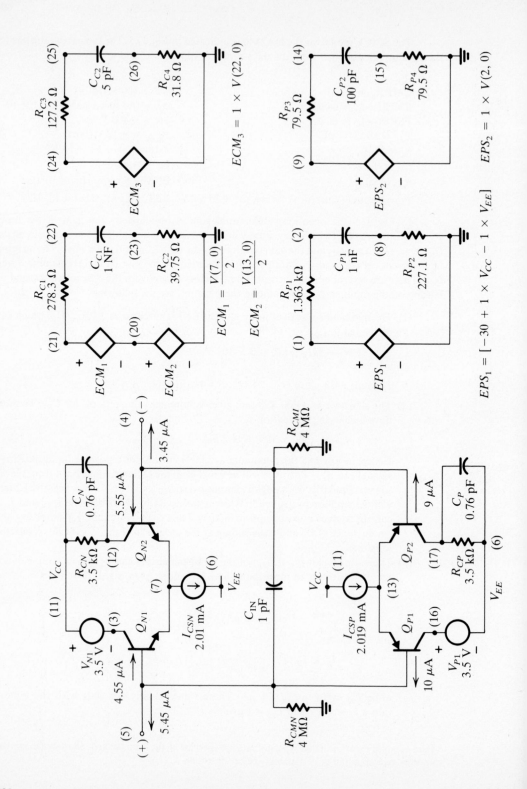

$ECM_3 = 1 \times V(22, 0)$

$EPS_2 = 1 \times V(2, 0)$

$ECM_1 = \dfrac{V(7, 0)}{2}$

$ECM_2 = \dfrac{V(13, 0)}{2}$

$EPS_1 = [-30 + 1 \times V_{CC} - 1 \times V_{EE}]$

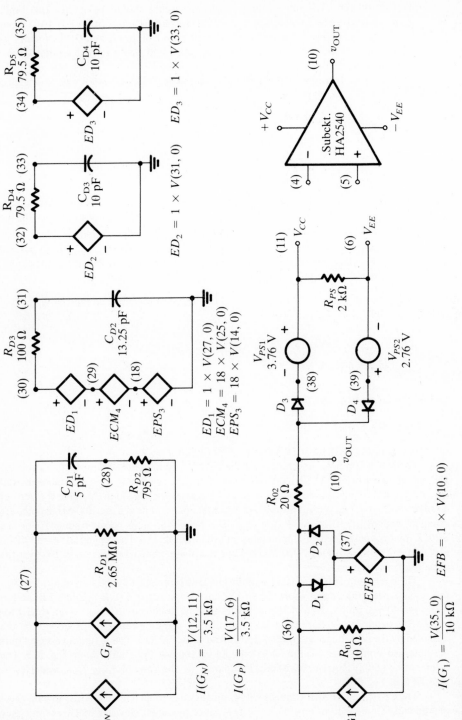

Figure D.5 SPICE model for the HA2540 op amp.

601

(4) The differential input resistance and capacitance should be 10 kΩ and 1 pF, respectively. The capacitance is easily obtained by C_{IN} in Fig. D.5, but the input resistance is a direct function of the current gain β of the Q_N and Q_P transistors, as well as the emitter current (of 1 mA each) and any external emitter ohmic resistance.

(5) The equivalent noise voltage of the circuit in the midband noise region is related to [see Eq. (4.15)]

$$(\text{ENV})^2 = 4kTR_n$$

where for a single transistor

$$R_n \approx r_b' + R_e + \frac{r_e}{2} \tag{D.5}$$

where r_e was defined earlier (in Chapter 4) by $r_e = kT/qI_E$, r_b' is the intrinsic base resistance and R_e is any ohmic intrinsic or extrinsic resistance in series with the emitter. From Eq. (D.5), for $\text{ENV} = 5 \text{ nV}/\sqrt{\text{Hz}}$, the total equivalent noise resistance R_n required would be 1.5 kΩ. However, since Q_{N1}, Q_{N2} are in *parallel* with Q_{P1}, Q_{P2}, then each transistor pair only contributes 1/2 the gain of the circuit, so the total required value of R_n must be increased.

The open-loop gain in the final circuit of Fig. D.5 is obtained by an input stage gain of [see, for example, Refs. 3.4 and 3.14]

$$A_1 \approx \frac{\alpha_{2N} R_{CN}}{2r_{eN} + 2R_{eN} + \dfrac{R_{BN1}}{\beta_{N1}} + \dfrac{R_{BN2}}{\beta_{N2}}} = 21.1 \tag{D.6}$$

and by the G_N and G_P network of

$$A_2 = (G_N + G_P)R_{D1} = 1.51 \times 10^3 \tag{D.7}$$

for a total gain of $(21.1)(1.5 \times 10^3) = 3.2 \times 10^4$ (90 dB).

The open-loop poles and zeroes for the HA2540 op amp are obtained from Table 3.1 and are modeled in Fig. D.5 by the $(RC)(CN)$ network producing a pole at 60 MHz and $(R_{D1})(C_{D1})$, producing the dominant pole at 12 kHz; while R_{D2} and C_{D1} give the zero at 40 MHz. Similarly, $(R_{D3})(C_{D2})$ produces a 120 MHz pole, while the two 200 MHz poles are obtained with $R_{D4} \times C_{D3}$ and $R_{D5} \times C_{D4}$. The open-loop gain versus frequency for the SPICE model is compared with manufacturer's data in Fig. D.6. The magnitude comparison is within ± 2 dB from 100 Hz–200 MHz, while the phase comparison is within 20° over the same frequency range.

The open-loop output resistance of the HA2540 is modeled by the sum of R_{01} and R_{02} in Fig. D.5. Also, the output short-circuit limiting circuit of $D1$, $D2$, R_{02}, and EFB models $I_{SC}(+)$ of 40 mA, and $I_{SC}(-)$ of 30 mA, with the same design equations as given earlier for the LF351 example. Similarly, the maximum input common-mode limits of ± 12 V are obtained by the dc voltages at nodes 3, 12, 16, and 17 in Fig. D.5. The $V_O(\text{max})$ voltage limits are obtained similarly as per the LF351 model by $D3$, $D4$, V_{PS1}, and V_{PS2} in Fig. D.5. The total power supply current of 20 mA is equated to the sum of I_{CSN}, I_{CSP}, and $|V_{CC} - V_{EE}|/RPS$ in Fig. D.5.

The CMRR and PSRR changes with frequency as shown from the HA2540 data sheet of Appendix C and also in Figs. D.7 and D.8. Since the actual device CMRR vs frequency curve has a slope of -12 dB/octave, instead of the usual gain vs frequency slope of -20 dB/

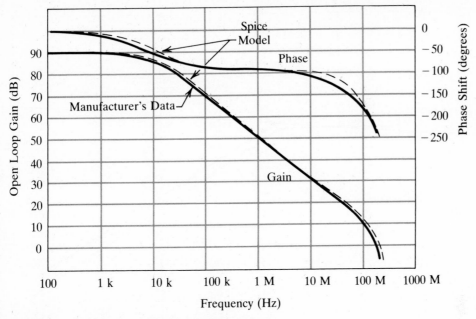

Figure D.6 Open-loop gain for the HA2540 op amp.

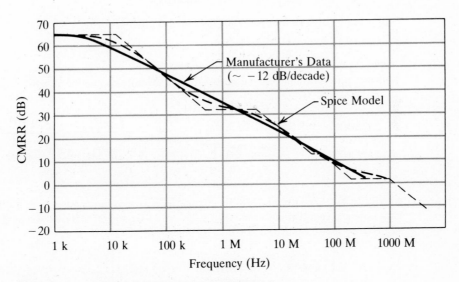

Figure D.7 CMRR vs frequency for the HA2540 op amp.

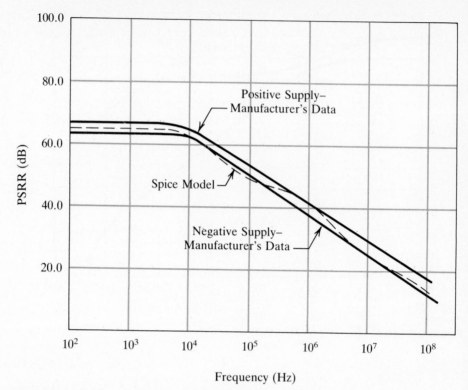

Figure D.8 PSRR vs frequency for the HA2540 op amp.

octave, the modeling can only be approximated by a piecewise linear combination of break frequencies. For example, from Fig. D.7 if we judiciously choose the approximation as

$$
\text{CMRR} = \frac{A_\text{diff}}{A_\text{CM}} = \frac{\text{CMRR}_o\left(1 + \dfrac{s}{500 \text{ kHz}}\right)\left(1 + \dfrac{s}{40 \text{ MHz}}\right)\left(1 + \dfrac{s}{200 \text{ MHz}}\right)}{\left(1 + \dfrac{s}{12 \text{ kHz}}\right)\left(1 + \dfrac{s}{4 \text{ MHz}}\right)\left(1 + \dfrac{s}{60 \text{ MHz}}\right)\left(1 + \dfrac{s}{1000 \text{ MHz}}\right)}
$$

(D.6)

where $\text{CMRR}_o = 65$ dB, or 1778, then from the pole-zero terms for A_diff in Table 3.1 we have obtained cancellations of the A_diff poles at 12 kHz and 60 MHz, as well as the zero at 40 MHz, so that the equation for A_CM becomes

$$
A_\text{CM} = \left[\frac{\left(\dfrac{A_\text{OL}}{\text{CMRR}_o}\right)\left(1 + \dfrac{s}{4 \text{ MHz}}\right)\left(1 + \dfrac{s}{1000 \text{ MHz}}\right)}{\left(1 + \dfrac{s}{500 \text{ MHz}}\right)\left(1 + \dfrac{s}{200 \text{ MHz}}\right)}\right]
$$

$$
\frac{1}{\left(1 + \dfrac{s}{120 \text{ MHz}}\right)\left(1 + \dfrac{s}{200 \text{ MHz}}\right)^2}
$$

(D.7)

with $(A_{OL}/\text{CMRR}_O) = 3.2 \times 10^4/1778 = 18$. Thus, in the circuit model of Fig. D.5 the common-mode voltage is obtained by the ECM_1 and ECM_2 voltage-controlled voltage sources that sample the input common-mode voltage at nodes 7 and 13. The gain A_{OL}/CMRR_O of 18 is furnished by ECM_4; the R_{C1}, C_{C1}, R_{C2} network provides a common-mode pole at 500 kHz and a zero at 4 MHz; and the R_{C3}, C_{C2}, R_{C4} network furnishes the remaining pole and zero at 200 MHz and 1000 MHz, respectively. The common-mode signal at $V(25, 0)$ is then inserted into the model (via ECM_4) such that only the differential gain poles at 120 MHz, and the two at 200 MHz are effective, as indicated by Eq. (D.7). The resulting SPICE piecewise approximation is within ± 2 dB of the actual CMRR curve over the frequency range from 1 kHz to 300 MHz, as indicated in Fig. D.7.

The PSRR is slightly different between the positive and negative power supplies for the HA2540 circuit. Thus, the average of the two PSRR curves was used to form a SPICE approximation, as indicated in Fig. D.8. The piecewise approximation used was

$$\text{PSRR} = \frac{\text{PSRR}_O\left(1 + \dfrac{s}{10^5}\right)\left(1 + \dfrac{s}{10 \text{ MHz}}\right)\left(1 + \dfrac{s}{40 \text{ MHz}}\right)}{\left(1 + \dfrac{s}{12 \text{ kHz}}\right)\left(1 + \dfrac{s}{700 \text{ kHz}}\right)\left(1 + \dfrac{s}{20 \text{ MHz}}\right)\left(1 + \dfrac{s}{60 \text{ MHz}}\right)} \tag{D.8}$$

where the average PSRR_O was 65 dB (1778). Since

$$\text{PSRR} = \frac{\Delta V_{\text{supply}}}{\Delta V_{\text{in}}} = \frac{\Delta V_{\text{supply}}(A_{\text{diff}})}{\Delta V_{\text{out}}} \tag{D.9}$$

the output-voltage change becomes, after substitution (and cancellation of poles with zeroes)

$$\frac{\Delta V_{\text{out}}}{\Delta V_{\text{supply}}} = \left[\frac{18\left(1 + \dfrac{s}{700 \text{ kHz}}\right)\left(1 + \dfrac{s}{20 \text{ MHz}}\right)}{\left(1 + \dfrac{s}{100 \text{ kHz}}\right)\left(1 + \dfrac{s}{10 \text{ MHz}}\right)}\right] \frac{1}{\left(1 + \dfrac{s}{120 \text{ MHz}}\right)\left(1 + \dfrac{s}{200 \text{ MHz}}\right)^2} \tag{D.9}$$

In the SPICE model of Fig. D.5 the R_{P1}, C_{P1}, R_{P2} network produces a pole at 100 kHz and a zero at 700 kHz, while the R_{P3}, C_{P2}, R_{P4} network gives the remaining pole at 10 MHz, and zero at 20 MHz, for the PSRR. Similar to the modeling for CMRR, the EPS3 VCVS is inserted in series with the differential signal to obtain the 120 MHz and two 200 MHz poles. Any change in the V_{CC} and V_{EE} power supply voltages is obtained from nodes (11) and (6) with the use of the second-degree polynomial voltage generator EPS_1 given by

$$\text{EPS}_1 = P_{OP} + P_{1P}V(11, 0) + P_{2P}V(6, 0) \tag{D.10}$$

here

$$P_{OP} = -30$$

$$P_{1P} = 1 = -P_{2P}$$

The PSRR for the SPICE piecewise model is compared in Fig. D.8 with values obtained from the manufacturer's data sheet.

The offset voltage specification of ± 3 mV has to be obtained by the input circuit of Fig. D.5. This is conveniently modeled by unequal reverse saturation currents I_S for Q_{N1} and Q_{N2} (and similarly, Q_{P1} and Q_{P2}). For example, if we specify the offset voltage between the noninverting and inverting input terminals to be $+3$ mV, then the Kirchhoff's Law voltage equation from input node 5 to node 4 in Fig. D.5. is

$$V_{OS} = 3 \text{ mV} = I_{B-QN1} r'_{b-QN1} + V_{BE-QN1} + I_{E-QN1} R_E$$

$$- I_{E-QN2} R_E - V_{BE-QN2} - I_{B-QN2} r'_{b-QN2} \tag{D.11}$$

or substituting values, we need

$$(V_{BE-QP1} - V_{BE-QN2}) = 3.8 \text{ mV} = \frac{kT}{q} \ln\left(\frac{I_{SN1}}{I_{SN2}}\right) \tag{D.12}$$

If we let $I_{SN1} = 10^{-15}$ A, therefore $I_{SN2} = 1.16 \times 10^{-15}$ A. In a similar fashion, by writing the voltage equation from node 5 to node 4 through the Q_{P1}-Q_{P2} path, one obtains

$$(V_{BE-QN2} - V_{BE-QP1}) = 3.67 \text{ mV} \tag{D.13}$$

or again if we choose $I_{SP2} = 10^{-15}$, then $I_{SP1} = 1.15 \times 10^{-15}$ A.

The complete SPICE input data describing the HA2540 model is as follows:

```
.SUBCKT HA2540 4 5 6 10 1 11
*
*NODES; INV IN=4, NON-INV IN=5, PS+=11, PS-=6,OUTPUT=10.
*DEVICE CHARACTERISTICS:
*       AOL=3.2E4; CMRR=65DB; ACMO=18; GB=400MHZ;
*       SR=400V/USEC;
*       VIN MAX=+,-12V; VO MAX=+12V,-13V; VOS=3.3MV;
*       IB(AVER)=-4.45UA;
*       IOS=2UA; ZIN=11.5K/1PF; RO=30; ISC(+)=30MA; ISC
*       (-)=40MA;
*       RN=1510 OHMS(5NV/RTHZ); IN=29UA(3PA/RTHZ); 1/FB=4KHZ.
*
*--- THE FOLLOWING MODELS THE INPUT STAGE ---
VN1    11 3 3.5
QN1     3 5 7 N1
RCMN   5 0 4MEG
ICSN    7 6 2.010MA
QN2    12 4 7 N2
RCN    11 12 3.5K
CN     11 12 0.757PF
CIN     5 4 1PF
VP1    16 6 3.5
QP1    16 5 13 P1
RCMI    4 0 4MEG
ICSP   11 13 2.019MA
QP2    17 4 13 P2
RCP    17 6 3.5K
CP     17 6 0.757PF
*--- THE FOLLOWING MODELS COMMON-MODE RESPONSE ---
ECM2 20 0 13 0 0.5
ECM1 21 20 7 0 0.5
RC1    21 22 278.3
```

```
CC1     22 23 1NF
RC2     23 0 39.75
ECM3 24 0 22 0 1
RC3     24 25 127.2
CC2     25 26 5PF
RC4     26 0 31.8
*--- THE FOLLOWING MODELS ADIFF ---
GN      0 27 12 11 2.857E-4
GP      0 27 17 6 2.857E-4
RD1     27 0 2.56E6
CD1     27 28 5PF
RD2     28 0 795
ECM4 29 0 25 0 18
ED1     30 29 27 0 1
RD3     30 31 100
CD2     31 0 13.25PF
ED2     32 0 31 0 1
RD4     32 33 79.5
CD3     33  0 10PF
ED3     34  0 33 0 1
RD5     34 35 79.5
CD5     35  0 10PF
*--- THE FOLLOWING MODELS THE OUTPUT STAGE ---
G1      0 36 35 0 0.10
RO1     36 0 10
D1      36 37 DIODE2
D2      37 36 DIODE1
EFB     37 0 10 0 1
RO2     36 10 20
D3      10 38 DIODE1
D4      39 10 DIODE1
VPS1 11 38 3.76
VPS2 39 6 2.76
RPS     11 6 2K
*
.MODEL DIODE1 D(IS = 1.45E-15)
.MODEL  DIODE2 D(IS = 2.5E-12)
.MODEL N1 NPN(IS = 1FA,BF = 220,RB = 750,RE = 52,6,KF = 1.28E-15)
.MODEL N2 NPN(IS = 1.159FA, BF = 180,RB = 750,RE = 52.6,KF = 1.28E-15)
.MODEL P1 PNP(IS = 1.153FA,BF = 100,RB = 620,RE = 50.25,KF = 1.28E-15)
.MODEL P2 PNP(IS = 1FA,BF = 111,RB = 620,RE = 50.25,KF = 1.28E-15)
.ENDS HA2540
```

The small-signal transient response for this HA2540 SPICE model was compared earlier (Fig. 3.17) with an experimental response. The slew-rate limited step response for a noninverting gain-of-ten circuit is illustrated in Fig. D.9 and compared with the manufacturer's data; it is apparent the SPICE approximation is quite good.

Similarly, the SPICE approximation to the values for ENV and ENI of the HA2540 op amp are reasonably close to the actual data, as indicated in Fig. D.10. From Eq. (D.5)

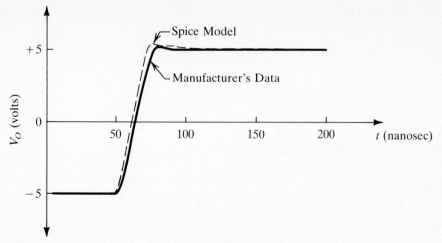

Figure D.9 Large-signal response for a noninverting gain of 10.

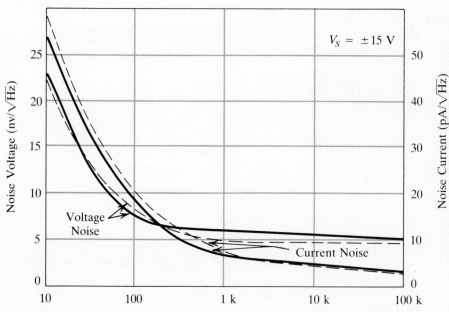

Figure D.10 Comparison of noise data for the HA2540 op amp. Solid lines are manufacturer's data, dashed lines are SPICE model.

and the data utilized for the Q_N and Q_P transistors, the theoretical value for ENV should be (in the midband region)

$$ENV \approx \frac{1}{2} \left\{ 4kT \left[2(750\ \Omega) + 2(52.6\ \Omega) + 2\left(\frac{26\ \Omega}{2}\right) \right] \right.$$

$$\left. + 4kT \left[2(620\ \Omega) + 2(50.25\ \Omega) + 2\left(\frac{26\ \Omega}{2}\right) \right] \right\}^{1/2} \tag{D.14}$$

or

$$ENV \approx \frac{1}{2} \left[4kT(3\ k\Omega) \right]^{1/2} = 3.5\ nV/\sqrt{Hz}$$

The actual SPICE result is slightly larger due to contributions from other noise sources in the model. The ENI midband value should be, from the SPICE model of Fig. D.5,

$$ENI \approx \left\{ 2q[I_B(\text{total})] \right\}^{1/2} = [2q(29\ \mu A)]^{1/2} = 2.5\ pA/\sqrt{Hz}$$

which is within 10% of the manufacturers data. The $1/f$ corner frequency was obtained from an asymptotic approximation to the manufacturer's data by using the SPICE equation for input equivalent noise current for a bipolar transistor

$$\frac{I_{BN2}}{\Delta F} = 2qI_B \left[1 + \left(\frac{KF}{2qf}\right) I_B^{AF-1} \right] \tag{D.15}$$

or, if we choose $AF = 1$, then the $1/f$ corner frequency f_b is defined by

$$\frac{I_{BN2}}{\Delta f} = 2qI_B \left[1 + \left(\frac{f_b}{f}\right) \right] \tag{D.16}$$

where now

$$KF \equiv 2qf_b$$

From the HA2540 data, $f_b \approx 4$ kHz, hence $KF = 1.28 \times 10^{-15}$ A.

D.2 Useful Programmable-Calculator Programs

Various programmable calculators are available, at reasonable costs, that are extremely useful for repetitive calculations, particularly those calculations involving frequency response of amplifiers, and also calculations for op amp filter networks. As an example, the program "BODEPL" below is very useful for calculating $T(j\omega)$ and $T(j\omega)/[1 + T(j\omega)]$ in the examples and problems of Chapter 3. The program is an adaptation of an earlier program "COMP" by Ward Helms [Ref. D.4]. The program is written for the HP41CV calculator, but is adaptable to the T159, and other programmable calculators.

STEP	ENTRY	COMMENTS
1.	LBL"BODEPL"	Initialize [SIZE should be ≥ 20]
2.	DEG	Put in degree mode
3.	FIX 1	
4.	"TO<MAG> =?"	Enter magnitude of T_O
5.	PROMPT	
6.	STO 12	Reg. 12 contains $|T_O|$
7.	"No. P/Z?"	Enter total number of poles and zeroes (max = 12)

8.	PROMPT	
9.	"P = +, Z = −"	Negative number indicates a zero
10.	AVIEW	
11.	PSE	
12.	STO 17	Reg. 17 contains Nos of P and Z
13.	1	
14.	−	
15.	12	
16.	X < = Y?	
17.	GTO "BODEPL"	If No. P + Z > 12, go back to start
18.	X < > Y	
19.	1000	Steps 18 through 32 read in all poles and zeroes, storing
20.	/	in registers 0 through 11
21.	.00001	
22.	+	
23.	STO 13	
24.	LBL 01	
25.	RCL 13	
26.	INT	
27.	"P/Z"	
28.	ARCL X	
29.	PROMPT	
30.	STO IND 13	
31.	ISG 13	
32.	GTO 01	
33.	CF 01	
34.	CF 02	
35.	"CALC. ACL"	Do you wish to calculate A_{CL}, or just
36.	AVIEW	form $T(j\omega)$ vs. frequency?
37.	PSE	
38.	PSE	
39.	2	
40.	"ENTER 1 = Y, 2 = N"	To calculate A_{CL} enter "1," otherwise
41.	PROMPT	enter "2"
42.	X = Y?	
43.	SF 02	If FLAG 2 set, indicates do not
44.	RCL 17	calculate A_{CL}
45.	STO-13	STEPS 44, 45 reset register 13
46.	LBL 06	
47.	"FREQ = ?"	Enter frequency for calculation of
48.	PROMPT	$T(j\omega)$
49.	STO 14	
50.	0	
51.	STO 15	Reg. 15 now contains 0 degrees
52.	RCL 12	
53.	STO 16	Reg. 16 now contains $|T_O|$
54.	LBL 05	
55.	RCL IND 13	[recalls first P or Z, in location 00]
56.	X > 0?	Tests for zero
57.	GTO 02	

58.	CHS	
59.	SF 01	FLAG 01 set indicates a zero
60.	LBL 02	
61.	RCL 14	
62.	X < > Y	
63.	/	
64.	1	
65.	R → P	
66.	FS? 01	Tests for a zero
67.	GTO 03	
68.	STO/16	Reg. 16 $= |T_O|/|1 + j(f/f_p)|$
69.	X < > Y	
70.	STO-15	Reg. 15 $= 0° - \angle$ pole
71.	GTO 04	
72.	LBL 03	
73.	STO*16	Reg. 16 $= |T_O| \times |1 + j(f/f_z)|$
74.	X < > Y	
75.	STO + 15	Reg. 16 $= 0° + \angle$ zero
76.	CF 01	
77.	LBL 04	
78.	ISG 13	Process the rest of the P and Z
79.	GTO 05	
80.	RCL 15	
81.	"$\angle T(j\omega) = $"	
82.	ARCL X	$\angle T(j\omega) = $ NN.N°
83.	AVIEW	
84.	PSE	
85.	PSE	
86.	RCL 16	
87.	SCI 2	
88.	"$|T(j\omega)| = $"	
89.	ARCL X	$|T(j\omega)| = $ K.KK EKK
90.	AVIEW	
91.	PSE	
92.	PSE	
93.	XEQ "DB"	
94.	"T(DB) = "	
95.	ARCL X	$|T(j\omega)| = $ MM.M (dB)
96.	AVIEW	
97.	PSE	
98.	PSE	
99.	FS ? 02	If FLAG 2 set, indicates do not
100.	GTO 07	calculate A_{CL}, so go to LBL 07.
101.	X < > Y	If FLAG 2 not set, then calculate
102.	RCL 16	closed-loop gain as $T(j\omega)/[1 + T(j\omega)]$
103.	P → R	
104.	1	
105.	+	
106.	R → P	
107.	X < > Y	
108.	RCL 15	

109.	-
110.	CHS
111.	X < > Y
112.	RCL 16
113.	/
114.	1/X
115.	X < > Y
116.	STO 18
117.	"∠T/1 + T = "
118.	ARCL X
119.	AVIEW
120.	PSE
121.	PSE
122.	X < > Y
123.	SCI 3
124.	STO 19
125.	"|T|/|1 + T| = "
126.	ARCL X
127.	AVIEW
128.	PSE
129.	PSE
130.	XEQ "DB"
131.	"T/1 + T<DB> = "
132.	ARCL X
133.	PROMPT
134.	LBL 07
135.	RCL 17
136.	STO-13
137.	GTO 06
138.	LBL "DB"
139.	LOG
140.	20
141.	*
142.	FIX 1
143.	RTN
144.	END

Line 118: $\angle T/1 + T = NN.N°$

Line 126: $|T(j\omega)/[1 + T(j\omega)]| = K.KK\ EKK$

Line 131: $20 \log_{10} |T/1 + T| = MM.M$ (dB)

Line 136: Resets Register 13
Line 137: Go back for next frequency
Line 138: Convert from magnitude to dB subroutine

DATA REGISTERS

00	P/Z 0.0	10	P/Z 10.0
01	P/Z 1.0	11	P/Z 11.0
02	P/Z 2.0	12	T_0 (magnitude)
03	P/Z 3.0	13	Counter
04	P/Z 4.0	14	Frequency (Hz)
05	P/Z 5.0	15	$\angle T(j\omega)$
06	P/Z 6.0	16	$|T(j\omega)|$
07	P/Z 7.0	17	No. P/Z
08	P/Z 8.0	18	$\angle T/1 + T$ (degrees)
09	P/Z 9.0	19	$|T/1 + T|$ (magnitude)

Several other programs available for use with the HP41 [see Ref. D.5] are also particularly applicable for op amp circuits. Some of the more important are:

NUMBER	TITLE
41-00477-7	Curve-fitting
41-00596-4	"ANAP," Active (op amp) Analysis
41-00761-4	"Trap," Transient Analysis
41-00798-6	Filter Function Noise Bandwidth
41-00849-7	"ORDER," Butterworth & Chebyshev Filters
41-00860-4	Least Squares Polynomial Curve Fit
41-01196-2	Bode Plot of a General Transfer Function
41-01733-2	Numerical Integration

Appendix  E

Resistor and Capacitor Tables

In this appendix several useful tables indicating important characteristics of resistors and capacitors are presented. The author has found that most undergraduates, and often graduate students as well, have little concept of the differences between one type resistor and another, and likewise for capacitors. The educational process for engineers is really to blame, since technology moves so rapidly we seldom have time to include such practical matters in the curriculum. Instead, we hope that industry addresses these problems in the first few years of practical job training.

The student should find the listing of standard resistance values (for $\pm 0.1\%$ to $\pm 10\%$ tolerances) in Table E.1 useful in choosing components for active filters in Chapter 6. For larger resistors, the listed values in the tables are merely multiplied by an appropriate scale factor, i.e., a $\pm 1\%$ resistor closest to 39 kΩ would be specified as 39.2×10^3, or 39.2 kΩ. The standard values also apply to available capacitors; thus, a $\pm 5\%$ capacitor near a 2600 pF required value could be chosen from 2200 pF, 2400 pF, 2700 pF, etc.

The listing in Table E.2 compares the advantages and disadvantages of the various *types* of resistors, such as carbon, wire-wound, metal-film, etc. For precision requirements (such as filters, A/D and D/A converters, and precision references) the carbon resistors should be avoided, and the metal or bulk metal-film resistors used. The wire-wound resistor offers excellent tolerance and stability, but should be avoided for higher frequency applications due to the large series inductance obtained by concentrically winding the resistance wire on a cylindrical form. For lowest $1/f$ noise (we referred to this as as excess

RESISTANCE TOLERANCE (±%)

0.1% 0.25% 0.5%	1%	2% 5% 10%	0.1% 0.25% 0.5%	1%	2% 5% 10%	0.1% 0.25% 0.5%	1%	2% 5% 10%	0.1% 0.25% 0.5%	1%	2% 5% 10%	0.1% 0.25% 0.5%	1%	2% 5% 10%	0.1% 0.25% 0.5%	1%	2% 5% 10%
10.0	10.0	10	14.7	14.7	—	21.5	21.5	—	31.6	31.6	—	46.4	46.4	—	68.1	68.1	68
10.1	—	—	14.9	—	—	21.8	—	—	32.0	—	—	47.0	—	47	69.0	—	—
10.2	10.2	—	15.0	15.0	15	22.1	22.1	22	32.4	32.4	—	47.5	47.5	—	69.8	69.8	—
10.4	—	—	15.2	—	—	22.3	—	—	32.8	—	—	48.1	—	—	70.6	—	—
10.5	10.5	—	15.4	15.4	—	22.6	22.6	—	33.2	33.2	33	48.7	48.7	—	71.5	71.5	—
10.6	—	—	15.6	—	—	22.9	—	—	33.6	—	—	49.3	—	—	72.3	—	—
10.7	10.7	—	15.8	15.8	—	23.2	23.2	—	34.0	34.0	—	49.9	49.9	—	73.2	73.2	—
10.9	—	—	16.0	—	16	23.4	—	—	34.4	—	—	50.5	—	—	74.1	—	—
11.0	11.0	11	16.2	16.2	—	23.7	23.7	—	34.8	34.8	—	51.1	51.1	51	75.0	75.0	75
11.1	—	—	16.4	—	—	24.0	—	24	35.2	—	—	51.7	—	—	75.9	—	—
11.3	11.3	—	16.5	16.5	—	24.3	24.3	—	35.7	35.7	—	52.3	52.3	—	76.8	76.8	—
11.4	—	—	16.7	—	—	24.6	—	—	36.1	—	36	53.0	—	—	77.7	—	—
11.5	11.5	—	16.9	16.9	—	24.9	24.9	—	36.5	36.5	—	53.6	53.6	—	78.7	78.7	—
11.7	—	—	17.2	—	—	25.2	—	—	37.0	—	—	54.2	—	—	79.6	—	—
11.8	11.8	—	17.4	17.4	—	25.5	25.5	—	37.4	37.4	—	54.9	54.9	—	80.6	80.6	—
12.0	—	12	17.6	17.6	—	25.8	—	—	37.9	—	—	55.6	—	—	81.6	—	—
12.1	12.1	—	17.8	17.8	—	26.1	26.1	—	38.3	38.3	—	56.2	56.2	56	82.5	82.5	82
12.3	—	—	18.0	—	18	26.4	—	—	38.8	—	—	56.9	—	—	83.5	—	—
12.4	12.4	—	18.2	18.2	—	26.7	26.7	—	39.2	39.2	39	57.6	57.6	—	84.5	84.5	—
12.6	—	—	18.4	—	—	27.1	—	27	39.7	—	—	58.3	—	—	85.6	—	—
12.7	12.7	—	18.7	18.7	—	27.4	27.4	—	40.2	40.2	—	59.0	59.0	—	86.6	86.6	—
12.9	—	—	18.9	—	—	27.7	—	—	40.7	—	—	59.7	—	—	87.6	—	—
13.0	13.0	13	19.1	19.1	—	28.0	28.0	—	41.2	41.2	—	60.4	60.4	—	88.7	88.7	—
13.2	—	—	19.3	—	—	28.4	—	—	41.7	—	—	61.2	—	—	89.8	—	—
13.3	13.3	—	19.6	19.6	—	28.7	28.7	—	42.2	42.2	—	61.9	61.9	62	90.9	90.9	91
13.5	—	—	19.8	—	—	29.1	—	—	42.7	—	—	62.6	—	—	92.0	—	—
13.7	13.7	—	20.0	20.0	20	29.4	29.4	—	43.2	43.2	43	63.4	63.4	—	93.1	93.1	—
13.8	—	—	20.3	—	—	29.8	—	—	43.7	—	—	64.2	—	—	94.2	—	—
14.0	14.0	—	20.5	20.5	—	30.1	30.1	30	44.2	44.2	—	64.9	64.9	—	95.3	95.3	—
14.2	—	—	20.8	—	—	30.5	—	—	44.8	—	—	65.7	—	—	96.5	—	—
14.3	14.3	—	21.0	21.0	—	30.9	30.9	—	45.3	45.3	—	66.5	66.5	—	97.6	97.6	—
14.5	—	—	21.3	—	—	31.2	—	—	45.9	—	—	67.3	—	—	98.8	—	—

Table E.2 COMPARISON OF DIFFERENT TYPES OF RESISTOR[1]

	Advantages	Disadvantages
DISCRETE		
Carbon Composition	Low Cost High Power/Small Case Size	Poor Tolerance (5%) Poor Temperature Coefficient (1500 ppm/°C)
Carbon Film	Lowest Cost TC -200 ppm/°C	Poor Tolerance (5%)
Wirewound	Excellent Tolerance (0.01%) Excellent TC (1 ppm/°C) High Power	Reactance may be a problem Large Case Size Most Expensive
Metal-Film	Good Tolerance (0.1%) Good TC (<1 to 100 ppm/°C) Moderate Cost	Must be Stabilized with Burn-in Low Power
Bulk Metal or Metal Foil	Excellent Tollerance (to 0.005%) Excellent TC (to <1 ppm/°C) Low Reactance	Low Power Very Expensive
High Megohm	Very high Values (10^8–10^{14} Ω) Only Choice for Some Circuits	High Voltage Coefficient (200 ppm/V) Fragile Glass Case Expensive
NETWORKS		
Thick Film	Low Cost High Power Laser Trimmable Readily Available Suitable for Hybrid IC Substrate	Fair Matching (0.1%) Poor TC (>100 ppm/°C) Poor Tracking TC (10 ppm/°C)
Thin Film on Glass	Good Matching (<0.01%) Good TC (<100 ppm/°C) Good Tracking TC (2 ppm/°C) Moderate Cost Laser Trimmable Low Capacitance	Not Suitable for Monolithic IC Construction Delicate Often Large Geometry Low Power
Thin Film on Ceramic	Good Matching (<0.01%) Good TC (<100 ppm/°C) Good Tracking TC (2 ppm/°C) Moderate Cost Laser Trimmable Low Capacitance Suitable for Hybrid IC Substrate	Often Large Geometry Not Suitable for Monolithic IC Construction

[1] Adapted from *Analog Circuit Design Seminar Notes*, July 1984, with permission of Analog Devices, Inc., Norwood, MA.

Thin Film on Silicon	Good Matching ($<0.01\%$)	Not Suitable for Hybrid IC Substrate
	Good TC (<100 ppm/°C)	Some Capacitance to Substrate
	Good Tracking TC (2 ppm/°C)	Low Power
	Moderate Cost	
	Laser Trimmable	
	Suitable for Monolithic IC Construction	
Thin Film on Sapphire	Good Matching ($<0.01\%$)	Higher Cost
	Good TC (<100 ppm/°C)	Low Power
	Good Tracking TC (2 ppm/°C)	
	Laser Trimmable	
	Low Capacitance	
	Suitable for Monolithic IC Construction	

noise in Chapter 4; see Section 4.1.3) one should use wirewound or metal-film type resistors, since carbon resistors can generate excess noise to as high as 50 kHz when dc current flows in the resistor.

A short summary and comparison of various capacitor types is illustrated in Table E.3. In general the polarity-sensitive capacitor [such as aluminum foil (often referred to as aluminum-electrolytic) or tantalum] should be avoided in signal-processing circuits, unless the relative large leakage currents can be tolerated. For active filter applications the plastic capacitors (polyester, polystyrene, etc.) or the COG (often referred to as NPO) through COK ceramic capacitors are preferred due to their low temperature coefficient and high resistance. For data-acquisition circuits, such as S/H, T/H, A/D, and D/A applications, we need capacitors with high resistance (very low leakage currents) and, most important, low dielectric absorption values (dielectric absorption was discussed in Chapter 7, Section 7.6). The data of Table E.4 suggests thast polystyrene, polypropylene, or Teflon capacitors would be preferred.

Table E.3 COMPARISON OF DIFFERENT TYPES OF CAPACITORS[1]

Type	Capacitance Range	Voltage Range	Temperature Coefficient (ppm/°C)	Dielectric Absorption (%)	Leakage (Ω − uF)
Ceramic—COG	1 pF–0.1 μF	50–600	0 ± 30	0.2	5×10^8
COH	1 pF–0.01 μF	50–600	0 ± 60	0.2	5×10^8
COJ	1 pF–0.01 μF	50–600	0 ± 120	0.2	5×10^8
COK	1 pF–0.01 μF	50–600	0 ± 250	0.2	5×10^8
U2J	1 pF–0.01 μF	50–600	-750 ± 120	0.2	5×10^8
P3K	100 pF–0.01 μF	50–600	-1500 ± 250	0.2	5×10^8
X7R	10 pF–2.7 μF	50–100	$+1000 \pm 3000$	0.2	10^8–10^9
Y5F	0.01–2.2 μF	3–50	± 2500	0.2	10^5–10^8
Y5R	0.01–2.2 μF	3–50	± 3000	0.2	10^5–10^8
Y5T	0.01–2.2 μF	3–50	$+1000 \pm 4000$	0.2	10^5–10^8
Y5V	470 pF–4.7 μF	50–100	$\pm 20,000$	0.2	10^9
S2L	3–200 pF	1k–6k	-330 ± 500	0.2	8×10^7
S3N	3–200 pF	1k–6k	-3300 ± 2500	0.2	8×10^7
X5F	100 pF–0.01 μF	50–600	-500 ± 2500	0.2	5×10^4–10^{10}
X5U	100 pF–0.01 μF	50–600	± 7500	0.2	5×10^4–10^{10}
Z5F	100 pF–0.01 μF	50–6k	± 2000	0.2	5×10^4–10^{10}
Z5P	0.001–0.01 μF	50–6k	$+2500 \pm 2500$	0.2	5×10^4–10^{10}
Z5R	0.005–0.1 μF	50–6k	$+2500 \pm 2500$	0.2	5×10^4–10^{10}
Z5U	0.001–4.7 μF	50–6k	$\pm 10,000$	0.2	5×10^4–10^{10}
Z5V	0.001–0.1 μF	50–600	$\pm 10,000$	0.2	5×10^4–10^{10}
Silver Mica	1 pF–0.1 μF	100–2k	± 500 to ± 10	1.0	10^9–10^{11}
Polyester (mylar)	0.001–10 μF	50–1600	$+400 \pm 200$	0.5	5×10^9–10^{11}
Polystyrene	20 pF–30 μF	30–600	-120 ± 30	0.02	10^{11}–10^{12}
Polycarbonate	0.001–25 μF	50–400	0 ± 100	0.2	10^{10}–10^{11}
Polypropylene	100 pF–0.15 μF	200–1600	-450 ± 300	0.02	10^{10}–10^{12}
Parylene	0.001–1 μF	30–100	$0 \pm 50, -200$	0.05	10^{10}–10^{12}
Teflon	0.001–1 μF	50–600	-200	0.02	10^{10}–10^{12}
Paper Impregnated	0.0005–100 μF	200–15k	0 ± 500	2.0	10^9–5×10^{10}
Glass	0.5 pF–0.01 μF	300–1k	$+140 \pm 25$	2.0	10^9
High K Glass	10 pF–0.01 μF	50–100	± 4500	5.0	10^9
Aluminum Foil	0.5 μF–1 F	3–500	$+10,000$	10	0.01–10 μA/μF
Solid Tantalum	0.001–1000 μF	3–125	$+1000$	2	0.01–1 μA/μF
Tantalum Foil	0.1–10,000 μF	3–500	$+2500$		0.01–1 μA/μF

All values shown are representative figures.

[1] Adapted from *Analog Circuit Design Seminar Notes*, July 1984, with permission of Analog Devices, Inc., Norwood, MA.

Table E.4 CAPACITORS FOR SWITCHED DATA-ACQUISITION APPLICATIONS[1]

Type	Typical Dielectric Absorption	Advantages	Disadvantages
NPO Ceramic (COG)	0.1%	Small Case Size Inexpensive Good Stability Wide Range of Values Many Vendors Available in Chip Form	DA too High for More than 8-Bit Applications
Polystyrene	0.001% to 0.02%	Inexpensive Low DA Available Wide Range of Values Good Stability	Destroyed by Temperature $> +85°C$ Large Case Size Not Available in Chip Form
Polypropylene	0.001% to 0.02%	Inexpensive Low DA Available Wide Range of Values	Destroyed by Temperature $> +105°C$ Large Case Size
Teflon	0.003% to 0.02%	Low DA Available Good Stability Operational Above $+125°C$ Wide Range of Values	Relatively Expensive Large Not Available in Chip Form
MOS	0.01%	Good DA Small Operational Above $+125°C$ Available in Chip Form	Limited Availability Available only in Small Capacitance Values
Polycarbonate	0.1%	Good Stability Low Cost Wide Temperature Range	Large Not Available in Chip Form DA Limits to 8-Bit Applications
Polysulfone	0.1%	Good Stability Low Cost Wide Temperature Range	Large Not Available in Chip Form DA Limits to 8-Bit Applications

Adapted from *Analog Circuit Design Seminar Notes*, July 1984, with permission of Analog Devices, Inc., Norwood, MA.

Index